Religion in the Lands That Became America

Religion in the Lands That Became America

A New History

THOMAS A. TWEED

Yale
UNIVERSITY PRESS
New Haven and London

Published with assistance from the foundation established
in memory of William McKean Brown.

Yale University Press books may be purchased in quantity for educational, business, or promotional use. For information, please email sales.press@yale.edu (U.S. office) or sales@yaleup.co.uk (U.K. office).

Set in Minion Pro type by Westchester Publishing Services.
Printed in the United States of America.

Library of Congress Control Number: 2024942004
ISBN 978-0-300-22148-0 (hardcover : alk. paper)

A catalogue record for this book is available from the British Library.

This paper meets the requirements of ANSI/NISO Z39.48-1992
(Permanence of Paper).

10 9 8 7 6 5 4 3 2 1

For Margaret L. McNamee

Contents

A Note on Terms

Since almost every word for a place, a group, or a practice has a long and contested history, I should say something about my use of terms. Places had been named long before Columbus, but an early European map introduced the word *America,* and its meaning has been contested ever since, referring alternately to the United States, North America, or the Western Hemisphere. I sometimes give Indigenous place-names, but more often use geographical terms, referring to the hemisphere or the continent. Or I refer to the *Eastern Woodlands* and the *Atlantic World.* I use cultural referents like the *Mississippian Interaction Sphere* and political categories like the *Spanish Empire* too. When it applies, I say "the lands that became America," meaning locales that would become part of the United States—its commonwealths (Puerto Rico and Northern Mariana Islands) and territories (Guam, American Samoa, and US Virgin Islands), as well as the District of Columbia and the fifty states.

I use varied terms to describe the inhabitants of those locales. When chronicling early events, I borrow labels from those who study the distant past, including *Paleoindian,* which some readers might find offensive. The adjective *American* is contested too. In a strict sense, it applies to citizens of the United States, but in a loose sense it can refer to all the land's inhabitants, both those who lived before the US formed and those granted—or denied—citizenship after 1789. When quoting historical documents about those inhabitants, I often retain the labels, including dismissive religious terms like *Heathen* and racial descriptors like *Red.* I use *White* to describe people who identified that way or were classified that way in the color-coded scheme of the day. I capitalize *White* to avoid presuming whiteness as the unacknowledged norm. I also capitalize *Black* and related labels. Used as a noun, Black often is a synonym for *African American.* I use *Asian* or *Asian American* to refer to inhabitants who trace their descent to Asia. When interpreting historical sources, I choose terms that would be recognized today, like *Chinese* or *Vietnamese.* More than 62 million residents identified as *Hispanic* or *Latino* in the latest US Census, but scholars debate the best label for native Spanish speakers and those who trace their ancestry to the Iberian Peninsula or to Latin America. To be gender inclusive—and avoid *Latina/o*—many specialists prefer *Latinx.* My usage varies according to the period and the context. When possible, I use self-descriptors and specific terms like *Cuban* or *Mexican.*

European settlers talked about *Indians,* perpetuating Columbus's misunderstanding about who greeted him, though the term became a self-descriptor too. I use *Native, Indigenous,* and *Indian* interchangeably—and use *First Nations* for inhabitants of the lands that became Canada. The US Census employs broad categories like *American Indian and Alaska Native* or *Native Hawaiian and Pacific Islander.* I usually mention specific Native Nations, giving both the term preferred today and the term in the documents, as with *Diné* (Navajo) and *Haudenosaunee* (Iroquois). In general I follow Gregory Younging's *Elements of Indigenous Style,* which suggests that scholars capitalize *Indigenous Peoples* and *Native Nations,* as I do here.

I use *religion* when referring to Indigenous sacred stories, objects, and ceremonies. Some might not prefer that term, but it has advantages. It reminds readers that Indigenous activists sometimes strategically employed *religion* to assert their rights and, by emphasizing continuities, that usage also makes it harder to exclude Indigenous Peoples from the story. To avoid repetition, I sometimes use *faith* as a synonym. Some Americans now say they are *spiritual* but not *religious.* I use the terms as synonyms when discussing earlier periods, although in contemporary speech *spiritual* often signals a person who might believe in God but does not affiliate with a church, synagogue, or mosque. When describing religious communities, I usually use the group's preferred name, as with *Roman Catholics* or *Latter-day Saints,* but when quoting archival sources or reconstructing historical context, I sometimes retain unwelcome descriptors like *Papists* or *Mormons.*

Preface

Americans have been telling stories about the nation's religious history for a long time. One much revered—and much debated—story begins on a chilly day in 1620 when the Pilgrims came ashore at Plymouth Rock. Most of those Pilgrims, who became linked with Thanksgiving, had left England for Holland in 1607. For a variety of motives—including religious freedom—they set out again, crossing the Atlantic on the *Mayflower* in 1620. The Pilgrims' landing site, Plymouth Rock, became especially important to many White Protestant New Englanders between 1820 and 1920, a time when immigration was transforming America.

That narrative tradition owes a great deal to Daniel Webster, the skilled political orator who gave a speech in 1820 commemorating the two hundredth anniversary of the Pilgrims' arrival. Webster, a spiritual descendent of those Protestants, urged the crowd at Plymouth Rock to remember the nation's religious character, including how the Pilgrims' piety had influenced society and government: in fact, those passengers had brought "the first footsteps of civilized man!" That's why, he said, the place still inspires awe. It's the spot where national history began, amid "the hearths and altars of New England." There Christianity and civilization came to a land "covered with a wilderness and peopled by roving barbarians."

We're not sure those "civilizing" Protestants actually stepped on the small rock now displayed in the coastal Massachusetts monument; but that didn't discourage countless representations by artists, writers, and even living history reenactors by the 1960s, when Plymouth also had Jewish and Catholic houses of worship.

Of course, those representations don't all tell the same story or make the same point. One nineteenth-century lithograph includes a peaceful Indigenous resident unnoticed by the landing party's leader, William Bradford, who looks out to the unfamiliar land as a companion kneels in gratitude by the iconic rock (fig. 1). But not everyone would give thanks or pay homage. In his 1963 "Letter from Birmingham Jail," Martin Luther King Jr. reminded Americans that "before the Pilgrims landed at Plymouth we were here," and the Muslim convert Malcolm X challenged the narrative by claiming in a 1964 speech that the Pilgrims didn't land on that rock. Bemoaning America's long

Figure 1. *The Landing of the Pilgrims at Plymouth, Massachusetts, December 22nd, 1620.* Lithograph published by Currier and Ives (1876). Courtesy of Yale University Art Gallery, Mabel Brady Garvan Collection.

history of spiritually sanctioned racial violence, he suggested "the rock was landed on us."

Even Protestants in Webster's generation, the first after the Revolution, didn't agree among themselves. Compare Webster's oration with an 1836 speech by William Apess, a Pequot minister, in Boston. A descendant of the "roving barbarians" Webster denigrated, Apess used the same narrative motifs—*liberty* and *civilization*—but cast Indigenous Peoples as the story's heroic characters. It was the Pilgrims and their descendants who had acted like barbarians and devalued liberty. "Our groves and hunting grounds are gone, our dead are dug up," he reminded listeners. America had deprived Natives of their rights, blocking them from citizenship and driving them from their lands. Comparing Indigenous Peoples to enslaved Africans, Apess suggested the real national story was about barbaric newcomers who failed to live up to their own religious ideals. So Americans shouldn't celebrate the Pilgrims' landing—or the Fourth of July. Instead, "let the children of the pilgrims blush, while the son of the forest sheds a tear." "Every man of color" should mourn on those civic holidays and "pray to the great Spirit, the Indian's God, who deals out mercy to his red children, and not destruction."

Whether or not you're ready to mourn on the next anniversary of the Plymouth landing or the Declaration's signing, perhaps these accounts have reminded you that stories about the past can stir passions. That's because stories matter, especially for those who are left out.

In this book I want to tell a new story that includes more characters and more places. We'll meet familiar figures like Bradford and those transatlantic migrants gathered around New England's "hearths and altars" but also notice destroyed hunting grounds and farmlands as we trace how religion inspired the European colonists' plantations and shaped the Native habitats of Apess's ancestors. That means starting our story earlier, long before the Pilgrims, and following all the migrants—Indigenous and African as well as Asian and European—as they move across oceans and lands to make and remake environments. Along the way we'll meet memorable people and places omitted from the usual tales: Horn Shelter Man, a medicine man buried with 100 grave gifts in a rock shelter in Texas about 11,000 years ago; a small band of Louisiana hunter-gatherers who built a ritual plaza inside a ring of earthen mounds about 3000 BCE, before the Egyptian pyramids; and a Mississippian priest who presided at elaborate harvest festivals and lived on a ten-story mound in a cornfield chiefdom near St. Louis, long before Bradford called on the Bible's God in the Mayflower Compact or Thomas Jefferson celebrated "Nature's God" in the Declaration of Independence.

And there are more gripping stories of people and places after Plymouth's planting: Jemmy, the Portuguese-speaking Catholic slave from the Congo who led a rebellion so he could join Spanish Catholics in St. Augustine, Florida, the oldest European settlement in the lands that became America; Mike Abdallah, the Syrian migrant who helped establish an early mosque in the remote farming town of Ross, North Dakota; and Shigeo Kikuchi, a Japanese Buddhist woman in Hawai'i who stood at a port during World War II to send off each young Japanese American headed to fight by offering Buddhist prayer beads and a whispered reminder that "the Buddha is always with you."

This story also introduces a new plot with different turning points. If you like histories that foreground presidents and wars, you'll find elected leaders and armed battles. However, for the religious history of the lands that became America, other long-term processes and short-term events had as much influence. For example, the Revolutionary War and the Civil War transformed the political landscape, but the aftermath of those conflicts was more decisive for religious history: the drafting of the First Amendment and the "conquest" of the West, as well as the racist exclusions of the post-Reconstruction Era and the imperial ambitions of the late Gilded Age. And, as Apess sensed, other long-term processes had influence. The decimation of Indigenous habitats and the construction of slave plantations would set the stage for the religious drama that would play out in the years ahead.

Before we set out to follow the twists and turns in that drama, it might help to have a bit more orientation. The introduction explains more about why we need a new story and how we might tell it.

Religion in the Lands That Became America

Introduction

Toward New Narratives

There were no Puritans on my street in Philadelphia. That was my reaction when, as an undergraduate, I first read Sydney Ahlstrom's *A Religious History of the American People,* winner of the 1973 National Book Award in Philosophy and Religion and still a widely respected overview.[1] His story about the rise and fall of "Puritan America," which foregrounded theological ideas and Protestant churches, was impressive. It just didn't have much to do with religion as I encountered it in my Catholic parish and my friends' synagogues. Where were the incense and May processions? The Torah pointers and bar mitzvahs? The story also said little about ordinary people, including women, and everyday life, including private devotions. It mentioned Natives but focused on efforts to convert them; it discussed slavery but said more about how it divided Protestant churches than how it affected enslaved people.[2] It noted that ministers addressed inequities in nineteenth-century cities, and at the end, while lamenting Puritan America's decline, Ahlstrom mentioned some twentieth-century social problems.[3] But, I wondered, could a religious history offer a fuller account of how more people confronted more problems? By the time I entered graduate school, I had other questions about Ahlstrom's story, since I had decided I would specialize in—of all things—US religion. And someday, I told myself, I would write my own story. Well, that day has come.

I still admire Ahlstrom's book—and appreciate the subsequent surveys—but the most celebrated historical overviews of US religion have obscured important features of the past and failed to speak to many in the present. I first said so at a conference in 1988, when I wondered aloud if those of us teaching American religion might profit from a sustained conversation about how we narrate that history. Soon my initial resolve became a concrete plan. I would give it a try. I then spent decades preparing to write this book, because I had to learn things I never imagined I would need to know. As you'll notice, I crossed disciplinary boundaries as I tried to learn about everything from the flow of genes into ancient North America to the flow of information across fiber cables in the twenty-first century. Then a global pandemic reminded me I had still more to learn, including about how religion has brought people together and pulled them apart during moments of shared suffering. By then I was more aware than ever of what I didn't know and what I couldn't see. But from the start I considered different ways of recounting the past and sought help from colleagues who might correct my blind spots. I invited a group of scholars to collaborate, since the task seemed so formidable. In 1997 we published *Retelling U.S. Religious History* as our attempt to imagine new stories. I made other attempts after that too, experimenting with new chronologies in the classroom and proposing new narrative strategies in books.[4]

I was so persistent because I had become even more convinced it was important to change the narrative. In that sense, the story I tell in this book also makes an argument. But so do all histories. "History," after all, "is the art of making an argument about the past by telling a story accountable to evidence."[5] Historians don't agree about what evidence to consider or how to interpret it. And different motifs or themes orient their tales, just as narrators start their stories in different times and places. Those varied stories also enact different moral values and have different social consequences. Historical narratives have affected how citizens voted and politicians justified war. They have determined where commuters sat on the bus, what work women could do, which migrants crossed the border—and who was sent back, as with the more than 50 million deported from the US since 1945.[6] When it comes to national narratives, there's no such thing as *just* a story. Stories dictate whom we'll remember and forget. Tales about the past have real effects in everyday life since they propose answers to crucial questions: What is America? Who is American? Those answers determine not only the central characters in the story but also the social power of contemporary residents. That's why we should pay attention to the stories we tell and hear.

Toward New Stories

At least since the first scholars began writing overviews of American religion during the 1920s, the most popular surveys have been historically constricting.[7] Their plots have placed White British Protestants along the North

Atlantic coast at the start of the narrative and then traced how increasingly diverse faiths confronted Protestant dominance. That plot about the rise and fall of Protestant public power has relied on presuppositions about the beginning, the setting, and the scope.[8] When combined with assumptions about the centrality of theology and churches, the presuppositions generated plots that highlight White male Protestants, especially preachers in the pulpits of mainline denominations in the Northeast.[9] Those plots have recounted parts of the story but haven't fully situated religious history in terms of the "big changes," revealing less about how religion shaped the ways ordinary people as well as cultural elites experienced the forces that transformed daily life in the modern world, including capitalism and nationalism.[10] The surveys also have obscured other regions, as well as the roles of women and of Americans of diverse ethnic heritages and religious backgrounds—not to mention those who have practiced no religion, mixed faiths, or, more recently, proclaimed themselves "spiritual but not religious."[11] Further, despite the significance of migration—forced and voluntary—most surveys have favored the settled over the itinerant, minimizing the decisive historical roles of the displaced—including Native Peoples, enslaved persons, and transnational migrants. At the same time, there has been an enduring habit of minimizing emplacement, the process of place-making. The overviews tell us too little about how the devout employed spiritual resources to reimagine and transform local environments.

I also worried about other blind spots. Migration to and across the hemisphere started long before Columbus sailed and the Pilgrims landed, and beginning the story with European settlement erases more than ten thousand years of the continent's religious history, obscuring how Native Americans' ancestors experienced big changes in the distant past, including the transition from foraging to farming.[12] The preoccupation with the British origins of the nation-state, and the conviction that the US is "exceptional," has hidden from view the ways in which religion in the lands that became America has been shaped by practices in other parts of the world.[13] Finally, survey writers haven't always acknowledged their presuppositions and values. They have employed the authorial voice of the value-free narrator who enjoys a god's-eye view. I try to acknowledge my vantage point and say a little about my values and assumptions because I think I owe you, the reader, an account of what I'm doing and why I'm doing it. In other words, I believe histories are situated stories written by limited scholars with particular viewpoints.[14]

My aim in this situated story is to change the plot, so I can include some of what has been obscured about the past and alter the tale's social effects in the present. But changing the plot is difficult. Learned, well-intentioned narrators have added characters—women and slaves, for example—and then celebrated those chronicles, without really changing the roles the characters play and the argument the story makes. To more fully revise the plot, I believe it's important to change the story's starting point, spatial scope, and organizing motif.

Changing the Starting Point

Most surveys of US religion have presupposed that the story must begin with and focus on the British colonies—as opposed to starting, as I do, with ancient Indigenous practices in the territory now within national borders, and then chronicling the history of those locales, from Florida to Alaska and Maine to Hawai'i. That presupposition commits narrators to focusing on Anglo-Protestant men who had political and ecclesiastical power in Britain's Atlantic colonies. In turn, everyone else—Protestant women as well as racial and religious others—appear as supporting actors with bit parts. More recent survey writers have enriched the story. But the plot hasn't changed; nor have the supporting players' roles. Everyone who isn't an Anglo-Protestant man becomes defined by her or his relation to those with political or ecclesiastical authority during a relatively brief period, 1607–1776, on a strip of land along the North Atlantic coast. To alter this pattern, I start by narrating the religious history of the continent and consider all locales now part of the United States—its commonwealths (Puerto Rico and Northern Mariana Islands) and territories (Guam, American Samoa, and US Virgin Islands) as well as the District of Columbia and the fifty states.[15] And I try to expand the scope in other ways too.

Expanding the Narrative Scope

Stories "serve as a mean of mass transportation."[16] They take us somewhere and propel us across time, backward and forward. Yet most historical overviews of US religion haven't carried us far enough, so I try to range further in time and space. The action starts earlier, when we can detect the first signs of religious practice in the archaeological record, and the scope expands to include influences that converged in the territory that now lies within contemporary US borders, as in the Polynesian Pacific, where ancient Indigenous mariners settled islands that would become American Samoa and Hawai'i.

Long History

Some scholars have suggested we start the story much earlier: when the cosmos began 13 billion years ago, when the earth formed about 4.5 billion years ago, when human history began about 200,000 years ago, or at least when *Homo sapiens* started transcontinental migrations tens of thousands of years ago.[17] I start only with the first signs of humans in the Americas, but this approach still requires cross-disciplinary explorations at a time when it seems impossible to know all that's required to cover such an enormous temporal span.

Given the challenges, it's not surprising specialists in US religious history haven't recounted the long-term history of inhabitants in the lands that became America.[18] But there are precedents for considering this approach. From the late eighteenth century to the late nineteenth century, some writers in the Americas and Europe assumed an earlier starting point. By the 1780s, timelines representing an extended past had become popular, and histories and geographies started the story with the early migrations to the hemisphere.[19] The entry on "América" in *Diccionario geográfico-histórico de las Indias Occidentales ó América* (1786–1789) by Antonio de Alcedo, who identified as "American" because he was born in Ecuador, suggested that "the earliest settlers and inhabitants of the hemisphere" entered North America "by sea from Ramstchaia."[20] He meant Kamchatka, the site in present-day Russia where Captain James Cook's ships anchored during his 1779 voyage around the North Pacific. It's a site that archaeologists still consider a possible origin of one of the migrant streams to the Americas.[21] William Robertson, who exchanged letters with Alcedo, wrote his *History of America* in Scotland, and that learned interpreter also started his account with the peopling of the Americas from "the northeast of Asia."[22] Writing from Virginia, the equally learned Thomas Jefferson noted "the great question has arisen from whence came these aboriginals of America?" And he too wrote that Cook's discoveries proved inhabitants may have passed into America from Asia, since the two continents are separated "only by a narrow strait."[23]

Just as mariners' reports expanded the chronological span of historical narratives in the late eighteenth century, new scholarly fields pushed back the starting point for some later interpreters, including US historian James Robinson, who in 1912 cited new archaeological findings to reject the distinction between the "historic" and "prehistoric" eras. He suggested history includes "all we know of the past of mankind."[24]

Yet the authors of overviews of religion didn't follow his lead, or recall the arguments of Alcedo, Robertson, and Jefferson.[25] Major surveys published since 1920 acknowledge that inhabitants greeted disembarking European colonizers, but say little about the peopling of the hemisphere and ignore thousands of years of subsequent history.

No one could recount all the immense past, but there are ways to extend the story a bit. Like an 1883 chronological chart that depicted "faith streams," we might use aquatic metaphors to understand the task of writing long history.[26] Scholars who study ancient practices for which they have little evidence engage in *upstreaming*, using more reliable evidence about a later period to interpret earlier practices. When the evidentiary stream slows to a trickle, I sometimes resort to upstreaming, including by consulting Native oral traditions.[27] And I do a lot of *downstreaming*, following history's converging and diverging streams as they flow forward from the distant past to the present. Sometimes I go against the current, to seek the headwaters of a less charted tributary or pause at a point of confluence, where converging spiritual streams meet. The episodes I narrate present only a partial view of this long expanse of time, of course, but I hope my imperfect attempt to expand the temporal scope opens new vistas that hint at fuller histories.

Broad History

The narrative also needs a wider geographical frame. Humanities scholars have been making this argument at least since the 1990s' "transnational turn."[28] One distinguished British historian announced that "all local, national, and regional histories must, in important ways, therefore, be global histories. It is no longer really possible to write 'European' or 'American' history in a narrow sense."[29] A prominent US scholar agreed, condemning the "narrow parochialism" of those who assume the nation-state as the unit of analysis and arguing "American history cannot be adequately understood unless it is incorporated into [a] global context."[30]

These appeals for a wider geographical framework also have precedents. Many late-eighteenth-century histories and geographies situated national plots within global stories.[31] Nineteenth-century interpreters relied on botanical metaphors to document the "growth" of religions and cultures around the world; in the early twentieth century, a time of worldwide migrations and US imperialism, some advocated a wider spatial span.[32] Anticipating the field of Atlantic history, early sociologist W. E. B. Du Bois, who was born in Massachusetts and died in Ghana, wrote about "the souls of Black Folk" in a transnational context. He noted in 1903 that "the Negro church of today is the social center of Negro life in the United States" but also looked to Africa's coast to discern "the shadow of a mighty Negro past."[33] Anticipating transhemispheric and circum-Pacific history, Berkeley professor Herbert E. Bolton pioneered the study of the southwestern borderlands, encouraging US historians to gaze south of the border to discern patterns in the Americas, and, looking farther west, he published a 1917 volume on *The Pacific Ocean in History*.[34] Both scholars called for a broader geographical frame.

Most overviews of US religion have shown less sympathy with transnational and comparative perspectives, even if rich case studies have broken new ground by tracing connections with the rest of the world.[35] To a great extent "the world" has meant western Europe.[36] For me, the world means, well, the world. So I aim for a *broad* history, a deceptively simple term for a complex approach that traces historical forces wherever they lead.[37] Since nonlocal influences are always lived out in distinctive environments, broad history always keeps both the global and the local in view. In other words, I tell the story of grounded globalism.[38]

Those grounded global flows were transoceanic and transhemispheric. Any narrative of religion that considers the converging influences on the lands that became the United States must expand the setting to include the Atlantic World, the vast transoceanic space extending to the West African coast. But the wider setting extends also to the Indo-Pacific World—back to the Indian Ocean, up to northeast Asia, and down the hemisphere's Pacific coastline from northern Canada to southern Chile. The connections between North and South America began long before the European colonial conquests. Genetic analysis of the remains of an infant in western Montana about 12,500 years ago shows he was closely related to contemporary Indigenous groups from Central and South America, especially Brazil.[39] The groups from ancient Montana and contemporary Brazil seem to have descended from common ancestral migrants. And Asia and the Indo-Pacific World have been more important than narrators have acknowledged, from the peopling of the hemisphere to the present.[40] Columbus's famous 1493 letter reported he had reached China and the islands of India, and Alcedo was still using orientalized geographical labels in the 1780s.[41] Some of the eighteenth-century US founders—like Jefferson, John Adams, and Benjamin Franklin—looked to Chinese Confucianism for models of "natural religion." Between the 1840s and the 1890s, and again after 1965, Asian migration further shaped the US religious landscape.[42] Charting Pacific as well as Atlantic currents and following along the coastlines provides a way to map border crossings and reconstruct cultural exchanges in varied local and regional environments.

The narrative's widened spatial frame is also transcontinental. It stretches to North America's geographical corners, and I note how transportation technologies (from canoes and horse-drawn wagons to steamships and gas-powered cars) affected travel.[43] I notice how people and practices moved up and down the aquatic dividing line, the Mississippi and its tributaries, and consider what happened as residents navigated other north–south waterways, from the St. Lawrence in the Northeast to the Rio Grande in the Southwest, the corridors of transcontinental travel before jet planes began leaving wisps of smoke across the sky in the middle of the continent. And that vast middle is as noteworthy as the jagged edges of the Atlantic, Pacific, and Gulf coastlines. It's as important as the lines in the sand along the borders, which officials marked after wars with Mexico and Canada.[44]

In an interesting coincidence, many prominent authors of popular historical surveys published between 1930 and 1990 were born in the middle of the continent, including William Warren Sweet (Kansas), Winthrop Hudson (Michigan), Edwin Gaustad (Iowa), Ahlstrom (Minnesota), and Martin Marty (Nebraska).[45] Sweet, the first scholar to teach "American church history," was born not far from the diminutive roadside chapel that consecrates the US's "geographic center," and the name of Ahlstrom's birthplace, Cokato, derives from a Dakota word, *çoka,* meaning in "the middle or center."[46]

But that's not what Ahlstrom meant when he confessed "I exist in the middle of things."[47] He was humbly acknowledging the shortcomings afforded by his position: the sentence continued "and inherit the limitations of my situation." "Not only the inadequacy of my knowledge," Ahlstrom graciously predicted, "but also my hidden presuppositions and my unexamined major premises will in due course be exposed." The inadequacy of my premises eventually will be exposed too. Like all historians, I too stand in the middle of things—and, in my case, in the homeland of the Pokégnek Bodéwadmik, the Pokagon Band of Potawatomi.[48] I too have blind spots. But I hope that by positioning myself alternately near the middle and along the edges, I can tell a bigger story that accounts for more evidence.

Changing the Organizing Motifs

To tell that bigger story, the usual narrative motifs need to change too. Survey writers have employed multiple guiding themes. *Frontier,* which Sweet highlighted, was prominent from the 1920s to the 1950s; *Puritanism,* which Ahlstrom emphasized, wielded influence from the 1970s to the 1990s; and plots about *unity and diversity,* or the one and the many, have predominated in recent decades.[49] Sweet's and Ahlstrom's accounts continue to inform the stories Americans tell, but few scholarly interpreters today would choose *frontier* or *Puritanism* as guiding themes. Even the unity/diversity motif illumines some things and obscures others.[50] One element of the thematic pair acknowledges heterogeneity and invites narrators to foreground the diversifying role of immigration and church–state separation. That's helpful. And plots fashioned with the motif have other advantages. Protestant political and cultural clout has been real. For those who have experienced marginalization, it's been all too real. Yet the presumed sources of unity—Protestant influence and civil religion—have been more contested than some suggest.[51] Further, whether narrators rely on spatial metaphors (*center* and *periphery*) or aquatic images (*mainstream* and *tributaries*), the unity/diversity motif can't overcome the embedded implication: there are insiders and outsiders in US religious history. So those without public power in the former British colonies are forever relegated to the narrative's margins. Natives, Hispanics, Africans, and Asians—along with Catholics, Jews, Muslims, Hindus, Buddhists, and the irreligious—appear only as minor characters in subplots affixed to the main story. Women enter the story only when they elbow their way into White male public spaces. We lose sight of private spaces, like the home, as well as the wider built environment, and the motif doesn't incline narrators to chronicle the continent's long spiritual history or recount residents' experience of the big lifeway transitions.

So which motifs might be better? After experimenting with alternatives, I decided the paired themes of *displacement* and *emplacement* (or crossing and dwelling), when combined with a focus on *sustainability* (or individual, communal, and environmental flourishing), might allow a history that accounts for more of the past and that speaks to the present, by recounting the longer history of problems we still face today, and showing how religion made some things better and made other things worse. Before foreshadowing the narrative, let me say more about those motifs, explain how I use *religion,* and introduce other terms (*figurative tools* and *niche construction*) that describe how emplacement works, or how the devout have used spiritual resources to make the more or less sustainable worlds they inherit, modify, and bequeath.[52]

Displacement and Emplacement

As I understand it, religion is about *crossing,* or moving. It propels and constrains devotees as they move across all sorts of boundaries—terrestrial, corporeal, and cosmic. Terrestrial or aquatic crossings include foreign missions, holy wars, and pilgrimages as well as spiritually motivated migration. More metaphorically, spiritual crossings are also corporeal and cosmic. The pious mark and cross stages in the life cycle, as with burial rituals, and they chart and traverse a path to *flourishing,* or well-being. Yet most religious traditions say complete well-being requires seeking the highest good or final end, whether that is achieved in this life or after death. Some traditions have imagined the end as a change in condition, like union with God or release from the cycles of birth, death, and rebirth. Others have seen it as a change in location, a journey toward the ultimate horizon of human life or across the threshold between this world and the next. Final spiritual flourishing, then, has meant joining the ancestors or ascending to heaven.[53]

Religion is also about *dwelling,* or place-making. It's about mapping, building, and inhabiting lived worlds. As humans settled, they used not only utilitarian tools (an axe or a plow) but also *figurative tools* (analogical language like metaphors, symbolic actions like burials, and sacred structures like churches) to transform the local ecology and construct a symbolic world. In this sense, religion is homemaking. To reconstruct the history of homemaking in North America I sought aid from niche construction theory, which posits multiple forms of inheritance—not just from genes; that framework proved useful for analyzing long-term changes. Just as other animals construct a niche—think of a bird's nest or a beaver's dam—humans modify their environment. The transformed environment, niche theory suggests, becomes part of what humans bequeath to the next generation. In this expansive view, then, inheritance is genetic, cultural, and environmental. Genes and cultures interact, as when the practice of dairy farming led to an increase in residents with a genetically inherited lactose tolerance. Cultures and environments interact too. Hunter-gatherers in small-scale North American societies engaged in niche construction or ecosystem engineering—from controlled burning to seed scattering—to increase the abundance of wild species of plants and animals. Farmers, who cleared brush and planted crops, created agricultural niches. Then modern industrial lifeways generated cityscapes crowded with smokestacks, skyscrapers, and steeples. In each case, the next generation inherited not just genetic codes but cultural lifeways and modified landscapes. That insight provides a conceptual frame for a new history of religion, a story that begins with the notion that humans inherit, modify, and bequeath an *eco-cultural niche,* a lived world with shared symbols, communal ceremonies, special objects, and sacred landscapes.[54] So we can talk about a generation's "symbolic inheritance" and trace how it used religion's figurative tools to preserve or transform what it received.[55]

Sustainable Niches and Human Flourishing

The lived worlds the religious inherit can be more sustainable or less sustainable. An eco-cultural niche can meet the minimal needs for mere survival or offer the optimal conditions for full flourishing—providing environmental goods (renewable resources, favorable climate, biodiversity), communal goods (equity, freedom, political participation), and individual goods (health, meaning, and belonging). In either case, *sustainability* implies a long temporal frame. To say a farming village or an industrial city is sustainable is to suggest residents have met their transgenerational obligations. Both Indigenous leaders and US founders pondered those obligations. The Haudenosaunee Confederacy's Great Law of Peace advised Council members to consider "not only the present but also the coming generations," and Jefferson suggested in 1789 that the earth belongs to the living and "no generation can contract debts greater than may be paid during the course of its own existence." Applying a similar principle, we might say that a narrow niche or broad habitat is sustainable when a community's symbolic endowment, transmitted lifeway, and modified environment enables residents to meet "the needs of the present without compromising the ability of future generations to meet their own needs." In other words, the bequeathed niche can sustain human and nonhuman life and, if optimal conditions are met, can foster ecological, communal, and individual well-being (fig. 2).[56]

But human flourishing sometimes has been stifled or restricted to a segment of the population, and a niche can become stressed when the conditions for sustainability aren't met. Eventually, a lived world can become so unstable—so unjust, violent, unhealthy, and environmentally degraded—that it "breaks" and requires collective efforts to repair or restore it. In that sense, there can be "crises of sustainability."[57] But crisis hasn't come only when climatic conditions or food security declined. Sustainability isn't only about the natural environment. As I use the term, it has a broader meaning. The sources of crisis—and the conditions for well-being—are individual and communal as well as environmental. Others have made this point. The Protestant activist who first proposed the idea of an "Earth Day" in 1968 and the Wisconsin senator who coordinated the nationwide celebration that attracted 20 million Americans in 1970 both identified converging social, economic, and environmental problems. They noted problems in the "ecosystem" and the "social environment," including racism, poverty, and war.[58] And to make sense of the long historical record, we need to broaden the meaning of *sustainability* even more. For an eco-cultural niche to be fully sustainable and

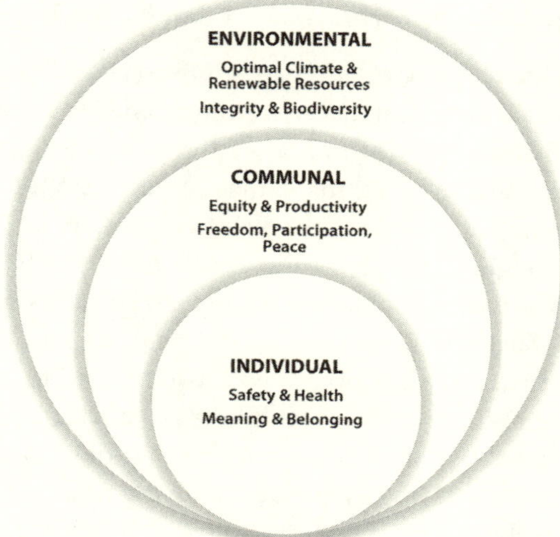

Figure 2. Optimal conditions for sustainable eco-cultural niches to meet basic needs and allow full flourishing.

able to promote human flourishing, it must provide suitable climate and renewable resources, safety and health, equity and productivity, meaning and belonging, and as much individual freedom and political participation as the common good allows. In turn, niches can become stressed if some needs aren't met, and increasingly unsustainable if multiple stressors converge—as when resources diminish, climate changes, disease devastates, injustice pervades, violence mounts, and religious worldviews no longer provide personal meaning and collective belonging.

This broader notion of sustainability—and the talk of making and breaking niches—can clear a path to new religious histories by recognizing religion's role in environmental and economic changes as well as in social, political, and intellectual shifts. Most important, considering niche construction as well as nation building can provide language for chronicling how inhabitants have conceptualized and experienced big lifeway transitions, like the onset of colonialism and the rise of industrialization, crisis points when lived worlds became less stable. The narrative focus on human flourishing in sustainable niches also reminds us that dwelling, or place-making, sometimes affects crossing, or moving. Medieval migrants in North America resettled after climate variability caused crops to fail, and Africans and Natives appealed to spiritual resources as they resiliently regrouped after colonialism destroyed niches and displaced communities. Industrialization also spurred movement and altered landscapes—as rural transplants and transnational migrants sought to thrive materially and spiritually in grimy factory towns and crowded urban neighborhoods.

The Story and the Argument

Foregrounding religion's role in fostering and hindering sustainability as residents have negotiated lifeway transitions, this book recounts how devotees in the lands that became America moved across and settled down from the end of the Ice Age to the start of the Information Age, from foraging religion to digital religion—or from the time when hunter-gatherers' modifications of the environment were local, short-term, and minimal to the time when modern human communities became the predominant force modifying earth systems and the ecological effects were global, long-term, and hard to reverse.[59] The focus on crossing restores the itinerant to a central place in the narrative, attending to how migration quickened and slowed as multiple forces—not just spiritual motives, but climate and conflict as well as famine and enslavement—constrained and propelled movement. But since itinerants ultimately sought a place of their own—a home and a homeland, a place to flourish—in the end this book chronicles dwelling or place-making. It shows how communities used utilitarian technologies and figurative tools to make, break, and sometimes restore eco-cultural niches.[60]

The book's four parts trace changes in those eco-cultural niches as ways of life transitioned from foraging to farming to factories to fiber optics—and communities bequeathed their unresolved crises as well as their resilient adaptations to the next generation.[61] This story opens with foraging religion at the Horn Shelter, a rock shelter overlooking the Brazos River in present-day Texas, where mourners placed more than 100 burial offerings in a shaman's grave 11,100 years ago.[62] Horn Shelter Man's hunter-gatherer community was already modifying the environment by spearing animals and starting fires, but the impact was minimal. The human impact was slightly greater in the next period, during the transition to agriculture—and farming religion—between 100 BCE and 550 CE along the Mississippi and in the Southwest. However, eco-cultural niches started to change even more after Columbus brought not only a cross, the symbol of a foreign religion, but also new seeds, animals, and germs. The social, cultural, and environmental transformations increased in scale, scope, and duration during the seventeenth and eighteenth centuries as competing Catholic and Protestant empires "planted" colonies and tried to "harvest" Native souls, while imported diseases shattered Indigenous niches and a new social space, the slave plantation, hindered Africans' efforts to flourish. Farming religion continued during the transition to a new form of democratic governance, an agrarian "empire of liberty," after the American Revolution. And the nation's founders and framers bequeathed moral compromises on slavery and aspirations for continental conquest, along with inspiring political documents that championed religious tolerance, declared universal equality, and presented a vision of human flourishing in both the Constitution's concern to promote justice, liberty, and "the general welfare" and the Declaration's assertion of God-endowed rights, including the right to "Life, Liberty, and the pursuit of Happiness."[63]

The same year Jefferson was in Philadelphia drafting a Declaration that challenged tyrannical political power, the inventor James Watt was commodifying steam power at a "manufactory" near Birmingham, England.[64] By the time the Continental Congress ratified the treaty that ended the American Revolution in 1784, an Industrial Revolution had begun in Britain as Watt perfected the steam engine that would power the mills importing bales of slave-picked cotton. As church-sanctioned slave plantations caused human trauma and soil depletion in the agricultural South, a shift to factory religion began in the urban industrial North by 1848 and intensified after 1873, when Andrew Carnegie's use of a new process for making steel initiated the coal-powered Second Industrial Revolution.[65] By 1920 America was an urban industrial nation, and religion continued to shape—and be shaped by—manufacturing and agribusiness during the Great Depression and World War II, when America's dependence on oil increased.[66] The early 1950s saw an acceleration of human-induced impact, and the long-term ecological changes began to be more evident by the oil crisis of 1973.[67] The mid-Seventies also witnessed the transition to a post-industrial lifeway that inspired varied forms of postindustrial religion and quasi religion, including digital religion, as the first sale of personal computers in 1977 heralded the onset of an Information Age that would bring environmental and communal costs, despite Silicon Valley's "digital utopianism."[68]

Reminders of technology's peril and promise converged in 2007, when the Nobel Peace Prize was awarded to the United Nations Panel on Climate Change and Al Gore Jr. for increasing knowledge about "man-made climate change," and, at the same time, Apple introduced the iPhone, which one blogger sarcastically called the "Jesus phone" because techies greeted it as a savior that would bring everyone together. The new technologies also pulled people apart, it turned out, but mobile phones did mediate new kinds of ritual. So this story ends with digital religion, not far from where it began with foraging religion—in Clifton, Texas, about twenty-miles east of the ancient rock shelter burial, where the town's fiber-optic Internet services enabled access to a local museum's web page commemorating Horn Shelter Man, while the Find-a-Grave phone app memorialized the working-class Baptist couple, Adeline and Herman Horn, who had allowed excavators to cross their land and unearth that holy man's grave, with its shamanic medicine bundle and shell bead offerings.[69]

Like all historians, I enact values in how I tell this story. I've already hinted at some of those values by emphasizing the individual, communal, and ecological conditions for human flourishing. I've also hinted at answers to foundational questions, including What is America? and Who is American? My answers will be expansive, since any narrative that restricts authentic Americanness to a single faith or ethnic heritage rests on unsteady historical grounds. Diverse devotees have been moving and mixing for a long time.

This narrative also shows that the eco-cultural niches those diverse inhabitants inherited and bequeathed have changed dramatically. America can't be linked solely with any spiritually figured way of life—foraging, farming, factories, or fiber optics—and this historical narrative doesn't offer a simple story of linear progress or precipitous decline. It hasn't all gone downhill, tumbling toward hell in a handbasket. This tale doesn't suggest we emulate the "ecological saints" who inhabited the landscape before Columbus or that we return to the Garden, some imagined agrarian paradise before industrialization.[70] But the moral also isn't that all things have gotten better and better. We can't allow ourselves to forget the niches broken—and the people broken too.

So this story suggests that religion has played a complex role, both escalating and easing major crises of sustainability (see appendix). First, religion supported elite practices and popular revitalization movements in stressed cornfield cultures at Cahokia along the Central Mississippi Valley and at Chaco and Mesa Verde in the San Juan Basin of the Southwest before and after about 1300, when weather changed, crops failed, devotees clashed, and violence spiked (chapter 2).[71] Second, during the colonial exchange of biota—of germs as well as seeds—competing religious empires triggered demographic decimation, environmental stress, social inequality, and psychic trauma between 1565 and 1776 as settlers displaced Native Peoples and introduced the slave plantation (chapters 3 and 4).[72] An urban industrial crisis intensified between 1873 and 1920, when fossil-fuel dependency started to increase pollution, and income inequality and health disparity in crowded northern cities signaled a wider decline in well-being (chapter 7).[73] The global environmental effects of industrialization, urbanization, and rising population accelerated by the 1950s, when evidence of humans' destabilizing impact on earth systems mounted (chapter 8).[74] The rise in carbon dioxide, methane, and nitrates signaled significant and long-term global ecological damage. That damage, in turn, threatened dramatic social and economic disruptions from climate migrations to food scarcity, and presented new challenges for religious communities, which also struggled to respond to deepening economic inequalities, continuing racial tensions, and intensifying political polarization (chapters 9 and 10).

Descendants of the thirteenth-century cornfield cultures eventually confronted their difficulties by scaling down, managing resources, and reducing hierarchy, but the unresolved Colonial and Industrial Era crises were passed on to future generations. Americans now face the legacy of those social problems, including racial and economic inequality, while they also confront the unprecedented challenges of a global environmental crisis.

At each moment of crisis, spiritual and political leaders used religion's figurative tools to sanctify the lifeway of an unstable niche. That happened with the *symbolic surplus* on display in the burial of a leader at Cahokia's maize-dependent ceremonial center along the Mississippi in medieval America; with the *planter piety* of the mid-nineteenth-century South, where a hierarchical worldview and paternalistic ethic guided slaveholding landowners and fortified the plantation complex; and with the *industrial religion* that shaped the late-nineteenth-century factory North, where an elite discourse attributed superhuman power to raw materials, mechanical technologies, and consumer goods. In each case, however, dissenters used religion's figurative tools to reimagine just, peaceful, and healthy habitats. They founded revitalization movements or created alternative niches to encourage individual, communal, and environmental well-being. Yet nonadaptive and unjust religious worlds have stubbornly persisted. Unresolved ecological problems remain, and the legacies of Indigenous displacement and African enslavement continue to haunt the contemporary American landscape.[75]

Some readers might find this plot gloomy, since I call attention to inspiring spiritual and political principles but also note how Americans sometimes haven't lived up to them.[76] I offer no apologies for that. In this book I've tried to recount how religion has functioned, for good and ill, and let the reader decide whether to throw a party or organize a protest, whether to celebrate or mourn. All historians disrupt the dead, unearthing their grief and joy, and in return they promise to bear witness—to all of it. For me, that means trying to follow the advice of James Baldwin, who suggested writers should "tell as much of the truth as one can bear, and then a little more."[77]

While telling a bit more than I can bear, I also try to recover historical sources of hope. At the end of this story I'll ask if looking back suggests ways to move forward. Can contemporary faith communities use religion's figurative tools to restore broken niches and remake sustainable worlds—just, peaceful, and healthy habitats where everyone can flourish?[78]

PART ONE
FORAGING

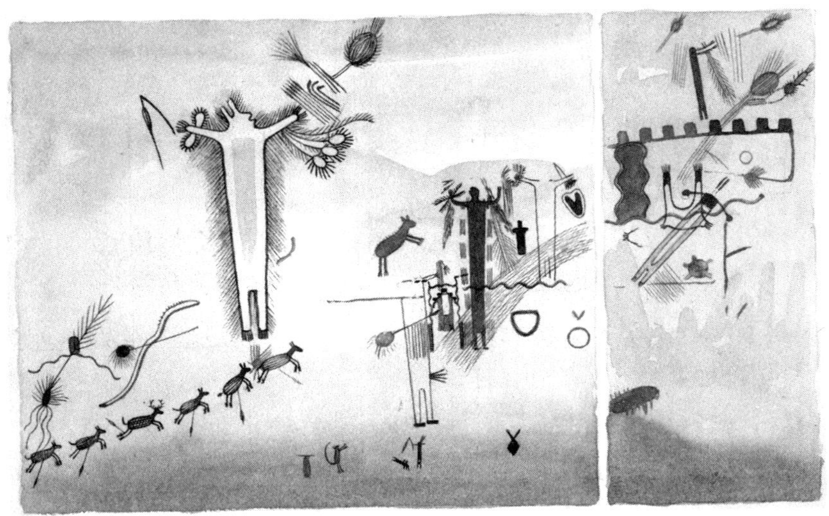

Figure 3. Representation of a rock shelter pictograph in the Lower Pecos Canyon. A shaman hovers over deer pierced by spears thrown by Archaic hunter-gatherers in western Texas. In *The Rock Art of Texas Indians,* watercolor by Forrest Kirkland, July 1937. Courtesy of the Texas Archaeological Research Laboratory, University of Texas at Austin, TMM 2261-23.

CHAPTER 1
Foraging Religion
Ancient Crossings and Mobile Niches,
9200 BCE–1100 BCE

About 11,100 years ago a group of hunter-gatherers took time out from catching turtles and sewing hides to stand around an oval hole in the dirt under an overhanging rock near a riverbank about eighteen miles upstream from what is now Waco, Texas. They came to express grief and find hope. As the mourners looked down on two lifeless bodies, both with their knees flexed and facing the same direction, they used their available cultural tools, material objects, and ritual performance to confront "metaphysical anguish."[1] It wasn't the quotidian worries that occupied most of their time and labor—finding food and seeking shelter—but a particular form of anxiety that has shaken and inspired humans for thousands of years. Maybe some of the graveside group secretly entertained irreverent thoughts—"I never liked them anyway"—or got distracted during the ritual by mundane matters—"The fire needs more wood." But by that relatively late moment in human history, they would have long had the cognitive capacity to worry about the big questions that such moments can prompt, including "What happens after death?" Without romanticizing or denigrating those foragers, I see no reason to presume—as some do—that humans would have to await the great prophets and sages of Israel, China, and India for the ritual participants to have formulated even bigger questions, such as "Why do bad things happen?" Or perhaps, with a flash of realization that I exist and I know it, even generated nagging queries about meaning: "Why are we here? How did all this come to be?"[2]

Don't get me wrong. Those foragers didn't hang framed theology diplomas on that rock shelter wall. They didn't codify their answers to such worrisome questions in doctrinal treatises. In fact, those concerns might not have bubbled to the surface of consciousness for any of them that day. But considering the special objects they placed in the carefully prepared grave, it certainly seems they had ways of answering the big questions, including by telling stories about the deceased's postmortem journey and by modifying objects and performing rituals that helped them remember and transmit the group's views about its shared purpose, future destiny, and ancient origin.

So what *was* their origin? And what happened before they appeared? Zooming out to get the widest angle of vision on that rock shelter community, what happened before the peopling of the hemisphere, before the earliest inhabitants created an eco-cultural niche that called for ritualized burials, before those ancient devotees transformed the landscape of that river valley by digging holes for graves?

Before Metaphysical Anguish

We can start that long history by considering the hole in the dirt. If you went there today to dig another hole for another burial, the soil would be mostly black. That's because you would literally only be scratching the surface. That dark dirt is the uppermost layer. Scholars who surveyed the rock shelter called it Stratum 14. There they found traces of nineteenth- and twentieth-century locals who left artifacts from a very different eco-cultural niche: bicycle spoke bolts, metal tobacco cans, and rifle firing pins.[3] The dirt farther down at Stratum 5, where excavators found the double burial that dates to 11,100 years ago, is mostly red clay. A bit lower than that on Stratum 3 rests the earliest layer with evidence of human occupation, dating to 13,200 years ago, where there are the remains of a large (and extinct) species of turtle, whose bones had been carefully arranged in the yellow clay. And at the deepest level of the rock shelter, on Stratum 1, there is a fine, dark red sand that washed there when the river flooded, though only nonhuman animals were around to notice.

Actually, our species, *Homo sapiens sapiens,* wasn't around to notice most of the history of that place, the earth, or the universe. How you recount the story of the long past varies depending on how you think about the passage of time.

Some religious stories say before human emergence and metaphysical anguish the gods or spirits were setting the stage for their plan to unfold. So religious traditions have their own long histories and chronological divisions. Consider three examples. Christians borrow the Jewish creation story from the Hebrew Bible—God created the heavens and the earth out of "a formless void" (Genesis 1:1–2)—and their calendar starts with Jesus. All time is measured as before or after his appearance (AD, from the Latin for "year of our Lord"). The Islamic creation account shares much with the Christian one (Qur'an 2:29, 2:117, 35:1), though Muslims begin their spiritual timetable more than six centuries later, the year of Muhammad's journey from Mecca to Medina (AH, in the year of the Hijra). Buddhists, who don't believe in a personal creator of the universe, either sidestep questions about creation or retell earlier Indian myths about immense cycles of existence, and their followers start the religious clock about five centuries before the Christian calendar (BE, or the Buddhist Era).[4] In one way or another, the storyline of many religious myths concerns the unfolding of a meaningful sacred cosmos that reserves a special place for humans.

The natural scientists' narrative, on the other hand, recounts how natural forces have driven the universe's initial surge, continuing expansion, and increasing complexity.[5] During that vast time before humans emerged to worry and wonder, the universe seemed quite indifferent to the possibility of such surprisingly inquisitive and oddly anguished life-forms. If the mythic gods greeted the arrival of humans and our capacity for engaging the transcendent with a knowing nod of approval, the scientific story of the universe, with its recounting of more than 100 billion galaxies, offers no more than a cosmic shrug. *Homo sapiens* appeared very late in the history of the cosmos and the earth, long after the universe began. Most narrators of cosmological time use an inconspicuously sad metaphor from the post–World War II era to describe the origin point, a term coined by an English astronomer only three years after the US dropped two atomic bombs on Japan: he told a BBC radio audience that some believe the universe "was created in a big bang."[6] Within a second of that event 13.7 billion years ago, the universe's cooling and expanding began, even if it was not cool enough for atoms of hydrogen and helium to form until about 300,000 years later. The first stars appeared about 12 billion years ago, but the next major episode in the cosmic story only happened about 4.6 billion years ago, when earth and our solar system appeared. Using mitochondrial DNA evidence, some scientists have proposed that all life on earth came from a hypothetical last universal common ancestor that lived about 3.5 to 3.8 billion years ago. The first organism with more than one cell emerged 600 million years ago, and the branches of chimp and human family trees can be traced to a shared ancestor about

6 million years ago. The continents as we know them only formed about 200 million years ago, when the supercontinent Pangaea broke apart and North America appeared, though that landmass looked quite different as recently as 75 million years ago. But North America still doesn't enter the story, since all the skeletal remains found in the Americas are anatomically modern *Homo sapiens.*[7] Evidence for the first member of our genus, *Homo habilis,* which appeared about 2.5 million years ago, and for our other relatives—*Homo erectus, Homo heidelbergensis,* and *Homo neanderthalensis*—has all been found outside the Americas, although all non-Africans in the Western Hemisphere retain genetic marks of human interbreeding with Neanderthals 50,000 to 60,000 years ago.[8] In any case, genetic analysis suggests that those we now call human emerged at least 150,000 years ago from a human ancestor in Africa.

The scale of that long history can be difficult to fathom, so some scientists have used the helpful strategy of imagining the 13-billion-year history of the universe as compressed into thirteen years.[9] If the universe had begun thirteen years ago, the earth would have existed for about five years. Multicelled organisms would have been around for seven months. Hominines—big-brained primates like chimps, gorillas, and early humans—would have existed for three days and *Homo sapiens,* with our capacity for religion, for only about fifty-three minutes. (And since we're interested in American religious history, we might add that about five or six seconds ago Thomas Jefferson would have penned the Declaration of Independence, with its appeal to citizens' "inalienable rights" endowed by "Nature's God.")

In both cosmological narratives, the sacred plan story and the cosmic shrug tale, humans have some significance, even if their value is relative to a grander purpose, such as divine will or evolutionary advantage. "Where were you when I laid the foundation of the earth?" God asks Job in the Hebrew Bible after he questioned ultimate meaning and complained about evil (Job 38:4).[10] In the end, Job comes to see God's point: no, he wasn't around then. So, he apologizes and reaffirms the meaning of things: "I know that you can do all things, and that no purpose of yours can be thwarted." (Job 42:2). Some Jewish, Christian, and Muslim environmental ethicists have worried that their traditions make humans too central by misreading scriptural passages about "dominion" over the earth to mean that environmental destruction is divinely sanctioned. But in most ways monotheistic traditions have imagined humans as significant while also setting limits on anthropocentrism. Scientific accounts decenter humans even more, though some proponents of long history argue that doesn't mean the narrative has no coherent plot or that humans aren't noteworthy: One scholar proposed that "intelligent, networked life forms such as ourselves that can adapt through collective learning may be extraordinarily rare," and modern human societies "arise close to the limit of our universe's capacity to generate complexity."[11]

Even if it might be reassuring to imagine humans as nature's finest accomplishment or the divine's loftiest creatures, a little decentering might help at the start of this account of religion in the lands that became America. *Homo sapiens* are the story's inevitable protagonists, but we can't lose sight of humanity's place in the wider biosphere. It's fine to center the Americas, the inevitable focus of a story about US religion, but we shouldn't overlook the long history of global interconnections and the African starting place for all stories of human beginnings. It's important to recognize dwelling—*Homo sapiens'* modifying of the environment to create eco-cultural niches—but not to the extent that we forget crossing also has been as important a part of human history, including the first dispersions from Africa.[12]

The Late Pleistocene Peopling of the Americas

Scientists disagree about the date of *Homo sapiens'* first migrations out of Africa, though most think it was more than 100,000 years ago. The journeys that led to permanent populations began at least 60,000 years ago as modern humans spread to Europe, Eurasia, and East Asia.[13] Migrants headed toward North and South America by at least 30,000 years ago. That means during the Late Pleistocene Epoch (2 million to 11,700 years ago) in geologic time, or the Upper Paleolithic Period (40,000 to 10,000 years ago) in terms of cultural change. But when did they leave and how did they travel? The old scholarly account, called the "Clovis First Model" for the New Mexican town where archaeologists found biface spear points in 1932, proposed that a single group of tundra-dwelling big game hunters from Asia walked across the land bridge that connected Siberia to Alaska. The sites in New Mexico were about 13,000 years old, and archaeologists found similar stone hunting tools across the continent. So, scholars had their origin story: the Clovis people came first. They then spread their culture: Clovis artifacts have been found in the forty-eight lower states as well as Canada, Mexico, Costa Rica, Guatemala, and northern South America.[14]

But specialists in a variety of fields started to challenge this narrative. Population geneticists, who trace the circulation of mitochondrial DNA and Y chromosomes, said the date of first settlement couldn't have been more recent than 15,000 years ago, and maybe thousands of years before that.[15] Linguists reasoned that for 1,000 languages and 150 language families to appear in the Americas by 1492 the first entry into the hemisphere must have been pre-Clovis. The linguistic diversity also suggests more than one migrant stream. There is a connection to languages from southeastern Asia and Near Oceania.[16] Some Siberian transcontinental migrants, whose ancestors originated farther south in Asia, might have spoken a language that was ancestral to modern Amerind languages; other migrants probably brought other language families, including Eskimo-Aleut and Na-Dene.[17] Climatologists joined the conversation. They proposed that the first migrations could have started as early as 25,000 years ago, when gradual warming began, and suggested the melting of the North American ice sheets that stretched as far south as Cincinnati happened earlier than we thought, perhaps about 17,000 years ago.[18] Some final evidence—from stones and bones rather than genes and glaciers—led archaeologists to change their minds: researchers unearthed objects dated before Clovis culture.[19] Paisley Caves in Oregon included signs of human habitation about 14,000 years ago, and the oldest artifacts at Buttermilk Creek in central Texas, not far from the rock shelter burial, were 16,000 years old.[20] Evidence from South America was as exciting, and even more perplexing: on a creek bank at Monte Verde in southern Chile, archaeologists found a long, hide-roof dwelling with artifacts that dated to 14,800 years ago, predating Clovis by more than one thousand years.[21] There were uniface pebble tools but no Clovis biface points. That meant the Monte Verde community was probably a distinct culture that settled in South America before the Clovis hunters spread their tool-making culture in North America.

Scholars still debate the evidence from Monte Verde, but many find the excavations from the southernmost reaches of the hemisphere convincing. In other words, if you accept the dating of Monte Verde and still want to hold on to the Clovis First story you have problems.[22] You need to explain how Siberian hunters walked 8,000 miles down the hemisphere in a relatively short period of time. You could presume other modes of transportation and suggest that Paleolithic mariners traveled in boats down the Pacific coast "kelp highway," eating seaweed and hunting seals along the way.[23] The discovery of a 13,000-year-old femur on an island off the California coast supports that explanation.[24] But you still have to assume a much earlier entry point into the Americas. As one scholar put it, "You've got people in South America at the same time as Clovis, and the only way they could have gotten there that fast is if they transported like 'Star Trek.'"[25]

If we exclude God's providential activity from our historical explanations, we probably also should rule out Captain Kirk's technological wizardry, so that leaves an exciting but still developing story of the peopling of the Americas. Or, actually, multiple competing stories. Scientists tell stories of ancient migrant journeys. Christians have origin stories, both the biblical one about Yahweh creating heaven and earth in seven days and the textbook one about Europeans "discovering" the hemisphere in 1492. Contemporary Indigenous Peoples have origin stories too, like the Potawatomi tale explaining how humans emerged when Ki-ji Man-i-to waw quin, the Creator, called a great council of the spirits before making two-legged creatures who had "the soul of the Divine shining in their faces."[26] A Cree-Métis archaeologist welcomes both ancestral stories and excavated evidence, "the histories held in the land," and celebrates the elongated scholarly timelines as a recovery of "the deep Indigenous past."[27] Other Native narrators challenge scholarly tales, as with Lipan Apache elders who say "the Bering Strait story is wrong," and Indigenous scholars who say researchers' methods are wrong, like the Dakota anthropologist who laments geneticists' "ethical lapses," their insensitivity to the sacred worldviews and ancestral values of the peoples they study.[28] Another Native scholar, a Potawatomi historian who acknowledges the competing stories—including those his grandmother told—avoids trying to reconcile them and urges a generous respect for diverse accounts: "we are all entitled to our stories, particularly regarding our origins and creation."[29]

That seems right. Generosity toward diverse stories seems helpful, and if you prefer scientific accounts of the peopling of the Americas, humility seems indispensable too, since new findings continually force interpreters to rethink things. With those cautions in mind, what does the best evidence suggest? Most scholars think the earliest inhabitants of the Americas hailed from eastern Asia and ultimately descended from a population of modern humans who dispersed from Africa by 60,000 years ago and appeared in central Asia by 45,000 years ago.[30] About 30,000 years ago, Siberian hunter-gatherers started their eastern trek toward Beringia, the landmass that connected eastern Asia and western Alaska. Scholars aren't sure when and how humans first arrived in the Western Hemisphere, since new research keeps pushing back the date of initial entry. There are now intriguing pre-Clovis sites, including Miles Point in Maryland (31,000–25,000 years ago), Cactus Hill in Virginia (18,400–17,100 years ago), and Cooper's Ferry in Idaho (16,560–15,280 years ago).[31] And the discovery of preserved human footprints in New Mexico's White Sands National Park suggests mammoth-hunting humans were already in southwestern North America 23,000 to 21,000 years

Figure 4. Footprints found in White Sands National Park dated to 23,000 to 21,000 years ago. Courtesy of the National Park Service.

ago, during the Last Glacial Maximum, when continental ice sheets prevented migration from Asia (fig. 4).[32] But how and when did they get there? A statistical model that uses archaeological data along with genetic and climatic evidence proposes an explanation: people were present in North America before and during the peak of the Ice Age (26,500 to 19,000 years ago), even if widespread occupation began during a period of abrupt warming between 14,700 and 12,900 years ago.[33] The earliest Pleistocene explorers probably traveled along the Pacific coast, though later migrants also could have walked down an interior corridor.[34] By 15,000 years ago—and maybe earlier—there were signs of human habitation in the full expanse of the Americas.

As researchers trace the migratory paths that converge at sites from southern California's Channel Islands to eastern Maryland's continental shelf, many accept the Pacific coastal route as most likely, but some propose other entry routes and migrant streams (fig. 5).[35] Some say itinerants came from Iberia before they came from Siberia. This controversial account, which geneticists challenge, suggests the first Americans came from southwestern Europe, traveling along the Atlantic ice sheets about 19,000 and 23,000 years ago.[36] If so, we would expect to find human habitation from the period along the eastern coast, and in the Chesapeake Bay region archaeologists did uncover a spear point near a mastodon tusk not

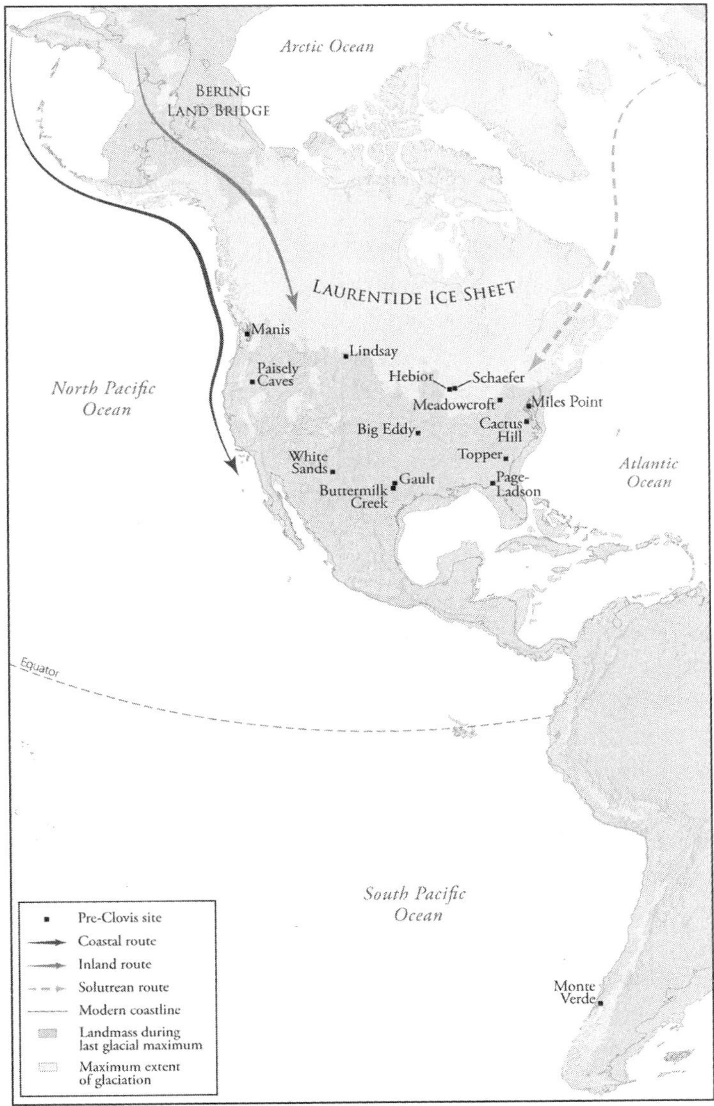

Figure 5. Map of possible entry routes and early sites. Beehive Mapping.

far from Jamestown, Virginia, where Native Peoples would encounter British colonists in the seventeenth century.[37] While some don't rule out a northern Atlantic journey, others say island-hopping seafarers also could have traversed the southern Pacific.[38] Whichever story of Paleolithic crossings eventually wins out, it appears multiple peoples came at different times.[39] Migration and diversity, it seems, have been part of the story for as long as there have been humans in the Americas.

Metaphysical Anguish and Ancient Religion

Tracing the possible migrant routes into the Americas provides some sense of the early pathways, but what about the eco-cultural niches that itinerants inherited, transported, and created?[40] Some traces of cultural practices, unearthed signs of humans intentionally transforming the environment, can be minuscule. At Texas's Gault site archaeologists found tiny geometric patterns and animal shapes on small incised limestones. That representational art, dating to about 13,000 years ago, shows that even minute cultural traces can be exhilarating if you're trying to understand the distant past. You could encounter another minute trace if you visited Blackwater Draw, a site southwest of Clovis, New Mexico, which has an excavated mammoth tusk on display.[41] If you pressed your face to the glass case, you would notice that the 10,000-year-old tusk has a few parallel lines scratched onto it. Those incised grooves are indisputable marks of intentional cultural activity, a decorative flourish.[42] They signal that the ancient inhabitants of that area of eastern New Mexico had been busy imagining their world and transforming their niche.

Yet not all intentional activity that imagines and transforms the environment is religious. We can confidently say that *culture* had emerged by the time those hunter-gatherers used a sharp-edged tool to decorate that tusk—or made arrow points and cooking utensils. The intriguing material evidence might be interpreted as *technology* or *art,* but it doesn't clearly signal that *religion* had emerged. So when did religion emerge historically? Framed that way, the question is difficult, even impossible, to answer, even for those who specialize in studying humanity's distant past. There is no unambivalent material evidence of a single historical starting point. Perhaps our long history of religion can have a different kind of beginning, one that starts by answering two other questions.[43] First, what are the *conditions* for the appearance of what we're calling religion? Second, when in the history of the territory that became America can we first find reliable *evidence* of those conditions in the archaeological record?

What Are the Conditions for the Emergence of Religion?

Those who get paid to teach about religion can't agree what the term means, and I'm not going to settle the long-standing debate here.[44] But I can say a little about how I'm using the term. Religious action is always mediated by technology and institutions, constrained by human biology and the local ecology, and enacted with collectively transmitted but creatively appropriated cultural resources such as figurative language, ceremonial artifacts, and ritual practices. What does that mean for when we start our story? It seems reasonable to assume that the historical emergence of religion required certain biological capacities, environmental conditions, and social forms; most important, it required certain cognitive and affective capacities—and their neural correlates in the brain.[45] The surviving material evidence can't settle when those conditions first emerged or whether they arose abruptly or gradually. But we can try to identify some of those capacities. Religions label and shape the emotions that frame experience, including valued "transformative experiences," by providing devotees with a linguistic network of assertions and associations that present an authoritative picture of the way the world is and the way it should be. That picture has implications for identity, for how individuals and groups understand who they are. But religion involves doing as well as feeling and believing. Religious communities make signifying artifacts, patterned sounds, and meaningful gestures that enable their always contested but mostly shared picture of the world to be remembered, enacted, and transmitted.[46] Those practices—ritual performance, material creativity, and moral action—depend on other emergent capacities: for example, empathy (the ability to detect what others feel) and imitation (the ability to do what others do). Religion also presupposes devotees can cooperate closely and communicate skillfully in extrafamilial groups, so that social institutions can circulate moral guidelines and ritual practices within (and beyond) the group and pass them down the generations, although it doesn't require "ultrasociability," the ability to cooperate in huge groups of genetically unrelated individuals.[47]

However, if I'm right that religion is about crossing and dwelling—or routes and roots—and that we can distinguish it from other cultural practices like art, technology, or science by devotees' appeal to *suprahuman forces* (spirits or gods) and their imagining of an *ultimate horizon* (an ideal condition or a final destination), then two other cognitive processes are also crucial.[48] First, religions ask and answer big questions: for example, not When was I born? but How did all things begin? and What happens when we die? The religious imagine ultimate beginnings and endings, a chronologically or geographically distant threshold of human flourishing beyond the here and now, and that requires the capacity for complex spatial and temporal representation. For religious practice, humans must have what some have called a "higher order consciousness."[49] They have to be able to imagine the space beyond the body's immediate surroundings and the group's eco-cultural niche and to project a time before and after the particular moment.[50] Those capacities, in turn, have neural correlates in the brain: they involve the basal ganglia, the frontal cortex, and the cerebellum, areas of the brain most responsible for representing temporal intervals, especially the distant past and the imagined future. Those orienting mechanisms also involve the parietal neocortex for the mapping of space around the embodied individual, and, more important for religious practice, the hippocampus and adjacent cortical and subcortical structures that map long distances beyond the immediate environment, including imagined places beyond the individual's multisensorial experience. The neural networks in those regions of the brain enable the devout to conceptualize distant centers, holy sites like Mecca or Jerusalem, and, even more important, to imagine an ultimate horizon of human life, a threshold beyond this world and after their death, where they might achieve a state of being like nirvana or travel to a subterranean or celestial place like heaven.[51]

With those orienting capacities we see most of the conditions for religion's emergence, but there's one more. The religious also appeal to suprahuman forces or beings by employing tropes, figurative or nonliteral language, including metaphor, simile, metonymy, narrative, and symbol. Religions, in other words, provide devotees with *figurative tools* for making and remaking imagined worlds. Playfully repurposing a colloquial expression, we might say the religious imaginatively use tropes to "figure out" themselves and the world around them.[52] Others have made a similar point. Some have proposed that "symbolic behavior" is the key criterion for deciding when "modern human behavior" began, and others have taken that approach as they engage the related question of when religion began.[53] Two anthropologists, for example, have suggested that the evolution of "the capacity to think and communicate symbolically" led to the generation of "something like a religious predisposition," because symbolization led to the tendency to seek "systemic relationships that are hidden behind surface appearances" and "the tendency to give narrative explanations of the world."[54] Narrative is important, yet as we ponder when to begin this account, focusing on storytelling can be limiting because we have little evidence about modern humans' earliest narratives. And other figurative processes seem just as important for religious practice—and somewhat easier to detect in the archaeological record.

So it's helpful to focus instead on the more fundamental capacity that seems to be at work in religion's nonliteral language usage, including in metaphor, simile, metonymy, and symbol: the capacity for analogical reasoning. Scientists who study thinking describe this capacity in slightly different ways. Some propose that every concept is a "tightly packed bundle of analogies," and thinking analogically involves leaping from one "analogy bundle" to another.[55] Others delineate different "cognitive domains," or areas of knowledge, and in those terms religious practice seems to require the ability to cross domains and associate unlike things. Christians, for example, say Jesus is the Lamb (*amnos*) of God and, thereby, move between how they think about animals and how they think about humans, imagining Jesus as a sacrificial offering. Buddhists draw on medical analogies to interpret the Buddha as the Great Physician (*bhisakka*) who diagnoses and cures spiritual maladies. Muslims declare that Muhammad is the Seal (*khātam*) of the Prophets and, thereby, they move between how they think about documents and how they think about humans, imagining Muhammad as a waxy sealant that closes and authenticates a prophetic lineage.[56] Scientists aren't sure how analogical reasoning works or how the brain's neural networks interact, but most agree that the prefrontal cortex (PFC) is crucial.[57] Some research even suggests that activation of PFC neurons involved in visuospatial reasoning and analogical reasoning—both important for religion—overlap.[58] Whatever further research shows, it seems religion requires not only neural compasses and biological clocks but also the capacity to speak and act as if something—for example, a lamb, or anything else in the mundane world's literal referents—can be something else too. A lamb sometimes can be just a lamb; but analogical artifacts, ritual performance, and transmitted stories can also cross cognitive domains. The devout can suggest that a man was sacrificially slaughtered like a literal lamb: Jesus is the *Lamb of God.* Followers can say that a man without medical training provided the cure they sought: Buddha is the *Great Physician.* The pious can suggest that a man was a waxy sealant on an important document: Muhammad is the *Seal of the Prophets.* Elaborate doctrinal systems, with intricate interlocking claims about what the metaphors mean, need not be present, of course, but when humans can say things like that—and enact them in ritual, materialize them in objects, recount them in narrative, and transmit them in institutions—they can be religious.[59]

The First Signs of Religion in the Archaeological Record

When do we first see evidence of that figurative capacity—along with the other cognitive, ecological, and social conditions for religion's emergence? We can't identify the exact moment when "cognitive fluidity," or domain crossing, first appeared. Until recent findings changed the chronology, it had been common to point to grave goods, personal adornment, and cave art in the Upper Paleolithic Period and argue for a "symbolic explosion" between 40,000 and 50,000 years ago: "If we hoped to find evidence in the archaeological record for the first appearance of the human soul," one scholar suggested, "this would be the place for it."[60] While the capacity for religion had emerged by then, before the dispersals from Africa, a few earlier behavioral milestones widen the scope to other *Homo* species and push back the timetable hundreds of thousands of years. Hominines applied natural pigment to decorate bodies and caves, and also used red ochre in the disposal of remains, as early as 300,000 years ago, and some date "the first incontestable signs of symbolic thought" to then. In a *Homo heidelbergensis* burial in a Spanish sinkhole, excavators found a funerary gift—a pink hand axe—with the remains. Even more signs of "metaphysical anguish" in more purposeful burials appear somewhat later, in Neanderthal and *Homo sapiens* graves in Europe and central Asia a little less than 100,000 years ago.[61] Scholars of the distant past find "symbolically mediated communication" in the incised ochre, shell beads, and painted images in Blombos Cave on the western cape of South Africa from 75,000 years ago.[62]

So there is evidence of nonliteral communication and action quite early, and the excavated traces of religion really start to accumulate in the archaeological record after 40,000 years ago. By 30,000 years ago, *Homo sapiens* were the only surviving member of the wider human family, and their symbolic communication, moral guidelines, and ritual action had helped strengthen the bonds of small hunter-gatherer bands and probably even afforded them an evolutionary advantage.[63] They had built eco-cultural niches in varied ecological settings in Africa, Europe, and Asia that allowed for greater innovation and cooperation than other primates. We could start the story of *Homo sapiens'* religion, or full-blown metaphysical anguish, at a number of sites around the world after that moment of cultural change. On the plains of Russia the Sunghir children rest in a long shallow grave that dates to about 26,000 years ago: a boy and girl covered with red ochre, or hematite, the natural pigment also found at Blombos and other ancient burial sites, and adorned with an extraordinary array of grave goods, including 5,000 perforated ivory beads, hundreds of perforated fox teeth, and ivory animal carvings.[64] The tale could start closer to the present, in southern Turkey with 11,600-year-old Göbekli Tepe, an early example of monumental architecture, a structure of concentric circles that included carved representations of animals on its impressive stone pillars.[65] Or there is the 12,000-year-old grave of an elderly woman at Hilazon Tachtit. That funerary cave is about eight miles from the Mediterranean in northern Israel, where excavators found evidence of ritual feasting and a large number of grave goods, not only red ochre but also fifty complete tortoise carapaces and the parts of local and rare animals, including a wild boar, an eagle, and a leopard. In fact, that woman's elaborate grave, some suggest, represents one of the earliest burials of a shaman, a ritual specialist responsible for healing the ill and communicating with nonterrestrial worlds.[66] So the broader narrative of global religion begins at those places and at other African, European, and Asian sites in the distant past.

But where do we start the story of religion in the lands that became the United States? The earliest sites testify to human habitation and suggest a diversity of ethnic origins and a spectrum of foraging behaviors. Excavations have yielded few clues, however, about the spiritual life of the earliest inhabitants.[67] Religious practice might have begun earlier—and the red pigment on the remains of the Anzick infant (12,707 cal yr BP or 10,807 BCE) in Montana suggests symbolic behavior—but archaeologists have not unearthed enough to make confident interpretations.[68] The clearest signs of religion's analogical reasoning and spatiotemporal orientation appear a little later, toward the end of the first Ice Age, in gravesites that date to the period of climatic volatility, species extinction, and niche adaptations during the transition from Pleistocene Paleoindian environments to Holocene Archaic habitats.[69]

Mortuary practices during this transitional period, especially around 11,000 years ago (or 9250 BCE), provide the best place to look for our narrative's starting point because we have a number of graves from that time, and they often provide evidence of the figurative action and cosmic mapping that eases metaphysical anguish. Consider Arch Lake Woman, whose interred remains suggest that red ochre might have been sprinkled over her corpse during a burial ceremony.[70] She was between the ages of seventeen and twenty-one when mourners laid her to rest in New Mexico about 11,260 years ago, making her grave among the earliest scholars have found.[71] Yet she was buried with only a few ornamental and symbolic objects—a beaded necklace, a thin bone tool, and some other beads—so there aren't many clear signs of religion's figurative imagination and spatial orientation at work. Archaeologists have excavated other Paleoindian burial sites with intriguing grave goods in diverse eco-cultural niches—including incised and ochre-covered antler shafts in two infant burials in Alaska's Upward Sun River site; elk teeth in the grave of a twenty-five-year-old woman at Gordon Creek in Colorado; a badger bone in the Buhl female burial on the Snake River Plain in Idaho;

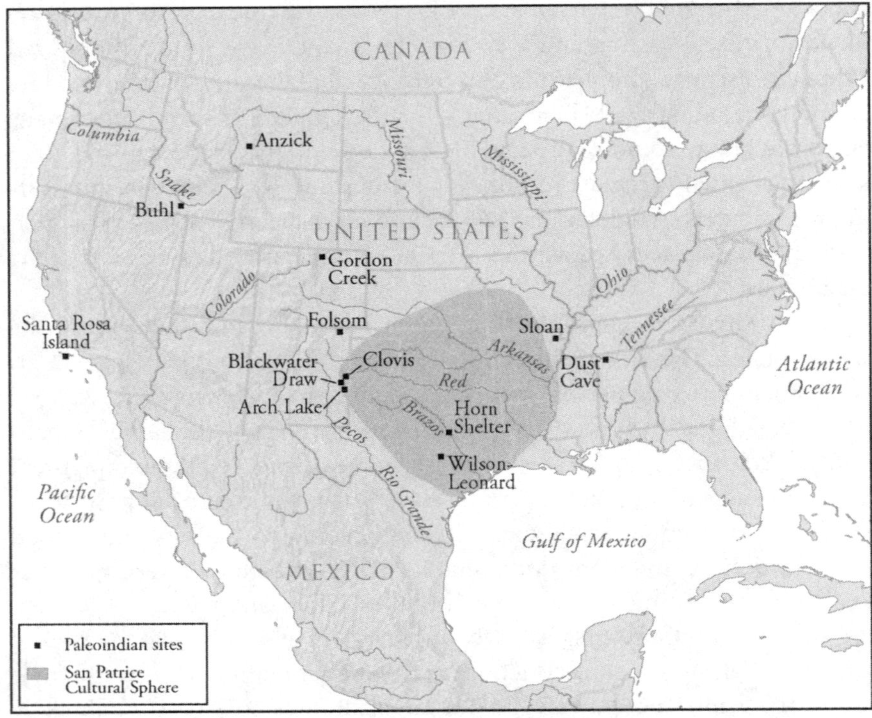

Figure 6. The Horn Shelter and other Paleoindian sites. Beehive Mapping.

and a shark's tooth around the neck of a female skeleton at the Wilson-Leonard site in Texas's Brushy Creek Valley.[72] Those sites tell us about memorial practices during this transitional period, including about the use of animal symbolism. But the Texas rock shelter this chapter opened with stands out for the abundance and clarity of its material evidence. So that's where our story starts (fig. 6).

A Shaman's Burial along the Brazos

We can see the clearest evidence of the figurative imagination and other features of religion at that shelter overlooking a bend in the Brazos River.[73] The site, called Horn Shelter No. 2, is one of the earliest burials excavated in the lands that became America, and it's the Paleoindian grave with the largest number of mortuary goods, more than 100 objects. Two avocational archaeologists excavated it in 1970 on property owned by Herman (1919–2007) and Adeline Horn (1925–2006), a Baptist couple who had farmed that land in Bosque County. There excavators discovered the interred remains of a 5′4″ adult male (called Burial 1 or Horn Shelter Man) and a 4′ girl (called Burial 2 or Horn Shelter Girl), which date to about 11,100 years ago, the end of the last Ice Age in North America (11,158 cal yr BP or 9208 BCE).[74]

Because this burial is the starting point for our story, we need to know more about what the excavators found and what it means. They discovered that the hunting-gathering community who used the shelter had placed the deceased beside each other, with the girl behind, and aligned them so they both faced westward and toward the setting sun. Both rested on their left side with knees flexed, and flat limestone slabs covered their torsos. Like the woman buried in Idaho about 500 years later, the ten- to eleven-year-old girl, who still had a baby tooth but also osteological features that appear at puberty, had only a bone needle nearby, suggesting she probably had sewn hides or fibers. Yet survivors placed many objects on and around the male, who was between thirty-seven and forty-four years old. This late Paleoindian grave contained about eighty small beads made of Gulf Coast snail shells, and decorative beads lay near his arm, head, and neck. Three perforated coyote tooth pendants also rested near his neck, suggesting they had been strung on a necklace or fastened to his clothing. Clustered under or touching his head, excavators found some used stone and bone tools. Near his waist, and apparently originally in a bundle, were several objects, including a nodule of red ochre that most likely had been used as pigment to mark bodies and natural surfaces and, as at other ancient sites, to ritually sprinkle over the dead. That nodule showed signs of use: both of its flat sides had fine straight indentations, suggesting that the deceased—or someone else—had scraped off small powdered grains of red ochre.[75] Three carefully arranged turtle shells (*Terrapene ornate*) formed an enclosure under Horn Shelter Man's head, with "the bottom shell upside down and the other two nested within each other in the opposite direction."[76] Two other carapaces from the ornate box turtle rested nearby: one covered his face and another, upside down under his pelvis, contained two shell beads and an antler fragment. The interior surface of two turtle shells showed residue of red pigment, as did the sandstone abrader and deer bone stylus in the bundle. Adding more animal species to the array of grave gifts—and more information for an interpretation—inside his mouth cavity lay the claw of a badger and the talon of a hawk.

What can these evidentiary fragments reveal about these foraging Paleoindians? The gravesite offers several hints about culture and ethnicity. The San Patrice projectile points found in the fifth level disclose their cultural affiliation. Those stone tools suggest the Horn Shelter community shared technologies and practices with other groups within a cultural sphere that stretched from the southern plains to the eastern woodlands, from the San Patrice heartland in eastern Texas and Louisiana and east into Mississippi, north into Arkansas and Missouri, and west into Oklahoma and western Texas. Scientists studying the remains of the San Patrice people in central Texas suggest the Horn Shelter Man and Girl might have been genetically distinct from other Indigenous groups in the hemisphere and contemporary American Indians. Like some other Paleoindians—Arch Lake Woman and Spirit Cave Man—they might have had more in common with the peoples of Eastern Polynesia and the Ainu of Japan.[77] So they offer intriguing hints of even greater diversity among early residents of the lands that became America.[78]

But who were those two members of that small San Patrice community? Horn Shelter Girl might not have been related to the man, and that raises questions about her presence. Why was she buried beside him? Who was she? The quantity, significance, and rarity of objects associated with a person, in a grave or other space, reveal something about social status and spiritual standing.[79] The girl had only a bone needle. The older man, on the other hand, was abundantly adorned with special things, some of them not found in the local environment. That *symbolic surplus,* large quantities of culturally significant exotic objects, signals his higher status.

To be more specific, the grave objects suggest he was a medicine man or shaman, the community's ritual specialist, who was responsible for healing the ill, divining the future, communicating with spirits, and traveling between cosmic realms. The bundle by his waist seems to be a shamanic tool kit: the stains on the inside of the two turtle shells indicate that the carapaces were used as bowls, so that the ritual specialist used the sandstone abrader to grind the ochre and the spatula-like tip of the deer bone stylus to apply it. He probably applied the red ochre in burials, flaking it over the corpse. And hematite had other uses. It was applied to the skin, ingested for healing, and used for body painting and tattooing. The sharp biface point and coyote tooth in the bundle hints that Horn Shelter Man might have ritually incised and marked bodies—to apply medicine, release blood, decorate skin, commemorate a life cycle transition, or identify a spiritual kinship affiliation. The sonorous elements of religious practice are often silenced in the archaeological record—it's difficult to know which surviving objects might have been used to produce patterned sound—but chanting, dancing, and drumming also might have been an important part of the holy man's performative role. Other evidence—an analysis of his bones—offers hints about that role. His "robust hands and lower arms" might have come from tool making or another repetitive utilitarian task, or, like later ritual specialists, he could have spent long hours drumming at healing rites or community celebrations.

So the strength of Horn Shelter Man's forearm, together with the red ochre nodule and associated ritual implements, gives us reason to think "he may have been a healer or a shaman."[80] It seems likely he served as the community's spiritual leader and health care specialist—and maybe as philosopher, educator, historian, therapist, and entertainer too. The community would have come to him when things went wrong, seeking explanation and remedy, and asking him to serve as their intermediary between this and other worlds. Seeking aid from animal spirit guides, and perhaps entranced by emotionally intense rituals, he would have been transported to other cosmic realms to communicate with spirits. Given all those important social roles, perhaps it's not surprising the respected man's passing evoked elaborate commemoration and warranted symbolic surplus.

But what about Horn Shelter Girl, who stood on the threshold between childhood and adulthood? Did those gathered for the burial view the shaman's female companion as his selected mate? Was she a relative? Since we have evidence of female shamans in that period, could she have been an apprentice or co-worker, someone learning the shamanic craft or assisting at ritual performances? And there's another possibility: was she another burial offering that marked his social status, even though there's no evidence she died from trauma? "It is possible," one interpreter suggests, "that she was sacrificed and placed in the grave, perhaps as someone to help in the next world, after death."[81] Whichever interpretation wins out in the end, the gravesite provides some clues about the foraging niche and their place in it.

This Horn Shelter burial also offers hints about crossings—across life stages and cosmic realms as well as land and water. The projectile points and other artifacts suggest terrestrial and aquatic travel, including *micro-scale mobility* (the lived world of daily life), *mesoscale mobility* (trips taken every few months or years), and *macroscale mobility* (special trips taken only every few years or once in a generation).[82] The San Patrice people in Texas quarried stone for their tools nearby in Edwards Plateau, and they moved up and down the region now and again to find other resources they needed, including red ochre. They also took occasional round-trip journeys for other cultural motives—to maintain interband relations and secure special materials for communal rituals. The Horn Shelter community traded with similar groups in Oklahoma, and, like other San Patrice people, once in a while they also might have traveled hundreds of miles north to meet others at Big Eddy, a site in Missouri.[83] The grave goods also point to regular and intermittent aquatic travel that extended the boundaries of that lived world. Those Gulf Coast shells in the grave demonstrate the regional circulation of things, practices, and people up and down the 1,000-mile Brazos River Valley from New Mexico to Texas. The Horn Shelter's location on the longest watercourse in Texas made it an "important corridor of travel, social interaction, and information flow connecting the Gulf Coast and the Southern Plains."[84]

The burial site also shows evidence of spatial thinking that imagined an ultimate horizon, a final crossing place, and figurative thinking that crossed cognitive domains as it appealed to suprahuman beings. It suggests analogical rituals and artifacts—and implied symbols and myths—that incorporate spirits linked with animals like the turtle, badger, and hawk. Those animals probably played roles in stories told among San Patrice people, or at least those in the local area. Consider the turtle. One specialist in comparative mythology has identified two main story lines about the world's origin and destruction, and in the narrative system that extends to 40,000 years ago and spans Indigenous groups in Eurasia, Polynesia, and the Americas the turtle plays a few different cosmic roles.[85] In some story lines, for example, a turtle dives down beneath the primordial waters to bring up the earth. In other accounts, which are repeated later by some Indigenous Nations, the unstable earth rests on the back of a giant turtle.[86] Eastern Woodland Peoples like the Anishinaabe (Chippewa) and Haudenosaunee (Iroquois) even have imagined North America as "Turtle Island."[87] We can't know what role the turtle played in the stories that the San Patrice community told. And, of course, the gravesite turtle shells might have served some unknown utilitarian function, but a plausible interpretation that fits the material evidence—and what we know about other sites—suggests the animal referents played some mythic roles and functioned as "symbolic locatives," material or linguistic tropes that signaled a particular geographical and cosmological location.[88] In other words, the community's thinking about the spirits intertwined with their thinking about the cosmos, even if we cannot know all the details of their religious cartography. The Ainu, who imagined the land of the dead as lying in the West, have pictured the universe as having a horizontal and vertical plane, with the vertical sphere including six skies piled on top of one another, like layers of a cake.[89] Many Indigenous Peoples on the other side of the Pacific, in North America, have imagined a three-tiered universe, with travel across the sky after death leading to a final destination in the underworld, from which all things originally emerged.[90] If the Horn Shelter community made similar analogical connections—and the mortuary gifts suggest they did—it might have associated the zoomorphic grave objects with those different cosmic realms: the earth-burrowing badger with the underworld, the sky-soaring hawk with the celestial world, and the crawling, swimming, and burrowing turtle with both this world and the subterranean world from which the community came and hoped to return.

In any case, even if we can't confidently decode all the animal analogies or be sure that they function as "spirit emblems," the evidence demonstrates emotionally evocative, cognitively complex, and collectively performed ritual practice.[91] The carefully arranged grave demonstrates the survivors' concern about the deceased's final fate, their crossing of the threshold between life and death. The placement of so many objects to convey the deceased man's social standing and to equip him for the afterlife journey suggests that the mourners were interested in more than the hygienic disposal of remains. They could have casually dumped the corpses in a remote hole—and without the 100 grave objects, some of which originated hundreds of miles away—if waste disposal had been their concern. Further, those carefully stacked turtle carapaces served no utilitarian function, and other ancient burials from around the world also included symbolic use of shells: that 12,000-year-old shaman's grave in Israel contained carefully arranged turtle shells, as did another female shaman's grave in Germany that dates to about 7,500 years ago.[92] We can't confidently decipher the meaning of those zoomorphic grave objects in widely disparate places. Nor can we assume, without more evidence, that there was historical contact among those communities. But whatever turtles—and hawks and badgers—meant to mourners at the Horn Shelter burial, they probably served as metaphors, symbols, and mythic characters in the foraging community's figurative world. They were, we might say, "analogy bundles," a bit like the bundle containing red ochre at Horn Shelter Man's waist. Like the abrader and stylus used to crush and ritually apply the ochre, they were figurative tools. And with the abundant metaphorical adornments found in that grave—especially the turtle, badger, and hawk—we have the evidence we sought: we have early signs of religion in the lands that became America.

So this historical narrative doesn't begin in Plymouth or Jamestown. It begins more than nine thousand years earlier in the dirt beneath an overhanging rock in central Texas, far from the northern Atlantic coast.

Paleoindian to Archaic Forager Niches, 9300 BCE–8000 BCE

Fertile Crescent farmers halfway around the world soon would begin to plant seeds and build villages where residents would honor local ancestors and use agricultural symbols, but foraging religion continued among the San Patrice people in central Texas around 9200 BCE, when the area was cool, wet, and green. Graves again offer clues about how other Paleoindians used figurative tools to transform their habitats and craft imagined worlds during this transitional period.[93] About two hundred years after Horn Shelter Girl was interred, another San Patrice group in south central Texas dug an oval hole to carefully place the body of a young Paleoindian woman near a small stream at the Wilson-Leonard site.[94] Leanne (named for the nearby town of Leander) was also buried in a flexed position with a limestone slab covering her body. The mourners placed some grave goods: a worn stone tool for grinding food and a decorative necklace with a shark's tooth, which community members presumably retrieved or traded from along the Gulf Coast.

Other communities performed mortuary rites around this time and during the next thousand years in other eco-cultural niches across North America. Rock shelters continued to be important ritual spaces. Like the Horn Shelter couple, some of those interred Paleoindians faced their postmortem futures in the flexed position under the natural roof of a rock shelter, including an adult man in Spirit Cave in the Great Basin, an adult woman at the Modoc Rock Shelter in the Upper Midwest, and a five-year-old child at Dust Cave in the Southeast.[95] There are no signs of symbolic surplus at those burials of community members—just some clothing and textile bags—but the mortuary practices display and confront metaphysical anguish.

Even more elaborate communal strategies for dealing with the big questions can be found at a cemetery in the Mid-South, along the Cache River drainage in Arkansas not far from the Mississippi River. Confounding assumptions about itinerant Paleoindian foragers and heralding the shift to Archaic patterns, starting in about 8500 BCE the Dalton people at the Sloan site created the oldest cemetery in North America.[96] The 211 excavated bone fragments don't enable us to recall particular people, so the vivifying details we hope for are elusive, but scholars found twenty-nine clusters of grave goods, several associated with red ochre. Most mortuary offerings were one- and two-sided stone tools, including points for killing animals and adzes for carving wood. Most of the burial clusters—including Cluster 11, which had the most diverse objects—contained several different tools.[97] Yet those tools weren't restricted to quotidian uses and literal meanings. They weren't just for killing, chopping, or scraping. They also were for imagining, mourning, and remembering. One of the locals had used two uniface blades to engrave bone or antler. Even more significant, many tools were unused. The community had crafted them for ritual purposes, to serve as grave goods. As at other Paleoindian sites, utilitarian implements offered as grave objects became figurative tools, artifacts for making spiritual worlds.

There were burial rites and grave goods at earlier Paleoindian sites, including the Horn Shelter, but the Sloan site is a more complex and segmented built environment. The itinerant Dalton community, which had occupied the region for about five hundred years, regularly used hunting and butchering camps, food collecting and processing sites, and nearby quarries where they secured the stone needed for tool making. Then there is that unexpected cemetery, which marked off sacred from profane space. The Dalton built environment was not as complex as the larger forager-farming villages starting to appear at this time in China and the Middle East—including in what is now Turkey, Syria, and Israel—where there were house burials and reburials of plastered skulls in communal memorials.[98] Nor was it as elaborate as some later farming settlements in Arkansas, such as the Toltec Mounds (700 and 1050 CE) that the Plum Bayou people would construct in the Mississippi River Valley about a thousand years later.[99] But the Sloan foragers transformed the local landscape more fully than some might expect, given the previous picture of Paleoindians as mobile big game hunters.

That scholarly picture rested on presuppositions about the defining features of the Paleoindian and the Archaic that now seem oversimplified.[100] It's true that the climate changed and the large mammals died out, and Paleoindians did live in smaller mobile bands with less hierarchical social organization. Some of them used very similar weapons to kill and prepare mammoths and other large game. But that picture fits the Great Plains better than other regions in North America. It's the regional variability that now seems most striking, along with the findings that Paleoindian hunter-gatherers ate a more varied diet than we thought, killing small animals and gathering some plants. There was a spectrum or continuum of foraging behaviors in the Paleoindian era, and some of the widely accepted features of the next cultural period, the Archaic—varied food sources and diverse tool manufacture—seem to have begun earlier. Most important for discerning religious shifts, some features attributed to Archaic cultures after 8000 BCE appear in limited form earlier, including evidence of "greater population stability" and "systematic burial of the dead."[101] The semisedentary Dalton

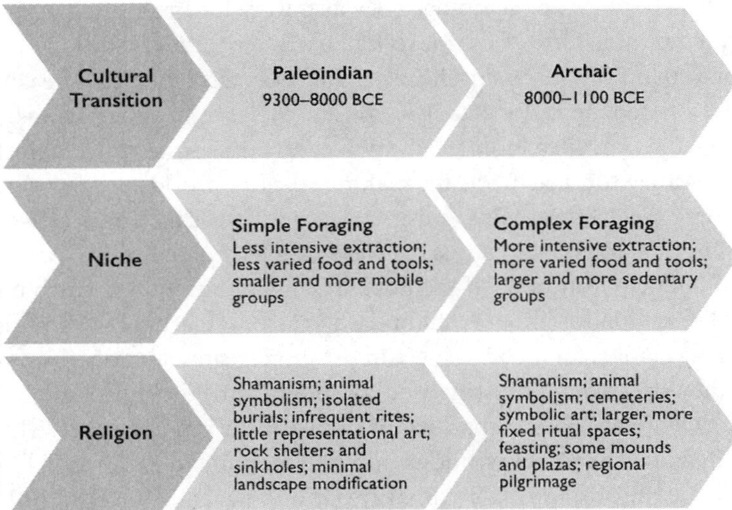

Figure 7. Transition from Paleoindian to Archaic religion.

people certainly buried their dead systematically at Sloan. And the San Patrice people of the Horn Shelter, and other Paleoindians of Texas and the Southern Plains, already ate a diverse diet and ritually interred corpses. The Horn Shelter community had status markers, as the display of excess at the shaman's grave shows. To acknowledge the fuzziness of the periodization, some suggest we name this transitional period in the region the *Protoarchaic,* meaning before but leading to the Archaic.[102]

Whatever we call the regionally diverse and culturally rich transformations occurring between about 9300 BCE and 8000 BCE, those shifts still couldn't anticipate the changes to come. Shamanic practice, animal symbolism, and ritual burial continued, and there's still red ochre in graves. But increasingly larger and more sedentary Archaic communities used familiar and new figurative tools to transform their eco-cultural niches in more elaborate ways (fig. 7).

The Archaic Foraging Spectrum, 8000 BCE–1100 BCE

Those niches varied dramatically, with shifts happening at different times and in different ways across North America. The varied religious practices of those living in the marine ecosystems on the North Atlantic and North Pacific coasts differed from those in the Southwest, Midwest, and South.[103] The figurative tools of foraging peoples of the Pacific Northwest, for example, incorporated imagery from salmon fisheries, early systems of aquaculture. Those had few exact parallels in the religious life of archaic riverine cultures in Texas and Louisiana, which introduced some of the most striking innovations of the period—including increasingly elaborate material culture (such as representational art) and ritual practice (like larger communal rites).[104] Archaic Peoples continued to take advantage of evocative landscape features, using rock shelters, hilltops, and sinkholes as ritual spaces, but they also painted rock and moved earth, not just digging oval burial holes but dramatically reshaping the environments of their slightly larger, more differentiated, and more sedentary communities.[105]

Two Archaic communities in Texas, one in the borderlands between southwestern Texas and central Mexico and the other near the southeastern Gulf Coast, show these new patterns and suggest interregional exchanges. In the Lower Pecos Canyonlands, where Paleoindians had roamed at that climatic crossroads between the humid east and the arid west, researchers found Archaic cemeteries and rock art. Seminole Sink, which dates to about 2050 BCE, is a vertical shaft burial that includes the remains of at least eleven children and ten adults.[106] There was only one grave gift, a point, but the site shows special concern for the dead, since community members had to carry the corpses across the canyon and some distance from where they spent most of their daily life in that rocky and dry terrain.

The same cultural region also has vivid evidence of the beliefs and practices of Archaic Pecos Peoples in the multicolored pictograph panels on rock shelter walls. One panel at Fate Bell Rock Shelter (2020 BCE) stood across the canyon from Seminole Sink.[107] Its painted wall seems difficult to decipher: just lines and curves and dots, with deceptively simple renderings of humans and animals. Yet some of those figures combine human and animal features, as with a winged and antlered figure, suggesting ritually mediated transformations. Several motifs recur on the rock art panels in that shelter and at others in the Lower Pecos Canyonlands, including at Rattlesnake Canyon, Mystic Shelter, and White Shaman (see fig. 3). As that last rock shelter's name indicates, the key characters in those visual narratives are shamans, the community's spiritual leaders. At the Horn Shelter burial there was only the tool kit bundle to identify the shaman's social role and reconstruct his religious practice. But these Archaic sites yield more metaphors, symbols, and narratives to ground an interpretation.

What do they tell us? It seems that the rock art created and transmitted group knowledge about the ecology of that hunting-gathering niche, pictured proper social relations, and conveyed important religious practices, especially the ecstatic communal rituals led by shamans.[108] These Early Archaic foragers hunted small animals and gathered plants, living in encampments of small conical huts built from fibers and hides or residing in rock shelters, which had spaces designated for different activities—a latrine area and an oven area.[109] Deer were the largest game animal, and other animals inhabited that hot, dry niche, all of them depicted in the rock art and associated with shamanic practice: panthers, birds, rabbits, and snakes.[110] Deer seemed especially important: shamans in the Lower Pecos wore deer antler headdresses and the anthropomorph at the Fate Bell Shelter had the head of a deer. The Fate Bell shaman, and other leaders in nearby communities, probably induced altered states that allowed ritual travel to other worlds by fasting, dancing, and drumming, like the Horn Shelter medicine man. But local ritual specialists also ingested psychoactive plants found in the rock shelters and pictured in the drawings: mescal beans (*Sophora secundiflora*), jimson weed (*Datura*), and peyote (*Lophophora williamsii*).[111] In the rock shelter images—and in stories of the Huichol of Mexico—deer and peyote were linked metaphorically. That made sense ecologically too, since locals would have seen peyote and deer at the same time, after a rain: peyote was hard to find in drier times, hidden underground, but it would swell when downpours came, just as deer appeared quickly after a rain too. It would not have been a big causal leap to associate one with the other. Those associations, which transmitted useful ecological as well as spiritual information, appear in the pictograph panels: the Fate Bell flying deer shaman is painted with black dots on his antlers and near his transfigured ritual body. Those dots are likely peyote buttons, the hallucinogen that induced the shaman's trance and otherworldly journey. The visual vocabulary of that painted narrative, known as the peyotism motif, was one of the recurring themes in the rock art panels.[112]

Similar visual elements appear at White Shaman, along with a second pictorial pattern, the otherworld journey motif, which portrays a skeletonized figure that endures a ritual death as it passes a serpent and, with the help of guiding animals, travels through an arch, the portal that leads from this world to the other world below.[113] Those standardized pictographic elements convey information about shamanic practice and shared cosmology. The tiered universe hinted at in the symbolic locatives found among the Horn Shelter grave goods—the badger, hawk, and turtle—become vividly re-created in representational art in the Lower Pecos. That cosmology also might explain why they buried their dead in vertical shafts, cemetery-like spaces for returning the deceased to the place of origin in the subterranean realm.

Another funeral landscape shows some of the religiously inspired niche transformations of the period.[114] At Buckeye Knoll in southeastern Texas, an Early Archaic knoll top cemetery dated to 5350–4250 BCE includes the remains of at least 116 individuals whom the survivors had interred alone or together in flexed, semiflexed, or seated positions.[115] The scale of that separate ritual space is especially striking, but the grave goods also provide an angle of vision on the community and their possible connections to other regions. There are an extraordinary array of burial offerings—projectile points, grooved stones, stone plummets, and seashells, as well as chunks of red ochre, and yellow ochre too. There are also nonlocal objects, showing that residents traded or traveled. Buckeye Knoll's ritual offerings reveal a bit about the otherwise anonymous community members. The tool kits interred with Burial 8 and Burial 49 suggest they were flint knappers, skilled at striking stone to craft tools, and some community members were mourned and celebrated more elaborately.[116] Excavators found symbolic surplus in Burial 59, where a child was buried with a cluster of seventy-eight marine shell beads, and in Burial 74, where a forty-five-year-old went into the earth with 604 beads beside him.[117] Next to the bead pile were two bannerstones, crafted limestone objects that had both a utilitarian purpose and a social function: they would have served as a weight on the shaft of a spear-thrower (atlatl), so it could be hurled farther, but they also served as emblems of personal status or communal identity, enabling the deceased to stand out or fit in.[118] Some of those grave goods, including the bannerstones, also are intriguing because they "suggest connections to Middle Archaic cultures of the Mississippi region and beyond."[119]

In the Lower Mississippi Valley, Middle and Late Archaic sites display another surprising religious innovation—foragers constructing impressive earthen mounds. The earliest Archaic mound complex was at Watson Brake, near the Ouachita River in northeastern Louisiana. There archaeologists unearthed intriguing details about the culture of those broad-spectrum foragers who ate fish, nuts, and deer during their periodic stays throughout the year.[120] At that site built about 5,400 years ago, they found no burials with grave goods, though Mound B included some remains.[121] No ritual offerings appear nearby, so they disclose little. Some cultural artifacts such as fire-cracked rock and fired-earthen objects in varied shapes—cuboidal, cylindrical, and spherical—are attention grabbing, as are the many ornamental chert beads produced there.[122] However, only a few objects clearly suggest the symbolic meanings associated with shamanic practice—quartz crystal and red ochre. Most revealing, there is a bone shaft fragment stained with red pigment, suggesting the community's ritual specialist might have used the implement to apply ochre for decorating or healing.[123]

If those objects were the only evidence, we wouldn't linger long at Watson Brake. But the Middle Archaic site is crucial because it's the earliest mound complex in the Americas, and mounds became a crucial part of the spiritual built environment.[124] Later mounds were built on higher ground in floodplain habitats along the Mississippi, and in wetland areas from Florida to California, as well as in the Caribbean, Central America, and South America.[125] The mounds at Watson Brake were started earlier than other historic sites in the hemisphere—before the shell and dirt mounds at Puerto Rico's Angostura site (2700–1500 BCE), before the stone mounds at Sechín Alto (1600–1400 BCE) in Peru, and before the stone mounds at Paso de la Amada (1800–1200 BCE), the earliest ceremonial center in Mexico.[126] We can't know if the Lower Mississippi mound complex was a model for all the transhemispheric mound building—though some say the mounds at Sechín Alto, Paso de la Amada, and Watson Brake used the same measurement system and geometric forms.[127] In any case, Watson Brake is the earliest.

The Watson Brake mound complex could fit inside the plaza formed by the earthworks built at Poverty Point between about 1700 and 1100 BCE (fig. 8).[128] Contemporaneous with the stone mounds at Peru's Sechín Alto and Mexico's Paso de la Amada, the earthen mounds at Poverty Point had no burials with grave goods on that 400-acre Eastern Woodland site overlooking the Mississippi River floodplain. The few bone fragments excavators found were burnt, showing evidence of cremation, as with a charred femur interred in Mound B.[129] The minimal traces of mortuary practices don't provide a window into the worldview of the Late Archaic fisher-hunter-gatherer communities who valued the place.[130] Yet other features make it a striking setting for the early history of religion in the lands that became America.

First, there were symbolic objects. Some artifacts resemble those at earlier Archaic sites, like the bannerstones from Buckeye Knoll cemetery, but Poverty Point foragers also made many more—and more elaborate—symbolic objects, some of them from exotic materials acquired in a long-distance trade network. This network—in effect an import business—stretched from the Great Lakes to the Gulf of Mexico. Local artisans used nearby clay and imported material—copper from the Great Lakes, obsidian from Wyoming, and red hematite from Arkansas—to craft ritual implements like cylindrical stone pipes.[131] They also made small zoomorphic and anthropomorphic objects that materialized their figurative world and marked their collective identity—and

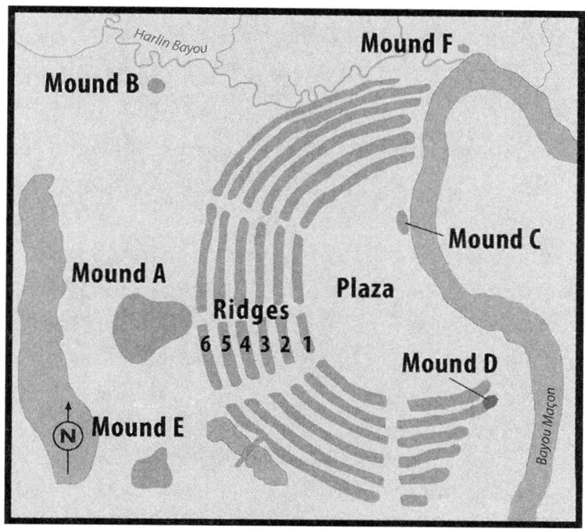

Figure 8. Map of the earthworks at Poverty Point in West Carroll Parish, Louisiana. Courtesy of the Louisiana Division of Archaeology.

also might have served as amulets, powerful objects to ward off bad things, and talismans, powerful objects to bring on good things.[132]

Ceramic objects represented humans, including one-inch or two-inch torsos made of clay, small enough to carry. The rare figurines seemed androgynous, though breasts, wide hips, and distended bellies marked some as female.[133] These figurines might not have been fertility goddesses, as scholars might guess if they had been found in a contemporaneous foraging-farming community in the Middle East or the Andes, since Poverty Point residents and visitors weren't farmers, though they intensively extracted lots of fish and acorns. Still, the objects must have served a purpose, even if they weren't for scaling fish or cracking acorns. Perhaps they memorialized distant ancestors or venerated communal gods, beings they approached to express gratitude or seek favors.

The more abundant animal representations might have functioned in similar ways. There were ground stone pendants shaped like animal talons, paws, and claws—in other words, the crafted equivalent of the actual claws and talons ritually placed in the Horn Shelter Man's mouth. There also was a panther etched on a soapstone vessel and a turtle shell carved on a gorget, an oval shell worn as a necklace. As at the mounds at Mexico's Paso de la Amada, birds also were important at Poverty Point.[134] In particular, owls played a prominent role in the community's analogical imagination, in both personal ritual practice and shamanic communal ceremony.[135] Individuals wore red owl pendants around their necks, keeping protection nearby. Owls played varied roles in later myths, including in a Choctaw story suggesting that one of the deceased person's two spirits—yes, there are two—changes into an owl that frightens anyone who approaches the corpse. Those stories associate owls both with negative things like death and bad luck and with positive things like kindness and divination.[136] Whatever the associations for those at Poverty Point, it seems likely that owls were cast as lead characters in the community's ritually enacted stories. And they were linked with shamanic practice: excavators found an owl carved with deer antlers, like the painted shaman at Fate Bell, and another owl-human image seems to represent a dancing shaman.[137]

The symbolic artifacts are intriguing, but a second feature strikes any Poverty Point visitor: the enormous scale and figurative significance of the built environment, which includes five Late Archaic mounds and six semielliptical nested earthen ridges that partially enclose a forty-three-acre plaza.[138] Now a World Heritage site, Poverty Point impresses scientists and tourists alike. To grasp the scale, consider some numbers: a cubic foot of soil weighs almost 100 pounds, and Poverty Point laborers moved as much as 53 million cubic feet of dirt in baskets that held about fifty pounds per load. Mound A, the largest, was built rather quickly around 1300 BCE, with more than 1,000 laborers working for less than a year.[139] The second largest earthen mound in the lands that became America, it stands 72 feet high and stretches 710 feet long, several times larger than the big mound at Watson Brake. Mound A is a surprisingly large and place-centered monument for a foraging community.

Most scholars think the monumental earthen architecture has some spiritual significance but disagree about why it was built and what it means.[140] Mound A, some suggest, is an effigy of a bird flying west.[141] A visitor can't make out that avian shape from ground level or standing on the mound. Yet a bird's-eye view offered by an aerial photograph suggests wings off to the right and left, and the abundance of excavated avian imagery, including the owl beads, makes this account plausible. In this reading, the mound depicts a mythic bird that played a crucial role in their narratives about the origin and destiny of humans and the world. Or, other interpreters propose, perhaps the mound is a representation of "earth-island," the center of creation. One proponent notes that the sequence of mound building, which began with wet, dark swamp and continued with light colored sediments, was a ritual recounting of the myth of emergence, the Earth Diver story, which in other cultures has been associated with animals like turtles or birds: "the building of this earthwork represents an enactment of ritual where the builders covered the watery chaos of precreation and erected a monument symbolizing the triumph of creation over the forces of chaos."[142] Both accounts suggest that the analogical imagination was at work: Mound A is either a mythic bird or a terrestrial symbol. In either case, dirt was more than dirt.

A third interpretation has gained increasing support: Poverty Point was a major pilgrimage center.[143] It's not clear why pilgrimage practices began, proponents say. It might have been an inspiring prophet or reorienting experience that attracted culturally diverse communities to the site, but the massive construction projects, the importing of exotic nonutilitarian items like quartz crystals, and the absence of export trade goods, except the red-jasper owl beads, suggest devotees made the round-trip journey to engage in rituals that crafted identities, created alliances, and reinforced shared stories about the world and their place in it. Mound A, a ceremonial site that remained free of debris, was spiritually significant, and so was the plaza created by the half circle of mounds. The edges of the earthen forms created a large ritual space that might have served multiple functions but was more than a site of commercial exchange or secular entertainment. It's likely the plaza teemed with activity during ritual events that attracted nearby residents and regional pilgrims, and the emergence of large fixed spaces for public ritual marked an important moment in the history of North American religion. Poverty Point wasn't a 16,000-seat megachurch near a highway off-ramp. But the pilgrims who gathered in that cleared space below the half circle of symbolic mounds had a very different experience than the small group of mourners arranging turtle shells at the burial beneath the overhanging rock at the Horn Shelter. The vast scale, fixed location, and symbolic complexity of the ritual space changed things.

By 1100 BCE the foragers' ceremonial space at Poverty Point no longer was being used. But in the centuries ahead, foragers who began to introduce small-scale farming moved more dirt to make other plazas in other mound complexes in the South and Midwest, and new kinds of ritual spaces appeared in the Southwest among forager-farmers. Crop cultivation had started earlier in South and Central America. When Poverty Point was reaching its peak about 1500 BCE, the community at the mound complex on Mexico's Pacific Coast already had small-scale farming, and the Peruvian mound complex in the Casma Valley was a large agricultural center with 18,000 residents, maybe the earliest Andean state.[144] Eventually, maize cultivation—and greater symbolic complexity—could be found throughout the hemisphere. By 800 CE more place-centered and socially differentiated eco-cultural niches emerged in communities that came to rely more on farming the seas and the land. It wasn't as if all the fisher-hunter-gatherers picking acorns, netting bass, and killing deer simultaneously checked their watches and said, "Oh, it's time for agriculture. Let's cultivate maize today—and, while we're at it, let's start planning the Corn Goddess festival." As chapter 2 shows, it happened more slowly and sporadically than that. While some of the farmers' figurative tools may look familiar, a major shift began with the introduction of farming. Many spiritual niches from the eastern woodlands to the southwestern plateaus would never be the same again.

PART TWO

FARMING

Figure 9. An Algonquian village in present-day North Carolina, showing bark and reed dwellings, fields of corn, and a ceremonial dance. Watercolor by John White (1585). Courtesy of the Trustees of the British Museum, London.

CHAPTER 2
Farming Religion
Sedentary Villages and the First Sustainability Crisis, 1100 BCE–1492

Long after Poverty Point pilgrims abandoned their ceremonial plaza, dense crowds of mound-building farmers gathered in another plaza across the Mississippi from present-day St. Louis.[1] There in Greater Cahokia, the largest population center north of Mexico before the American Revolution, festival-goers congregated during a few successive years in the late eleventh century. We know from the trash in a nearby pit that they came in late summer or early autumn to give deities thanks, use medicinal plants, smoke ritual tobacco, and eat special food—lots of food. Those harvest festival celebrants didn't eat corn, their dietary staple, but gorged themselves on animals and plants that were less locally abundant and more ritually significant, from white swans to white tail deer. The ceremonial spectacle disrupted daily routine, and some of the pageantry derived from the monumental architecture that surrounded them. Those standing shoulder to shoulder in the fifty-acre Grand Plaza looked up toward Monks Mound, a looming ten-story earthen structure with a thatched palace and temple on top. The crowd below could watch the priest theatrically gesture from that elevated perch, the largest earthen structure in the Americas.

Yet the corn harvest rite was about more than the crowd, mound, and performance. Even if the crowd included unknowing infants carried by parents and ambivalent adults motivated by obligation, the public rituals probably stirred emotions and created bonds for most attendees, producing what some call "collective effervescence."[2] In that agricultural niche, which depended on crops and the rituals that sustained them, almost everyone would have found meaning in the symbols of renewal, even if some attendees might have taken more delight in the chance to eat their fill of charred deer amid the choreographed commotion of that communal rite.

Dazzling public rituals in massive agricultural communities didn't appear suddenly. There was no straight line from forager religion at Poverty Point to farming religion at Cahokia. As with the transition from simple to complex foraging, the religious life of farming niches didn't emerge in the same way or at the same rate in all the lands that would become America. Maritime communities that hugged the Atlantic and Pacific coastlines venerated seawater spirits as they monitored the tides and followed the fish, while more sedentary coastal peoples intensely extracted resources through mariculture—clam gardens and salmon fisheries—and eventually started to farm the nearby land, with maize cultivation appearing on the northeastern Atlantic coast as early as 260 CE.[3] In the Lower Mississippi Valley, the transition from the Late Archaic to the Early Woodland period was complicated, including around Poverty Point.[4] Ceramic styles suggest cultures overlapped there. More intriguing for our story, Poverty Point's import business in exotic raw materials fell on hard times, but some Early and Middle Woodland foragers continued to build earthen mounds in present-day Louisiana, most notably at the Marksville mound complex, which had at least two earthen enclosures and eight mounds.[5] Marksville's ritual landscape resembled that of the Hopewell, the Middle Woodland Peoples who began to cultivate crops near midwestern rivers, and the wider Hopewell Interaction Sphere, which stretched from the Gulf of Mexico to the Great Lakes and from the Great Plains to the Appalachian Mountains (fig. 10). In that region and farther southwest, sedentary peoples in farming villages began to do what devout American farmers have done ever since—pray for not too much or too little rain. That was especially true in the semiarid valleys and plateaus of the Southwest, where Basketmaker Era Peoples—including maize-growing migrants from Mesoamerica—began to take advantage of a drought-free period to construct farming villages with slightly larger domestic and ritual spaces.[6] A few hundred years later, those southwestern and midwestern agricultural niches would become even more densely populated and even more elaborately figured.

During this initial period of farming religions, which lasted until European Christian settlers imperiled Native niches, devotees in the Midwest and Southwest cultivated an even more place-centered piety in larger interconnected settlements. Animal tropes persisted, and those were even more

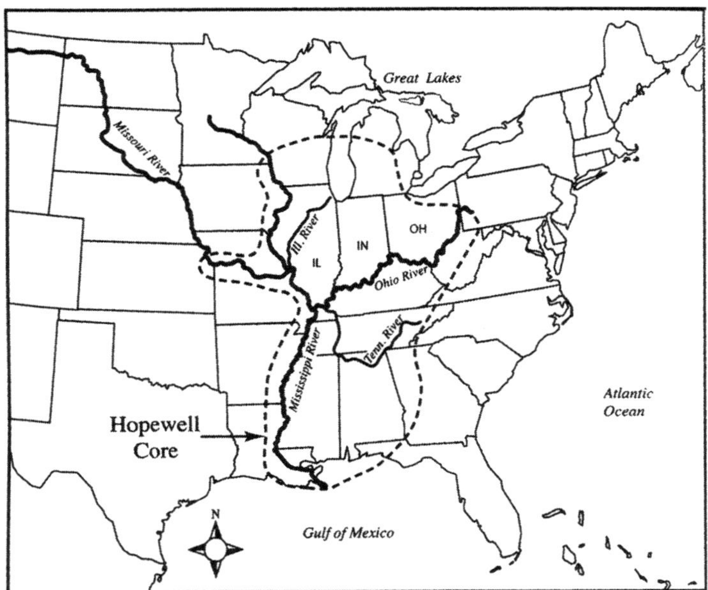

Figure 10. Core area of the Hopewell Interaction Sphere about 1,800 years ago. From Timothy Pauketat, ed., *The Oxford Handbook of North American Archaeology.* © 2015, Oxford University Press. Reproduced with permission of the Licensor through PLSclear.

clearly associated with clan identities and social roles. Early in this period, shamans remained linked with some of those zoomorphic images. Turtles appear again in graves, and precious materials too, some ochre but also mica, shell, quartz, turquoise, and copper. But new types of ritual specialists and new forms of religious organization developed. By about 900 CE, farming communities increasingly turned to agricultural metaphors to understand the world, associating seeding and sprouting with their priests' generative rituals and their rulers' sustaining power.[7] Those cultivators used more complex figurative tools, conducted more ornate mortuary rites, made more intricate symbolic objects, and built more elaborate ritual spaces. The new utilitarian and symbolic technologies that swelled the populations—and produced great kivas in the Southwest and platform mounds in the Midwest—eventually generated more unhealthy living environments and more inequitable social divisions than in Archaic foraging habitats.[8] By 1000 CE, agricultural niches already had formed on the continent. Those eco-cultural niches prompted more competition and conflict, even violence, and by about 1300 CE a crisis of sustainability erupted in the ceremonial centers of the Midwest and Southwest (see appendix). Those communities became more vulnerable to climatic and cultural forces that threatened the harvests, making farmers and their neighbors ever more reliant on the religio-political rituals that sustained the crops and safeguarded the cosmic order.[9]

The Transition to Farming Niches

Before those multifaceted maize niches appeared, inhabitants of the lands that became America began to introduce some cultivated crops as part of their diet, and the early shift in resources as well as the changes in religion emerged most clearly in the dry plateaus of the Southwest and the humid woodlands of the Midwest.

The Hopewell in Ohio, 100 BCE–400 CE

Inhabitants in the interconnected Hopewell communities picked nuts and berries and hunted deer and turkeys. They also supplemented their diet by removing trees to plant sunflowers and goosefoot. Like the Poverty Point mound builders, the Hopewell traded for exotic raw materials that were visually compelling and spiritually powerful: copper from the Great Lakes, mica from the Carolinas, shells from the Gulf of Mexico, and obsidian from the Rockies. Those materials became figurative tools in their *symbolic sphere,* the communal ritual space positioned beyond their *residential sphere,* where they lived in hamlets with thatched dwellings, and their *subsistence sphere,* where they sought what they needed to get by—not just plants and animals for food but stones for tools and mates for marriage.[10]

To get by—and ease worry and enhance wonder—the Hopewell apparently needed ceremonial spaces like the earthworks they built throughout the Midwest. The most elaborate symbolic enclosures and mounds were in present-day Ohio, and the Scioto Hopewell at the Hopewell Mound Group provide an especially revealing glimpse of what persisted and changed in early agricultural habitats. There were familiar Archaic features—earthworks, art, and burials—but they were more plentiful and variegated than at Poverty Point. The Hopewell site's earthen-walled enclosure spanned 130 acres, and its two-mile-long wall created a massive sacred space with four enclosures and forty mounds, including twenty-nine burial mounds.[11] The site mapped cosmic space as it connected local communities. Architects used contrasting soil colors to enhance devotees' experience: yellow soil marked the interior side of the walls, and red soil covered the outer surfaces. The sequencing of contrasting soil colors in the mortuary mounds—for those who knew the sacred stories—re-created the structure of the universe and reenacted the process of creation.[12] The earthworks also linked the residential and subsistence spheres, which extended outward for several miles, and connected the Hopewell Mound Group with the nearby hamlets of Siep and Liberty, forming a regional symbolic community. Members of that ceremonial alliance buried their most prestigious residents at the Hopewell site, and devotees gathered for annual performances, seasonal rites, and life-cycle rituals, especially mortuary ceremonies.[13]

The largest burial mound (Mound 25) reveals a good deal about Hopewell religion—as well as their politics, economy, and society. That mound, which laborers formed by covering smaller burial mounds in a D-shaped enclosure, was 500 feet long and 33 feet high.[14] It was the scene of mortuary rites, including cremated and uncremated interments and multi-stage burials and reburials as early as 40 BCE and as late as 398 CE—in other words, from just before Jesus's birth to just after Christianity became the official religion of the Roman Empire.[15] The graves of many Hopewell elites had mortuary offerings, including the symbolic surplus seen in Paleoindian and Archaic graves. DNA analysis shows they were a diverse and expanding group with genetic connections to four of the five lineages found among the First Peoples of the Americas.[16] It seems to have been a relatively healthy and peaceful eco-cultural niche, with more cooperation than competition: skeletal remains show few marks of trauma. In terms of political power and social stratification, it was a middle-range society, neither as egalitarian as Paleoindian foraging groups nor as stratified as later agricultural chiefdoms, with their more centralized political authority.[17] In this mid-scale Woodland society, inhabitants formed alliances by inherited lineages and chosen associations. Nine animal symbols identified nine clans, including bear and canine clans, and funereal objects suggest organizations called "sodalities," cross-village guilds dedicated to a shared religious or social purpose.[18] We're left to speculate about the sodalities' purposes and the clans' practices, but residents' identities live on in the grave offerings: sodality members wore breastplates and earspools, and clan members were accompanied by signifying animal parts, like bear claws or canine teeth. In these and other ways, mortuary goods point to both ascribed (given) and achieved (earned) status among the Scioto Hopewell. There seems to have been some social mobility and several kinds of communal leadership, with prestigious roles open to different clans and both men and women, though not equally.

For Scioto women there was a bit of a glass—or quartz—ceiling, but they crafted most of the clay figurines used for domestic and communal rituals and performed roles in mortuary ceremonies and other rituals.[19] Women and men probably had shared and separate ritual spaces. The cradle board and medicinal plants found at an Early Woodland rock shelter about 100 miles south suggest it provided a secluded spot where female ritual specialists performed rites in that menstrual retreat, healing space, and birthing center.[20] Scioto women might have conducted similar gender-segregated rituals in the hilly terrain beyond the Ohio mounds, but Mound 25's deposits show women also had some communal spiritual roles. At other Hopewellian sites, female shamans were buried with tortoise shell ornaments, translucent quartz bifaces, and—as at the Horn Shelter—clumps of red ochre. At Mound 25 wind instruments appear in female shamans' graves.[21] A panpipe, or multitubed instrument, was found with Skeleton 249, and a copper flute appeared with Burial 12, a female shaman whose grave offerings included other high-prestige artifacts: copper plates and pearl beads.[22] The instruments were ritual implements, as at the Early Nasca mounds in southern Peru.[23] But we are not certain of the instruments' exact function. In later periods, flutes served ritual purposes, as its high-pitched sound could be heard across distances and amid crowds.[24] So Burial 12's flute might have been used in secluded rites of passage, like puberty rituals, or in multivillage ceremonies to welcome visitors, summon spirits, or accompany processions.[25] In any case, more than 1,500 years before ordained women ministers ascended Ohio pulpits, the flute's inclusion in Mound 25 identified that female shaman as a revered ritual specialist.

The shaman's traditional duties continued, but novel forms of religio-political leadership also began to appear by the end of the Middle Woodland period. Excavations have uncovered the first traces of the priest, a settled ritual caretaker who tends a farming community's sanctuary, but priests didn't predominate. Rather, shamans specialized, performing different roles—healing the ill, divining the future, processing the corpses, and convening the ceremonies.[26] Grave offerings suggest that male shamans tended to deal with death—funerals and battles—while women took on other roles, including healing.[27] Yet even though we don't see evidence of a male priest-chief, the task of presiding at community-wide Scioto ceremonies seems to have been reserved mostly for men. Funereal gifts hint at some ceremonial roles for women, but the highest-prestige items (like headplates) are found only in male burials at Mound 25.[28]

Two male burials, for instance, included earspools, breastplates, and smoking pipes made from exotic materials, as well as animal-themed ceremonial headdresses.[29] Resembling the antler-wearing shaman pictured at the

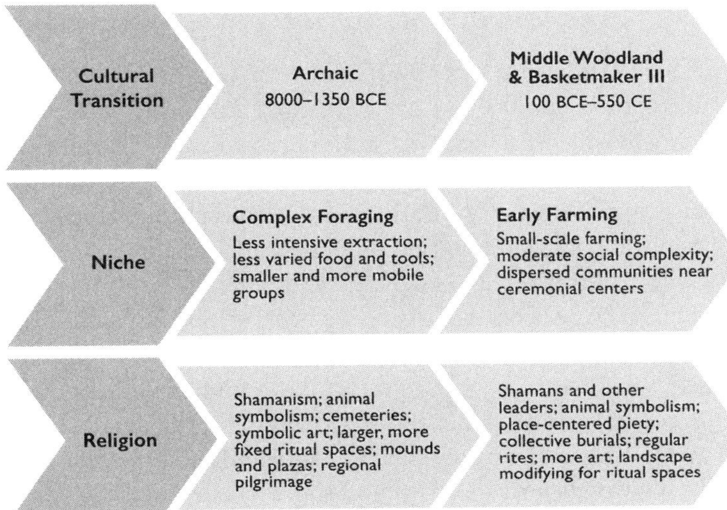

Figure 11. Transition from Archaic to Middle Woodland and Basketmaker III religion.

Pecos rock shelter, Skeleton 248 wore a cloth stitched with thousands of pearl and shell beads. The 5′11″ male also was adorned with a carved headdress of antlers covered with copper.[30] Recalling the avian images at Poverty Point and anticipating those at Cahokia, the headdress on Burial 11 is especially striking.[31] The man might have had sodality and clan associations: he wore copper earspools and held bear incisors. The deer bone awls suggest his shamanic duties might have included preparing corpses for the afterlife. Preparations for his own postmortem transit involved pomp: ritual specialists displayed his ostentatiously adorned body in a log crypt about ten feet long by six feet wide and placed it on an earthen platform; they then capped his grave by a small mound and covered it again later when they completed Mound 25. But pomp wasn't the whole story. The grave's avian headdress communicated his status as the presider at communal gatherings. Extending from the headdress's round base was a rectangular copper, pearl, and mica headplate with large copper flaps on both sides. The wings suggest avian analogies, and other Mound 25 funereal objects confirm that this head covering represented a bird, a double-headed raptor.[32]

Avian images recur later, and features associated with the transition to the religion of early agriculturalists also can be found among the Ancestral Puebloans in Chaco Canyon a century and a half later, even if their domestic dwellings and ritual spaces were quite different (fig. 11).

Ancestral Puebloans in Chaco Canyon, 550 CE

The peoples of the North American Southwest, a cultural sphere that extended north to Colorado and south to northern Mexico, included the Ancestral Puebloans, who lived where the current states of Utah, Colorado, Arizona, and New Mexico converge (fig. 12).[33] Some lived in New Mexico's Chaco Canyon, and during the Basketmaker III Period (especially 550–700 CE) the basin was home to pithouses, dwellings built near a kiva, a round subterranean ritual space. Those residential-symbolic communities clustered at either end of the canyon, and the eastern settlement, Shabik'eshchee, has been excavated.[34] The village's name probably came from a later mangling of the Diné phrase *Tsé Bik e'eschi,* or graven rock, and we know a little about the built landscape and the local residents, though in this period Chacoans didn't offer durable mortuary goods that revealed the deceased's social standing.[35]

As in the woods near the Hopewell site, this sandstone canyon habitat supported a middle-range society that relied on small-scale agriculture supplemented by foraging forays. Maize agriculture had begun in Chaco much earlier. But Shabik'eshchee's farmers, who built their village where rainwater accumulated, had fewer local resources than the Hopewell. The Chacoans adapted, however. They built fifty storage bins to conserve maize for the winter—and for the years with meager harvests. They followed the canyon's seasonal rhythms, gathering pinyon nuts in the fall and widening their subsistence sphere when the agricultural yield demanded it. Specialists debate how many residents remained year-round, since the ruins show that Chacoans sometimes abandoned, burned, and repurposed pithouses. All agree, however, that Shabik'eshchee was one of the largest settlements in the region, with more than seventy structures up and down the Chaco Basin.[36]

Women apparently had increased workloads in that household-centered economy, as the pithouses were not only zones for sleeping and cooking but also for food processing and tool making.[37] Domestic rituals were part of Chaco religious life, and each pithouse had an architectural feature that marked the dwelling as a sacred center.[38] House F's interior had four wooden posts along the four cardinal directions; in the center was the fire pit and, nearby, a small hole, a sipapu, marking the mythic spot where the ancestors ascended as they crossed from the underworld to this world. In this sense, Chaco homes opened to the sacred.

Those householders also gathered for communal rituals at the kiva they built by 550 CE.[39] We can't recover the sounds participants heard or the accessories presiders wore. But locals made whistles, and ritual specialists might

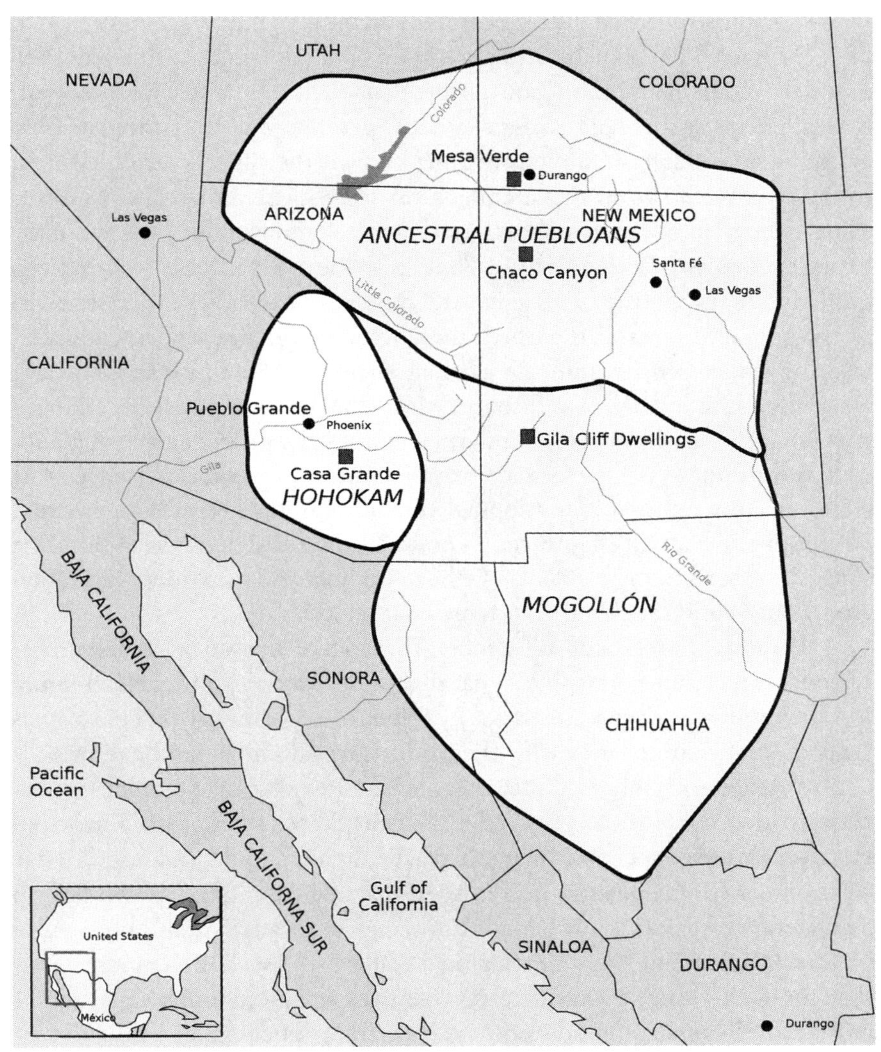

Figure 12. Map of the North American Southwest, including the cultural region of the Ancestral Puebloans around 1350 CE. Yuchitown / Wikimedia Commons.

have used those notched tubes as ceremonial implements, as the Zuni would later.[40] Chaco Canyon artisans crafted personal adornments too, like shell bracelets and hematite and turquoise pendants. The hematite, or ochre, is intriguing because it recalls earlier shamanic practice, and the turquoise is an arresting new material, though we don't know if the ritual specialist wore it in the kiva. We do know that architectural designs encourage distinct devotional experiences, and therefore the structure's contours offer clues about the experience during a ceremony at Shabik'eshchee's kiva. It must have been quite different than the experience at a daytime ceremony at the Hopewell site, where attendees at the open-air sanctuary watched their headdress-wearing leader process into the earthen enclosure. By contrast, Chacoans descended into a dark, round space, where the encircling benches allowed participants to look across at familiar faces lit by the pit fire and then glance back toward the ritual performance in the center. The kiva experience must have been more intimate, enveloping, and perhaps just as emotionally evocative and communally significant—or so all the subsequent kiva-building suggests. After 800 CE, residents of Chaco Canyon and the wider cultural region would build many more and much larger kivas.

Despite the regional differences, there were also unexplained cross-regional, even transhemispheric, parallels. For example, a bird-head figure in Canyon de Chelly, an Ancestral Puebloan site northwest of Chaco, suggests thematic similarities with the Middle Woodland avian headdress in Ohio.[41] Religious symbols in the two communities also have perplexing parallels beyond those areas.[42] Consider the swastika, or swirl cross. The Scioto Hopewell made copper swastikas and placed them in burial mounds.[43] Today we're blinded to the positive meanings of that ancient talismanic symbol, an equilateral cross with arms bent at right angles, because Adolf Hitler put it on the Nazi flag. But it has a long global history. The *svastika,* from the Sanskrit for "well-being" or "auspicious," goes back at least to Indus Valley towns in India and Pakistan (2600–1900 BCE), where it appeared on seals and tablets, and it became a symbol of good fortune in Hindu, Jain, and Buddhist art and architecture.[44] So how did it get to ancient Ohio? Anthropologist Thomas Wilson, who worked for the Smithsonian Institution, was obsessed with that question. His 1896 report listed examples from around the world, including Asian Buddha statues that have the *svastika* on them, and some interpreters even claimed Chinese Buddhists journeyed to America and evangelized the Ohio "mound builders."[45] That's an entertaining account, but until we unearth an ancient bronze Buddha in the Midwest, you might accept a contemporary archaeologist's take—that the swirl cross went through "regional adaptations," including in ancient North America—or ponder Wilson's conclusion: that we can't reconstruct the symbol's path, but it might have migrated across the Pacific or the Atlantic before the Scioto Hopewell made their copper swastikas and before Indigenous ancestors put it on everything from southwestern rock art to southeastern pottery.[46]

Pacific and Atlantic Crossings

We can set aside that question, but an expanded narrative must consider other transoceanic migrations which affected the Pacific islands that would become US territory, American Samoa and Hawai'i, and show how tattooed voyagers from forager-farming cultures, North Atlantic Norse as well as South Pacific Polynesians, reached the hemisphere, leaving traces that recall earlier Paleolithic transits and anticipate later colonial contacts.

The Polynesian Pacific, 750 BCE–1300 CE

It might seem odd to look for American religion in the vast aquatic space called Oceania, but some of the earliest religious practitioners—including Horn Shelter Man—had ancient links with Island Southeast Asia and Oceania, and Hawaiians and other contemporary citizens and US nationals trace their ancestral homelands to there. The earliest migration into Near Oceania began about 40,000 years ago, when humans were already using figurative tools to make symbolic worlds.[47] By 4,000 years ago, Austronesian speakers created an Oceanic inter-island sphere—the Lapita cultural complex—and about 1200 BCE their outrigger canoes began transporting cultivated crops and domesticated animals to Remote Oceania. Those forager-fisher-farmers reached Western Polynesia (Tonga and Samoa) by 800 BCE. Settlers near Samoa's Pulemelei site then built coastal dwellings with stone walkways, storage pits, and boundary fences, and created ceremonial spaces in the island's interior.[48] In those spaces they used stone tools and high-temperature ovens to caramelize the roots of the *tī* plant (*Cordyline fruticosa*), a delicacy that would be associated with chiefly and ceremonial activities after Samoans began constructing large earth and stone mounds about 900 years ago.[49]

Perhaps driven by prolonged drought and social tensions, some Western Polynesian seafarers began exploring Eastern Polynesia, including the remote Hawaiian archipelago, which they settled between about 1000 and 1300.[50] By then, Samoa-Tonga mariners had replaced the outrigger canoe with the double-hulled sailing canoe, which expanded the ships' cargo capacity and oceanic range, and that boat made settlement easier. Soon after those mariners settled Hawai'i, they began making the tropical archipelago their own. Polynesians transported their early agricultural way of life, while discovering new ways to take advantage of the islands' marine resources, and they brought ritual practices as well as crop seeds, carrying old gods on their canoes and finding new ones on Hawaiian shores. For instance, they transformed the landscape at a sand dune on the windward coast of O'ahu, where that small community started digging burial pits sometime after 1040 CE.[51] The grave of Burial 4 was the most elaborate. The sand around the nine-year-old was red, probably because a mourner wrapped her in colored bark cloth (*kapa*).[52] She also wore an anklet of tusk pieces and an oyster shell on her chest. Another mortuary offering signaled her high status, and perhaps her kinship with kings: around her neck hung a *lei niho palaoa,* a whale tooth pendant, which symbolized religious power and political status.[53]

By the time those O'ahu mourners placed that pendant around her neck, voyaging Polynesians probably had already discovered the Pacific coastline of the Americas. Evidence suggests that by about 1000 CE Polynesian sailing canoes had reached the coast of South America, where locals borrowed the Polynesians' short axe and took a liking to Pacific Islander chicken.[54] In turn, the explorers carried back the sweet potato and the bottle gourd to Eastern Polynesia, including the Hawaiian Islands.[55] There are chicken remains with a Polynesian DNA signature at ancient coastal sites in Chile, scholars point out, and the word *kumara* means sweet potato in both Peru and Polynesia. Polynesians even might have reached California's coast, since the Chumash who settled around the Santa Barbara Channel had sewn-plank canoes (*tomolo*) and bone fishhooks that resembled those in Hawai'i and Eastern Polynesia.[56]

Pacific islanders had interhemispheric contacts, then, and those exchanges also shaped Hawaiian religion. Consider the objects and rituals associated with Lono, one of the gods Oceanic sailors discovered in Hawai'i. By analyzing that devotion we can detect how two South American borrowings—the sweet potato and the bottle gourd—shaped Hawaiian ritual life and, at the same time, explain the O'ahu girl's whale tooth necklace. Lono, one of Hawaiians' primary deities, brought the rains and was associated with agriculture, healing, and fertility.[57] Rituals also linked him with those imported sweet potatoes and bottle gourds. Farming households would offer Lono the first fruits of the annual harvest, and daily household devotions involved offering him the first portion of cooked sweet potato by placing it in a gourd (*ipu-o-lono*).[58] Island leaders expressed thanks too, including in ways that explain the girl's grave goods: during feasts the ruler's wife draped Lono's image with red bark cloth while the ruler placed a whale tooth pendant around the god's neck.[59] Devotees also consecrated agricultural temples, called the Temple of Lono's Gourd (*waihau ipu-o-Lono*). So the transplanted bottle gourd became linked with Lono more than 6,000 miles from its South American source. Along the way, that imported plant had become part of a local devotion. The gourd, devotees came to believe, is Lono's body, with its roundness suggesting a rain-bearing cloud and a pregnant woman's abdomen. Those life-sustaining themes materialize at the Temple of Lono's Gourd, where devotees place kava (*'awa*), a beverage made from a calming medicinal root, in the gourd around the god's neck. It's not just disquieted relatives at sand dune graves or worried farmers in sweet potato fields who need help; gods apparently need calming too.

Lono's gourd, which stored that drink, had become a ritual object that memorialized an earlier transoceanic transit. Polynesians, however, weren't the only voyagers who found their way to the Americas.

The Norse Atlantic, 800–1100 CE

Tropical Hawaiians west of the North American mainland associated Lono with rain-bearing clouds and thunder, and the arctic Norse east of the mainland carried their own thunder god, Thor, on maritime voyages, although by the time the Vikings established an exploration base and winter camp in the North Atlantic around 1000 CE, most had given up Thor's hammer for Christ's cross.

Just as scholars have proposed ancient Pacific migrations to explain the peopling of the Americas and legends have circulated about a fifth-century Chinese Buddhist journey to the coast, a few scholars have claimed that Paleolithic migrants from Europe followed the ice across the Atlantic, and legends have circulated about a sixth-century Irish monk, St. Brendan, crossing the Atlantic to discover a promised land he would never reach.[60] But the Vikings did reach it.

Scandinavian Vikings, who cultivated crops and domesticated animals, left their farmlands on longboats to discover, colonize, and establish communities between 800 and 1000 CE.[61] Those journeys took the Norse east to the Caspian Sea, south to the Mediterranean, and west across the Atlantic as they played a role in the tumultuous religious history of the Early Medieval Period (750–1050).[62] Religiously inflected reports about the Viking diaspora appeared in several languages—Icelandic, Latin, and Arabic—and most classified them as part of the pagan world.[63] European Christians saw the Vikings as violent heathens who raided their markets and monasteries, marauders as ungodly as the Muslims pressing in from the south and the east. And those seafaring devotees of Thor and Odin retained some of their vernacular symbols and practices during the transitional period when they began embracing the Christian faith.

Erik the Red (950–1004), the Norwegian-born Viking who would lead the economically driven colonization of Greenland, resisted a dunking in baptismal waters, even though most of his family and colony converted.[64] The Icelandic sagas say his family sailed to Iceland, which the Norse had colonized around 874. Before Christianity became the law of the land in Iceland, Erik sailed farther west. In 986 he became the first to colonize Greenland, setting up an eastern farming settlement with 500 colonists. That's where Erik's family lived, and later he encouraged a smaller western settlement there. That Arctic island is important for this story because geologically Greenland is part of North America. An underwater ridge connects the island to the mainland, and it was from Greenland that Erik's son Leif led the party that established a base camp in present-day Canada.

Before 1000, settlers on Iceland performed traditional Viking rituals, including burials with sacrificed horses.[65] At Erik's settlement in Greenland, the Norse sometimes still asked shamans to divine the future, though only one older woman could remember the chants for summoning the spirits and only two symbolic objects were non-Christian, including an image of Thor's hammer on a loom weight.[66] But there were Christian crosses, burials, and even the first church in the hemisphere. At Brattahlíð, Erik's estate in Greenland, he built a sod-covered chapel for his wife. Their son Leif knew that chapel and probably attended mass there. He had returned as a Christian from a trip to Norway in 999—and with a mandate from King Olaf to spread the faith, or so the sagas suggest. In any case, by the time Leif and his party sailed toward the Atlantic coast most on board might have identified as Christians.

The Icelandic sagas and the Latin account by Adam of Bremen, the first surviving European mention of North America, yield hints about Leif Erikson's journey.[67] But readers who've been waiting for written texts—sources for *reliable* history—might be disappointed. Christians with pious motives penned those accounts, and they are vague and contradictory.[68] But if the *Grænlendinga saga* is right, Leif's crew first spotted Hellundland, probably Baffin Island, where a thirteenth-century Thule Inuit figurine of a man with a European tunic suggests later intercultural contact.[69] Leif's party then came upon a tree-filled land they called Markland, perhaps the coast of Labrador, and spotted an area in Newfoundland they called Vinland, probably because it had wild grapes (*vín*) for making wine.

Archaic Peoples had settled there around 4000 BCE, but there is little evidence the Vikings encountered locals while constructing at least one and maybe two bases at Newfoundland.[70] The northern site, L'Anse aux Meadows (The Bay by the Meadows), offers indisputable evidence of Viking colonization, even if it lasted only a few years or was used only sporadically after that.[71] L'Anse aux Meadows was a winter base camp where the Norse fixed ships, stored food, and prepared wood for export to Greenland. The three building complexes might have housed the chief and crew of three ships, and the turf-topped structures suggest a somewhat stratified society, with small huts for slaves and a six-room building with a traditional Norse hall for communal gatherings in the center. The building's remnants didn't include a single amulet, neither hammer nor cross, even if locals might have blended Christian and Norse practices in daily life.[72]

Some scholars suggest the settlement's name (Vinland) and the butternuts unearthed there indicate that the Vikings probably sailed down the Gulf of St. Lawrence toward present-day New Brunswick, since that's as far north as butternuts and wild grapes grew. It's possible they also explored the St. Lawrence River, which connects with the Great Lakes, or traveled down the coast to present-day Maine. An eleventh-century Norwegian coin found in Maine suggests some First Nations people traded with the settlers or that the Norse sailed south to the lands that became America.[73]

The Vikings would play a role in later US debates about national belonging, including when xenophobic leaders reasserted America's White Protestant origins by dedicating a Boston statue honoring "Leif the Discoverer" in 1887, and marginalized Catholic immigrants claimed legitimacy by embracing a fraudulent 1898 "runestone" describing a Viking Christian expedition to Minnesota.[74] But—more important for the hemisphere's medieval history—by 1100 mariners from both the Pacific and the Atlantic had come to the Americas.

Large-Scale Farming Niches, 800–1300

There's little direct evidence of sustained contacts with Scandinavians or Polynesians during the next few centuries. Global travelers—soldiers and traders as well as pilgrims and missionaries—had appallingly violent and surprisingly generous exchanges, from Christian–Muslim battles for Jerusalem during and after the First Crusade (1096–1099) to the Flemish Franciscan William of Rubruk's interfaith debates with Muslims and Buddhists in thirteenth-century Mongolia.[75] Travelers enjoyed warmer weather during this period because of the Medieval Climatic Anomaly (900–1300), even if some agricultural villages didn't always get the rain they wanted.[76] That climate shift meant improved conditions for farming in many places, however, with surpluses in Europe's wheatfields, China's ricefields, and America's cornfields. There was a cultural flowering too, with shrewd technological innovations and grand religious spaces, from Song China's Iron Pagoda in Kaifeng (1049) to the Gothic cathedral at Chartres (1260). In their more modest island temples, Hawaiian chiefs attended rituals for farming communities, and converted Norse chiefs gathered near fields for worship in Greenland's churches, just as the Europeans who converted them continued their practice of consecrating kings. Political forms that resembled agricultural chiefdoms flourished between 1000 and 1300 in the Caribbean: the ceremonial center at Tibes in Puerto Rico had twelve stone structures and stone-lined ceremonial plazas.[77] On the North American continent, the warmer seas affected the eco-cultural niches of maritime peoples from the northern Pacific coast to the eastern Subarctic near Newfoundland. Coastal peoples who didn't turn to agriculture still developed intricate symbol systems. Thule hunters who had colonized lands from Alaska to Greenland by the 1200s revered the whaling crew leader (*umialgit*) and his wife as they performed whaling rituals in homes and kiva-like structures (*qargit*) with benches along the walls, and the Chumash of southern California, who navigated their resource-rich marine environment in Polynesian-style canoes, established ritually encoded chiefdoms.[78] But the striking change in this period was more farmers planting more seeds. The temple pyramids in the plaza at Tula, the Toltec capital, showed how religion buttressed Mesoamerican states that profited from surplus bean and maize crops.[79] Most important for our story, large-scale maize farmers also transformed symbolically mediated environments in the Southwest, Southeast, and Midwest.

Making and Breaking a Maize Niche in the Chaco Symbolic Sphere, 750–1285

Two hundred years after Basketmaker Chacoans built small pithouses and intimate kivas, canyon residents scaled things up.[80] In the Pueblo I and II periods (750–1150), they continued to mix farming with hunting and foraging, but added more maize, beans, and squash to their diet. Elites consumed more animal protein than villagers, but everyone ate a lot of corn. Somewhat improbably, the drought-endangered cultural area became a niche dependent on corn agriculture and the symbol system that sustained it. Chacoans harvested some corn locally and imported the rest.[81] With sufficient food and occasional surplus, the local population expanded: there were as many as 2,700 canyon inhabitants at Chaco's peak. Elite households grew larger and society more stratified. The built environment reflected the social inequality, with scattered small houses for those in the lower social levels and "great houses" for the upper social rung.[82] Laborers began constructing the larger edifices before 850, consolidated the architectural practice by 1000, and building boomed between 1020 and 1125.[83] The three primary great houses in Chaco's core (Pueblo Bonito, Chetro Ketl, and Pueblo Alto) either accommodated distinct lineages competing for control or stood united against the other great houses.[84] Either way, the canyon sometimes saw more competition than cooperation. Factions struggled, and great house elites might have used episodic violence to intimidate local villagers and outlier communities.[85]

Chaco's great houses stood at the center of a regional symbolic community where people and practices crossed.[86] The canyon was home to twelve great houses, and neighbors built similar structures east and west of the canyon, areas that contributed laborers, brought tribute, and gathered for communal rituals at Chaco. From that residential and ceremonial core, some influence radiated outward about 100 miles north and south, with occasional contacts as far as 150 miles away.[87] Chaco's reach, stronger to the north than the south, was limited because travel was foot-driven.[88] Communication was limited too in the San Juan Basin, where mesas and buttes rise above the valley floor, even if signalers could flash reflectors or build fires to invite or warn neighbors. Those distant communities could see back toward Chaco's great houses and sacred spaces from those elevated vantage points.[89] Symbolically placed roadways connected them. In lean years, Chacoan leaders exported stored crops—perhaps part of a bargain struck with satellite communities—as well as ideas and practices. For the most part, however, goods and people flowed into that religious center. Chacoans needed wood for the roofs of great houses and kivas, so workers lugged thousands of tree planks from the western Chuska Mountains. Some goods came from Puebloans to the north and the desert Hohokam to the west.

And there was a good deal of exchange with the maize-growing religious cultures to the south. Chaco's elites procured status-enhancing materials and artifacts favored by Mesoamerican political rulers and ritual specialists, including the scarlet macaw feathers rulers wore, the copper bells priests struck, and the cacao used in their chocolate ceremonial drink.[90] Mesoamericans stored cacao in ceremonial jars, and designs on the jars at Pueblo Bonito suggest that Chacoans incorporated ritual objects and ceremonial practices of the Mesoamerican "corn lifeway."[91] Farmers to the south venerated gods associated with the sun, the rains, and the cornfields.[92] They also posited parallels between the stages of growth in corn and in humans, and artisans represented those stages in ceramic designs, as in the bent-hook pattern on Mesoamerican and Chacoan pottery, including at Pueblo Bonito. Agricultural analogies even informed their understanding of the creation of the universe, the movement of celestial bodies, and the daily rising and setting of the sun.

But Chacoans didn't just transplant that corn lifeworld; they scratched away at the parched dirt to generate cultural hybrids in the starkly beautiful but inhospitable canyon. Unlike Mesoamericans, for example, they interred macaw skeletons in elites' graves, and they developed distinctive architectural designs. Yet, like their southern neighbors, Chacoan elites' political power rested on their ability to assert religious authority by claiming access to sacred objects, revered ancestry, and hidden knowledge. Architectural design enabled the great house priestly elite to claim they were in harmony with cosmic forces like the movements of the sun, moon, and stars.[93] Pueblo Bonito's south wall aligned with the solstice marker carved on Fajada Butte, and a priest observing how the light fell on the great house wall could predict when to harvest crops and when to hold the seasonal ceremonies, including those at the fall equinox.[94] Predicting that timing might have been crucial if Pueblo Bonito's female residents had begun conducting versions of later Hopi equinox rituals.[95] In any case, whether the solar calculations supported gendered rites or communal celebrations, the wider community would have depended on Pueblo Bonito priests to predict and convene those calendric rites.

Even if Chacoan piety also extended to villagers' modest residences, which had interred relatives and family kivas, the local religion and society come into focus most clearly in the dazzling artifacts and monumental architecture of the great houses, especially the earliest and largest one, Pueblo Bonito. It was four stories tall, with 650 rooms, and took about 805,000 person-hours to complete.[96] The D-shaped masonry and wood structure resembled an apartment building, but it was more like a palace with chapels, a posh royal residence near an impressive cathedral.[97] It included thirty-two small-group kivas and three communal great kivas, and a road linked it with another great kiva, Casa Rinconada.

The building's entrance opened onto a plaza with a ponderosa pine—perhaps of symbolic significance like the Mesoamerican cosmic tree—and nearby was one of the five kivas made during the earliest construction phase.[98] But Pueblo Bonito's northern wing reveals more about residents' religious life, since it contains mortuary chambers honoring twenty-four ancestors, including ritual specialists and community leaders.[99] Room 32 contained the partial remains of an adult who might have been a priest. Near him was a crafted hematite bird with turquoise and shell inlay, and beneath him was a ceremonial cactus stick ritual specialists held. There were also eye-catching materials—galena, gypsum, and blue turquoise—as well as vessels for chocolate and 300 more ceremonial sticks. Among the 30,000 objects in Room 33 were many prized accessories, including more than 500 turquoise pendants and more than 24,000 turquoise beads. Forty-two ceremonial sticks rested near the deceased leaders, perhaps Bonito's ancestral priests or founding fathers. There were other ritual items like a shell trumpet and wooden flutes, which were rare in the Southwest. Burial 14 might have died about 817, and about four years later family members interred Burial 13 in the same chamber.[100] Burial 14, who died violently, enjoyed the more lavish funeral goods.[101] It's hard to say whether the display honored his social role or commemorated him because he died defending sacred spaces or important people. In any case, the signs of esteem are indisputable: on his chest lay turquoise pendants and a turquoise ornament with almost 2,000 beads; more imported turquoise items, including 168 pendants and 2,642 beads, rested on his abdomen. Crafted ornaments encircled his ankles and wrists, including a turquoise bird pendant.

For several hundred years Pueblo Bonito priests continued to maintain this mortuary chamber—and bury elites in nearby rooms—but construction had stopped in the canyon by 1120. By 1200 most residents had left. Some Chacoans may have migrated to the Zuni area near the New Mexico–Arizona border, and their ideas certainly had arrived between 1200 and 1250, as a Chaco-style great house there shows.[102] Others fled to the northern San Juan Basin, including Mesa Verde residents who had migrated to Chaco in the late tenth and early eleventh centuries.[103] During Chaco's heyday, the influences went back and forth: locals built Chaco-style great houses in Mesa Verde between 1075 and 1150, including Far View House. Emigrants and emulators to the north built other structures with familiar features: multiple stories, enclosed plazas, and blocked-in kivas. About two days' foot travel north of Chaco, they constructed a three-story great house at Salmon Ruins about 1090 and four more great houses at Aztec Ruins, including a 400-room structure with kivas erected between 1100 and 1130. Chacoan priests and masons must have helped plan those communities, and in the years ahead the memory of Chaco's religious vision and architectural style would become a source of impassioned disagreement at Mesa Verde.

A great deal changed in the northern San Juan after Chaco's decline in 1150. Religious shifts coincided with ecological strains and social strife. It happened about the time the basin suffered a major drought, between 1130 and 1180, which anticipated the Great Drought of the late 1270s. But the dramatic regional changes between 1150 and 1285 were about more than reduced rain and failing crops, since northern Pueblo people sometimes migrated to areas with less reliable rainfall and less agricultural potential. Cultural factors, especially religion, played a decisive role.[104] During this post-Chaco period there was mounting violence: skeletal remains from Mesa Verde sites tell a grim story. Soil depletion and population growth played a role, but tensions also arose from inhabitants' varying assessments of the rise and fall of Chaco's farming faith. Diverging attitudes toward that symbol system produced competing responses to the ecological and social stresses.[105] Religious worldviews and ritual practices must seem plausible to motivate devotees, and Chaco's priestly elites had promised to make the crops grow. When their seasonal rites didn't work, it threatened everything from notions about how to organize themselves politically to judgments about how to perform rituals in kivas. This eco-cultural niche, it seems, wasn't resilient enough to adapt to the conditions, and the new cultural capital at Aztec didn't have a prayer of long-term success, since it was too closely tied to the controversial Chacoan symbolic world.

Mesa Verde lasted more than a century after Chaco's demise, though locals continually modified how they lived and worshipped during that time of crisis. The evidence from architecture and pottery suggests that competing new religious movements sought either to nostalgically recover Chaco's faded glory or to emphatically distance devotees from its failed symbolic system.[106] Mesa Verde planners kept constructing Chaco-style kivas, but by about 1200 many locals started moving from their mesa-top cornfields to seek refuge in sheltered cliffside alcoves. Those cliff dwellings were much more richly configured than the rock shelters along the Brazos and the Pecos. Beneath the sandstone overhang at Cliff Palace (1209–1280), one of the largest cliff dwellings in North America, they built a ceremonial and political center

Figure 13. Cliff Palace at Mesa Verde. Courtesy of the National Park Service.

with towers for detecting intruders and kivas for spiritual gatherings (fig. 13). It was there that kin groups, religious societies, and visiting dignitaries performed secluded ceremonies aimed at unifying the fragmenting social order and revitalizing the drought-stubbled fields.

But the cliffside communities didn't endure. By 1285 everyone left Mesa Verde and the surrounding area. Tens of thousands of migrants fled in different directions. Some headed toward the Northern Rio Grande, including the Parajito Plateau, though that area would be abandoned after a devastating drought in the 1500s. Near Zuni in western New Mexico, earlier Chacoan migrants and their diverse neighbors fared better, as at the Hinkson site, where residents shifted from hierarchical communities organized around the roofed kivas of a great house to densely populated towns organized around large central plazas.[107] Just south of that stood a striking innovation: a Chaco-style great kiva that was much bigger, more than two and a half times larger than the one across from Pueblo Bonito. Zuni planners also didn't add a roof. So the traditional intimacy and exclusivity of the dark enclosure opened up and out, allowing more participants inside and offering a clear view to anyone who wanted to watch the sacred performances. This open, oversized kiva didn't find many imitators, but it eventually morphed into the public ceremonial plazas of the more egalitarian and less violent Pueblo IV settlements

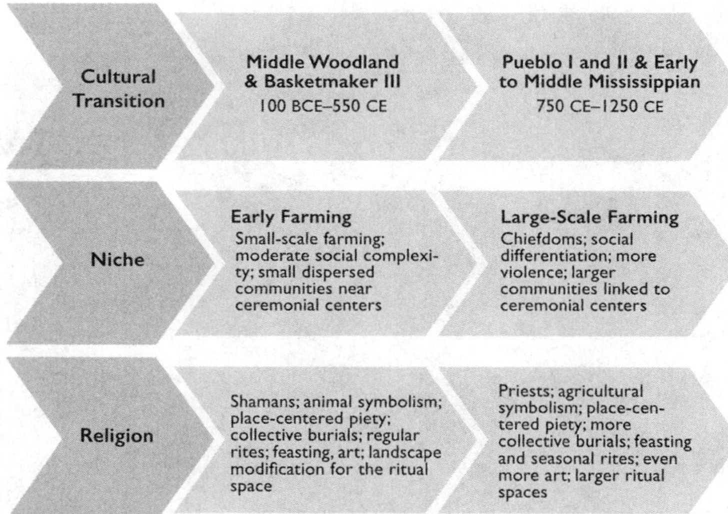

Figure 14. Transition to Pueblo religion at Chaco and Mississippian piety at Cahokia.

(1300–1600). Pueblo oral histories about the Chacoan experiment in hierarchy tell a tale about a mistaken turn corrected by a circling back to egalitarian piety and society. Scholars who concur have called it a "spiritual renaissance" or "religio-political reformation."[108] However we describe the change, a more socially and ecologically sustainable corn lifeway emerged in the plaza-oriented pueblos, a reimagined eco-cultural niche that honored Earth Mother and Sun Father and ritually negotiated with the intermediary spirits (*katsinim*) that seasonally visited those large farming towns.

Cahokia and the Mississippian Interaction Sphere, 900–1300

Back in the woodlands where the Hopewell had flourished centuries earlier, there were even more farming settlements connected in a symbolic interaction sphere about the time Chaco was peaking. Some similar cultural features appeared in that large-scale agricultural niche, including priestly elites, celestial alignments, elaborate burials, and large ritual spaces (fig. 14). While eleventh-century Ancestral Puebloans were lugging lumber to build the great houses and kivas, midwestern Mississippian Peoples stirred by a new religious movement were moving vast quantities of dirt to create earthen mounds like Cahokia's Monks Mound, the largest in North America, and

Figure 15. Pictorial reconstruction of Cahokia Mounds. Photo courtesy of Cahokia Mounds State Historic Site, artist: William Iseminger.

Mound 72, which contained the remains of almost three hundred people and tens of thousands of grave offerings, from pottery vessels and projectile points to sacrificed young women and ritually decapitated men.[109]

If you strolled Cahokia's grounds and approached the six-foot Mound 72, which was built between about 900 and 1150 CE, you might not be impressed.[110] It looks like a baby whale from an aquatic park had burrowed under a grass carpet to hide. It's a barely visible green bump. You might wonder why I'm not focusing on one of the other 120 mounds, especially the 100-foot-tall earthen monument on the other side of the Grand Plaza, Monks Mound (fig. 15). The first European American to record his reactions told Thomas Jefferson in 1811, "I was struck with a degree of astonishment. . . . What a stupendous pile of earth!"[111] Others who saw the structure named for the nineteenth-century monks who lived there found it so amazing they couldn't believe that Indians' ancestors built it. As with New Mexico's "Aztec Ruins," nineteenth-century observers assumed that Monks Mound must have been constructed by the Vikings, the Maya, or the lost tribes of Israel. More than two centuries later, most contemporary visitors who ascend that pile of earth still find it astonishing. It's not just because the posted signs say that about

1,200 years ago Cahokia's chief presided as priests performed rituals in the temple and palace that stood on its highest terrace. It's also the vista the elevated ceremonial space provides. From there you can see much of Cahokia's 5.1 square miles, looking south toward the Grand Plaza and east toward St. Louis's Gateway Arch, which is visible from the mound top. There's no doubt, if you want grandeur, Monks Mound is hard to beat.

Cahokia's population grew rapidly after 1050. Improved climatic conditions yielded larger maize harvests, which could sustain more residents. Locals grew corn on the Mississippian floodplain when the water level was right, and gathered it from upland farming communities in present-day Illinois and Missouri, at least until drought hit.[112] But neither corn nor climate explains why so many people wanted to move there. Religion, some scholars suggest, had something to do with it. Cahokia's early mortuary landscape, which included Mound 72, attracted devotees, and a prophetic new religious movement that flourished at a nearby shrine center drew pilgrims who eventually moved to Cahokia, joining migrants from near and far who relocated to the vibrant ceremonial center around 1050.[113]

Southern Caddo potters who made ritual objects for public ceremonies arrived, for instance, while locals were displaced to a nearby "suburb" so laborers could transform the landscape.[114] When the mound builders were finished, the ceremonial complex had become the center of a metropolitan area that stretched eight miles on both sides of the Mississippi. About twenty-six mounds stood across the Mississippi in present-day St. Louis, and at least forty-five more were in the Illinois town of East St. Louis. Almost 50,000 people also lived within a day's travel, and pilgrims from those satellite communities also attended communal rituals, either traveling on foot or paddling on the creek that snaked along Cahokia's eastern border.[115]

Greater Cahokia, which had a population of between 10,000 and 20,000 people, functioned as a political capital as well as a ceremonial center, and the built environment of that regional state or complex chiefdom—some call it a city—oriented residents in time and space.[116] In some ways its downtown core resembled the National Mall in Washington, DC. Both civic spaces form a rough diamond shape of similar dimensions, each with a large plaza along the central pathway. In Washington, which is oriented on an east-west axis, the Capitol building rests at the diamond's head and the Lincoln Memorial stands across from it. Cahokia was oriented along a north-south axis, and Monks Mound stands toward the northern point while Mound 72 is aligned about 1,000 yards south of it.[117] In Washington, later leaders would allow "free exercise" of religion while prohibiting the "establishment" of any faith, but the two urban designs were not that different, since the original plan for the District of Columbia called for a "national church" for civic rituals. That's similar to what happened on Monks Mound, as the chief and the priest performed rites aimed at solidifying political power and reinforcing religious meaning.

Yet the top-down civil religion on Monks Mound obscures a good deal about devotional life at Cahokia. Mound 72, which offers clues about the diverse community's contested but compelling worldview, provides a more useful vantage for understanding Mississippian piety.

Located halfway between the Mississippi's source and its delta, Cahokia had wide influence. Its symbols circulated throughout the Mississippian Interaction Sphere, just as the mound–plaza pattern recurred from Wisconsin to Louisiana, and as far as the Caddo Mounds in eastern Texas.[118] In turn, people and objects also traveled to Cahokia by canoe from long distances, even hundreds of miles. Some of the young women and men ritually sacrificed and interred at Mound 72—perhaps as political tribute and spiritual offerings—were not from Cahokia. The grave objects included special raw materials (like mica and copper) and skillfully crafted artifacts (like arrow points and shell beads) that originated east and west of the Mississippi or along the riverine basin that stretched from the Great Lakes to the Gulf of Mexico.[119] As with the Archaic mound complexes in Louisiana, some specialists think the parallels with Mexican imagery and architectural design are too close to rule out shared heritage or cultural exchange. Chaco had items of indisputable Mesoamerican origin, like macaws, chocolate, and copper bells. The connections are less clear but still intriguing in the Midwest. In the archaeological record of the Early and Middle Mississippian Eras, there are architectural parallels and iconographic similarities but not the trade goods that would settle the debate. So until more evidence surfaces, it's probably safest to say that crossings went up and down the hemisphere and there was "a pattern of interaction through many centuries, perhaps millennia."[120]

Cahokia's mental map extended even further: Mound 72's spatial alignment and burial objects represent the whole universe. Cahokia's designers laid out the communal landscape in terms of the four directions, and symbols mapped a cosmos with three realms—the Middle World, the Upper World, and the Underworld. They aligned Mound 72 with the north-south axis of the ceremonial center and the astronomical movements of the celestial realm.[121] The axis of the mound's ridgetop is angled northwest to southeast, which aligns with the winter solstice sunrise and the summer solstice sunset.

That alignment recalls an individual's lifespan and mirrors the world's death at sunset and rebirth at sunrise. The symbolization about cosmic and earthly renewal is vividly portrayed in the "Beaded Burial" complex in Submound 1, which got its name because of all the shell beads around a young adult male (Burial 13) and overlying a young adult female (Burial 14), who both rested close to an apparently sacrificed man (Burial 16) and another male-female pair.[122] Scholars who unearthed those remains called Mound 72 the "summer solstice sunrise mound" because Burials 13 and 14 lie near a post in a circle of cedar posts marking the position of the sunrise, with their feet pointing northwest. Interpreters agree about the spatial orientation and concur that the grave goods function as symbolic locatives pointing to cosmic realms. Yet they disagree about whether the grave offerings signal the Upper World, with male warrior imagery linked with falcons and the Morning Star, or the Underworld, with Earth Mother fertility imagery and the creative coupling of Morning Star and Evening Star.[123]

The first interpretation presumes that the male (Burial 13) is the central figure, and that the arc of beads extending out from his shoulder and face formed the shape of a bird's head. The beads do look like an avian symbol, whether that was intended or not, but it turns out that his mortuary mate (Burial 14) was female. That identification, together with the discovery of other male-female pairs—and the comingled child—has challenged the male-centered warrior account of the Beaded Burial, which relied on later Indigenous hero myths associated with falcon figures. The burial sequence, which began around 1000, suggests that the alternate interpretation emphasizing creation and fertility is plausible, and might fit better with what we know about that eco-cultural niche's dependence on cornfields. The caretakers of the dead first lowered the woman on a layer of marine shell beads and placed beads over her thighs and lower legs. They then placed the male, Burial 13, on top of her, covering her right side. Then—in the crucial step—they placed more beads near his shoulder and face. Later excavators would be struck by the effect: he resembled the bird-man figure that has parallels in earlier and later Central and North American cultural history.

Interpreters who emphasize the male-female pairs point out that the bird symbol, if it was intended, still might have referred to the Underworld. The reverse side of Cahokia's Birdman Tablet includes snakeskin cross-hatching signaling the lower realm, and marine shells usually signal the lower realm too. If those interpretations are right, they argue, the gravesite coupling of Burial 13 and 14 might evoke mythic parallels with later Native tales about the first man and the first woman; it even might mean those grave goods functioned as "votive offerings for celestial beings."[124] In turn, this might suggest that early Cahokia symbolization, as with these burials and female figurines, reflect a female-centered or dual-gendered religio-political system that later changed into a more male-centered political order, with the authority of male chiefs and priests sanctioned by male imagery, including the bird-man symbol and its associations with falcon-like warriors.[125]

Whichever account eventually proves more persuasive, there is a good deal we can say with some certainty. As with the ancestral interments in Pueblo Bonito's Room 33, the Beaded Burial offers evidence of funeral rituals that "likely represent foundational events both for Mound 72 and for the creation of Cahokia itself."[126] The 20,000 Gulf shell beads stage a spectacular display of symbolic surplus, the recurring inclination to bury important people with an extraordinary number of special objects and with an extraordinary level of communal contribution.[127] The long-distance goods near them in the mound also send a signal. There was rolled copper from the Great Lakes region, shell beads from the Gulf of Mexico, bushels of mica from the Appalachians, and 800 unused projectile points made of chert from across the midcontinent. The goods' stunning quantity and distant origin show the elite status of Burial 13 and Burial 14. The mortuary excess and exotic goods signal—to local observers and to spiritual beings encountered on their postmortem journey—that they were special.

The mortuary objects and corpse position also offer hints about how locals might have imagined what happened after death, if later sacred myths offer relevant clues.[128] Their feet pointed in the direction they would travel: like all of Cahokia's dead, they would start their final journey when their "free soul," the soul not constrained by their lifeless body, took the westward trek along the earth disk and toward the setting sun, the transition point between night and day. Then a carefully timed leap from the terrestrial to the celestial realm would lead them across the night sky to the Path of Souls, the Milky Way. From there their free souls would travel south toward the Realm of the Dead. Traversing a bridge to cross the river bordering the underworld, the successful traveler—sometimes souls get stuck—would reach a perfected analog of the everyday world that those two elites had known during their lifetimes of privilege.

Wherever the locative symbols pointed, the gathering mourners might have found some comfort in the symbolism of regeneration. We can't reconstruct what the sacrificed man or the dirt-moving laborers thought about the social hierarchy enacted so starkly in that public communal rite, but participants would have understood the figurative logic that aimed to reassure the community that the celestial, terrestrial, and subterranean realms were in order—whether they imagined the beaded bird-man corpse ascending to the celestial realm and reaching the Realm of the Dead or whether they imagined the male-female pair replicating the primal creative act of intercourse between Morning Star and Evening Star. In any case, it seems that the commemorative rite concerned the community more than those individuals. The ritual not only sent a message about communal and cosmological roles but also assured mourners that all things will be regenerated: those elites will find a new life in the realm of the dead, their descendants will continue their ancestral lineage, successors will assume their vacated social positions, another morning sun will rise on another day's horizon, the seasons will change, the corn stalks will grow, and all will be right in the heavens.

After Chaco and Cahokia, 1300–1492

But all would not be right forever. Regeneration at Cahokia had its limits. Because of escalating social conflict, heightened spiritual controversy, rising floodwaters, and the onset of the Little Ice Age, a sustainability crisis broke out near the Mississippi, just as it had in the Southwest (see appendix).[129] The ceremonial center began to be abandoned about 1300, a few years after migrants fled Mesa Verde. There would never be another Cahokia, a congested ceremonial center almost as big as London, and after 1300 those dispersing Mississippian Peoples tended to relocate in small, clustered villages with local chiefs. Yet just as resilient Pueblo farming communities near Zuni modified the southwestern landscape after 1300 by retaining some Chacoan traditions and inventing new ones, some communities kept alive the memory of Mississippian maize niches and mounds. In the Upper Mississippi, mound builders in the LaCrosse area of Wisconsin abandoned that complex by about 1250, but they took their lifeways with them as they migrated to the Great Plains, where centuries later they prompted a surprising revival of mound ceremonialism in Iowa.[130] In the Lower Mississippi Valley, near the Natchez Bluffs, locals kept traditions alive after 1200. For several centuries residents adapted to the new conditions but continued to organize themselves in chiefdoms, and continued to move dirt to build platform mounds encircling ceremonial plazas.[131]

Varied religious practices and political forms flourished among the Algonquian, Iroquoian, and Siouan speakers of the northeastern Atlantic Coast, from the Mi'kmaq on the upper St. Lawrence River, near where Vikings explored, to the Tuscarora near North Carolina's Roanoke Island. Not all were large-scale farmers, but shellfish-loving residents of Cape Cod were sedentary enough to create elaborate burial spaces by 1000, and by 1500 they consumed a diet rich in maize, beans, and squash.[132] Political arrangements included confederacies among the Haudenosaunee (Iroquois), who were agriculturalists, and farther south there were symbolically inflected eco-cultural niches among the Arawak-speaking Taíno of the Caribbean, including in future US territories (Puerto Rico and the Virgin Islands) where Columbus anchored.[133] The Taínos' religion, art, and architecture displayed continuing connections to South America and possible contacts with Mesoamerica, where regional interaction spheres emerged in this period. The Incas of coastal Peru were expanding their Andean control, and the Mexica (Aztecs) established the capital of their maize niche in the Basin of Mexico at Tenochtitlán, where rulers and priests performed ceremonies, including ritual killings, at the Great Temple. The temple and leaders are depicted in a 1542 image of the city. The temple stands near the top, and scattered maize plants proclaim the city's agricultural plenty. The chief speaker, who would have conducted rites at the temple, stands to the left of the religio-political symbols with which he is associated: a blooming cactus and a giant eagle.[134]

Metropolitan Tenochtitlán might have been one of the largest urban areas in the world in 1491, with as many as 100,000 residents at a time when the continental population north of Mesoamerica might have numbered no more than 6 million.[135] The world's two largest cities, Beijing and Cairo, were still recovering from the devastating impact of lethal microbes during the Black Death (1320–1355). Cairo, the culturally rich but politically declining Islamic center, would be seized in 1517 by the Ottoman Turks, whose fifteenth-century resurgence panicked some Europeans, including the Portuguese rulers who sponsored Late Medieval Europe's earliest and most successful imperial seafaring. Beijing developed navigational technology that could have allowed more protocolonizing than their maritime emissaries accomplished in the first quarter of the fifteenth century.[136] Yet after 1424, increasingly isolationist China didn't try to discover new lands. The Chinese withdrew from the global transoceanic competition they might have won. Inspired more by pragmatic Confucian statecraft than speculative Buddhist philosophy—or stories about Buddha's Pure Land in the West—they focused on homeland security and political consolidation, fortifying the Great Wall and battling the Mongols. The Confucian elite also didn't compete with Iberian Christian rulers because they were less preoccupied with religiously inspired efforts to conquer Muslim infidels. Most important, Ming ships were already trading with Indians, and the Chinese already had found Cathay, the term that Marco

Polo had used for northern China, the imagined destination of many fifteenth-century European explorers.[137] Iberian elites didn't care only about China and India, to be sure. Portugal's Prince Henry also explored Africa to secure financial gain, slow Islam's spread, and convert the heathen. Most important for North America's religious history, the Portuguese had begun transporting enslaved people from West Africa by the 1440s and converted the Congo's king in 1491.[138] Yet the quest to find an Asian sea route consumed Portuguese and Spanish monarchs. It wasn't just the silk and spices; they also hoped to resist the Muslim crescent and raise the Christian cross. The royal launchers of the Spanish Inquisition, Ferdinand and Isabella, as well as their devout Italian discoverer, imagined themselves as divinely sanctioned crusaders. Spain, in turn, was their reconquered holy land providentially expanding eastward.[139]

So, emboldened by his sacred charge and protected by the Virgin Mary and other holy intercessors, Saint Francis and Saint Christopher, Columbus sailed in August 1492 from Palos, Spain. He and the crew marked the time by prayers: a boy recited a prayer while turning the timer every thirty minutes, and they sang the Salve Regina every sunset, a hymn asking Mary to assist those "exiles" from the Garden. More than two months later, they found a garden of sorts, though it wasn't Eden. Instead Columbus strode ashore on a Caribbean beach near a Taíno farming village. The village's chieftain and priest had their own spiritual guardians (*zemis*)—including Yúcahu, the god of the sea, and Atabey, the goddess of fertility—and they all welcomed their European guests to Guanahani.[140] Columbus promptly claimed the island for the Spanish crown and renamed it for the Redeemer. It would now be *San Salvador,* Holy Savior. The saving of Chinese and Indian heathens had begun. He said so in a letter, reporting he had reached China (*la provincia Catayo*) and had found "Indians" (*los Indios*) from "the Indies" (*las Indias*).[141] After that portentous misunderstanding and asymmetrical exchange, some Taínos on other islands would begin telling stories about how after the Christians came some gods "escaped and went into the lagoon."[142] The gods who stayed and the islanders who venerated them also would discover what Columbus's crew already knew—they had a cannon as well as a cross—and, as exploration became settlement, they all would learn what no one then suspected. The Europeans also carried fatal germs, and the later settlers would follow the Portuguese pattern of displacing and transporting West Africans, including Yorùbá diviners, Muslim scholars, and even Congolese Catholics, whose faith couldn't save them from being sold to Protestant planters on South Carolina plantations. With those intended and unintended forces unleashed on that tropical beach, those farther north in the lands that would become America were poised to learn—or learn again—that figured habitats can prompt wonder and ease suffering, but sometimes can grow socially and ecologically unsustainable. At those times, spiritual flourishing—even mere survival—requires the resilience to repair eco-cultural niches, welcome displaced newcomers, and reimagine shared futures. That was a lesson that wouldn't be learned quickly or easily, however, and only long after Europeans began to uproot Native niches, establish slave plantations, and plant Christian colonies in a world that only seemed "new" to the late-arriving Europeans.

CHAPTER 3

Imperial Religion

Agricultural Metaphors, Catholic Missions, and the Second Sustainability Crisis, 1565–1756

Exploration continued for a half century after 1492, as other empires joined the Spanish in launching marine expeditions. By 1550, crews had sailed to the tips of North and South America and sent reports that raised European expectations and increased imperial competition.[1] The reports persuaded kings—and the kings of commerce—they could expect precious resources, fertile soil, a route to Asia, and willing converts. The first map of that land to mention "America," a 1507 image, showed a long sliver of a continent, but cartographers gradually filled in the landmass on colonial maps as exploration led to settlement (fig. 16).

Sustained European settlement in the Americas began in 1493, when Columbus returned with carpenters and farmers as well as priests and soldiers, and the papal bull *Inter Caetera* sanctioned Spanish territorial ambitions by introducing what came to be called the "Doctrine of Discovery," which held that any land not inhabited by Christians could be claimed to save the souls of its inhabitants.[2] The Spaniards then conquered Native Peoples and established settlements in Mexico in 1519 and Peru in 1533. Using the same theological justifications and military strategies, they founded towns and built churches north of the Rio Grande. In 1565 Spanish Catholic soldiers killed Protestants and subdued Native Peoples at St. Augustine, Florida, the first permanent settlement in the lands that became the United States.[3] It was not until 1607 that English Protestants founded a permanent settlement in Virginia, and the French Catholic empire got a continental foothold the next year with the

Figure 16. Universalis cosmographia secundum Ptholomaei traditionem et Americi Vespucii alioru[m]que lustrationes, by Martin Waldseemüller (1507). Library of Congress, Geography and Map Division, G3200 1507W3.

founding of Quebec. Dutch Protestants built a trading post on the Hudson River in 1614, and Swedish Lutherans erected a fort near Delaware Bay in 1638. The imperial contest for souls and soil was underway by 1650.

As isolated settler outposts became interconnected imperial provinces, a second crisis of sustainability flared up between 1650 and 1750, when empires' emissaries sanctioned the displacement of Natives and the enslavement of Africans. A few religiously inspired dissenters spoke out, but the imperial church and state mostly made things worse. Most European newcomers did little to defend Native Peoples, resist African enslavement, or restore damaged niches. Leaders had sacralized the status quo around 1300 too, but dispersing groups eventually resolved the cornfield crises by continuing some ancestral practices while altering others in scaled-down farming villages where everyone still gathered to pray for rain. The colonial crisis, however, would remain unresolved as stressed spaces like the mission and the plantation became increasingly unsustainable (see appendix).[4] Colonial agriculture and merchant capitalism depended on forced labor, unrestrained extraction, and inequitable distribution.[5] Early settlers unwittingly spread germs and intentionally used force. Few colonists and even fewer Natives wielded political power or enjoyed individual freedom, even if before 1756 some Indigenous communities on the edges of settlements negotiated as almost equals in trade agreements and military alliances, and inspiring but partial efforts to defend religious liberty emerged in colonial Rhode Island, Maryland, and Pennsylvania.[6]

Colonial eco-cultural niches also were unsustainable because the trauma of Indigenous decimation and African enslavement diminished religion's ability to provide the meaning and belonging necessary for full human flourishing. Colonists sometimes listened to Indigenous or African practical knowledge—about planting corn or cultivating rice—but surviving records suggest they rarely questioned whether God was on their side.[7] To be sure, early European settlers suffered bouts of despair as the chill of cropless winters loomed or the pile of unburied corpses grew—often without clergy to comfort them or church bells to call them.[8] But colonialism's impact on Natives and Africans was worse. Depopulation and displacement destabilized priestly and shamanic traditions, including mechanisms for creating symbolic artifacts, training ritual specialists, and convening communal rituals. In response, Natives tried to restore the broken traditions and heal the "historical trauma."[9] Exiled Africans suffered trauma too, and those who had practiced Indigenous, Muslim, or Christian faiths also struggled to reconstitute their traditions after the uprooting that began in the sixteenth century. Some scholars think that by 1700 war and disease had reduced the Western Hemisphere's Indigenous population to about one-tenth of precontact numbers. High estimates say there may have been as many as 50 to 100 million people in the Americas in 1492, and about 5 to 10 million north of Mexico.[10] Whether we trust the "low counters" or the "high counters"—or the conservative estimate of 1 million north of the Rio Grande—many Natives died and survivors relocated, even if most territory west of the Mississippi remained Indian Country into the 1750s.[11]

To replace the forced labor of dwindling Indigenous populations, Europeans imported enslaved Africans. In 1510 the Spanish king approved the shipment of fifty captives to Santo Domingo in Hispaniola, and the transatlantic trade escalated in the centuries ahead. By the time it ended in the nineteenth century, the English, French, Dutch, Danes, and Americans had joined the circum-Atlantic slave trade, with its vast network of complicit agents in Africa.[12] About 45 percent of the captives were taken from Congo and Angola, with others departing from farther north along the West African shore, from the Bight of Biafra to the Gold Coast (fig. 17).[13] Violence, and often death, awaited captives. Two-thirds had been seized in local wars or by roaming bandits, and not all survived the trek to port. Further, even though captains' logbooks often opened by appealing for God's guidance during the

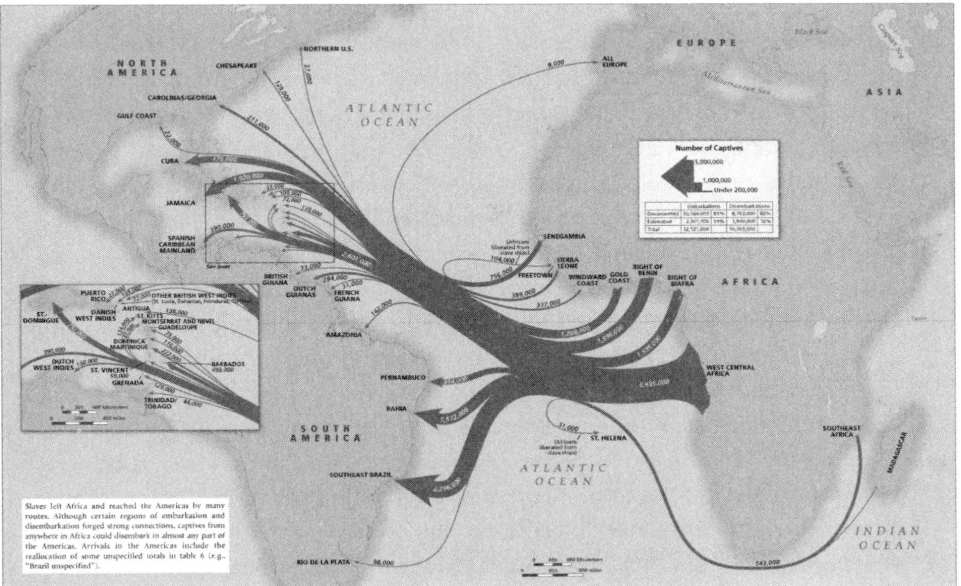

Figure 17. The flows of the slave trade from African ports to the Americas. From Eltis and Richardson, *Atlas of the Transatlantic Slave Trade*, map 11, "Overview of the Slave Trade out of Africa, 1500–1900," 18–19. © 2010 by Yale University. Courtesy of Yale University Press.

voyage, many who embarked didn't make it across.[14] That's why Portuguese and French vessels carried chaplains to perform the last rites for African Catholics who—if the sharks didn't get them—would slowly sink to an aquatic grave. Between 1501 and 1867 at least 15 percent of the 12.5 million Africans destined for the two-month journey in leg irons died before docking.[15]

All this upheaval altered religiously figured niches—but not everything and not all at once. The standard narrative, which starts with Christians arriving, blinds us to continuities with the Indigenous past—and not only the spiritual responses to earlier sustainability crises. If you were skeptically awaiting an intellectual payoff for starting with that ancient rock shelter burial, here's a first installment: now that our story of how religion promoted and hindered flourishing has arrived at the colonial period, we can notice what *didn't* change, or least not right away. We still see red ochre and bird symbols, ritual hallucinogens and shamanic trances, burial offerings and harvest festivals, as well as worship spaces like mounds, plazas, and kivas. Farming lifeways continued for many Native Peoples, who struggled to tell the old stories and conduct the old rituals in new places. As they did their best to remake their homes and restore their homelands, Indigenous exiles still told tales about how they got maize. They still celebrated the seasonal rites. Even Natives who did more hunting than farming continued to ritually mark the transitions from birth to death, including in mortuary ceremonies that confronted metaphysical anguish. The red ochre that recurred in those burials also explains one small change—how Natives came to be called "red." The presence of newcomers who called themselves *White* and described their enslaved laborers as *Black* led some Indigenous leaders and colonial elites to start using a color-coded descriptor—*Red*—to identify locals who adorned themselves with red ochre and were tanned from exposure to the sun. The chromatic label, which appeared in early explorers' and travelers' accounts, began to take hold by the 1750s.[16]

There were other changes in this era of spiritual boundary crossing (fig. 18). One White captive, Esther Wheelwright, was an English Protestant infant in Massachusetts in 1696, an adopted daughter in a Wabanaki village in 1703, and a nun in a French Catholic convent in Quebec by 1713.[17] Few experienced such dramatic changes, but the contacts affected almost everyone in the eastern woodlands and the southwestern borderlands. The newcomers introduced the printing press—and religion of the book—to Natives who had rich oral traditions. Locals had practiced long-distance trading for thousands of years, but Europeans created transoceanic networks that imported new symbolic artifacts, religious organizations, and sacred rituals. Natives already had known violence, both intercommunity warfare and ritualized human sacrifice, but the Europeans gave them more lethal weapons. Indigenous Peoples had taken captives, but the colonists instituted more dehumanizing forms of slavery. Natives had cleared the land for planting and preached their faith to neighbors, but Europeans built new worship spaces like the church and established new social spaces like the plantation and the mission.

Europeans' demand for tobacco, sugar, and cotton altered bioregions—as the search for precious metals honeycombed southwestern terrain and the quest for lumber deforested northeastern hillsides—but the continent also became an arena for an imperial struggle for heathen souls.[18] Christians kept one eye on their old foes as they continued holy wars and resumed religious reformations on the other side of the Atlantic, and traditional rivalries and alliances shifted as Indigenous communities fiercely resisted, pragmatically joined, or ritually incorporated newcomers. With communities swapping mates and exchanging goods, peoples mixed and practices merged. And almost everyone felt a need for more fortifications, material and spiritual. The

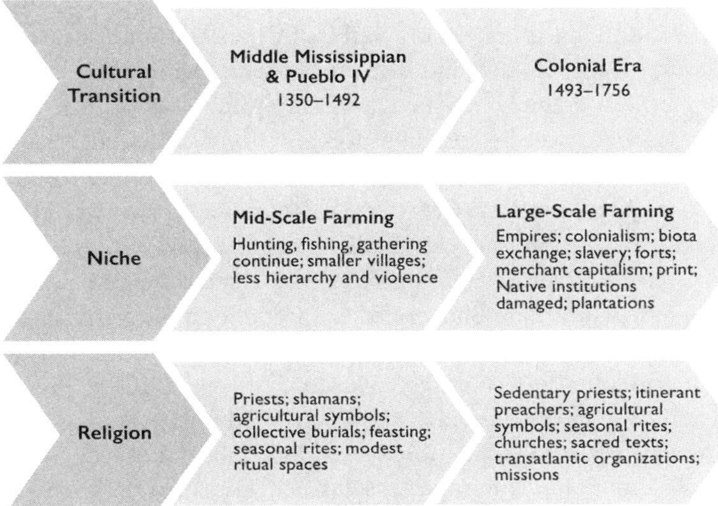

Figure 18. Transition from Pre-Columbian piety to religion of the Imperial Era.

Europeans built chapels near forts, just as Mesa Verde's residents had retreated to kivas beneath the southwestern cliffs. In the colonial period, Natives and newcomers turned to religion to make sense of the new forms of wonder and worry. And contact did produce some wonder, even if worry sometimes won in the end. Natives and Europeans initially marveled at new crops and technologies and expressed curiosity about each other's origin stories and death rituals.[19] At least at first, they were "capable of genuine wonder and even delight in the recognition of differences."[20] Later participants in cross-cultural exchanges even created mixed practices in zones where the colonizers and the colonized met.[21] Muskets and cannons gave European Christians the upper hand in those encounters, yet settlers still worried. They took comfort in their royal mandate and repeated timeworn explanations for suffering: it's a spiritual test, a divine retribution, or beyond human comprehension. For practitioners of Native and African Indigenous traditions, contact brought more worry than wonder: the displaced asked why their diviners hadn't foreseen these misfortunes and why their ceremonies hadn't protected them. They sought answers in the continent's imperiled agricultural habitats and in the new colonial niches. There they turned to familiar figurative tools—and borrowed or crafted new ones—to describe the newfound wonders and, most of all, to relieve the new forms of anguish, physical and metaphysical.

The imperial struggle for territory and converts intensified during the 1750s, a transition in the history of religion. By then the Spanish and French claimed wide swaths of land, and their missionaries had established Catholic identity among some Native Peoples in the Midwest and Southwest, but the religious identity of the continent was still hotly contested. That decade witnessed the first world war, which was also the last of the European wars of religion.[22] That Protestant-Catholic conflict, called the Seven Years' War or the French and Indian War, eventually redrew the borders of the lands that became America. Transoceanic currents also carried new rationalist and revivalist pieties that altered how residents in the English colonies, the Anglophone Caribbean, and Protestant Europe mapped the *interior* landscape. Transatlantic Protestant revivals, which emphasized experience and situated authority in the individual, had enlivened many towns in the 1730s and 1740s but began to divide them by midcentury. Those divisions, and transplanted Protestant denominations, further diversified the colonies. Both Congregationalist Boston and Quaker Philadelphia, the two largest cities, were changing, and splintering sects and new denominations foreshadowed the nation's future religious diversity.

Europeans and Africans also outnumbered Native Peoples east of the Mississippi for the first time by the 1750s, when encroaching settlers forced tribes westward while pan-Indian religious movements arose to reassert Native sovereignty.[23] Enslaved Africans also staged revolts, yet by the 1750s the slave plantation and rural chapel were reshaping the southern landscape, and the limited religious liberty enjoyed in some British colonies began to erode as lawmakers excluded Jews, Catholics, and atheists from full political participation.[24] Even residents of Pennsylvania, home to pacifist Quakers, joined the British colonial campaign to fight Natives and their French confederates, in order to prevent Catholic tyranny and preserve Protestant liberty.[25]

That's the grander sweep of the story from the onset of colonial settlement in 1565 to the start of the Seven Years' War in 1756. But let's take a fine-grained view of how farming metaphors seeded the fields of imperial religious discourse and how the religiously figured "planting" of colonies transformed local landscapes, while acknowledging Natives' and Africans' resilient responses to the displacement of peoples and the uprooting of traditions.

Farming Faiths, Agricultural Metaphors, and Imperial Struggles

Imperial officials came from the Dutch and Swedish, who influenced the future Middle Colonies, as well as from the Danish, who settled terrain that would become the US Virgin Islands, and from the Russians, who colonized

Alaska.[26] However, the Spanish, French, and English most fully transformed the colonial landscape, and religious and political elites from those wheat-field empires advocated an agricultural lifestyle and used figurative language about farming to make sense of themselves and their world.[27]

Missionaries came with a plow as well as a cross. They believed in both, even if the cross sometimes consecrated unsustainable lifeways and the plow depleted the soil and polluted the air. Environmental scientists tell us tilling the earth to bury crop residue and control unwanted weeds increases carbon emissions.[28] But Franciscan Alonso de Benavides had no way of knowing that. His caravan to New Mexico carried tilling tools as well as altar cloths, and he reported in 1630 that the Natives "used to live like savages."[29] He praised the Pueblo women who built more than fifty churches with "amazing ceilings" and "painted walls" in the new towns the Franciscans established, but he didn't seem to notice that the locals already had agricultural towns. Even when the friar reluctantly acknowledged the fields, he claimed Natives were farming in the wrong way with the wrong crops. So the missionaries introduced plows and raised cattle to pull them. Indigenous Peoples in the Southwest only needed instruction, those Franciscans reasoned, "in our way of doing things."[30] Similarly, John Eliot, a Puritan minister in seventeenth-century New England, created fourteen agricultural "praying towns" because he thought Natives needed enclosed fields and household lots as much as baptism and Bible reading. French missionaries sometimes followed hunter-gatherers tracking game, but they too preferred farmers to foragers.[31] That's clear, for instance, in missionary Jean de Brébeuf's assessment of the sedentary, corn-growing Wendat (Huron), as opposed to the mobile hunting Innu (Montagnais): "I do not claim here to put our Indians on the same level as the Chinese, Japanese and other perfectly civilized nations," he wrote in 1636, "but only to rank them among men." As evidence of their humanity, he noted that the Wendat "live assembled in villages" and "cultivate the fields."[32]

Leaders of the main colonial powers also used agricultural analogies to understand their colonizing activity and devotional practice. They talked about "planting" colonies and establishing "plantations." They used metaphors about domestication to understand settlers' spiritual life and interpret efforts to tame the landscape and evangelize the heathen.[33] Early observers noticed stores of Indian maize, but many settlers still saw the terrain as barren and barbaric, absent the marks of Christian civilization. It needed cultivating. Despite praising Natives' care for the dead and their natural generosity, many settlers also saw them as untamed and untutored. They were sprouts in an untended garden.[34] They needed spiritual cultivating. Relying on agricultural images from the New Testament, which assumes familiarity with farming, and drawing on their observation of tilling fields, Spanish, French, and English elites used a shared language about sowing seeds, tending crops, and reaping harvests to describe their colonizing efforts.

They debated whether Native Peoples were the lost tribes of Israel or the demonic allies of Satan. Most concluded they were either heathens with the wrong religion or people without religion. In either case, most missionaries and monarchs thought there was hope for Native souls. A Protestant lawyer and member of Parliament, Richard Hakluyt, wrote *A Discourse on Western Planting* in 1584 to convince Queen Elizabeth I to support colonial ventures, like the (doomed) one then setting out for Roanoke Island. He suggested that such ventures provided a chance to spread the gospel by converting those who practice "idolatrie."[35] Quoting Jacques Cartier's report for the French crown, he reminded her there was reason to think evangelization might bear fruit, because Natives are "very easie to be perswaded." Many English Protestant settlers were less focused on conversions but still discussed cultivating souls and planting colonies. William Bradford's journal about "Plimoth Plantation" used farming metaphors to understand religious as well as political life, and American Quaker followers of George Fox were advised to tend to their "inner plantations" as they built "outer plantations."[36] French Catholic missionaries planted the "seeds" of the gospel among Native Peoples: the Jesuit Paul Le Jeune argued that the Native soul is "naturally fertile soil," even if it contains "all the evils that a land abandoned since birth" might have.[37] Those French Jesuits hoped effort might yield "a harvest of souls."[38] Spanish Franciscans in New Mexico, using the same phrase, reported that the "harvest of souls" had been "abundant" in the "mission fields" among the Pueblo and other idolaters in the Southwest.[39]

Roaming evangelists and settled preachers also used farming metaphors to interpret the variety of peoples in the land and the diversity of faiths taking root. Many who pondered the practical challenges of peaceful coexistence reflected on the Parable of the Tares and the Wheat in the Gospel of Matthew (Matt. 13:24–30).[40] That biblical story proved popular as ecclesial and government leaders thought about diversity, liberty, and the end of time.

> The kingdom of heaven may be compared to someone who sowed good seed in his field; but . . . an enemy came and sowed weeds among the wheat. . . . And the slaves of the householder came and said to him, "Master, did you not sow good seed in your field? Where then, did these weeds come from?" He answered: "An enemy has done this." The slaves said to him, "Then do you want

> us to go and gather them?" But he replied, "No; for in gathering the weeds you would uproot the wheat along them with them. Let both of them grow together until the harvest; and at harvest time I will tell the reapers, Collect the weeds first and then bind them in bundles to be burned, but gather the wheat into my barn."

Europeans debated whether the "field" referred to the church building or the political realm.[41] Yet all interpreters confronted the story's pragmatic proposal: leave the "weeds," the heretics and heathens, so you don't accidently pull up the "wheat," faithful Christians. Many Protestants and Catholics in early modern Europe were sure they could tell weeds from wheat and were happy to do the sorting. Some Catholics in early modern France, and even in Spain and its colonies, quietly ignored the Catholic teaching that "there is no salvation outside the church" and advocated a softer view expressed in the common phrase, "Each person can be saved in his or her own religion."[42] Some English Protestants came to a softer view too. Some reasoned their way to toleration by articulating moral principles like liberty of conscience, as in John Locke's *A Letter Concerning Toleration* (1689).[43] Yet most, like William Penn, arrived at toleration as a strategic solution to a practical problem. In England that future founder of Pennsylvania rejected the "forced uniformity" demanded by the Church of England. To defend himself and other nonconformists, Penn argued that "a Kingdom of many Minds" must respect liberty of conscience, just as Jesus instructed his followers not to persecute those of differing opinions because "the Tares should grow with the Wheat."[44]

The parable came up in disputes in the American colonies too, as when the dissenter Roger Williams complained that Massachusetts Bay Colony had unfairly chased him out. The founder of Rhode Island appealed to that biblical passage when conveying his reluctant conclusion—that you could condemn a weed-choked congregation but, at least until the reaper burns the weeds, believers must be resigned to live with unbelievers in the wider civic community.[45] Others would continue to ponder that parable, including eighteenth-century churchmen like the Catholic John Carroll, the first US bishop, and the Congregationalist Jonathan Edwards, the respected Protestant minister.[46] Edwards's hesitation arose from the similarity between the weeds and the wheat, the sinners and the saints: it was "next to impossible to distinguish them." The botanical features of that particular weed, sometimes called darnel or false wheat, support his interpretation. The Greek word in the gospel passage (*zizania*), which was translated as *tares* in the King James Bible and as *cockles* in the Douay-Rheims Catholic Bible, referred to a weed well-known to farmers of Jesus's day as closely resembling wheat.[47] Botanists call that process "mimicry," whereby an invasive species copies nearby crops.[48] Unaware of the botanical science but aware of the scriptural caution, some colonial Christians used the parable to explain their practical solution to the plurality of peoples and perspectives.

Religious diversity and competition were familiar to the arriving European Christians. The era of colonial planting in the Americas coincided with a fractious—and violent—time in European history. There was an Age of Reformations between 1450, when the invention of the printing press allowed dissent to circulate, and 1648, when a bloody war among Christians ended.[49] The complaints—and reforming impulse—had begun earlier, but in 1517 a scrupulous German monk named Martin Luther circulated ninety-five theological propositions challenging the late medieval practice of selling indulgences, the merciful reduction of a sinner's punishment. Printed copies of that document unleashed impassioned disputes about the nature of salvation and the role of the church. Those disputes continued when the pope, who initially dismissed Luther's complaints as "monkish squabble," finally kicked him out of the church.[50] To make things more tense, those "protesting" Catholicism didn't agree among themselves. Multiple Protestant reformations emerged in the sixteenth century, not only Lutheran but also Swiss Reformed, Radical, Calvinist, and Anglican. As Protestant–Catholic divisions deepened and Protestant movements splintered, Christians fought religious wars in Europe.[51] The pious disagreed about matters that today might seem minor—what is the Eucharist?—but the divergent interpretations became fighting words. Disputants shed blood because almost all European Christians became more confessional, fervently defending a particular understanding of the gospel. And those stridently confessional churches were conjoined with the state. As in pre-Columbian polities from Cahokia to Cuzco, religious establishments flourished across early modern Europe. In that context, religious dissent became political dissent. Heresy was treason.[52]

Across the Atlantic, those rivalries spurred the planting of colonies—and the uprooting of Natives. Rivalries intensified the contests for soil and souls. Hakluyt, the Elizabethan Protestant, urged "speedy planting" between Florida and Nova Scotia to slow the advance of the Spanish king and the "popish" clergy.[53] The English were reacting to the Spanish, just as the French were pushing the English and the Spanish were countering the French. In 1717, two years before New Spain's viceroy appointed Don Juan de Oliván de Rebolledo governor of Texas, that appointee described French territory, indicating where presidios and missions should be established to stop France's westward "incursions."[54] Most Protestant and Catholic leaders had hopes of establishing conformity in their new "plantations," even if that didn't always work as they had hoped.[55] Native and African spiritual difference was hard to miss, and the plural forms of European piety proved a nuisance. Despite evangelists' efforts, spiritual weeds sprouted, just as unwanted plants choked the wheat. Colonial farmers found more weeds in their fields than they could pull, historians of agriculture tell us, so they adjusted. "As in the meeting house, so in the fields: weeds would have to be tolerated."[56]

Not all Natives tolerated the invasive species of Christians. But just as native plants can fend off exotic invaders and show "biological resilience," Indigenous Peoples adapted.[57] Everyone did. Sometimes that meant mixing or mimicry, strategies employed in the ecology of cross-cultural contact: Europeans, Africans, and Natives imitated each other, sometimes consciously and sometimes not. Francisco Vázquez de Coronado, the conquistador who invaded the Southwest in 1540, reported that Zuni women in New Mexico made "the best tortillas I have seen anywhere."[58] That casual judgment unwittingly revealed an adaptation: he, like other Spanish, ate corn and liked tortillas. Indigenous food had become his own. And there was a lot of borrowing. Seeds of new crops arrived with the slave ships and the colonizers' provisions. African okra and watermelon as well as European wheat and barley grew near indigenous plants in colonial fields.[59] Contiguity produced mixing, in agriculture and in religion. As botanists tell us, plants also adapt by forming hybrids, mixtures that create something new.[60] There was gene flow in the planted fields and culture flow in the built environment. Clergy sometimes pragmatically accepted the adaptive hybrids, like the Pueblo Catholics worshipping in a kiva beside a church, and sometimes they condemned the mixing. Yet mimicry and mixing created new niches that wouldn't be exclusively European, African, or Indian. Colonial Americans of European heritage eventually would come to terms with that variegated landscape, in both the fields and the churches. Sometimes they would confidently pull up the weeds. Often they impatiently awaited the harvest. That didn't mean, however, that while they awaited the final sorting out, rival religious empires wouldn't try to win the race to plant the flag and raise the cross.

For almost two centuries, colonizers would use their imperial faith's figurative tools—its guiding metaphors, justifying beliefs, and perpetuating rituals—to claim their God-given right to plant colonies and, if necessary, uproot Natives. In turn, Natives and Africans repurposed borrowed symbols or dusted off ancient ones to unsettle the settlers, to push back and rise up.[61] By the middle of the eighteenth century, there would be stressed eco-cultural niches across the continent. Interactions with the agents of empires centered in Mexico City, Quebec, and London would transform the lands that became America, from the Gulf to the Great Lakes, from Savannah to Salem, and from Florida to New Mexico.

Mixing and Mimicry in the Spanish Empire

The religious history of the Spanish colonies north of the Rio Grande starts in the Caribbean and Latin America, because that's where the patterns were set that would shape the first settlements and missions in the lands that became the US.

In September 1493 Columbus returned to Hispaniola with seventeen ships and 1,200 men, as well as horses, cattle, and farm tools. He also brought seeds and cuttings: sugar for profit and wheat and grapes for faith as well as food, since the host consecrated during mass must be made from wheat and the wine transformed into Christ's blood had to be made from grapes.[62] While farmers toiled to produce wheat and wine, his craftsmen built the first settlement, La Isabella, named for the Catholic queen. On the land that became the Dominican Republic, settlers had not only ritual food but ceremonial artifacts like crucifixes and statues.[63] Thirteen clerics had come to preside at those rituals, serve the settlers, and evangelize the Natives.[64] And to provide a space for communal worship, Columbus's masons built a church and a cemetery, which rested on an earlier Taíno burial ground.[65] That first colonial metropolis, then, was built on a Native necropolis.[66]

Both the town and its burial ground were abandoned by the end of 1497, but the Spanish remained convinced of their God-given mandate and established other settlements, starting with Santo Domingo in 1496.[67] The processes that would characterize Spanish settler colonialism on the mainland were already becoming evident.[68] Columbus enslaved 1,500 Taínos and transported 500 more to Spain.[69] The remaining islanders' susceptibility to imported pathogens increased because of the living and working conditions. Most of the Taínos on Hispaniola fled, blended, or died. Those who stayed, mated with the Spanish and produced mixed offspring.[70] The 300,000 islanders who greeted Columbus had become 33,000 in less than two decades, and only 500 remained by 1548.[71] To replace those laborers, the Spanish initiated a strategy their compatriots to the North would imitate: the crown contracted to transport enslaved Africans.[72] After that, the uprooting of Africans and Natives went hand in hand.

Mexico and Peru

Native maltreatment continued in the Aztec ceremonial center in the Valley of Mexico and the Incan ceremonial center in the Andes Mountains. When Hernán Cortés arrived in Tenochtitlán in 1519 and Francisco Pizarro marched into Cuzco in 1533, colonizers were meeting colonizers in those high-altitude capital cities. Like the Spanish, both the Aztecs and the Incas had conquered peoples and established religiously figured interaction spheres where outliers paid tribute and sent crops to the capital.[73] They both used a capital-centered civic religion, legitimated by cherished myths and elaborate rites, to justify the tribute, control the territories, and unify worldviews.[74] European–Indigenous encounters in both capitals started with Native attempts to establish alliances by exchanging goods and mates. In the first exchanges, elite Indigenous women like the Incan Doña Inés and the Aztec Doña Marina played important roles as interpreters and brokers—and, in time, gave birth to the mixed offspring who created blended religious cultures in Mexico and Peru.[75]

But Native efforts to establish diplomatic relations didn't succeed. Within a few years the Incan and Aztec religio-political capitals fell, and the invaders suppressed ritual life. Soldiers, for instance, attacked participants in a festival ceremony at the Great Temple in the place the Spanish called Mexico City.[76] More than a thousand elite Aztecs gathered in the temple's courtyard for that 1521 ceremony. The paper lanterns remained from the night before, when devotees had adorned a statue of the Aztecs' divine patron who led them on their southward journey to the Basin of Mexico.[77] Earlier Chaco elites to the north would have recognized the symbolic materials: the Aztecs fashioned the god's image from chocolate and gave him turquoise earrings. His headdress, necklace, and belt included brightly colored bird feathers. The following day, the statue's face was uncovered, and the warriors danced. Then the soldier in charge ordered his men to rush the celebrants. They stabbed and beheaded them until, as one Native narrative put it, "the blood flowed like water and gathered into pools."[78]

Some Catholics condemned this maltreatment of Indigenous Peoples between 1500 and 1550. Bartolomé de las Casas, a famous critic, complained that Christians "have uprooted these pitiful peoples and wiped them from the face of the earth."[79] In a series of reports the Dominican priest documented the depopulation and displacement in gruesome detail. He noted, for example, that soldiers on Hispaniola had hacked villagers to death and sliced open their bellies. They hurled infants against the rocks. Christians grilled shamans until they "howled in agony."[80] His protests had some influence. By 1537 the pope would declare that Natives were "truly men" who ought to be instructed in the faith and not deprived of their liberty.[81] It might seem astonishing that a church leader believed it necessary to declare Natives were human beings, but apparently it needed to be said.

Explorations above the Rio Grande

While that intra-Catholic debate about the status of Indigenous Peoples raged between 1500 and 1550, the Spanish also were encountering Natives in the lands that became the mainland US. Ponce de León, who had settled La Isabella with Columbus, spotted the East Coast on Easter Sunday in 1513 and named the lush land La Florida for the Spaniards' Easter festival of flowers (Pascua Florida). Sailing around the peninsula, his crew then had skirmishes with canoe-paddling Calusa along the shell-covered Gulf shore.[82] Álvar Núñez Cabeza de Vaca also landed on Florida's western coast but then hugged the shoreline from Tampa Bay to present-day Texas. With 296 shipmates gone, Cabeza de Vaca then wandered for years with two Spanish Catholic survivors and Estebanico, a Black, Arabic-speaking slave from Morocco who, at some point, had been asked to relinquish his Muslim identity and adopt a Christian baptismal name.[83] In the region that became northern Mexico and southern Texas, Cabeza de Vaca noticed "fruit-like beans" used in local "dances" and "festivals"—probably like the mescaline beans and peyote buttons the Pecos shaman had ingested centuries earlier—and red ochre, the natural pigment we've encountered repeatedly, including at the Horn Shelter grave, which remained undisturbed about three hundred miles to the north.[84] After Cabeza de Vaca's party made it to Mexico in 1536, they could brag they were the first non-Indigenous people to see the Mississippi River. Four years later, Hernando De Soto, who had refined his brutal techniques by terrorizing the Peruvian Incas, battled the Natchez, a Native People who had kept alive Cahokia's mound-building culture along the Mississippi.

Spanish Catholic excursions reached ancestral lands in the Southwest too. A fighting force led by Coronado clashed with locals in the 1540s.[85] After hearing tall tales about southwestern riches and cities, Coronado left Mexico City to seek the Seven Cities of Gold.[86] However, when Coronado's conquistadors, friars, and Native slaves arrived in July 1540 at a New Mexican town, they were greeted by a line of sacred corn the Zuni priests had used to mark the boundary of sacred time and space.[87] The priests and the warriors behind them assumed the intruders would understand they should wait until their summer solstice festival was completed. Coronado couldn't decipher the symbolic code, however, and his soldiers crossed the line to attack. When the battle dust cleared, Coronado looked around at what they had captured. The Zuni's multistory adobe pueblos disappointed him, though he marveled at their corn storehouses—and emptied them to feed his army. Soon after, he demanded the Zuni accept "the true God" and acknowledge the Spanish king as their "earthly master."[88] Many Natives refused and fled, and the Spanish didn't establish a permanent settlement. The invading party instead pressed on to the Wichita's grass-hut villages in present-day Kansas, but the Spanish didn't find the mythic Seven Cities there either.[89] So they returned to Mexico City disappointed, with tales about strange people and customs. The southwestern Natives had new stories too—about the bearded men who misunderstood the rules of diplomatic exchange and risked ill fortune by not performing the solstice rites. There would be more spiritual misunderstandings, and some accommodations, in the next two centuries as the Spanish returned to settle the land.

Florida

Starting in 1565 the Spanish forcibly established towns and missions north of the Rio Grande, and they won the imperial contest for Florida after attacking French Protestants, the Huguenots, who had established a fledgling colony near the St. Johns River. Eight years earlier other Huguenots had founded the first Protestant mission in the Americas in Brazil, and those who settled in Florida hoped to slow Spanish territorial gain and find refuge from persecution during France's First War of Religion. The French followers of John Calvin condemned the Catholic veneration of saints as idolatrous, but in Florida they allied themselves with less culpable idolaters, the Timucua and their chief, Saturiwa.[90] One of the Protestants, a royally commissioned artist, pictured them as idol worshippers, like the Catholics back home, but with some signs of cultivated feelings, as with the mourners' shorn hair and the ceremonial wailing at the chief's funeral.[91] The new Timucua chief would have to deal with the Spanish instead of the French, however, since the Spanish crown heard about the Protestant colonizers and commissioned a hardened naval officer, Pedro Menéndez de Avilés, to settle the religious rivalry. In September 1565 Menéndez and 500 soldiers killed most of the Huguenots and then enslaved or executed most of the rest.[92]

Menéndez, who apparently hadn't contemplated the parable of the weeds, defended his actions to Spain's King Philip II: God had called him to "chastise" the Huguenots and render the Catholic realm "free from this wicked sect."[93] The Huguenot artist, who managed to survive, had his own theological interpretation. The Spanish were the "rod" God used to "scourge" them for some transgression.[94] Few Protestants who learned of the massacre agreed. They condemned the Spanish Catholic brutality and used the massacre—and maltreatment of the Indians—to justify later French colonization. In turn, the English took the incident as another reason to dislike Spanish "papists" and accelerate their own American colonization.[95]

The English would settle the eastern coast as far south as Charles Town by 1680, but in 1565 the Spanish had managed to secure a hold on the southeastern Atlantic coast they wouldn't relinquish until 1763.[96] Forty-two years before English Protestants settled Jamestown, St. Augustine was the first permanent European settlement in the lands that became the US. In the years ahead, the Spanish built a fort and a town. After 1587 Franciscans established an Indian mission church and village called Nombre de Dios on the town's northern periphery. In time the St. Augustine region became the hub of a terrestrial network of royal roads, military presidios, and Catholic missions—and of a maritime trade network linked with the farther reaches of empire from the Philippines to Spain.

The new built environment of the mission, the fort, and the cornfield was nutritionally deficient, and the overworked Timucua ate a less diverse diet than before.[97] The Spanish also exerted disproportionate power, but St. Augustine's creole community was not as violent as some seventeenth-century southwestern settlements would be.[98] There the Spanish and the Indigenous exchanged food and mates as well as religion. Blended households meant disease spread easily, and the Native community suffered smallpox and measles epidemics. There were declines in the first generation after contact, and susceptibility to illness continued. The Native Christian population at Nombre de Dios, for example, dwindled from 216 in 1606 to only 35 in 1655, though the total population at Indian towns around St. Augustine would rise to almost 1,000 by 1717.[99]

The creole colonial niche around St. Augustine was not fully sustainable, but lifeways survived.[100] The *caciques* or hereditary chiefs maintained power and held council meetings. The Spanish made alliances that rewarded the chiefs and kept the peace. Their ritual specialists continued to be respected, or at least tolerated.[101] And Native women with inherited status found their standing in colonial society elevated by intermarriage and conversion, as with Doña María Meléndez, the chieftainess (*cacica*) of Nombre de Dios, where she lived with her children and husband, a Spanish soldier.[102] She had respect at the mission and political power among Indigenous mission villages up the Atlantic coast in the early seventeenth century. Natives like María who identified as Christian retained the standing afforded by the hereditary chiefdom but gave up traditional mortuary practices.[103] They would be memorialized in death according to Spanish Catholic custom, as with the more than 100 unadorned corpses in the Nombre de Dios cemetery who faced east with their legs extended and hands folded.[104]

Other Franciscan missions stretched westward along the "royal road" that spanned northern Florida, and those sites also showed signs of both religious persistence and accommodation. For instance, persistence and accommodation are visible in the design of the mission village of San Luis, the capital of the Spanish settlements among the Apalachee in western Florida between 1656 and 1704, when there were more than 1,400 Indian and Spanish residents.[105] The Indigenous devotees descended from those who had lived at the Mississippian chiefdom at Lake Jackson before 1500 and then abandoned that complex with its central plaza and earthen mounds.[106] At their new town, Anhaica, the Apalachee constructed a moundless village with thatch-roofed buildings surrounding a plaza sometime before De Soto appropriated it.[107] Driven by sincere spiritual longing or shrewd political maneuvering, Apalachee chiefs later asked Spanish administrators to send friars, and by 1656 Natives and Franciscans had moved to the hilltop mission and administrative capital near present-day Tallahassee. From there they would export wheat and pork to St. Augustine and Cuba, and import European goods including religious artifacts.[108] The San Luis site didn't have traditional mounds, but the layout reveals both the continuation of Apalachee ritual life and the introduction of Catholic devotional practice. The two cultural traditions faced each other across that plaza.[109] On one side stood the mission church and friary, where Catholic ritual specialists presided; on the other side stood the chief's house and the council house, where Native chiefs and priests presided.

The council house, a circular thatched building, was the gathering place for the Indigenous community. Probably the largest Native building in the Southeast at the time, it had two rows of benches around the crackling central hearth, where they prepared the ceremonial "black drink" from the roasted leaves of the yaupon holly (*Ilex vomitoria*).[110] The chief took a sip and passed around that vomit-inducing stimulant. Continuing a ritual tradition we can trace at least as far back as Cahokia—one that would reappear in eighteenth-century Indigenous resistance movements—the chief circulated that tea each morning after the council discussed the day's business, and he also presided at purification ceremonies where anxious warriors or ecstatic priests drank and danced.[111] To the left of that council house was the chief's circular home. It too had a row of benches and a central hearth. The building's style and contents were Native, and objects unearthed there show the Apalachee chief's religious as well as political role, including quartz beads and pendants, material associated with shamanic and priestly ritual in pre-Columbian Indigenous communities.[112]

There also was quartz in the church grounds across the plaza, where Apalachee and Spanish symbols mingled.[113] On one hand, the material culture was Christian. The rectangular church was oriented on a traditional east-west axis. Near the entrance was a baptismal font. The nave was smaller than those of Europe's great cathedrals, and stained glass windows didn't adorn its steeply inclined walls. But the building's proportions replicated those used in grand churches. Further, glancing toward the altar a European visitor would have noticed a familiar scene—a priest standing over an altar cloth with a cross and statue. As in Spain, local Native Christians came to the San Luis church for the weekly sacraments, annual feast-day celebrations, and rites of passage like baptisms, marriages, and burials. Even the positioning of the corpses beneath the church was Christian: the extended bodies faced east with hands on chests.[114]

Yet Native and Christian meanings mixed at San Luis. The Catholic Church prohibited grave goods, but the long-standing Indigenous practice of adorning the deceased continued at the San Luis church. Apparently the friars tolerated that ancestral mortuary practice. Some of the 161 Indigenous Christian burials beneath the church floor included rosary beads and crosses.[115] Other graves had many objects, as with a child adorned with 659 glass beads, a Spanish brass cross, and a quartzite pendant.[116] That interment recalls the symbolic surplus of ancient elite burials, though the grave offerings were both Apalachee and Spanish. Quartz, a traditional material, prevented evil and brought good fortune. Shamans used it in divination, but no ancient shaman could have foreseen that one day cherished Apalachee artifacts would include a quartz cross.[117] Its form points to Christian acculturation. It's a cross, after all: Christianity's central symbol. Yet the material also recalls long-standing practices among the Apalachee and other Indigenous People. That ritual artifact, then, serves as a reminder of how Natives incorporated Spanish devotions and friars accommodated Native customs.

The Spanish imperial administration and the Apalachee traditional chiefdom adjusted, and religious leaders negotiated on the Florida panhandle. That cooperation, and the productivity of the farms and ranches, led to some short-term stability in the precarious mission network. At the peak of the Florida missions around 1675, 40 friars served 20,000 Native devotees in 36 churches—and 1,400 Apalachee lived at San Luis, the most populous mission.[118] Yet for all the mixing—and the beauty of that translucent cross—the mission couldn't endure because of internal and external stresses. A brutal colonial governor strained relations in 1685, reminding the Apalachee that the threat of the soldier's sword and the friar's whip meant that the Catholic–Native agricultural niche was, in the end, a coercive community. Their nearby rivals, the Apalachicola, became furious when the Spanish imposed trading limits and destroyed a nearby mission in 1703. The next year the English and their Muscogee allies destroyed San Luis, forcing the Apalachee to seek refuge in Mobile, then the capital of French Catholic Louisiana. The Apalachee, who probably blended into Native and European communities, wouldn't be heard from again.

Texas

The proximity of the French along the Mississippi and the encroachment of horse-mounted Natives on the Plains prompted Spanish administrators to extend their network of presidios and missions. The French explorer René-Robert Cavalier de La Salle had panicked New Spain's viceroy by building a fort on the Texas Gulf Coast in 1685. Its subsequent failure was a sign of "divine aid," administrators in Mexico City concluded, but it was still too close for comfort.[119] To prevent more incursions, Franciscans began to establish Texas missions to entice the Caddo, "the most socially complex Native American communities living between the Mississippi River and the Ancestral Puebloan Peoples of the American Southwest."[120] Those mound-building farmers might have been more open to Spanish farming and faith—both of which they already had—if soldiers hadn't killed the villagers, friars hadn't criticized their healers, and baptismal water hadn't caused a smallpox epidemic. Either that, they reasoned, or the missionaries' god was battling their god.[121] Within three years the friars despaired of success at that first mission, San Francisco de los Tejas, so they buried the bells, burned the church, and ran for safety.[122] There would be renewed evangelizing efforts later, though never with great success.[123]

Of the thirty-seven Texas missions Franciscans established, the most successful were five along the San Antonio River. By 1750 they included a thousand Natives affiliated with Catholicism, including descendants of the Coahuiltecan speakers Cabeza de Vaca had watched using hallucinogenic plants.[124] The first and most famous of those five missions, San Antonio de Valero, was founded in 1718, and by 1740 a friar was celebrating the "harvest of converted souls."[125]

That mission's abandoned chapel, called the Alamo, would be remembered later by Texas patriots as the site of a mythic battle for independence from Mexico, but the surviving records reveal three important things about that mission in its eighteenth-century heyday. First, the friars and Natives accommodated one another.[126] San Antonio's friars reported that in their dances the Coahuiltecan "drink something prepared from the peyote and other herbs . . . from which visions and hallucinations result," but a manual for missionaries advised them to let Natives have their dances.[127] The guidebook noted that the Spanish had their "diverting" dances too and encouraged new pastors to recall that "the missionary does make allowances." Second, the records show that many Natives seem to have been Christianized, and the regional population was transformed by intermarriage. In 1727 a Franciscan visitor at San Antonio counted "70 native families, totaling 273 Indians of whom two-thirds were converts," and they participated in elaborate Holy Week processions and received chocolate on Easter.[128] The friars' records also show that Natives wed in Catholic ceremonies with mates from other Indigenous communities and that Native-Spanish couples also sealed their unions in the church: Hermenegildo Puente, a Papanac Indian, pledged fidelity to Candelaría Trabieso, a Lipan Apache; Melchor de Medina, a Muruame, married Juana Rodríguez, a Spaniard.[129] Finally, the mission transformed the environment. Records show it had 439 head of cattle and 542 sheep and goats, for example.[130] By the 1720s it ran three fenced farms with irrigation ditches and a ranch with more than 4,000 cattle.[131] So the labor of the Spanish and the Indians left terrestrial traces—not just churches and houses but fences and ditches, and sloping hills altered by grazing cattle.

New Mexico

The friars and the mission system, with its emphasis on livestock and crops, already had transformed the parched New Mexican landscape between 1610 and 1680, but missions there showed fewer signs of accommodation. There were exceptions. One Franciscan built his church next to an existing kiva and then looked the other way as Indigenous devotees used both, and a kiva was constructed outside the friar's quarters at the Mission of San Gregorio de Abó, perhaps to ease Natives' transition to worshipping at the church next door.[132] Overall, however, the Spanish administrators were ruthless, the soldiers brutal, and many friars sincere but condescending, especially in the northern Rio Grande Valley.

In the 1100s the Valley had been home to Chaco "outliers," and by the fourteenth century some Ancestral Puebloans who fled Mesa Verde settled along the Rio Grande.[133] That's where Spanish soldiers had encountered their descendants in the 1540s. It took a half century after Coronado's disastrous journey across New Mexico for a Spanish king, Philip II, to risk colonizing the area, but in 1598 Juan de Oñate, a conquistador married to Cortés's granddaughter, led an expedition up the royal road from Mexico City and toward the pueblos that Coronado had rampaged. The governor of New Spain's northernmost province, Santa Fe de Nuevo México, still hoped resplendent cities of gold might be found. They weren't. But Oñate and the 500 colonists, 129 soldiers, and seven Franciscans would establish missions and farms amid the pueblos—the multistoried adobe dwellings bordering central plazas. In the plaza and the kivas, residents convened for communal ceremonies that petitioned the spirits to make the rain fall and the crops grow, as their maize-growing ancestors in the region had done.[134]

Yet tensions mounted soon after Oñate started colonization. In 1599 he authorized brutality at Acoma Pueblo. That upset the friars and infuriated the Native residents. Acoma warriors had grown annoyed by the Spaniards' inordinate demands for labor, maize, and flour, so they killed the patrol sent to exact more tribute.[135] In response the governor made a show of force. Spanish soldiers killed 800 Acoma residents. Five hundred survivors were tried in royal court. Those over twelve were consigned to slavery and—this is the atrocity the Pueblo can't forget—the governor sentenced the men over twenty-five to amputation as well as enslavement: they each would have one foot severed, so they wouldn't resist again.[136] A month later Oñate wrote to Mexico City to beg for more men to "pacify" the Natives and "develop" the land by "the preaching of the gospel and the founding of the government."[137] But friars wrote to the capital too, complaining about the "outrages" perpetrated by Oñate and his men.[138] In 1681 Brother Juan de Escalona reported that soldiers had burned houses, killed villagers, and "plundered their pueblos of the corn . . . and here corn is God." So Natives "drop dead from starvation." In short, "we cannot preach the gospel now because it is despised on account of our great offenses." Oñate resigned, and eventually more Natives would be baptized, married, and buried in the missions along the Rio Grande Valley in the years ahead.

Some Puebloan converts sided with the Christians when all-out revolt started in 1680—after eight earlier uprisings. Most, however, supported the insurgents in that unsafe, unhealthy, and coercive eco-cultural niche.[139] Memory of the Acoma tragedy hadn't faded, and famine, violence, and epidemics had reduced the Pueblo population from 40,000 in 1638 to 17,000 in 1680.[140] Two other events intensified dissent. First, there was religious suppression in 1675.[141] The Spanish imprisoned forty-seven medicine men accused of being *hechiceros,* or sorcerers, killing ten of them.[142] Three Indigenous healers were hanged in their pueblo's plaza. Another killed himself before they could execute him, resorting to a tactic that colonized Natives and captured slaves sometimes felt was the only way out.[143] The other medicine men were sold into slavery or imprisoned. In response, seventy warriors stormed the governor's home in Santa Fe to demand their release, and the surprised governor backed down. That concession planted a thought: armed resistance might work. Then a second event, a failed summer crop in 1680, escalated tensions more. Two nights of freezing summer temperatures destroyed the crops and foreshadowed more famine to come.[144] After years of drought and disease, the colonial farming niche protected by the Spanish God seemed broken. But one of the religious leaders who had been imprisoned in 1675 was readying himself to use the ancestral Puebloan religion to restore that eco-cultural niche. Po'pay, the leader of the Pueblo Revolt of 1680, prayed in a kiva at Taos Pueblo. There he received messages from spirits, including Po'se yemu, the rain-giving spirit recognized by all Pueblo in the northern Rio Grande.[145] The spirit told him to reject Catholic rituals in the churches and restore Pueblo ceremonies in the kivas. Po'pay told others about his vision, first at Taos and then at more than thirty other participating pueblos.

The war captains that planned the rebellion included *mestizos* (Indian and European descent), *coyotes* (Native American and African American descent), and *indios ladinos* (Spanish-speaking Natives educated by the friars).[146] They all believed the revelations that legitimated Po'pay's revitalization movement and promised an era of peace and plenty. There had been religious revitalization movements before on the continent. Reformers at Mesa Verde who blamed the Chaco symbol system for the crop shortage had started one. There would be more to come, including the prophecy-inspired insurgency called Pontiac's Rebellion in the eighteenth-century Great Lakes region, the Indigenous Ghost Dance movement that swept the Plains in the nineteenth, and the American Indian Movement that advocated "spiritual renewal" and political rights in the twentieth.[147] But this seventeenth-century pan-Pueblo insurgency was probably the most notable Native uprising in American history. The Pueblo warriors and their short-term allies, the Apache, killed almost four in ten colonists. Most of the Franciscans died, some dismembered in grisly public displays.[148] The insurgents put Po'pay in charge. They then smashed bells, shattered statues, and burned churches to usher in the promised restoration. Puebloans who identified as Catholic preserved some crucifixes and chalices, and some Franciscans were spared.[149] But at one pueblo where ritual suppression had been especially intense, locals hacked the arms off a Saint Francis statue in a grim memorialization of Oñate's amputations, and one insurgent defecated on the altar and set the church ablaze.[150] To ready themselves for the return to Pueblo lifeways, they renounced their Christian names and invented a ritual to undo the sacramental incorporation into the ecclesiastical community, dipping themselves into the Rio Grande to reverse their baptisms.[151] With most churches emptied or burned, including the one at Taos Pueblo, Native worshippers returned to the kivas to openly perform the ceremonies the friars had banned.

Neither the insurrection's fury nor its euphoria lasted. The drought persisted, inter-Pueblo tensions resurfaced, and Apache raids returned. The expected era of peace and prosperity hadn't begun. By the end of the first year, Po'pay was ousted. The Spanish fled south to El Paso, where they would remain in exile for twelve years. The pueblos enjoyed self-rule until Governor Diego de Vargas, forty soldiers, fifty Indians, and two Franciscans retook the town. Nuestra Señora del Rosario got credit for the "bloodless reconquest," and ever since she has been venerated as La Conquistadora, the victorious intercessor, in an annual festival in Santa Fe.[152] Another uprising, the Second Pueblo Revolt of 1696, didn't unseat the Spanish. After that, however, civic administrators softened their demands on the locals, and the friars allowed more mixing of faiths in kivas as well as churches. The hard-earned compromises would continue into the 1760s, when the Franciscans' power started to wane. In 1760 a bishop inspecting Acoma Pueblo disapproved of the Natives' continued use of the kiva, "that dark and strange receptacle."[153] But there had not been another revolt, in part because of those compromises—and because the colonists and the Natives joined forces to fight back the encroaching Comanche, who would keep the Spanish from moving farther north into the Plains and also prevent the French from spreading west from Louisiana.[154]

Those skilled equestrians had acquired Spanish horses after the 1680 revolt, and in the next century the Comanche traded with the French, who were skilled at forging alliances and content to trade guns for beaver pelts—and for the chance to preach the gospel.[155]

Furs, Farming, and Faith in the French Empire

The French sent those pelts to Europe, where artisans made them into hats. Native Peoples, in turn, knew what to do with the guns the French gave them. Not everyone was sure what to make of the missionaries' gospel, however. The brutal deaths suffered by some seventeenth-century Jesuits in New France attest to the initial resistance, and a century later some Native residents in and around French settlements farther south still found the gospel of little use.[156]

Natchez

Consider, for example, Natchez, the mound-building chiefdom on the Lower Mississippi that had sustained Mississippian spiritual life after the collapse of Cahokia and the arrival of Christians. The first intercultural encounter with De Soto in 1542 had ended in conflict.[157] Warriors chased off that Spanish expedition. There was less violence when the French explorer La Salle followed the Mississippi up from the Gulf in 1682. A priest in La Salle's party celebrated the first mass there, and French officials would send more traders, planters, and priests in the years ahead. By 1716 the French had built a fort, and a small Catholic church stood on the river landing just below the steep bluffs. By the 1720s there were about 1,800 Natives, 500 colonists, and 200 enslaved persons living near the French church and the Natchez mounds.[158] Most Natchez still told their sacred stories, including one about the Great Sun's descent from two luminous ancestral beings, Thé and White Woman, and remained mostly indifferent to the missionaries' offer of a sacred book containing more stories.[159] They welcomed other trade goods, however: not only hoes and muskets but religious medals symbolizing the Holy Family.[160] Some even tried to incorporate the French Catholics, as they would any newcomers, by exchanging mates to solidify bonds and establish new kin relations.[161]

As a memorial address at a chief's funeral in 1725 suggests, some elite Natives tried to prevent further conflict in their increasingly stressed environment. A grieving Native woman spoke to Indigenous and French mourners in the plaza of the Natchez Grand Village that day.[162] We don't know her name, but a French-speaking planter, Antoine Le Page du Pratz, observed the scene.[163] He watched the festivities from the mound that housed the peace chief or Great Sun, the leader who oversaw civic affairs and convened religious rituals. From there Le Page could see the adjacent mound where the speaker's mate, the war chief or Tattooed Serpent, would be interred. Elite women among the People of the Sun, whom the Europeans called the Natchez, often functioned as diplomats. So the local community would not have been surprised at her public role that day. The French also had heard her speak at the memorial dance, when she praised her husband as a friend to the French: "he walked the same road." If Le Page's account is right, she urged the Native residents to "walk in peace with the French" and, in a final gesture of peacemaking and cultural brokering, encouraged French leaders to "be friends always with the Natchez."[164] The men carrying the chief's corpse turned the body to the four directions, first to the south and finally to the east. Then the procession, led by a ritual presider whose upper body was painted ochre red, wound its way to the top of the temple mound. There the Tattooed Serpent was laid to rest.[165]

But conflict couldn't be laid to rest quite as easily. Things took a turn for the worse four years after the chief's mate pleaded for peace. On 28 November 1729 the Natchez responded violently when an insensitive fort commander demanded a village relocate so he could clear the ground for a plantation worked by his enslaved laborers. The outraged Natchez, who had welcomed the French by sharing their soil, their daughters, and their corn, killed 150 men, 36 women, and 56 children. That amounted to one-tenth of Louisiana's White population and included the local Jesuit missionary but not Le Page, who had left the previous year to supervise a New Orleans plantation.[166] Native allies of the French, the Choctaw, launched a retaliatory attack. With about two hundred slaves siding with the Natchez, the mound builders and Africans fled.[167] The French sent their recently orphaned children downriver to New Orleans and ordered troops and Native allies to respond even more forcefully. By 1731 hundreds of Natchez had been killed, and the French had enslaved the Great Sun. He and five hundred others were shipped to West Indian sugar plantations.[168] The escapees sought refuge among other southeastern Indigenous communities, mostly Cherokee and Muscogee (Creek), just as Natives fleeing English slave raids had previously found refuge in that mound-building chiefdom near the Mississippi.

Things didn't go well at Natchez, but missionaries had some success elsewhere in France's overseas empire, which reached its peak by the 1690s and contracted by the 1760s. At its height, that vast mercantile empire included trading posts in India and along the northern coast of South America.[169] The African trading posts procured slaves for France's profitable plantations in the West Indies, especially Saint-Domingue, a colony with 27,000 enslaved workers and 21,000 Whites at the start of the eighteenth century. That island's plantations would produce more sugar and coffee than any others in the world during the 1700s.[170] Starting with the founding of Quebec in 1608, small numbers of French colonists also settled the varied ecological niches in mainland North America, where they emphasized extraction economies in the woodland North, like fur trading near Detroit, and production economies in the riverine South, like farming near Natchez.[171] In all those territories, missionaries either led or followed expansion.[172] In the fur-trading and crop-growing outposts of New France and Upper Louisiana missionaries brought the gospel's light to those in "savage" darkness—and challenged Spaniards' assumption that all heathen souls were theirs to win. In Lower Louisiana, especially the fertile Mississippi Valley, church representatives reached out more to Africans, since the crown was (unsuccessfully) trying to replicate the flourishing slave-dependent West Indian plantations. And in Louisiana's unruly capital of New Orleans—filled with male ex-convicts, women from Parisian asylums, and poorly trained soldiers—priests and nuns found they had a hard row to hoe since, as they saw it, almost everyone needed spiritual cultivation.

Three sites between the headwaters of the St. Lawrence and the mouth of the Mississippi offer a snapshot of religious life in France's mainland empire: the Jesuit-Haudenosaunee community at Kahnawake in New France, the Jesuit Illiniwek (Illinois) community at Kaskaskia in Upper Louisiana, and the Ursuline nuns' community in colonial New Orleans.

New France

Kahnawake (meaning "on the rapids") was one of the missions Jesuits had established as they edged southwestward from Quebec. One resident in that mission village was an unusual but pious young woman who would become America's first Indigenous saint, Catherine Tekawitha. She was born among the Kanien'kehá:ka (Mohawk), the easternmost of the Five Nations of the Haudenosaunee or Iroquois Confederacy, in what is now northern New York, where an early bout with smallpox left her face scarred and her vision impaired.[173] It was in her home village in 1676 that she also added her baptismal name, Catherine.[174] The next year the twenty-year-old followed other baptized Natives who had moved to Kahnawake, a village below Montreal on the St. Lawrence.[175] In that bankside community, the chapel and clerical quarters stood beside two rows of longhouses, narrow log structures housing multigenerational groups of kin.[176] The patchwork fields for growing corn, squash, and beans stood behind the dwellings and in front of the tree-covered hills. In that chapel Catherine received her First Holy Communion a few months after her arrival. She soon joined a group of Haudenosaunee Catholic women who abstained from sex and engaged in ascetic practices like fasting and self-flagellation.[177] Catherine's demanding bodily "mortifications" and apparent therapeutic talents impressed the three Jesuits at the mission they called Sault St. Louis. When she grew severely ill, one of them proclaimed her "the most fervent" of the locals affiliated with Catholicism, and after Catherine's untimely death in 1680 two of them penned biographies portraying her as a devout woman gifted with revelatory visions and healing powers.[178]

When that future saint from Kahnawake died, the Jesuits put her to rest in a coffin and memorialized her in a mass in the mission chapel. But some Haudenosaunee Catholics at Kahnawake created a blended devotional life. After her conversion, Catherine had endured the jabs of traditionalists and "the jeers of the shamans in her home village."[179] But Jesuits who served Kahnawake in the years ahead reported that Native villagers continued to value dreams as conduits of revelations and perpetuated traditional mortuary practices such as the Feast of the Dead, a ritual in which the recently deceased are collectively honored so their second souls can continue their journey to the ancestors.[180] Shamans at Kahnawake also continued to offer wampum, maize, and animals to the sun and still ritually visited other realms. "The shamans have some innate quality which partakes still more of the divine," one Jesuit observed. "We see them go visibly into that state of ecstasy which binds all the senses."[181] Native spiritual intermediaries also continued to perform divination and healing rites for those who went to mass, knew the prayers, and adorned themselves with crucifix pendants and rosary beads.

Upper Louisiana

There weren't overt signs of Indigenous practice in the Upper Louisiana mission in 1694, when Marie Rouensa, another rosary-praying and marriage-renouncing devotee reluctantly wed a colonist selected by her father, the chief.[182] The success of that alliance-forming bond between a devout Indian convert and a half-hearted French Catholic would convince the discouraged second-generation missionaries in Kaskaskia that intermarriage might "Frenchify" and evangelize the Natives more effectively than the first-generation missionary emphasis on cultural accommodation, which had accelerated after Father Jacques Marquette entered the village on his 1673 journey to find a path down the Mississippi.[183] Marquette initially discovered the 300 cabins of the Peoria, another Illiniwek (Illinois) group, and two elders came out to greet him carrying long "calumets" that were "trimmed with many kinds of feathers."[184] After ritually establishing peaceful relations by smoking tobacco from that ceremonial pipe—actually only the stem was called a calumet—Marquette told council members about "the Great Spirit" and attended a communal feast.[185] Then the locals gave him a young Indigenous slave and his own ritual pipe, which he carried down the Mississippi. On the return, his party's two canoes also pulled ashore near the larger Illinois town of Kaskaskia. After doing his best to communicate by relying on his knowledge of other Algonquian dialects, the Jesuit promised to return and tell them more about Jesus, Mary, and the saints. When Marquette did come back, despite a recurring illness, he was greeted "as an angel from heaven."[186] Uplifted by that reception, he approached the chiefs and elders "to sow in their minds the first seed of the gospel." Then he tried scattering seeds in a larger field, preaching to a crowd of 500 by holding up "four large pictures of the Blessed Virgin," to compensate for his imperfect grasp of their language. Marquette distributed presents, a ritual requirement, and, without locals grasping the implications of his solemn verbal performance, he "took possession of the land in the name of Jesus Christ, and gave this mission the name of the Immaculate Conception of the Virgin," as he had promised Mary he would do if she guided him safely downriver.

The "Ave Maria" was one of the prayers Marquette had asked a colleague to include in the prayer book Natives would use in the decades ahead, and he would have been pleased to learn that the next generation of Illiniwek professed devotion to Mary.[187] Rouensa, for example, taught other Kaskaskia women about Mary when they came to her house to pray. She even invoked the Virgin in the will she executed just before her death in the summer of 1725.[188] In that legal document the "Frenchified" woman commended her soul to Mary and God, and requested memorial prayers in the original mission church and in Kaskaskia's worship space, the Church of the Immaculate Conception, where she had attended mass and soon would be honored as the only woman, French or Native, interred beneath its floor. Marquette and his Jesuit collaborators in the first generation had seemed content that Indigenous People honored God "in their own way," but Rouensa's Jesuit tutors came to learn the language more fully and highlight the differences more often.[189] Medicine men living near the Immaculate Conception mission, a Jesuit complained, had proven "a great obstacle in the conversion of the Indians." Those "imposters," who pretended to honor the spirits and heal the infirm, threatened the newly affiliated Catholics, but "thanks to God, our village is now purged" of them.[190] Rouensa must have retained some Native beliefs—no "conversion" is a full erasure of old ways of thinking, feeling, and acting—but there is evidence of her Catholic identity and cultural standing in that Franco-Illinois community by the time she died in 1725.[191] She left her children houses, barns, and a good deal of land. They also received pigs and chickens, sickles and plows, French wheat and Indigenous maize—and, like Lower Louisiana planters, Rouensa had owned six enslaved servants, five of them African, which she also bequeathed.[192]

Lower Louisiana

Five years after Rouensa's funeral, a delegation of Kaskaskia Catholics canoed down the Mississippi to New Orleans to express their solidarity with the faith and the French at a time of rising Native dissent in Lower Louisiana.[193] In that year after the Natchez revolt, the Illinois delegates presented the governor with two calumets, one to symbolize their shared faith and one to reaffirm their military alliance. The delegation's leader, Chicagou, already knew both cultures. He had interacted with the Jesuits in Illinois County, and five years earlier had visited the "great chiefs" in Paris to agree that the French crown could have their land at Kaskaskia but "you must leave us masters of the land where we have placed our fire."[194] It's probably not surprising, then, that during their three-week stay in New Orleans in 1730 the delegation not only used that Native ceremonial artifact but also demonstrated familiarity with French Catholic ritual. "They charmed us by their piety," a Jesuit said, noting that they recited the rosary every evening and attended mass every morning.[195] They even knew sacred choral music. As French nuns from the Ursuline convent "chanted the first Latin couplet . . . the Illinois continued the other couplets in their language in the same tone."

Those chanting nuns, who had arrived in 1727, also won over the New Orleans community. They did so by staffing a hospital, sheltering orphans, and teaching girls. The Ursulines, the first nuns to arrive in the lands north of New Spain, were a religious order of women founded in the sixteenth-century Catholic Reformation under the protection of Saint Ursula, an early missionary and martyr. Active nuns like the Ursulines wielded more social power than was available to most Protestant women until at least the late nineteenth century, and so the colonial convent attracted talented women, including the New Orleans community's first mother superior. She had been raised as a Huguenot until, as her obituary put it, "God made his conquest by his strokes of grace."[196] She and the other French nuns who left for Lower Louisiana had read tales of Jesuit missionaries in New France and wanted to evangelize and teach Natives, as Ursulines in Quebec City had done.

The New Orleans sisters tutored some Indigenous students, but since 6,000 enslaved Africans had arrived in Lower Louisiana during the 1720s, the Ursulines spent more time instructing African and French girls. One of the order's teachers, Marie Madeleine Hachard, the youngest of the twelve who arrived in 1727, could write home since she had not taken her final vows. Letters reveal she found the city "charming," even if the devil enjoyed "a great empire" there. Yet she held out hope that "God's love"—and hard work—might turn things around.[197] Hachard told her father, "we do not have a minute to ourselves," and the sisters certainly worked hard instructing boarders and day students of all colors and classes. In 1727 the Ursulines had twenty boarders and "a great number of day students, female Blacks and female savages who come for two hours a day for instruction." They also owned slaves and tutored their servants and those of other Louisiana residents. The legal status of Africans, and all residents, was determined by the "Black Code." Drafted by planters in the French West Indies and enacted in New Orleans in 1724, it prohibited enslaved persons from working on Sundays and required that they be baptized Catholic.[198] Unlike some ambivalent English planters who worried that evangelizing slaves would give them dangerous notions about liberty, the French insisted the enslaved join the ecclesiastical community. The sisters didn't see the gospel's potential for challenging slavery, but their missionary zeal did motivate them to incorporate slaves into the church. In 1727, when about half of the New Orleans population was Black, they had seven enslaved boarders. That May they received two more girls "to instruct in our religion."

The Ursulines also cared for a few orphans they "took through charity," and three years later thirty girls orphaned by the Natchez revolt arrived.[199] The young French exiles would be among the diverse contingent processing through New Orleans's streets in July 1734 to transport the Eucharist to their newly completed convent across town, a ritual that claimed public space for women and displayed the nuns' commitment to serve all colors and classes.[200] After a benediction in the nuns' old chapel, participants started their measured walk through the muddy streets. The governor and inhabitants led the way and, as was customary in France, the clergy brought up the rear. A viewer who noticed the soldiers marching in single file on each side of the procession might have concluded this was a routine masculine tribute to church and state. But the diverse marchers in the middle signaled something different, even transgressive, about the sisters' spectacle. After the governor's lead party came the diverse women and girls associated with the convent. First were the destitute orphans and then female students who were White, Black, and Native. They were followed by forty women of the confraternity, the lay association called the "Ladies Congregation of the Children of Mary."[201] Those Marian devotees represented the full spectrum of colonial New Orleans: poor White widows and women of color walked beside soldiers' wives and wealthy plantation mistresses like Marie Payen Dubreuil, niece of the city's founder and spiritual tutor to 106 enslaved workers on their farm upriver from New Orleans.[202] Led by a silver-cloaked girl portraying Saint Ursula, the nine Ursulines were next in line, marching "with veils lowered," while the mother superior stepped beside the canopied Blessed Sacrament. Their new bell tolled as the nuns reached their three-story convent, the town's largest building, and the priest placed the Blessed Sacrament on the altar of their new chapel.[203]

Farther north, the British would gain ground by the 1750s. Catholic Kanien'kehá:ka (Mohawk) at Kahnawake would lose their pastors. So would the Catholic Illiniwek (Illinois) at Kaskaskia. The British invaders would use the chapel as a storehouse and the cemetery as a garden, and when they got their worship space back, lay devotees, not priests, would ring the bell to call the community to prayer.[204] In the decades after the New Orleans procession, the Ursulines fared well. The number of nuns would double, and the sisters would continue to serve the city's diverse population, including the confraternity. The group of Marian devotees would expand to at least eighty-five members. It still attracted women of color and those of limited means, but about 40 percent of the confraternity members were wealthy planters like Dubreuil.

The French and the British

French officials yearned for more rich planter families. The extraction of fur and lumber helped, and colonial leaders appreciated that the alliance-savvy Jesuits had convinced some Native Peoples to add Catholic practices to their ritual life. Yet New France's trading posts and small farms couldn't attract colonists: in 1660 the English mainland colonies had over 70,000 people while New France had a population of only 3,000.[205] And in the next century, New France couldn't replicate the relatively healthy and well-populated agricultural towns of New England, which was becoming "a world of fields and fences" dependent on family farms and centered on meetinghouses. Upper Louisiana settlements near the Mississippi didn't enjoy the religious diversity and rising prosperity of Philadelphia, that vibrant city on the Delaware River. And farmers in Lower Louisiana couldn't create profitable—if unhealthy and unjust—rice plantations like those in the Carolina Lowcountry, where the Protestant churches justified that way of life and its seaport, Charles Town, imported slaves from the African coast and sent cash crops to the wider Atlantic world.[206]

There were multiple reasons for the differences between French and British colonies, but religion was key. The less systematic English colonial system never exercised as much state or church control as the Spanish wielded in their colonies, and the charters and constitutions the English negotiated with the provincial proprietors and stock companies varied more than the uniform French law. The Catholic French, like the inquisitorial Spanish, insisted on allegiance to a single faith. The Black Code banned even French Huguenots who might have settled in Detroit, St. Louis, or New Orleans but instead ended up in Boston, New York, and Charles Town.[207] Most French Catholics remained in Europe, and religious restrictions in the empire's mainland colonies discouraged non-Catholic migration. Protestants from Europe were enticed to settle in British America by the fewer spiritual constraints and, by the 1750s, consoled by the promise of joining fellow combatants in the struggle against French Catholics and their Indigenous allies.

CHAPTER 4

Plantation Religion

The Meetinghouse, the Multi-Steeple City, and the British Slave Plantation, 1607–1756

Hostility to Catholics pervaded Britain's American colonies.[1] Seventeenth-century Congregationalists migrated to Massachusetts to save themselves and their descendants—but also to defend the hemisphere against Catholics who were winning Native souls in territory claimed by the Spanish and the French. They came, as John Winthrop put it, "to raise a Bulworke against the kingdome of the Ante-Christ."[2] Continuing the Reformation's unfinished business, these Calvinists believed the Catholic Church was an evil force that must be defeated before Jesus returned. They were doing their part by scrubbing Catholicism's residue from altars and from hearts.[3] Protestant-affiliated Natives helped too, as when Haudenosaunee "kings" traveled to London to request missionaries to counter Jesuit influence and seek protection from Catholics' "tyrannical" power.[4] Anti-Catholicism intensified again after the 1720s, when Catholic-aligned Natives were pressuring New England from the west and north. Protestants up and down the coast reinforced spiritual boundaries by celebrating Pope's Day every November 5th to express gratitude for the thwarting of a 1605 Catholic plot to blow up King James I and the House of Commons.[5] It was a religious occasion, a day of public thanksgiving and, in New England, a day for sermons, parades, bonfires, and the crowd-pleasing torching of the pope's effigy.

But the mainland English colonies also had to resolve the broader issue of the relationship between the church and the state. They were connected to an empire with a state church (Church of England), but policies varied across regions and changed over time.[6] Tolerance of diverse Protestant faiths increased after 1689 and became common by 1756 with the onset of the Seven Years' War, a Protestant–Catholic world war. Like Massachusetts, some seventeenth-century English colonies had begun as restrictive religious establishments; in 1680, 90 percent of all congregations in the mainland colonies were either Anglican, as in Virginia, or Congregationalist, as in New England.[7] Rhode Island, Maryland, Pennsylvania, and New Jersey had no officially established denomination at some moments, and some colonies with official establishments—Carolina and New York—tolerated all faiths or all Christians for a time. Subsequent changes in England affected the colonies. In 1689 James II, a Catholic sympathizer with a Catholic heir, was replaced by a Dutch Protestant king (William) and an English Protestant queen (Mary), and the 1690 Toleration Act granted freedom of worship to non-Anglican Protestants. In the colonies some New England Congregationalists, who continued their regional dominance, began to see the advantage of a pan-Protestant alliance against Catholics' imperial plans. Soon Massachusetts, Connecticut, and New Hampshire officially tolerated all Protestants.[8] By the 1720s every colony, including liberty-loving Rhode Island, allowed diverse Protestant faiths but required anti-Catholic oaths or prohibited Catholics from voting and office, while Jews and atheists also had less political power.[9] Legal and de facto establishments gave a few churches political clout—Congregationalists in New England, Quakers in Pennsylvania, and Anglicans in the South—but the more fluid religious situation in the English colonies attracted Protestants, and some persecuted Jews.[10] After 1700 the influx of non-English migrants altered the religious landscape, and denominations splintered, faiths mixed, and occult practices thrived.[11] Those converging forces in the decades ahead began to create two distinguishing features of American religious life: notable ethnic and spiritual diversity and negotiated experiments in church–state relations.[12]

The planting of colonies—from Virginia in 1607 to Georgia in 1732—left enduring marks on the land by 1750. Settlers cut trees, fenced lots, planted fields, and built churches. European migration heightened competition for land and resources in the stressed coastal colonies and forced Native Peoples to seek new hunting grounds and cornfields. As many Eastern Woodland Peoples moved westward beyond British rule, the colonial population swelled to 1.2 million, outpacing the stagnating French colonies.[13] The major North American population center was still Mexico City, which had more than 100,000 residents. But Boston (16,000) and Philadelphia (13,000) finally equaled Cahokia's population, and urban centers were expanding. Only

5 percent of colonial settlers were urban dwellers, but seaport cities from Boston to Charles Town became nodes in a consumer network by midcentury: wharf workers loaded crops and timber and unloaded everything from Chinese-inspired wallpaper to spirit-inspired sermons.[14] Those cities also furthered the transatlantic slave trade. Commerce in human cargo linked the mainland colonies to island plantations and African ports, and that affected religious life.[15] British imperial religion and commercial interests shaped personal devotion, collective belonging, church–state relations, and the built environment in regional eco-cultural niches from New England and the Middle Colonies to the mainland South and the Caribbean.

New England

Settler–Indigenous interactions altered the landscape from the "middle ground" of backcountry villages in the Connecticut River Valley to the "muddy ground" of ports opening onto the briny seawater of the Atlantic.[16] For New England Congregationalists, that sea seemed as dark, mysterious, and unchanging as their Calvinist God. In the end, colonists would transform coastal spaces too, even redirecting tides to create Boston Harbor. But first they would follow the estuaries from the boundless ocean, under God's jurisdiction, to the bounded land, under their control. Native residents' mental maps included sacred spaces, hunting grounds, cornfields, and dwellings, but they didn't think an individual could *own* land. A few Europeans, like Jean-Jacques Rousseau, agreed: he traced the origins of inequality and war to "the first person who, having fenced off a plot of ground, took it into his head to say *this is mine*."[17] But New England settlers believed they had a biblical command to "subdue" the earth and a natural right to compensate for the lack of land by finding "uncultivated" and "unenclosed" terrain ready to be cleared and seeded.[18] In other words, British Protestant colonists claimed land by planting crops, not flags. John Winthrop, the first governor of Massachusetts, promoted that view, and so did others in England and its mainland colonies. For example, the philosopher John Locke proposed in an analysis of "property," which he wrote while editing Carolina's 1682 Constitution, that "as much land as a man tills, plants, improves, cultivates and can use the product of, so much is his property. He by his labour does, as it were, enclose it from the common."[19]

As New Englanders enclosed private lots and shaped communal space, they created a distinctive regional niche that featured a Congregational meetinghouse on the town common or green. As a 1748 map of New Haven,

Connecticut, shows, most New England towns included houses surrounded by outlying fields, individual lots with a barn, house, and cornfield where "husbandmen" and their families could harvest crops and domesticate livestock (fig. 19).[20] Some space was shared, including the common, the cemetery, the school, and the meetinghouse. The roads connected inhabitants and linked towns. The schools produced literate young people who encountered God's word in the Bible, and at the cemetery ministers put residents to rest in the hope they were among the preordained elect who would rise again.

The meetinghouse was the communal ritual space. The first ones were square, hipped-roof structures with four planes sloping from the roof's horizontal ridge, like Hingham's Old Ship Meetinghouse (1681) on the shore south of Boston.[21] Its curved roof beams made the interior look like an upturned hull, and its red oak interior was intimate—smaller, for example, than the Apalachee council house and the Franciscan church in Florida's Mission San Luis. But First Parish was big enough for Hingham's residents, where 90 percent of the 105 families had joined the Congregational church by the time they started raising construction funds. When the faithful entered the new building, women and men used separate doors and sat on opposite sides of the aisle.[22] Indentured servants, boys, African Americans, and Natives sat upstairs in the second story galleries and faced the high pulpit, which focused congregants' attention on the spoken word.[23] But more than preaching went on there. The seventeenth-century meetinghouse, a sort of Congregationalist kiva or Puritan council house, was used for civic and religious gatherings. It reflected the community's sense of itself as the New Israel, a "Bible Commonwealth" where church and state entwined. White male residents went there to vote on municipal matters, and the whole community heard lengthy sermons on urgent spiritual issues.

By the eighteenth century, builders had added exterior coloring—they weren't only white—and the worship spaces became oblong, steepled churches, the now iconic American image.[24] Their interior design revealed Congregationalists' changing social views. Boston's Old South Meetinghouse (1730), twice as wide as Old Ship, was one of the first oblong structures.[25] Historians remember the congregation, first organized in 1669, as the place where Benjamin Franklin was baptized, the Boston Tea Party began, and the poet Phillis Wheatley worshipped. In Wheatley's day, enslaved persons like her still sat in the balcony, but the congregation had moved to a new seating system for everyone else. Men and women worshipped together in box pews "owned" by families, and the pew's placement signaled the seating committee's judgment about their standing.[26] The box pews and gallery seats

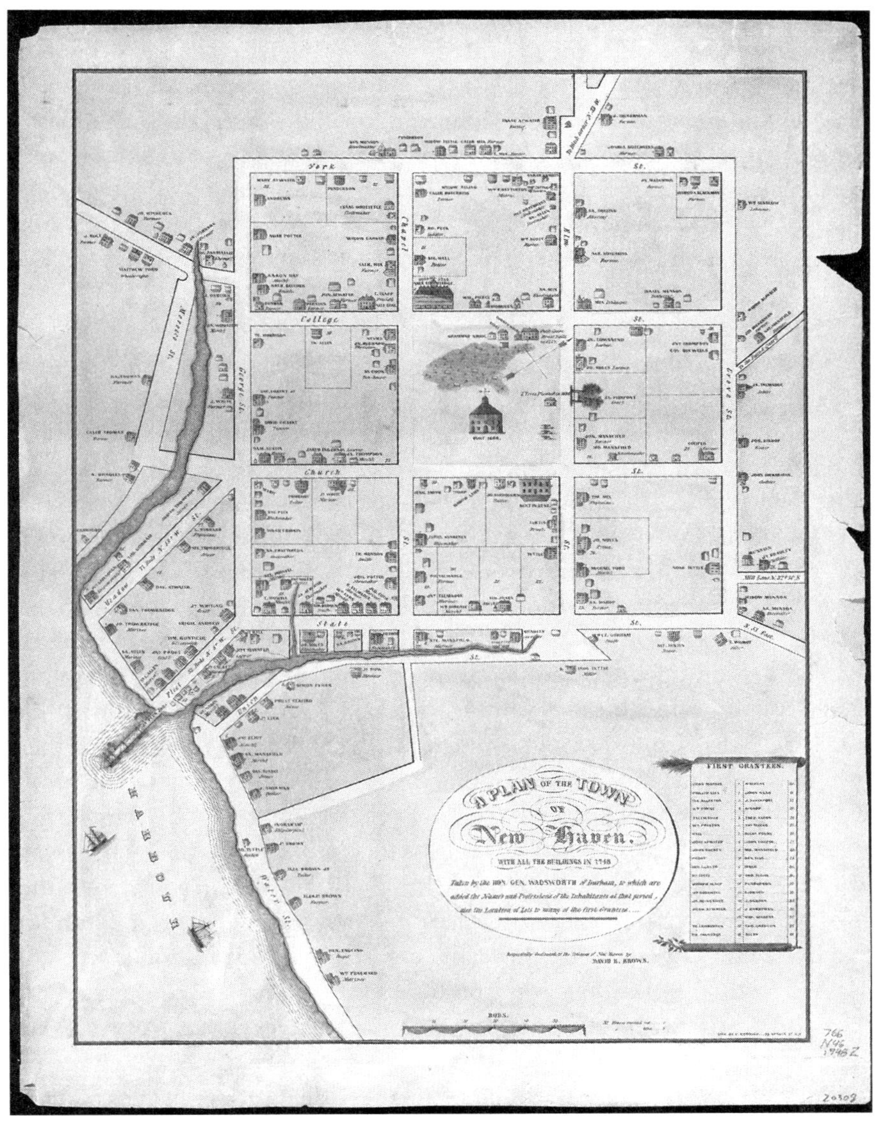

Figure 19. *A Plan of the Town of New Haven in 1748.* Artist: Charles Currier. Courtesy of Yale University Art Gallery, Mabel Brady Garvan Collection.

sorted congregants, with elites enjoying the places of honor, though the attempts to manage difference eventually led to bickering—and a different seating strategy.

In this and other ways, the Congregationalists who planted colonies in New England struggled with difference within and beyond their scrupulously unadorned meetinghouses, and those encounters produced new social spaces: the Indian praying town, an English Protestant version of the Catholic mission, and the multi-steeple towns of the dissenters' refuge, Rhode Island.

The confrontation with Indigenous religious difference began as early as 1620, when William Bradford's Plymouth party dug up a grave with burial offerings and red ochre. They decided the Native inhabitants might be offended—because they would be.[27] So the colonists returned the grave goods but kept the corn and settled the land, even though it already had been "enclosed" by planting. Their defenders would point out they were doing what survival demanded that first year, when half of the Pilgrims would die.[28] Many Natives also had died recently in an epidemic, as the English could tell from the hurried burials and abandoned fields. The settlers' theology suggested that God had cleared the ground for them—though it might have been the French, who landed on Cape Cod earlier and circulated germs. Of course, no one talked about germs in the seventeenth century, and settlers assumed that English deaths also were God's work, a just retribution. Convinced of their own unworthiness but grateful for the Native corn, settlers focused on growing food, building shelter, and avoiding their neighbors, the Wampanoag. Arrows flew in their first halting encounters, but in time their hosts were welcoming, a decimated community sharing diminished resources. In that stressed eco-cultural niche, there wasn't much evangelizing, even if London had hoped for converts, and the leaders of Plymouth Plantation (1620) and Massachusetts Bay Colony (1630) both said they came in part to evangelize the "heathen." Their provincial seals even pictured receptive Natives awaiting the gospel of English agriculture and Christian scripture. In the Bay Colony's image, for instance, a ribbon of text recorded a Native's plea, "Come Over and Help Us."[29]

Missionary efforts picked up between the 1640s and the 1670s, as leaders urged more attention to Natives' spiritual needs. Thomas Mayhew, for example, had some success preaching to the Wampanoag on Noëpe, an island the English called Martha's Vineyard.[30] His great-grandson, Experience Mayhew, would continue that ministry and publish spiritual biographies of four generations of Indigenous women and men who lived a faithful Christian life, including Hannah Ahhunnut, "a person of good Knowledge in the things of God" who read the Bible and visited the sick.[31] And John Eliot established the first of fourteen agricultural "praying towns" at Natick, Massachusetts, in 1652. Over the next two decades Eliot and his colleagues strove to make Natives Protestant by making them English. They set up towns on the New England model, complete with a common and meetinghouse, and hoped Indigenous residents would join the church. Because Congregational church membership required public testimony of one's experience of Christ's saving grace, Eliot asked potential converts to recount that experience and read the Bible.[32] In this and other ways, their interactions with Algonquians showed less accommodation than the Franciscans among the Apalachee or the Jesuits among the Illinois. In praying town services Eliot read biblical passages, gave an Algonquian translation, preached for an hour, and then quizzed Native worshippers on their theological understanding.[33] Most rejected Eliot and shunned the praying towns. Small numbers did embrace the gospel, even if they continued traditional spiritual practice out of the minister's sight: Algonquian-English praying towns would claim about 1,100 residents at their peak.[34] Some who affiliated with Protestantism, like Waban, chief of the village of Cohannet, hoped the arrangement would secure their remaining land.[35] They didn't realize at first, however, that they would have to move to a missionary village, and later resented the misunderstanding. As tensions mounted, King Philip's War broke out in 1675, and only four praying towns remained by the end of that assault, organized by the Wampanoag sachem Metacom, son of the chief who had befriended the Pilgrims.[36] Those who collaborated with missionaries were reserved a place just up the Charles River from Cambridge, but it didn't go well for Indigenous resisters. The English killed Metacom and displayed his severed head in Plymouth.

Yet some Natives in New England continued to incorporate Christian symbols after 1675. Consider the grave of an eleven-year-old Mashantucket Pequot girl who died sometime between 1680 and 1720.[37] Her interment on land in present-day Connecticut was traditional: the mourners placed her in an oval grave in the flexed position, knees to her chest, her head facing the direction her soul would travel on its way to Cautantowwit's house, the afterworld where the creator lives. Her forehead was adorned with beads and sprinkled with red ochre. Shell necklaces with effigies of turtles and birds adorned her neck, and there were tools for tending fields. Only the medicine bundle complicated the religious identity of the deceased girl: it contained a bear paw and a Bible page. The bear, able to move between terrestrial and celestial realms, was a guide for afterlife transit. The page with Psalm 98 from the King James Bible—"O sing unto the Lord a new song; for he hath done marvelous things"—is harder to explain. She spoke Pequot, and we can't know how much she understood. She might have been told the psalm's meaning, and it resonated. Perhaps she liked the sound of Christian hymns. Or maybe the girl saw the biblical page as infused with *manitou,* the animating spiritual force in special things. Whatever the significance, at least fragments of Christian practice survived the war's destruction. After that—and especially between the 1720s and the 1760s—there would be more attempts to encourage Indigenous reverence for the Bible, as with the contracts for Native indentured servants like Rebeckah Chin.[38] In 1731, that young girl's impoverished parents signed her over to a Barnstable family until her eighteenth birthday. Until then Rebeckah would work for them; in turn, the Massachusetts family promised to teach her to read the Bible—and give her one when her service ended.

Congregationalists' encounters with Protestant dissenters also generated new spaces, including a new colony where those who challenged the established church could practice their faith. There was a long list of the spiritually unwelcome: in 1652 Massachusetts's governor petitioned Parliament for permission to exclude ten groups—not only Catholics but also Jews, Muslims, Quakers, atheists, and "what not." Massachusetts wouldn't see a lot of "what not" for a while, but the seventeenth-century colony did confront some religious dissent. In 1635 Salem's minister, Roger Williams, told colonial leaders they shouldn't steal Indian land. And, he warned, coerced conversions don't last and state churches don't work; to keep the church free from the state's defiling influence, the two should be separated. It's not surprising, then, that the colony's General Court convicted Williams of sedition and heresy. After securing a deed from the Narragansett, he moved to present-day Rhode Island in 1636.[39] There at the place he called "Providence Plantation," Williams established his colony, where he welcomed dissenters. By 1663 residents were promised "a full libertie," or what he called "soul liberty," since everyone has a conscience, including "Jews, Turks, Papists, Protestants, pagans."[40]

Others who appealed to conscience—and the indwelling spirit—threatened Massachusetts authorities by claiming direct access to the transcendent, a bit like the experiential piety that inspired Po'pay's Pueblo rebellion. Just after Williams left, locals worried about how they might know if they were saved.[41] They couldn't know by following the "covenant of works," Anne Hutchison told the sixty women and men who gathered regularly in her home. She suggested the colony's ministers were like Catholics who mistakenly thought it was "works" that brought divine reconciliation. Instead, Hutchison proposed, only a "covenant of grace" animated by an experience of the Spirit could comfort them. In response, the General Court read a list of accusations, including that "you have stepped out of your place," acting more like a husband than a wife, more like a preacher than a congregant.[42] She shouldn't have been preaching, especially to men, and certainly not criticizing ministers. Hutchison also claimed she could discern religious truth "by an immediate revelation."[43] That went too far. After the court banished her, Hutchison left for Williams's new colony, though other dissenters, like the Quaker Mary Dyer, who was hanged on Boston Common for her unrepentant spiritual nonconformity, never got the chance.[44] Neither did the twenty executed during the 1692 Salem witch trials.[45]

Social and ecological stressors amplified the religious tensions.[46] There was more political participation for landowning men than almost anywhere else in the world, but in most ways Congregational New England was a hierarchical and sexist society that insisted on consensus in religion and all things. It was a regional niche where the tragic loss of Indigenous life had allowed a precipitous rise in the colonial population. The decimated and displaced hadn't gone away, however, lingering in the collective imagination and just beyond the edges of settlement, where the threat of retribution loomed. Meanwhile, expanding New England colonial families squabbled as their neighbors' cow trampled their corn, their self-scrutinizing piety couldn't bring assurance, and everyone competed for shrinking resources, especially fertile fields to plant.

The Middle Colonies

There was more land for farms in the Middle Colonies, which were settled by the Dutch (New Netherland, 1614–1664) and Swedes (New Sweden, 1638–1654) and then conquered and chartered by the English starting in 1664.[47] There also was less pressure to conform and more freedom to worship in the lands that became New York, Delaware, New Jersey, and Pennsylvania. That's because the English Mid-Atlantic provinces arose between 1664 and 1681 under the patronage of Charles II, who didn't insist on establishing the Church of England.[48] He allowed "liberty of conscience" and even chartered three Quaker-influenced colonies. As they did elsewhere in their global empire, the Dutch in New Netherland made the Reformed Church the only official place of public worship. They hoped everyone would join but reluctantly tolerated dissenters—except Catholics—as long as they kept their beliefs to themselves and confined worship to the home. New Netherland's leader Peter Stuyvesant also accepted Jewish migrants, who had enjoyed financial standing and religious protection in the pluralistic Dutch colony in Brazil.[49] So there was some ethnic and religious diversity, not only Jews and non-Reformed Protestants but settlers like Anthony Jansen van Salee, an African-born farmer of Dutch-Moroccan heritage raised as a Muslim and known as "Anthony the Turk."[50] Yet Stuyvesant banned non-Reformed worship. And the 1657 Flushing Remonstrance, an unsuccessful petition asking him to extend "love, peace, and liberty" to "Jews, Turks, and Egyptians" as well as Quakers, had no impact on colonial policy, though it led to jail time for four petitioners.[51] Dutch Calvinists, then, played only a limited and indirect role in the emergence of liberty and diversity in the Middle Colonies and the later nation.[52] Charles II and the Quakers get most of the credit. The three Quaker-influenced provinces—West Jersey (1676), East Jersey (1683), and Pennsylvania (1681)—institutionalized the "liberty of conscience" that led to a diversity of faiths.[53]

Once in place, heterogeneity couldn't be reversed, even when the religious situation in England changed. European visitors to early Pennsylvania noted the diversity, and by 1700 Delaware had Swedish and Finnish Lutherans as well as Dutch Reformed, English Quakers, and Welsh Baptists.[54] A member of the Church of England complained that New Jersey was a "Hotch Potch of all Religions."[55] New York's governor lamented the presence of Catholics, Jews, Anabaptists, and "Ranting Quakers," while an Anglican priest warned London about the colony's "difference of opinion in religion."[56] Those differences characterized many locales in the English Middle Colonies, and the region's multi-steeple hamlets and seaports looked quite different from the classic New England town, which centered on a single state-sponsored church. The decentered Mid-Atlantic landscape included cities planned in linear grids with sites for churches, like Philadelphia, and rural hamlets where well-spaced farms dotted the terrain and congregations popped up to meet—or spark—the locals' spiritual interest, as in Chester County, one of the three original Pennsylvania counties established by the colony's founder, William Penn.

Penn loved wooded terrain and cultivated plots—and he imported seeds of his favorite trees—but it was "liberty of conscience" that seeded "Penn's Woods."[57] He was five when Puritan rebels chopped off the head of King Charles I, and Penn sided with the Puritans by 1656, at age twelve. But the seed of conscience sprouted a few years later while he strolled the quadrangle of Oxford's Christ Church College in 1660, as students attended Anglican services in that year when the monarchy—and the state church—was restored.[58] He attended discussions at the home of Christ Church's ousted Puritan dean, and that earned Penn a fine and a reprimand.[59] By 1622 spiritual dissent got him expelled from college and "banished" from home.[60] Four years later he joined the Quakers, whose worship entailed sitting silently to await the Spirit's inspiration. The Spirit soon moved Penn to preach and promote Quakerism, which got him arrested, and he wrote his most famous book from the Tower of London in 1669.[61] By 1682, Penn's quest to secure "liberty of conscience"—and financial reward—spurred a transoceanic journey to the land he had received to settle a debt Charles II owed his father.[62] At the confluence of the Delaware and Schuylkill Rivers, Penn planted a different sort of community, what he called a "holy experiment." He wrote "a charter of liberties" and crafted a "frame of government" to promote the public good, at least for White Christian "freemen and planters," creating a political culture that afforded Europeans who believed in God the protections Penn had been denied.[63]

Those liberties did not apply to everyone equally, however. Penn's holy experiment required replotting the land and removing the residents, the Lenni Lenape (Delaware), who had farmed and hunted the land for thousands of years, and the province also allowed the slavery of Africans. Penn negotiated land deals with the Lenape. Although a Wampum Belt with an image of a colonist and a Native holding hands is the only surviving evidence of the mythic first treaty, Penn did engage with Natives more humanely than most provincial proprietors.[64] But he expected them to submit to imperial authority, and there were misunderstandings and inequities. The Lenape probably presumed they were granting access, not ownership, and Penn sometimes sold tracts to settlers before Indigenous deals had been negotiated.[65] But the province's leader believed he had respectfully acquired the 10,000 wooded acres surrounding the commercial port of Philadelphia, City of Brotherly Love, since he had signed agreements and had assigned them plots.[66] The Lenape soon found themselves crowded out of their cornfields, however. Many left by the 1730s, moving westward beyond frontier settlement.[67]

The liberties also didn't apply equally to enslaved Africans. By the 1750s, for example, Chester County's 3,000 landowners used the labor of 231 Africans, who worked beside their owners in the fields.[68] Slaveholding presented a moral quandary for many Mid-Atlantic Friends or Quakers, however.[69] Some spoke out: in 1688 four Germantown Quakers used the Golden Rule—"we shall doe to all men licke as we will be done ourselves"—to craft the first organized antislavery protest in the English colonies, and John Wollman, who visited the Chester Quaker meeting, wrote a 1754 antislavery essay that Philadelphia Quakers would endorse.[70]

Many Pennsylvania residents did enjoy religious liberty. In Chester County, a major wheat-producing region by 1750, most residents were rural "yeomen" who worked their own land, but above the yeoman majority was an upper middle class that included clergymen who served a variety of denominations in the county's multi-steeple hamlets.[71] The Church of England established multiple congregations. Swedish and Finish Lutherans and Dutch Calvinists were already there when Penn mapped the county's boundaries. The Presbyterians had the second greatest presence, and Welsh Baptists added a log church. German-speaking migrants like the Mennonites and German Reformed came, and so did the Baptist Brethren or Dunkers. Henry Melchior Muhlenberg, a prominent Lutheran missionary, organized churches too.[72] Yet the Quakers had the most worship spaces.[73] By 1750 English, Welsh, and Irish settlers had established "plain style" Quaker meetinghouses across the county's rolling farmland, staring with the first one in Chester in 1676.

Quaker egalitarianism did allow some social mobility and gender equity. White women benefited from the Friends' egalitarian theology. After Penn suffered a stroke, his wife Hannah took over as Pennsylvania's proprietor, and, unlike in Massachusetts, women in the Quaker colony could offer public testimony about matters of faith, a sight that surprised European travelers.[74] George Fox, the founder of the Friends, had said women and men enjoyed equal access to the Spirit. The Quakers rejected paid university-trained clergy—like the "learned ministry" educated at Harvard—but acknowledged that some men and women had the gift to preach, like Jane Fenn Hoskens, who had left London for Philadelphia in 1712.[75] Thrown in a debtors' prison after arrival, Jane was rescued by Pennsylvania Quakers who employed her as a schoolteacher. By 1719 she was worshipping in Chester's meetinghouse.[76] As in other Quaker worship spaces, there was an elevated bench for those running the meeting and rows of unpainted benches where the devout sat facing each other.[77] Hoskens, who worked as a housekeeper, grew more confident at speaking up, and her witness was well received, to her surprise: "tho' I was but in the station of a servant yet was taken great notice of by them."[78] Like other Quaker women of the period, she also began traveling to preach. Going first to meetinghouses in Philadelphia and New York, by 1722 she was embarking on "religious visits" to New England and the South. In 1725 she went on a preaching tour of Barbados, the former home of some Pennsylvania Quakers, and then on to Ireland and England.[79]

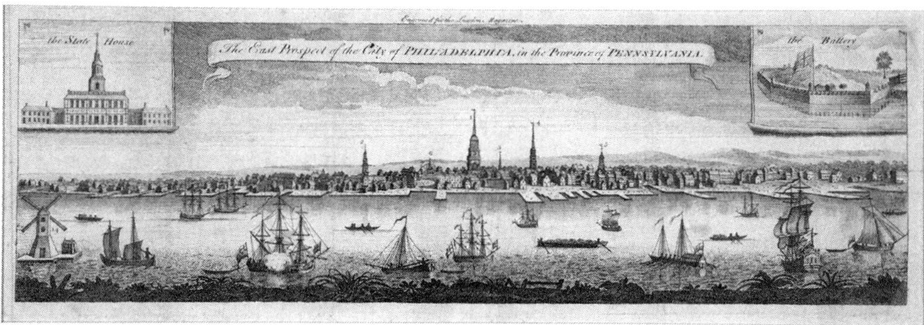

Figure 20. *East Prospect of the City of Philadelphia.* Representation of the city in 1755, with Christ Church in the center, the steepleless Quaker meetinghouse hidden to the left, and Presbyterian and Dutch Calvinist churches to the right. Courtesy of Yale University Art Gallery, Mabel Brady Garvan Collection.

Jane and her husband, a merchant, also traveled the valley road to Philadelphia, where he conducted business and she attended the Philadelphia Yearly Meeting, the regional gathering for Quakers. By the 1750s, denominational associations of Quakers, Baptists, Presbyterians, Reformed, and Lutherans also were headquartered there, and the city displayed the ethnic and religious diversity that characterized the Middle Colonies and that would define the future nation.[80] A surprised Maryland visitor noted the multiplicity he found around a tavern table one night in 1744: "a very mixed company of different nations and religions," with Scots, English, Dutch, Germans, and Irish as well as Catholics, Presbyterians, Quakers, Methodists, Moravians, Anabaptists, and Jews.[81] Out on the streets, the tallest building by the mid-1750s was the Anglicans' Christ Church, as a 1755 image of the city's skyline shows (fig. 20). The Quakers' steeple-less meetinghouse is harder to spot at the left of that building, but the spires of the Presbyterian and Dutch Calvinist churches rise skyward on the right. Elsewhere in town, a Jewish community had begun, and some of the province's 1,365 Catholics could gather to worship.[82] When they founded Philadelphia's St. Joseph's Church in 1733, it became the only place in the seaboard colonies—and the British empire—where the public celebration of Catholic mass was permitted by law. By 1750 the cityscape also included the oldest church in Pennsylvania, Gloria Dei, a Swedish Lutheran church, as well as buildings for German Lutheran, Baptist, and Moravian churchgoers.[83]

The Lenape, who were evangelized by the Moravians, kept moving westward, and 787 enslaved Africans lived in Philadelphia in 1750, fewer than in New York but more than the principle of brotherly love might suggest.[84] Some of those Philadelphia slaves were buried in First Baptist Church cemetery, and colonial New York City, also home to diversity, had an African burial ground that offers clues about their presence in the Middle Colonies.[85]

By 1750 New York City had nine spaces for public worship, including for Huguenots and Quakers, and Anglican, Presbyterian, and Dutch Calvinist churches had steeples visible to approaching ships.[86] Unlike in Philadelphia, there was no Catholic church, but by 1730 there was a synagogue, Shearith Israel, built by Spanish and Portuguese Jews who had first arrived in 1654. Africans arrived earlier, in 1626, and slaves of the Dutch India Company could own property and be baptized. A few won partial freedom. Those Africans began burying their dead in Lower Manhattan while the Dutch still controlled the area, and they continued interments there through the end of the eighteenth century. Harsher English slavery codes restricted Africans' public gatherings for funerals, but the community continued to ritually mark the passing of those who died, often after years of malnourishment and bone-stressing labor. The thousands of graves at the "Negros Buriel Ground," as it was called in a 1755 map, show a blending of Christian and African practices. Like other colonial Christians, most baptized slaves were buried face up in a coffin with their head toward the west, but an African heart-shaped symbol decorated one man's coffin lid, and a woman from West Africa, whose body showed signs of too much work and too little food, went to her rest with "an African-style strand of beads around her waist."[87]

Diverging Devotional Styles and Deepening Transregional Connections

African influences shaped religious practice throughout the British colonies, especially in the mainland South and the Caribbean, which were nodes in an imperial commercial network that linked New England and the Middle Colonies with the wider British empire. Transregional spiritual networks mediated by print culture and denominational ties also connected Britain's colonies. By the 1750s, for instance, itinerant preachers like George Whitefield had riled listeners at revival meetings up and down the coast. This new ritual form, the revival meeting, shook the Mid-Atlantic and New England but also reverberated in Virginia and South Carolina. Most narratives of American religion have highlighted revivalism, which makes sense since it would become an enduring devotional style. However, eighteenth-century revivalism is best situated on a continuum of transatlantic pieties shaped by the Great Awakening, the midcentury revivals that stirred passions, and the

Enlightenment, the intellectual movement that emphasized reason. Elite disputants disagreed about which authorities to trust, which metaphors to use, and which spiritual path to take.[88] To oversimplify the diverging devotional styles: some inclined toward a religion of the head that situated authority outside the self and used metaphors about cultivation or domestication to suggest that the spiritual path was gradual; others emphasized a religion of the heart that seated authority in the individual and used metaphors about light, sex, or birth to capture their sense that the path was sudden.[89] Most ordinary devotees fell somewhere along that continuum, not at the extremes, though contemporaries could be forgiven for being blinded by the polarizing public rhetoric that exaggerated differences.

Itinerant and settled ministers played a role in stirring the cross-colony revivalist fervor, including Jonathan Edwards, who spread news of conversions in a 1737 book about God's "surprising work" in Massachusetts.[90] Sinners were "brought out of darkness into the marvelous light," he reported, and were "so suddenly and yet so greatly changed."[91] Whitefield's tours between 1739 and 1743 prompted thousands of conversions.[92] The tremors, which had begun in the Middle Colonies in the 1720s, shook nearly every New England town by the 1740s. Colonists were moved by the indwelling Spirit or appalled by the emotional excesses. Rationalist critics like Boston's Charles Chauncy lamented the shrieking, swooning, and "convulsion-like Tremblings," and in 1743 James Davenport scandalized New London, Connecticut, observers by removing his pants to show his dedication to God and disdain for fancy clothes.[93] He apologized later and explained his excesses as the effects of a "long fever" and a "false spirit."[94] Revivalists found it hard to support Davenport after 1743, but Whitefield defended himself in an exchange of public letters with Chauncy.[95]

Even Whitefield's critics admitted his skill in affecting crowds in packed churches and open-air gatherings, where he stood on a portable pulpit (fig. 21). Benjamin Franklin, the rationalist who printed his sermons but resisted his appeals, described "the multitudes"—perhaps 10,000—who heard Whitefield in Philadelphia in 1739, when "it seemed as if all the world were growing religious."[96] During a 1740 visit to Boston, Whitefield reported that most of his 6,000 hearers "wept for a considerable time," and an attendee captured the crowd's alternating emotions: "O how dreadful was the place, and yet how delightful!" At a meeting that afternoon it was mostly dreadful, since the gallery collapsed. Some leapt from windows, and five died before Whitefield moved the gathering to the Boston Common.[97] About a month later Nathan Cole learned that Whitefield would be preaching near his farm in

Figure 21. George Whitefield, published by Carington Bowles, after a Nathaniel Hone mezzotint (1769). Courtesy of the National Portrait Gallery, London.

the Connecticut River Valley. He threw down his hoe and jumped on his horse. When Cole arrived, he found "a great multitude" of about 3,000 people at the meetinghouse. But Whitefield's preaching didn't provide comfort: it started him "quarrelling with God," though later his spiritual crisis resolved in a conversion experience, when his dark despair "was gone in the twinkling of an Eye, as quick as a flash of lightening."[98]

The revivals—and the impulse to tend to "inner landscapes" as well as outer landscapes—are important for our story.[99] First, they reveal transatlantic as well as intercolonial crossings. Itinerant preachers like Whitefield traversed the colonies and sailed the Atlantic. Influences from German Pietism entered the seaboard colonies.[100] Jonathan Edwards's *Faithful Narrative of the Surprising Work of God* (1737) was translated into German the next year, and mainland colonists read news of later revivals in Scotland, Ireland, Switzerland, and Holland.[101] Further, since opposing voices also found expression in the circulating media, a revival-influenced "religion of the heart" competed with an Enlightenment-influenced "religion of the head." Ebenezer Gay, the reason-guided minister at Hingham's Old Ship Meetinghouse, noted that rituals intended to unify congregations had "changed into a ruinous War." Splits started during the mid-1740s, and New England religious life fragmented more after 1750.[102] Towns divided, congregations fractured, and families split. When the fires of revival burned out, some wives and husbands walked to different meetinghouses on Sunday. Cole's wife, Anne, for instance, didn't follow when he joined the Baptists.[103]

The revivals also show that the prevailing way of life, farming, couldn't always provide the appropriate spiritual vocabulary. New experiences required different analogies. Two models of Protestant piety—the gradualist gospel of the word and the sudden gospel of the spirit—had comingled in the same congregation, even the same person, and only occasionally clashed, as with the uproar over Hutchison's claim to "immediate revelation." The Bible-focused gradualists relied on the analogy with agriculture's regulated cycles and labor-intensive duties—the clearing, seeding, and weeding. They imagined spiritual cultivation as a steady process that would cease when the saved would be united with Christ in the final harvest. Yet some spirit-focused Protestants, who emphasized the sudden experience of redemptive grace, searched for other images to capture the contrast they felt before and after that time-stamped event: I was in darkness, but now there's light. I was born once, but now I am born again. I was asleep, and now I am awake. Cole, for example, wrote in his diary that he was born in February 1711 and "born again" in October 1741. His lightning-quick experience of God was like "the Clear light of the sun."[104] He was familiar with the steady toil required to make things grow but abandoned agricultural analogies in his conversion narrative, partly because he was performing a learned script and partly because it fit his experience. However, the awakened returned to organic images when they assessed the revivals' effects. They talked about the revivals' "fruits" as they considered what had been gained and lost, and, as with Edwards's *Distinguishing Marks of a Work of the Spirit of God,* they noted that "the Fruits of the Earth are first green before they . . . come to their proper Perfection gradually."[105]

The 1740 revivals are also important for understanding collective belonging and human flourishing, because they touched the socially marginalized, including women, children, Natives, and Africans. The Spirit couldn't hurdle all social barriers, but the revivals reached the propertyless poor as well as the profit-chasing merchants. Young people joined the ranks of the awakened, and so did women. In 1743 Sarah Osborn was "ravished by his love," and that Rhode Island Congregationalist hosted prayer meetings at her house for years, welcoming the free and the enslaved.[106] About 1739 Samson Occom, a Mohegan, felt "the great stir of Religion" in Connecticut, and he would be ordained twenty years later.[107] Some free and enslaved Africans were touched too, and Occom's acquaintance Phillis Wheatley, the Boston slave who wrote poetry, would compose a memorial tribute to George Whitefield, asking the "Impartial Savior" to welcome him home.[108]

The sudden and gradualist gospels also reached the commercial seaports and backcountry farms of the mainland South, where Whitefield sparked episodic Lowcountry revivals, even if the published sermons of rationalist Archbishop of Canterbury John Tillotson, the most popular clerical author before 1750, elicited continuing appreciation from slaveholding planters.[109] Whitefield preached to sizable crowds in Savannah and Charles Town, and publications praising and criticizing his tours prompted debate.[110] While in Charles Town, Whitefield was irked because he noticed that Tillotson's restrained sermons remained highly esteemed.[111] In turn, elite residents attacked Whitefield in newspapers and pamphlets. One antirevivalist leader of South Carolina's Anglicans charged that the enthusiasts' unfounded claims were beyond "the Reach of all the Arguments and Conclusions of Reason and Revelation."[112] He also insisted that regeneration is not "the Work of a Moment" but "a gradual and co-operative work of the Holy Spirit." What he didn't say was that some southern critics also worried that lightning-quick awakenings might upend the plantation system so central to the local economy and the global market. Whitefield, who supported slavery in Georgia and would later own slaves, didn't want to do away with enslaved labor.[113] But South Carolinians couldn't be sure, since he had condemned planters' "cruel" treatment of their laborers and had preached to slaves.[114] Almost as worrisome, he converted a few slaveholding planters, including Catherine and Hugh Bryan, who began evangelizing their slaves after Whitefield's tour. Fears spiked, and in 1742 the Carolina Assembly asked the lieutenant governor to prevent the Bryans from continuing their religious gatherings for slaves.[115] It turns out that the legislators had little to worry about. There would be a few dissenting White voices—and Black resistance—but religion mostly supported the stressed slave plantation, the defining eco-cultural niche that emerged in the Caribbean and the mainland South.

The Greater South

The slave plantation, the defining niche of the mainland South, would go on to change US history, and to understand it requires tracing links with the Caribbean and analyzing religion's role in transforming the habitats that Southerners inherited and bequeathed.[116]

The major southern seaport, Charles Town, was more like Bridgetown, Barbados's island capital, than New York, Boston, or Philadelphia. In Charles Town and Bridgetown, two "hubs of empire" in the region I'll call the *Greater South,* the state-sponsored Anglican Church and the large slave plantation developed together, reconfiguring the population and modifying the landscape.[117] The Greater South had subregions: the Chesapeake Bay, English Caribbean, and southeastern Lowcountry, which stretched from the Cape Fear River in North Carolina to the Atamha River in Georgia.[118] In terms of religious history, Maryland's early experiment with religious freedom and surprising mix of denominations was noteworthy.[119] Yet Virginia and eighteenth-century Maryland were somewhat less representative. It was the Anglican plantation provinces of Barbados, Jamaica, and South Carolina that exhibited the ethnic, linguistic, and religious diversity found in the Middle Colonies and, later, the new nation.[120] So it helps to include the Caribbean as well as the mainland. That enlarged scope captures the shared history and striking parallels, and it better represents the perceptions of contemporaries—chained slaves crossing the Atlantic, captive Natives shipped to the Caribbean, and those who left Britain or stayed home.[121] For all of them, it was difficult to tell where the continent's southeastern edges ended and the Caribbean colonies and global empire began, as a 1700 map depicting the colonies or "plantations" of English America shows (fig. 22).[122]

"English America" included Barbados, Bermuda, and Jamaica—just as Spanish and French maps claimed hemispheric terrain—and the island settlements were linked with the mainland provinces.[123] The English slave plantation took form as an eco-cultural niche in the tobacco-growing Chesapeake colonies of Virginia (1607) and Maryland (1634).[124] Between 1612 and 1684 Virginia also included Bermuda, because a 1609 storm diverted some Jamestown passengers who landed on that archipelago. After the shipwrecked made it to Virginia, the hemispheric interconnections persisted. One of those shipwrecked Virginians was John Rolfe, who gained fame for marrying Pocahontas but also changed regional history in 1612 by experimenting with Spanish tobacco seeds (*Nicotiana tabacum*) imported from the Orinoco Valley in South

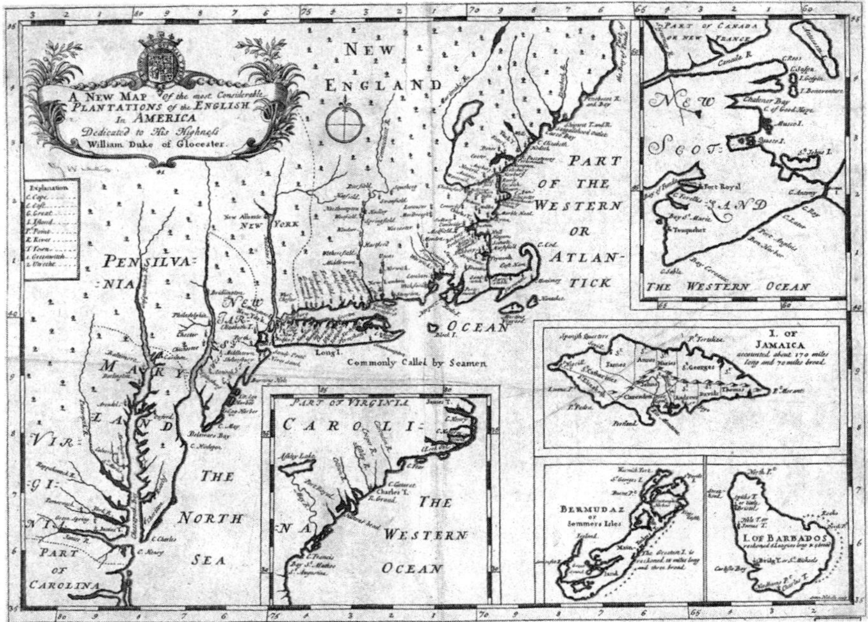

Figure 22. *A New Map of the Most Considerable Plantations of the English in America* by Edward Wells (1700). The four boxed maps along the bottom depict, from left to right, the Carolina Lowcountry and the islands of Jamaica, Bermuda, and Barbados. Library of Congress, Geography and Maps Division, G3300 1722.N5.

America.[125] The English agreed it was milder than the species Natives smoked. Virginia, which shipped England millions of pounds of that tobacco every year, became the model for Barbados (1627). Yet when tobacco proved unprofitable there, Dutch migrants who had farmed in Brazil taught Barbados planters how to grow sugarcane, and sugar made Barbados the richest English colony. Barbados in turn became the model and sent settlers to Jamaica (1655) and Carolina (1663). Continuing the chain of connections, in 1725 South Carolina rice planters introduced slave plantations to North Carolina's Cape Fear region. Finally, after the Georgia Assembly abandoned James Oglethorpe's founding vision of the colony and lifted its ban on slavery, wealthy rice planters replicated the Carolina slave plantation along coastal Georgia starting in the 1750s.

Religion played a key role by justifying—and sometimes condemning—the region's stressed eco-cultural niche, the Anglican slave plantation.[126] *Planter piety,* the hierarchical worldview and paternalistic ethic that guided slaveholding landowners and fortified the plantation complex, began in the seventeenth century, when there was a good deal of spiritual practice in the home—including as Anglican planters in Virginia baptized infants in their houses and Maryland Catholics attended mass at manor chapels.[127] The Christianization and Anglicization of the landscape accelerated in the eighteenth century.[128] London's Society for the Propagation of the Gospel in Foreign Parts (SPG) sent both missionaries and money after 1701, and colonies from the Chesapeake to the Caribbean had statutory Anglican establishments by 1715.[129] In the next four decades, civil and ecclesiastical bodies constructed more worship spaces to meet settlers' spiritual needs. For most planters, however, their livelihood was too reliant on enslaved labor to risk exposing field hands to biblical prophets and egalitarian messages, including the notion that everyone—even the slave—was created in God's image. Maryland's Catholics, like the French and Spanish, evangelized slaves as well as Natives. But most Anglicans and dissenting Protestants weren't focused on baptizing the Indigenous and didn't welcome the enslaved into the ecclesiastical community.

The demography changed with the topography: the number of Natives declined and the proportion of Africans increased across the Greater South as elite plantation owners bought more slaves to harvest Caribbean sugar, Chesapeake tobacco, and Carolina rice. By the 1750s farming faiths had sanctioned chattel slavery and deforested river valleys. But the unjust conditions and environmental degradation weren't only the Anglicans' fault. Quakers in Barbados, Catholics in Maryland, and Huguenots in South Carolina owned slave plantations. And those plantations became socially and ecologically unstable—more violent, less healthy, and more inequitable than the smaller farming communities and expanding commercial centers north of the Chesapeake.

The Anglican establishment and the slave plantation didn't arise fully formed in the Chesapeake Bay, a region of dispersed farms along a 200-mile aquatic system interrupted by small towns like Virginia's first settlement at Jamestown and Maryland's first capital at St. Mary's City—but without a port city rivaling Charles Town. There were differences between the two colonies, but by the 1750s the Church of England had more of a presence across the Chesapeake, and spiritually diverse African workers were cutting more and more tobacco for Protestant and Catholic planters.

Maryland

Maryland was established in 1632 as a proprietary colony, a grant of land and authority to a single person, the Catholic Cecil Calvert. His deceased father, the first Lord Baltimore, had befriended Charles I, and the king and the proprietor named the province for the king's French Catholic wife, Henrietta Maria.[130] So it became "Mary land," in honor of the English queen. Calvert, with help from the Jesuit Andrew White, then planned the province and advertised for settlers. The campaign enticed Catholic gentlemen and indentured servants (mostly Protestants) to join Leonard Calvert, the colony's first governor.[131] The passengers aboard the first two ships arrived in 1634—after stopping in Barbados, the initial landing for many transatlantic travelers. That March, White's journal tells us, they came ashore at a waterway they called St. Mary's River, where they celebrated the first mass. White and the other Catholics then planted a wooden cross, "a monument to Christ, our Savior."[132] The Spanish had tried to plant a Catholic colony there earlier, but the English Catholics aimed for less and accomplished more. White and the Calvert family wanted more freedom to worship. They knew English law couldn't allow an official Catholic realm, but Marylanders could at least minimize interfaith conflict. That's why Calvert instructed provincial Catholics to worship "privately" and treat Protestants with "mildness."[133] The ordinance of 1639, the first official statement on the issue, made it policy: "Holy Churches" shall have "rights and liberties."[134]

White and the Calverts had other spiritual goals in that era of Native contact and Protestant–Catholic coexistence (1634–1645). White, like Calvert, cared about "sowing the seeds of Religion" among Natives.[135] Another Jesuit imagined "the hope of the Indian harvest" but also "reaping" Protestant converts.[136] Catholics did convert some, including "nearly all" of the non-Catholics who landed in 1638.[137] They also had some spiritual success among Algonquian communities in the province, where there was less interpersonal violence and more intercultural openness than might be expected.[138] That was partly because Kittamaquund, the leader of the Piscataway confederacy, wrongly assumed that a strategic alliance with the Jesuits might shelter them from their enemies, the Susquehannock.[139] The chief also believed White had healed him in 1639, so he agreed to be baptized. Mass conversions didn't follow, but the missionary managed to live in the Piscataway village and translate part of the catechism into their language.[140] A few years earlier White also had contact with the Yaocomaco, who greeted the first landing party, but to avoid intertribal aggression and European intrusion many Natives left by the end of the first year.[141] White in turn appropriated an abandoned longhouse to serve as a chapel.

White and his fellow Jesuits replaced the longhouse chapel with a wooden church at St. Mary's City, but tensions with Protestants intensified between 1642 (the start of the English Civil War) and 1660 (the restoration of the monarchy). The battle between the Parliament and the Crown reached Chesapeake Bay when anti-Catholics plotted to overthrow Calvert's government, and in 1645 Richard Ingle and like-minded Protestants sailed into St. Mary's City. That tobacco trader chained the five resident Jesuits and burned the "papist" chapel. White would stand trial in London for violating England's law prohibiting priests. He spent three years in prison and never returned to the Maryland mission, which wouldn't recover for decades. Some persecuted Catholics left, just as Virginia Catholics headed for the Leeward Islands, where Irish Catholics would constitute about one-third of the White population by the late seventeenth century.[142] Most in Maryland laid low or made compromises. The proprietor and the legislators responded by trying to re-create the earlier coexistence.[143] Cecil Calvert had welcomed Virginia Puritans to Maryland, and, because he hoped it might ease interfaith tension, the proprietor installed one of them as governor. With Calvert's blessing, the assembly then passed "An Act Concerning Religion," better known as the Maryland Toleration Act, in 1649. Anticipating the First Amendment, it promised "free exercise" to all Christians, but also prohibited negative religious speech. Offending terms warranting a ten-shilling fine included not only "popish priest" but also "heretic" and "puritan."[144] But the assembly rescinded that act a few years later.

The situation improved somewhat for Catholics between the 1660s and the 1680s, as political changes across the Atlantic affected the coastal colony. Soon after the Catholic sympathizer Charles II was restored to the throne in 1660, the Jesuits felt able to erect a brick chapel in their modest capital.[145] For a time there was less strife, and migration diversified the religious landscape. Maryland had Catholics and Anglicans, but most residents were Protestant dissenters, including Presbyterians, Anabaptists, and Quakers.[146] A promotional pamphlet published in this peaceful period claimed spiritually harmonious Maryland was "the miracle of the age."[147] The Jesuits agreed: "the Maryland mission flourishes; the seed which our fathers sowed there is growing up into a copious crop."[148]

There would be a smaller yield than they hoped. The non-Catholic assembly curtailed Catholics' political participation and religious freedom, and Anglicanism became the official faith between 1689 and 1704. With Catholics banned from the assembly and the capital moved to Annapolis, eighteenth-century Maryland became a royal colony divided into Anglican parishes governed by lay vestries responsible to the Bishop of London.[149] More Anglican church buildings were constructed, and there were some signs of lay devotional practice. A 1724 survey complained about the "papists" and

Quakers but boasted that 58 percent of Anglicans attended worship regularly.[150] Still, the Anglican churches had problems. Vestries—lay groups charged with deciding civic and spiritual matters—had almost no power to choose their rectors.[151] There was a shortage of clerics too, at least good ones. In a pastorless parish a lay parishioner was paid in tobacco to read from the *Book of Common Prayer* on Sundays.[152] Anglican parishes that had rectors sometimes wished they didn't. St. Paul's in Baltimore County complained that their rector rarely attended the church and refused to bury the dead.[153] A "habitual Drunkard" served one parish, and parishioners accused another of murdering one of his slaves.[154]

As with that rector, Anglicans in the pulpit and in the pews owned slaves who worked their tobacco fields. The landowners believed they were enacting a divinely sanctioned code that affirmed their superiority, sanctioned their lifeway, and demanded slave obedience. Enslaved workers were God's property "entrusted" to masters' and mistresses' use, as planters entrusted overseers with their laborers, Rev. Thomas Bacon suggested at St. Peter's parish in Talbot County around 1750.[155] In turn, what the enslaved did for the enslavers, they did for God. Some of those Maryland slaves were Christians, as at St. Peter's, and others observed African Indigenous traditions. A minority were Muslims who strove to meet their spiritual obligations by facing Mecca five times a day to pray. That could cause problems, as Ayuba Suleiman Diallo found at a tobacco plantation near Talbot County.[156] A Fulani Muslim, portrayed with a Qur'an around his neck in an eighteenth-century painting, he was the son of a respected imam from present-day Senegal, and he could write in Arabic and recite the Qur'an. After he was found ill-equipped for tobacco farming, he was assigned to tend cattle. But one day Diallo abandoned the herd to pray in the field, as a nearby White boy hurled insults and threw dirt. Unable to explain because he knew no English, he ran, but he soon found himself in jail. We know all that because an SPG missionary published a biography of him in 1734, the year after an influential English translation of the Qur'an appeared.[157] The Anglican priest also arranged a trip to London, and that helped Diallo win his freedom. Unlike most of the enslaved in Maryland, he managed to return to Africa, though as an agent of the imperial trading company that had shackled, shipped, and sold him.[158]

Catholics also traded with the agents of the Royal African Company, which had been chartered in 1672 to protect the English empire's slave trade, and, like their Anglican neighbors, they also housed enslaved workers on tobacco plantations.[159] But they faced different spiritual challenges. A priest was arrested for saying mass at the Great Brick Chapel in St. Mary's City in

1704, and officials closed the chapel and prohibited public worship.[160] Despite the restrictions, women in religious orders made strides: in 1702 Elizabeth Carberry became the first nun to be professed in England's mainland colonies, and Mary Digges was the first to cross the Atlantic to enter a European convent in 1721.[161] The Jesuits also continued their work. They used bricks from their shuttered chapel to construct a manor house, Bohemia Manor, where America's first bishop and his cousin, the only Catholic signer of the Declaration of Independence, would attend school.[162] There were fourteen Maryland chapels by 1700 and fifty six decades later, some on Jesuit land and some on lay manors.[163] Charles Carroll the Settler (grandfather of the Declaration signer) hosted masses at his Annapolis mansion, and a chapel was added to his tobacco plantation.[164] Catholic landowner Henrietta Maria (Neale) Bennett Lloyd erected a chapel on one of her Talbot estates and supported another nearby.[165] So Catholics didn't stop practicing their faith. They just did it out of sight, and because of the paucity of priests—one for every 650 adherents—they also received the sacraments less regularly, even if horse-riding Jesuits with saddlebag chalices tried to reach them, often riding "about 300 miles a week."[166] So for Catholic tenants, servants, and slaves, devotional practice meant receiving the sacraments in someone's house or at one of the dispersed planters' chapels.

Catholic planters' wealth buffered them from provincial leaders' ire, but they had a moral problem: Catholic devotion, tobacco cultivation, and African enslavement all grew together on their manors. Henrietta Maria Lloyd's will instructed relatives to ensure her children were "brought up Godily & Virtuously," while also bequeathing her land and slaves.[167] She had shrewdly consolidated the holdings of her two deceased husbands and used a high-status, mixed-faith marriage to gain security.[168] Her land included the main plantation at Wye House, which grew corn and wheat as well as tobacco and had at least twenty slaves by 1700.[169] Many more would sweat in those fields in the decades ahead. By 1770 a male descendant owned 174 slaves, and the future abolitionist Frederick Douglass would grow up at Wye House during the 1820s, before later documenting plantation slavery's horrors.[170] Doohoregan Manor, a Catholic slave plantation in Baltimore County owned by Charles Carroll the Settler, was named after his family's confiscated land back in Ireland.[171] The Irish-born tobacco planter was determined to recover what his family had lost, even if it was on the other side of the Atlantic.[172] He also brought over countrymen, recruiting Irish Catholic servants to plant his fields. Carroll had acquired the land by working hard and, like Henrietta Lloyd, "marrying well."[173] With property added from his deceased wives' estates, the Settler acquired so much land that when he died in 1720, he owned more than anyone in the colony. By the 1770s, 330 slaves toiled at Doohoregan Manor, where his prominent grandson Charles Carroll of Carrolton housed them at the main plantation and across his 10,000-acre tract.[174]

The Jesuits also owned farmland where both indentured servants and, after 1717, enslaved Africans cut and cured tobacco.[175] By buying or inheriting land, they would oversee sixteen manors covering 31,000 acres by 1642.[176] Banned from political office and public worship, jittery Catholics gathered for mass in posh plantation chapels and intimate domestic spaces, and they continued to mix faith and farming in the decades ahead, as at Bohemia Manor, the Jesuit plantation on the Eastern Shore that owned twenty-six slaves by the 1760s.[177] By 1838, financial need would prompt the Jesuits to sell the remaining 272 slaves working on their six plantations.[178]

Virginia

Slaveholding Anglican landowners in Virginia also came to believe they were "God's overseers," charged with a sacred duty to discipline and "civilize" the slaves in their care. The plantation niche and its justifying planter piety only began to appear in Virginia between the 1660s and the 1720s. Yet from 1607 to 1657 some important processes got underway: the importation of enslaved Africans, the exportation of tobacco, and the establishment of the Anglican parish system, which meant legally excluding Catholics and violently displacing Natives.

Like John Winthrop in Massachusetts, some of the Virginia Company's London investors and settlers imagined themselves as participants in a cosmic spiritual battle against Catholicism. Robert Rich, for example, acknowledged commercial interests but also hoped Virginia would defeat the "popish" antichrist and his champion, the Spanish king.[179] There were a few Catholics among Jamestown's earliest settlers, and within the first two years Virginia's leaders exiled one suspected Catholic and executed another.[180] Anti-Catholicism even played a role in the first slaves coming to Virginia in 1619. English and Dutch Protestants cooperated to steal those captives from a Portuguese ship bound for Catholic Mexico. The vessels, including one commanded by a Calvinist minister, attacked the Portuguese ship, confiscating more than twenty Africans and transporting them to Virginia.[181] And anti-Catholicism then intensified. By 1643 colonial law required attendance at the Anglican Church, and after 1689 officeholders took an anti-Catholic oath, swearing they had no allegiance to the pope and rejecting transubstantiation, the Catholic belief that the consecrated host is the real presence of the divine.

Establishing the plantation niche also required displacing the Natives some hoped to convert. Early documents proclaimed that Jamestown's 1607 settlers came to convert the heathens, but in the end Virginia was an investment, not a mission. James I had granted a charter to the Virginia Company, London investors seeking wealth, even if the king hoped they also might expand the empire's reach to the homeland of the 15,000 Algonquian speakers. Some of those Native Peoples were led by Wahunsunacock, the chief whom the English called Powhatan.[182] But colonization led to a series of wars between 1607 and 1646. By 1650 Powhatan's chiefdom had lost power, though some Indigenous Virginians were granted rights to Pamunkey Neck, a patch of land that included their holiest sacred site.[183]

It was not obvious at first that the English would displace the Indigenous. In 1585 Sir Walter Raleigh secured a short-term settlement on Roanoke, but those hungry would-be colonists sailed back, and the second group, the so-called Lost Colony, was never heard from again. The English tried again, landing farther south at Jamestown in April 1607. By June they had built a triangular fort with a modest garden and makeshift church. It would be a harsh winter, with armed Native resisters threatening outside and famished colonists dying inside, but the survivors made Jamestown the first permanent English settlement.

Excavations at the Jamestown fort reveal evidence of mimicry—colonists borrowed strategies for growing crops and techniques for making pipes—but there were a lot of missed cultural signals too.[184] Jamestown's residents didn't understand the Powhatan stories and ceremonies.[185] Most important, they didn't understand incorporation rituals and diplomatic customs. When Captain John Smith was captured, he thought he had been saved from death by a girl known by her nickname, Pocahontas, and not her given name, Matoaka.[186] But the incident he described was probably an incorporation rite, and the chief probably assumed that Smith, an English representative, had promised his allegiance in exchange for a new Native identity.[187] Smith and Virginia's settlers couldn't imagine "heathens" as equal partners in a diplomatic agreement, but there would be another opportunity when Pocahontas accepted a hurried baptismal rite and married Rolfe in 1614.[188] Pocahontas, one of the chief's daughters, had been kidnapped the year before, and during her captivity the Anglican minister, Rolfe, became enamored. It's difficult to know if the eighteen-year-old felt the same way, but both communities understood the union as a diplomatic alliance.[189] The Powhatan community saw a second chance for incorporation; the vice governor saw a chance to stop the fighting. Rolfe did too but said the union also was "for the glory of God, for my owne salvation, and for [saving] . . . an unbelieving creature."[190] The convert, who took the name Rebecca, was then invited to London to solidify support for Virginia.[191] She delighted royals and investors and was welcomed as an Indian princess, as a 1616 portrait with native feathers and European dress suggested—even though the Powhatans' matrilineal succession rules meant she would never lead the chiefdom. But she got a chance to see London and even a performance of Shakespeare's *The Tempest,* which the Bard wrote after hearing about the hurricane that had stranded her husband's party on Bermuda in 1609.[192] She never made it home, dying in Kent, where she was buried in an Anglican churchyard. Her death didn't help intercultural relations. War broke out, and clashes continued off and on until 1677, when thousands of Native Peoples in the region fled.

The importation of slave laborers and the formulation of planter piety also began during Virginia's first fifty years, when Africans worked in a somewhat less constricting system of servitude.[193] There were between 300 and 500 Africans in Virginia by 1650, but elite officeholders with London commercial connections owned about 70 percent of them. Those planters began purchasing African slaves rather than procuring fixed-term servants because tobacco had emerged as a profitable crop.[194] Some of the enslaved were baptized Catholics, though most Protestant planters might have preferred "heathen" talk of spirit possession and protective objects to "papist" talk of rosary beads and patron saints.[195] In that less dense and less constraining system of servitude—the laborers didn't live in separate quarters—some Africans like John Pedro, a Kongolese Catholic, managed to gain freedom, find a trade, and buy some land.[196] But when he denounced Maryland's anti-Catholic governor decades later, Pedro's hard-earned status as a landowner couldn't protect him; he was executed in 1655. The plantation generation began to emerge the following year, as one Virginia family imported forty-one Africans in a single shipment. The religious situation changed too, since the newcomers practiced different faiths: some from the Bight of Benin blended veneration of Catholic saints and Indigenous spirits, while others embraced the Efik belief in the high god and a variety of lesser gods.[197] As African spiritual life in the colony diversified, planter piety solidified. Planter piety needed pulpits and pews, and many Anglican churches were built during Virginia's first fifty years. A 1643 law mandated and empowered vestries, and a 1656 statute required that parish boundaries be drawn. Not every parish had a rector and some residents traveled for services, but Virginia was becoming "as much a colony of churches as it was a colony of tobacco farms and courthouses."[198]

With those processes underway, planter piety and the slave plantation emerged more fully between 1650 and 1750, as changes in the law, the church, and the market converged. The General Assembly passed a law in 1662 proclaiming that baptism would not bring freedom—a key doctrine in the planters' catechism. Separate slave quarters appeared in 1670, and slave codes got harsher in the next decades.[199] Increased density and separate housing on tobacco plantations had an unplanned benefit—it allowed space for the enslaved to build a distinctive communal culture.[200] In most ways, however, conditions got worse. With the Virginia slave codes of 1680 and 1705, Africans became chattel, "movable property" that could be owned for life and legally killed if they became disruptive—and records show there was "disruption," from news of runaways to whispers of insurrections.

England's imperial religion also maintained order. There was an expansion of the local Anglican parish's authority after 1650, making the church somewhat stronger and giving it more authority to support the plantation niche. Each neighborhood parish had a "miniature hierarchy" that included the vestrymen and churchwarden, or lay leader.[201] Those vestries dealt with everything from public roads to orphan welfare, and between 1662 and 1705 the churchwardens took on crucial secular duties. Churchwardens, not surveyors or justices, determined property lines.[202] Quite literally, then, religion mapped the boundaries of the slave plantation.

But market forces, not ecclesiastical structures, controlled the flow of enslaved workers to those religiously figured habitats. When the Royal African Company had a monopoly on the English slave trade, only gentry with London connections had access to African laborers. However, the supply increased for both middling farmers and elite planters after 1698, when the company no longer channeled the flow of slaves.[203] By then the gentry plantations were staffed almost entirely by slaves, not indentured servants, and during the first decades of the eighteenth century tobacco plantations added more enslaved workers, with officeholders wielding disproportionate power to acquire them: one country justice owned eighty-six slaves in 1724, and a well-connected planter, William Byrd II, had accumulated 220 by 1716.

The devotional life of slaves also continued to change. Byrd confided to his diary that reading a Tillotson sermon made him "shed some tears of repentance," and when he sought forgiveness, he could ride to his parish church.[204] It was much more difficult for enslaved Africans, since worries about revolts led the Virginia Council to prohibit communal worship in

1687.[205] That didn't prevent nighttime gatherings of enslaved Christians, Muslims, and devotees of African Indigenous traditions, but pious Africans faced daunting challenges. The shackles of slavery seemed to break the chain of memory. Scholars debate whether it amounted to a "spiritual holocaust," a destruction of the institutions that had mediated devotional life in the homeland, or whether ancestral religious practices persisted.[206] Sidestepping that either-or question, it seems more useful to note that, like everyone else, Africans were born into an eco-cultural niche, and they too left their mark on the landscape, bequeathing not only rows of tobacco plants in the fields but also scattered footprints in the brush where boisterous worshippers danced. Enslavers snatched devotees from urban hubs where residents venerated ancestors at nearby shrines, and from rural farms where locals celebrated yam harvests in communal rituals. Plantation owners also didn't allow traditional spiritual tools—Ifá divination trays or Muslim prayer beads—after they arrived.[207] But planters couldn't suppress all collective memory, ritual practice, and vernacular creativity. Reports of noisy celebrations and "frequent meetings of considerable numbers of Negro slaves" suggest there was both continuity and creativity in Africans' religious life in Virginia.[208]

The slave plantation found its justification in the planter piety preached by wealthy vestrymen and acquiescent rectors between the 1650s and the 1750s. Almost no White Virginians protested slaveholding itself, although a few challenged the power of the slaveholding parish vestry, the neglect of slaves' spiritual needs, and the clergy's misguided materialism. Rev. Morgan Godwyn, who owned slaves while he pastored an Anglican church in Virginia between 1665 and 1670, didn't question the superiority of Christianity or the need for enslaved labor, but he criticized "the religion of the plantation." He thought planters should treat slaves better and teach Christian principles, because the Creator had "planted" a sense of right even in "barbarous" heathen souls. The planter class, who controlled the vestry, however, demanded that rectors preach a profit-seeking gospel. Those planters, Godwyn said in a later sermon at Westminster Abbey, put trade before religion. They knew no God but money.[209] Other White Christian critics used light verse to complain about rectors, as in the satirical "Loyal Address of the Clergy of Virginia," which suggested that clergy paid themselves tithes and "prayed for Tobacco."[210]

The few opposing voices didn't dissuade slaveholding and churchgoing planters like Robert "King" Carter. He probably didn't pray for tobacco—he had plenty—though he hoped his public displays of fortune and faith elicited the approval of the king, the bishop, and the guardians of gentry culture.[211]

He was born in 1663 at Corotoman, his father's plantation near the Chesapeake Bay, and rose to prominence in the local church, the colonial government, and international commerce. Carter served as speaker of the House of Burgesses and governor of the colony. He was chosen vestryman and warden of the parish church, Christ Church, near present-day Kilmarnock. In business he would surpass most Virginians, owning 300,000 acres, 45 plantations, and 750 slaves. And Carter could be brutal, as when he tortured the recaptured "runaway" Madagascar Jack, cutting off his toes to punish him and terrify others.[212] There is no evidence such brutality caused him any spiritual disquiet. Carter often sold slaves on Friday and then on Sunday attended the wooden church his father had commissioned.[213] To secure his own spiritual legacy, Carter began building a brick church, though he died in 1732, the year his children finished that stately building, with its vaulted ceilings and walnut altarpiece.[214]

The Latin inscription on Carter's churchyard tombstone insisted his "ample wealth" was "honorably acquired," and he wasn't alone in his "honorable" pursuits, though he stood out. In the 1720s two-thirds of the landowners in Lancaster County had working slaves, but only two owned more than twenty.[215] His eldest son would build a Georgian mansion on Shirley Plantation, a tobacco-growing and slaveholding estate on the James River.[216] Well-connected planters like Carter who paraded their profits and piety secured their offspring's futures.[217] Excessive ritual and architectural displays have a long history, and in the eighteenth century symbolic surplus still could elevate the giver's status and boost the offspring's prospects, as with Carter's descendants, who would include Revolutionary patriots, Civil War generals, and even governors and presidents.

But Carter also bequeathed an inequitable and coercive social world and an increasingly stressed eco-cultural niche. The tobacco plantation changed the people and the place. Africans, who numbered less than 10 percent of Virginians in 1680, would be 44 percent by 1750.[218] The plow's more destructive effects didn't take hold until the late eighteenth century, when Virginians started planting more wheat. Tidewater farmers had done less ecological damage in the seventeenth and early eighteenth centuries because they relied on native crops (corn and tobacco) and used axes to clear the fields and hoes to prepare the soil. Unlike sugar cultivation, tobacco growing didn't require enslaved workers, but large tracts of land were needed—about fifty acres per laborer—so one depleted field could be abandoned and the next one cleared. That ecological balance got disrupted by the middle of the eighteenth century. Slave populations increased and crop rotations shortened, which degraded the soil. By the 1750s the landscape had a more open look. Hardwood forests became fenced fields, and the ancestral lands of corn-growing Tidewater Natives became tobacco farms, county courthouses, and Anglican churches, a royal colony where slaves suffered daily indignities, imperial representatives distributed land inequitably, voting was restricted to landowning White men, and almost everyone, especially slaves, died too young.[219]

Barbados, Jamaica, and the Leeward Islands

As some Virginians learned when they sailed south to Barbados, the religiously figured environment could be even worse elsewhere in the Greater South. Virginia's connections to Barbados began during the 1640s sugar boom, when a Norfolk planter bought four Black islanders. About 6,200 more Barbados slaves arrived between 1670 and 1700, when seventy ships sailed to the Chesapeake each year.[220] The commercial and cultural flows went the other way too. The quest for arable land led islanders to fell trees and plant sugar. That helped the export economy but depleted resources the residents then had to import, from wood shingles to dairy cattle.[221]

Some Virginians landed on that island in the Caribbean. The disgruntled Reverend Godwyn departed for a Barbados parish in 1670 but soon decided the sugar planters were greedier and the slaves' conditions harsher. It was his experience in Barbados that nudged him to pen his critique, an attempt to convince London officials and Bridgetown planters to evangelize slaves and improve conditions on the island, where the average sugar plantation had eighty enslaved laborers, more than most Chesapeake tobacco farms at the time.

George Washington, a slaveholding Anglican born on a Virginia farm, left Chesapeake Bay for Carlisle Bay in 1751, and the "pleasant" vista from his rented house above Bridgetown looked out on a scene that seemed both familiar and foreign.[222] Unlike in Virginia, there were few signs of Native presence. Barbados had been settled about 2000 BCE, and in later centuries the Arawak caught fish, grew crops, and made pottery, living along the coast in oval houses, where they performed ceremonies and buried ancestors.[223] They used red ochre to divine futures, adorn bodies, and paint pots.[224] The Arawak never numbered more than 500 after 1600, but they exerted influence—teaching the English to trap local crabs and make cotton hammocks, showing them how to grow maize, cassava, and tobacco. They modified the landscape too, erecting a bridge not far from where Washington stayed. However, the English colonists had replaced the native bridge that gave the capital its name, so Washington never saw it. Signs of the chromatic symbolic world of the Arawak had disappeared too.[225] By 1750 English settlers were using the island's red ochre deposits for profane purposes: when their paint ran out, they would dab it on windmills.[226]

The precolonial past wasn't in view, then, as Washington looked out toward Bridgetown, one of the largest urban centers in the plantation region that included Kingston, St. John's, Basseterre, Charles Town, and Savannah. Barbados's capital was the most populous town Washington had seen, and that lover of agriculture was "enraptured" by the "the delightful green" of the fields. The hue came from cane fields, and the island's sugar plantations were larger and the planters richer, as Washington noted in his journal: islanders "are either very rich or very poor." The island also had more slaves, and a steadier flow of them. Some stopped for a few days and then continued on the same slave ship. Others were sold in Bridgetown and then rerouted, as with the ten-year old Venture Smith, who came ashore in August 1739 and eventually ended up in Rhode Island. Many, however, stayed on Barbados—like Ashy, who insisted that their traditional rituals involved praying to "de same dat you call God."[227] That shared ritual knowledge, and the cascade of disembarking slaves, made it easier to maintain West African traditions, as shown in the African-inspired burial goods interred with a revered healer at Newton Plantation.[228] And creole cultures formed. The nineteen-year-old Washington expressed no qualms about slavery—he would later—but complained about the cultural mixing on the island: "by ill custom [the women] affect the Negro Style."

Washington was also a churchgoing Anglican, and he worshipped during his stay.[229] He would have noticed that Barbados had more ethnic and religious diversity than Virginia. There was an early synagogue, and the Quakers had six meetinghouses by 1680. Irish Catholics, Dutch Calvinists, free Blacks, and Brazilian Jews owned property in Bridgetown.[230] But the Anglican establishment also was slightly stronger there because the island's population was denser—400 persons per square mile—and the farms less dispersed. That meant residents lived nearer a church, though Barbadian parishes still had trouble finding rectors.[231] In 1680 there were only eleven Anglican clergymen, one for every 1,800 persons, and decades later some still thought the ministers' low salaries and the government's shaky support put them "at the mercy of their parishioners.[232]

Yet the strain of planter piety that grew on that limestone island was hardy, as adapted to the tropical climate as the domestic architecture, even if gusts of opposition blew now and then.[233] A few critics advocated better conditions for enslaved workers, or more spiritual outreach. Richard Ligon, who had lived on a local plantation, criticized planters' cruelty and encouraged missionary efforts. God initiated that outreach, Ligon suggested, when he made bananas a tool of evangelization, since if you cut a banana crosswise you see "Christ upon the Crosse."[234] The fruit prompted no documented conversions, but Quakers successfully evangelized some Blacks after Anne Austin and Mary Fisher carried their faith to the island in 1655. Two years later the Quaker founder, George Fox, reminded sugar planters to love everyone as Christ had, and some baptized their slaves.[235] That got the Quaker community in trouble after a failed slave insurrection in 1676, which authorities blamed on them. Yet even after officials forbade Quakers from ritually incorporating Blacks, a few chose to incur the fines. Anglican parish registers also record the baptisms of free and enslaved Blacks, and one planter asked the executor of his estate to raise his two slaves as Christians.[236] Christopher Codrington, an Anglican landowner who served as governor of the Leeward Islands, consulted with SPG preachers and French priests about how to evangelize slaves.[237] Yet he didn't reject the institution of slavery, even bequeathing SPG missionaries two sugar plantations and 300 slaves.[238] Like Codrington, other Anglicans in Barbados had large plantations and hundreds of slaves, while Quakers owned 3,254 enslaved laborers in 1680 and had freed only twenty by 1720.[239] No one, it seems, had taken an axe to the problem's root—the planter piety of the profit-loving gentry.

In fact, sugar planters and their spiritual advisors employed faith to justify "the most brutal labor regime in the Atlantic basin."[240] The regime was brutal for several reasons. The year after Barbados became the first English colony with a Black majority, unnerved legislators passed the slave code of 1661, which marked African slaves as "heathenish" and "dangerous," and deprived them of political rights.[241] Slaves had no recourse; planters had no restraints. Part of the problem was the labor-intensive process of sugar production.[242] It required cutting the cane and then boiling it within hours so it wouldn't spoil, grueling work in a hot climate. One sugar planter wondered privately if he was killing his slaves.[243] He was. The long hours, poor nutrition, and cramped housing lowered resistance to diseases. On one Barbadian plantation enslaved workers lived only to about twenty.[244] The hazardous conditions also affected fertility rates. The appalling result: planters brought 130,000 Africans to that port city between 1649 and 1700, but only

50,000 were still alive at the end of the century.[245] Almost two-thirds had died. By the time Pennsylvania Quaker Jane Hoskins arrived to preach there in 1725, many Quakers had left for the Middle Colonies or Carolina, though she still encountered slaveholding sugar planters. By then Barbados's plantation niche and slave code also had become the model for the Leeward Islands—St. Christopher (1624), Nevis (1628), Monserrat (1632), and Antigua (1632)—as well as Jamaica (1655) and Carolina (1663).

The Leeward Islands transplanted the sugar plantation and the Anglican church, though those institutions took root there somewhat differently. The Leeward residents battled their French Catholic neighbors from 1666 to 1713 and suffered devastating earthquakes and hurricanes that forced them to rebuild. And sugar production never made them as rich. The Leeward Church of England had familiar struggles, though the English, Irish, and Scottish settlers expressed more resistance to the church tax, even if Anglicanism still became a central part of the built environment by the middle of the eighteenth century. Nevis, the largest and most populated island, had three churches by the 1690s, and even Quakers, Huguenots, and lukewarm Anglicans accepted the Church of England as a venue for displaying their English imperial identity and defending the slave society hierarchy.[246] The most famous American born on Nevis, Alexander Hamilton, had been tutored there by a Sephardic Jewish woman before his family moved to the Danish West Indies, where Black Moravian missionaries like Rebecca Proten were becoming transatlantic preachers.[247] British leaders in the Leewards were more suspicious of African congregants but reluctantly tolerated some non-Anglicans, as long as they shared their anti-Catholic sentiment and supported the parish church.

Jamaica also experienced natural disasters, which clergy interpreted as divine punishment, but it would become Britain's richest eighteenth-century colony.[248] And its lucrative slave plantations would be as cruel as those in the "culture hearth" of Barbados.[249] To keep slaves in line, for example, Jamaican landowners would sever a runaway's head and affix it to a post, warning those who pondered escape or resistance.[250] Some did flee or fight back: Jamaica's larger size meant there was a mountainous interior where escaped slaves formed isolated communities. Those maroons or "wild ones" would eventually negotiate a treaty with authorities. But the island's colonial leaders still had reason to worry, because Afro-Jamaican religious movements recovered familiar ritual forms, like spirit possession and ritual dance, and sanctioned resistance, from sabotaging work to running away.[251] Despite such challenges, the church and the crown still managed to create public spaces that reinforced their authority. St. Catherine Parish Church in Spanish Town communicated public power in its masonry exterior, while the interior's cruciform shape enabled the architect to map degrees of social distance by the placement of the pews.[252] Some residents were more equal than others, and Jamaican church buildings made that clear.

The Carolina Lowcountry

"Very elegant" St. Philip's (1711), another Anglican monument to hierarchy, would be erected in another plantation port, Charles Town, where migrants would extend Barbadian influence to Carolina's coastal plain and would exchange commodities—human and nonhuman—in the global market.[253] By the 1750s the southeastern "shatter zone" had expanded, the rice plantation had formed, and the colonial crisis of sustainability had quickened. To follow some twists and turns in that tale, consider one family, the Bulls, who played key roles in colonial governance, Anglican establishment, rice cultivation, Native relations, and even slave rebellion.[254]

Stephen Bull traveled on a ship that anchored in Barbados before carrying the first settlers to "Carolina," a territory that extended from Virginia to Florida. It had been chartered in 1663, and its harbor town (named after Charles II) would be the only walled city in British North America.[255] That's because planners viewed it as a fortress against the Indians and a barrier against the Spanish. Of course the king and the proprietors hoped it also would be a profit-yielding plantation colony like Virginia and especially Barbados.[256] Bull arrived as the deputy of Anthony Ashley Cooper (later the Earl of Shaftesbury), a proprietor. Cooper would come to write a treatise arguing all humans have an innate moral sense, but at the start of this colonial venture he just hoped that civic peace could be maintained amid the diversity.[257] In early Carolina that meant ensuring Anglican Barbados planters—about half the early population—didn't squabble with the non-Anglicans. Cooper and his secretary John Locke had helped draft the *Fundamental Constitutions of Carolina* (1669), which recognized the Church of England as "the national religion of all the King's dominions" and demanded inhabitants affirm "that there is a God" and "that God is publicly to be worshipped." Yet that document acknowledged residents might have "different opinions concerning matters of religion" and, if they stayed out of trouble, they could enjoy "liberty."[258]

The policy allowed an array of spiritual communities. Presbyterians, Baptists, and Quakers could meet for worship, and an entire Congregational church group moved from Massachusetts to Carolina in 1696.[259] Persecuted Huguenots like Judith Giton Manigault were among the early settlers.[260] A small Sephardic Jewish community took refuge there, even if Irish Catholic residents were still under suspicion. Stephen Bull affiliated with the Church of England but favored the somewhat inclusive Carolina constitution, siding with dissenting Protestant denominations on some issues. On pragmatic grounds, it seems, Bull favored leaving the weeds.

Bull took on varied tasks Cooper assigned him—negotiating with the Natives, protecting against the Spanish, and finding a cash crop.[261] In the first two decades, as Carolinians experimented with crops, they raised cattle and cut lumber, exporting beef and barrels to the Caribbean. It was only in the 1690s that planters agreed on rice, and Bull helped establish the first rice-growing plantations in Charles Town's core settlement along the Ashley and Cooper Rivers.[262] He acquired a 400-acre tract along the Ashley and called it Ashley Hall.[263] It was slightly smaller than the average Carolina rice plantation but much larger than the plots Massachusetts farmers were cultivating.[264] He also built a brick home and prepared the land for growing rice, a crop that requires arduous labor. Bull had help, thanks to the colony's constitution, which gave planters "absolute power and authority" over slaves. At first he depended on five White indentured servants who arrived with him in 1670, and he sent for more. But starting in the 1690s he added enslaved Africans, as did the Draytons, the Bulls' prosperous kinfolk, who helped transform the Ashley riverbank into a showcase for the local gentry.[265] The Blacks who constructed that showcase would constitute 56 percent of that parish's population by the 1720s, and they would modify the terrain by clearing swamps to create a grid of raised ridges for rice cultivation, just as Barbadians had deforested the island to impose rows of tall cane.[266] The historical record doesn't indicate whether Bull's particular fieldworkers had prior experience with rice cultivation in Africa, but those who did used their expertise to change how Carolinians sowed, threshed, and winnowed the crop.[267]

Other slaves kept arriving, and by the middle of the eighteenth century Charles Town would be the primary entry point for Africans coming to the mainland. By then settlements north and south of the port were being integrated into the stressed plantation region, which was somewhat more sustainable than Barbados but had shocking disparities in labor conditions and legal rights. It also was a place where life expectancy was remarkably low for everyone, partly because the swampy rice fields bred mosquito-borne diseases like malaria.[268] In Charles Town's St. Philip's Parish, for example, burials outnumbered baptisms by a ratio of 3.5 to 1, almost as bad as Bridgetown's

St. Michael's Parish. At a time when most New Englanders lived until sixty, 86 percent of residents in Christ Church Parish died before twenty.[269] Anglican ministers, in turn, attempted to console parishioners, as when St. Philip's pastor spoke about "The Duty and Benefit of Bearing Afflictions."[270] Slaves were among those who died young, and they bore many more "afflictions." Carolina's task system (laborers were finished when they completed the day's task) gave them more autonomy than the gang system, which required they work in groups, but rice plantation slaves endured horrible conditions.[271]

So did Natives. Traders enslaved them, disease stalked them, and the militia attacked them. We can't blame Stephen Bull and his son William for the Great Southeastern Smallpox Epidemic (1696–1700).[272] But the Bulls had a hand in the bartering and the battling between 1670, when the Carolina Grand Council asked Stephen to get food from the Cusabo, and 1715, when William led a Cherokee expedition as a militia captain in the Yamasee War.[273] The beleaguered Cusabo had welcomed the English, Stephen explained, because they saw them as allies against the Spanish and the Westo, who "strike a great feare" among "our neighboring Indians."[274] Within a few years an English–Native trade network formed.[275] Stephen sent his furs and skins to London, and his brother sent back goods to trade with the Natives.[276] Yet it soon became a market in people as well as products—in "deare skins, furrs, and Younge Indian slaves."[277] Traders like Bull received Native women and children captured by their Indigenous collaborators in exchange for rum and guns, thereby undermining ancestral rules about captives, who were no longer ritually integrated into a community but callously exchanged as commodities. The global market was centered at Charles Town, and many Indigenous slaves departed its port for Chesapeake and Caribbean plantations, but Carolina rice planters kept some too. Stephen probably owned Native slaves, and he certainly profited from the slave-raiding system, which affected both the plantation niche and the Native villages. By 1715, 25 percent of all South Carolina households owned a Native slave.[278] In turn, desperate Indigenous communities jostled for favor with the British and planned attacks on their neighbors. The Westo enslaved the coastal Cusabo. The interior dwelling Savannah (Shawnee), who were armed by Barbadian migrants, captured the Westo. Siouan-speaking Peoples from the Piedmont region, in turn, enslaved the Savannah.[279] And farther south, Muskogean-speaking British allies, the Yamasee and the Muscogee, conducted slave raids among Florida Natives. One tragic episode there picks up a dangling narrative thread by revealing more about the fate of the mission at Apalachee: in 1702, a 3,000-member force of the Alabama and the Coushatta, former slaves themselves, stormed the Spanish and Apalachee, and the survivors were sold to the English at Charles Town and shipped to Caribbean sugar plantations.[280]

By the time William Bull and his Native soldiers celebrated their victories in the Tuscarora War of 1711–1712 and the Yamasee War of 1715–1716, Natives' southeastern homelands had been devasted. In the Tuscarora villages of North Carolina, 1,000 had been killed and 700 enslaved.[281] Some nearby Englishmen, like John Lawson, implored Carolinians to avoid setting up "our Christian Banner in a Field of Blood."[282] But it was too late—for both Lawson and the ceremonial chiefdoms. The Tuscarora killed Lawson in 1711, and the "field of blood"—as well as the scourge of pathogens and the indignity of slave raids—was devastating. Native priests lost their ceremonial centers, chiefs lost their tribute, and Indigenous exchange networks collapsed.[283] The polity and the piety shattered, even if some religious practices continued and the Muscogee and the Cherokee retained some communal identity.[284] William Bull dealt with both groups after he was appointed Commissioner of Indian Affairs in 1721, and the familial legacy continued: six years after William died, his namesake signed a treaty with the Cherokee at Ashley Hall Plantation.[285]

William, who had been born there, enjoyed prominence as a planter and politician, and also played a role in building the Anglican church and defending the slave plantation. He was later South Carolina's lieutenant governor and acting governor, but he began by serving in the Carolina Assembly in 1706, the year it banned Catholics and established the Church of England.[286] Bull ended up fortifying Anglican institutions.[287] He became a church commissioner when the assembly started constructing sixteen churches, including the one serving Ashley River planters—St. Andrew's.[288] Of the parish's hundred families, only thirty were Anglican. The others were mostly Presbyterians and Baptists. So it's not surprising they had trouble agreeing on a rector. One pastor arrived with plans to evangelize the parish's slaves, for instance.[289] Some Carolina slaves, like the Kongolese Catholic fieldworkers who recited prayers in Kikongo, were already Christian, but most planters in Bull's congregation vigorously denounced the plan.[290] St. Andrew's ill-fated rector found only one congregant, a recently arrived Barbadian planter, who would allow him to preach on his plantation. The rest, including Bull, resisted. After that SPG missionary left for another assignment, William continued to uphold the local variant of planter piety as vestryman and churchwarden, including after he moved to another parish, where he built a new plantation on confiscated Yamasee land and funded an elaborate Anglican church.[291]

William Bull also defended the slave plantation as a member of the king's council from 1721 to 1738 and after he was appointed lieutenant governor and acting governor in 1738. The following year he also took credit for suppressing the only large-scale slave revolt in the mainland British colonies, the Stono Rebellion, which sparked stricter codes and widespread White anxiety. The surviving sources are scarce and slanted, like Bull's self-serving report, so historians have debated the sequence of events and the motives of the rebels.[292] But it seems that a drainage crew of twenty led by a slave named Jemmy went to a store near the Stono River on Saturday night, 8 September, and—whether by accident or plan—ended up taking guns, drums, and cloth and killing the shopkeepers.[293] The next day, the rebels went to nearby plantations, sparing some owners and killing others. Altogether about twenty-one White residents died, Bull reported. The group then marched with two drummers and a white banner down the King's Highway that linked Charles Town and Savannah—and led to St. Augustine. As the resisters headed south shouting "Liberty," they came upon Bull and four other riders.[294] One of those men sounded the militia alarm at—where else?—a church. He had hurried to a Presbyterian church, and a militia contingent of twenty rode out from there. One hundred planters joined the irate pursuers.[295] They then encountered between sixty and one hundred jubilant resisters drumming and dancing in an open field. After an exchange of musket fire, some slaves were killed. A month later Bull told his London superiors he had sent for Chickasaw and Catawba allies to capture those still "concealed in the Woods," but the militia had killed enough "to stop any further mischief."[296] Some escapees continued south toward St. Augustine but were eventually overtaken, and the mounted militia would kill the others in the next days and weeks—all but one, who was hanged three years later.

If that's the approximate sequence of events, questions remain: why did the rebels choose that weekend, and why were they marching south? The historical record doesn't say, but the timing and destination invite a religious interpretation. The Congo's king had been baptized by the Portuguese, and a creole Kongolese Catholicism was still practiced there in the 1720s, when slaves from that area began arriving in South Carolina. It seems likely that Jemmy, the alleged leader, was a Kongolese Catholic, and if other rebels shared that religious background, then they might have started on Saturday, 8 September, because it was the feast of the Nativity of the Virgin Mary.[297] Marian devotion had been important in the Congo, where it also was associated with Saturdays. And seeking Mary's protection in a rebellion would not have been odd for African Catholics in the Americas: Marian devotion had animated an earlier slave revolt in Portuguese-speaking Brazil.[298] More broadly, some scholars think the chanted word might have been the Kingongo term *lukangu*, whose root (*kanga*) also would have meant "salvation" to the Catholics.[299] So the impending liberation could have been understood as political and spiritual, a view that accords with practices in the Congo, where Portuguese priests blessed warriors' weapons before battle.[300] The rebellion's link with royal Catholicism and Marian devotion is possible, then, though far from certain.

But we do know why they went south. The Spanish had posted a notice in St. Augustine welcoming runaways who swore allegiance to the Catholic Church, and more than 100 African fugitives arrived in 1738. To accommodate them, Spanish officials established Fort Mose.[301] It's likely that some of the Carolina rebels had heard about the town, the first for free Blacks in the lands that became the US. It's almost certain that the resisters who did the planning or the leaders who emerged along the route had heard about Catholic Florida's offer of freedom. In fact, Governor Bull proposed that as the cause: it was St. Augustine officials' "declaring freedom to all Negroes," and at least 251 British slaves did find their way to Fort Mose. Whether or not the Stono rebels timed their escape to align with the Marian feast day, it seems likely that many marchers were attracted by the Spanish invitation, and for the Kongolese Catholics that welcome would have been even more compelling. It offered a chance to join fellow Catholics at Fort Mose, with its thatched church and resident priest. There they might have found familiarity and freedom. In that sense, the Stono Rebellion reveals as much about the motivating power of transplanted religion and the competition between religious empires as it does about the instability of the plantation niche.

In the decades ahead, the slave plantation would become more entrenched, religious empires would fight a world war, and religion would spark more rebellions—by colonists as well as Natives and slaves.

CHAPTER 5

Rebellious Religion

Tyranny, Liberty, and the "Pursuit of Happiness," 1756–1791

The lands that became America. That phrase has recurred to acknowledge the long history of religion on the continent before the emergence of the United States as a constitutional democracy. That form of governance appeared in the second half of the eighteenth century, however, as did new ways of imagining collective belonging and practicing communal religion. It might seem odd to have taken so long to get to this historic moment. After all, this chapter appears at the book's midpoint, and it picks up the story almost 1,000 years after the rise of fertility goddess veneration at maize-growing Cahokia and more than 500 years after Columbus brought the cross and the plow to the Americas. But this chapter and those that follow show the continuing relevance of pre-Columbian and colonial religious history by noting, for example, the enduring presence of farming religion, from Native harvest festivals to Protestant planter piety; the continuities in Indigenous spirituality, including vision-inspired revitalization movements; and the impact of the unresolved colonial crisis on slaves' and Natives' ability to meet the individual, communal, and ecological conditions for flourishing (see fig. 2).[1]

It's also important to notice what's new in this period. The political changes started with the Seven Years' War (1756–1763), the last global religious war. It redrew the continental map, diminished Indigenous sovereignty, and established rhetorical themes (*tyranny* and *liberty*) that patriots would use in the American Revolution, the religiously sanctioned rebellion against imperial Britain (1775–1783). Thomas Paine claimed the Revolution was "the birthday of a new world," and it did have continental, hemispheric, and global causes and consequences.[2] Along the Gulf of Mexico, Spanish officials, enslaved Blacks, and Chickasaw chiefs affected the war's outcome. And, as would happen up and down the hemisphere, the US Congress initiated a "landward turn" toward the interior.[3] The Revolution also had wider impact. Tsarist Russia and Qing China were reluctant to follow America's political lead.[4] Yet the founders' embrace of liberty helped to inspire a global Age of Revolution that would oust Christian monarchies and create new republics, and some Muslim states would sign treaties with US representatives who distanced themselves from the Crusader past by saying America was "not in any sense founded on the Christian Religion."[5]

Since the founders and framers rejected the term "nation," and a new state emerged before national consciousness or nationalist sentiment, the US became a "state-nation," a confederation of states, a constitutional republic with limited federal power and only a nascent collective identity.[6] Empires didn't disappear. In fact, imperial Britain would peak in the next century, but the nature of sea and land empires was changing. And many elites in the new republic presumed or declared America's imperial ambitions. Officials, pamphleteers, and ministers imagined America as an expanding transcontinental empire or, as Thomas Jefferson called it, an agrarian "empire of liberty," a democracy preserved by the God-fearing farmers who cultivated the moral virtues a republic required.[7]

The Revolutionary Era also would bring religious changes. With the addition of the First Amendment in 1791, constitutional grounds for a spiritually diverse nation would be in place, as legislators modeled the federal system on multi-steeple Pennsylvania rather than meetinghouse Massachusetts.[8] Most Anglo-American elites believed religion was socially useful, and many attended worship services, but the founders and framers wouldn't establish a Protestant, or even a Christian, state.[9] The new republic prohibited a religious "establishment," an official state church, although its explicit protection of "free exercise" and implicit acceptance of spiritual imagery complicated the religious situation. By the time the armed defense of "liberty" had ended in 1783, the founders had appealed to "Nature's God" to assert natural rights, and within a few years a *civil religion* would start to emerge, a piety found outside the churches and associated with the political realm.[10] It would incorporate Enlightenment beliefs about God as Creator and biblical metaphors about America as the New Israel, and it was on display as citizens staged parades to celebrate the Constitution in 1788 and, the next year, when George Washington put his hand on a Bible as he promised to protect constitutional principles.[11] Soon a new pattern of church–state interaction began to appear: the First Amendment's ban on religious establishment kept religion at a distance in the federal government, while civil religion's blending of piety and politics pulled it closer. In the years ahead that ongoing oscillation would become a distinctive feature of US religion.

The Revolutionary Era would have other consequences, intended and unintended, and to assess those it helps to consider niche construction as well as nation building, visions of flourishing as well as mechanisms of governance.[12] That means asking how the revolutionary generation transformed regional eco-cultural niches, the material and symbolic worlds they inherited and bequeathed, from Native villages to slave plantations and from commercial port cities to inland farming towns. It also means asking whether those niches provided the minimal conditions for mere subsistence or the optimal conditions for full flourishing. Did they offer the necessary environmental goods (renewable resources, favorable climate, biodiversity), communal goods (equity, freedom, political participation), and individual goods (meaning, health, and belonging)? To answer those questions requires looking forward as well as backward. It means analyzing what residents did with what they inherited and assessing the legacy they left their descendants.

That framework—and the questions it prompts—would have been familiar to some eighteenth-century Indigenous leaders and US founders who thought about the good life or well-being, and pondered transgenerational obligations. Jefferson ventured one guiding principle for a transgenerational ethic of sustainability in a letter to James Madison in 1789—that the earth belongs to the living and "no generation can contract debts greater than may be paid during the course of its own existence."[13] The Haudenosaunee Confederacy's solemn covenant or Great Law of Peace included this advice to the council of the Six Nations: "Look and listen for the welfare of the whole people and have always in view not only the present but also the coming generations."[14] Native Nations had conceptions of well-being or flourishing. For instance, Anishinaabe traditional religion emphasized the concept of *bimaadizwin* or "the good life," which included personal, social, and environmental obligations.[15] US founders and framers thought about rights and obligations too. Congress not only championed religious liberty and declared universal equality but also passed down a vision of human flourishing in the Constitution's call to "promote the general Welfare" and the Declaration's assertion of God-endowed rights, including the right to "Life, Liberty, and the pursuit of Happiness."[16]

Attending to the environmental conditions for well-being also alerts historians to some hard-to-notice changes during the period. It doesn't just invite questions about how that generation dealt with short-term ecological problems, like the species decimation in New England, the soil exhaustion on southern tobacco farms, and the scarcity of wood almost everywhere soldiers camped during the Revolutionary War.[17] It also encourages a longer and broader view. Although contemporaries could not have divined its devastating long-term environmental effects, a second "revolution" was just beginning in 1776. In the same year Jefferson was in Philadelphia drafting a Declaration that challenged tyrannical political power, the inventor James Watt and his business partner were commodifying steam power at a "manufactory" near Birmingham, England.[18] By the time the Continental Congress ratified the treaty that ended the American Revolution, an Industrial Revolution had begun in England, as Watt perfected his double-acting steam engine, which would power the mills that imported millions of bales of slave-picked cotton. The shift from an agricultural to an industrial lifeway would begin to have a regional ecological impact in America's urban North by the late nineteenth century and its hard-to-reverse global effects would accelerate by the mid-twentieth century (see appendix).

Considering the individual and communal conditions for flourishing provides new language for asking whether the Declaration's promise of liberty, equality, and the chance at a good life would be extended to all. Would the Constitution actually "promote the general Welfare," as its preamble announced? More specifically, would all residents enjoy safety and health? Would everyone have a sense of belonging? Would White male property owners be the only ones to gain political participation, another condition for well-being? If so, would the tension between the ideal and the real inspire justice-seeking dissent, and would the period's spiritually inspired rebellions—by Natives and Blacks as well as Whites—repair broken niches? Most important, would the sons and daughters of the Revolution confront the Colonial Era's moral wrongs or bequeath an unresolved social crisis to their descendants?

To begin to answer some of those questions, let's start before the American Revolution, with the global religious war that had such wide-ranging impact.

Catholic "Tyranny" and the Seven Years' War, 1756–1763

The Seven Years' War officially started in 1756, but the first battles began the year before in Ohio, near where the earthwork-building Hopewell had cooperated with neighbors to extend their symbolic interaction sphere.[19] Interaction spheres expanded in the mid-eighteenth century too, but there was more conflict than cooperation—and the conflict crossed the globe, reaching Europe, Africa, India, and the Caribbean. Fighting broke out in 1755 between the Protestant British and the French Catholics and their Indian allies as expansion-minded traders in Pennsylvania and land-hungry planters in Virginia yearned for territory beyond the Appalachians, though preachers employed paired metaphors about constraint and autonomy—*tyranny* and *liberty* as well as *bondage* and *freedom*—as they described the present autocratic Catholic threat and imagined a Protestant imperial future.[20]

Philip Reading, an Anglican pastor from Delaware, climbed the pulpit of Philadelphia's Christ Church to issue a spiritual call to arms in June 1755. French Catholics had built Fort Duquesne near present-day Pittsburgh, and the minister explained "The Protestant's Danger and the Protestant's Duty" as the British army marched westward.[21] Reading couldn't know those soldiers would suffer a stunning defeat a few weeks later, as French and Native combatants inflicted almost 1,000 casualties.[22] Yet he was already worried. He had been preoccupied with safeguarding his Delaware parish from the "popish religion" at nearby Bohemia, the Maryland Catholic school.[23] With the "armies now invading our Borders," Catholic power posed an even greater threat. "Love of Freedom inflames us," he said, "while we behold . . . the Inquisitors of Rome approaching to crush us." In turn, colonists must confront those trying "to deprive us of our religious and civil Liberties." To dramatize the stakes, the preacher encouraged congregants to envision the horrors if popery's "arbitrary power" won: the "tyrannical" Catholic ruler would enjoy the fruits of "our cultivated fields," the "lustful Ravisher" would rape "shrieking" virgins, and British mothers would grieve for sons "hurried into Slavery."[24] Reverend Reading's rhetoric about the looming loss of freedom is striking, particularly since he held slaves on his Delaware plantation and preached to them on Sundays. More than a dozen attended regularly, though he had a dim view, saying that "they seem to be of a different species" and warning that Africans religious beliefs cause trouble.[25] Africans believed they would be freed at death, so some "idolaters" committed suicide, and even converts displayed "rebellious behavior after baptism."[26] Reading would later bequeath most of his "rebellious" slaves to his children and leave three to his wife.[27] But he didn't seem to notice the inconsistency in his distress about White colonists' impending "bondage," or perhaps he feared it precisely because he had seen slavery's degradation up close.[28]

Ministers in multi-steeple Rhode Island also feared Catholic constraint, and some, like Newport's Ezra Stiles, also owned enslaved laborers.[29] For Stiles, a learned Congregational minister, Christian history was the saga of reformers freeing themselves from Catholicism's ecclesiastical and civil tyranny. That's also how he viewed the Seven Years' War, which affected Newport when the French blockaded the port.[30] The "corrupting" influence of British soldiers' "infidel" religion, deism, concerned him, but he worried more about Catholic tyranny.[31] In 1759, when the British captured Quebec, he still believed "American Morals and Religion have never been so much in danger," but with Canada secured and Catholicism conquered, he turned his attention to the future.[32] Stiles, who thought of himself as British, suspected the colonies might become independent, and after the providential northern victories, also seemed to think of the continental provinces as a new empire: "We are planting an Empire of better Laws and Religion," he told his Newport congregation in 1760, one that would be better adapted to "the present age."[33] As Stiles foresaw, an empire would rise from the mounting tensions between ill-adapted British dictates and emerging American values, but—as with that slaveholding preacher of liberty—it wouldn't be without its moral compromises.

Boston's Jonathan Mayhew, George Whitefield's old opponent, didn't own slaves, though enslaved Africans constituted between 10 and 15 percent of city's population by midcentury.[34] Yet he too relied on imagery about tyranny and liberty as well as bondage and freedom to describe the war and imagine its aftermath. Massachusetts residents had split during the 1740s about whether to favor his gradual religion of the head or Whitefield's sudden religion of the heart, but Mayhew hoped they might come together to confront the common enemy—Catholicism.[35] He suggested that God-given liberties, civil and religious, should be defended, and tyrants need not be obeyed. That argument would resurface two decades later as John Adams consulted Mayhew's revolutionary "catechism" to justify rebellion against the British.[36] The enemy of the moment, however, was Catholicism, and in a 1754 sermon Mayhew contemplated a bleak future, in which "all liberty, property, religion, happiness changed, or rather transubstantiated into slavery, poverty, superstition, wretchedness!" He ended by saying he hoped his vision wasn't prophetic.[37]

It wasn't. The British would suffer some defeats, but divine vindication came in 1759 with the conquest of Quebec, the political and religious capital of New France. Quebec's Catholic bishop said the battle had left the city and its people devastated. Fire had consumed farms and churches; British soldiers had smashed statues and "thrown the consecrated Hosts on the ground."[38] Even though the global war's official end wouldn't come until 1763, the bishop sensed a shift. Protestants did too. Mayhew's tone had changed when he preached after the fall of Quebec, since "the British American plantations had never so much cause for general joy."[39] Mayhew favored retaining Quebec and used his sermon to again imagine the future, a happier one.[40] "By the continued blessing of heaven," the colonies could "become a mighty empire," with "cities rising on every hill; happy fields and villages" and "a vastly extended territory" where true religion would be practiced.[41] Others shared Mayhew's delight in that year when Britons enjoyed military victories in the West Indies, Germany, and India, as well as Quebec, the most celebrated.[42] London, Boston, and Philadelphia threw parties, and so did coastal towns.[43] In Portsmouth, New Hampshire, "an unfeigned joy appeared in every Face," the paper reported, as residents heard sermons, fired cannons, rang church bells, lit bonfires, and gave thanks that liberty had been preserved.[44]

Africans and Natives had less to celebrate. The war had rerouted some slave ships, but Africans were still arriving. The shackled also still used their spiritual resources to resist during the journey and hatch plots in the fields.[45] But Africans got drawn into the Protestant–Catholic global conflict. Most in eastern North America bet on the British, but free and enslaved Africans fought for both sides around the Great Lakes and across the Eastern Woodlands. Those abroad sometimes were captured as prisoners of war. An Algerian Muslim named Selim was seized in the 1750s by Spanish Catholics in Constantinople, transferred to French New Orleans, and sent to their Ohio allies, the Shawnee, though he ultimately found refuge in Virginia by criticizing his Catholic captors' "idol-worship" and accepting the baptismal water offered by his Protestant rescuers.[46] Meanwhile, Natives made various alliances, stayed neutral, or, like the Nations of the Haudenosaunee (Iroquois), switched from the French to the British side during the war. For decades, Indigenous communities had played the French, Spanish, and British against each other to maintain control of sacred sites, cherished farmland, and hunting grounds, but their limited independence broke down during the Seven Years' War.[47] Africans and Natives hoped for liberty like everyone else but settled for smaller victories, like achieving some spiritual autonomy. Southern Blacks inspired by revivals began to gather in African-majority congregations, including the African Baptist church that formed in 1758 on the tobacco plantation of William Byrd III.[48] New England Natives who identified with Protestantism created autonomous worship spaces too. By the 1750s and 1760s, some who had affiliated with churches or attended missionary schools began to favor separatist congregations led by Indigenous clerics like the Narragansett minister Samuel Niles and the Mohegan preacher Samuel Ashpo.[49]

The official end of the Seven Years' War in 1763 established Britain as a major Christian imperial power and added vast territory to its continental empire (figs. 23 and 24). Yet residents of eastern North America experienced the conflict's conclusion differently. It depended on where they lived, who they were, and how they worshipped. Esther Edwards Burr, an elite White Protestant and devout daughter of Jonathan Edwards, spent the war in Princeton, New Jersey, where she was preoccupied with household labor, child-rearing, and spiritual self-scrutiny. Esther told her friend she felt so isolated from "publick news" that "if the French were to take Boston, we should not hear of it so soon as they would in London."[50] Boston was spared, and life didn't change much for her when the 1763 treaty ended the hostilities. Esther Wheelwright, the Catholic convert introduced earlier, had a very different experience.[51] She spent the war in prayer and service in Quebec's Ursuline convent, where she was elected mother superior. There she devoured every morsel of news, suffered through the siege on the city, and then led the community's rebuilding. For her, material and spiritual conditions worsened after the war.

The war's end also made things worse for most Africans and Natives—by removing the obstacles to intensifying the slave trade and reducing the imperial competition Indigenous leaders had used to their advantage.[52] British, French, and Spanish negotiators didn't worry much about the other combatants—including the Haudenosaunee—as they hammered out the Treaty of Paris in February 1763.[53] In the largest land transfer in history, the French retained all but two of the sugar islands they lost during the war, and the Spanish got Cuba back, added New Orleans, and the following year England returned Manila, the center of Spain's Pacific presence.[54] The British, the big winners, received all of France's North American possessions east of the Mississippi, as well as Catholic Florida, which had lured the Stono rebels and worried the Protestant planters.[55] So slaves who were willing to convert to Catholicism lost the promise of freedom to the north in Quebec and to the south in St. Augustine. The redrawn imperial map also positioned some communities on the edge between empires, like the town of Natchez, which had few remaining Natives but hundreds of enslaved Africans on plantations. Most important, the new map placed diverse eco-cultural niches from the St. Lawrence River to the Florida Everglades in British Protestant control, while Spanish Catholics were left to contest Indigenous claims to the western mountains and plains, most of which was still Indian Country.

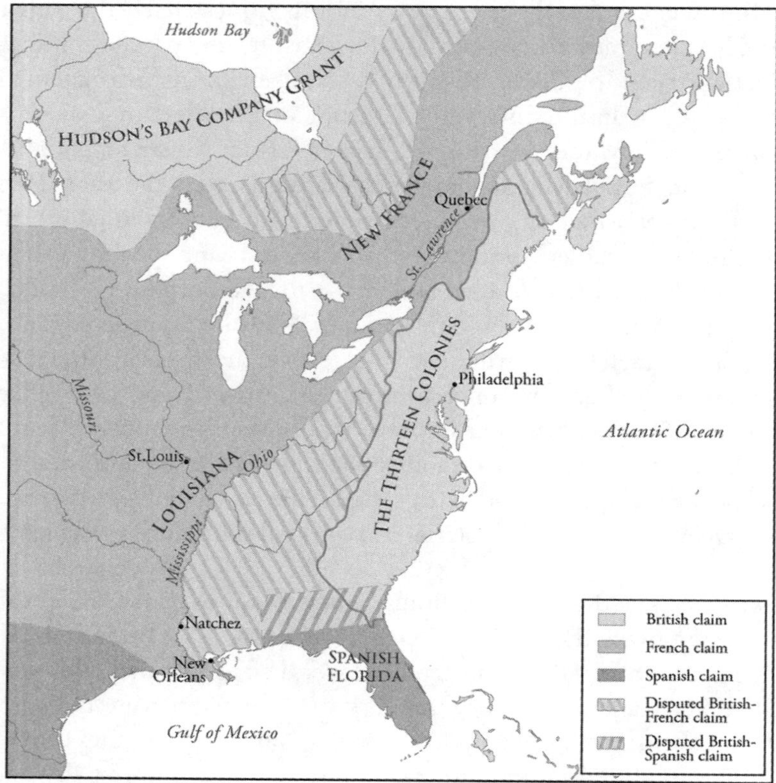

Figure 23. Map showing territorial claims before the Seven Years' War. Beehive Mapping.

British "Tyranny" and the Onset of Rebellions, 1763–1774

Some Indigenous communities on the Northern Plains soon would feel the effects of the border making, and in 1769 Catholics in Mexico City would respond to various threats (attacks on vessels traveling from the Philippines, British claims east of the Mississippi, and Russian encroachment in the Northwest) by evangelizing and "civilizing" Pacific Coast Natives and establishing Franciscan missions that eventually would stretch from San Diego to San Francisco.[56] But the Treaty of Paris's impact on the Eastern Woodlands Natives was immediate. Despite the peace pipes smoked and the Wampum Belts exchanged, they very quickly realized their place on the new imperial map. Soon after the

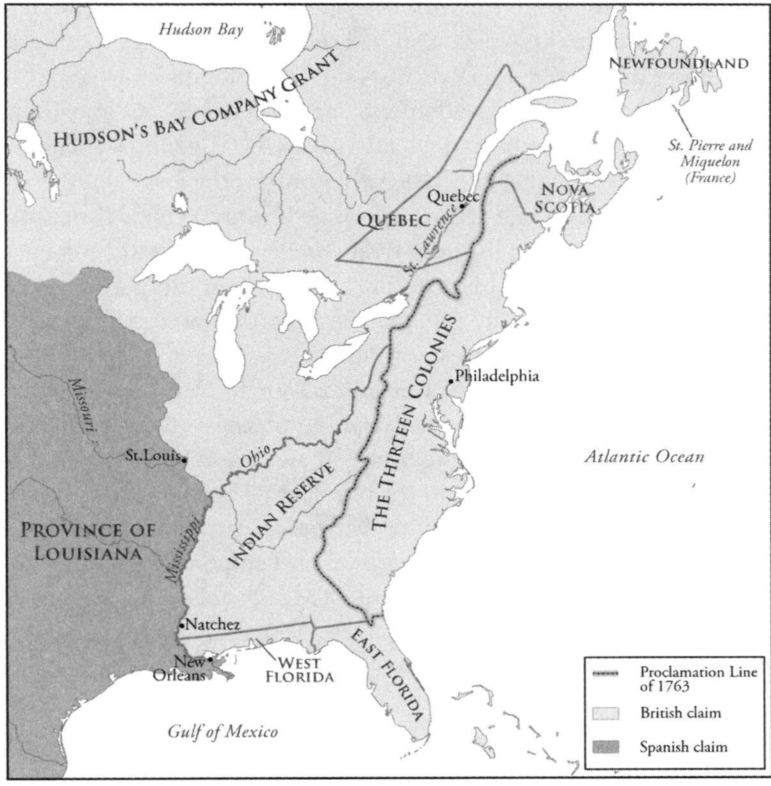

Figure 24. Map showing territorial claims after the Seven Years' War. Beehive Mapping.

superpowers signed the February 1763 treaty, multiple Indigenous communities turned to religion to foment armed rebellion—the *first* American Revolution.

Their Native ancestors had bequeathed two broad paths of spiritual resistance to mid-eighteenth-century woodland communities.[57] We might call them scripture-focused and vision-centered strategies. On one hand, there were indigenized Christian practices encouraged by Bible-quoting missionaries and grounded in gospel messages about equality; on the other hand, some used Christianized Native practices transmitted orally and grounded in purifying rituals and religious visions.[58] Both had deep roots and new shoots. Resisters might prefer the old ways or the new ways, but they couldn't completely disentangle the two. As Blacks in the Greater South made their choices within the constraints of the slave plantation niche they had inherited, post-treaty Natives in the North also had the range of choices set for them by the mission, the other colonial niche—and by the long history of territorial dispossession and resilient resettlement. Samson Occom, the most famous ordained Native clergyman and an advocate of Indigenous villages with British-style farming, chose the first path; Pontiac, the leader of the armed resistance and advocate of a return to Native lifeways, chose the second.

Historians have called the post-treaty battles Pontiac's Rebellion (1763–1765), and that Odawa war chief and intertribal leader did play a key role.[59] However, the fighting actually was part of a pan-Indian rebellion, the first successful one since the southwestern Pueblo Revolt of 1680, which also began with a spiritual vision. Just as Pueblo resisters in New Mexico had challenged the lifeway of the Franciscan farming mission, eighteenth-century rebels around the Great Lakes and Ohio Valley were challenging the Christian colonial lifeway—its agricultural, commercial, and spiritual practices.[60] In that sense, it was a Mississippian revitalization movement, with combatants hoping to restore subsistence practices and communal rituals that had circulated from the Great Lakes to the Gulf of Mexico.[61] Pontiac and his armed coalition used warfare practices, racial categories, and religious beliefs to disrupt the unsustainable colonial habitat and, they hoped, repair the broken niche. As a Quaker in the Ohio Valley reported, "it grieves ye Indians to see ye White People Settle on these Lands & follow Hunting or Planting."[62] Grief at the loss of their traditional habitat—and outrage at settler advances—mounted after the February 1763 treaty. Pontiac convened a war council in April, and by the end of May a coalition of Natives from Lake Superior to the Lower Mississippi—including the Odawa, Shawnee, Potawatomi, Huron-Wendat, and Lenape—had captured three forts and begun the siege of Detroit and Fort Pitt. They captured more forts in June and won a battle in July. Only the British victory at Fort Pitt in August and the October conclusion of Pontiac's six-month siege of Detroit eased White worries temporarily, though skirmishes continued into the next year.[63]

Whatever we call this conflict, it's important to recognize its spiritual origins and ecological significance. Pontiac acknowledged his debt to a 1761 vision of Neolin, an Ohio Valley Lenape prophet who, in turn, had learned from three earlier visionaries.[64] The teachings of Neolin, who was called the Delaware Prophet, spread from the 3,500 Lenape of the Ohio Valley to Native communities from New York to Minnesota.[65] We have some sense of what he said and how he preached from several unsympathetic observers, including a Moravian missionary and a Quaker trading-post attendant.[66]

Neolin reported a "Vission of Heaven, where there was no White people but all Indians," and preached by using a visual aid, a deerskin pictographic chart showing the Native path to heaven. Just as the Catholic Marquette had held up an image of Mary and Protestant missionaries used diagrams, Neolin pointed to the map as he recounted what the Master of Life had told him of the spiritual path.[67] So Lenape traditionalists had their own revealed guide to right living, a sort of Native *Pilgrim's Progress.*

The chart provided guidelines for living and praying. The path for Natives, the map showed, required turning away from Whites' trade goods, teaching boys to use the bow and arrow again, and encouraging women to grow corn. Meanwhile, the men would temporarily avoid hunting so the decimated game would return and the community could again live "as their forefathers did." In this seven-year plan, everyone would exchange imported textiles for animal skins. The boys would refuse rum and renew the ritual of ingesting the "black drink," the vomit-inducing tea the chief had passed around in the Apalachee council house and other Natives had used for a long time.[68] The rejuvenated Lenape added the practice and were performing their new devotions "by Dancing, Singing, & sometimes all Kneeling and Praying" to supernatural intercessors who conveyed their requests to the "Great Being."[69] Those rituals would return them to the divinely ordained path, a separate route to heaven, and the drink would cleanse them, "purge out all that they got of ye White peoples ways."[70] The renewed beliefs and rituals provided an explanation for their present suffering, a justification for armed rebellion, and a blueprint for future regeneration. They would repair their God-given homeland and reclaim their rightful place on the continent and in the cosmos.

Soon White British colonists started their own rebellion in the name of liberty. This time they complained that the tyrannical king and Parliament, not the autocratic pope and Catholic Church, was shackling them. Unlike Pontiac's rebels, the colonists weren't rejecting all things British, just laws limiting their freedom to consume, sell, settle, farm, govern, and worship. As Pontiac's Rebellion raged, a panicked Parliament asked King George III to sign the Royal Proclamation of 1763, which redrew the imperial map again, reserving the province of Quebec for Catholics, who weren't allowed to seek election or worship freely, and setting aside a Native reserve stretching from Canada to Florida and prohibiting settlers from crossing the new boundary, the Appalachian Mountains.[71] Settlers already there had to leave. The statute encouraged some Natives—and some still argue it established their land rights—though it didn't bring peaceful relations. Chiefs couldn't control resentful young warriors; colonial administrators couldn't curb backcountry farmers, who resented the restrictions on westward movement. London had assumed that separating the squabbling subjects would help. It didn't. In fact, things got uglier. Pontiac's spiritually sanctioned and grievance-focused violence against Whites found its mirror image in the spiritually sanctioned and grievance-focused violence of the Paxton Boys, a self-appointed backcountry militia Benjamin Franklin would condemn as "White Christian Savages."[72]

In December 1763 fifty Presbyterians from the central Pennsylvania town of Paxton marched on the twenty remaining Susquehannock residents of a Christian Indian town. The armed men, who had fought on the frontier, killed six of those "Moravian Indians," and others murdered the remaining fourteen residents. Five weeks later, about 250 marched toward Philadelphia to kill the Natives that Quaker officials were harboring, although the mob turned back after provincial representatives, including Franklin, heard their complaints. Two Paxton spokesmen then sent the governor, John Penn, nine "grievances," which lamented their wartime suffering and decried legislators' failure to help.[73] During the Seven Years' War, Pennsylvania's governor had asked the pastor of Paxton Presbyterian Church, John Elder, to recruit a militia, and it was that fighting force, the Paxton Rangers, who carried out the Indian attack.[74] Reverend Elder alerted Philadelphia authorities about the advancing rioters, but he refused to identify his congregants, explaining that the backcountry residents felt unrepresented in the provincial government and unsupported during their wartime battles with "Savages."[75] Other Paxton advocates justified the violence on religious as well as political grounds: God had called them to punish those Natives because they had aided Lenape war parties.[76]

The murdered Natives had lived on land granted them by the Penn family, and one can only imagine what the colony's pacifist founder might have thought of recent events: first a disillusioned Lenape prophet displaced from his Delaware Valley homeland preached a separatist religious message that inspired armed revolt, and then a mob of Christ-professing Pennsylvanians struck back with more violence.[77] Fortunately, because a "pamphlet war" broke out and sixty-three authors took sides, we know the diverging views.[78] In this 1764 debate, a coalition of Presbyterians, Anglicans, and Lutherans united against the Quakers, whom they criticized for ignoring the frontier, supporting the Indians, and promoting self-interest.[79] They divided along religious, not regional, lines, and more than half of Philadelphia sided with the Paxton Boys. That might have surprised William Penn, and the vitriolic support for vigilantism might have troubled him. Yet he also might have been reassured that many Philadelphia elites—not just Quakers but also deists like Franklin—expressed alarm. So did London officials, who misjudged the situation. They had underestimated the war-weariness and righteous rage on the bloody frontier, where most of the fighting had been happening.[80]

The misperception didn't prevent Parliament from further efforts to establish order and raise funds, since the war had been expensive and so was the frontier's continuing defense. In 1765 it passed the Stamp Act, which taxed all forms of paper, from newspapers to marriage certificates. Britain's Caribbean subjects paid it without protest, except for the Whites who rioted in the Leeward Islands.[81] The most vigorous resistance occurred in the mainland colonies, so vigorous that observers in Barbados accused Americans of "rebellion." Pennsylvania's delegate to the Stamp Act Congress, the Quaker-influenced lawyer John Dickinson, refuted that charge by suggesting the "popular fury" arose from a sense of natural rights implanted by "the King of Kings" and not by any worldly monarch.[82] The law was repealed, and in his 1766 sermon about the decision Mayhew linked British and Catholic tyranny, using the same metaphors he had employed in his sermon celebrating the fall of Quebec.[83]

The Stamp Act resistance didn't lead inevitably to the American Revolution.[84] After all, the Leeward Islands malcontents didn't declare independence.[85] However, the mainland civil disobedience did set patterns of rhetoric, modes of communication, and forms of protest the patriots would use later.[86] They also introduced new forms of association: colonists gathered in that the Stamp Act Congress to coordinate their response, a document Dickinson drafted. And there were shared themes in the protesters' messages: from Maine to Georgia, colonists claimed London had constrained their liberty by imposing a tax without the consent of the governed.[87] New symbols and figures appeared, and older ones were used for new ends. Lady Liberty still symbolized their cause, but the Indian came to stand for the American colonies in the transatlantic imagination, as in *The Deplorable State of America*, the first British image to protest the Stamp Act.[88] In the engraving, kneeling Britain offers the Stamp Act to America, the headdress-wearing Indian at the center. In turn the barbaric but virile colonies seek the aid of Wisdom, standing to the far left, who advises "take it not." That advice seems wise, since both commerce and liberty are endangered: Commerce, represented by Mercury, says he must leave, and Liberty, the fallen figure at America's feet, reports "It's all Over with me." In a surprising development, the

London satirist's image of America as an Indian came to be accepted by colonists, who circulated this print and similar visual declarations of protest.

Colonial critics of the Stamp Act also expressed their opposition by turning to other media and different strategies—from writing and speaking to boycotting and parading. Sermons protested the law and celebrated its repeal. Newspaper essayists expressed opposition. The outraged also organized economic boycotts, which had intended and unintended effects. It was during the 1760s that White women began to think more about their role in public affairs, partly because the household became a site of resistance during and after the Stamp Act crisis, when male leaders asked women to eschew British-made goods and produce American-made alternatives.[89] One Philadelphia woman who favored boycotts didn't have to imagine what the colony's founder might have said about the debate: Elizabeth Graeme Fergusson composed a 698-line poem that told of an angel descending to deliver a scroll with Penn's advice. His posthumous message said Pennsylvanians should avoid foreign imports, seek God in Nature, and value the "rural manners" of self-sufficient farmers.[90] Dissent also reached beyond the farm. Some urban protesters—mostly men—staged public displays. They hung or burned effigies of the tax collectors. Urban rebels also repurposed anti-Catholic holidays like Pope's Day, which included the tradition of burning the pope's effigy. In Boston's 1765 Pope's Day celebration, Stamp Act opponents added even more effigies to condemn British "tyranny, oppression, and slavery."[91]

British "tyranny" took other forms after the Stamp Act, and so did colonists' defense of liberty. Americans continued to recycle rhetoric from the anti-Catholic battle to defy Parliament's taxation. Dickinson criticized the 1767 Townshend Acts, which taxed paint, glass, lead, and tea, in *Letters from a Farmer in Pennsylvania* (1768), perhaps the most widely acclaimed colonial document before the Revolution, and that text returned to the themes of slavery and freedom.[92] The Quaker-inspired proponent of civil disobedience reminded colonists they were "bound together by the same rights," which included the right to freedom in religion, trade, and government. But the Townshend Acts had shackled them: "Those who are taxed without their own consent, expressed by themselves or their representatives, are slaves." Dickinson's message reached colonists who ignored pamphlets but frequented taverns: newspapers printed "The Liberty Song" (1768), Dickinson's musical call for resistance and America's first patriotic song.[93] Sung to a familiar British naval tune, its chorus urged colonists to battle bondage ("In Freedom we're born and in Freedom we'll live"). One stanza introduced a now-famous phrase and assured agitators of divine favor: "Then join hand in hand brave AMERICANS all, / By uniting we stand, by dividing we fall; / in SO RIGHTEOUS a cause let us hope to succeed, / For Heaven approves of each generous deed."

The Tea Act of 1773 elicited similar rhetorical responses, and colonists again used ritualized protests and Indian symbols in the Boston Tea Party.[94] Bostonians dressed in Native garb boarded the docked ships of the British East India Company and threw 342 chests of tea into the harbor. Not all colonists thought it was prudent to toss forty-two tons of tea—Washington condemned the tactic and tea-laden ships in Philadelphia were turned back peacefully—but that public theater got Britain's attention.[95] And it drew immediate retribution. Parliament passed three acts in 1774 known collectively as the Intolerable Acts. Those laws closed the Boston Harbor, prevented free elections, and required that locals house British troops. A fourth law enacted almost at the same time, the Quebec Act, offered freedom of worship to Canadian Catholics. That went too far. With this 1774 law one tyrant, Britain, was siding with the other, Catholicism.

In that year when liberty sounded in raucous taverns and solemn churches, the laws did prove "intolerable," and in response colonial assemblies sent delegates to Philadelphia for the First Continental Congress, which met from 5 September to 26 October 1774.[96] The advisory group hoped to formulate a joint response to the laws. Even if the political crisis brought the delegates together, religion was never far from their minds.[97] For the delegates, however, religion didn't mean *all* religions. It didn't mean southeastern Natives' Green Corn Festival or West African divination practices. It didn't mean Buddhism or Hinduism, which were not yet widely understood in the West. There were no devotees of Chinese religions at the Congress, even if several founders admired Confucius's teachings, which Franklin excerpted in the *Pennsylvania Gazette* and John Adams mentioned in *Thoughts on Government*.[98] Confucianism was closer to what Franklin and Jefferson had in mind, but it didn't exhaust what they meant by religion. And the delegates certainly didn't mean Islam, which came up mostly when a speaker wanted to dismiss a suggestion by comparing it to the tradition's inauthentic prophet or the aggressive practices of the Ottoman Empire. Jews, who numbered between one and two thousand and boasted small congregations in Newport, New York, and Charles Town, also weren't discussed much—except when delegates compared America to the biblical Israel and Americans to God's chosen people. It was the symbol of Israel, not actual Jews, they referenced.[99] As you might guess, Catholicism didn't have many fans in the hall. The delegates summoned the usual rhetoric about Catholic tyranny to condemn the Quebec Act. It endangered "the civil rights and liberties of all America" and would "reduce the ancient and free Protestant Colonies to the same state of slavery."[100] Maryland's Charles Carroll, who would eventually sign the Declaration, had assured Protestant readers of the *Maryland Gazette* that Catholicism sided with liberty, but, at least at first, the delegates in Philadelphia weren't buying it, even if they occasionally gathered for worship at St. Mary's or took a trip there for "entertainment." John Adams, who visited the Catholic church in 1774, for example, couldn't hide his disdain for "the poor wretches fingering their beads."[101] Yet he reluctantly acknowledged the aesthetic charm—the flickering candles, ornate altar, and "exquisite" music. He left so enchanted that he wondered "how Luther ever broke the spell." But Adams, a loyal Congregationalist, was glad the reformers had broken free. So were most White colonists, who then affiliated with one brand of Protestantism or another.

If *religion* didn't mean Catholicism, Judaism, Islam, or Indigenous faiths, then what did it mean? That was an issue the delegates confronted, and it arose on the second day. A Massachusetts delegate moved that a minister open their next session with prayer, but two delegates objected. The South Carolina delegate looked around at the Episcopalians, Quakers, Anabaptists, Presbyterians, and Congregationalists and suggested that prayer was "rendered impossible by the diversity of religious sentiments represented in Congress."[102] Samuel Adams from Massachusetts rose to speak in favor of the motion and nominated the Reverend Jacob Duché, pastor of Philadelphia's Christ Church, where Reading had preached his Seven Years' War sermon. The motion was approved, and on the third day the Anglican read a scriptural passage and prayed for ten minutes.[103] Surviving accounts say it was well received, partly because of his shrewd choice of the scriptural passage, Psalm 35.[104] It begins, "Plead thou my cause, O Lord, with them that strive with me, and fight thou against them that fight against me." Adams, who could be grumpy, told his wife, Abigail, that he "never heard a better prayer"—even though the preacher was Anglican. The former governor of Rhode Island, Samuel Ward, agreed: it was "one of the most sublime, catholic, well-adapted prayers I ever heard."[105] The Continental Congress would appoint Duché legislative chaplain and would assign army chaplains, hear political sermons, and declare days of fasting and thanksgiving.[106] In contrast to the anticlerical tone of the French revolutionaries of 1789, religion had a notable presence at the Congress.[107]

Yet diversity continued to test their dedication to liberty. By 1774 there were signs of some spiritual opportunities for women. Sarah Osborn had already published a spiritual memoir and preached to Blacks and Whites at a revival in Newport, with as many as 500 people gathering at her house each week by 1767.[108] Jane Hoskins's autobiography about "a Public Preacher among the People Called Quakers" announced a precedent for women who felt called to preach, and in 1774 Ann Lee and her English followers arrived in New York.[109] A former mill worker, Lee would establish a new religious movement, the United Society of Believers in Christ's Second Appearing. The Shakers, as they came to be called, taught that Jesus would come again as a woman—since the divine had appeared first as a man—and gender parity should be reflected in everything from church architecture to community leadership. Women and men entered the worship space through separate doors, and each community had a male and a female leader.

Ethnic and racial difference also would test congressional delegates as they used language about bondage and freedom to advocate resistance. They were making that case during the 1770s, the numerical peak of the slave trade and a time of increased disruption in Indigenous communities. However, it was also a moment when some elite Natives and northern slaves were achieving small gains in social status. To get some sense of how the talk about liberty played out among those excluded from political participation in 1774, consider the letters exchanged that year between Phillis Wheatley, the Black poet, and Samson Occom, the Mohegan preacher (figs. 25 and 26).[110]

Both were gaining notoriety. Wheatley had just returned from England in 1773, the year she gained freedom and published a book of poetry. In that work she commented on the issues of the day, composing poems about deism (1767), slavery (1768), the Stamp Act (1768), George Whitefield (1770), and even an ambitiously titled poem, "America" (1768), which employed the twin themes of "tyranny" and "liberty."[111] Occom toured England too, and his best-selling 1772 sermon yielded regular preaching invitations by 1774, when he was planning an independent Native Christian community and preaching to large crowds of Whites and Indians in New York and Connecticut.[112] If we could overhear any conversation in that momentous year when the Continental Congress began to debate the meaning of liberty, we might choose listening in on those two. Fortunately, we can. Reverend Occom's letter to Wheatley suggested that Africans and Natives had "natural rights." Wheatley agreed: "In every human Breast, God has implanted a Principle, which we call Love of Freedom; it is impatient of Oppression, and pants for Deliverance."[113] The African-born poet condemned "the strange Absurdity" of those who "cry for Liberty" but exercise "oppressive Power." That problem, like the question of religious liberty, would recur when the Continental Congress met again in 1775, and the Revolutionary War began in earnest.

Figure 25. Jonathan Spilsbury, after Mason Chamberlin, *The Reverend Samson Occom (1723–1792)*, 1768, mezzotint on laid paper. Courtesy of the Hood Museum of Art, Dartmouth, Gift of Mrs. Robert White Birch, Class of 1927W.

Figure 26. *Phillis Wheatley, Negro Servant to Mr. John Wheatley, of Boston.* Engraving by Scipio Moorhead, in Phillis Wheatley, *Poems on Various Subjects, Religious and Moral* (A. Bell, 1773). Library of Congress, Rare Book and Special Collections, LC-USZCNA 12533.

Rhetoric, Ritual, and Rebellion, 1775–1791

War might have been avoided in 1774. By 1775 that didn't seem possible. The inertial force of insurrection had been set in motion by the Stamp Act resistance. That force could have been slowed if Britain had granted parliamentary representation and eased up on taxation. King George III ignored the efforts by the Continental Congress and their British allies to find a solution, however, and by the spring of 1775 all that remained to be seen was which kind of battle they would wage and, if victorious, which kind of government they would form. Some delegates, like Dickinson, pushed for peace until the end, but that strategy looked noble but futile after fighting broke out that April at Lexington and Concord, where 93 militiamen and 273 British soldiers lost their lives.[114] In response, the Second Continental Congress, which convened in May and governed until 1789, appointed George Washington commander of the Continental Army. More combatants would die that June in the Battle of Bunker Hill, with Britain losing more than 1,000 men. Congress would offer a last olive branch in July 1775, but when the king rejected the overture, there was no turning back from rebellion.

All who lived in eastern North America had to take sides, and, as with the revivals, those decisions sometimes divided families, communities, and congregations. Several thousand slaves won their freedom by fighting in the war, and some Blacks began to think the British afforded a better chance of securing their own liberty.[115] At least 20,000 African Americans and many Native Nations, like the Kanien'kehá:ka (Mohawk), sided with the Crown. About one-quarter of White colonists did too.[116] After 1776 most loyalists not in British enclaves like New York City took off, laid low, or found themselves imprisoned in guardhouses.[117] The majority of Jews sided with the patriot cause, with about 100 fighting in the Revolution, but some remained loyal to Britain. For example, Isaac Touro, the cantor of Newport's congregation, headed for Jamaica.[118] The Lutheran Henry Muhlenberg stayed but watched for signs of God's will. Some were "down in the mouth," he reported in his journal, while others joyfully talked of independence. He decided to leave the outcome to God, who "has never yet made a mistake in his government," and eventually the pastor concluded that Washington was "a genuine Christian."[119] Many Quakers remained grateful to Charles II for granting them religious liberty and were reluctant to disavow the king. So was John Wesley, founder of the Methodist movement, who sided with the Crown.[120] All Methodist pastors except Francis Asbury joined Wesley in England. Anglican clergy had especially difficult choices to make after 1776. Their Sunday worship services included a prayer for the king. Should they keep it, cut it, or shut down their church? Some Anglicans, like Reverend Reading, persisted through the Revolution and then helped establish the new Episcopal Church. Others, like Duché, the congressional chaplain, switched sides and headed for England.[121]

The Revolution eventually would impact almost everyone, though in varied ways. The mapmaker Thomas Hutchins, who was in London when the war broke out, stayed until 1779, the year after he published a map of the western frontier.[122] Upon his return, Hutchins was suspected of being a British spy, but Franklin convinced Congress of his patriotism, and by 1781 he had been appointed the official geographer of the United States. John Spaulding, a farmer who gave up the plow for the pulpit, noted that the war left almost no one rich, except in the "principles which were the seed-corn of a Republican Government."[123] But the Massachusetts Congregationalist Hannah Adams, who began her *Alphabetical Compendium of the Various Sects* in 1778, found that her financial situation improved slightly during the war: she learned to weave "bobbin lace," more profitable than the spinning and sewing she did before fighting broke out.[124] Religious pacifists who valued republicanism but refused to take up arms—Quakers, Mennonites, and Moravians—initiated an American tradition of conscientious objection. Some Moravians even tried to avoid all news of the war.[125] While Haudenosaunee sachems observed congressional deliberations forty miles away in Philadelphia, Sister Susel advised unmarried Moravian women in Bethlehem, Pennsylvania, to ignore anything they heard about "affairs in the country," so they might "remain in communion with the Savior."[126] On 4 July 1776, as the founders were declaring independence, those young pacifists marked a seasonal change, not a political shift, attending a "Harvest Blessing" before heading to the fields for the day.

Patriot intellectuals who supported the armed struggle headed for the podium, the pulpit, or the writing desk. While the Continental Army fought with muskets, others blended religious and political rhetoric to wage a war with words. Those intellectuals weren't a uniform group, though they all rejected the loyalist charge that rebellion was "unnatural" and framed the uprising as grounded in divinely sanctioned natural rights.[127] Combining references to the natural and the supernatural as they defended resistance and imagined government, they suggested the capacity to recognize rights was "implanted" by the creator, as Wheatley had put it. In other words, God gifted creatures with the capacity to discern their rights and detect when they've been infringed. In that sense, elite defenders of rebellion consecrated natural rights. They made them at once both universally human and God-given. In short, they made them American.

Of course, there was no America. Not yet. That would come after the signing of the Declaration and the ratifying of the Constitution. But resolutions, speeches, and sermons on the eve of Revolution not only mentioned divinely implanted rights and universally available sensibilities, but also condemned "tyranny" and warned of "enslavement," as resisters had done during the Seven Years' War and the Stamp Act crisis. Patrick Henry's famous "Give me liberty, or give me death!" speech repeated those motifs.[128] In March 1775 the Virginian told fellow legislators in a Richmond church that if they used the reasoning powers imparted by the "God of Nature" they would vote for war because the "tyrannical" Parliament gave them no other way to avoid "chains and slavery." Congress's "Necessity for Taking up Arms," issued later that year, made the case for force by employing "common sense" and celebrating "divine favor" but also presented colonists' decision as a choice between an armed rebellion to preserve their "liberties" or an unconditional submission to "tyranny."[129] Thomas Paine's *Common Sense,* which sold more than 100,000 copies, also repeated the thematic pattern.[130] Paine appealed to "natural rights" and recounted the king's abuse of power, comparing monarchical Britain to authoritarian Catholicism: "For monarchy in every instance is the Popery of government." Shifting to a biblical metaphor, he suggested that "the Pharaoh of England" enslaved colonists but the Almighty implanted "feelings for good and wise purpose."[131] Paine, a rationalist who would offend churchgoers' sensibilities by the 1790s, even asked God to preserve the continent's "peace and happiness."[132]

American Scripture

All those themes were present in the Declaration of Independence (1776), which called on "Nature's God" as it announced America's entry into the order of nations.[133] The document, which would become one of the sacred texts of US civil religion, began with presuppositions: "All men are created equal" and "endowed by their Creator with certain unalienable rights." For Jefferson, who drafted the document, and Adams and Franklin, who served on the committee that edited it, those rights were both natural and supernatural, arising from both the "Laws of Nature and Nature's God." The Declaration then defended independence by listing grievances, noting how Britain had trampled on their rights. King George had established an "Absolute Tyranny," and subjects of a despotic ruler have a right, even a duty, to "throw off such Government." The right of rebellion, then, is grounded in divine will as well as human nature. Appealing to "the Supreme Judge of the world" to vouch for their good intentions as well as to the authority of "the good people of these colonies" the fifty-six signers announced the colonies were no longer tied to Britain but "FREE AND INDEPENDENT STATES." That phrase was capitalized to make sure no one missed the point.

The document makes other less obvious points about the theology, geography, economy, and demography of the new state. But what the Declaration doesn't say is as important as what it does say.[134] First, the founders appealed to "Divine Providence" and "Nature's God," but not to the Trinitarian God. They did not invoke Christ. The language is generically theist, with an emphasis on the Creator rather than the second person of the Trinity. Later readers who have wanted to use the document to insist America is a Christian nation have faced an unsurmountable challenge. That word, *Christ,* isn't there. Even the Southerners who approved the Constitution of the Confederate States in 1861 would settle on the broadly theistic language of the Declaration and not the narrowly sectarian language of the revival.[135] Leaders would add biblical images, like the trope of America as God's New Israel, but the incipient civil religion was loosely deistic, not boldly Christian.[136]

Second, the Declaration didn't specify the boundaries of the new nation.[137] Since the fall of Quebec, American commentators had projected a future empire that was continental in scope, as Paine did in *Common Sense.* He used the words *continent* and *continental* dozens of times in his popular pamphlet. More important, the new governing body was also called the Continental Congress. Delegates might have chosen a more modest modifier: "continental" is a rather capacious word—more aspirational than actualized—for what amounted to the eastern coast. In any case, the new independent states had no announced borders in 1776, and even the first map published after the end of the war in 1783 wasn't clear: the western boundaries of many states extended to the Mississippi.[138] Boundaries—and intentions—would be clearer by 1787, however, as federal lawmakers and church leaders planned for transcontinental expansion. A Congregational minister and land speculator explained the 1787 map of lands around the Ohio River and predicted the region would become "the garden of the world, the seat of wealth, and the centre of a great Empire."[139] Even before the maps were drawn and plans were made, Natives like Occom who scanned the Declaration for hints about territorial limits in 1776 might have been alarmed. It decried "insurrections" among "the inhabitants of our frontiers, the merciless Indian Savages, whose known rule of warfare, is an undistinguished destruction of all ages, sexes, and conditions." The Declaration stopped short of saying settlers were legally entitled to the frontier territory. That was the good news. The bad news? Transcontinental creep wasn't ruled out by that dismissive reference to Natives.

Third, what's not in the Declaration also reveals predominant attitudes about Blacks and the slave-based economy. Jefferson's document went through several drafts, and a passage about slavery was removed by Adams, who didn't own slaves, and Franklin, who did. Like the slaveholding Jefferson, they recognized that the exalted rhetoric about equality and rights was in tension with the South's slave-based economy and the practice of complicit northern traders who depended on commerce with plantation owners. Adding to the list of colonists' grievances, Jefferson's original passage had claimed the king provoked slave insurrections and "refused us permission" to ban the slave trade. Further, the tyrannical monarch had violated Africans' "most sacred rights of life and liberty" by "captivating and carrying them into slavery in another hemisphere."[140] The excised text recognized Africans' rights, but didn't urge the abolition of slavery. By blaming the slave trade on the king, it exonerated Southern planters. Adams and Franklin didn't buy it, and cut the passage. Nineteenth-century abolitionists still would find some aid for their cause in the document, however, using the passage about equality as a tool for resistance. Abraham Lincoln would call the Declaration "a rebuke and a stumbling-block to tyranny and oppression."[141] Yet the Continental Congress valued sectional unity more highly than moral consistency, thereby postponing America's reckoning with the practice of owning human beings.

Despite what the Declaration said—and didn't say—after it was printed as a broadside, read to the troops, and translated in a Philadelphia German newspaper, it didn't ease all the concerns of patriots who supported the separation, or of loyalists in England who condemned it.[142] One 1776 British sermon reversed the accusations: the London preacher prayed that God might deliver colonial loyalists "from the violence, injustice, and tyranny of those daring Rebels who have assumed to themselves the exercise of arbitrary power."[143] Another London sermon appealed to the parable of the tares and wheat to suggest the rebels were intrusive weeds, "oppressing the fine fruits" the colonial field might have yielded.[144] That biblical parable suggested Christians should leave the weeds until the final sorting, but in 1776 loyalist clergy seemed sure they could spot them. On the other side of the Atlantic, John Adams was less sure, and he turned to a different metaphor to understand the dangers and uncertainties of the revolutionary project. He hoped the new "confederation" might preserve "the Principles of Virtue and Freedom in the World," but imagined the path to independence not as a field they were cultivating but a maritime journey they were undertaking, with God's help: "We must be content to trust, to Winds and Currents with the best Skill We have, under a kind Providence to land us in a Port of Peace, Liberty and Safety."[145]

Peace and safety weren't in sight, and Americans were still far from the port of liberty in 1776. Elite White men were gaining more political participation, but the displacement of Natives would continue, and so would the spread of slavery. The Revolution temporarily interrupted the slave trade, and talk of freedom did stir some to condemn the practice as unjust. Yet the greatest change would come in terms of religious and political debate. As one historian has suggested, "the revolution generated clashing contagions, of slavery and liberty, and pitted them against one another."[146] In the fifteen years after the Declaration, America's political elites would work out the meaning of liberty by creating new symbols (the Great Seal), passing new statutes (the Northwest Ordinance), and staging new rituals (the Constitutional Procession) that would provide the spiritual tools and set the conditions for freedom seekers in the nascent agrarian empire.

Birds Again

Before they adjourned on 4 July 1776, the founders decided the new state needed a new symbol, a Great Seal.[147] So Congress asked Adams, Franklin, and Jefferson to design the emblem. The committee proposed classical, Masonic, and biblical themes, like the Children of Israel in the wilderness, and suggested a few features that would appear in the final version: the Eye of Providence and the motto *E pluribus unum*, or Out of Many, One.[148] When their design failed to win congressional approval, two more committees would try. Still not satisfied, in 1782 Congress reassigned the task to Charles Thomson, secretary of the Continental Congress. A rationalist Presbyterian who knew Greek and Latin, Thomson had no special skills in heraldry.[149] He did have a reputation for getting things done, however, and he accomplished the task. In June 1782 Congress adopted Thomson's two-sided emblem, a composite of earlier suggestions that created a visual vocabulary for America's budding civil religion.[150] The reverse had an unfinished pyramid topped by the Eye of Providence, and the obverse included the first committee's Latin motto, the second committee's olive branch, and the third committee's eagle.[151] Yet Thomson had made changes. He replaced the imperial eagle with the bald eagle, a native species, and placed symbols of peace and war (the olive branch and bundle of arrows) in the raptor's talons. Most important, he made the avian symbol more prominent.[152]

Eagles and other raptors had a long history as religio-political symbols, both on the continent and around the world.[153] Raptors recurred in pre-Columbian material culture. Horn Shelter Man had a hawk's talon in his mouth. The bird-man symbolism on the Cahokian tablet was striking. So was the giant eagle on the Aztec *Codex Mendoza.*[154] The Mandan of the Dakota Plains revered eagles and their feathers as sacred.[155] And the thunderbird, often represented as an eagle, appeared across Indigenous North America, from wooden carvings in the Northwest to rock art in the Northeast.[156] It was associated with the sky and often portrayed as battling a serpent from the lower world, as in the Cahokia tablet, whose reverse side included hatched lines symbolizing snakes and their subterranean realm.[157]

When Thomson made the final revisions to the Great Seal in 1782 some of that figurative history was remembered and some forgotten. As a former teacher of Latin and later translator of the Greek New Testament, he knew the classical referents.[158] He also would have been familiar with eagles on European emblems, including Holy Roman Emperor Charles V's.[159] In Charles V's symbol, the eagle held a thunderbolt, invoking unintended parallels with North American thunderbird iconography. Thomson replaced the thunderbolt with arrows, though it's unclear if Thomson knew the Native precedents. He had negotiated Lenape treaties and defended them in print, lamenting "the Abuses the Indians had received."[160] The Lenape even ritually adopted him. Yet he apparently didn't know that thunderbird motifs appeared on nearby rock art and in the stories of diverse Algonquian Peoples. Even some Natives of his time seem to have forgotten the eagle's continental history and figurative significance, though they would recover avian imagery and non-Native leaders would appropriate it for diverse causes: in 1933 the National Recovery Administration would use a blue thunderbird as the symbol of industrial recovery during the Great Depression, and César Chávez would put it in the United Farm Workers logo, inviting laborers "to join under the symbol of the thunderbird and fight for our rights."[161] The Great Seal's eagle would have even more uses: Rutherford B. Hayes used it for the presidential seal in 1877, Franklin D. Roosevelt put it on the $1 bill in 1935, and twenty years later the eagle appeared on the stained-glass window in the Capitol's prayer room.[162]

We don't know what most Native people thought about the Great Seal's eagle, but some of the 1,800 Shawnee who had been pushed westward by the

1780s weren't pleased.[163] We know that because in 1789 a Congregationalist land speculator in the Ohio territories asked two Shawnee leaders what they thought of the Great Seal and its centrally placed eagle.[164] The wealthy landowner believed it was proof of America's peaceful intentions toward the Indians, but one of his Shawnee guests found the symbolization unsettling: "If the United States were such lovers of peace as you describe them to be, they would have chosen for their coat of arms something more appropriate and expressive of it."[165] The Shawnee chief suggested the designers could have chosen a more peaceful bird, like the dove; the eagle is large, proud, even condescending: it "looks down disparagingly upon all the birds." And the Great Seal's rendering made things worse: "You have not only put one of the implements of war, a bundle of arrows, into one of his talons . . . but have painted the bird in the most fearful manner, and in a position of attack upon his prey." The Shawnee, who had sided with the British during the Revolution, were already suspicious of American intentions. The new federal symbol didn't reassure them.

Imperial Intentions

The Northwest Ordinance, which passed two years before that conversation, might not have reassured them either. Jefferson drafted the law's first version in 1784, setting guidelines for land distribution and regional governance that would inform the 1787 statute crafted by two Massachusetts delegates, an antislavery Congregationalist and a bishop-wary Episcopalian.[166] Those guidelines eventually would be used to add states north of the Ohio River, and the Northwest Territory's official seal provided more evidence of expansionist aims. It depicted an axe-felled tree and declared "from the fallen tree, a better one has grown." The 1787 law it symbolized did seem better in some ways. Whether the Shawnee knew or trusted its provisions, the act not only prohibited slavery in the new territory but also mandated fair relations with Native Nations: "The utmost good faith shall always be observed towards the Indians; their lands and property shall never be taken from them without their consent; and . . . they shall never be invaded or disturbed, unless in just and lawful wars authorized by Congress."[167] Article 3 also proclaimed religion was "necessary to good government and the happiness of mankind." The contract negotiated between the US Treasury and the Ohio Company didn't identify an official territorial church, but it ignored the example of Virginia's Statute for Establishing Religious Freedom (1786) and proposed a Massachusetts model of state-supported clergy.[168] The Congregationalist minister who negotiated it insisted on providing land for "the support of an educated ministry," and starting in 1788 the government paid Rev. Daniel Story, a Boston-born clergyman, to paddle a thirty-mile pastoral route to combat frontier irreligion.[169] Congress later would reject plans for other sponsored ministers in the territory, but Americans would continue to both entangle and disentangle religion and the state as they imagined their new empire.[170]

Consider *Vision of Columbus*, an epic poem Joel Barlow published the year the Northwest Ordinance passed. Barlow, a revolutionary war chaplain and Ohio land speculator, praised the new republic's championing of religion: "In no blest land has fair Religion shone / And fix'd so firm her everlasting throne."[171] America is poised, an angel tells Columbus, to "harmonize mankind" and serve as a global model because it emulated "the Immortal Penn," allowing liberty of conscience and, in turn, fostering spiritual diversity. Yet unity would arise from plurality, as the "mingling rays" of faiths—"the lights of the world"—would converge in America, which Barlow imagined as a rising empire. Looking to earlier hemispheric civilizations to prove US cultural superiority, the poet suggested America would be better than Europe because it was built upon glorious empires that flourished before Rome. He didn't mention the political-spiritual centers farther north, at Chaco and Cahokia, because he didn't know about them, but Barlow suggested the splendid cities with impressive temples to the south, Aztec Tenochtitlán and Incan Cuzco, showed that America wasn't new or barbaric, as Europeans said. Rather, Americans were building on an ancient heritage, far older than Europe's, as "new temples rise and splendid towers increase." The imperial built environment had started with Penn's Philadelphia, the "wonder of mankind," and continued in Boston, New York, and Charleston.

Revolutionary America's heroes—"sage Franklin" and "great Washington"—had inspired this angelic vision, but Barlow believed much still depended on the outcome of the Constitutional Convention deliberating in Philadelphia that year.[172] To his delight, in September 1787 delegates sent the new Constitution to the states for ratification. And some in Philadelphia read Barlow's patriotic poem. Franklin read it, and Washington did too. He even sent a copy to a friend, the wife of the Philadelphia Agricultural Society's president. The following year that group's president would have a prominent place in the Grand Federal Procession, the July Fourth parade that celebrated the Constitution's ratification, reinforced the emerging civil religion, and announced the rising agrarian empire.

Venerating the Plough

In 1788 delegates ratified the Constitution, which guaranteed political offices would be open to citizens of any faith, and about two weeks later Philadelphians staged a public festival that both celebrated religious liberty and deepened the symbolic connection between the religious and civic realms. The city had hosted parades before, as when White Freemasons, members of a fraternal society, walked the streets to mark the opening of the first Masonic Hall in America.[173] But nothing matched the scope and spectacle of the 1788 event. As many as 22,000 residents, half the population of America's largest city, attended that parade on the Fourth of July.[174] About 5,000 walked the grid of streets settlers had imposed on the ancestral homeland of the Lenape, who, as Penn observed, had staged impressive festivals of their own in nearby farming towns—feasting, drumming, and dancing "with great appearance of Joy."[175] There were plenty of farmers at the 1788 rite, but less joy among Native Peoples. By then most Lenape had migrated to the Ohio Valley. Some displaced elders could still recall being in Philadelphia "when the first houses were built," but there is no evidence any Natives attended the parade.[176] Indigenous traces on the cityscape in 1788 included only the inconspicuous graves of Lenape Christians like Johannes and Sophia, siblings buried by Moravian missionaries; the Indian Queen Tavern, where convention delegates stayed; and a costumed White Indian, who rode in a carriage and passed a peace pipe with a performer in Quaker attire to reenact the founding myth of Penn's "holy experiment" in peace and diversity.[177] Even if there were only faint traces of Indigenous presence that day, some free Blacks and enslaved Africans probably watched the festivities from "the footways, the windows, and the roofs of houses."[178] African Americans in the urban North, including Philadelphia, held funeral processions and staged parades.[179] Yet they didn't walk the parade route in 1788. And only six White women, all textile workers, processed that July Fourth. So it was mostly White men of Protestant heritage who passed the white-steepled churches and brick Georgian buildings in the open-air ritual that sacralized the city's agricultural and commercial activity—and sanctified the rising American empire.

Parade organizers conjoined piety and politics in multiple ways. An ode composed and distributed for the occasion said attendees were witnessing "an empire rise," one that would enjoy "the numerous blessings Heav'n decrees."[180] Local experts on Heaven's decrees played a part, as Declaration signer Benjamin Rush noted. Rush, a "friend" of all sects, was delighted the clergy affirmed the "connection between religion and good government."[181] Rabbi

Jacob Cohen and sixteen other congregational leaders marched "arm in arm" to celebrate the Constitution's opening of political offices "to worthy men of every religion."[182] The First Amendment's extension of religious liberty would follow three years later, but the public performance of clerical cooperation gave hope that the new political order might overcome the long history of interreligious strife. And the blending of piety and politics found expression in other ways that day. The 1788 ritual commenced with a ship's cannon firing, signaling military might, and a church bell tolling, affirming Christian clout; it ended three hours later with a patriotic speech and communal feast. To accommodate religious difference, Jewish attendees "ate separately at a special kosher table prepared on their behalf."[183] The other revelers consumed 4,000 pounds of beef and 2,600 pounds of ham, washing it down with locally brewed beer.[184] The speech by James Wilson, another Declaration signer, praised the Constitution but insisted "liberty, virtue, and religion go hand in hand."[185]

Religion also goes "hand in hand" with agriculture, he said. In fact, farming ranked first among worldly pursuits because communal well-being "springs originally from the soil." The parade reinforced that message.[186] Signs along the route boasted about nearby fields and orchards, the sources of Philadelphia's exports, as well as imported sugarcane, the crop processed on Caribbean slave plantations. But at that moment of patriotic self-congratulation, organizers showed little remorse about African slavery. Nor did they seem conflicted about Native displacement: leading the procession were twelve "axe men," symbolizing the settlers who had cleared Lenape land to plant the colony. Then came men on horseback carrying flags celebrating the Declaration of 1776 and George Washington. The main cause for celebration followed: six white horses pulled an eagle-shaped carriage, as Pennsylvania's chief justice lofted a banner announcing "The New Constitution." Following the carriage, men raised flags of five allied countries, including Muslim Morocco, the first to recognize the US. The parade also displayed the local social hierarchy: marchers included the "better sort" (merchants and professionals), the "middling sort" (prosperous artisans and shopkeepers), and the "lower sort" (poor artisans and wage earners).[187] Boat builders and brick makers walked, for instance. But, reasserting agriculture's primacy, Philadelphia Agricultural Society members led the way, with farmers from the countryside close behind. Leading the contingent was mayor Samuel Powel, the society's affluent president, who was a guest at Washington's plantation and a pallbearer at Franklin's funeral. Just behind Powel another member lifted a banner with the society's motto (fig. 27). In its vivid representation of

Figure 27. "Venerate the Plough." James Trenchard's 1786 rendering of the motto of the Philadelphia Agricultural Society. Library of Congress, Prints and Photographs Division, LC-DIG-ds-04633.

farming religion, a man pushes a plough driven by oxen across a sun-drenched field. The goddess of plenty trails behind, as the motto encourages citizens of the new agrarian empire to "venerate the plough."[188]

Faith and Flourishing in 1791

Enslaved laborers who planted their masters' crops had little reverence for the plough, even if many Europeans and some Natives did venerate farm tools. However, almost everyone in the lands that became America reached for figurative tools, including agricultural metaphors and seasonal rituals, as they made sense of the political changes of the Revolutionary Era.

By 1791, on the eve of the Columbian tercentennial, Natives had preserved the tradition of vision-based spiritual resistance for the next generation, while Christian-identified Natives used other implements—the plough and the pen—to ease anguish and to repair, even reconstitute, broken niches.[189] Occom visited and eventually moved to Brothertown, the pan-Indian settlement in New York, where the community blended Indigenous and Christian practices to make an alternative space. In October 1785, Occom reported, one Native farmer celebrated the traditional Green Corn Festival with a Christian twist: he gathered his corn in the morning and the huskers sang Protestant hymns that afternoon.[190] Natives also turned to the pen, writing sermons, letters, declarations, and petitions to reclaim land and lifeways. "With hearts full of sorrow and grief," Mohegan leaders Henry Quaquaquid and Robert Ashpo sent a petition to the Connecticut Assembly in 1789 to describe their "concerns."[191] They described the history of their ancestral niche, with its central plaza for the corn festival, its hunting grounds toward the northwest, and its planting grounds along the river. They told a strategic story of precolonial sustainability and postcolonial declension, recalling that "our forefathers lived in peace, love and great harmony, and had everything in great plenty." They shared the land. Meat, fish, and nuts were so abundant their northeastern ancestors "planted but little corn and beans." Colonial control of their villages, however, had reduced hunting and farming resources and set Indigenous communities against each other. The Native petitioners asked legislators to restore equity among the villages so that "everyone may have its own fire."

In Indian Country, where 150,000 Natives lived west of the Appalachians and east of the Great Plains, locals still tended their own fires.[192] But even Indigenous communities in Alaska and Hawai'i already had experienced colonial contact. Russians colonized Kodiak by 1784, and in 1779 the British explorer Captain James Cook sailed into the Hawaiian bay named for Lono, their god of agriculture.[193] After Hawaiians discovered Cook's colonial aspirations, they killed him. The European effort to settle the islands was off to a bad start, but American mariners hoped the 1784 inauguration of trade with China and India might go better, as the *Empress of China* sailed into Canton and the *United States* anchored off Pondicherry.[194] Back home, converging imperial forces had transformed much of the landscape on the mainland. New figured niches like the mission and the plantation had emerged, and spiritually diverse urban centers like Philadelphia arose along the Eastern Seaboard and in the cultural centers from Quebec to Mexico City.

In all those places, the devout employed religion for contradictory ends. Faith earnestly sanctioned and prophetically challenged inequity. By 1791 the features of American religion had begun to take shape. Forced and voluntary migrants spoke many languages and worshipped at many altars—enriching the continent's long-standing diversity. For Americans who seemed too different, a vast landscape awaited religious dissenters fleeing hostility. The continent also was home to diverse eco-cultural regions, and, despite the displacements, regional variation still characterized America's piety, Native and non-Native. By 1791 a federal commitment to disestablishment and free exercise coexisted with some state-level Protestant establishments and an emerging civil religion, as at that 1788 Philadelphia procession.[195]

We're tempted to tell stories teleologically, reading the end back into the beginning. We know how things turned out. But in 1791 Americans didn't know.[196] Anna Clifford, a wealthy Quaker loyalist who had attended the Grand Federal Procession three years earlier, confidently predicted the parade's "pageantry" would be remembered but wasn't sure if the political changes would "produce happiness or misery."[197] For those who cherished liberty, hope alternated with anxiety. George Washington felt both. He had done his part for religious liberty—and would do more—but as early as 1775 he had announced his own civic principle. As Washington instructed an officer to seek an alliance with Canadian Catholics and First Nations, especially the Wendat, he ordered troops to respect residents' religions: "While we are Contending for our own Liberty," he warned, "we should be very cautious of violating the Rights of Conscience in others."[198] Would Americans follow that advice in the decades ahead? Would religious liberty—and other liberties—extend to Catholics and Jews, heathens and atheists, and to the women who filled the pews and cleaned the altars but couldn't ascend the pulpit? By 1791 American Catholics had their first bishop, John Carroll, who warned the laity to avoid "pernicious" Protestant texts, which cause the "weed of infidelity" to sprout. A Protestant reply cited the parable of the weeds to imply the devil had sown Catholic teachings, and urged Protestants to separate the "good grain from the chaff."[199] Even if Catholics weren't warmly embraced, the situation had improved: Carroll wasn't marched off to prison like the Maryland Jesuits. Jews also took advantage of the new liberties. They had more synagogues by 1791 and felt secure enough to ask Christians to help them pay off a building debt for their Philadelphia congregation.[200]

Women saw a few signs of progress too. In spring 1776 Abigail Adams, who hoped for legal protections against domestic violence, suggested the delegates "remember the ladies." Congress didn't pass protective legislation, or even ask whether self-evident truths applied to women too. But the idea of liberty had been unleashed. A few months later Abigail's husband, John, complained "our Struggle" prompted challenges to authority from all segments of society, even women, "who will demand a Vote."[201] They wouldn't get the vote until 1920, but elite women like Philadelphia's Elizabeth Powel, the mayor's wife and Washington's friend, had clout, orchestrating political conversations and entertaining power brokers in their fashionable homes.[202] As important, White and Black women in the churches had begun to publish, organize, and preach.

The view from Charleston still looked bleak, but some slaves and former slaves in Boston and Philadelphia saw reason for hope. Appealing to the talk of liberty, Africans in Boston petitioned the Massachusetts legislature for their freedom or even for reparations, as with Belinda, who fondly recalled visits to "a sacred grove" in Ghana before slavers sent her to Massachusetts.[203] After her loyalist master fled to England, the petition noted, the aged woman lacked the resources to care for her disabled daughter. So, to compensate for decades of forced labor, Belinda asked for a pension paid from her master's estate, and legislators awarded her a modest annual payment. Slaves also "stole themselves," as advertisements for runaways in Franklin's *Pennsylvania Gazette* show, and in Philadelphia, the seaboard city with the most free Blacks, some saw encouraging signs.[204] White Protestants formed the Pennsylvania Abolition Society in 1775, the Gradual Abolition Act passed in 1780, and future church leaders Absalom Jones and Richard Allen established the Free African Society in 1787.[205] Passages in America's founding documents and federal laws also inspired hope of religious liberty.[206] Some even hoped Americans might repair the niches broken by enslaving Africans and maltreating Natives. After all, the optimistic could point out, the 1787 Northwest Ordinance prohibited slavery in the new Great Lakes states and demanded the respectful treatment of Native communities. Yet the Great Seal's designer, who was less optimistic, made a chilling but prescient prediction: Slavery, Thomson wrote in a 1785 letter to Jefferson, "is a blot on our character that must be wiped out. If it cannot be done by religion, reason, and philosophy, confident I am that it will one day be by blood."[207] Sadly, there would be blood—and anguish—soon after the exhilaration of the Constitutional Procession and well before the bloodbath of the Civil War.[208] Some spiritually figured niches in the agrarian empire would grow more stressed, and the Naturalization Act of 1790, which limited citizenship to free Whites, didn't help. To enslaved Blacks and displaced Natives who insisted the gospel of liberty was meant for all, there seemed to be more weeds than wheat in the American garden. And Judgment Day, the final sorting out, seemed a long way off.

CHAPTER 6

Expansionist Religion

Expanding and Contracting Worlds in the Agrarian "Empire of Liberty," 1792–1848

In 1792 the Revolutionary War general Rufus Putnam and the Kaskaskia chief John Baptist de Coigne passed the peace pipe to open a treaty meeting beside the Wabash River.[1] The Catholic chief traveled to Indiana from his village on the Mississippi; the Protestant Ohio Company executive came from Marietta, a settlement built around a 2,000-year-old burial mound that would eventually adorn the town's cemetery and appear on promotional material (fig. 28).[2] Putnam worried about violence destabilizing the region and knew the Northwest Ordinance promised to respect Indigenous "property, rights, and liberty."[3] So to address their grievances—and protect his investment—he negotiated the return of Native prisoners. Putnam's respectful treatment of the traumatized women and children led to a treaty, which included an article admitting the land was "originally" theirs. But the US Senate refused to ratify it. So Indigenous grievances remained unaddressed two years later when settlers resumed the westward trek to Marietta, a town with a government-paid minister but no church buildings. While settlers negotiated church–state arrangements and reimagined Native relations, they confronted another issue—slavery. Putnam and the other delegates drafting the Ohio Constitution kept slavery out but failed to grant Blacks access to the ballot.[4]

By the time Putnam was interred in Mound Cemetery in 1824, he had confronted the Early Republic's most pressing issues, and, as in Ohio, leaders faced two crucial questions by 1792, the tercentenary of European

Figure 28. A representation of the burial mound at "Mound Cemetery," Marietta, Ohio. From Henry Howe, *Historical Collections*, vol. 1 (J. W. Barber and Howe, 1846), 516. Courtesy of the Mennonite Historical Library, Goshen College, Indiana.

colonialism and a year after the First Amendment's ratification.[5] Federal legislators had prohibited a religious establishment but approved a congressional chaplain and enacted a civil religion. So first, how would Americans work out the relation between religion and the state? Second, the founders and framers, who assumed slavery would end and the "empire of liberty" would be transcontinental, bequeathed an unresolved crisis caused by African enslavement and Native displacement.[6] How would the postrevolutionary generation handle the sectional divisions that prompted constitutional compromises on slavery, and how would they treat Indigenous Peoples as US territory expanded?

This chapter's opening section addresses the first question, sketching America's emerging solution to church–state relations. The remainder focuses on the second question and acknowledges that US political borders expanded and church buildings proliferated as settlers moved westward, but suggests that migrants didn't just transplant the New England village in an uninhabited wilderness, as you might conclude after reading about Marietta's founding in classic religious surveys.[7] Natives were there, slaves were nearby, and the new settlements were initially unchurched and increasingly diverse. The traditional theme of expansion captures some of the period's changes. Mental maps expanded for elite readers introduced to India's religions, especially

Hinduism, and, as in Marietta, some Americans' sense of time elongated as they encountered the continent's ancient mounds, even if that didn't improve their assessments of contemporary Natives.[8] Further, while westward-moving Whites experienced a widening world, the slave system expanded too, as did efforts to control enslaved laborers and displace Indigenous Peoples. The crossings went in multiple directions—eastward from the Pacific, westward to Indian Territory, and southward to the Cotton Belt. Most important, there was contraction as well as expansion. "My land is but small," one chief told President Washington in 1793, and "if any more [land] be taken from us . . . we shall not be able to live."[9] Despite such pleas, lived worlds contracted as imperial borders expanded, even if spiritually inspired movements for Indigenous revitalization, social reform, soil restoration, and slave resistance emerged.[10] By sacralizing territorial expansion—as well as slavery's extension and Natives' "removal"—religious and political leaders intensified the lingering Colonial Era crisis of sustainability and made it harder for the enslaved and the displaced to meet the minimal needs for subsistence, much less the optimal conditions for full flourishing.

While President Washington was in the capital (Philadelphia) and awaiting a meeting with Putnam and Native chiefs, New Yorkers were attending the first Columbus Day celebration on 12 October 1792.[11] Not everyone would celebrate colonialism during the next five decades, however, since psychic trauma, social inequity, and ecological stress intensified as US borders expanded. While the number of states doubled from fifteen to thirty, things got worse for most Blacks and Natives, and, despite a movement for gender equity, White women still didn't enjoy "the full blessings of liberty." The lived world felt smaller for those shackled on the plantation, confined to "woman's sphere," or exiled to a tract in Indian Territory. By 1848 many White Christians still had not confronted the colonial crisis, and, to make things worse, signs of a looming industrial crisis started to appear in northeastern cities (see appendix).[12]

Religion and the New Republic

Americans offered a complex answer to the question about religion and the state. The First Amendment had defined the legal rules for religious competition, but that didn't stop diverse communities from claiming national belonging or prevent Protestants from presuming they played the central role in God's plan for the country.[13] In this period, however, those claims to national primacy would be limited by the disestablishment of denominations in the states, challenged by the plurality of worldviews, and offset by the consolidation of civil religion.

Within a few decades of the Revolution, the landscape looked more Christian, and residents were more churchgoing, though there also was more occult dabbling and rationalist freethinking.[14] A hierarchical planter piety justified southern slavery and Native dispersal, but a populist impulse and democratic spirit also emerged among some Protestants.[15] Most important, the statutory disestablishment that began at the federal level in 1791 culminated at the state level in 1833, when Massachusetts ended financial support for the Congregational Church. That didn't mean, however, that the federal government sought to safeguard First Amendment rights in local communities. That wouldn't happen until the mid-twentieth century. The responsibility for working out the meaning of disestablishment fell to state legislators, who focused on protecting the individual's spiritual liberty by requiring lay congregational control and limiting religious groups' annual incomes and land holdings.[16] A Maryland congregation, for instance, couldn't bring in more than $2,000 or own more than two acres. These legal changes—as well as federal statutes guiding western and southern settlement—benefited the agile upstart denominations like the Methodists, Disciples of Christ, and Baptists and not the status-guarding churches that predominated on the eve of the Revolution. Jews and Catholics made small advances too. Influential Jews used "a mobile assemblage" of spiritual tools to accommodate the western movement and Protestant nationalism of the age.[17] Catholics' patriot credentials insulated them from hostility before the 1820s, though anti-Catholicism spiked again as new migrants began worrying Protestants, who responded with alarmist books and violent riots.[18]

It was a time when almost everyone looked to the past to secure their place in the present: descendants of Massachusetts's "Pilgrims" (Daniel Webster), Maryland's "Catholic Pilgrims" (John McCaffrey), Virginia's plantation slaves (William Grimes), and New England's Aboriginal inhabitants (William Apess).[19] Authors crafted competing historical narratives that exalted or lamented colonialism's legacy—and disputed who had been "civilized" and "savage." The plural plots widened or narrowed "American" identity, and—like the scenes John Trumbull painted for the Capitol, the national history Emma Willard penned for the schoolroom, and the patriotic quilt Susan Strong stitched for her home—the narratives provided resources for contemporaries to begin to transform the state-nation, the loose confederation of states, into a nation-state, a unified republic with a shared story.[20]

Religion was the first language of American nationalism, and the patriotic could appeal to civil religion, which solidified after George Washington's death in 1799, when the displays of symbolic surplus recalled lavish pre-Columbian interments.[21] Philadelphia's worship service and memorial procession was the largest public event since the Constitutional parade, and more than 300 clerical eulogies appeared within months of the president's death.[22] Indigenous leaders frustrated by Washington's broken promises said little, but tributes included a printed sermon by the African Methodist Episcopal (AME) Church's founder, Richard Allen. He praised the "country's deliverer" for freeing his slaves in his will and assured Whites that Blacks mourned too.[23] The over-the-top verbal, visual, and performative expressions provided a toolbox of symbols that citizens used to consecrate Washington as America's first civic saint, as popular representations of his ascension to heaven suggest (fig. 29). A version of that scene later would adorn the Capitol rotunda's canopy, and by 1848 the blending of God and country already had become commonplace in inaugural addresses, state funerals, and Fourth of July celebrations.[24] Civic piety also found expression in the churches and memorials being erected in the new federal capital. The original plan for the District of Columbia proposed a nonsectarian church "for national purposes."[25] That never materialized, but St. John's Episcopal (1816), across from the White House, claimed to be the "church of presidents."[26] James Monroe did sit in the "presidential pew" during his years in office and every president since James Madison has attended a worship service there.

The civil religion that would inform the "redeemer nation's" domestic and foreign policy couldn't be associated with any single religious institution.[27] Yet some White Protestants still made aspirational claims, suggesting the US was a Protestant nation, even though the constitutional battle had been waged and lost. The Continental Congress and Constitutional delegates had settled the matter—and the states reaffirmed that solution when they ratified the First Amendment. To be sure, disestablishment's meaning would continue to be debated and, even if Catholics would outnumber Presbyterians by 1848, signs of Protestant power were indisputable. East of the Mississippi and places farther west a de facto or unofficial establishment was emerging.[28] Thousands of new Protestant churches also dotted the terrain. Yet Protestant claims on the nation's identity remained assertions in the subjunctive mood: they expressed a wish more than they stated a fact. By 1848, as construction was underway on the Washington Monument, Pacific islanders had sailed to Oregon and Russian Orthodox adherents had settled in Alaska.[29] Irish Catholics were crossing the Atlantic to flee the potato fam-

Figure 29. John James Barralet's *Apotheosis of Washington* (1800–1802). Washington rises from a tomb, signifying his divinity. In the lower right, a Native American mourns. To his left are Liberty, the American eagle, and the Great Seal's motto, "E pluribus unum." Engraving and etching on plate. Courtesy of the Metropolitan Museum of Art.

ine as Chinese "heathens" were crossing the Pacific to seek California gold. The victory over Mexico brought more southwestern Catholics and Natives within America's political borders. By the end of this period, the proliferation of spiritual pluralism and consolidation of civil religion were as noteworthy as Protestants' ecclesiastical advances and transcontinental aspirations.

Expansionist Religion and Regional Niches

But those transcontinental aspirations did shape religious history between 1792 and 1848. Americans glorified farmers, spread slavery, displaced Natives, and appealed to divine sanction, as political borders expanded with the purchase of Louisiana (1803), the negotiation for Florida (1819), the annexation of Texas (1845), the treaty for Oregon (1846), and the victory over Mexico (1848). A journalist first used the phrase "manifest destiny" in 1845 to suggest God favored continental expansion, yet many Whites already had sanctified the impulse to move and the right to displace.[30] Many also continued to believe democratic citizenship required the moral virtues agriculture instilled. The expanding agrarian empire required, in Jefferson's phrase, "virtuous cultivators" who tended the seeds of virtue in the pews and in the fields. After the 1820s, expansionists still agreed about all that, but two divergent conceptions of divinely favored expansion fought for dominance.[31] The first, affirmed by the Jeffersonians and grounded in the Enlightenment, venerated the rationalism and egalitarianism of the Declaration of Independence and affirmed the antislavery and church–state separation clauses in the Northwest Ordinance. The second, exemplified by Andrew Jackson and stirred by the sentiments celebrated by "Romantic nationalism," emphasized social hierarchy and White superiority, favored the Constitution's proslavery clauses, and revered the Bible (or, more accurately, a status quo–conserving interpretation of it).[32] Except for the most cynically self-interested, expansionists of both sorts believed they were doing the right thing. Yet both camps compromised cherished principles and shared responsibility for expansion's high moral cost, especially its limiting of Blacks' and Natives' ability to meet the conditions for full flourishing in the stressed eco-cultural niches along the Ohio River, around the Great Lakes, across the South, and in the West.

The initial justification for expansion was articulated during Jefferson's presidency (1801–1809), and that rationalist rhetoric continued with his protégé and fellow planter, the Episcopalian James Monroe (1817–1825), who negotiated the "compromise" extending slavery into Missouri.[33] Expansionist rhetoric escalated during the administrations of two cotton-growing Presbyterian presidents from Tennessee—Andrew Jackson (1829–1837) and James Polk (1845–1849). Those slaveholding planters embraced the second version of manifest destiny. But, like Jefferson, they also appealed to the emerging civil religion, as their inaugural addresses show. Jefferson's second address had imagined the US as a New Israel, even if his own miracle-less spirituality inclined toward deism.[34] Jackson and Polk, who were more conventionally religious, also relied on the imperialist aspirations of a blustery nationalist Protestantism. And those presidents would be emboldened by military incursions and legal decisions that accelerated expansion. Jefferson had ordered militia to battle "Indian savages" on the western frontier to "add to the Empire of liberty an extensive and fertile Country" for farmers.[35] By 1819 Jackson had invaded Florida to conquer unfriendly Natives, recover fugitive slaves, and acquire Spanish land. By 1823 the US Supreme Court had applied the 1493 papal "discovery doctrine" to Native homelands and classified Indigenous Peoples as "domestic, dependent nations," thereby claiming contested territory and erasing Indigenous borders.[36] Jackson's 1830 State of the Union address trumpeted religious nationalism and justified Indian removal by pointing to the need for "prosperous farms."[37] Polk, who owned a Mississippi cotton plantation and favored displacing local tribes, actualized an aggressive and divisive imperialist vision.[38] He extended slavery's western reach, gained territory by defeating Mexico, and claimed the Pacific Coast by adding Oregon and California.

To enact this expansionist creed—or just make a fresh start—about 1.5 million persons born in the East would head West by 1850.[39] Spiritually diverse settlers and horse-riding preachers crossed a boundary to the south, the Tennessee River, and headed for the Cotton Kingdom's cultural hearth along the Mississippi, while others traversed western barriers—the Appalachians, the Mississippi, and the Rockies. Interacting with Natives already there, settlers transformed the landscape. Together they made and remade a patchwork quilt of spiritually inflected niches. Quilt making, a popular women's craft at the time, is a useful analogy for interpreting settler place-making, as long as we remember that the Indigenous had already stitched "blocks" onto the landscape.[40] Resilient Native communities also retained mental maps or, as with the Minnesota Anishinaabe (Ojibwe), birch bark scrolls showing migration routes and ceremonial sites.[41] The southeastern Cherokee also had mental maps, and, for them, Appalachia's Great Smoky Mountains weren't a barrier to be crossed.[42] Those peaks were the center of the world, a site for communal veneration and world renewal. That's why some refused to leave, even when threatened with military force.

Seeing settler place-making as akin to quilt making reminds us that women participated, just as they made patchwork blankets. Mining, whaling, and fur-trading niches attracted mostly men—even if a few women went on whaling voyages.[43] But women were important historical actors as farming and ranching families went west along the Ohio River, trekked southward to the Cotton Belt, or staked out pastures on the Plains. Settlements, like quilts, were communal ventures that welcomed all hands. In 1847 female members of a Presbyterian Church in upstate New York gifted the departing minister's wife with a quilt of sixty signed blocks.[44] Even that "album quilt," all the rage at the time, followed a pattern. There was a semifixed design transmitted orally that allowed for creativity, as with Susan Strong's decision to place vines, not arrows, in the eagle's talons in her patriotic quilt.

Well-known quilt styles such as "Jacob's Ladder" referenced biblical themes, just as some settlers, like the planners of not only Marietta but Connecticut's Western Reserve, tried to reproduce eastern spiritual patterns.[45] There in present-day Ohio, the Connecticut Missionary Society and Connecticut Land Company imagined a New England village along the shores of Lake Erie. A 1796 map of Cleveland, for example, mostly erased Native presence.[46] Two Indigenous men stand by the river, but the design positioned two-acre lots around a New England village green. That church–state pattern couldn't be replicated, however; the spiritual descendants of the Puritans had to accept a reduced role in Cleveland. Episcopalians would build the first church in 1816, three years before the Congregationalists in 1819. Next came the Presbyterians (1820), Methodists (1827), the African American Episcopal Church (1830), Baptists (1833), Universalists (1834), and Unitarians (1836). The Shakers erected a meetinghouse in their North Union community (1822) southeast of town, and the Latter-day Saints (LDS), a new religious movement organized in New York by Joseph Smith, built a temple in nearby Kirtland (1836). By the 1840s the Congregationalist dream of a homogeneous New England village seemed even harder to realize, as Catholics and Jews also arrived.[47]

Diverse migrants and local circumstances forced spiritual leaders and town planners to alter the pattern elsewhere too. Just as patchwork quilts revealed unexpected detail—frayed homespun fabric here and factory-made broadcloth there—the settler landscape included a variety of regional ecocultural niches.[48] Those habitats were transformed by residents' lifeways—fur trading or farming, for instance—and affected by climate and terrain. Many locales, like Cleveland, were so diverse they defied spiritual classification, while a distinctive experiential Protestantism developed in the Appalachian Mountains.[49] A string of Catholic Indigenous farming missions stretched along El Camino Real from San Diego to San Francisco, and a Russian Orthodox domain, an icon zone, was forming in Alaska, where locals trapped furs and caught fish. A patchwork of fields marked the Moravian farming enclave in central North Carolina as well as the Methodist-Baptist rural South. A Latter-day Saints region started to form in the Intermountain

West, as their temple-centered plan overlaid a Shoshone landscape where ancient worshippers had placed prayer stones in caves.[50] That Great Basin area was north of the Comanche horse culture that dominated the southwestern Plains, south of the Lakota horse culture that dominated the northern Plains, and west of the Pueblo Catholic agricultural communities in New Mexico, which became US territory in 1848.[51]

Christianizing the Ohio River Valley

An earlier historian offered advice for those hoping to understand the trans-Appalachian region: "Stand at Cumberland Gap and watch the procession of civilization marching, single file—the buffalo following the trail to the salt springs, the Indian, the fur-trader and hunter, the cattle-raiser, the pioneer farmer."[52] As Western historians and Indigenous Peoples have noted, it wasn't "civilization" marching past.[53] It was militia, officials, and land speculators who would dispossess many midwestern Natives and create a Great Lakes "scatter zone."[54] The Wilderness Road from Cumberland Gap, an opening between Appalachian ridges, was a well-worn path for west-moving wagons, and it did provide a glimpse of settler colonialism's advance. Yet if you wanted the perfect vantage for glimpsing the region's religious life it might be better to board a flatboat—or, after 1830, a steamboat—along the Ohio River, as it crossed six states, connected to the Mississippi, and from there allowed access to St. Louis and New Orleans.

By 1800 the river valley, transformed by ancient earthwork designs and French Catholic missions, had become a "middle kingdom" between east and west as well north and south.[55] Or, to return to quilt imagery, it was a *seam,* a thread stitching together regional niches, a transition area between climatic regions, a jagged space where plants and animals from distinct bioregions mixed.[56] Congress stitched borders there by defining the Northwest Territory as land north and west of the Ohio River, so the river became a north-south dividing line, slavery's frayed edge, since the slaveholding zone began on the Kentucky side of the river.[57] The Ohio was a spiritual seam too. There the planter piety of the South met the abolitionist religion of the North; the church-steeple piety of the East met the log-cabin piety of the West. By positioning our narrative there on the seam, new ritual spaces, spiritual styles, and institutional forms come into view (fig. 30).

Considering Cincinnati, an Ohio city with more than 100 congregations, would offer a glimpse of the region's spiritual diversity, but religious influences on the southern side of the river, in Kentucky, also were

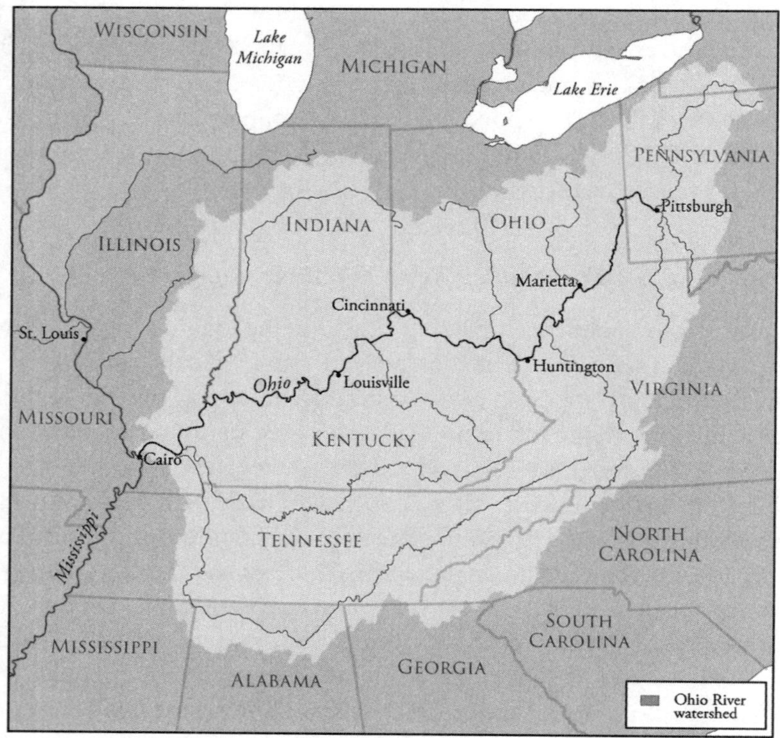

Figure 30. Map of the Ohio River Valley, with key Early National towns, including Marietta, Louisville, and Cincinnati. Beehive Mapping.

important.[58] Vibrant but volatile Kentucky was the origin of camp-meeting Protestantism and fiddle-dancing Catholicism—as well as new denominations and dioceses. It was admitted to the Union in 1792 as the first state west of the Appalachians, but settlers started arriving while it was still part of Virginia. With the soil depleted in tobacco fields, some growers like James Monroe planted clover to restore nitrogen levels, but other Protestants from Virginia and Catholics from Maryland headed for Kentucky.[59] The settling process was more haphazard than in Marietta and Cleveland, with no plotted grid. Kentucky was also spiritually untamed. Amid the region's fighting, swearing, and drinking, a Presbyterian observer found few in 1783 who made "a credible profession of religion."[60] David Barrow, a Baptist, had only a slightly better impression in 1795.[61] He was enthralled by the ancient mounds, but contemporary piety elicited only qualified praise. Barrow found little "vital religion" anywhere during the mid-1790s, as deistic "infidelity" peaked.

Popular occult traditions also heightened the spiritual confusion. Kentuckians' *Farmer's Almanac,* for example, displayed an astrological chart of "Man's Body" as governed by the constellations.[62] But Barrow did notice a Christianization of the landscape. He found "almost all denominations," including Methodists, Universalists, and Catholics, even if "Deists, Nothingarians, and anythingerians" predominated. The rationalist "nothingarians" disrespected the Bible, while the credulous "anythingerians" accepted every prophet who floated down river. Deism remained popular until 1810, but spiritual options proliferated and sources of authority corroded.[63] Many felt what Latter-day Saints founder Joseph Smith called a spiritual agitation due to the "war of words."[64] Smith would find clarity when two "personages" appeared to him, but backwoods Kentuckians without private revelations remained confused. Barrow didn't help the situation when he moved to Kentucky, adding an abolitionist Baptist voice to the shrill debates in that slave state.[65]

The clamor presented pastoral problems, but most Indigenous and Christian leaders agreed on the solution: a spiritual revitalization, a vibrant personal piety, was needed, though renewal took different forms. Among the Shawnee, the vision-seeing prophet Tenskwatawa urged alcohol-drinking Natives along the Ohio to return to traditional holy ways. Among the fiddle-loving Catholics on the Kentucky side of the river, priests discouraged raucous dances and introduced a catechism that invited devotees to "a holy life," while Protestant revivalists in Kentucky invited enlivened camp meeting attendees to accept Jesus's offer of salvation.[66]

A Protestant religion of the heart returned, generating sudden conversions at Cane Ridge, Kentucky, in August 1801. Richard McNemar and other log cabin preachers had been prompting emotional outbursts since 1797, so when Barton Stone of Cane Ridge Meeting House planned the 1801 event, he knew how to spread the word, arrange the space, and provoke the hearers, who came from Ohio, Tennessee, and Indiana as well as Kentucky. They arrived in a thousand wagons, as 20,000 attendees heard preachers gesturing from stumps, wagons, or makeshift altars.[67] Most also noticed worshippers' "bodily agitations."[68] McNemar saw rolling, when devotees "rolled over and over like a wheel"; jerking, when they twitched as if prodded "with a piece of red-hot iron"; and barking, as the Spirit moved them to get on all fours and bark like a dog.[69]

There wasn't a lot of barking in New Haven, Connecticut, where Yale's learned president Timothy Dwight prompted more decorous conversions, but news of the great Kentucky revival, the "holy fire," reached there and spread south and west, provoking critics and prompting imitators.[70] Cane Ridge continued to have an impact long after the wagons had left.[71] Diverse people mixed at later camp meetings, attracting women and men, the young and the elderly, Blacks and Whites—and sometimes Natives too. In the summer of 1819, 100 Wendat and their Methodist pastor attended an Ohio camp meeting.[72] African Americans also preached at camp meetings, and some revivalists criticized slavery, intensifying North–South divisions and increasing intradenominational tensions. In fact, Cane Ridge prompted religious switching and denominational splits.[73] McNemar joined the Shakers, and Barton cofounded a new denomination, the Disciples of Christ.[74] Presbyterians lost interest, and soon it was mostly Methodists organizing camp meetings. A decade after Cane Ridge, 3 million Americans were attending camp meetings each year.[75] This new kind of worship space prompted different ways of arranging the service and the site, even a designated area where the spirit-filled could roll and jerk without harming anyone.[76] How-to manuals explained how to replicate the space and the experience.[77] In the decades ahead, influential preachers like Charles G. Finney would modify the arrangement and codify the methods—and clear the path for twentieth-century evangelists like Billy Graham.[78]

Kentucky's Catholic clergy, who derided Cane Ridge's "contagious frenzy" and struggled to tame their congregants' emotional excesses, made their own enduring contributions.[79] Father Stephen Badin, the first priest ordained in the US, hoped for spiritual revitalization too, but he worried about the fiddle-induced ecstasy at church dances in central Kentucky. In 1796 he complained about the drinking, fighting, and sexual intimacy at a congregational dance near Bardstown.[80] That happened, another priest explained, because of "the practice of electrifying the feet of the guests by the sounds of the fiddle."[81] The all-night dances were "delirium and madness," and fiddle Catholicism—which mixed Blacks and Whites as well as women and men—couldn't be easily stopped, though the clergy tried.[82] In 1819, for instance, ecstatic dancers stepped energetically at Holy Mary Church as three enslaved fiddlers played "Turkey in the Straw" for an hour, until the perturbed priest announced, "We will now have the rosary until sundown."[83]

Congregants didn't recite the rosary as enthusiastically as they danced, but lay Catholics adapted to the priests, who tried to contain the spiritual frenzy and build an ecclesial infrastructure. Kentucky's Catholics had hailed from slaveholding Maryland, including sixty families who relocated to Bardstown in 1785, and more came later to central Kentucky's "Holy Land," where Catholics catechized slaves but didn't free them.[84] By 1810 Father Badin had been given ten enslaved laborers, who worked his farm while he was off building church institutions.[85] And institutions did grow. Baltimore had become a node in Rome's transnational network when John Carroll was named its first bishop in 1789. The massive first US diocese included the trans-Appalachian "frontier," and it was Carroll who asked Badin to move to Kentucky, where the priest was still serving in 1808 when dioceses were added in Bardstown as well as in Boston, New York, and Philadelphia.[86] Sprawling Bardstown, which the Vatican would subdivide to create dioceses in Cincinnati (1821), St. Louis (1826), and Chicago (1843), stretched from the Appalachians to the Mississippi.

Back in Baltimore, Carroll spent a good deal of time building churches and encouraging seminaries, schools, and orders. He helped Georgetown College, for instance, and he encouraged America's first native-born saint, Elizabeth Seton, as she established the first parish school and founded the Sisters of Charity. Carroll was especially interested in church building—more than 100 were constructed by 1809—though he cared most about the Baltimore Cathedral (1821), a neoclassical structure planned by Benjamin Latrobe, an architect who designed sections of the White House and Capitol.[87] It inaugurated an American tradition of using monumental churches to claim civic space, a practice that culminated in the twentieth century with Washington's National Cathedral and the National Shrine of the Immaculate Conception.[88] Baltimore's hilltop cathedral was visible to approaching wagons and ships, and to worshippers entering the city's Protestant churches. Early-nineteenth-century Catholics, then, had their own expansionist vision, as clerics tried to demonstrate their faith's superiority by building churches, convents, seminaries, schools, orphanages, and hospitals—in short, by transforming the built environment.[89] In that sense, the cathedral buttressed Catholic claims to American presence and global reach.[90] The hilltop sanctuary loomed over multi-steeple Baltimore but also sent a signal across the continent and around the world.

The message was received in Kentucky, where Bardstown's bishop built the first "western" cathedral, and by 1815 Kentucky's Catholics worshipped in nineteen church structures.[91] They also celebrated other firsts by establishing schools, seminaries, colleges, and religious orders.[92] The Sisters of Loretto was the first women's religious order in the US not founded on European communal rules, and the Trappists made two attempts to establish monasteries in Kentucky.[93]

Their second attempt yielded the Cistercian Abbey of Our Lady of Gethsemane, which Thomas Merton would enter later, but the earlier Trappist group deserves mention because its leader established a monastic community

(1809–1813) beside Cahokia's largest mound, which was named "Monks Mound" in their honor in 1811, a time when Euro-Americans were "discovering" the continent's ancient religious past.[94] Between 1775, when a Boston magazine circulated the first map of an Ohio earthwork, and 1848, when the Smithsonian Institution's *Ancient Monuments of the Mississippi Valley* published an image of Marietta's mounds, elites celebrated "American antiquities" as rivals of the ancient temples of Egypt and Rome.[95] Marietta's leaders even gave the mounds Latin names to reaffirm the classical associations, and town planners in Circleville, Ohio, and Moundsville, West Virginia, linked their communities' identity with the ceremonial spaces and mortuary mounds of the Adena and Hopewell Peoples who lived in the Ohio Valley between 1000 BCE and 500 CE.[96] Travelers also gushed about those ancient structures, as when Lewis and Clark praised the "remarkable artificial mound" they saw near Wheeling: a seventy-foot-tall mound dating to 100 BCE.[97] Travelers who followed the Ohio west to the Mississippi also marveled at the later Mississippian Era mound complex at Cahokia, which the Trappists reconsecrated in the name of a very different farming faith, one that used a red sacramental wine instead of a ritual black drink and venerated a Virgin intercessor instead of a Corn Goddess.[98]

Those self-supporting Trappists planted wheat on Monks Mound and made watches they sold across the river in St. Louis, where a Cahokian "Big Mound" was still visible in the 1840s (fig. 31).[99] By then the riverside outpost in Indian country had become a gateway city in a slaveholding state that opened to the trans-Mississippi West.[100] The French had founded colonial St. Louis as a fur trading post with a log cabin Catholic church. In an 1804 ceremony marking the political change after the Louisiana Purchase, the outgoing Spanish administrator told residents they no longer needed to show allegiance to "his Catholic majesty." With that pronouncement and a few signatures, the terrain transferred from Spain to France to the US.[101] In many ways, however, it retained its French Catholic character until Missouri entered the Union in 1821. After statehood, that city on the National Road welcomed more domestic and foreign-born migrants. By 1848 the foreign-born outnumbered the native-born.[102] Many newcomers, including transplanted Yankees, were Protestant. In 1817 Baptists founded a congregation, and that would be joined by Presbyterian, Methodist, and Lutheran congregations, though Catholics still predominated in 1834, when the bishop opened a new cathedral, the first west of the Mississippi.

From the riverbank, St. Louis residents looked east and south as well as west. Enslaved churchgoers looked east as they reimagined the Mississippi

Figure 31. View of St. Louis with the "Big Mound" off to the right. John Caspar Wild, *North East View of St. Louis from the Illinois Shore,* lithograph, ca. 1839. Courtesy of the American Antiquarian Society, call no. Lithf Wild Nort.

as the biblical River Jordan, which the Israelites crossed to enter the Promised Land, and some Blacks actually crossed over to make a legal claim to freedom in Illinois.[103] Antislavery Whites like the Reverend Elijah Lovejoy, editor of the *St. Louis Observer,* had to cross the Mississippi to escape mob violence, only to be shot as he defended his abolitionist newspaper.[104] St. Louis Whites who loathed Lovejoy and traded with slaveholders looked downriver, where by the 1840s the power of the plantation had grown and slaves' and Natives' ability to flourish had diminished.

Expansion and Contraction in the Cotton South

Congress outlawed foreign importation of slaves in 1808, the first year the Constitution allowed a ban, but the plantation system was still thriving four decades later. In fact, the number in bondage swelled from almost 700,000 in 1790 to more than 3 million in 1850.[105] There was a slight increase in the largest slaveholding state, Virginia, where about one in three residents lived in bondage at midcentury, but a steep rise in Mississippi, the heart of the Cotton South, where the percentage of slaves jumped more than 300 percent from 1800 to 1810. By 1850 more than half of the state's population was enslaved.

The plantation system's expansion—and the contraction of Blacks' and Natives' lived worlds—happened for several reasons. The planter class gained political clout because of compromises made during the Constitutional Convention in Philadelphia. The Constitution delayed the date when Congress could ban importing human cargo (Article 1, Section 9); other clauses perpetuated bondage, including provisions mandating escaped "servants" be returned (Article 4, Section 2) and calculating representation by including slaves, even if they only counted as three-fifths of a person (Article 1, Section 2).[106] The lure of cotton profits also prompted change. By midcentury, cotton would become more valuable than tobacco, sugar, or rice. More land, therefore, was devoted to its cultivation. The textile network also extended to Europe and Asia and touched every US region. Bankers in New York City financed cotton planters, and the city exported manufactured textiles. Western and northern farmers earned cash for food shipped to the Cotton Belt. New England mills received bales from New Orleans, and more went to Liverpool and then on to British manufacturers. From England, merchants shipped the yarn to distant ports like Calcutta, and it might be woven into a shirt in rural India.[107] This global commodity chain impacted the Upper South too, as overseers from tobacco-growing Virginia and Maryland marched slaves south to sell them, prompting an "African-American trail of tears," with 1 million shackled Blacks going south by 1860.[108] Natives on cotton-growing land also would be displaced, a process that intensified with the Indian Removal Act of 1830, which forced the Southeast's "Five Civilized Tribes" (Cherokee, Chickasaw, Choctaw, Muskogee, and Seminole) to relocate to smaller parcels with inferior soil in Indian Territory. Finally, religion played a key role. In response to spiritually framed resistance to slavery, elite Southerners fortified their conscience-soothing planter piety.

RELIGIOUS RESISTANCE

The enslaved continued to use religion to assert dignity and nurture hope. Charms and beads excavated from slave cabins on Andrew Jackson's plantation show that traditional African practices for promoting good fortune survived into the mid-nineteenth century.[109] So did Islam. African-born Muslims continued solitary devotions, even if their children no longer identified with the tradition.[110] Plantation records and runaway notices mention Muslim names like Mahomet and Fatima, and some slaves prayed daily and fasted during Ramadan, the holy month. 'Umar ibn Said, who was born in modern-day Senegal and knew Arabic Islamic sources, escaped from the abusive owner of a South Carolina plantation before a North Carolina Protestant bought him and tried to convert him.[111] Yet in a later autobiography Said claimed Christian identity without severing his connection to Islam, as he opened by quoting *al-Mulk,* the Qur'an's sixty-seventh chapter.[112]

Some used Christianity to resist. Charleston's bishop John England stopped short of proclaiming a gospel of equality, even though Pope Gregory XVI condemned the slave trade in 1839 and southern Catholic slaves participated in the liturgical community.[113] After the rise of the camp meeting, some Blacks expected to be included in worship, and weekly services and intermittent revivals were rarely all-White affairs.[114] Some Blacks complained when treated disrespectfully. A Georgia slave wrote an 1821 protest letter to an itinerant White preacher, for example, asking why "you always preach to the white folks and keep you back to us" and suggesting Whites pretended to care about slaves' spiritual state but "never once inquire whither you sold to a heathon or a christian."[115] Some Blacks also felt called to preach. Free Black women in the North risked their safety to bring the gospel to southern slaves, as with Zilpha Elaw, who had been "overpowered with the presence of God" at an 1817 camp meeting and then took multiple mission trips to the South.[116] Southern slaves preached too. In 1822 a Baptist in Virginia named Old Jerry conducted an outdoor slave funeral with such "a clear and impressive tone of voice" that a White passerby felt moved to repent his "unmerited prejudice."[117]

Others looked to the African homeland. A new position in the national debate emerged in 1816 with the founding of the American Colonization Society (ACS), which favored the return of free Blacks to Africa.[118] The idea came from a Quaker who was the son of a Black father and an Indigenous mother, and it was embraced by both gradual abolitionists and slavery apologists, who argued that emigration would reduce the free Black population and thereby the risks of racial mixing and violent rebellion.[119] In 1824 the ACS purchased land to found Liberia, where 4,291 African Americans would emigrate by 1843. Six northern states and four in the Upper South embraced the ACS strategy, and governing bodies of the Presbyterian, Methodist, Baptist, and Episcopalian churches endorsed it too. Support for the African colonization movement waned, however. Richard Allen argued against it in 1827, suggesting that "this land, which we have watered with our tears, and our blood, is now our mother country."[120] Such critiques convinced many of slavery's opponents, White and Black, to seek other solutions after 1831.

That was the year when antislavery agitation turned up the heat on Southern planters and ministers. Denmark Vesey, a free Black AME member who believed the Bible taught equality, had been falsely accused of plotting to overthrow Charleston's planter society in 1822. The cooked-up charges—and subsequent execution of thirty-five Blacks—provided fuel for the fire.[121] Three years later William Grimes fanned the flames by publishing the first fugitive slave narrative, which condemned America's failure to live up to its principles: "If it were not for the stripes on my back which were made while I was a slave, I would leave my skin as a legacy to the government, desiring that it might be made into parchment, and then bind the constitution of glorious, happy, and *free* America."[122] Ten years after the AME Church established the first Black publishing house, the first Black newspaper (*Freedom's Journal*) appeared in 1827.[123] Two years later a contributing editor, David Walker, published his *Appeal* to "coloured citizens." He warned planters that God would not tolerate slavery: "your DESTRUCTION is at hand, and will be speedily consummated unless you REPENT."[124] And in 1831 the Lord's patience ran out. The enslaved preacher Nat Turner led a widely publicized uprising in Virginia. The Spirit told him to proclaim liberty to slaves and deliver judgment to Whites, so Turner led about sixty enslaved and free Blacks wielding axes during a two-day uprising that killed fifty-seven Whites, many of whom were decapitated.[125] Word of the insurrection spread hope to slave quarters, though it ended with Turner's severed head on a stake, a warning to would-be rebels. In Jamaica the Baptist War, an 1831 insurrection involving nearly 60,000 enslaved workers, tilted British public opinion toward antislavery and attracted attention in the South.[126] Northern abolitionists attracted attention that year too. White reformer William Lloyd Garrison, who communicated with Black activists and favored immediate abolition, tended the fires of resistance through his newly launched antislavery newspaper, the *Liberator*.[127]

PLANTER PIETY

Southerners shaken by Turner's revolt and Garrison's abolitionism responded by tightening control on their plantations and adding more patrols. But they also advocated slave evangelization and reformulated planter piety. A hierarchical Christianity that encouraged subordination, they hoped, might challenge slaves' subversive religion and abolitionists' haughty humanitarianism. When conscience generated doubt or guilt, plantation owners and their clerical defenders could seek comfort in their evangelizing effort and reinvigorated theology.[128] Systematized planter piety would peak with *Cotton*

Is King (1860), the "*summa theologica* of pro-slavery thought," but similar views appeared as early as 1831, when Rev. Charles Jones urged planters to evangelize slaves while cultivating in them "a greater subordination."[129] Jones, the slaveholding pastor of a Savannah church, was well positioned to serve as a leading spokesman for the spiritual training of slaves.[130] He shared other planters' indignation at abolitionists' "incendiary publications" but suggested the best response was inviting preachers who taught "subordination" to evangelize their slaves.[131]

Slave evangelization was good Christian practice and sound economic policy, he suggested in *Religious Instruction of the Negroes* and in his "slave catechism."[132] Jones's *Catechism of Scripture, Doctrine, and Practice* appeared a year after Unitarian Lydia Maria Child published her *Anti-Slavery Catechism,* which cited Jones and argued that Christian values and democratic principles demanded Americans embrace "abolition doctrines."[133] Jones's popular catechism, which planters read aloud to their enslaved workers, countered the abolitionist critique by selectively citing scripture. In discussing church membership standards, for example, it cited Paul's letter to the Galatians (5:16–26), but conveniently omitted the chapter's opening: "For freedom Christ has set us free. Stand firm, therefore, and do not submit again to a yoke of slavery" (Galatians 5:1).[134] It also ignored the baptismal equality of all Christians announced two chapters earlier: "There is no longer Jew or Greek, there is no longer slave or free, there is no longer male and female, for all of you are one in Christ Jesus" (Galatians 3:28). By ignoring these and other hope-inspiring biblical passages, including the much-loved Exodus story, Jones's *Catechism* helped slaveholders erect a sacred hierarchy: God is the "Master in Heaven" to whom "Earthly Masters" are responsible; in turn, slaves must obey their masters, even "taking it patiently" when owners are cruel. If field hands missed the point, the *Catechism* made it clear: "Q. Is it right for the Servant to run away, or is it right to harbor a runaway? A: No."[135] Some slaves did run away, and some who stayed rejected the gospel of subservience. Jones's plantation supervisor assured him that his churchgoing slaves knew they could not be faithful to their "Heavenly Master" and unfaithful to their "Earthly Master."[136] But a married couple, Phoebe and Cash, denounced that theology and caused so much trouble that Jones sold them.[137]

Jones's foreman also reported agricultural news, telling him "we have all the women picking cotton . . . very white and pretty cotton."[138] Farther west, eye-catching cotton spurred expansion, contraction, and multidirectional movements. White settlers rushed to the Cotton Belt, which included

Figure 32. Picking cotton in the Cotton Belt. Photographic print by Josephus Holtzclaw Lakin, taken near Montgomery around 1860. Library of Congress reproduction LC-USZ62-16156.

South Carolina, Alabama, Louisiana, and Mississippi. They hoped to claim cheap land, as future president James Polk did in 1834 when he moved to the fertile plain between the Yazoo and Mississippi Rivers, an area that became the chief grower of the world's most important commodity, producing 66 million pounds of slave-grown cotton in a single year.[139] A slave-owning observer noted the rapid changes: "forests were swept away in a week; labor came in crowds to the South to produce cotton; and where yesterday the wilderness darkened over the land with her wild forests, to-day the cotton plantation *whitened* the earth."[140] He was describing the cotton fields' visual effect, but there also was a blackening of the fields (fig. 32). He mentioned "labor" but not the slave system that—along with the cotton gin—powered the Cotton South. He also didn't mention the theology that justified displacement as well as enslavement, as cotton planters advocated Indian removal and transformed daily life in inland plantations and river towns.

BACK TO NATCHEZ

Cotton transformed Natchez, for example, and the Mississippi town illustrates broader patterns and local variations between the 1790s, when plantation agriculture began, and the 1840s, when planter piety had solidified, restrictions on the enslaved had intensified, and many Natives had left. By the time Mississippi became a state in 1817, the town named for the Natives who built the Grand Village's mounds already had a history of slavery, but the cotton boom was as sudden, lucrative, and transformative as anywhere in the South. Natchez had the largest slave market outside New Orleans, and slaves outnumbered settlers by the 1820s. With its lavish planter mansions, Natchez became the heart of the Cotton Kingdom, where religion accommodated the slave plantation economy. The town's richest planter, Dr. Stephen Duncan, helped build Trinity Episcopal Church (1823) and invited the minister who conducted its first service. After 1831, planters recruited clergy to preach subordination on the plantation, slave-picked cotton funded churches in town, and cotton-bale religion justified increased slave patrols and restrictions on Black worship.[141]

Natchez came to symbolize antebellum cotton culture, but its religious life and planter elite were distinctive.[142] Between 1798 and 1816, Natchez was more unchurched than many places in the South, and it had more racial mixing in worship. It would become a Protestant-majority community, with Catholics and Jews in town and Muslims on the plantations, but early-nineteenth-century Natchez also had as many "nothingarians" as Kentucky.[143] Lorenzo Dow, who addressed more people than any preacher of his day, participated in Mississippi's first camp meeting in 1804 but found it impossible "to get the people out to meeting" in Natchez, which didn't have a major church building until 1817.[144] The local landscape would be Christianized by the 1840s, but there were more racially mixed congregations than one might expect. Natchez Baptist Church, for instance, would become a Black-majority congregation by 1846, with only 62 Whites among its 442 members.[145] Natchez's elite White planters also were richer—the highest per-capita wealth in the US—and they maintained unusually close ties with the North. Those ties complicated regional identity: Duncan, for instance, even would move to New York during the Civil War.[146]

Almost as surprising, Natchez's newspaper editor criticized Indian removal, and a local planter argued that America shouldn't break treaties' "sacred" pledges.[147] But dissenting elites lost that fight when most of the Choctaw and Chickasaw, Mississippi's largest remaining groups, were forced to relocate, and the Natchez who had found refuge among the Muskogee and the Cherokee after their 1729 revolt also left for Indian Territory. Some area residents still remembered the Natchez, however. By the 1840s the Grand Village mounds rested on a cotton plantation owned by Duncan's in-laws, and its slaves were using timeworn Natchez pottery they unearthed while working the fields. Even the planter who celebrated the landscape's "whitening" recalled Native presence, though he predicted "soon these mounds will be all that is left . . . of the once powerful Natchez."[148]

INDIAN REMOVAL

Southern Native niches contracted in this period. As a Cherokee women's petition put it in 1818, "the land was given to us by the Great Spirit," and our formerly extensive country "has become circumscribed to the very narrow limits we have at present."[149] It got even more "circumscribed" in the next three decades. President Jefferson had pressured southeastern tribes to relocate to land acquired in the 1803 Louisiana Purchase, and some Cherokees of Georgia and Choctaws of Mississippi headed west. In 1818 President Monroe warned that Natives in "the hunter state" faced extinction and needed "civilizing."[150] With the support of Thomas McKenney, the Quaker superintendent of the Office of Indian Trade, Congress responded by passing the 1819 Indian Civilization Act. It charged benevolent organizations with changing Natives' way of life by introducing literacy, so they could read the Bible and understand democracy, and by teaching agriculture, so they could cultivate the requisite moral virtues. Missionaries then rushed south with plows, Bibles, and spelling books.[151] Yet they were ignoring both historical reality and contemporary practice. Southeastern Natives had been farming the land and celebrating the Green Corn Festival for centuries. Some had developed commercial agriculture and, like other Southerners, used enslaved laborers on their farms. What did the critics mean, then? They meant that Native *men* didn't farm.[152] Cherokee women followed the example of Selu, the First Parent who gave them corn, as they tended the fields, but that provided officials with a gendered religious motive for removal, as they argued the practice violated natural and divine law.[153]

Protestants who worked with the government offered other justifications. Isaac McCoy, a Baptist missionary who evangelized the Miami, Odawa, and Potawatomi, became convinced by 1823 that Natives should be moved west to escape the corrupting influences of land-hungry, whiskey-peddling Whites, and he convinced Monroe's secretary of war, who created the Office of Indian Affairs.[154] McKenney, who would lead that office, agreed with

McCoy and those in the administration of John Quincy Adams (1825–1829) who argued that the civilizing process couldn't succeed in the East.[155] McKenney, like McCoy, believed he was helping Natives, of course, but we're reminded of Henry David Thoreau's warning: "If I knew for a certainty that a man was coming to my house with the conscious design of doing me good, I should run for my life."[156]

The targets of that benevolence had nowhere to run after 1828, when gold was discovered on Cherokee land, cotton production was booming, and Andrew Jackson, the slaveholding "Indian fighter" who campaigned on western expansion and Indigenous removal, was elected president. Few supporters of removal went as far as "Sharp Knife," as southeastern Natives called him, though many were complicit in the spiritual condescension and false information that grounded lawmakers' arguments. A racialized Protestantism buttressed the case for removal, and so did the new pseudoscience of phrenology, which analyzed cranial "bumps" to claim that Natives (like Africans) were inferior.[157] Constitutional clauses played a role too, as sectional loyalties produced the tight House vote (102 to 97). Free states opposed removal, but Southern legislators sided with the planter class to expel Natives from the cotton-growing South. Jackson's legislative victory could not have happened without the Constitution's three-fifths rule enlarging Southern representation; the bill would have failed.[158] In the end, however, removal was driven by President Jackson, who deceived Congress as he promoted the policy (promising removal would not be forced and treaties would not be broken) and abused power as he implemented it (negotiating with unauthorized chiefs, ignoring the act's provisions, and defying a Supreme Court decision).[159]

Jackson did all that because he knew there was opposition to the Indian Removal Act. New Jersey Senator Theodore Frelinghuysen, great-grandson of a colonial revivalist; Edward Everett, Unitarian congressman from Massachusetts; and Tennessee Representative Davy Crockett, whose district bordered Chickasaw country, spoke against the bill in Congress.[160] Protestant women like Catherine Beecher, who felt for "the distressed," organized petition drives.[161] White and Black abolitionists expressed opposition.[162] So did Northern missionaries who lived with Indigenous Peoples. Quakers and Unitarians dissented too.[163] There was especially vigorous dissent about the Cherokee removal in 1838–1839, including a public protest letter by Ralph Waldo Emerson.[164]

Resistance also came from Native communities.[165] Some fled, including the Seminole who went to the Everglades and the Cherokee who went to the Blue Ridge Mountains. The Seminole fought a second war with the federal government, and, after their own battle, the Muskogee began removal in 1834.[166] The next year a small faction of the Cherokee negotiated an unauthorized treaty that accepted removal, but Principal Chief John Ross, a Methodist, condemned the agreement and tried public persuasion and legal action.[167] By 1838 Ross concluded that for the safety of their loved ones the Cherokee had to leave "the land of our Fathers."[168] Most stayed, however, so government soldiers initiated forced removal. Six hundred wagons made their way to eastern Oklahoma, a path soon known as the Trail of Tears because about 4,000 Natives died along the way. Chief Whitepath, who supported Ross, died at the farm of a Kentucky couple who opened their home to the weary itinerants. Cherokee mourners marked his grave with a tall pole with black streamers—to memorialize him and remember "the trail where they cried."[169]

The exiles who arrived in eastern Oklahoma made a new life in that constricted territory, reconstructing communal life far from their ancestors—but not quite far enough from the settlers who continued to stream into the trans-Mississippi West.

Expansion and Contraction in the West

To illustrate this period's territorial and ecclesiastical expansion—and the corresponding contraction of western Native worlds—let's go back to St. Louis. Long before the government established the Jefferson National Expansion Memorial and built the arch marking the "gateway" to the West, St. Louis had been a staging ground for westward-facing imperial initiatives. The Jesuits, so important during the Colonial Era, became a presence again after 1814, and by the 1830s new Protestant congregations hosted missionaries heading west. Settlers bound for the Oregon Trail also left from there by boat, and St. Louis–based steamboats transported goods up the Missouri, sometimes with tragic consequences. In 1837 one steamboat spread smallpox to the Mandan, the Indigenous community that had greeted Lewis and Clark in 1804. They lost 90 percent of their population, including Chief Four Bears, who denounced the "Black hearted Dogs" who infected them.[170]

St. Louis also became a western gateway because it was the home of the Indian Affairs superintendent, and he worked closely with the missionaries who lived there or passed through.[171] John Dunbar, a Presbyterian, stayed several days before deciding he would convert and civilize the "ferocious" Pawnee at a village in present-day Nebraska, where he met Shón-ka-ki-he-ga

(Horse Chief) and attended a buffalo hunt.[172] In the years ahead, the Pawnee ceded land for "civilizing" goods and services but resisted Christian conversion and settled agrarianism—at least until the herds shrunk and epidemics struck—since, as Dunbar sensed when he left in 1846, they had more interest in literacy and horseshoes than plows and Bibles.[173] Pierre-Jean De Smet, a Belgian Catholic priest who lived in St. Louis but evangelized Natives in the West, had more success. One 1842 mission trip, for example, included a worship service with 3,000 Apsáalooke (Crow) on the northern Plains, an area destabilized by disease as well as Lakota and US incursions.[174] The crowd, which included the sick carried in on animal-skin stretchers, assembled to hear of the Christian God's "wonders," especially healing, since they heard he had protected Whites while Natives succumbed to epidemics.[175]

Disease struck Indigenous Peoples farther west too, including in Oregon Country. An earlier smallpox pandemic had devastated Native residents, and the sea otter fur trade—driven by Chinese demand—had destabilized the maritime habitat by the time Lewis and Clark arrived in 1805.[176] In that stressed eco-cultural niche Natives interacted with British and American fur traders, who made competing land claims. But humans had been in Oregon's Paisley Caves 14,000 years ago, and locals had put Kennewick Man to rest along the Columbia River about 9,500 years ago.[177] Native Oregonians were still practicing their rituals and transforming the landscape in the nineteenth century. Chinookan people along the Columbia celebrated the First Salmon Ceremony, while the Kalapuyan in Willamette Valley built burial mounds and staged field-burning rituals, which exposed the deer they hunted and regenerated the plants they gathered.[178] Those rituals couldn't regenerate their communities, however. Epidemics decimated the valley's Kalapuyan-speaking residents, which plummeted to only 600 by 1841.[179] By the late 1850s the remaining Kalapuyan and Chinook would be removed to a reservation.

Yet between the 1810s and the 1840s Indigenous Peoples helped build fur-trading niches in the Willamette Valley and along the Columbia River, the principal destination for trappers in the 1820s, missionaries in the 1830s, and settlers after Oregon became US territory in 1846.[180] Two Catholic missionaries arrived in 1838 to nurture French Catholics and evangelize Natives, and six years later De Smet escorted four Jesuits and six sisters to the Columbia River, where they enjoyed surprising success among the blended trader families and the local Indigenous communities.[181] Protestant missionaries made conversions too, though Marcus and Narcissa Whitman got a chillier reception on the Columbian Plateau, where the Cayuse killed the couple after concluding they had spread the measles that devastated their community.[182] Yet before tensions escalated and removal accelerated, the Cayuse, Chinook, and Kalapuya provided crucial labor as river boatmen, travel guides, fieldworkers, domestic help, and missionary assistants.

Other Indigenous Peoples had a presence in Oregon's missionary outposts and trading towns. An American fur magnate sent ships to establish a trading post on the Columbia, but the crew stopped in the kingdom of Hawai'i, where US Protestants had begun preaching. With the approval of King Kamehameha, the party brought forty Kānaka Maoli or Native Hawaiians to work in Oregon Country, and more followed.[183] The Whitmans had Native Hawaiians in their household, for example. Hawaiians also worked in the fur trading outposts and at Fort Vancouver in present-day Portland. By the 1840s there were so many Hawaiians at the fort—which also had Haudenosaunee and Nehiyawak workers—the company requested an islander to "assemble his people for public worship."[184] The lay preacher William Kaulehelehe and his wife Mary Kaai arrived in 1845 to found Owyhee Church, where William urged his congregants to avoid alcohol and love Jesus.

Indigenous Peoples also had a presence in Spanish and Russian settlements along the Pacific Coast from San Diego Bay to the Aleutian Islands, where evangelization and imperial incursion yielded Native baptisms but destabilized fisher-hunter-gatherer niches. Russian traders had been clubbing seals and shipping pelts from the Aleutians since 1741, and they brought back an Unangax̂ (Aleut) islander to be baptized six years later.[185] However, Russian Orthodoxy's presence in the lands that became America really began in 1793, when St. Petersburg officials sent missionaries to Kodiak Island, a Russian colony on the coast of present-day Alaska.[186] Within nine months, missionaries reported they had baptized more than 7,000 "Americans," who "take baptism so much to heart that they smash and burn all the magic charms given them by the shamans."[187] It seems unlikely the "Americans"—they meant the Sugpiaq (Alutiiq)—instantly stopped wearing talismans to ward off evil. They probably added Orthodox icon veneration to Sugpiaq talismanic use. But Orthodoxy had taken root in the areas settled by the Russian American Company (1799), including at New Archangel, the ancestral land the Tlingit called Aani and the capital of Russian America after 1808.[188] A second wave of Orthodox missionaries included Father Ioann Veniaminov, who began evangelizing Natives in 1824. A decade later he moved to New Archangel, where he baptized a few Tlingit before a smallpox epidemic struck in 1836. The shamans' healing rituals proved less effective than the Russians' immunization program, so more Tlingit accepted baptism after that.[189] By

1848, when Veniaminov was bishop, fifty Orthodox priests attended the consecration of the new St. Michael's Cathedral.

Veniaminov's duties extended south to Fort Ross, a Russian outpost in California, where Franciscans had established Catholic missions along the coast. Finns and Native Hawaiians joined Russians and Pacific Coast Peoples at the fort, which provided Russia's Alaskan settlements with grain and livestock but depended on the forced labor of the Pomo and Miwok, as Russians kidnapped Native women and children to coerce male laborers to harvest crops. Despite the company's inhumane practices, Orthodox missionaries made some spiritual progress before Veniaminov's 1836 pastoral visit to Fort Ross.[190] Some of the baptized had a Russian Orthodox father and a Native mother, but most were offspring of Alutiiq Alaskan men and Pomo California women.[191] Reflecting that diversity, Fort Ross had Native Alaskan and Native Californian neighborhoods as well as a Russian village and an Orthodox chapel with two icons overlooking the Pacific.[192] So Veniaminov, who would be revered as Saint Innocent of Alaska, encountered Native laborers who had ritually affiliated with Orthodoxy through baptism and marriage, even if they perpetuated Indigenous spiritual traditions too.

Veniaminov also toured San Francisco Bay missions. He praised San Jose's Spanish-speaking pastor for preserving "the old right of ruling and managing the Indians as their slaves."[193] But Veniaminov, who had learned Alutiiq and studied Tlingit, couldn't master California Natives' sixty-four languages. Nor did he know that most locals ingested *Datura,* a vision-producing hallucinogen—or that the Kuksu religion practiced there was one of several regional traditions.[194] The northern California tradition diverged from the beliefs and practices of the Luiseño, who lived at San Luis Rey, and the Chumash around Mission Santa Barbara. As in Russia's settlements, there was dual belonging and blended practices at the missions, where brutal treatment and demographic decimation made Indigenous resilience even more remarkable. California's Natives declined to 150,000 by 1846, but they found ways to keep traditions alive.[195] The Chumash near Santa Barbara preserved traditional artifacts by wearing the shaman's talisman under their shirt and the priest's rosary on top, for instance, and the Ohlone performed their dances at Mission San Francisco.[196]

The situation worsened for Indigenous Peoples and Hispanic Catholics after 1846. Polk, who wanted to control California's ports and build a transcontinental railroad, provoked the Mexican–American War (1846–1848), and religion played a role.[197] Mexican Catholic clergy in the Southwest resisted US expansion during the war and undermined conquest afterward, performing marriages between Anglo men and Mexican women and serving Catholics on both sides of the river separating Ciudad Juárez and El Paso.[198] Some US Catholic soldiers even switched sides, as Antonio López de Santa Anna recruited Irish Americans by reminding them they were fighting with torch-carrying Protestants "who put fire to your temples in Boston and Philadelphia."[199] About 200 Irish Catholic soldiers joined Mexico's St. Patrick's Battalion.[200] But Mexico lost the war, and the 1848 treaty signed "in the name of Almighty God" confirmed the annexation of Texas and established the Rio Grande as the border.[201] Mexico also ceded more than 500,000 square miles of territory, including Arizona, Utah, Nevada, New Mexico, and California. Miners discovered gold that year in California, and the state entered the Union two years later. Over the next two decades Hispanic residents would lose rights and the Native population would plunge to 30,000.[202] Military conquests and missionary practices had contracted and destabilized the eco-cultural niches of Indigenous Peoples and Mexican Catholics along the Pacific and in the Southwest.

Expanding Contracted Worlds and Creating Alternative Niches

Between the 1810s and the 1840s many Protestants felt called to usher in the coming Kingdom of God by converting souls, defending morality, and reforming society.[203] United by their apocalyptic urgency, Catholic fear, and nationalist fervor, Protestant do-gooders cooperated until the 1830s, when debates over slavery polarized politics and split denominations. Targeting personal failings and social ills, Protestant activists fought not only slavery but drunkenness, gambling, and dueling. They ran orphanages and prisons. They tried to improve the artisan's conditions and meet the seaman's needs.[204] A few Catholics supported Protestant causes, including abolition: two Catholics aided the Quaker "station master" of Wilmington's Underground Railroad, and parishioners in upstate New York traveled to hear a Baptist antislavery preacher.[205] Most, however, couldn't see past the insults and mob violence to join Protestant causes. Jews felt the sting of discrimination too, but reform-minded congregants sometimes followed the Protestant model, as when Philadelphia's Rebecca Gratz established the Female Hebrew Benevolent Society.[206] Rationalist reformers promoted deistic visions too. However, an optimistic Protestantism provided the moral and institutional resources for most humanitarian ventures before 1848, as churchgoers tried to expand constricted worlds and repair damaged niches.

The biracial antislavery movement, the most widespread Protestant reform effort, informed attempts to improve agriculture and empower women. Antislavery advocates inadvertently sparked debates about gender equity.[207] The Quaker Elizabeth Heyrick, who called for *Immediate, Not Gradual Abolition* (1824), had influence in Great Britain, which passed an Abolition Act in 1833, and female abolitionists in the US were drawn into the cause for women's rights as they spoke to mixed-gender audiences about emancipation.[208] Some men supported them. William Lloyd Garrison encouraged female attendees of the American Anti-Slavery Society to form a women's auxiliary, which Lucretia Mott, a White Quaker, and Charlotte Forten, a Black Methodist, established. But not all men were welcoming, as antislavery lecturers like Sojourner Truth and the Grimké sisters learned.[209] Sarah and her sister Angelina Grimké had seen slavery's trauma on their family's Charleston plantation, and they invited others to the abolitionist cause by speaking and writing, as with Angelina's 1836 *Appeal to the Christian Women of the South.*[210] But when they spoke publicly, some men tried to silence them.[211] Angelina confided to her future husband and fellow abolitionist, Theodore Weld, that the harsh reaction to their "stepping so far out of the bounds of female propriety" nudged them toward another cause: "We are placed very unexpectedly . . . in the forefront of an entirely new contest . . . for the *rights of woman.*"[212] Sarah would write *Letters on the Equality of the Sexes,* the first book-length argument for women's rights by an American, though after 1839 the Grimké sisters would step aside as Mott and others continued the battle for racial and gender equality.[213]

Mott traveled to the 1840 World Anti-Slavery Convention, but the London organizers refused to seat her with the delegates.[214] Yet she met a new ally, Elizabeth Cady Stanton, and they would plan America's first women's rights convention, which would be held at a Methodist chapel in Seneca Falls, New York, in 1848.[215] The convention's Declaration of Sentiments, which Stanton drafted, implied it was 1776 again, time to throw off another form of patriarchal tyranny. Appealing to "Nature's God," it announced, "We hold these truths to be self-evident; that all men *and women* are created equal."[216]

Other reformers focused on restoring depleted soil and "improving" agricultural practices to morally uplift farmers and invigorate the agrarian nation.[217] Short-sighted practices had deforested the landscape, washed away topsoil, and robbed the dirt of nutrients. In turn, Northern reformers like Jesse Buel encouraged farmers to use fertilizer and rotate crops. The Dutch Reformed writer saw soil as "a gift of the beneficent Creator" to be safeguarded for future generations, and judicious management of farmland, he assured readers, could restore the environmental conditions for well-being.[218] Southern planters needed no convincing about the soil's poor condition but adapted the message to their region's ecological and political climate. They struggled to defend their use of enslaved labor, as Northern critics said that even if planters restored fertility to the soil, they couldn't restore fairness to the plantation system.[219]

Some gave up on repairing things and tried to establish new communities, alternative agrarian niches. In 1836 the Pequot clergyman William Apess helped the Mashpee Wampanoag win a Massachusetts legal battle to govern themselves and choose their own minister.[220] However, Indian removal policies disrupted Native plans to build counter-niches, even among those who adopted plow agriculture and Christian hymn singing, like the residents of Stockbridge and Brothertown.[221] During the 1830s those New York residents first relocated to Wisconsin and then were forced to go to Kansas and Oklahoma. Black utopians had a bit more success, as long as they left the US. Some welcomed the creation of Liberia, the African colony that became a republic in 1847. For many exiles, however, Liberia was more dystopian than utopian since mortality rates there were even higher than on Southern slave plantations: almost half of the 4,442 early migrants died.[222] Thousands of US slaves headed for Canada, which Black Christians called Canaan, invoking the biblical story of the Promised Land.[223] In 1830 Josiah Henson, a Methodist preacher and escaped slave, followed the North Star, his "God-given guide to the land of promise," to help establish Dawn, a Black settlement in Upper Canada where 500 residents planted wheat and oats and became well-known producers of finished lumber.[224]

Smaller alternative spaces, such as two-story Grahamite boardinghouses, attracted activists working on other US social reforms, including Grimké and Weld. The health movement's founder Sylvester Graham, a Congregationalist, advocated vegetarianism and teetotalism as a way of returning to the natural and biblical laws that govern the body. By avoiding meat, alcohol, and caffeine, Grahamites hoped to further the "blessed cause of improvement, the spread of the gospel, and the universal regeneration of the world."[225] During the 1830s and 1840s they maintained boardinghouses in New York City, Rochester, and Cambridge, where proprietors would ring the bell early each morning to awaken the boarders.[226] Then all would exercise and bathe, return for a vegetarian meal, and be in bed by ten.

Alternative spaces also included larger agrarian communities with dozens of buildings and hundreds of residents. Many of them challenged prevailing norms about gender, family, sexuality, dress, property, and war—almost everything except the value of religion and the importance of farming.[227] There were celibate Catholic communities established by religious orders, like the Loretto convent and Trappist monastery in Kentucky, but also Protestant experiments in agrarian communal living. Persecuted Protestants who challenged Germany's official Lutheran Church founded seventeen agrarian communes, including Zoar, a prosperous eastern Ohio community.[228] By 1838 about 500 celibate and pacifist residents lived there on 12,000 acres of farmland, and they worshipped by singing hymns and hearing "discourses" by their founder, Joseph Bäumeler, who believed the world was corrupt and the end was near.[229]

The Shakers agreed about celibacy and pacifism but developed a spirit-focused theology that inspired a more ecstatic worship style and a loftier view of women.[230] Adherents believed Ann Lee, the illiterate daughter of a Manchester blacksmith, was the chosen vessel for Christ's second coming.[231] That teaching, along with the Shakers' affecting rituals and tidy communities, attracted conversions as well as condemnations. In fact, the nineteen Shaker villages established by 1827 were the largest and most dispersed planned communities in the US.[232] New York's Mount Lebanon, the "Mother Church," was the administrative center and architectural blueprint, and in 1823 it had more than 500 residents in self-sustaining "families" of 50 to 100. By midcentury almost 4,000 followers, including some Black devotees, lived in eighteen villages.[233] By then the Shakers had become famous for their seeds as well as their celibacy, their unadorned furniture as well as their unconventional rituals.

Brook Farm, a commune nine miles from Boston, offered a different kind of agrarian spiritual experiment.[234] Its Transcendentalist cofounders were George Ripley, a Unitarian minister who preached "the divinity of labor," and his wife, Sophia Ripley, a Unitarian and future Catholic who exhorted female readers to resist being a "possession."[235] She offered that advice the year Brook Farm began, in 1841, and the commune's aim was to unite "intellectual and manual labor," extend the benefits of education to all, and seek "a more simple and wholesome life" beyond the reach of capitalism's "competition." Its original thirty-two "associates" included the novelist Nathaniel Hawthorne and three Unitarian ministers.[236] There were a few farmers, and shoemakers perused Ripley's library as intellectuals worked the fields. But Brook Farm didn't achieve class mobility. Despite its many well-educated and independent-minded women, it also didn't usher in an egalitarian society, although mothers could drop off their children for communal childcare. A steady stream of curious visitors stopped by to observe this "Republic of lovable fools," including Transcendentalists like Emerson and Margaret Fuller and Catholic converts Orestes Brownson and Isaac Hecker.[237]

Henry David Thoreau visited Brook Farm too. He commiserated with commune residents who traveled to Boston for antislavery meetings, and, by refusing to pay the tax that supported the Mexican war, he cleared a path for civil disobedience, advocating a protest strategy that would exert global influence. Thoreau also tried his hand at restoring old niches and building new ones.[238] As Brook Farm neared its end, he headed to Walden for a solitary experiment in simple agrarian living and organized his book of the same name according to the agricultural clock—by the seasons. Even his last writing used farming metaphors about "seeds" and "growth."[239] But Thoreau noticed the increasingly intrusive industrial world. The railroad cut across the corner of the property where he built his Walden Pond cabin, and he condemned the upstream industrial causes of the problems facing Massachusetts fishermen and farmers.[240]

Toward Another Lifeway Transition

Despite these utopian experiments and reform efforts, by 1848 Americans had not resolved their inherited Colonial Era crisis. Inequities persisted as plantation slavery spread and Indigenous displacement accelerated. And new problems loomed. There were signs of another major lifeway transition, the momentous shift from farming to factories—and from farming religion to factory religion. As with the earlier transition to agriculture, elites would use religion to sanction industrialization, which produced a regional social and environmental crisis by the late nineteenth century and a global ecological crisis by the mid-twentieth. But the first human-made rise in global warming dates to the 1840s, when the gospel of "improvement" constructed a fossil fuel infrastructure in the Mid-Atlantic and factory religion emerged in Philadelphia manufacturing hamlets and New England mill towns, including Lowell, America's first factory town.

"Christian Industrialism" in Philadelphia

Wood, water, and muscle provided the energy that ran daily life in 1800, but by midcentury coal was starting to be burned in Philadelphia's homes, iron forges, and textile factories.[241] Native Peoples had known about coal, and so had Revolutionary Era settlers.[242] But in the early nineteenth century Josiah White, a Quaker engineer who hoped for prosperity so he could work "for

God and my brothers," strove to make "improvements" in transportation technology.[243] He designed and built the Lehigh Valley coal canal, which would carry tons of hot-burning anthracite from northeastern Pennsylvania.[244] By 1850 more than 700,000 tons floated down the Lehigh River.[245] Other canals linked the upstate anthracite region to ports in New Jersey and New York as well as Philadelphia. Before long, city dwellers began to become more dependent on that cheap and abundant energy source for heating homes and powering industry, and workers and owners started to live closer to the new infrastructure that linked mineral power and urban life. By midcentury the gospel of improvement had created a new energy landscape, an anthracite niche, in the eastern Mid-Atlantic.[246]

Coal wasn't the main source of power in Philadelphia factories between the 1820s and 1840s, when waterwheels propelled the small-scale cotton mills southwest and northeast of center city, and varied forms of "Christian industrialism" sacralized everyday life in those manufacturing hamlets. In Rockdale, a southwestern district, Protestant churches served the 2,006 persons living in seven mill villages, and local elites embraced the "Christian industrialism" of political economists like Henry Carey, an Episcopalian convert who argued that protective tariffs and the golden rule could create a utopian Christian empire that optimized the natural harmony of agricultural, commercial, and manufacturing interests.[247] In Cedar Grove, a northeastern district, a few laborers tended the farm that supplied corn and wheat, but most of the eighty-eight women, men, and children employed during the factory's peak in 1840 worked at the four-story mill, which took bales of raw southern cotton and produced finished textiles, including mattress ticking, the tightly woven covers for mattresses.[248] Many workers who produced that consumer comfort couldn't afford it themselves, but they could turn to the comfort of religion.[249] The mill neighborhood included Quaker, Presbyterian, Baptist, Methodist, and Episcopalian congregations in 1840, when at least half of the mill households affiliated with a church. The McMillan family, for example, attended Frankford Presbyterian (1770), and five households sang hymns in the Methodist church (1816) across from the mill. The family of Henry Whitaker, the factory owner, worshipped with other mill families at Trinity Church (1711), the Episcopalian congregation.[250] The owners also built a company chapel and closed the mill each summer for a revival and picnic they called the annual "camp meeting."[251]

New England textile mills, which also had company-supported churches, were the main competition for Philadelphia's small-scale factories, and one mill town became especially notable for its interweaving of the economic and the spiritual.

Early Factory Religion in Lowell

Natives would gather at Pawtucket Falls each spring to catch salmon and shad along the Merrimack River, but in 1826 Boston investors decided to use the site—and the power of the falls—for other purposes.[252] They established Lowell, a planned town of water-powered cotton mills, women's boarding-houses, and diverse Christian churches.[253] It would be America's first industrial city. The age of factories had begun with the founding of the Derby silk mill in 1721, but England's early industrial cities like Birmingham and Manchester drew criticism for their grimy appearance and inhumane conditions.[254] Lowell would be better, its absentee investors and local promoters hoped, because it would attract a rotating supply of young women raised on the farm and formed in the church.[255]

Lowell was incorporated in the same year Thomas Jefferson died, and if he could have seen all those churchgoing farmers' daughters in the mills he might have been comforted.[256] When Samuel Slater built a cotton mill in Rhode Island during the 1790s and early signs of industrialization appeared during his presidency, Jefferson persisted in imagining America as an agrarian empire.[257] But he changed his mind. Trade interruptions during the War of 1812 convinced him that the nation's hard-won independence rested on Americans' ability to make their own goods. "We must now place the manufacturer by the side of the agriculturist," he argued by 1816.[258] Lifeways had already begun to change. There were about 243 cotton mills in fifteen US states.[259] Then Lowell took off. By midcentury the obscure village of 2,500 had become a famous manufacturing city of 33,000—and the nation's major industrial center. The First Industrial Revolution, which used water, steam, and some coal to mechanize production, had begun in America. As with the shift from foraging to farming, it wasn't as if every cozy agricultural hamlet instantly became a midsized factory city. The transition was slow, and it happened differently in the South. But Lowell foreshadowed what was to come.[260]

Most observers thought things looked promising in Lowell at midcentury. Promoters believed it had avoided the problems facing English factory cities, even if the news wasn't all rosy. When the bosses lowered wages in 1836, Lowell's female workers announced a strike—in the name of "liberty"—and "the girls in the Weave Room all went out at once."[261] There was an official investigation of labor conditions in 1845, and the next year a visitor warned about the long workdays and the looms' "din and clatter."[262] Factory bells woke the "mill girls" at 4:30 a.m. and sounded again at 7 p.m. so they could return to their overcrowded boardinghouse. Some critics, like Thoreau, noticed that the mills changed the river's course. The dams endangered the shad and salmon fishermen depended on. In the Merrimack watershed, fishers had caught 840,000 shad in 1784, but by the 1840s dams had depleted the region's fish species.[263] Few worried about the long-term environmental toll of fossil fuels, even though the Merrimack Company annually used 5,000 tons of coal and 13,000 gallons of oil and would use much more in later years.[264] For most observers, Lowell's industrial experiment was a source of pride. After all, the town and its mills kept expanding. The population had increased to 17,000 a decade after incorporation, and Lowell's residents grew to 33,000 by 1850, when each week 40 mills and 10,100 workers converted 56,000 pounds of cotton into 250,000 yards of finished cloth.[265] Many visitors came to see the marvels of the nation's first industrial city, with its multistory brick factories along the waterfront. Four current or future presidents (Jackson, Tyler, Polk, and Lincoln) joined pilgrims like Charles Dickens, who compared Lowell favorably to English factory towns like Manchester. The contrast, that novelist suggested after his 1842 visit, was between "Good and Evil, the living light and the darkest shadow."[266]

One local Thanksgiving sermon expressed gratitude for that light: "Lowell has demonstrated that a Manufacturing city need not be a place of helpless dependency, abject poverty, abandoned corruption and sin."[267] And clerics had an explanation for Lowell's success. Unitarian Henry Miles suggested it was not only the trees planted along the streets and the wholesome rural workers. Lowell was also better than Manchester because of the "moral machinery of the mills."[268] The "machinery" included overseers who supervised the women, "improvement circles" that refined them, and boardinghouse rules that mandated churchgoing.[269] Christian investors and clergy believed those rural refugees who worked twelve-hour shifts needed religion, and by 1846 clergymen served worshippers in nineteen churches. There were Congregationalist, Methodist, Presbyterian, Baptist, Universalist, and Unitarian churches, as well as an Episcopalian congregation its pastor called "the company church" because the corporation's pragmatic Unitarian leaders funded it. They even donated a plot for St. Patrick's, the city's first Roman Catholic church.[270] An image of the city around midcentury showed some of the steeples (fig. 33).

Letters, memoirs, and diaries provide more evidence of mill workers' devotional life. One woman told a friend that "there has been quite a revival here among the Methodist."[271] A contrite Congregationalist weaver sent a confession to her Lowell church: "To save my reputation as a weaver, I have

Figure 33. View of Lowell, Massachusetts, with textile factories along the Merrimack River and church steeples in the background. Library of Congress, Prints and Photographs Division, LC-USZ62-16156.

taken the ticket from cloth woven by another person and placed it upon that done by myself . . . thereby practicing dishonesty, and sinning against God and the church."[272] So there were new kinds of sin—factory sins—and new kinds of salvation, or so she hoped. She asked to be "remembered in their prayers" so she might more consistently live out the gospel.

There were many ways to live out the gospel in Lowell, but the community's church hopping was especially striking. Some transplanted farm girls remained loyal to their childhood faith, while others asked relatives at home to decide.[273] Yet some visited an array of churches. One mill worker attended a Congregational church in the morning and a Methodist service in the afternoon, and then decided to continue sampling the options. The next week she would visit the Episcopalians and Catholics, because she experienced a "strange but not unhallowed sensation" when she first saw a church spire with a cross.[274] Another worker reported no "hallowed sensations" when she visited Catholic churches.[275] She preferred Miles's Unitarian Church and the Second Congregational Church, but also worshipped in the Episcopalian "company church" as well as in two Universalist churches, two Baptist fellowships, and two Methodist congregations.[276]

The mill girls, it seems, searched for a worship space that suited their shifting sensibilities and made sense of the changing times. The memoir of Lucy Larcom illustrates how one worker, a Congregationalist from Massachusetts, experienced the shifts.[277] She remembered it as a time when "people were guessing and experimenting and wondering and prophesizing about . . . almost everything." There was the telegraph, which sped up communication, and folks "were only beginning to get accustomed to steamboats and railroads," which accelerated travel. Mesmerists brought some under "uncanny influence," phrenologists discerned character by interpreting "cranial bumps," and Millerites warned the end of the world was coming. But Larcom preferred Emerson's emphasis on experience—encountering the divine "without mediator or veil"—and, though she was raised on "grim" Calvinist principles, she would end up worshipping in an Episcopalian congregation where starch-collared Bostonians raved about Buddha's teachings more than they worried about divine election.[278] She compared the experience of rapid change to a child's wonder at a traveling show: it was like children climbing a fence "to watch an approaching show, and to conjecture what more remarkable spectacle could be following behind." She suggested that little had changed in "the first fifty years of the Republic." Yet all was "expectancy" by midcentury: "Changes were coming. Things were going to happen. Nobody could guess what."

PART THREE

FACTORIES

Figure 34. The Pittsburgh Steel Company blast furnaces in Monessen, Pennsylvania, stand across from St. Leonard Catholic Church and parochial school in this factory town that had about 10,000 residents in 1906. John T. "Jet" Lowe, photographer. Historic American Engineering Record, Library of Congress.

CHAPTER 7

Industrial Religion

The Sharecropper South, the Reservation West, and the Sustainability Crisis in the Urban Industrial North, 1848–1920

Lucy Larcom, the former Lowell factory worker, sensed that "things were going to happen" after the 1840s, and when she died as a well-known writer in 1893, she had witnessed a few of the period's momentous changes.[1] She observed the rise of industry and the move to cities. She took sides during the Civil War and saw the completion of the transcontinental railroad.[2] She witnessed religious changes too, including new forms of postwar civil religion and new religious movements like spiritualism and Christian Science, which valued the spiritual over the material.[3] She read about Asian religions and heard that Protestant missionaries went abroad to save the "heathen."[4] Closer to home, Larcom saw how surging immigration was diversifying US religion. Like other White Protestants, she worried about foreign laborers and lamented that Irish Catholics had replaced Protestant women at the Lowell mills after 1850, as the town's population rose from about 33,000 in 1850 to almost 77,000 in 1890—as in nearby Boston, where the foreign-born population increased as Italian Catholics and Russian Jews arrived.[5] Intellectual challenges like Darwinian biology and biblical scholarship also shook the faith of middle-class Protestants like Larcom.[6] In turn, she strove to understand the "unseen," the spiritual realm, and sought aid at Boston's Trinity Church, where Philips Brooks's soothing preaching and H. H. Richardson's stately architecture brought some comfort.[7] Yet in her final poem she suggested there was no hope for those who seek heaven above but fail to see that earth below is "holy ground."[8]

Not everyone could find holy ground in America's increasingly grimy industrial cities. Larcom, who hated machinery's "oily smell" and suffered respiratory problems, experienced some of the mounting social and environmental problems.[9] The US was still rural and agricultural in 1848, and farming religion and planting metaphors predominated. But the nation was becoming more urban and industrial, with signs of the shift from an organic to a mineral economy. As this major lifeway transition approached, political and religious leaders began to address one source of the Colonial Era crisis the post-1848 generation had inherited. The North's victory in the Civil War emancipated slaves and shuttered the plantation, the unjust and stressed niche that planter piety sanctioned. Yet the postwar period brought reunion without reconciliation. After securing constitutional gains and founding independent churches, ex-slaves in the South found themselves "resubjugated" in a new agricultural space, the sharecropper's patch. The period saw even fewer successful attempts to redress moral wrongs and lingering inequities arising from Indigenous displacement. In fact, assimilation-minded "friends of the Indian" made things worse in the western reservations, creating new spaces like the allotment, the family homestead intended to remake mobile heathen hunters into settled Christian farmers, and the Indian boarding school, designed to "kill the Indian, but save the man."[10]

With the Colonial Era crisis unresolved, a third sustainability crisis began between 1873 and 1920 in the urban industrial North, limiting some city dwellers' abilities to meet the conditions for individual, communal, and ecological flourishing (see appendix). The industry-generated ecological effects that began in the 1780s and increased by the 1840s started to intensify after the 1870s. Industrial processes and fossil-fuel dependency started to degrade the land, air, and water. Even if raw materials came from the hinterlands and extractive industries scarred rural landscapes, the effects were mostly regional, as urban factories started to pollute the industrial North. Those regional and (mostly) reversible environmental effects were accompanied by a decline in well-being precipitated by urban crowding, health disparity, and income inequality—and exacerbated by spiritually sanctioned hostility to those who were not White, native-born Protestants.[11] As the US became a carbon-dependent industrial nation, varieties of *industrial religion* sanctified the stressed regional niche.[12] Yet the religious both accelerated and slowed the crisis. Some spiritual reformers and utopian planners would try to address the problems by 1920, when the US Census showed more Americans lived in the city than the country, and the factory had become more important than the farm.[13]

Diverging Lifeways and the Belated Battle over Slavery

The Civil War, which confronted one source of the inherited crisis, had roots in the interdependent lifeways of the manufacturing North and the plantation South, and it affected how Americans would experience the later Industrial Era crisis.[14] The regional tensions evident by 1787, when most congressional delegates saw slavery as a necessary but temporary evil, became cultural divisions by 1831, when Southern preachers started defending the slave plantation system as a positive good while Northern abolitionists began condemning it as an unqualified evil. By 1850, contrasting aspirations deepened the tensions as Congress debated the future of western lands and Southerners argued that the slave labor system was better than the wage-earning system of the industrializing North. Mounting tensions erupted into war by 1861, when both the Cotton South and the Industrial North appealed to the Bible as well as the Declaration and Constitution, with Northern ministers emphasizing scripture's emancipatory spirit and Southerners highlighting references to ancient slaveholding.

Even if religion did not *cause* the war, it sanctified the sectional divisions of the 1850s, sacralized the bloodshed of 1861–1865, and consecrated the contrasting worldviews after the fighting stopped.[15]

Mounting Divisions, 1850–1860

Diverging lifeways deepened divisions as Southerners and Northerners made competing plans for the continent's western lands—plans that did not include Indigenous inhabitants.[16] In the North, which had much more industry, small farmers raised enough wheat, corn, potatoes, and cows to feed families and allow exports, as wageworkers manufactured goods, dug coal, and refined iron.[17] Wealth distribution was more unequal in the rural South. Rich planters profited from cash crops like cotton, as New York banks mediated the transactions and Massachusetts mills processed the bales. But those planters depleted the soil by failing to rotate crops, and the resulting ecological stress prompted slaveholding Southerners to covet the prairie plains out West.[18] The Cotton South sought nutrient-rich soil for plantations and new markets for crops, while Yankees hoped to populate the West with small farmers and free laborers.[19]

As Southerners claimed divine favor for their expansionist hopes, they applied proslavery defenses crafted by thinkers like George Fitzhugh and Rev. James Thornwell.[20] A month before South Carolina seceded, Thornwell, the son of a plantation overseer, delivered a widely circulated sermon, "Our National Sins" (1860). After defending secession, Thornwell then explained the Presbyterians' 1861 split from the Northern denomination. Yet it was his 1850 sermon "The Christian Doctrine of Slavery" that refined planter piety, a hierarchical worldview and paternalistic ethic that guided slaveholding landowners and fortified the plantation complex. Thornwell didn't just cite biblical passages to show God approved of slavery. He argued that God imposed inequity as retribution for humanity's sin, including "the curse of Ham," which made Blacks inferior. Thornwell also compared the regions' diverging lifeways. In 1841 he had witnessed the ill effects of Britain's coal-fueled industrial economy, its "smoky and dingy" buildings and "ragged and dirty" poor. Those observations informed his defense when abolitionists attacked the Southern way of life. He claimed the slave economy's divinely ordained hierarchy was better. Unprotected by the Christian slave owner's paternalism, Northern wage earners toiled in "involuntary servitude," constrained by the whims of the factory boss and the capitalist market.[21]

These competing theological and economic visions informed the political debates of the 1850s. A divided Congress agreed California could be a free state, for example, but authorized tribunals that returned runaways without testimony or trial. Using a phrase Southern Democrats loved, the Kansas–Nebraska Act said "popular sovereignty" would decide slavery's status on the Plains. The prospects for African Americans, free and enslaved, seemed even dimmer when the Supreme Court's Dred Scott decision of 1857 declared Blacks naturally inferior and ineligible for citizenship.[22]

Meanwhile, abolitionists increased their public attacks on slavery and clandestine efforts to aid runaways. Harriet Tubman, the "Black Moses," led slaves to freedom along the Underground Railroad, and in 1855 Frederick Douglass, the "Black Jeremiah," documented slavery's effects in his second autobiography, which sold 5,000 copies in the first two days.[23] Three years earlier, Harriet Beecher Stowe's popular novel *Uncle Tom's Cabin* had highlighted slavery's destructive effects on the family by appealing to Protestant values about the sanctity of the home.[24] By the end of 1859, Virginia had hanged John Brown for his God-sanctioned slave insurrection, but not before the White Congregationalist predicted "the crimes of this guilty land will never be purged away but with blood."[25] Northerners compared Brown's hanging to Jesus's crucifixion.[26] Douglass, who admired Brown but didn't support the raid, fled to Canada to avoid being charged as a co-conspirator, and Abraham Lincoln, who would be elected president the next year on the promise to prevent slavery's spread, condemned Brown's use of violence. Yet Brown's execution in December 1859 and Lincoln's election in November 1860 hardened resolve on both sides and made Brown's prediction seem more likely. Soon there would be blood, lots of it. More than 750,000 would die in the Civil War and both sides would insist that those deaths, like Christ's, were redemptive.[27]

Wartime Piety, 1861–1865

The path to war's redemptive suffering started in South Carolina, which seceded in December 1860. In January 1861 its militia fired the first shot, a cannonball aimed at a federal ship.[28] By midsummer 1861, blood stained Virginia's soil in the first major battle, but before that confrontation the North's diverse constituencies began to use spiritual rhetoric about deliverance, saying God called them to preserve the Union and save the South, while Southern elites emphasized their righteous effort to preserve their lifeway and defend state sovereignty.[29] Some officials did care about states' rights, but it was not a squabble about abstract principles. Secession, a rebellion driven by the desire to protect slavery, escalated the conflict. As secession sermons and speeches show, slavery had become the basis for Southerners' way of life and collective identity.[30] So South Carolina and ten other slaveholding states left the Union. Without "the heresy of secession," as one Northern industrialist put it, there would have been no war.[31] The desire to defend the slave plantation niche led to a new nation, the Confederate States of America, and a new constitution calling on "Almighty God" to sanction its efforts.[32]

As fighting intensified, fatalistic combatants and anguished civilians pondered their mortality, and the Civil War became the holiest as well as the bloodiest war in US history.[33] There were religiously inspired dissenters on both sides, but both governments endorsed religious patriotism.[34] They appointed chaplains for lawmakers in Washington and Richmond, and approved regimental and hospital chaplains. More than 2,000 served the Union army, including fourteen Black ministers, and more than 1,000 supported Confederate troops. When chaplains weren't available, units got creative, as when a Confederate regiment asked Louis Nelson, an enslaved cook, to lead a worship service, and a Yankee artillery unit elected the spiritualist Ella Gibson Hobart as chaplain.[35]

Both US President Abraham Lincoln, who read the Bible but never joined a church, and Confederate President Jefferson Davis, a churchgoing Episcopalian, also called for National Days of Fasting, Prayer, and Thanksgiving. Some immigrant Catholic and Jewish leaders who had seen nationalism abused in Europe hesitated to align religion and the state. Rabbi Isaac Wise of Cincinnati refused to speak on a National Day of Prayer because it violated his policy of "no political preaching."[36] Yet many ministers, priests, and rabbis endorsed the governments' appeals for prayer, and assured listeners in each region that God was on their side. A rabbi, for example, told his Philadelphia congregation in an 1863 Thanksgiving Day sermon that Providence was guiding them and, despite predictions of economic collapse, the war had brought Northern prosperity because "God is king, not cotton."[37]

Regional loyalties split Protestant church institutions and strained Catholic and Jewish communities. Baptist, Methodist, Episcopalian, and Presbyterian denominations divided along sectional lines by December 1861.[38] The Presbyterian Church in the Confederate States of America, the last to split, acknowledged its decision arose from disagreements over slavery.[39] Catholics and Jews avoided institutional splits and fought for both sides. Most Jews in uniform fought for the Union.[40] And rabbis, including Jacob Frankel, the first Jewish military chaplain, nurtured those soldiers.[41] Catholic leaders disagreed about the Civil War, and those in the pews fought for both the blue and the gray.[42] They could express contrasting positions because Pope Pius IX, who privately favored the Confederacy, was officially neutral.[43] Nuns, who ignored uniform color as they tended the wounded, made up about 20 percent of the Civil War nurses, and seventy Catholic chaplains served the two armies, including a young Union chaplain named James Gibbons, the son of Irish immigrants, who would become the American church's most influential leader.[44]

During the brutal conflict, when both sides violated just war principles by targeting civilians and retaliating disproportionately, personal devotion increased.[45] While women at home prayed for the troops, soldiers attended services with more frequency and fervor. Among Union troops, Jews took leaves for the High Holy Days, and Irish Catholics attended large open-air masses.[46] The Confederate Army of Northern Virginia, led by Episcopalian Robert E. Lee, experienced the first of several revivals in 1862, as soldiers "prayed fervently to the God of battles."[47] Black religious devotion increased too. Some of the South's 3.9 million enslaved workers continued African-inspired practices, like the "conjure doctor" Aunt Darkas, who healed ailing slaves with roots from the woods.[48] Others attended secret prayer meetings in slave cabins.[49] Inspired by their "soul-hungering desire" for freedom, attendees worshipped all night and dispersed after singing "The Gospel Train," which cautioned sinners that the train might leave without them.[50] Many Blacks did leave, and more than 500,000 ended up in one of the Union-run refugee camps, where those who died of disease were memorialized at torch-lit funerals where attendees danced, clapped, and prayed.[51] Spiritual renewal also reached the Union's 149 "colored" units.[52] Rev. Garland White, an AME chaplain, baptized forty members of Indiana's 28th US Colored Infantry, and one wounded soldier in his unit marveled that, "by the Lord's will," he had survived, though he took comfort in knowing that if the next battle brought death, "the generations to come will receive the blessing of it."[53]

But time would pass before later generations received the blessing of his service. Lincoln had looked toward that day in his address at Gettysburg, the Pennsylvania battleground where more than 7,000 died in 1863. He suggested that the divinely protected nation conceived in liberty and dedicated to equality had unfinished work as it progressed toward "a new birth of freedom."[54] The work remained unfinished in March 1865 when Lincoln delivered his second inaugural address, which called for binding the nation's wounds. But the president worried that the two sides who "read the same Bible and prayed to the same God" might have to endure more suffering, "until every drop of blood drawn from the lash, shall be paid by another drawn with the sword."[55] And there would be more suffering that year. Confederates opened a prisoner-of-war camp where nearly 13,000 diseased and malnourished Yankees would die, and Union troops captured Atlanta, destroying its rail lines and much of the city, as General William Sherman enacted the new Northern tactic of demoralizing the Confederacy and decimating its resources. By early April 1865 Reverend White's Colored Infantry marched into Richmond, and six days later, on 9 April, General Lee surrendered to General Ulysses S. Grant. That ended the war, but not the suffering. Five days later a self-professed instrument of God, John Wilkes Booth, a Confederate sympathizer who had witnessed John Brown's hanging and mourned Richmond's fall, assassinated Lincoln on Good Friday. As the president's lifeless body traveled by train to Illinois and crowds paid their respects, Northern preachers said Lincoln's death, a final sacrifice, was redemptive too.[56]

Confederates didn't agree, of course, and, unlike the Union soldiers who paraded past President Andrew Johnson on Pennsylvania Avenue in May 1865 as a "benediction" on the War, dispersing Confederate soldiers staged no satisfying end to the fighting and—at least at first—couldn't see anything redemptive about it.[57]

Reunion without Reconciliation

In the postwar decades, when Americans had a chance to confront the sustainability crisis generated by slavery, almost everyone found something redemptive about the Civil War—except the Plains Indians subdued by war-hardened veterans and the indentured Chinese who replaced Southern slaves.[58] Frederick Douglass was as hopeful as anyone, even after Lincoln's assassination. Less than twenty-four hours later on that Easter weekend, Douglass suggested Lincoln's blood would bring "salvation to our country." He added a warning, however. Northerners must recognize that the South's leaders had committed "crimes of treason and slavery," and, anticipating peace studies experts' advice about post-conflict reconciliation, Douglass suggested they shouldn't move too quickly to restore the Union.[59]

Unfortunately, war-weary politicians did move quickly, valuing political reunion more than restorative justice. That hampered efforts to restructure the prewar plantation niche and address the wartime wrongs. Northern churches educated freed slaves, and Republican legislators established justice-promoting institutions, like the Freedmen's Bureau (1865–1870), while passing laws that widened political participation.[60] But leaders failed to meet other conditions necessary for ex-slaves to flourish. By abolishing slavery, Americans had begun to resolve the Colonial Era crisis, but few Whites challenged the racist theology that sanctified the slave plantation. They also didn't redistribute slaveholders' land to create Black-owned homesteads, and they ignored the Civil War's environmental and social impact. The reconciliation process, which began when Lincoln granted Confederates property rights and a "full pardon," continued with lenient decisions by Presidents Johnson and Grant after the war.[61] They demanded only that Southerners pledge loyalty to the Union and accept freed slaves' new legal standing. They didn't punish either Confederate President Jefferson Davis, who had led a rebellion against the US, or Union General William Sherman, who had fired on Atlanta's residential districts for almost three weeks.[62] Nor did the rush to political reunion allow other restorative practices that could have brought a more just and enduring reconciliation: there were neither apologies for prewar inequities nor reparations for wartime wrongs.[63] Farmers who had their fences burned for firewood and their fields trampled by soldiers got little help. Most White Southern elites refused to admit that slavery was wrong, and neither side acknowledged they had violated long-standing principles guiding soldiers' conduct. To make things worse, flag-waving faith justified their intransigence.

The postwar dismantling of the plantation niche had not gone far enough when US troops left the South in 1877. It had brought neither economic equity nor environmental revitalization, even if most ex-slaves found a modest improvement in their way of life—at least compared with the slave system's brutality. In 1865 the emancipated had faced two choices—stay or leave—and they could employ biblical images to imagine it as a Jubilee year, a time of liberation when they could return home, or as an Exile, a time to journey toward the promised land.[64] Some Southern Blacks went West, which they imagined as a utopian space, and, reconsidering a prewar option, some left for Liberia. Later, millions would take part in the Great Migration, moving to Northern cities for factory work. But just after the war most freed slaves stayed in the South. Some found jobs on the railroads or in the coal mines of the industrializing "New South," but most remained in rural areas and worked the land.[65]

Even if some White planters were slow to accept it, the postwar agricultural niche had changed. Landowners who grew export crops like cotton or sugarcane couldn't rely on forced labor. What to do? At first planters hired wage hands, even paying former slaves, but found they couldn't demand the same backbreaking hours without the threat of the whip. So, in an agrarian experiment, some sugar and cotton planters replaced enslaved Africans with indentured Chinese, who signed multiyear contracts that promised rice and lodging in exchange for long hours. A Mississippi preacher saw "the hand of God in this Chinese immigration," though one pious planter complained that these unmanageable workers had to be whipped "within an inch of [their] life."[66] A small portion of the 2.3 million Chinese who went abroad between 1840 and 1900 settled in Louisiana.[67] But the newcomers added religious and ethnic diversity. In East Carroll Parish, which had seventy-nine Chinese residents by 1875, Pat Low and thirteen other "heathen Chinee" worked the fields for an Episcopalian planter and sometimes gathered for public ceremonies, as when "quite a concourse of Chinamen" rode in rented carriages to a friend's funeral.[68]

However, by the 1870s most planters settled on another agricultural system that would transform the rural landscape. In a compromise between landlords' desire for permanent labor and workers' desire to own land, planters subdivided their acres for tenant farming.[69] The tenant workers included renters, who owned animals and equipment, paid a fixed lease rate, and kept their harvest, and sharecroppers, who used the landlord's animals and equipment, worked without supervision, but had to share the owner-mandated crop, usually cotton, even when profits plummeted. The sharecropping landscape included the small, often unsanitary cabins of ex-slaves and poor Whites, and the soil they hoed became degraded because most landholders forbade crop rotation and erosion control.[70] For White families who had lost their farm in the war, sharecropping was a step down. For former slaves, it was a small step up since it allowed some autonomy. Black sharecropper families could work twenty acres without supervision. Yet they still didn't own the land they tilled, and they paid high interest to secure credit for provisions at the planter's store. This coercive economic scheme, which involved three-quarters of Southern Black farmers by 1900, trapped African Americans in debt. Economically and ecologically, the region's long-standing sustainability crisis remained mostly unresolved.

The postwar period brought less ambivalent political gains. The states-nation became a nation-state. Before 1861 the two words *United States* were often used as a plural noun: "the United States *are* a republic." After 1865 the United States became a singular noun. The divided nation reunited, the federal government strengthened, and, as one historian proposed, "the incarnation of a national American civil religion may have been the final great legacy of the Civil War." That's right, though it began as early as Philadelphia's 1788 Grand Federal Procession, and there wasn't a single civil religion. Three overlapping but distinct civil religions emerged in the postwar period: a *prospective* Northern variant focused on the restored Union and its divinely directed future; a *retrospective* White Southern piety focused on preserving prewar distinctiveness and explaining wartime defeat; and a *circumspective* African American alternative performed in Black-owned spaces and focused on seeking God's aid in the ongoing struggle for freedom. Only the third variant, the Black public religion, frankly faced slavery's horrors and actively sought restorative justice.[71]

Postwar Civil Religions

White Northerners' civil religion, which often deemphasized emancipation and sometimes excluded Blacks, emerged from interpretations of Lincoln's death and the South's "ruins." A former Union chaplain suggested that the "divine will" had been revealed in "word" (Lincoln's second inaugural address) and "deed" (Richmond's fall), and Lincoln's sacrificial death had prepared the nation to become a "harmonious whole."[72] Northerners awaiting unification saw evidence of spiritual victory and future progress in the representations of Southern ruins. One Union veteran and Protestant minister who visited Charleston's "hideous ruins" said the rubble proved that "God guided the missiles of war" (fig. 35).[73]

Figure 35. *View of Ruined Buildings.* Photograph by George Barnard of Charleston, South Carolina, in 1865. Collection: Civil War Photographs, 1861–1865, Library of Congress Prints and Photographs Division, reproduction LC-DIG-ewpb-03049.

General Sherman's photographer staged a shot of Charleston in 1865 to show the accuracy of God's aim. As with similar images of devastation in Atlanta and Richmond, such ruins came to signify divine vindication of the Northern cause, righteous destruction of the South's lifeway, and the North's opportunity to remake the region.[74] Henry Ward Beecher, the Northern preacher, interpreted it that way when he visited Charleston's rubble on his way to the 1865 flag-raising ceremony at Fort Sumter, where he proclaimed the South was "no longer a land of plantations, but of farms; no longer filled by slaves, but freemen."[75]

Northerners expressed their patriotic piety in multiple ways. Congress added "In God We Trust" to US currency in 1864, and the civil religious landscape expanded: federal officials dedicated the Washington Monument in 1888, completed the US Capitol's enlargement in 1892, and began the Lincoln Memorial in 1914. White Northerners revered George Washington, and Blacks continued to emphasize the posthumous freeing of his slaves.[76] Lincoln also entered the pantheon of American saints. A painting of the "martyred" Lincoln portrayed his heavenly ascent exactly as artists had depicted Washington.[77] Sacred rituals and texts were added too. Decoration Day, known eventually as Memorial Day, joined Fourth of July festivities and presidential inaugurations on America's ritual calendar. Eventually, Lincoln's Gettysburg Address and second inaugural address—and Julia Ward Howe's "Battle Hymn of the Republic" (1862), a Union hymn—became sacred texts of US civil religion.[78] The Grand Army of the Republic (GAR), a Northern veterans' organization, transmitted this public faith as it fought the battle for memory. It organized a Memorial Day event in 1868, where the Ohio congressman and Protestant minister James Garfield spoke.[79] Garfield also dedicated a Union memorial in 1880, the year he was elected president, and four years later the GAR sponsored Kentucky and Indiana memorials that inscribed a moral claim made at their annual "encampment," where a Union veteran said his fellow combatants were willing to "thank the God of battles" for preserving the nation. However, using a phrase later chiseled on those monuments, he also said future generations must be reminded "that we were eternally right and that they were eternally wrong."[80]

African Americans agreed, and, as with Martin Luther King Jr.'s 1963 "I Have a Dream" speech at the Lincoln Memorial, a "hallowed spot," they also would employ the symbols, texts, and shrines of Northern civil religion "to make real the promises of democracy."[81] Even before the GAR set aside a day to commemorate fallen soldiers, Black South Carolinians and their White Northern allies organized the first Decoration Day celebration amid Charleston's ruins on 1 May 1865.[82] The public parade and grave decoration attracted about 10,000 people, many of them former slaves. In the years ahead, a distinctive Black civil religion set aside other ritual occasions, including Emancipation Day, Frederick Douglass's birthday, and Juneteenth ceremonies on the date (19 June) when enslaved Texans learned they were free. New civic saints, like Douglass, were added. Harriet Tubman, slave rescuer and Union spy, joined the venerated after her 1913 funeral.[83] Music was part of this prophetic nationalism too. Many African Americans loved the "Battle Hymn of the Republic," but they also embraced a Black patriotic song, "Lift Every Voice and Sing," written by James and John Johnson in 1900.[84] The lyrics asked "the God of our weary years" to continue to reveal the path to freedom as Black citizens, in turn, remained "True to our God / True to our native land." The hymn would be sung in Black churches, schools, and civic organizations in the years ahead. In 1903 it concluded the Emancipation Day program at Atlanta's Ebenezer Baptist Church, King's future pulpit, and in 1905 a glee club performed "Lift Every Voice" at a meeting of Booker T. Washington's National Negro in Business League. By then, the song hailed as "the Negro national anthem" was becoming part of a distinctive public religion.

To respond to Black and Yankee claims on national identity—and ease their psychic distress—unrepentant Southern elites refashioned their prewar planter piety into a White civil religion that undercut efforts to confront wrongdoing and make reparations.[85] Adjusting to war's aftermath proved difficult for White Christian Southerners.[86] One Episcopalian, a slaveholding planter, wrote in his journal for 30 May 1865, the day after President Andrew Johnson granted amnesty to most Confederates, that "it has pleased God that we should fail in our efforts for independence."[87] Few Providence-affirming Southerners moved on as quickly. James Tillman, a South Carolina soldier, first dismissed the "humiliating rumors" of Lee's surrender. When indisputable evidence reached his unit on 29 April, the captain admitted it "tried" his faith.[88] By mid-May he was back on the plantation but had "feelings of despair." In the spring of 1866 he returned to church, though he heard a "poor" sermon. James, who died that June, wouldn't live to hear a good one: a theological explanation for the Confederate loss, a sermon that might ease his despair, soften the humiliation, and revive his faith.

Yet Southern preachers were already giving sermons like that. By the summer of 1865 Episcopalian and Presbyterian leaders reluctantly acknowledged freed slaves' changed *legal* status but defiantly insisted that Southerners had been *spiritually* right about slavery. Abolitionist claims about the sinfulness of slavery remained "unscriptural and fanatical," and God-fearing Southerners had no reason to apologize. The Confederate dead need not be "covered with shame."[89] From soldiers' graves and urban ruins a renewed faith, a religion of the Lost Cause, would rise, as the Yankee photograph of postwar Charleston inadvertently suggested. It showed that St. Philip's Episcopal Church, symbol of prewar planter piety, survived the battle (see fig. 35). At the 1866 reopening of the church, which had recast its steeple bells to make Confederate canons, the pastor assured parishioners that righteousness would eventually win.[90] Abram Ryan, the "poet-priest of the Confederacy," consoled more Southerners, encouraging them to welcome the ruins. They could find redemption, Father Ryan proposed, by gathering the "sacred dust" of those who "fell in a cause, though lost, still just / and died for me and you."[91]

The phrase about the lost-but-just cause would adorn a North Carolina courthouse memorial sponsored by the United Daughters of the Confederacy, who published a "catechism" and erected monuments to give a "truthful" account of the war.[92] After 1885 Dixie's increasingly defiant defenders placed memorials at county courthouses and state capitals.[93] This religion of the Lost Cause included rituals and saints, and the South added its own Confederate Memorial Day, choosing Jefferson Davis's birthday. It was also on display at Davis's 1889 funeral, when 150,000 mourners passed his casket, and at sites venerating Lee, who was honored by many memorials, and General Stonewall Jackson, whose "shrine" stood near Fredericksburg, Virginia.[94] In the decades ahead, even former slave plantations became shrines, as hoop skirt–wearing women of the Natchez Garden Club organized annual "pilgrimages," so visitors could tour a master's house, attend a ball, and return to "the golden days of the Old South."[95]

Redeeming the South

Unfortunately, those "golden days" started to return by the mid-1870s in a process that historians describe as the "re-subjugation" of African Americans but White Democrats saw as the South's "redemption" from Black and federal control.[96]

Blacks had secured important political victories in the decade after the war. In 1865 Congress passed the Thirteenth Amendment, which abolished slavery. The Civil Rights Act of 1866 promised equality before the law, and the Civil Rights Act of 1875 forbade discrimination in public accommodations. The Equal Protection and Due Process Clauses of the Fourteenth Amendment (1868) laid the foundation for the later "rights revolution," but its Citizenship Clause had immediate effects, granting citizenship to all African Americans. The amendment didn't apply to Natives or Chinese, but it seemed to prepare the way for the diverse "composite nation" Frederick Douglass imagined.[97] The Fifteenth Amendment of 1870, the final constitutional change, prohibited the government from denying any male citizen the right to vote.

The enfranchisement of African American men had direct, if short-term, effects: about 2,000 Blacks held public office in the postwar period, including in Southern states with the largest African American populations: South Carolina and Mississippi. Fourteen Blacks were elected to the US House of Representatives, and in 1870 two joined the US Senate, including Mississippi's Hiram Revels, an AME preacher who had served the Union army as a chaplain.[98] Enjoying political advances that had seemed unimaginable a decade earlier, Black men also gained seats in local government. In 1870 Natchez elected an African American mayor. Men of color held half of Charleston's city council seats between 1867 and 1877, and South Carolina voters sent Blacks to the state legislature too.[99] Spiritual ties fostered political gains, including for the 250 Black ministers who held public office by 1877. Seven officials elected to South Carolina's legislature were AME ministers, for instance, and church attendance helped laymen like Natchez's mayor, who made political connections at the Black Catholic church.

African Americans made ecclesiastical gains too. Lay devotees convened "Colored Catholic Congresses," and religious orders sought converts. But like the Protestants who sent missionaries and opened schools, Catholics attracted few Blacks.[100] Most of the freed congregants also left White-led churches, making Sunday morning more segregated but giving Blacks spiritual autonomy. In Charleston the Methodist Church South had claimed 40,000 Black members in 1860; by 1873 that had plummeted to 653.[101] Across the South, African American Christians welcomed sincere collaboration but preferred to worship in independent institutions. They joined older denominations such as the African Methodist Episcopal Church and African Methodist Episcopal Zion Church or affiliated with those organized between 1870 and 1915, like the Colored (later Christian) Methodist Episcopal Church and the National Baptist Convention. The AME Church grew to almost half a million by the close of the nineteenth century.[102] Ministers like Daniel Payne became important public figures. There were also female preachers, like Jarena Lee, and women's ecclesiastical organizations provided opportunities to exert public power. Many now forgotten church women prodded and protested, as did well-known suffragists and antilynching activists like Ida B. Wells-Barnett.[103] In short, the Black Church emerged as the community's most important institution, providing psychic relief from trauma and social refuge from racism.[104]

While a potentially unifying civil religion splintered and a new theological racism circulated—a theology portraying Blacks as soulless beasts rather than as cursed humans—African American political gains were reversed between 1876, when Lost Cause religion and renewed White violence shaped many election campaigns, and 1896, when the Supreme Court's *Plessy v. Ferguson* ruling endorsed "separate but equal" railway accommodations.[105] Black congregations continued to provide protection, one former slave recalled: "I just built a wall of the Lord 'round me so they couldn't get at me."[106] And Southern Blacks needed spiritual bulwarks. By 1908, when every Southern state had ratified a restrictive constitution, resurgent Christian racism was supporting disenfranchisement, segregation, and violence—and Douglass's hope of an egalitarian America seemed further away than ever.[107]

To understand how that happened, consider the case of Confederate soldier James Tillman's younger brother, Ben, who believed that "the White man has the God-given right to govern this country."[108] Postwar federal legislation and Congressional investigations had tried to check the Ku Klux Klan, though White mobs still lynched more than 2,000 Blacks between 1865 and 1877. Things got even worse after federal troops left in 1877, and Ben Tillman played a role.[109] Tillman proudly admitted he used violence, intimidation, and fraud to suppress Black voting and enforce racial segregation when he rode with the paramilitary arm of the Democratic Party (1873–1876), served as South Carolina's governor (1890–1894), and moved to the US Senate (1895–1918). During the 1876 election, Tillman supported a Democrat who used Lost Cause symbols to frame his campaign as a religious crusade, and whose followers engaged in organized violence in the town of Hamburg.[110] Whites disrupted an African American parade on the Fourth of July that year, America's centennial, and a few days later Tillman and other Democrats killed seven Blacks to "strike terror."[111] That terrorism—and cheating at the polls—assured Democratic victory and elevated Tillman's political stature. In 1890 he was elected governor. In his second term he abolished elected local government and introduced a governor-appointed system. He unseated Black officials and secured disenfranchisement when he called for a state constitutional convention. South Carolina's 1895 constitution raised discriminatory obstacles—like a poll tax and literacy test—for Black voters.[112] Tillman defended these tactics, saying "we of the South have never recognized the right of the Negro to govern White men, and we never will."[113]

Tillman played a minor role elsewhere as violence—and voter suppression—spread. In Wilmington, North Carolina, where Tillman had stirred up locals at an October 1898 election rally, Democrats again used violent intimidation and ballot stuffing in a coordinated riot. On election day Whites pointed pistols at Black poll workers, who fled in fear.[114] That enabled Democrats to win more seats, and locals then endorsed a White Declaration of Independence, announcing they would "no longer be ruled by men of African origin."[115] An African American newspaper editor who had condemned lynching and defended Blacks was given twenty-four hours to leave town, and a White mob burned the newspaper office. That group, which included gun-toting White ministers, killed scores of African Americans and forced the mayor, aldermen, and sheriff to step down. Some townspeople hid in the swamp while others, like the leading Black Baptist minister, left the city. So there were few dissenting voices the following Sunday, when White preachers assured congregants that God sided with the rioters. The mob, one pastor said, was "doing God's service."[116]

Redeeming the West, 1869–1898

Preachers also reassured White Protestants in the West, as residents debated whether to remove or assimilate those whose worship and morality didn't conform to Protestant notions of "religion," whose color and customs didn't pass the test for "Whiteness," and whose lifeways and family relations didn't fit Victorian norms of "civilization." As the South again postponed its racial reckoning, elite White Protestants from the Plains to the Pacific waged struggles for national belonging with Natives, Catholics, Latter-day Saints, and Chinese, who used spiritual resources to adapt to the ecological and social changes that followed the westward "course of empire," as the title of a popular 1868 lithograph put it (fig. 36).[117]

As the print suggested, Natives' niches would be stressed as continental imperialism peaked between 1869, when a Congregational minister "consecrated" the completed Pacific railroad, and 1898, when US spiritual and economic imperialism went global. America's first environmental protest—over the cutting of a giant redwood—had erupted more than a decade earlier, but Fanny Palmer, the print's lithographer, didn't aim to provoke ecological outrage in 1868.[118] After all, she had to sell prints to support her children. Yet the Episcopalian artist subtly illustrated the gains and losses of industry's march across the continent. Her 1868 print foresaw profits for eastern factory owners who made locomotives and rails. Telegraph lines ran along the tracks, suggesting railroad towns would enjoy the latest communication and transportation technologies. To the left of the tracks, farmers clear new fields and public schoolchildren greet the train's arrival. Behind the school stands a church, signaling that the gospel would come west too. To the right of the tracks, the artist foreshadowed damage to western habitats and Native lifeways. Two mounted Indians are stopped by the billowing smoke from the coal-powered locomotive while, in the distance, a buffalo herd awaits impending doom.

The image omitted some features of the postwar West, including the ways Native Peoples initially resisted but later used the railroad and the industrial economy. Some Paiute, Shoshone, and Pawnee relied on the railroad for wage-paying labor, for instance, and in the 1870s and 1880s trains helped spread Native religious practices.[119] The print, which pictured a railroad settlement, also ignored other social spaces—not just the Indian reservation, but also the mining camp and the cattle town—and it failed to capture the West's ethno-religious diversity, including the role that Chinese, Irish, Mexican, and

Figure 36. *Across the Continent: Westward the Course of Empire Takes Its Way* (1868) by Frances Flora Bond Palmer. Colored lithograph, published in New York by Currier and Ives. Courtesy of Yale University Art Gallery, Mabel Brady Garvan Collection.

LDS laborers played in building the railroad.[120] Nor can the viewer sense the prejudice those diverse workers faced as White Protestants pressured them to acculturate or leave. Despite the lobbying by Protestants like Jee Gam, who argued that his fellow Chinese could become "real" Americans, preachers and politicians decided Asians were too different to become the citizens of an Anglo-Saxon Protestant nation, and in 1882 Congress passed the Chinese Exclusion Act, which restricted migration.[121] Five years later Congress banned polygamy, a statute directed at Latter-day Saints, who had graded soil for the railroad tracks.[122] Irish and Mexican Catholics had built the railroad too, and that same year, 1887, the American Protective Association argued that Catholics followed an undemocratic faith. The hostility continued, even if there were a few expressions of appreciation, as when Irish and Chinese workers were given the honor of laying the final section of track in 1869.

Fanny Palmer couldn't have foreseen that symbolic inclusion, but her print did anticipate the devastation to peoples and lifeways. By the end of the century, the Indigenous population would plummet to 250,000, and Natives would lose more land. Before 1880, Natives had 138 million acres of reservation land; that would eventually dwindle to 48 million acres. Overhunting and disease continued to decimate the spiritually and economically significant buffalo, as about 5 million vanished from the Southern Plains between 1871 and 1878. By 1889 a naturalist counted only 20 bison in Colorado and 236 in Wyoming.[123] The environmental revolution of the horse, which the Spanish brought, led to Plains Peoples' regional ascendency, and the "iron horse," which the Americans brought, triggered regional decline.

President Grant's Protestant-run "Peace Policy" of the 1870s also stressed Native eco-cultural niches. Self-designated "friends of the Indians" proposed nonmilitary solutions to the "Indian problem."[124] Like their military-minded opponents, they affirmed the government's right to redistribute Native land to White Protestant settlers who would fence a plot, plant a crop, and raise a Bible-reading family. But they worried about the heathens' spiritual condition, and hoped Natives could accept the gospel of property-owning, land-cultivating Christianity. These Protestants were well represented on the congressionally appointed committee that concluded Christian civilization's westward push shouldn't be slowed "by a handful of savages," although the US should "conquer by kindness."[125] And Grant, who attended his wife's Methodist church, agreed. He hinted at the new policy in his first inaugural address. Congress then created a Board of Indian Commissioners, which assigned each reservation to a denomination and charged missionaries with civilizing the Natives.[126]

By the 1880s, however, even supporters agreed Grant's Peace Policy had failed. Helen Hunt Jackson's *Century of Dishonor* (1881) condemned federal policy, and White Protestants founded the Indian Rights Association (1882) to protest conditions on the reservations. A few who had tried to enact Grant's plan complained that the nation had not actually implemented a nonviolent approach: "while offering peace with one hand," a Quaker missionary observed, the US "grasped the sword with the other."[127] Former Union generals had applied the same brutal tactics they had used in the South, including attacking and starving noncombatants.[128] By the end of military action after the 1890 Wounded Knee Massacre, Natives had become individual wards of the government rather than citizens of sovereign nations, and the assimilationist strategy of the de facto Protestant establishment had brought disastrous consequences.[129] Government boarding schools like the Carlisle Indian School (1879–1918) separated traumatized children from their families to cultivate marketable skills and instill Protestant beliefs.[130] The 1887

General Allotment Act, which subdivided reservations into individual plots, caused more trauma. It didn't affect northern New Mexico's Pueblo Peoples, who were assigned Presbyterian missionaries but stayed on their land. Yet all those on the western reservations lost territory and endured challenges to their way of life. The 1883 Code of Indian Offenses (or Civilization Code) also caused trauma by criminalizing medicine men and Indigenous rituals. Natives could be jailed for seeking shamanic healing or performing a ceremonial dance.[131]

Indigenous Peoples responded in various ways to imperialism's effects between the 1870s and the 1890s. Some turned again to the psychoactive plant the shaman at Fate Bell Rock Shelter had ingested around 2020 BCE.[132] Adapting that ancient practice to serve modern ends, a new Peyote religion emerged, despite governmental and ecclesiastical opposition. To fend off critics, a pan-tribal coalition of Peyotists insisted their ancient rite was a "sacrament" and sought government protection by incorporating as the Native American Church in 1918.[133]

Others turned to the Ghost Dance movement, which began on Nevada's Walker Lake Reservation.[134] A Paiute elder, Wodziwob, had a vision in 1869, when workers finished the transcontinental railroad. He predicted the buffalo would come back. So would dead relatives, or ghosts, riding from the East on a train. The movement reemerged in 1889, when Wovoka, a Paiute ranch hand and holy man, also had a vision of a future restoration, a time when the buffalo and the ancestors would return. He stood in a lineage of vision-inspired prophets that went back to Po'pay in the seventeenth century and Neolin in the eighteenth, but he called for more than nostalgia. Wokova preached an adaptive social gospel for the industrializing West. Ghosters could live better now—while hastening the restoration—by avoiding immorality, making peace, and finding wage-earning employment. And, of course, Natives should gather for the Ghost Dance, singing sacred songs and performing circle dances. By 1890 the movement had spread, and in October the Lakota chief Sitting Bull (Tatanka Iyotake) sponsored a Ghost Dance on the Dakota plains. Convinced the ritual would spark rebellion, however, US officials used the Civilization Code's rules against ceremonial dancing to justify the military intervention that led to Sitting Bull's death and the massacre of 150 men and 250 women and children at Wounded Knee Creek. Despite the tragedy, Indigenous groups kept the Ghost Dance alive, just as Natives and non-Natives preserved Sitting Bull's memory.[135]

Figure 37. Éttàlyi̊dònmàui, *Night of the Surrender* (1877). Graphite and color pencil on paper. Courtesy of Richard Henry Pratt Papers, Yale Collection of Western Americana, Beinecke Rare Book and Manuscript Library, Yale University.

Some Natives in the West also affiliated with Christianity. The Pueblo in New Mexico associated with Catholicism, while others used Protestant or Orthodox traditions to push back and blend in. Éttàlyi̊dònmàui, a captured Kiowa warrior from the Southern Plains, accepted baptism at St. Augustine's Fort Marion, but also joined a failed plot to escape. His mixed allegiances surfaced in his art, which recalled sacred sites and chronicled tragic events, as with a sketch of the Kiowa camp on the night before surrender (fig. 37).[136] The Medicine Bluffs rising above the tipis were sacred, so the image documented his exile from that holy place. Captain Richard Pratt, who supervised the fort and wrote the caption, didn't mention the sacred landscape, but he came to respect the artist, asking him to recruit Native students for his boarding school at Carlisle, where Éttàlyi̊dònmàui would study and teach but live in a tipi, suggesting that Pratt's approach might have saved the man but hadn't killed *all* of the Indian. By 1888, when he took his last breath, Éttàlyi̊dònmàui had returned to his homeland near Medicine Bluffs, but as a Presbyterian missionary preaching the value of farming as well as "salvation."[137]

Stepan Katlan, a Tlingit-Orthodox man from Sitka, learned that the Russians had sold his Alaskan homeland to the US in 1867. Three decades later, in January 1897, he found himself dealing with government demands, church rivalries, and Tlingit customs when a controversy arose about how to bury his wife, Catherine.[138] Russian missionaries had persuaded more Tlingit to affiliate with the Orthodox Church, but US Presbyterians also claimed converts, including Stepan's two sons by another mother.[139] The controversy started when Stepan and Tlingit-Orthodox devotees placed Catherine in a coffin they had carved.[140] The next day he found his devout wife lying in *two* coffins because, the Orthodox priest said, his sons had been pressured by the US governor and Presbyterian minister. As the Protestant-government contingent was carrying Catherine for a Presbyterian burial, the priest complained that his congregants' rights to "liberty of worship" were being violated.[141] The judge sided with Stepan, who then insisted Catharine have an Orthodox funeral. But, as a compromise, Stepan buried her in *both* coffins, an apt symbol of Natives' strategic use of Christianity in this period of continental imperialism.

Global Crossings

The steamship and the telegraph made transoceanic contact easier and faster; using those technologies, America's economic and spiritual imperialism went global in 1898. As Theodore Roosevelt wrote in *The Winning of the West,* the Spanish–American War of 1898 "finished the work begun over a century before by the backwoodsman," an expansion that was "but a variant . . . of the great western movement."[142]

America Goes to the World

The "course of empire" took Americans abroad because leaders thought the nation had not met its spiritual obligations or solved its economic problems. The anthropological displays and religious speeches at the Chicago World's Fair of 1893 reminded the pious that most of the world remained unredeemed, and that year's economic depression led some to conclude overproducing US manufacturers and farmers needed new markets.[143] The forecast looked better by 1898, when America exported more manufactured goods than it imported and produced 32 percent of the world's food supply. But the US also eyed new mission fields and commercial markets. It annexed Hawai'i in 1898, while the Spanish–American War netted claims to Puerto Rico, Guam, and the Philippines.[144] Americans set up a military government in nearby Cuba (1899–1902) the next year. By 1900 distant Samoa became a US territory, and American troops helped suppress China's anti-foreigner Boxer Rebellion and kept the "heathen" nation open to traders and missionaries. In 1915 Americans occupied Haiti and sponsored a world's fair in San Francisco to commemorate the US-controlled Panama Canal, the massive engineering project that connected the Atlantic and the Pacific. In 1917 the United States entered World War I, and a disproportionate number of Indigenous, Jewish, and Catholic soldiers went abroad to fight.[145] In the same year, the government purchased the strategic Danish West Indies, which became the US Virgin Islands. By 1918 America led the world in industrial production, and it had become a global power with business investments from Cuba to Hawaiʻi and military bases from the Virgin Islands to American Samoa.[146]

Politicians and preachers also hoped to export religious values, as an interventionist civil religion and White Protestant nationalism shaped foreign policy. Between 1897 and 1913 three churchgoing Protestant presidents—William McKinley (Methodist), Theodore Roosevelt (Dutch Reformed), and William Taft (Unitarian)—championed expansion in their roles as chief architect of international policy and high priest of civil religion. Those presidents and their congressional and ecclesiastical boosters redirected civil religion's focus: an isolationist nation viewed as an example to the world, a city on a hill, became an expansionist power, a redeemer nation on a divine mission to convert and civilize. McKinley, for example, recalled the origin of his "benevolent assimilation" policy for the Philippines. He knelt to pray for God's guidance and concluded that since Indigenous and Catholic Filipinos were "unfit for self-government," America had a duty to "uplift and civilize and Christianize them."[147] McKinley's second inaugural address, which called on "Almighty God," defended the interventions in Cuba and the Philippines as part of the nation's sacred mission to secure "life, property, liberty, freedom of conscience, and the pursuit of happiness."[148]

Protestant foreign missions also increased. By the turn of the century, those who had seen themselves as "friends of the Indian" began to focus on "dependent peoples" in America's Caribbean and Pacific territories, and Protestants reinvigorated their decades-long interest in going abroad to save souls.[149] Congregationalists had founded the American Board of Commissioners for Foreign Missions (ABCFM) in 1810. Adoniram Judson left to save "the perishing millions" in Burma as early as 1813, and Pliny Fisk was preaching to Egypt's Muslims ten years later. Anna Tuttle Bullard explained what children "can do for the heathen" (1831) and wrote *Wife for a Missionary* (1835), encouraging women to join the effort.[150] By the century's end, denominations sponsored forty female missionary societies, and women like Lottie Moon, the iconic Baptist missionary to China, would be half the overseas workforce.[151] Mission leaders also enlisted thousands of young men in the Student Volunteer Movement after 1888, and John Mott's bestseller *The Evangelization of the World in This Generation* (1900) used the group's slogan to inspire more White mainline Protestants to civilize and convert the heathen.[152] Others felt called to preach the gospel abroad too. Gunnar Vingren, a Swedish-born pentecostal, left his Indiana pulpit to introduce speaking in tongues to Brazilians in 1910.[153] Black churches sponsored 108 foreign missionaries by then. Latter-day Saints were sending out missionaries, and Catholics would soon do the same.[154] Yet global evangelization was predominantly a White, mainline Protestant endeavor in 1910, when 120 missionary boards and agencies operated abroad, mostly in China, India, and Japan.[155] The four largest boards each sponsored more than 500 missionaries, including among the Japanese, who had "a high degree of civilization" but followed a misguided religion, Buddhism.[156]

Spiritual and economic imperialism converged in Hawai'i. The ABCFM had converted thousands of Native Hawaiians by 1840, and descendants of the US missionaries became the turn-of-the-century oligarchy. Their children, grandchildren, and in-laws owned the large plantations, like Ewa Plantation, where the sugar mill's smokestacks also signaled the planters' early acceptance of industrial agriculture's motto—"every farm a factory."[157] In 1887 the landowning Protestant elite imposed a disempowering constitution on King Kalākaua (r. 1874–1891), and in 1893 thirteen landowners overthrew Queen Lili'uokalani (r. 1891–1893) with the help of the US foreign minister, who ordered US Marines to aim their cannons at the queen's palace (fig. 38).[158] The queen aimed back, though with different weapons—an "imprisonment quilt," a Hawaiian creation story, and a history of Hawai'i that reasserted Indigenous sovereignty.[159] Despite her efforts, the islands became US territory in 1900, though the deposed monarch, who attended a Protestant church and revered Hawaiian tradition, would continue to use spiritual resources to resist.

She also would embrace the islands' increasing diversity. With her friend Mary Foster, a half-Hawaiian Buddhist sympathizer, Lili'uokalani attended a 1901 service at a Buddhist temple, where Hawai'i's religious and ethnic heterogeneity was on display.[160] In the 1850s, Kānaka Maoli or Native Hawaiians

Figure 38. Photograph of Queen Lili'uokalani (1891). Library of Congress, Prints and Photographs Division, LC-UCZ62-22488.

made up 97 percent of the islands' population, but it would be only 16 percent by the 1920s, when the Japanese, who were predominantly Buddhist, had become 44 percent of the residents. The first Buddhist missionary arrived from Japan in 1889, and the White Protestant growers, who hoped religion would increase productivity, began to subsidize plantation temples, including a Buddhist temple at Ewa Plantation in 1902.[161] After that, farmworkers who lost relatives could find comfort in "the smell of the incense, the temple gong, and chanting of the prayers at funerals."[162] Not everyone welcomed immigrant temples or celebrated Hawai'i's diversity, of course. One critic warned that their faith needed to be "Americanized," and the leading Japanese-born priest agreed.[163] So he shrewdly repurposed Christian terminology and strategically emphasized Buddhism's compatibility with American democracy.

The World Comes to America

America didn't just go to the world. The world also came to America, and the spiritually diverse newcomers transformed the mainland. Short-term visitors had some impact: westernized missionaries from Asia promoted decontextualized versions of Zen, Vedānta, and Sufism, traditions that had visibility in this period and even more influence later.[164] But it was immigrants who diversified the population and transformed the landscape, especially the tenement houses, industrial districts, and worship spaces of Northern metropolitan areas.

The rising migration began when the Great Potato Famine (1845–1849) prompted Irish Catholics to seek a better life, and by 1850 the proportion of US residents born in a foreign country rose to 9.7 percent.[165] Resistance to immigration rose too. The Know Nothing Party, a White Protestant political movement of the 1850s, symbolized the first wave of nativism, or opposition to minority groups because of their foreign connections.[166] Nativists worried because more than 2.5 million migrants arrived between 1851 and 1860, and hostility spiked again during the 1880s, when more than 5.2 million entered, many of them Catholics and Jews from eastern or southern Europe. In response, Josiah Strong published his 1885 manifesto *Our Country*, which insisted that America was an Anglo-Saxon Protestant nation and that those who sought citizenship should "assimilate."[167] New Yorkers dedicated the Statue of Liberty the following year, although not everyone welcomed the "huddled masses."[168] Eugenic nationalists even lobbied to legally exclude physically, mentally, and morally "defective" persons from the "lower" religions and races.[169] Boston Protestants challenged Catholics' claim to hemispheric primacy by dedicating a 1887 statue honoring "Leif the Discoverer," the Nordic Viking.[170] Despite the resistance, migration continued. The proportion of the foreign-born reached almost 15 percent in 1890 and was almost the same between 1901 and 1910, the peak decade, when more than 8.7 million newcomers entered. In turn, anti-Catholic sentiment surged again between 1910 and 1920.[171]

By the early twentieth century, immigration had realigned the religious population. In 1906 Methodists and Baptists remained the largest Protestant denominations, but Catholics boasted at least 12 million members, making them the nation's largest single religious group. That was a 93 percent increase since 1890.[172] Lutherans, the fourth largest denomination, had grown more than 70 percent, and both Eastern Orthodox Christians and Orthodox Jews increased too. Overall, there were about 1 million American Jews. A large portion of the 247,000 Chinese and Japanese would have been Buddhists, and approximately 60,000 Muslim migrants arrived between the 1890s and 1920s.[173]

The spiritually diverse newcomers sacralized the landscape, making new maps of meaning and constructing new sites for worship. Some changes were hidden from outsiders. European Muslim immigrants, who faced Mecca when they prayed, formed the American Mohammedan Society in Brooklyn, and Syrian Muslims in Ross, North Dakota, met in homes for Friday prayers, even if neither community would have a mosque until the 1930s.[174] On Manhattan's Lower East Side, where most Jews lived in 1900, Poles not only mapped sacred space in relation to Jerusalem, but a Polish-born rabbi re-imagined the neighborhood by creating an *eruv*, a symbolic boundary that allows the Orthodox to carry things on the Sabbath.[175] Other Jewish migrants created prayer groups or congregations in tenement houses, including on the top floor of a tenement owned by the wealthy Episcopal Trinity Church, whose impressive spire, once the city's tallest point, had become obscured by Wall Street skyscrapers.[176] Catholics, who looked to Rome and European shrines, got public attention by constructing a posh Gothic building on Manhattan's Fifth Avenue, St. Patrick's Cathedral (1879), and Orthodox Jews added a showpiece structure, the Eldridge Street Synagogue (1887).[177] Both immigrant faiths constructed new worship spaces in the next few decades and opened schools to help the next generation preserve their traditions and adjust to America. In 1884 the US Catholic bishops ordered all dioceses to build an elementary school in every parish, and that mandate changed the built environment. By 1900 New York City would have sixty parish schools where nuns taught immigrants and the children of immigrants, as the nationwide enrollment in Catholic elementary schools rose to more than 1.2 million.[178]

Immigration's diversifying effects were not evenly distributed, however. A small proportion of migrants went to southern locales like New Orleans, Birmingham, and Ybor City, a Florida town where Cubans toiled in cigar factories and worshipped in Catholic churches. Black Bahamian farmers sought opportunities in Miami, a segregated tourist city planned by a Presbyterian oil and railroad executive who built his first hotel over an ancient Tequesta cemetery.[179] Bahamians helped build that hotel as well as St. Agnes

Episcopal Church (1901), which provided respite from the unhealthy conditions and police brutality of Miami's "Colored Town." By 1920 one-quarter of Miami's population was foreign-born, yet most places in the South saw far fewer newcomers.[180]

Most went to the Midwest, West, or Northeast. Some settled in rural agricultural areas of the Midwest, as with the Dutch Calvinists who founded Holland, Michigan, where they planted Reformed Churches and organized a tulip festival.[181] Denver and San Francisco, the West's "instant cities," attracted diverse laborers during and after their Gold Rushes, and so did high-elevation mining villages like Georgetown, Colorado, where Frances Cabrini's Missionary Sisters of the Sacred Heart of Jesus served Italian silver miners.[182] "The West is being settled by well-nigh every variety of race," Josiah Strong warned, with migrants "representing every type of religion and irreligion."[183] He seemed especially worried about one "thoroughly heterogenous" Montana town, where 42 percent were Catholic and residents included Chinese Buddhists, Orthodox Christians, and even three Muslims. In California some newcomers settled in rural areas like Isleton, an asparagus-growing town in the Sacramento River Delta with a large Chinese and Japanese population. By 1909 the state also had Indian-born Hindus, who "built a huge funeral pyre on a raft" to send a deceased devotee down the Sacramento before the coroner stopped them, saying they could cremate their friend but had to do so "according to American ideas."[184]

Drawn by manufacturing jobs, most migrants ended up in northern cities. The cityscapes they encountered included soaring skyscrapers and huge factories as well as new styles of worship spaces, like the Richardsonian Romanesque architecture of Lucy Larcom's Boston church and the auditorium-style evangelical churches like Union Park Congregational in Chicago.[185] And they diversified the population as they changed the urban landscape. By 1880 over 60 percent of New York and San Francisco residents were foreign born. Disruptions in eastern Europe pushed many to leave for Chicago, and by 1890 an astonishing 77 percent of its 1 million residents were born outside the United States. Altogether, the US admitted over 23.5 million newcomers from the 1880s to the 1920s, and three-quarters would live in cities by 1920, including Syrian Muslims who found factory jobs at Ford Motor Company in Detroit.[186]

Some of the masses "huddled," and some didn't. Many lived down the street from neighbors who whispered their prayers in another language, like Gabriel Brillante, an Italian Catholic barber who lived on a block that included a German factory worker, an Irish dock worker, and a Hungarian

Jewish tailor.[187] Japanese Buddhists in San Francisco clustered in "Japan Town" after the 1906 earthquake, but Shūe Sonoda, a missionary who established the first mainland temple, lived on a street in 1900 that included Christian and Jewish migrants born in eight countries, including Russia, Sweden, and Germany.[188] Some newcomers did settle in residential districts where one ethno-religious group predominated. Joshua Seigel, the Polish-born rabbi who approved the New York *eruv,* lived on a block where every resident was either a Polish Jew or the child of one.[189]

Most of the 2 million Poles who emigrated between 1870 and 1920 were Catholic, and many headed to the steel mills and manufacturing plants of northern industrial cities. Chicago's Polish Catholics regularly encountered diverse residents, but some lived, worked, and prayed in industrial neighborhoods with others from their homeland. Rev. Paul Rhode, the immigrant pastor of St. Michael the Archangel Church (1909), lived on a block where all the residents were Polish Catholics, like Julian Ziuchkovski, who worked as a pipefitter at the steel mill down the street.[190] As in that neighborhood, immigration, urbanization, and industrialization converged to shape diasporic religious life. St. Michael's parishioners decorated their modest dwellings with images of their homeland's patroness, Our Lady of Częstochowska, and chatted in Polish after mass at their church, whose uneven steeples recalled St. Mary's Basilica in Krakow. But they also were fully immersed in Chicago's industrial landscape: the Polish congregants who worked at the mill even built St. Michael's—with steel donated by the factory.[191]

Religion and the Crisis of the Urban Industrial Niche

Even if the neighborhood church provided meaning and belonging, the urban industrial environment didn't always improve residents' well-being or give city dwellers a chance to fully flourish. As efforts to achieve restorative justice in the sharecropper South and the reservation West met with resistance, and the Colonial Era crisis remained mostly unresolved, a new Industrial Era crisis began around 1873, the year Andrew Carnegie first used the Bessemer process for making steel (see appendix).[192] Extractive industries degraded rural landscapes in mining towns and oil patches, but the effects were especially evident in the overcrowded immigrant neighborhoods and coal-burning factories of the urban North. The effects on the land, air, and water were accompanied by a decline in residents' well-being, with rising income inequity and health disparity the most important signs of decline.

Urbanization and immigration played a role, but industrialization was a primary source of this social and environmental crisis. Northeastern cities had become more industrial by 1848, when residents noticed the first signs of the shift to a mineral economy.[193] The early-nineteenth-century industrial niche had relied on solar energy, which generated wind gusts for sails and falling water for mills. The trees used as firewood for homes, steamboats, and factories also depended on the sun to grow. The emerging mineral niche relied indirectly on solar energy, which produced hydrocarbons from plant and animal remains, though proponents of natural theology in Britain, which had a head start on extracting coal and sanctifying industry, claimed God had created the conditions for coal to form millions of years ago.[194] In other words, God had made coal—and therefore the new industrial niche that depended on it. America's early mill villages weren't socially sustainable, since they relied on child labor, but water-powered mills emitted little pollution and, as long as no one upstream dammed the river, the factory's water wheel could have kept turning. So the mounting dependency on coal was still reversible in 1830, when the fossil-fuel infrastructure—and the "Christian industrialism" that justified it—wasn't fully in place in Philadelphia or Lowell.[195] Yet those industrial centers couldn't turn back after 1850, and by 1890 coal had surpassed wood as the nation's primary energy source. The US economy's manufacturing (30%) and mining (30%) sectors also surpassed agriculture (19%) for the first time, and the dependency on subsoil carbons—coal, oil, natural gas—had begun.[196]

Spiritually figured built environments became stressed as America transitioned from an agricultural to an industrial nation between 1873 and 1920 (fig. 39). Rural farming and ranching communities continued—and sometimes thrived—though industrialization affected them too.[197] Railroad track linked the hinterlands with urban centers, and mechanization transformed food production.[198] Industrialization's impact might not have been as evident at an Iowa farm as at a New Jersey factory, but the new mineral economy had widespread effects.

The fossil-fuel economy started to damage the environment. In the 1870s chemist Ellen Swallow Richards, who coined the phrase "human ecology," showed how industry tainted rivers along New England's industrial corridors.[199] Pollution reached Pittsburgh's Monongahela River Valley and the Great Lakes, where factories lined the shores of North America's largest freshwater source.[200] Factories also polluted the air, and by 1900 a scientist had proposed that carbon dioxide emissions from burning fossil fuels could lead to global

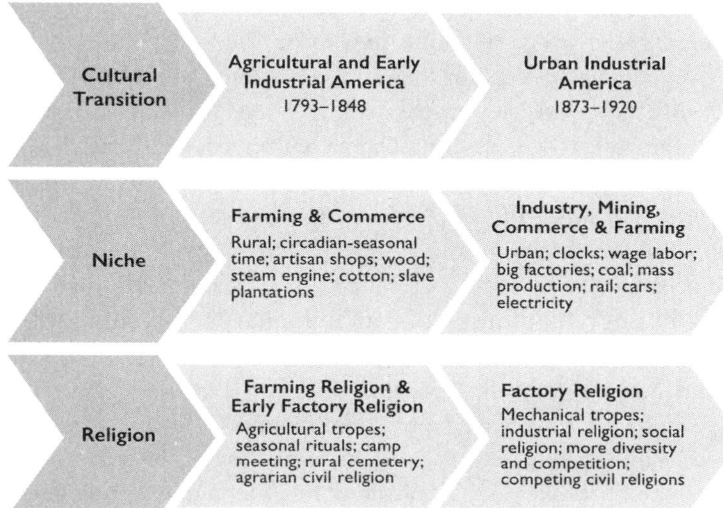

Figure 39. Transition from farming religion to factory religion.

warming, though few contemporaries listened.[201] As specialists now suggest, the warming trend started by the 1840s, during the First Industrial Revolution, and increased after 1880, during the coal-fueled Second Industrial Revolution. Technological wonders that filled investors' pockets and blackened workers' lungs made industrial communities less sustainable—as with one town south of Pittsburgh where a brick church and parish school stood across from a steel plant's smoke-emitting furnaces (see fig. 34).[202]

Contemporaries noticed the problems in factory towns and big cities. They debated income inequality, the gap between the poor and the rich, and during the long economic depression from 1873 to 1896, commentators complained about "tramps," jobless transients.[203] Politicians, journalists, and reformers also expressed alarm at health disparity. Some still thought divine Providence or moral character caused disease—or they blamed it on immigrants and the contagion of "foreign bodies."[204] But experts sought environmental explanations, applying the new germ theory of disease transmission. They emphasized population growth, suggesting that northern cities' density (persons per acre) and overcrowding (persons per housing unit) diminished health, including in New York City, the world's densest and most crowded city. An 1879 letter published in *Scientific American,* for example, warned that overcrowding was raising the mortality rate and lowering life expectancy.[205]

The decline in well-being had other causes and consequences.[206] Industrial accidents increased, signaling new workplace dangers; divorce rates went up, suggesting stresses on the family.[207] Adults weren't living as long, and more infants were dying. To make things worse, those who survived were smaller in stature. By the 1890s, municipal commissions and scientific reports began documenting the converging causes of health disparity.[208] Dilapidated tenements, contaminated food, piled garbage, and seeping sewage increased the urban poor's susceptibility to water-borne diseases like cholera and bacterial diseases like dysentery. Pollution also raised the risks in industrialized areas. Pittsburgh, for instance, had unsanitary tenements packed with poor European immigrants and Black southern newcomers. Its contaminated rivers contributed to nation-leading typhoid mortality rates between 1872 and 1908, and smoky air from coal-burning factories made residents more susceptible to respiratory complications during the flu pandemic of 1918–1919, when the Steel City's death rate was the highest in the country.[209]

This major lifeway transition also had spiritual effects. Industrialization restructured time and space, segmenting when and where wage workers prayed. Laborers worshipped when the factory whistle allowed it, and before 1900 they usually gathered for prayer near where they lived and worked. To increase company loyalty and reduce class conflict, some factory owners provided land for churches or donated construction materials, as at the Chicago steel mill that helped build St. Michael's, while other employers set aside devotional space at the workplace, as at a Brooklyn shipbuilding factory.[210] Industrialization even changed how the religious organized themselves. In an age when centralized corporate structures governed economic life, the pious worshipped in bureaucratic institutions and formed groups that targeted particular spiritual consumers or addressed particular social problems, from the Woman's Christian Temperance Union (1874) to the National Jewish Welfare Board (1917).[211] After 1900, electrified streetcars and urban railways enabled longer commutes, so laborers could worship farther from the workplace grime.[212] Improved transportation also heightened religious competition and multiplied Americans' "live options," their available spiritual choices, as suburban congregations proliferated and devotees could attend a wider array of services.[213]

Machine Age technologies also generated new figurative language for religious life. Organic tropes persisted, as intellectuals employed arboreal analogies, for example, to trace the seedlike "origin" and treelike "growth" of religions.[214] Some, however, started using the analogy of the steam engine, and mechanistic tropes gradually became more popular. Spiritualism, which gained attention during the 1850s, relied on the metaphor of the telegraph to describe how departed souls communicated with the living.[215] And evocative imagery from new technologies circulated after 1900.[216] Harriet Monroe, who worked at an evangelical rescue mission, talked of the mind's "machinery," for example, and used mechanistic analogies to describe religious experience. Scripture came to a convert, she observed, "like a wireless message to his soul," and, referring to the phonograph, Monroe proposed that scripture is "God's recorded message." She had seen electrified streetcars connected by an overhead wire to a power source, and Monroe used that imagery to explain religion's transformative effect. "The soul is as dead as a street car with the power gone," she wrote, "till it is touched by that special power."[217]

Industrial Religion

Wealthy industrialists, journalistic boosters, and Protestant preachers accelerated industrialization by sacralizing new technologies and the fossil fuels that powered them while, at the same time, minimizing their social and environmental costs.[218] When Queen Victoria sent a telegraph message to President James Buchanan in 1858, a New York reporter attributed it to "the directing hand of Providence."[219] In his opening prayer at Philadelphia's 1876 Centennial Exposition, where visitors marveled at Alexander Graham Bell's telephone, the Methodist who had preached Lincoln's funeral sermon thanked God for "the valuable discoveries and multiplied inventions."[220] That attitude was also on display at the Chicago World's Columbian Exposition in 1893, when fairgoers expressed wonder at electric lights and speakers praised industrial progress.[221] In 1904, the year after the Wright brothers' first flight, a Chicago minister said humans had asserted "dominion" over the land and sea, as God commanded, and soon would create a "highway over the earth."[222] Henry Ford cared about earthbound highways, and by 1906 he dreamt of a car that might enable families to enjoy "the blessing of hours of pleasure in God's great open spaces."[223] Less than a decade later, industry's devotees saw Ford's dream fulfilled at San Francisco's 1915 Panama–Pacific International Exposition. Its "Court of Abundance" displayed a tower of tiered altars depicting the "ascent of man," and organizers enshrined Ford's manufacturing process as well as his consumer products: Ford built an assembly line that turned out a Model T every ten minutes for three hours each day, except Sunday, the Christian day of rest.[224]

This industrial religion, which attributed "superhuman power to raw materials and the mechanical technologies employed to convert those

Table 1. Varieties of Industrial Religion, 1870–1920

FRAMEWORK	DIVINE	AUTHORITY	PATH	GOAL	EXEMPLAR
Liberal Protestant	theist: *God*	Bible, science, experts	gradual	accommodating gospel and culture	John D. Rockefeller
Conservative Evangelical	theist: *God*	Bible's "plain" meaning	sudden	obeying divine commands	Lyman Stewart
New Thought	pantheist: *Unseen*	hidden forces	gradual	harmonizing with eternal laws	Henry Ford
Spencerian	agnostic: *Unknown*	evolutionary sciences	gradual	recognizing evolutionary principles	Andrew Carnegie

materials into consumer goods," took different forms.[225] The spiritual language differed slightly among those who exalted the oil refinery, coal mine, steel mill, and auto plant, and advocates employed diverse spiritual frameworks to sacralize industrial progress (table 1).

Liberal Protestant and conservative evangelical theologies provided the most popular frameworks for industrial religion. Catholic clergy scrambled to serve the industrial underclass. Most of industry's boosters, then, were Protestants who advocated an updated version of the "Christian industrialism" of the early factory era. Holiness Pentecostal adherents who valued spirit-filled worship sacralized the minerals, processes, and products of industry, but most proponents of industrial religion were liberals or evangelicals in mainline denominations who disagreed about how to interpret the Bible and how much to accommodate modern culture.[226] Those theological differences arose even among Protestant business leaders who promoted the same industry. The evangelical Lyman Stewart and the liberal John D. Rockefeller both refined oil and funded evangelization but preached diverging carbon gospels. The sudden path to individual salvation mapped by boom-or-bust fundamentalists like Stewart of Union Oil of California differed from the gradual path to social salvation trod by monopoly-building liberal Protestants like Rockefeller of Standard Oil.[227] Despite the differences, they agreed that fossil fuels came from God. Like Stewart, Rockefeller believed oil deposits "were the beautiful gifts of the great Creator."[228] Coal was sacred too. Rev. Washington Gladden, a liberal Protestant who once rejected Rockefeller's "tainted" donation, didn't doubt coal's divine origin. It was "the handiwork of God." Even "mechanical devices," Gladden added, "are provided for in God's design."[229]

A few industry-celebrating factory owners embraced other spiritual worldviews. Protestant ministers baptized and buried Andrew Carnegie and Henry Ford, but each suffered a spiritual crisis they resolved by assembling a composite faith that didn't fit within the confines of the Christian church. Carnegie, the steel producer, admired his Scottish parents, who left Presbyterianism for Unitarianism and Swedenborgianism. But after rejecting those faiths, he found himself "at sea." He finally discovered Herbert Spencer, whose agnostic theory of natural and cultural evolution provided meaning and led him to venerate "the unknown but not unfelt something omnipotent beyond us," the "Eternal Energy from which all things proceed."[230] Carnegie continued to dismiss narrow creeds but appreciated diverse expressions of universal religious sentiment. He called his manuscript copy of Edwin Arnold's *Light of Asia*, a life of the Buddha, "one of my most precious treasures."[231] He praised an "inexpressibly sublime" Zoroastrian ritual he saw in Bombay, and hosted a tolerance-affirming leader of the Baha'i faith, which announced a new prophet for the new age.[232] Spencer's evolutionary framework also prompted "greater reverence" for the natural world and heightened wonder at technological advances.[233] One biographer even suggested that Carnegie's first encounter with "the dazzling brilliance of the Bessemer converter," which allowed inexpensive steel production, "resembled the religious experience known as conversion."[234]

Ford, a nominal Episcopalian who once worked for Thomas Edison, had his own light-bulb moments. But he built his industrial faith on the New Thought writings of Ralph Waldo Trine, an Emersonian pantheist who sought to live in harmony with the higher laws of the Unseen.[235] Ford's faith had its dark side—he was anti-Semitic—but his syncretic spirituality included a belief in reincarnation and an inclination toward mysticism. Those views surfaced in a conversation with the Sufi mystic Inayat Khan. Ford explained his industrial theology, noting "the power that makes the automobile go, is after all, invisible"; the Unseen force can be accessed if we seek "the unity of the soul with the Soul of the universe." Most important, unity-seeking mysticism, he believed, was compatible with profit-making industry. "Mastery and use of the material world need not interfere with our understanding and use of the spiritual."[236]

Ford's material "mastery" produced the assembly line, an epoch-changing tool, but he also suggested "faith is one of the most effective tools." "I believe," he said, "that faith works."[237] But how did industrial religion work—and for whom? It supported wealthy industrialists and those who managed plants and sold products, offering a sense of purpose, a code of conduct, and a justification for inequity. The trade magazine *Industrial World* assured hardware merchants they were entrusted with the "God-given powers of commerce" and offered moral guidelines: "Maintain your integrity as a sacred thing," and be prompt, avoid liquor, and work hard.[238] Wealthy factory owners recognized fewer moral constraints and offered more self-justifying explanations. Carnegie, the world's richest person and largest steel producer, said income inequality was good for the "future progress of the race." It was the "survival of the fittest" in the social realm.[239] Ford embraced reincarnation because "it offers an intelligible explanation of the inequalities of life" by positing that *karma,* or moral action, determines a person's social station.[240] Other evangelists of industrial religion saw profits as well-earned blessings from God. The Baptist Russell Conwell preached that everyone had "a duty to get rich," and corporate owners took that to heart, although they also donated to their favorite causes.[241] Carnegie built libraries and sponsored church organs. Ford funded a hospital and a home for orphan boys. Stewart established a Bible institute and a rescue mission. Rockefeller founded a university and supported Baptist churches. But like the early factory owners who cherished the mills' "moral machinery," industrialists and their ecclesiastical supporters also urged laborers to cultivate virtues like diligence and punctuality, habits that might increase wage earners' productivity and stifle labor unrest.[242]

Violent labor strikes still broke out between 1877 and 1894, and industrialists sometimes used spiritual resources as well as armed guards to quell dissent. Consider the Homestead strike of 1892, when steelworkers seeking reduced hours and higher wages were locked out of a Carnegie plant near Pittsburgh.[243] Carnegie condoned his manager's choice to use force, which left nine striking workers and seven hired guards dead. But a ritual staged during the strike showed how the company also wielded religion to sacralize the workspace, justify its actions, and disempower workers. One morning in July, Carnegie's plant manager arranged a Sunday service for the strikebreakers. With state militiamen and hired security standing guard, the fortified factory became a house of worship.[244] Replacement workers sat on beams, benches, and cranes as a Baptist minister presided, a small orchestra played, and a choir of company clerks sang. The service opened with "Nearer My God to Thee," a hymn retelling Jacob's dream of rising to heaven on a ladder, and then the beam-perched replacement workers heard a sermon describing the apostle Paul as "a workingman for Christ." The service ended with the company clerks singing "America," suggesting the replacements' union-busting labor was sanctified by both faith and flag.

Redeeming Urban Industrial America

After the strike, Pittsburgh's *National Labor Tribune* condemned Carnegie with a mocking prayer that began "Oh, Almighty Andrew Philanthropist Library Carnegie."[245] In this and other ways, some challenged industrial capitalists and defended urban workers. Journalists blasted the monopolistic practices of Cleveland's Standard Oil, and novelists detailed the hazards of Chicago's meatpacking industry.[246] Others employed spiritual rhetoric to "redeem" the factory and the city.[247] Contemporaries called this "social religion," since the reform-minded used the adjective *social* to describe problems they addressed, and many believed "there was something that could be done about everything."[248] Reformers disagreed, though, about exactly what could be done. Some focused more on the individual than the collective. They also held varied views about free-market capitalism and quarreled about government's role. To oversimplify the main positions on the continuum of social religion, religious conservatives hoped to rescue lost souls, moderates hoped to rectify social ills, and radicals hoped to restructure collective life.

The moderates included liberal Protestants, Reform Jews, and Roman Catholics. Protests emerged initially from the church pew and the factory floor, and not from the pulpit. A working-class Catholic led the first national industrial union, the Knights of Labor, from 1877 to 1893, and its constitution quoted scripture as it decried "the hopeless degradation of the toiling masses."[249] In Chicago, laborers forged a working-class faith that asserted their rights.[250] The ground-up effort, in turn, nudged a younger generation of Protestant and Catholic pastors to support demands for an eight-hour workday. The process happened elsewhere too as pressured clerics promoted a practical piety. Catholic leaders condemned capitalism's me-first ethic, but defended private property and social hierarchy against the atheistic socialism of Karl Marx. Cardinal James Gibbons denounced industrial monopolies and defended labor unions, and Father John A. Ryan advocated *A Living Wage* (1906) and drafted *Social Reconstruction* (1919), a pamphlet describing the US bishops' policy proposals, including unemployment insurance, a minimum wage, and health insurance.[251] Liberal Protestants embraced the "Social Gospel."[252] Pittsburgh's Calvary Episcopal Church aided wage workers and improved housing conditions, and novels by Rev. Charles Sheldon (1897) and Vida Dutton Scudder (1903) popularized the movement.[253] Settlement houses like Chicago's Hull House, cofounded by Episcopalian Ellen Gates Starr and Unitarian Jane Addams, encouraged immigrant acculturation and addressed community needs.[254] The Baptist Walter Rauschenbusch analyzed social sin and social salvation in treatises like *Christianity and the Social Crisis* (1907), and Methodists issued a Social Creed, which informed the Federal Council of Churches' advocacy of "industrial justice."[255] Rabbi Emil Hirsch convinced Reform Jews to add a plank to their Pittsburgh Platform (1885) calling for just relations between rich and poor, and by 1918 they condemned "social and economic evils."[256]

Conservatives endorsed free-market capitalism and prioritized individual regeneration. Rabbi Isaac Wise's successor in Cincinnati said synagogues and churches needed personal piety more than collective reform.[257] A conservative evangelical called the new social religion "a device of hell."[258] Revivalists Dwight Moody and Billy Sunday didn't go that far, but blamed personal sin and immoral living, not tenement conditions and worker exploitation. The world would get better, they said, by saving one soul at a time, even if conservatives endorsed organized action when a personal habit or public policy endangered the home. Evangelicals joined the Woman's Christian Temperance Union (WCTU) because men's drinking triggered domestic violence and drained household finances, and Frances Willard, WCTU president, even presented suffrage as a domestic issue, since it would allow wives and daughters to vote for temperance candidates. But most conservative evangelicals cared more about Salvation Army shelters, YMCA branches, and rescue missions, where evangelists offered slum dwellers "soap, soup, and salvation."[259]

Radicals who denounced capitalism favored more dramatic change, and, whether or not they affiliated with a tradition, many had religious roots and employed spiritual rhetoric. Christian socialist John Haynes Holmes saw Jesus as a working-class revolutionary and preached the funeral sermon for a radical cartoonist who had pictured the Christian savior as an agitator wanted by the police.[260] Episcopalian moral teachings influenced Henry George, author of *Progress and Poverty* (1879), and he later advocated a socialist religion as he criticized "the persistence of poverty amid advancing wealth."[261] Edward Bellamy, the son of a mill-town minister, published a futuristic novel that proposed nationalized industries but also imagined "a new phase of spiritual development."[262] He anticipated televangelism, as well as credit cards and shopping malls, and those eager to hasten that utopian future could join one of 162 Bellamy Clubs.

Like Bellamy, reformers imagined alternative niches, spaces of refuge within the industrial city or beyond its limits. Preservationists like John Muir, who believed "we may most easily see God" in the mountains, ignored Native land rights while campaigning to protect wilderness areas like Yellowstone (1872), the world's first national park, as sites for venerating Nature and escaping urban life.[263] The landscape architect Frederick Law Olmsted, a lapsed Congregationalist who admired New England village greens, suggested urban parks provided another way of "counteracting the evils of town life."[264] Green spaces like Central Park (1876), which Olmsted designed, could regenerate pedestrians wearied by the noxious cityscape and welcome the "poor and rich, young and old, Jew and Gentile." That strategy for unifying residents, improving health, and redeeming cities reached Lowell, where in 1910 locals dedicated Lucy Larcom Park.[265] A few industrialists even planned company towns. The Presbyterian Henry Disston established Tacony (1876), a factory town northeast of center city Philadelphia. The Disston family hoped to control environmental pollutants as well as moral temptations. They banned saloons but also built a water treatment plant and prohibited engines that caused loud noise, dirty air, and foul odors. Tacony, which also boasted diverse churches, was "a paradise for the working man of moderate means," a place where blue-collar families could enjoy "good air, pure water, and healthy surroundings."[266]

The spiritually inspired also looked back to a fading agrarian past. Handheld stereoscopes enabled nostalgic viewers to return to Plymouth Rock or even Mesa Verde, which became a national monument in 1906, and rural advocates of "old-time religion" embraced agrarian reform.[267] The Baptist Booker T. Washington was known for his industrial schools, but he also advocated "keeping the Negro on the soil . . . close in touch with Mother Earth."[268] And religious groups established utopian communities as havens from urban industrial life and as laboratories for reorganizing the social sphere.[269] Iowa's Amana Colonies (1856) included self-sufficient villages of German Lutheran farmers who ate in communal dining halls. Holiness healers offered the spirit-filled residents of Durham, Maine's Shiloh (1896) a place to await Christ's imminent return.[270] John Humphrey Noyes believed Christ had already initiated the New Heaven and Earth, so he founded a very different community of Oneida Perfectionists (1848–1881) in upstate New

York, where members practiced "Bible communism" (rejecting property) and "complex marriage" (rejecting monogamy).[271] Asian- and occult-inspired reformers also founded utopian communes, including the Theosophical community at San Diego's Point Loma (1897–1942), where upper-class spiritual seekers educated children and planted vegetables.

Others established agricultural colonies. To reform the moral character of the jobless, the Salvation Army founded farm colonies in the West.[272] Jews organized agricultural communities in New Jersey, where Russian Jewish immigrants "redeemed" the sparsely populated pinelands.[273] And Catholic leaders redirected immigrants to Minnesota farm colonies so they could avoid urban hazards and return to the land, since, as one bishop said, the agricultural life is more conducive to "happiness and morality."[274]

Faith and Flourishing in 1920

Americans, both rural and urban, seemed a bit better off by 1920. Prosperity came to the countryside during US agriculture's "golden age" between 1900 and 1920, when farm income doubled.[275] Religiously inspired reformers worried about *How the Other Half Lives* and pushed officials to clean up or tear down urban tenements.[276] Those troubled by corporate monopolies celebrated the Supreme Court's 1911 decision to break up Standard Oil, and industrial workers secured a few victories, as when railroad laborers won an eight-hour day.[277] The income gap between the rich and the poor began to narrow, and the declines in life span and physical stature started to reverse. Marginalized groups made minor legal gains, as when Indigenous and Asian American soldiers who fought in WWI gained citizenship by 1919.[278] African Americans continued to seek dignity in the Black Church, which had solidified by 1920. Natives raised on the reservation and in the boarding school joined advocacy groups like the Society of American Indians (1911) and creatively resisted pressures to assimilate while passing on ancestral practices. The Blackfoot (Niitsitapi) in Montana, for example, shrewdly rescheduled their prohibited Medicine Lodge ceremony on the Fourth of July.[279]

By 1920 women had gained access to the pulpit and the ballot. Elizabeth Cady Stanton, who left the Presbyterian Church, argued that all religions taught "the inferiority and subordination of women," but Frances Willard, the first woman honored with a statue in the Capitol, praised the Protestant women ordained since 1853 and supported Stanton's National American Woman Suffrage Association (1890).[280] Church women went to Washington, DC, for the 1913 Woman Suffrage Procession, when Rev. Anna Shaw, an ordained White minister, marched in front and the Anishinaabe Catholic Marie Bottineau Baldwin and the Black Presbyterian Ida Wells-Barnett paraded too.[281] The march helped to reinvigorate the movement, and women won the vote when the states ratified the Nineteenth Amendment in 1920.

Despite these gains, social inequalities lingered and environmental stresses deepened. Most Asian Americans still weren't citizens. Blacks had gained citizenship, but voter suppression limited their political participation. Starting around 1915, when a Methodist preacher founded a new Ku Klux Klan, racism prompted the Great Migration of Southern Blacks to the urban industrial North.[282] Industrialization's ecological degradation also accelerated, as most US households were using soot-generating coal by 1920.[283] Income inequality and health disparity persisted for many Blacks, Natives, and immigrants, and some health indicators were troubling, and not just the death toll (675,000) from the 1918–1919 flu pandemic. Suicide rates hit a historic high in 1910, and coal mining fatalities peaked too. Work conditions hadn't improved much, as adults in factories and mines worked long hours in dangerous conditions for low pay, and, despite religious protests, child labor continued.[284] As workers demanded change, class conflict and labor-related violence also rose sharply. About 4 million workers participated in unsuccessful strikes in 1919, and a lethal "mine war" broke out in West Virginia.[285] Violence even reached the White Protestant upper class in 1920, when a lunch-hour bomb on Wall Street killed thirty in New York's financial district.

Religion intensified the social and ecological crises—and not only because factory owners draped a sacred canopy over the new urban industrial niche. By 1920, the tercentenary of the Pilgrims' landing, a resurgent White Protestant nationalism constricted notions of what it meant to be an American.[286] As immigrants alarmed federal policy makers, Catholics continued to promote a Columbian narrative that began with the *Santa Maria* and highlighted early Maryland's tolerance. Jews told a Statue of Liberty tale about America as the migrant's refuge, though after 1908 they debated whether the metaphor of a *melting pot* (making uniformity out of difference) or an *orchestra* (creating harmony from discordant instruments) was best for national narratives.[287] The Great Seal's motto—*E pluribus unum*—hinted at an older narrative about the many becoming one, but by 1920 Protestant nationalists preferred the Plymouth Rock story, which honored the Mayflower Compact and claimed Anglo-Saxon Protestant priority.[288] It wasn't a new story. Daniel Webster had told it in his 1820 address at Plymouth. Josiah Strong alluded to it in *Our Country,* and the Congregationalist David Brewer repeated it in his 1892 Supreme Court decision that decreed the US was "a Christian nation."[289] The twentieth-century version, which commemorated able-bodied White Protestants who conquered wilderness and civilized Indians, had real-life consequences. It constructed an evolutionary ladder that subordinated religious outsiders (Catholics and Jews), "lower" races (Blacks and Natives), hereditary "defectives" (the deaf and the epileptic), and national groups (Italians and Chinese).[290] The implied social hierarchy informed public policy, as with the 1906 Naturalization Act's English requirement and polygamy ban, and the 1917 Immigration Act's barring of the "mentally and physically defective" and restricting of migrants from the "Asiatic" zone where Islam, Hinduism, and Buddhism predominated.[291] The narrative also produced material disadvantages and sustained lingering inequalities. Narrators' pejorative assessments, which claimed divine sanction, affected the self-perceptions of the maligned and restricted access to jobs, housing, health care, loans, and schools.

White Protestant nationalism found expression in varied cultural forms. Patriotic hereditary societies like the Sons of the American Revolution (1889), Daughters of the American Revolution (1890), and Society of Mayflower Descendants (1897) published immigrant assimilation manuals. Episcopalians built monumental architecture like the Washington National Cathedral, which Congress approved in 1893 and President Teddy Roosevelt endorsed in 1907, tapping in the cornerstone of the church with a "national" purpose. A new anti-Catholic nativism inspired combative Protestant periodicals like *The Menace* (1911), which echoed the anti-Catholic sentiment expressed in the fundamentalist paperbacks (1910–1915) that oilman Lyman Stewart financed.[292] The 1915 film *Birth of a Nation,* which President Woodrow Wilson screened at the White House, glorified the KKK.[293] It suggested that Jesus endorsed White supremacy, and it encouraged Northerners and Southerners to unite in a shared contempt for African Americans. Some did unite, as southern Whites warmed to northern civil religion by 1917, when Wilson, a minister's son from Virginia, led the US into WWI and assured Confederate veterans that Southerners would be "an instrument in the hands of God."[294]

Narrow nationalism was on display during the 1920 Pilgrim celebrations too. The government issued commemorative stamps and coins, and it sponsored monuments, parades, pageants, and speeches. Talk of Pilgrims echoed in the 1920 presidential election, as the Baptist Warren Harding and his vice presidential running mate, Congregationalist Calvin Coolidge, advocated "pious Americanism" and praised "Pilgrims' principles."[295] A month after their electoral victory, Plymouth's official celebration looked back to 1820 as well as 1620. Coolidge, the incoming vice president, began the commemoration at Plymouth Rock's "shrine" by telephoning California's governor to fulfill Webster's 1820 "prophecy" that the Pilgrims' voice would reach the Pacific. Senator Henry Cabot Lodge, an immigration foe, praised Webster's oration and celebrated the Pilgrims' "dream of empire," which began when English Protestants came ashore to "conquer the wilderness."[296]

Not everyone was celebrating—or sacralizing the same past. The local Wampanoag refused to join the commemorations, just as William Apess had countered Webster's oration by recasting the Pilgrims as barbarians.[297] Spanish-language newspapers in the Southwest mentioned the tercentenary but noted that St. Augustine was older than Plymouth and showed little enthusiasm for *los Padres Peregrinos,* the Pilgrim Fathers.[298] Catholic and Jewish leaders, who feared nativism, marked the anniversary, but Milwaukee's archbishop forbade Catholic children from attending a Pilgrim pageant until organizers agreed to change the script.[299] There were other scripts, other national myths, circulating in 1920.[300] Blacks told biblically figured tales about forced exile, emancipation from enslavement, and a continuing journey toward the promised land that Frederick Douglass had imagined in his depiction of the US as a "composite nation."

Debates about what it meant to be American raged in the capital, which took on more symbolic significance. Washington became the site for diverse civil religious rituals—Black and White, nativist and immigrant—and, spurred by the Episcopalians' architectural showcase, a new mode of interfaith rivalry emerged as the pious competed to erect "national churches" in the capital by 1920, when Cardinal Gibbons blessed the foundation stone of a Romanesque national shrine across town from the Episcopalians' Gothic National Cathedral.[301] The former Union chaplain would die soon after that ceremony, a time when thousands of aging Civil War veterans remained but shared memory of the bloody conflict was starting to fade.[302] By 1920, however, another conflict about national belonging was being waged in urban industrial America. And it wasn't clear which national myth would win, although those who favored an inclusive nation had reason to worry.[303]

CHAPTER 8

Reassuring Religion

Shifting Fears, Diverging Hopes, and Accelerating Crisis, 1921–1963

Social inequalities lingered, environmental stresses deepened, and conceptions of American identity narrowed after Warren Harding entered the White House in 1921. In his first year that pious Baptist would retell the Plymouth Rock story, preach free-market individualism, and—despite Catholic and Jewish opposition—appease nativist fears by restricting immigration. But the debate about what it means to be American would continue over the next four decades. This chapter traces religion's role in the ongoing debates, as it also documents the shifting sources of fear and the diverging visions of flourishing between 1921, when an industrial consumer culture was consolidating, and 1963, when the first signs of a postindustrial world began to appear.

Those changes unfolded in three periods: first, as borders closed, business boomed, and commercial religion prospered during the Twenties; second, as the pious and not so pious sought "freedom from want" and "freedom from fear" in an era of economic depression and world war between 1929 and 1945; and finally, when postwar leaders prescribed a tranquilizing national faith to calm Cold War anxieties about atomic bombs and atheistic communists while middle-class parents took refuge in the fallout shelter, the shopping center, the medicine cabinet, and the segregated suburb.[1] Despite the lingering problems, some spiritually inspired activists began to confront the legacy of earlier sustainability crises, which by the 1950s had dramatically accelerated environmental damage and prevented the socially marginalized from enjoying all the blessings of liberty and securing all the conditions for happiness (see appendix).

Believing, Belonging, and "Prosperity," 1921–1929

Fear-driven pieties emerged in the Twenties as public disputes about the meaning of "Americanism," or national belonging, and "prosperity," or economic well-being, intensified. Those discussions raged during the administrations of Harding (1921–1923) and Coolidge (1923–1929), and the "noise of conflict" was almost as great when Herbert Hoover, another probusiness Protestant, took the oath of office in March 1929 and the stock market crashed that October.[2]

As in earlier periods, disputes about belonging and prosperity reflected deeper disagreements, including about how founding political documents and familiar sacred texts should inform national conceptions of the good life. President Harding appealed to Micah 6:8, a biblical passage that has long been a favorite of US leaders.[3] As General George Washington did in his first message to the states in 1783 and President Jimmy Carter would do in his 1977 inaugural address, Harding recalled what the divine required of ancient Israel—and of the New Israel, America: "to do justly," "love mercy," and "walk humbly with your God."[4] But what do justice, mercy, and humility entail? And how should Americans understand passages in the Declaration and the Constitution about individual and communal flourishing? What does "equality" mean for those endowed with God-given rights to "Life, Liberty, and the pursuit of Happiness"? And how should they "establish justice," "promote the general Welfare," and "secure the Blessings of Liberty" for this and future generations? Can justice mean, as the *Plessy* decision said, "separate but equal"?[5] Could one generation's liberty come at the expense of the next? Which policies and practices contribute to "the general Welfare"? What is happiness and who has the right to pursue it? Americans asked, in particular, whether the nation's promises and principles applied to Blacks, Natives, Asians, Jews, and Catholics.

Competing Americanisms

A debate arose, for example, during Chicago's 1926 mayoral election. Indigenous voters, who had gained citizenship two years earlier, wrote to the eventual winner, William "Big Bill" Thompson, to denounce his campaign rhetoric.[6] The Protestant had praised the founders and repeated "America

First," Harding's phrase, but the Native group suggested that Thompson should emphasize instead "the First Americans."[7] They also challenged the prevailing talk of "100 percent Americanism," a slogan that reflected the wartime fear of Germans and "Reds" and came to be associated with the new Ku Klux Klan's motto of "Native, White, and Protestant supremacy."[8] Only Indigenous Peoples were "100% American," they insisted.[9]

The pragmatic three-term mayor did a better job of reaching out to others who felt under attack, because he recognized the city had been transformed by the arrival of Catholic and Jewish immigrants and the Great Migration of southern-born Black Protestants.[10] The Black community had suffered racial violence in the riot of 1919, and more harassment came with the Klan's arrival in 1921. As White Protestant fear increasingly focused on Catholic and Jewish migrants, Chicago's Klan membership swelled to 50,000, the largest among major cities, and Harding signed the Emergency Quota Act (1921), the first law to set numerical limits on immigration by establishing an annual quota for persons from each country.[11] As political cartoons pointed out, the 1921 law reduced the stream of new arrivals and narrowed the meaning of American identity. The restrictions got worse when President Coolidge signed the National Origins Act (1924), which reduced the quota to 2 percent of the total number of people of each nationality in the US as of the 1890 national census.[12] It barred almost all Asians and substantially reduced newcomers from eastern and southern Europe, religious and ethnic populations that some feared were sullying the purity of America's Anglo-Saxon Protestant heritage.

Some of Chicago's Catholics, Jews, and Blacks resisted this narrowing of national identity. They sometimes even joined forces. In 1922 Robert Abbott, the Presbyterian editor of the *Chicago Defender*, the nation's leading African American newspaper, proposed a Go-to-a-White-Church Sunday campaign, which, like the Federal Council of Churches' "Race Relations Sunday" in 1923, presumed interracial proximity would help.[13] Interracial worship services might have generated meaningful interpersonal encounters, but the American Unity League probably had more impact.[14] Founded in 1922 by an Irish Catholic layman, the Chicago-based group targeted the Ku Klux Klan, and many local Jewish rabbis and Black ministers signed on. So did Abbott, who urged readers "to join Catholics, Jews, and the Irish in the war against the Klan."[15] By publishing local Klan members' names in its newsletter, the league played a role in reducing Chicago's KKK membership by 1926, when thousands of emboldened Catholics gathered for the first International Eucharistic Congress held in the US.[16]

The struggles about national identity raged beyond Chicago, and combatants weaponized religion as they fought in churches, courtrooms, and streets as well as in government offices, voting booths, and print media. Some spiritual warriors battled in the shadows: J. Edgar Hoover, a churchgoing Presbyterian, became FBI director in 1924, and he slowly built up the agency "as a white Christian force that partnered with white evangelicals to aid and abet the rise of white Christian nationalism."[17] Other combatants went public, including advocates of Anglo-Saxon Protestantism who employed civil religion to vanquish what they feared and defend what they cherished. White Southerners erected a second wave of Confederate monuments, and the Natchez Garden Club sponsored nostalgic "pilgrimages" to the plantation South.[18] Led by President Harding and Vice President Coolidge, Northerners commemorated Pilgrim-inspired "Americanism" in 1921, and the next year the Greek temple enshrining Lincoln on the National Mall was finished.[19] Civil religion also found expression in presidential inaugurations. Harding's 1921 address called for "renewed devotion" and insisted God's hand was evident "in the making of this new-world Republic."[20] Three years later, Coolidge promoted "the advancement of religion" and said America's aims were of "divine origin." The Congregationalist, who had refused to condemn the Klan during his 1924 campaign, also praised "restrictive immigration."[21]

Others preached an even darker gospel of "Americanism." The American Eugenics Society used spiritual rhetoric to exclude "the biological ungodly," holding a sermon contest and publishing a *Eugenics Catechism*.[22] One member even proposed a new Ten Commandments that would ban migrants with defects and ensure that biologically superior races would enjoy the good life Jesus promised. Klan supporters used religious references to narrow national identity too. In *The Ku Klux Klan in Prophecy*, a Holiness denomination's founder suggested Klan initiates enjoyed the sanction of the Bible and the flag as well as the blessing of Washington and Lincoln (fig. 40).[23] The next year, the Klan's Imperial Wizard published "The Klan's Fight for Americanism" in a respected magazine, and his white-robed followers boldly paraded down Pennsylvania Avenue in the nation's capital.[24]

Yet, as in Chicago, this narrowly framed "Americanism" drew criticism. *The Forum*, a national magazine, held a contest in 1926 to define the contentious term. Some submissions emphasized the religious sources of shared identity, mentioning the motto "In God We Trust" or arguing that Americanism was "applied Christianity." Others quoted the Declaration's promise of "Life, Liberty, and the pursuit of Happiness" or suggested that narrow definitions didn't express "genuine Americanism."[25] But what did "genuine"

Figure 40. Depiction of a Ku Klux Klan initiation by Rev. Branford Clarke. In Alma White, *The Ku Klux Klan in Prophecy* (The Good Citizen, 1925), 24.

national belonging mean in 1926? A decade earlier, immigrant workers at Ford's English School graduation ceremony had walked into a "melting pot" onstage and emerged as Americans waving a flag.[26] The melting pot metaphor was declining in popularity during the Twenties, but whether religious and ethnic outsiders embraced the new talk of "pluralism" or the older image of many becoming one, most agreed it was important to challenge "percentage Americanism."[27]

The challenges met with mixed success. Advocates of a broad national identity learned that inclusion had its limits. Jews convinced a US president to attend the cornerstone ceremony for a new Jewish community center in Washington, but powerful industrialists like Ford still promoted anti-Semitism.[28] A nun and a priest joined the battle for collective memory by coauthoring *America's Story*, a history textbook that proudly listed eleven contributions Catholics made to America, but anti-Catholicism still surfaced during the unsuccessful 1928 presidential campaign of Al Smith.[29] Yet Catholic and Jewish leaders took comfort in small victories. About four months after Coolidge signed the restrictive 1924 immigration law, he told 100,000

Catholics gathered for a religious event near the Washington Monument they were "performing both a pious and patriotic service."[30] A month later he gave a speech by telephone to the Federation of Jewish Philanthropic Societies of New York and commended members for making good citizens and establishing God's Kingdom.[31]

Prosperity Gospels

Protestant politicians, worried about threats to industrial capitalism, talked about individualism and profit more than community and equity.[32] The government meets its constitutional duty to preserve the "common welfare," Harding said at his 1921 inauguration, by "maintaining American standards of living and opportunity." There couldn't be "equality of rewards or possessions," the Baptist president warned, but the new era of productivity would show that "wealth is not inimical to welfare."[33] Coolidge, the free-market Congregationalist who took office when Harding died in 1923, agreed. His 1925 inaugural address announced, "We appear to be entering an era of prosperity which is gradually reaching into every part of the nation."[34] Unlike his predecessor, who spoke of equal opportunity, Coolidge didn't mention equality and limited his talk of rights to the "right to earn a living" and "the right to hold property." His task as president, Coolidge believed, was to seek economic prosperity and develop natural resources, while reducing waste and cutting taxes. In other speeches, the business booster boasted about America's "higher standard of living" and, while acknowledging that accumulating wealth can't be the ultimate purpose of life, suggested that "the chief business of the American people is business." They care deeply about "producing, buying, selling, investing, and prospering in the world."[35]

But did prosperity and well-being reach "every part of the nation," as Coolidge claimed? The US had the highest gross domestic product (GDP) per capita in the world in 1925, and wage earners' pay went up. Many were healthier, too: infant mortality had decreased, as bodily stature and life expectancy improved. But continued reliance on high-polluting coal brought America's period of "dirty industrialism" to a peak, and the US led the world in carbon dioxide emissions per capita by 1925, when tailpipe exhaust from automobiles as well as smokestack discharge from factories were contributing to the long-term warming of the planet.[36] Further, prosperity didn't reach everyone. Farms were transitioning from horsepower to tractor power as industrial agriculture emerged, and many rural Whites struggled to make ends meet. Almost 1 million farmers lost their homesteads to foreclosures and bankruptcies in 1920 and 1921.[37] National prosperity also didn't improve life on western Native reservations, and it eluded Mexican and Asian farmworkers in California's agricultural valleys as well as Black sharecroppers in the South. African Americans who tried their luck in northern industrial cities found some improvements, but they lived in substandard, segregated housing and had higher mortality rates.[38] Income inequality also rose sharply during the Twenties. By 1929 the top 10 percent of the population received about 50 percent of the national income, a proportion not reached again until the Great Recession of 2007–2009.[39]

Despite the rising inequality, millions could afford coveted consumer products like autos, telephones, and radios, and many interpreted them in spiritual terms. White Protestants who worried about declining church attendance and rising mistrust of organized religion penned wistful reflections about what was being lost in the accelerating pace of modern life.[40] Or they protested the corrupting influence of jazz and the modern temptations of fast cars, unwholesome movies, and distracting radios.[41] An Episcopalian bishop in Los Angeles, for example, warned the new inventions tempted devotees to go from one thing to another seeking thrills, though he also unintentionally illustrated Protestant ambivalence toward modern consumer goods by broadcasting that warning on radio.[42] As Robert and Helen Lynd noted in their study of modernity's impact on religion in "Middletown," their fictitious name for Muncie, Indiana, young Protestants also noticed the new temptations. A Sunday school teacher asked her class in 1924 if they could "think of any temptation we have today that Jesus didn't have?" "Speed," a teenager replied.[43] He meant the temptation to drive fast in cars, which next to radios were the most coveted consumer products. By 1928, consumers had installed 6 million telephones, purchased 7 million radios, and bought 14 million automobiles, as the "consumption of goods increased by over 25 percent."[44]

And the religious did their share of this buying and selling. Christians disagreed about "modern" thought, especially Darwinian biology. But fundamentalists, who promoted biblical literalism and old-time religion, and modernists, who celebrated science and cultural progress, both embraced mass consumer culture, as cars became pulpits for itinerant evangelists and radios broadcast sermons to the isolated.[45] Applying new advertising strategies—and using radios, phonographs, and print to promote their brand—both fundamentalists and modernists mixed religion and commerce. Commercial activity commodified religion, while consumer capitalism's modes of organization created spiritual markets and, thereby, pious publics.[46] In the spiritual marketplace, which included church-owned publishing companies and radio stations, religion generated and was generated by commerce. This commercial religion emerged with the rise of consumer capitalism between 1893 and 1914. Trade periodicals preached the "God-given powers of commerce" during the 1890s, and business leaders used *Ben-Hur: A Tale of the Christ,* the best-selling book and popular play, to market everything from flour (1903) to perfume (1904).[47] But by 1925, when a film version of *Ben-Hur* appeared, it really took off. In *The Man Nobody Knows,* which sold 750,000 copies in two years and was adapted into a silent film, the ad executive Bruce Barton repackaged Jesus as a big-muscled businessman, the "founder of modern business."[48] Barton also suggested spiritual themes as he advised Coolidge's political campaign, consulted with Hollywood directors, and wrote copy for corporations, including a General Motors campaign entitled "Through the Eyes of Faith."[49]

The ad executive shaped Christianity's image in Washington and Hollywood as well as Madison Avenue, but not everyone bought Barton's Jesus.[50] Catholics criticized him. The Protestant theologian Reinhold Niebuhr, then a young Detroit pastor protesting working conditions at Ford and chairing a committee on race relations, condemned Barton's efficiency-loving Jesus, who endorsed business's "predatory practices."[51] Fundamentalists seemed more outraged by Barton's decentering of Christ's atoning death than his sacralization of marketing savvy. In fact, they enthusiastically deployed advertising that year. Modernist Protestants plotted to stimulate commercial activity in Dayton, Tennessee, by getting a local biology instructor arrested for teaching evolution in a public high school. During the subsequent Scopes Trial of 1925, fundamentalists countered with a media campaign, ridiculing the notion that humans descended from apes by, for example, staging photo ops with pious girls holding "monkey dolls."[52] Atheists seized the chance to market irreligion, founding the American Association for the Advancement of Atheism (4A) that year, while modernists dominated print media markets by promoting tolerant big-city religion and lampooning intolerant small-town fundamentalism.[53]

By 1929, embarrassed but undeterred conservative Protestants were fortifying the communication and institutional networks that would enable their postwar resurgence, while others hawked almost every brand of religion, quasi religion, and irreligion.[54] One block from Ford's Highland Park plant near Detroit, a Syrian-born imam marketed a new mosque as a national shrine, while the factory's owner, Henry Ford, endorsed Ralph Waldo Trine's New Thought gospel, which anticipated Norman Vincent Peale's *Power of Positive Thinking.*[55] From Boston to Los Angeles, Indian lecturers on the "swami circuit" publicized an occult-tinged Hinduism, while Christian critics warned of the "Oriental craze."[56] African American ministers in Chicago noticed "the yogi and the swami" but worried more about the spiritualist storefront church promising encounters with the unseen.[57] Timothy Drew's Moorish Science Temple also competed for disillusioned spiritual consumers in Chicago, where the Black nationalist group sold "Moorish Mineral Healing Oil."[58] Back east in New York City, White clergy promoted Protestantism, Catholicism, and Judaism on the radio, while Harlem record shops sold phonograph sermons to migrants who missed the cadence of lively Southern preaching.[59]

For some, the call for change was as powerful as the offer of comfort, and the change-minded sometimes employed a biblical image to express frustration and claim hope, predicting an impending "reckoning" with the costs of profit-first policies and narrow notions of Americanness.[60] A Georgian described a "ghastly" lynching and urged residents to prepare themselves "for a terrible day of reckoning," and a Californian who foresaw a "day of reckoning" condemned not only the racist lyncher but also the greedy capitalist, who ignored the poor, and the "cowardly preacher," who failed to denounce injustice.[61]

Depression Era Reckonings, 1929–1941

Some preachers, politicians, and ordinary people denounced injustice as the economy worsened after 1929. Father John Ryan, the Catholic moral theologian who advocated a living wage for industrial workers, was especially troubled by rising unemployment. In early 1929 he presciently warned that leaders needed to create more jobs to prevent "the hardships to be expected from the next industrial depression."[62] The Great Depression began a few months later as consumer demand fell, factory inventories swelled, stock values crashed, and Hoover, the first Quaker president, launched public works but failed to convince critics he had done enough to relieve the suffering. And there was suffering. By 1932, when Hoover ran for reelection, long "bread lines" made the news, including a story about a malnourished North Carolina woman who died while waiting in line for flour.[63] Almost 25 percent of the US workforce was unemployed, and the proportion reached 40 percent in steel-producing Pittsburgh and 50 percent in auto-making Detroit.[64] Even where the figures were slightly lower, patience with Hoover's policies was running out. An unemployed South Carolinian mailed Hoover's opponent, Franklin D. Roosevelt, a parody of the Twenty-Third Psalm to convey his frustration: "Hoover is my shepherd. I am in want. He maketh me to lie down on park benches."[65] FDR and his staff laughed, but the presidential hopeful also used spiritual language when he described the Depression as "retribution for our chasing after strange economic gods," and predicted "the day of reckoning will come."[66]

FDR and the "Life Abundant"

Political retribution arrived on election day, when Roosevelt won by a wide margin in 1932, but he and others who foresaw a reckoning weren't just condemning present policies. They were proposing alternative visions of well-being, or human flourishing, as they expressed hopes and imagined futures. Some who talked of reckonings hoped for "a higher standard of living for the average man," as one Boston editorial writer put it, while others expressed their aspirations in terms of "the American Dream," a phrase popularized by a 1931 book that hailed the "dream of a social order in which [everyone] shall be able to attain to the fullest stature of which they are innately capable."[67] But whether FDR and his administration was thinking of upwardly mobile dreams or higher living standards, they often used religious rhetoric to phrase their critiques and propose their solutions. Roosevelt, a biblically literate Episcopalian, compared profit-first tycoons to the "money changers" Jesus chased from the temple (John 2:15).[68] As he promised a "New Deal" to restore the "old standards of living," FDR said he and his supporters were "prophets of a new order" who sought a reappraisal of capitalism's individualistic values and a communalist redefinition of the rights promised in the Declaration of Independence.[69] FDR also reinterpreted a biblical phrase Republican politicians and Protestant pastors had used to tout free enterprise's blessings and trumpet the gospel's personal rewards: Roosevelt explained New Deal aims by invoking Jesus's promise of "life abundant" (John 10:10).[70] The goal, Roosevelt said, was not "mere subsistence" but "a more abundant life," and participants in the public debate repeated the phrase as they defended—or denounced—New Deal programs.[71]

FDR's spiritually figured reforms didn't go far enough in improving well-being for African Americans, Indigenous Peoples, and poor farmworkers.[72] Roosevelt tripled the number of Black civilian employees and mandated racial equity in wartime hiring. But he needed Southern White votes, so the president was slow to condemn lynching and battle segregation. Depression Era initiatives also had unintended effects. While the New Deal rescued struggling farmers, programs meant to improve rural life also accelerated migration from the farm to the city. While the Civilian Conservation Corps built terraces that restored the landscape, officials concerned to prevent soil erosion inadvertently smothered native plants by distributing millions of kudzu seedlings, "the vine that ate the South."[73]

But the president's programs did achieve some of his aims. FDR accused opponents of preaching "a gospel of fear," and in his 1933 inaugural address he assured Americans "the only thing we have to fear is fear itself," the paralyzing terror that prevents action. Roosevelt later listed "freedom from fear" as one of the "four freedoms" everyone should enjoy—along with "freedom from want," "freedom of speech," and "freedom of worship."[74] There was a bit more religious freedom. The Supreme Court extended First Amendment protections to the states in a decision defending Jehovah's Witnesses' right to proselytize, and even if many Natives still didn't feel free to practice their religions, FDR's "Indian New Deal," championed by John Collier, rescinded the "civilization codes" that had criminalized Native Americans' ceremonies for a half century.[75] Many Americans also felt more freedom from fear and want. "The falling economic tide of the Depression lowered all boats," and FDR's policies didn't bring opulence to the poor.[76] Income inequality decreased dramatically, however. And many employers and workers felt more security. New federal agencies secured depositors' savings and protected homeowners against foreclosure. New Deal policies stabilized the agricultural sector and brought rural families electricity, a feature of the "abundant life" FDR imagined.[77] When drought and hunger forced farmers to abandon the fields, the Farm Security Administration established migrant camps to shelter them. City-dwelling industrial workers enjoyed more workplace safety and long-term security too. New Deal legislation granted the right to form unions, and Roosevelt and fellow Episcopalian Frances Perkins, the first female cabinet member, advocated for child labor regulations and the Social Security Act, which provided a social safety net for many industrial wage workers.[78]

Those programs offered a stake in the country for the marginalized, and more Americans, including those in the churches and synagogues, felt included in national life. Franklin's "fireside chats" on radio and his wife Eleanor's syndicated columns both helped.[79] So did the "tolerance tours" of the National Conference of Christians and Jews, which intensified efforts to combat religious bigotry and broaden national identity.[80] The administration seemed to be listening to poor White Protestants in the South, and working-class Catholics and Jews gave the president their support. Modest homes and family businesses even displayed FDR's image, as if he were a national saint interceding for his suffering supplicants.[81] Elite lay Catholics and Jews moved closer to the center of political power, including a Jew and two Catholics who served in FDR's cabinet. And their spiritual leaders had the president's ear. Roosevelt added a phrase to his 1937 inaugural address suggested by Rabbi Stephen Wise, president of the American Jewish Congress, and FDR invited Father Ryan, "the Right Reverend New Dealer," to give the inaugural benediction.[82] Two years earlier, a majority of the 100,000 ministers, rabbis, and priests the White House surveyed admired Roosevelt, with less than 20 percent criticizing him and his policies.[83] Spiritual leaders continued to express admiration as the Depression continued. A rabbi in Charleston told FDR that Jews "look to you as our modern Moses sent by a kind Providence to deliver us from the present economic bondage," for example, and a Protestant minister in Kentucky proclaimed that "the principles of the New Deal are the Word of God."[84]

Not everyone saw New Deal legislation as divinely inspired scripture. Some Protestant preachers who initially urged federal intervention reversed course later in the 1930s, and the Lynds noted in their 1937 follow-up study that individualist values had persisted, even hardened, among churchgoers in "Middletown."[85] Prominent lay Protestants like Sun Oil's J. Howard Pew (Presbyterian) and General Motors' Alfred J. Sloan Jr. (Methodist) preached individualism and criticized Roosevelt.[86] Opposition surfaced among LDS, Jewish, and Catholic leaders too. Most Catholic clerics sided with the unions and supported the New Deal, but by 1935 Indiana's Bishop John Noll, who published *Our Sunday Visitor,* and Michigan's Charles Coughlin, the anti-Semitic "radio priest," accused union leaders of collaborating with communists and condemned the government's expanding power. Latter-day Saints regretted that unemployed adherents in Utah had accepted federal assistance, so to "help people to help themselves," officials announced a "Church Security Plan."[87] It looked a lot like a New Deal program but drew praise from anti-Roosevelt Protestants, and the acclaim, in turn, prompted a "reputational transformation" that nudged the Latter-day Saints toward the center of US political culture.[88] Jews supported federal relief programs, but rabbis focused on anti-Semitism, as European Nazis targeted Jews, and brainstormed solutions to secularization, as spiritual indifference spiked among young Jews and the new Reconstructionist movement reimagined Judaism as a "civilization," not a religion.[89]

African Americans were slow to join the New Deal coalition, but by the end of the Depression Era, a time of spiritual experimentation for Blacks, most embraced Roosevelt's economic agenda, even if they remained frustrated by the slow progress on racial justice. Their embrace of FDR's New Deal made sense since Blacks were hit hard by the economic crisis, although most Black congregations didn't experience the "spiritual depression" White Protestants reported.[90] Chicago's Olivet Baptist Church, one of the nation's largest congregations during the Twenties, was still thriving, even though half of the city's Black families relied on some government aid by 1939.[91] Large African American congregations had the resources to help, as with Harlem's Abyssinian Baptist Church, which sponsored health clinics and distributed free food. The Baha'i Fellowship served bread and soup to the destitute too, and prominent African American intellectuals like Robert Abbott, the Chicago editor, joined the faith in the 1930s because it provided a way to find dignity and fight inequity.[92] Other African Americans identified as Black Israelites or Black Muslims for similar reasons, while Howard and Sue Thurman, trailblazing Black Protestants, traveled to South Asia in 1936 to seek wisdom from the Hindu activist Mohandas K. Gandhi, who had led a nonviolent resistance movement in South Africa and had begun to do the same in India.[93]

Worker Religion during the Great Depression

Gandhi's spiritually inspired mode of resistance would play a crucial role in America's postwar reckoning with racism, but distressed coal miners, factory workers, and agricultural laborers also turned to religion as a source of comfort and a language for protest during the Depression. Prolonged drought, falling prices, and topsoil erosion brought hardship to many of the 30 million Americans who worked the land. Struggling agricultural laborers appreciated Shirley Temple's sunny movies and Will Rogers's folksy humor, but many also sought meaning in religion. A family of "fruit tramps," or migrant pickers, hung a calendar image of Jesus in the rickety truck they used for shelter and transportation as they moved from orchard to orchard in the Upper Midwest, and farm communities on the Southern Plains used Christian imagery to interpret the dust storms that frightened them on "Black Sunday" in 1935, when a sun-blotting storm swept in and prompted some to conclude "the end of the world was at hand."[94] On the day the Dust Bowl got its name, panicked attendees fainted in a Kansas church when the sky darkened and the dust swirled.[95] The dust then blew across the drought-stricken continent in the days ahead, even reaching Washington, where the Roosevelt administration used the apocalyptic spectacle to convince Congress to pass the Soil Conservation Act. The law helped, but didn't solve the problem. A hard-to-miss environmental reckoning was at hand. Dust storms were devastating the Plains because tractor-driving growers seeking short-term profits had ignored environmental conditions in that semiarid niche, plowing under 5 million acres of drought-tolerant grasses to plant cash crops. So when drought hit in 1932 there wasn't enough vegetation to hold the soil in place.[96]

By 1935 there wasn't much holding people in place either, as John Steinbeck showed in *The Grapes of Wrath,* his best-selling novel about an Oklahoma migrant family.[97] Within five years, more than 280,000 left the Southern Plains for California. Those Dust Bowl refugees included desperate farmers from adjacent states, "Arkies" as well as "Oakies," and they brought their old-time religion and free-market individualism with them as they sought shelter in federal migrant camps and work on California's industrialized farms, which had a legacy of exploiting Mexican and Asian field hands.[98] *Factories in the Field,* another bestseller, documented the exploitation and urged growers to repent, warning that "with the arrival of the dust-bowl refugees a day of reckoning approaches for the California farm industrialists."[99] But the day came and went; growers showed little remorse. The migrants, who made a life in California, transformed the state's political culture by fostering the rise of the religious right. But itinerant field hands were still fighting for their rights decades later, when César Chávez cofounded the United Farm Workers Union (1962) and aging Bible Belt transplants helped elect Governor Ronald Reagan (1966), an agrobusiness sympathizer.[100]

Yet during the 1930s Americans pursued agricultural reforms and imagined agrarian alternatives. Some, like the architect Frank Lloyd Wright, sketched individualist visions of the good life that drew on unconventional religious views while affirming traditional agrarian values. Wright's well-publicized but unrealized plan for "Broadacre City" (1932) included one-acre homes with garden plots and scaled-down spaces for "little farms" and "little factories," as well as a nonsectarian church. The plan, Wright hoped, would cultivate the true "individuality" that Jesus, Abdul Baha'i, and Laozi preached.[101] Others launched communal experiments, even as the few surviving Shaker villages lost members.[102] Father Divine's Peace Mission attracted 10,000 predominantly Black followers to 150 urban communal centers by the mid-1930s, but that African American leader also established agrarian homesteads for the poor like Promised Land, a racially integrated farm commune in upstate New York.[103] Few Catholics were planning interracial utopias, but priests associated with the National Catholic Rural Life Conference (NCRLC) explored the promise of reconnecting with the land. In his address "Life, Liberty, and the Pursuit of Happiness in Agriculture," Rev. John Rawe promoted a Catholic version of Jeffersonian agrarianism, a theology of land use that championed "the family-owned subsistence farm."[104] The NCRLC's social vision, a third way between capitalism and socialism, found expression in the Granger Homestead Project, which was organized by the conference's director, a parish priest in an Iowa coal mining town.[105] In 1933 he got a New Deal homestead loan to settle fifty families of unemployed miners on subsistence plots, an experiment that prompted a visit by Eleanor Roosevelt and attracted interest from the Vatican. The Catholic Worker Movement, which lay activists Dorothy Day and Peter Maurin founded in 1933, received less acclaim but had more influence. By the end of the Depression its one-penny periodical had promoted a vision of a new society, and the group had established not only thirty-two urban "houses of hospitality" but also twelve rural communal farms.[106]

Industrial workers and their allies also appealed to religion. Because of radio and movies—as well as union songs and labor sermons—those enduring the economic and environmental effects of industrial capitalism's excesses came to see themselves as united by a shared suffering, and new forms of worker religion emerged.[107]

Laborers in the Texas oil and gas fields attended lively services in revival tents and makeshift churches. The Baptist Herman Horn, who would own the central Texas tract where excavators discovered Horn Shelter Man in 1970, sought work in the northwestern Texas oil fields around Borger, a dirt-road town founded in 1926, when a refinery hit a gusher.[108] Congregations formed that year—including a revival-focused Baptist group that worshipped in a tent and a Catholic parish that met for mass in a tar-papered shack.[109] By the time Thomas Hart Benton depicted Borger in his 1928 painting *Boomtown,* locals had a few wooden churches, even though the artist's landscape showed no steeples.[110] Instead the viewer's eye is drawn to the gusher's thick dark cloud rising heavenward on the horizon. That remained a focus in the years ahead, as environmental conditions worsened by the time the Black Sunday duster hit Borger, and the plow-loosened soil mixed with petrochemical emissions to produce ominous—and toxic—"black blizzards."[111]

Lung-blackened coal miners and their defenders turned to religion too. Defenders included coal country pastors like J. J. Curran, a priest who received a mail bomb for his stance, and big-city ministers like Niebuhr, who after returning from the Kentucky mines in 1932 warned Manhattan seminarians that "religion has dulled the conscience" of self-satisfied Christians.[112] Eleanor Roosevelt, the Social Gospel Episcopalian, agreed. After visiting impoverished West Virginia miners, she said such "inequities" shouldn't exist in a country that claims to be religious.[113] Because Democratic legislation guaranteed collective bargaining and United Mine Workers (UMW) boss John Lewis told recruits that FDR wanted them to join, miners credited Eleanor's husband.[114] The 1935 song "Union Dues" expressed their gratitude.[115] But miners thanked God too. The National Miners Union had communist ties, for instance, and as soon as Kentucky miners realized its leaders didn't believe in God, they all quit.[116] Philip Murray, the United Mine Workers' vice president, shared their aversion to communism and devotion to Christianity. He kept prolabor encyclicals on his desk in the union's headquarters and argued workers' rights rested on the biblical view that humans are made in the image of God.[117] Union organizers also held meetings in worship spaces.[118] Meetings opened with hymns and prayers, and preachers' Sunday sermons confirmed the Bible was on the miners' side. Sometimes the sacralization of the miners' cause was hard to miss, as in one of Maxo Vanka's 1937 murals at St. Nicholas Croatian Church near Pittsburgh. It portrays a grief-stricken mother kneeling beside her son's corpse as more miners begin their daily descent into danger (fig. 41).[119] At other times the spiritual links were less obvious but still noteworthy, as when striking miners sang "We Shall Not Be Moved," a biblically inspired Black spiritual that organizers reappropriated for devout Appalachian workers.[120]

Union-joining factory workers in industrial belt cities like Pittsburgh, Chicago, and Detroit used religion for comfort and protest. They had made little progress during the probusiness Twenties. But the mood—and the laws—changed by the mid-Thirties, when the economy began to recover and the UMW created the Congress of Industrial Organizations (CIO) in 1935 to unionize steel and auto workers and challenge the American Federation of Labor (AFL). The AFL's Baptist president defended his organization in 1936 by claiming religious "precepts" informed their efforts, and Murray, who led the CIO's Steel Workers Organizing Committee, used religious rituals as well as political rhetoric to lure union recruits.[121] That July his committee staged a Sunday ritual at the Homestead plant where strikers had died and replacement workers had attended a company-run service in 1892.[122] But the union-organized event of 1936 showed how much the situation had changed. The 2,000 steelworkers and coal miners observed a moment of silence for the Homestead "martyrs," and endorsed a steelworkers' "Declaration of Independence," which proclaimed their right to "make real" the American dream.[123] The crowd then processed to the cemetery for a wreath-laying ceremony, where a union official prayed for the martyrs' souls and pledged "a better life for steel workers."[124] And life did get better: eight months later, US

Figure 41. Maxo Vanka, *The Immigrant Mother Raises Her Son for Industry* (1937). One of twenty-five murals painted by Croatian artist Maxo Vanka in the historic St. Nicholas Croatian Catholic Church in Millvale, Pennsylvania, in 1937 and 1941. Image courtesy of the Society to Preserve the Millvale Murals of Maxo Vanka (vankamurals.org).

Steel recognized Murray's union, guaranteed standard pay, and promised an eight-hour day.

Urban industrial laborers in the West, South, and Midwest also turned to religion. The industrial belt around Oakland employed diverse laborers, including the Portuguese migrant Maria Pinto, who marched each spring in the Holy Ghost Festival parade and worked fourteen-hour shifts in the cannery.[125] Birmingham, Alabama, attracted Blacks to its northside factories, including Will Prather, who worked at a hazardous iron furnace, lived in segregated company housing, and sang heartening hymns at Friendship Baptist Church.[126] In East Chicago, Indiana, the city's Mexican population grew when some who tried to overthrow Mexico's anticlerical government fled during the Cristero Rebellion (1926–1929).[127] Those exiles, called *Cristeros* for their battle cry of "Long live Christ the King," came north for steel jobs and religious freedoms. They found both. By 1928 they had a church, Santa María de Guadalupe, but the Depression's downturn worried nativists and disrupted resettlement, as the American Legion orchestrated a "repatriation" campaign that coerced half of the city's 6,000 Mexicans to return. Those who stayed built a vibrant religious community but would have to endure industrial pollutants, though the environmental and health dangers would remain hidden for decades.

Mexican factory workers also lived and worshipped in "Smeltertown," a border community near El Paso, Texas, that illustrates national themes as well as transnational connections and local variations.[128] The residential district near the American Smelting and Refining Company had impassioned Cristero exiles, unrecognized environmental dangers, and a Catholic church for working-class Mexicans. But the community also helped erect a twenty-six-foot statue of Christ the King about 4,000 feet above the Rio Grande Valley.[129] The parishioners cleared a pilgrimage path up the mountain in 1933, and six years later the sculptor finished the statue of a triumphant Christ, his arms outstretched on a limestone cross. The Cristero symbol faced Mexico, reclaiming the exiles' homeland while honoring their new land. The statue's dedication on 17 October 1940 saw US, Mexican, and Vatican flags flying, and the Vatican's delegate heard hilltop sermons by a Mexican bishop and Monsignor Fulton Sheen, the well-known priest who appeared on NBC radio's *Catholic Hour.* Sheen said the border monument was "neither American nor Mexican," but showed all are one in Christ.[130] FDR, who sent written reflections, emphasized spiritual unity too. He said the statue was a "witness to the eternal truths of religion," and those truths were crucial at that moment when the war news grew darker, since "only a spiritual awakening will save the world."[131]

Wartime Religion, 1941–1945

El Paso's monument-building factory workers had done their part for the awakening, and soon the nation would ask more of them. The same month FDR announced a draft lottery, and Smeltertown's sons were soon called to fight.[132] So were sons of coal miners, oil workers, and sharecroppers, many of them carrying wallet-sized images of Warner Sallman's *Head of Christ* (1941) distributed by the United Service Organizations (USO).[133] Even after the Japanese bombed Pearl Harbor on 7 December 1941 and Roosevelt invoked God as he declared war, some religious organizations opposed military action, including Dorothy Day's Catholic Worker Movement, the American Friends Service Committee, which organized public service for conscientious objectors, and the Fellowship of Reconciliation, an interfaith pacifist organization led by the Quaker A. J. Muste.[134] Yet most of the religiously inclined embraced the war effort, and Catholics and Jews, who saw a chance to fight aggressors abroad and secure belonging at home, joined in disproportionate numbers.[135]

Further, the vision of a tri-faith America, promoted in the Thirties by the National Conference of Christians and Jews and implemented in NBC's weekly radio programs, became more widely shared. A Catholic priest served as the Army's chief of chaplains, and tales of cross-faith tolerance circulated in the media, including the story of "The Four Chaplains."[136] A priest, a rabbi, and two Protestant ministers aboard the USAT *Dorchester* gave sailors their lifejackets, comforted shipmates of diverse faiths, and joined arms in solidarity as their Nazi-torpedoed ship sank in the icy Atlantic in 1943. By the end of the war, after the chaplains were awarded posthumous medals and a cartoon tribute proclaimed "bravery favors no religion," tri-faith tolerance had become civil religious dogma.[137]

US religious nationalism surfaced in other ways during World War II, as on D-Day, 6 June 1944.[138] After more than 150,000 American, Canadian, and British forces invaded a French beach to open a second front against Germany, worried loved ones visited churches and synagogues, and Roosevelt offered a prayer that evening in his radio address (fig. 42). Not since Lincoln spoke at Gettysburg had a president performed the role of America's high priest so solemnly. FDR said the operation had "success thus far" and asked the nation to join him in prayer. "Almighty Father," he began, our sons have gone abroad to "preserve our Republic, our religion, and our civilization, and to set free a suffering humanity." "With Thy blessing," he assured listeners, "we shall prevail over the unholy forces of our enemy." But those on the battlefield would need God's help, and Americans at home would too. So the president ended by asking for divine aid in "saving our country."

Roosevelt, who died in April 1945, wouldn't live to see that national salvation—or gauge its costs. Vice President Harry Truman, a Baptist from Missouri, assumed the presidency, and the victory FDR promised came when Germany surrendered in May and Emperor Hirohito, whom the Japanese revered as a Shintō god, went on the radio in August to tell his startled subjects they had lost. After the surrender ceremony in September, Americans of all faiths celebrated. But the conflict had cost the lives of 405,399 US soldiers, marines, and airmen. Global fatalities reached 60 million, including 10 to 20 million who died from famine or disease.[139]

A "Grave Injustice" at Home

Moral costs mounted too. Americans would remember World War II as a "good war" waged by a God-loving people reluctantly awakened from an isolationist slumber, but some denounced the era's intolerance at home.[140]

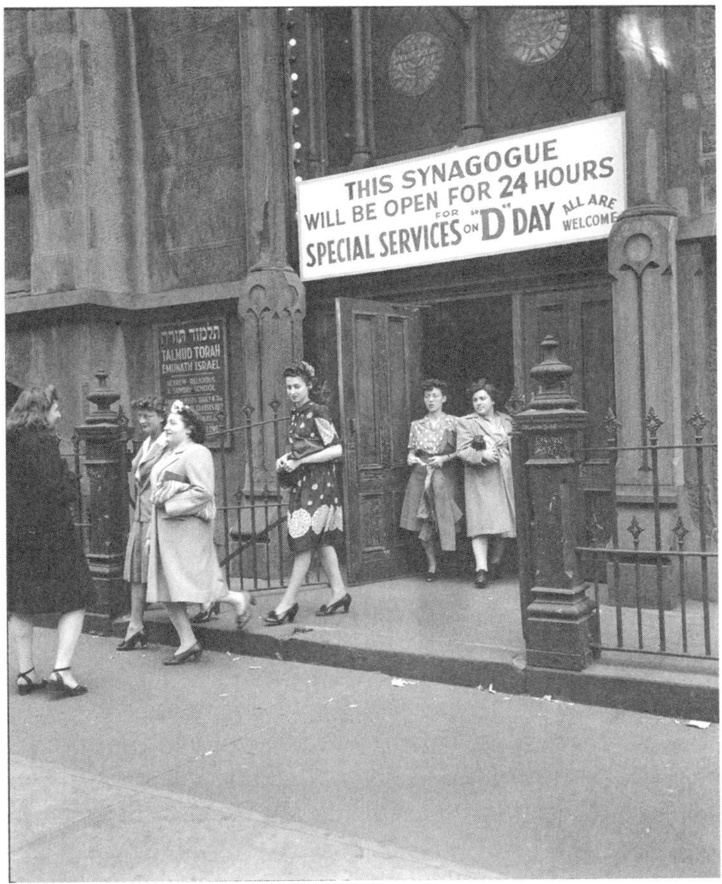

Figure 42. *Leaving the Synagogue on West Twenty-Third Street in New York after D-Day Services.* Howard R. Hollem, MacLaugharie, or Edward Meyer, photographer. 6 June 1944. Library of Congress, LC-USW3-054044-C.

Wartime reports described "mob outbursts" against religious and racial minorities, including Jews, Mexicans, Filipinos, Blacks, and Japanese, even though all those groups sent sons abroad to fight.[141] The rise of anti-Japanese sentiment after Pearl Harbor also pressured FDR's administration into a decision that would cause a "grave injustice."[142] In 1940 Roosevelt had urged Americans to celebrate July Fourth by banishing "every vestige of racial hatred and religious bigotry," but after Pearl Harbor he signed an executive order that would be used to perpetuate prejudice.[143] The 1942 order authorized the Secretary of War to prevent espionage and sabotage by excluding anyone who might threaten military areas. It didn't mention the Japanese or authorize imprisonment. However, partly because of Roosevelt's apparent bias against the "unassimilated" Japanese and his perplexing indifference to the order's consequences, his administration incarcerated over 110,000 residents of Japanese ancestry in ten barbwired concentration camps, remote compounds officials called "relocation centers."[144] Descendants of Germans and Italians, America's other wartime enemies, endured short-term scrutiny, but nothing like the sustained deprivations suffered by the Japanese, most of whom were US citizens.

Most Japanese also were Buddhist, not affiliated with a Judeo-Christian faith, and religious bigotry intensified racial prejudice in Hawai'i, where martial law was imposed, and on the mainland, where due process was ignored—even if White Protestants complained that incarceration without trial was unconstitutional, and White Buddhists visited the camps, bringing supplies and conducting services.[145] The imprisoned Japanese Buddhists lost livelihoods, belongings, and liberties, but they found ways to adapt—and challenge assumptions.[146] Thousands joined the US military, and Shin Buddhist clergy reaffirmed their allegiance by cutting ties with Kyoto and renaming their group the "Buddhist *Churches* of America." At Wyoming's Heart Mountain camp, the priest Nyogen Sensaki taught traditional Zen practices but also praised the "Land of Liberty" and hailed the Constitution as "scripture."[147] Spouses of Buddhist priests did their part too. Shigeo Kikuchi, who presided at funerals near their Hawaiian temple during her husband's incarceration, also organized send-off rituals for the young men who volunteered to fight for the US. As her former Sunday School pupils left for battle, she handed them Buddhist prayer beads and whispered, "The Buddha is always with you."[148]

Jewish Holocaust Abroad

As news of Nazi death camps circulated, some Jews began to wonder if God was with them. Most retained their faith but confronted a second moral cost of the war: Hitler killed 6 million Jews, and no one stopped him. Rabbi Wise, a leading anti-Nazi voice, knew FDR "loathed Hitler" and attributed his early inaction to domestic political divides.[149] Wise also praised Christians who protested Nazi anti-Semitism, including those who spoke at the anti-Hitler rally at Madison Square Garden in March 1933.[150] Despite Father Coughlin's anti-Semitic broadcasts and a disturbing pro-Nazi "Rally for True

Americanism," a few more Christians began to speak out, including Chicago's Cardinal George Mundelein.[151] Yet most pious Americans were slow to believe the horrific reports. In August 1942, however, European contacts sent Wise a telegram confirming the Nazi plan to "exterminate" Jews.[152] After waiting for State Department clearance, Wise held a November press conference to report that 2 million Jews already had been killed, and more would die if the world didn't act. In response, New Yorkers staged a "Day of Mourning." A few days later, Wise urged FDR to condemn the Nazi atrocities, and the president issued a statement. Six prominent Christians—including Ryan—contributed to Wise's 1943 volume *Never Again! Ten Years of Hitler.*[153] Yet the rabbi regretted that the US government didn't do more to stop the killing and rescue the refugees, and he admitted his "deep disappointment over the failure of American Christendom."[154] US Jews also began to ask why their own leaders didn't do more to prevent what they later would call "the Holocaust." And some American Jews would remain haunted by the Nazi ovens. Elie Wiesel, the Auschwitz survivor, recalled the protest that rose up in him as he watched children go to the camp's crematory, where their bodies were "turned into wreaths of smoke beneath a silent blue sky." Those moments, he confessed, "murdered my God and my soul."[155]

Wonder, Worry, and the Atomic Bomb

The atomic bomb also shook people of faith, even if eyewitnesses at the Trinity test site initially expressed spiritual wonder.[156] The Atomic Age began at dawn on 16 July 1945, when the US secretly tested a bomb in the New Mexican desert, just north of where mammoth-stalking humans had left their footprints at White Sands and near the path Spanish missionaries had trod to bring the Bible and the plow to Pueblo Peoples at the place they called *Santa Fe,* or Holy Faith.[157] Centuries later, scientists and soldiers went by bus for a rehearsal of the Hiroshima and Nagasaki attacks, and they too used spiritual language. Robert Oppenheimer, chief scientist, even named the test site Trinity, though scholars debate whether he meant the Christian Trinity or the three Hindu gods who create, sustain, and destroy the world.[158] The Hindu reference is plausible because Oppenheimer's Jewish parents reared him in the inclusive Ethical Culture Society, which preached "deed, not creed," and by the 1930s he was reading the Sanskrit original of the *Bhagavad Gita,* an epic poem recounting how a reluctant warrior recognized his duty to fight.[159] Given its message, it's not surprising the Hindu text was on Oppenheimer's mind in the war's final months. On detonation day he told William

Laurence, the only journalist there, that the bomb's flash made him think of a chapter in the *Gita* where a powerful god appears with "a thousand simultaneous suns arising in the sky" and says, "I am become Death, the shatterer of worlds."[160]

The allusion would become atomic lore, but most eyewitnesses thought of Western religious imagery. General Thomas Farrell heard an "awesome roar which warned of doomsday," and he wondered if the Manhattan Project team were blasphemous to tamper with forces "heretofore reserved to the Almighty."[161] Physicist Victor Weisskopf, an atheist Jew, said "when the brightness subsided we saw a blue halo surrounding the yellow and orange sphere," which brought to mind a painting he had seen of Christ's resurrection.[162] Laurence felt as if he had witnessed "the Birth of the World . . . at the moment of Creation when the Lord said: Let there be light!"[163]

And there would be more light. In August 1945 two atomic bombs killed 100,000 at Hiroshima and 35,000 at Nagasaki, and, by the end of 1946, commentators agreed the world had changed.[164] A son of Protestant missionaries, John Hersey, documented the weapon's devastating effects in his prize-winning journalism, and expressions of spiritual wonder faded as postwar anxiety set in and a commission appointed by the Federal Council of Churches asked if "the moral cost was too high."[165] Laurence, the *New York Times* reporter who witnessed the New Mexico test, also was at the Pacific airbase near Guam when the *Enola Gay* left for Hiroshima. Before its crew boarded, the base's Lutheran chaplain gathered the airmen for prayer, asking God to protect them.[166] Sixteen hours after they dropped the Hiroshima bomb—and while Truman returned from Europe—the White House issued a statement the president approved but didn't write. Laurence, who was paid by the War Department as well as the *Times,* drafted the statement that military leaders censored and a corporate public relations expert polished.[167] The final version thanked "Providence" for gifting the US with the bomb, and it celebrated the "new era in man's understanding of nature's forces," because atomic energy would one day supplement fossil fuels and bring world peace.[168] When the Japanese refused to surrender, Truman authorized a second bomb, which fell on Nagasaki three days later. Laurence watched from the air and reported it brought "good results."[169] Most Americans agreed; an August 1945 Gallup poll suggested that 85 percent approved of the bombings.[170] But as reports from the rubble circulated, some religious leaders spoke out. Catholics were initially divided, though some public figures like Sheen said the bombings were unjust because they targeted noncombatants.[171] Some Protestant clergy agreed. As early as August 1945 thirty-four New York ministers condemned the attacks as "an atrocity of a new magnitude."[172] By March 1946 the national ecclesiastical commission, which included Niebuhr, was "deeply penitent" about the "morally indefensible" bombings.[173]

Anxiety, Tranquility, and Religion in the Early Cold War, 1946–1963

The commission also noted that the prospect of nuclear destruction had spread "universal fear."[174] Even the persistently positive Norman Vincent Peale acknowledged "our philosophy seems to be shaken and our civilization seems to be at the edge of the abyss."[175] Contemporaries called the period the "Age of Anxiety," as postwar cultural elites struggled to find existential meaning, and political leaders stirred fear of "godless communists" who threatened imminent attack.[176] Weapons testing didn't help. The US military tested sixty-six devices in the Marshall Islands by 1958. Detonations also began at the Nevada Test Site, which saw twenty-nine blasts in 1957 alone. The Soviets were busy too. In 1949 the USSR detonated its first atomic bomb and accelerated its nuclear program in the years ahead. Concerned scientists introduced the Doomsday Clock to visualize their dismay. The cover image of the *Bulletin of the Atomic Scientists* set the time at seven minutes to midnight in 1947, and the editors reset it as tensions escalated.[177] Although Truman never regretted bombing Japan because "those bombs ended the war," in 1946 he announced that "all mankind now stands in the doorway to destruction."[178] Avoiding nuclear war, Truman told a national radio audience in fall 1952, had been his major accomplishment as president.[179] As Dwight D. Eisenhower began his term in 1953, his supporters in the Freedoms Foundation, a conservative group dedicated to free-market individualism, partnered with the Civil Defense Administration, the Ad Council, and the American Legion to launch the Alert America campaign.[180] Three convoys crossed the country to announce that, as their posters warned, civilians and their churches were in danger (fig. 43).

To assess the threat, Eisenhower commissioned a study, and the 1957 report recommended building more atomic bombs and more fallout shelters.[181] The government did both, and between 1961 and 1962, during John F. Kennedy's term, about 200,000 frightened families also bought fallout shelter kits from companies like Peace-O-Mind Shelter Corporation to fortify themselves against attack.[182]

Fear wasn't actually "universal," as the ministers claimed, and the bomb wasn't the only source of worry.[183] Middle-class Whites fretted about teenage

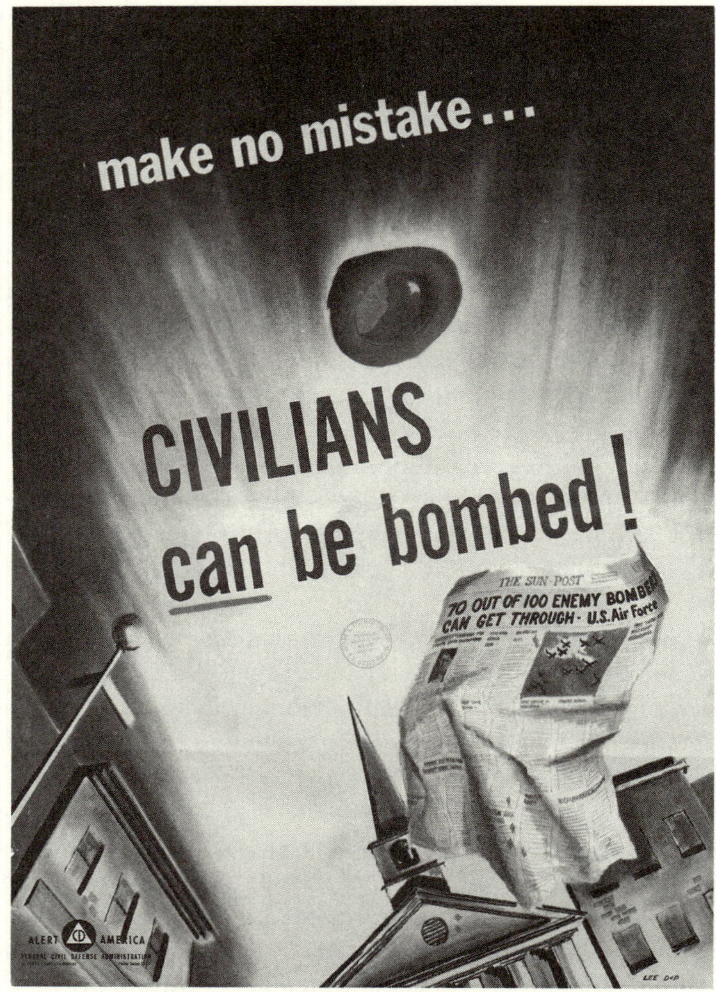

Figure 43. Federal Civil Defense Administration, *Alert America/Federal Civil Defense Administration/GPO* (1952). Poster by Lee Dap. Courtesy of the Harry S. Truman Presidential Library and Museum.

"delinquents," while poor Blacks in the segregated South still lived with the constant threat of violence.[184] And not everyone seemed jittery about nuclear attack. There were atomic-themed cocktails, toasters, and songs. The Atomic Energy Lab, a radioactive toy sold in 1950, came with uranium-bearing ores.[185] There was even atomic tourism: sightseers unaware of the link between radioactive fallout and cancer rates filled Las Vegas motels in 1951 to watch mushroom clouds rise in the desert sky.[186] Yet by 1959 two-thirds of Americans saw the threat of nuclear war as the nation's most pressing problem, including presumably the 500,000 consumers who bought the 1961 recording *If the Bomb Falls: A Recorded Guide to Survival.*[187]

Some of the anxious sought relief in the medicine cabinet, the shopping mall, and the suburban enclave. The instructional recording advised parents to stock their fallout shelters with Miltown (*meprobamate*), the nation's first prescription "tranquilizer," a shrewdly chosen name for a new class of drugs.[188] Within a year, one in twenty Americans had tried Miltown, and by 1957 pharmacists had filled 36 million prescriptions for executives and housewives. Those who eschewed "happy pills" could seek tranquility in the nearest shopping center. Postwar leaders said consumption was a patriotic duty since it increased national prosperity, but ads also hinted that a trip to the mall could bring peace of mind.[189] Developers built shopping centers near suburbs, another refuge for the anxious. Racially segregated suburbs like New York's and Pennsylvania's Levittowns distanced White homebuyers from the worrisome people and problems of cities, where most Americans still lived in 1963.[190]

Most of all, the anxious turned to religion. The narrator of *If the Bomb Falls* advised Americans to bring their Bible and "spiritual supplies" to the family fallout shelter, but Baby Boom parents needed no reminders about religion's reassuring effects. They had been turning to religion since the end of World War II. Some questioned the sincerity of the "surge" of piety, pointing to political pressures, sociological forces, or psychological needs.[191] Whatever the reasons, pollsters' statistical measures of piety peaked. A majority—75 percent—said religion was personally "very important," and more than eight in ten said it was increasingly influential and could solve contemporary problems.[192] Americans also trusted in and identified with institutions, including religious institutions. In a 1957 Census Bureau study, the last federal survey to ask about religion, 96 percent reported an affiliation, with two-thirds aligning with Protestantism, one-quarter with Roman Catholicism, and 3.3 percent with Judaism.[193] Americans also continued to join churches and synagogues. Membership figures reached an all-time high just after the war at 76 percent, and then remained steady at about 73 percent. Between 1955 and 1963 almost half also said they went to church or synagogue weekly. Those numbers might have been inflated, and the pollsters' questions may have obscured some patterns—like the proportion of evangelicals and spiritual seekers who identified as Protestant—but most agreed interest in religion had spiked.

The interest was bottom-up, a reflection of the lived religion of ordinary folks, but it also resulted from top-down promotional efforts, including several national faith drives.[194] The privately pious Truman supported those drives and developed his own civil religious rhetoric, evident in his 1949 inaugural address and 1952 Day of Prayer proclamation, while the USSR launched an unconvincing religious propaganda counteroffensive.[195] "Piety along the Potomac" intensified during the Eisenhower administration (1953–1961), with religious nationalists warning that victory over the atheistic Soviets depended on Americans' faith in God and trust in biblical principles.[196] That top-down effort began as Ike opened his 1953 inaugural address with a prayer, asking attendees to bow their heads as he petitioned "Almighty God."[197] Although he had been raised in strict, non-mainline denominations, the Brethren of Christ and Jehovah's Witnesses, he had not joined or attended a church as an adult. Advisors convinced him that would set a bad example for young people and limit his ability to lead. So ten days after the inauguration, Ike, at age sixty-three, was baptized at Washington's National Presbyterian Church, a prominent mainline congregation.[198]

During the next three years Eisenhower, his pastor, and a loose coalition of political, corporate, and ecclesial leaders vigorously promoted a theistic national faith. Ike endorsed two national campaigns for spiritual reinvigoration in 1953. First, in a recorded message for the televised launch of the American Legion's "Back to God" campaign, the president said belief in God is foundational to "Americanism," reaffirming the veteran group's commitments to "God and Country" and "one hundred percent Americanism."[199] Later that year he met with leaders of the National Association of Evangelicals (NAE) to support their "March for Freedom" and sign the brochure promoting the "Seven Freedoms" they claimed were implicit in Psalm 23 (which begins "The Lord is my shepherd, I shall not want").[200] Whether Eisenhower noticed it or not, the statement didn't include liberties named in the Constitution, and it challenged FDR's vision of national flourishing. It listed seven freedoms, not four: freedom from want and fear, as Roosevelt said, but also from hunger, thirst, sin, and enemies. The NAE's list didn't mention freedom of religion. It also omitted freedom of speech, then under attack in congressional hearings investigating communist sympathizers. Yet, gesturing to FDR's beloved biblical passage, the group added the freedom to "live abundantly," a theme that neo-Pentecostal preacher Oral Roberts would soon emphasize.[201] The NAE statement also implied that civic liberties rested on the authority of the Bible. To make America's spiritual foundation explicit, Eisenhower signed 1954 legislation that added "under

God" to the Pledge of Allegiance. In 1955 he put "In God We Trust" on postage stamps—as Coolidge did with a 1928 Valley Forge stamp—and Ike soon made the phrase the nation's motto.[202]

Potomac piety also found expression in the Congressional Prayer Room that opened in 1955. To aid lawmakers seeking divine guidance, the Bible on its oak altar opened to Psalm 23, and the stained glass featured Lincoln's phrase, "This Nation under God," as well the Great Seal's motto, "*E pluribus unum*."[203] Like the 1928 stamp, it also pictured a kneeling Washington, thereby perpetuating the fabricated claim that he knelt in prayer at Valley Forge and reimagining him as an orthodox Episcopalian and Cold War warrior.[204]

By the end of the decade a few Protestants, Catholics, and Jews complained that the top-down sacralization of the nation had stifled the Judeo-Christian tradition's prophetic impulse, violated the First Amendment's antiestablishment clause, and narrowed notions of what it meant to be American.[205] Nonetheless, with top-down and bottom-up impulses converging, religion was everywhere. It was on the jukebox, with songs like "The Man Upstairs" (1954), and in the theater, with films like *The Ten Commandments* (1956).[206] Evangelist Billy Graham brought it to the sports arena, filling Madison Square Garden for a sixteen-week "crusade" in 1957.[207] Inspired by a Catholic radio priest, an Oklahoma Protestant created a home altar and a prayer room at his roadside gas station.[208] Religion was on the factory floor too: by 1954 at least forty companies had hired "industrial chaplains."[209] Thanks to Boston Archbishop Richard Cushing, prayer found a place at the shopping center and the airport. He dedicated the nation's first airport worship space in 1952, and eight years later consecrated a chapel in a suburban shopping center that was "bringing the church to the people."[210] Sheen, the telegenic Catholic, was among those who brought religion into America's living rooms. Graham's *Hour of Decision*, a half-hour program on ABC, was carried on 150 TV stations, but Sheen's *Life Is Worth Living* (1952–1958) was even more popular, reaching 5.5 million households weekly in 1955.[211] The red-cloaked cleric opened with a homespun story and ended with a practical point, and the broadcast series, which attracted non-Catholic viewers as well, won its star a 1952 Emmy Award. The next year, Sheen's book of the same name, *Life Is Worth Living*, hit the bestseller list, and religion found its way onto bedroom nightstands.[212] Harry Emerson Fosdick, the modernist pastor of New York City's Riverside Church, published *On Being a Real Person* during World War II, and other therapeutic volumes that calmed fears took off after the war.[213] A Reform rabbi, Joshua Liebman, published *Peace of Mind* (1946), which sold a million copies in two years.[214] Sheen took his turn in 1949 with *Peace of Soul*, and Graham's *Peace with God*, coauthored with his wife, Ruth, and writer Janet Baird, appeared in 1953.[215]

Peale's 1952 volume *The Power of Positive Thinking* was the most popular of all.[216] It topped the bestseller list for two years, and its author became "the high priest of the cult of reassurance."[217] Peale served as pastor of Manhattan's Marble Collegiate Church, where Richard Nixon (who identified as a Quaker) started worshipping in 1962, and Donald Trump (who identified as a Presbyterian) would marry in 1977. The minister, who supported the Republican Party, would inspire new prosperity gospels like the "Christian libertarianism" of California televangelist Robert Schuller.[218] But Peale condemned tranquilizers, suggesting that "deep inner peace—real tranquility" can only be found through religion: "Turn your heart to God and you can live without pills in this tranquilizer age."[219] That meant—as Peale explained in columns, sermons, and books—using positive thinking and affirmative prayer to achieve inner peace and personal power. Problems, he proposed, arise from negative thinking, and the good life comes from thinking differently. In that sense, Peale's can-do piety resembled Trine's New Thought message more than Graham's sin-focused sermons, even if Peale quoted Jesus and courted evangelicals.[220] Spiritual alternatives in popular culture—including Zen and existentialism—also centered the self and promoted right thinking as the key to overcoming personal suffering, and a few White intellectuals even began to appropriate another class of drugs, hallucinogens, which charted an ancient Indigenous path to self-realization, as *Life*'s 1957 photo-essay about "divine mushrooms" showed.[221] Those countercultural pieties would soon have their day, but many middle-class Americans in the Fifties found Peale's positive thinking the right prescription for what ailed them.

If reassuring religion improved individual well-being, it seemed less useful for promoting communal and ecological flourishing. Consider one story Peale told in a 1957 bestseller. He described a young African American boy who asked a man blowing up balloons at the county fair if the black one could go as high as the rest. The fair employee told him, "It isn't the color that determines how high they go, but the stuff inside them that counts." Peale agreed; the boy only needed to dispel "self-doubt" and "think Big."[222] But as one 1958 interpreter observed, "The Negro lad showed himself painfully aware of the realities of contemporary American life . . . it *is* their color that determines how 'high Americans go.'"[223] Some "realities" required other remedies. They required, critics argued, a religion of resistance—and strategies for reparation—not just feel-good gospels that settled nerves.

Early Cold War Reckonings

By the end of 1963, conceptions of national belonging had begun to widen—in religion more than race—and income inequality lessened, labor unions strengthened, and the middle class grew, partly because the GI Bill (1944) had allowed veterans access to higher education and home loans.[224] It was for many a period of "plenty," as Eisenhower said, and a time when mainline ministers and liberal economists urged "corporate social responsibility."[225] Yet inequalities lingered: racial injustice, health disparities, gender inequity, and nativist suspicion. Despite some public protests, ecological stresses also deepened as urban-industrial America began to face an accelerating environmental crisis.

Religion and National Belonging

Religious belonging broadened, even if Graham condemned the "Sin of Tolerance," a Catholic found pluralism "pathological," and few praised Howard Thurman's interfaith and interracial Church for the Fellowship of All Peoples.[226] Belonging didn't extend to Natives. In 1949 Hopi elders sent President Truman a letter saying their prophets had predicted the atomic bomb and revealed the spiritual path forward. A Hopi read the letter at the National Congress of American Indians in Arizona that year, and President Kennedy hosted the organization at the White House in 1963.[227] However, Indigenous Peoples still didn't enjoy full religious freedom, as the 1962 conviction of three Diné (Navajo) men for using peyote made clear.[228] But Congress did end citizenship restrictions for Asians, granting full political participation to Asian Buddhists, Sikhs, Muslims, and Hindus in 1952.[229] Five years later, Eisenhower, who befriended oil magnates with interests in the Middle East, became the first president to visit a mosque when he attended the Islamic Center's dedication in DC.[230] Ike also appointed the first LDS cabinet member, Ezra Taft, later president of the Church of Latter-day Saints, and invited an Eastern Orthodox bishop to take part in the 1957 presidential inauguration.[231] Jews took comfort in the founding of Israel, and, despite continuing anti-Semitism, American civil religious discourse included Judaism.[232] Anti-Catholicism resurfaced, including during the 1960 presidential campaign, when Peale and an NAE group expressed alarm at the prospect of a "papal puppet" in the White House.[233] Nonetheless, voters elected the country's first Catholic president, John F. Kennedy. By 1963 Catholics also enjoyed proportional representation in Congress and got their own monumental Washington church with the dedication of the National Shrine of the Immaculate Conception.[234]

Cold War Protestants worried about this "pluralism," or religious diversity, as well as "secularism," or creeping irreligion.[235] Holy Spirit–filled pentecostals still struggled to gain wider cultural clout, but doctrinally focused "New Evangelicals," whom some called "neo-Fundamentalists," took their place beside mainline Protestants in the public arena.[236] They not only founded the NAE but established new seminaries and expanded media outlets, using Pew oil money to launch a competing magazine, *Christianity Today* (1956). One of its supporters, Graham, also had started advising postwar presidents, including Eisenhower. Yet White Protestants, who comprised 58 percent of the US population, continued their slow demographic decline, even if they remained overrepresented among corporate and cultural elites, and a de facto Protestant establishment persisted.[237] The religious right sometimes ignored the changes, though some, like Peale, decided it was "time to restrengthen the old time, if somewhat narrow, loyalties of Protestantism, or else we shall deteriorate altogether."[238] Mainline contributors to the moderate *Christian Century* and the progressive *Christianity and Crisis* confronted America's "pluralism" somewhat more fully, with the *Century*'s associate editor advising readers to accept their status in "pluralist Post-Protestant society."[239] Even if some Protestants acknowledged pluralism—or the "Triple Melting Pot," as sociologists called it—others remained ambivalent, as the design of the new Air Force Academy Chapel symbolized.[240] That 1962 Colorado chapel reserved its soaring upper sanctuary for Protestants, while relegating Catholics and Jews to subterranean entrances and smaller spaces. Airmen who didn't affiliate with those three faiths had to use the chapel's twenty-five-seat meeting room.

Various court decisions, however, defended spiritual diversity, protecting the rights of the atheist and agnostic as well as the Muslim and the Buddhist. By 1960 the Jesuit theologian John Courtney Murray and the Lutheran pastor Martin Marty had suggested that America's three mainstream faiths had been joined by a fourth stream, "secular humanism," a phrase that would appear in a 1961 Supreme Court decision and that evangelicals would weaponize in later battles.[241] But even in this period, public debates arose about the wall separating church and state. Church–state separationists cheered and Christian-nation advocates jeered when Chief Justice Earl Warren, a Republican who didn't attend church but sent his children to Sunday school, defended the establishment clause in a series of Supreme Court decisions.[242] The Court held in *Engle v. Vitale* (1962) that government-sponsored prayers in public schools were unconstitutional, and it extended the ban to devotional Bible reading in *Abington School District v. Schempp* (1963), a case involving a Unitarian high school junior reprimanded because he read from the Qur'an instead of the Bible.[243] Although fellow Unitarians supported Schempp's cause and some contemporaries sided with the disgruntled Jewish, Unitarian, and atheist parents in *Engle,* many religious groups denounced the decisions, which seemed to desacralize civic spaces like public schools at a moment when domestic leaders were emphasizing America's "Judeo-Christian" character.[244]

Global affairs also shaped domestic affairs, not only by keeping Americans on edge about nuclear attack but also by diversifying US religious life.[245] America had emerged from World War II as the global defender of democracy, promoter of capitalism, and exporter of values. Postwar Americans helped form global Christian organizations as well as North Atlantic military alliances. They helped establish not only global economic institutions but also the United Nations, with its religiously inspired Universal Declaration of Human Rights. The "America First" isolationism of the interwar years was over. Commodore Perry's fleet had steamed into Tokyo Bay in 1853 and, as the Japanese surrender ceremony aboard the *Missouri* hinted, America's spiritually figured imperialism had returned by 1945, when the Japanese delegation passed Perry's tattered thirty-one-star flag and heard General Douglas MacArthur's on-deck speech appeal to God.[246] Like other imperial powers, the US was affected by decolonization when the Philippines gained independence in 1946. Yet it retained Guam, Puerto Rico, and the Virgin Islands. Its borders even expanded when Alaska and Hawai'i became US states in 1959. Although few noticed at the time, that expansion also enriched America's ethnic and religious diversity. In the decades ahead, Hawai'i would give the US its first African American president and its first Buddhist and Hindu congressional members. Both states added sizable Indigenous populations. Alaska's Russian Orthodox heritage and Hawai'i's Japanese Buddhist heritage also diversified US spiritual life.

New migrants added to the postwar pluralism too. Truman and Eisenhower learned what US missionaries already knew: the 1924 immigration law, like Southern segregation, presented an obstacle for those promoting the moral superiority of the American way of life.[247] The 1952 McCarran–Walter Act did raise the numerical cap on "Old World" immigrants but, to Truman's embarrassment, it retained the internationally offensive racial and national exclusions.[248] Congressional leaders postponed the day of reckoning with Anglo-Saxon Protestant nativism, then, but some non-Protestants still entered the country. A portion of the millions of Mexican Catholics who came as seasonal farmworkers in the Bracero Program, including during the peak of 1956, stayed to make a life, and about 470,000 Puerto Rican Catholics, who had been citizens since 1917, moved to metropolitan New York in the Fifties.[249] Because Ike and JFK focused on the global battle against godless communists, they asked federal agencies and Catholic organizations to resettle refugees from the Soviet sphere, including 38,000 Hungarian Catholic "freedom fighters" who fled in 1956 and 258,000 Cuban refugees who arrived between 1959 and 1963.[250] The migrant flows added to America's pluralism, though immigration law revision remained on the nation's moral agenda.

Religion and the Black Freedom Movement

Race moved to the top of that agenda by 1963. Polls showed that—for the first time—Americans ranked civil rights as the most pressing problem.[251] The racial reckoning had yielded less than some hoped in the hundred years since the Emancipation Proclamation, but the optimistic recounted victories by the Civil Rights Movement, which used Gandhian nonviolent resistance, prophetic Black Church traditions, and shrewd legal strategies by the National Association for the Advancement of Colored People (NAACP) to challenge inequality.[252] An era of nonviolent protest began in 1941 when Philip Randolph, a Methodist-reared union leader, and Bayard Rustin, a Quaker pacifist, threatened FDR with a march on the capital, and the period ended when they co-organized the 1963 March on Washington, where 200,000 demonstrators gathered at the Lincoln Memorial to hear King's "I Have a Dream" speech.[253]

The earlier threat extracted a concession—FDR's executive order banning discrimination in war-related employment—and the NAACP's Thurgood Marshall, a Black Episcopalian, helped win a victory in the landmark case of *Brown v. Board of Education* (1954).[254] Its lead plaintiff, a Topeka welder and AME preacher, balked at sending his daughter across town to an inferior segregated school, and the Supreme Court sided with Reverend Brown, reversing *Plessy*'s "equal but separate" standard and declaring school segregation unconstitutional.[255] The decision sparked a "rights revolution" and provoked theological battles but also won some surprising endorsements, as with a Southern Baptist commission that concluded *Brown* reflected Christian principles.[256]

As theological segregationists and integrationists squared off, national attention turned to Montgomery, Alabama, where Rosa Parks, a fifty-seven-year-old Methodist seamstress, refused to move to the back of a bus in

December 1955. It was "a matter of dignity," she said, and a local women's group led by Jo Ann Robinson started a bus boycott.[257] Robinson's Baptist pastor, King, soon became the protest's public face. Segregationists, who believed God sanctioned separation, responded by bombing King's home in January 1956, and the next month Rustin, who had studied Gandhian nonviolence in India, arrived to brainstorm tactics and train protestors.[258] W. E. B. Du Bois telegrammed reassurance, urging King to "fear not . . . the foe," and the Supreme Court vanquished that foe when it declared Montgomery's bus law unconstitutional.[259] By late 1956, Montgomery's African Americans were boarding integrated buses. The victory earned King the cover of *Time* magazine in February and an opening prayer in July at Billy Graham's Manhattan crusade.[260] The same year, 1957, police had to protect the first Black family to desegregate Levittown, a Philadelphia suburb, and Eisenhower sent troops to Arkansas because its governor had blocked nine African American students from entering a Little Rock high school.[261] Ike did sign the Civil Rights Act of 1957, the first rights legislation since Reconstruction, but the law didn't go far enough.[262] So King's Southern Christian Leadership Conference (SCLC) continued its resistance, while he made a "pilgrimage" to meet with Gandhi's followers in India in 1959.[263] In the next few years, the SCLC endorsed other nonviolent campaigns, as when Black college students staged Sunday "kneel-ins" to desegregate White Protestant churches in Southern cities like Atlanta.[264]

King was serving an Atlanta congregation by 1963, when he accepted an invitation to return to Alabama. He joined Fred Shuttlesworth, the prominent pastor of a Northside church, who said it was "Birmingham's moment of truth."[265] The two joined hands to sing "We Shall Overcome" as protestors began a citywide desegregation campaign.[266] Before it ended, Shuttlesworth would be imprisoned and so would King, whose "Letter from Birmingham Jail" challenged clergy who asked him to slow down.[267] The sit-ins, pray-ins, and merchant boycotts undid racist laws, though only after Birmingham's police commissioner turned fire hoses and cattle prods on peaceful demonstrators. TV cameras captured that May violence, helping the cause, and networks broadcast the jubilant March on Washington for Jobs and Freedom in August (fig. 44).[268] Yet the joy subsided when the focus returned to Birmingham three weeks later. The Ku Klux Klan bombed a Baptist church, killing four girls between eleven and fourteen. President Kennedy, who had delivered a civil rights speech in June, expressed "outrage and grief."[269] In his final months he discussed racial justice, though Marshall and others weren't sure that JFK recognized "the urgency of it."[270]

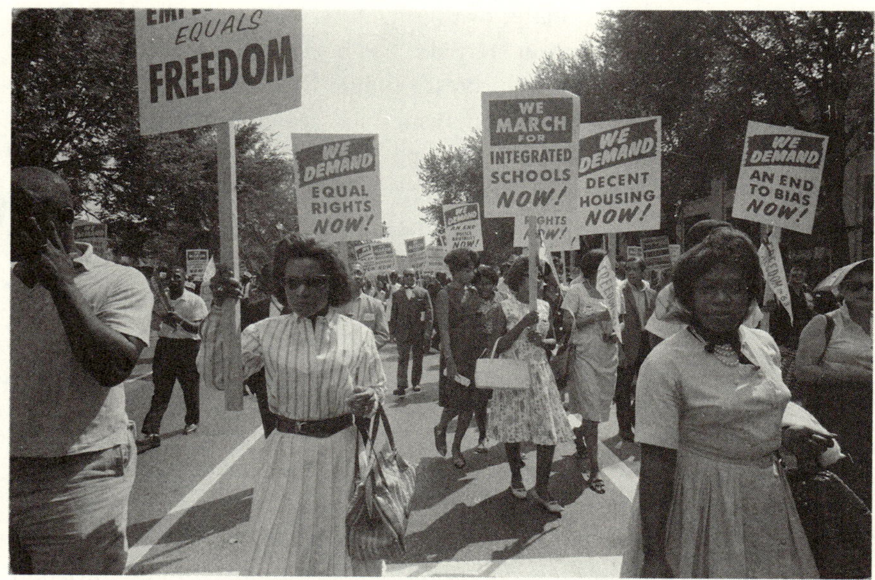

Figure 44. Demonstrators at the March on Washington on 28 August 1963 carrying signs demanding "equal rights," "integrated schools," and "decent housing." Library of Congress, Prints and Photographs Division, LC-DIG-ppmsca-03128.

The Great Acceleration and the Rise of Environmentalism

By the fall of 1963, Kennedy had conducted a fifty-day "conservation tour" and backed environmental legislation, but, like most Americans, the president didn't seem to fully recognize the urgency of the ecological crisis.[271] Human intervention in the natural environment had begun much earlier, as foragers and farmers made reversible small-scale modifications to local niches. However, the scale, magnitude, and pace of human impact increased with industrialization and escalated after World War II (see appendix). During the midcentury Great Acceleration, as some call it, human action became the main cause of earth-system disruptions, which included fallout radionuclides from bomb testing, spiking carbon dioxide and nitrate levels, and proliferating "technofossils" like aluminum and plastics.[272] This period saw the intensification of the urban industrial crisis that began in the 1780s and grew in the 1870s.[273] The acceleration began about 1950, when oil surpassed coal as the nation's main energy source, but the interconnected series of threats had converging causes and varied manifestations. The crisis was *environmental,* since it threatened the planetary ecosystem. At the same time, it was also *social,* because it disproportionately harmed the poor, the young, and the marginalized; *economic,* because industrial consumer capitalism drove it; *political,* because elected officials were slow to acknowledge harm and prevent damage; and *cultural,* because lifeway habits and religious worldviews intensified the problems.

A journalist who reported on postwar debates about nature warned that "a day of reckoning is at hand."[274] The "conservationist" vision articulated in *Our Plundered Planet,* an Episcopalian naturalist's 1948 book about population growth and shrinking resources, differed from the probusiness gospel favored by the "apostles of abundance."[275] Abundance-focused leaders delayed America's ecological reckoning by preaching a profit-first industrial religion that saw natural resources as God-given commodities available for unrestrained consumption. Promoters of this prosperity gospel used spiritual language, as when marketers hailed "petroleum's new miracles" in an oil company ad in *Fortune* magazine. It reminded executives that the "Petroleum Tree" had grown to include dozens of miraculous products, not only carbon black, which generated Borger's 1930s "black blizzards," and motor fuel, which triggered Los Angeles's 1950s smog, but also plastics, rubber, and asphalt.[276]

Industry executives also financed religious leaders who in turn sanctified fossil fuels as oil use tripled, automobile suburbs multiplied, and interstate highways expanded.[277] Conservative Protestants who welcomed oil money preached this gospel, including Graham, who starred as a revivalist in the 1953 film *Oiltown, USA,* which told the story of a Houston oilman converted by an evangelist.[278] Modernist Protestants supported by Rockefeller money preached their own gospel of crude. So did Catholic oil workers and their pastors. The Catholic Petroleum Guild sponsored Sunday masses during "Oil Progress Week" in 1949, and guild-supporting clerics officiated at annual communion breakfasts during the Fifties.[279] Even spiritual leaders known for their social conscience ignored environmental issues and, like Niebuhr, endorsed an anthropocentric ethic that stressed humans' God-given capacity to "transmute" and "transcend" nature.[280] As the biologist Rachel Carson observed, the public was "fed little tranquilizing pills of half-truth" by federal officials and corporate polluters, and anthropocentric visions of flourishing blinded many to the mounting ecological problems.[281]

Alternative theologies valuing nonhuman nature began to appear between 1945 and 1963.[282] Joseph Sittler, a Lutheran theologian in Chicago, published "A Theology for Earth" in 1954.[283] The next year the French Jesuit

Teilhard de Chardin died in New York City, but his posthumously published *The Divine Milieu* appeared in 1960.[284] Both thinkers imagined humans as embedded in an evolving natural world destined to be consummated by God. The biologist Aldo Leopold, author of "Thinking Like a Mountain," abandoned his theistic childhood faith but emphasized the interconnection of all things and expressed reverence for nonhuman nature.[285] So did Carson, a former churchgoer who was remembered as a "nun of nature" and memorialized at the National Cathedral.[286] Her 1956 article for the *Woman's Home Companion* urged mothers to pass on "a sense of awe and wonder" by teaching children to observe nature—as her devout Presbyterian mother did.[287] Reverence for nature drove various churched and unchurched activists, including the spiritual heirs of John Muir in the Sierra Club, who helped block the government-proposed "dinosaur dam" (Colorado's Echo Park Dam), which threatened revered ancient petroglyphs and cherished wilderness.[288]

A spiritually figured concern for public health also sparked protests about air pollution, nuclear fallout, and toxic pesticides. Scientists had begun reporting rising carbon dioxide levels and changing weather patterns, but smog alerts attracted more public attention.[289] Working-class families were distressed by the 1948 air pollution disaster in Donora, a valley mill town near Pittsburgh, where twenty died and 3,000 fell ill as a hazardous smog descended. The steel company dismissed it as "an act of God," while the local paper countered, "God Didn't Do It."[290] In fact, a physician told investigators that only a "God-sent rain" had prevented a thousand more deaths.[291] The next year, a Chicago Presbyterian church invited a speaker from the city's "cleaner air committee," and a Catholic grandfather wrote a letter to a Los Angeles newspaper saying that smog infringed "on our God-given basic human rights: the enjoyment of an atmosphere free from unnecessary contamination."[292]

Americans also worried about contamination from radiation. The US military knew the health effects of nuclear testing before the Trinity explosion, and officials continued to downplay them after the war.[293] Prominent scientists were the public face of dissent against nuclear proliferation and bomb testing, but grassroots groups like St. Louis's Eves against Atoms provided much of the movement's energy. Another St. Louis organization began a drive with "religious overtones" to inform the public about bomb testing.[294] Its founding members included a Congregationalist minister, two Quakers, and three members of the Ethical Culture Society, and in April 1958 they met at a church to formally establish the group. They soon circulated their newsletter, *Nuclear Information,* and by December launched the Baby Tooth Survey to study radioactive strontium-90 levels in the teeth of children born since atomic bomb testing started.[295] With the help of Protestant churches and Catholic schools, the project catalogued almost 15,000 baby teeth the first year, and results revealed increases in childhood cancer. The study—and a one-day national protest of strontium-90 tainted milk in 1961—helped convince the Kennedy administration to negotiate a 1963 treaty with the Soviets to end above-ground testing of atomic weapons.[296]

Carson mentioned radiation's dangers in *Silent Spring* but focused on pesticides, a topic that came up during a 1962 White House press conference, where Kennedy responded to a question about pesticides like DDT by mentioning "Miss Carson's book" and revealing his staff were discussing the topic.[297] That surprised observers, since few politicians publicly discussed pesticides' dangers, even though US scientists planning wartime troop invasions had learned that DDT killed wildlife as well as insects. A few ordinary citizens voiced alarm, as when Mamie Plyler, a rural Georgian, complained that chemical spraying on nearby fields was harming her family's health. Her letters yielded little, though the scriptural passage on her tombstone conveyed no regret: "I have fought a good fight" (2 Timothy 4:7).[298] Others fought spraying in farm fields and suburban gardens in the years ahead. Nationwide outrage erupted during the "cranberry crisis" of 1959, when the FDA removed pesticide-tainted berries from grocers' shelves during the Christmas season.[299] Public alarm intensified after the 1962 publication of *Silent Spring,* which convinced many of DDT's dangers. The chemical industry responded by ridiculing Carson, but the Kennedy administration's scientific advisors supported her claim that pesticides harmed birds as well as humans. Interior Secretary Stewart Udall led the administration's defense of Carson, and the less active Latter-day Saint would publish his own environmental warning, *The Quiet Crisis.*[300] Evangelical "apostles of abundance" who wrote for *Christianity Today* said little, but mainline Protestants and Catholics praised *Silent Spring.* A Protestant reviewer praised the book's analysis of nature's "network of interdependence" and its call to share the earth.[301] The well-known Trappist monk Thomas Merton sent fan mail in January 1963, saying that nature manifests the divine and thanking Carson for her "important warning" about the dangers of "our whole way of life."[302]

DDT would be banned in the Seventies, but JFK wouldn't live to see it. He died that November, when a Castro sympathizer shot him as his motorcade drove through downtown Dallas.[303] Kennedy also didn't get to sign the Clean Air Act his administration supported, an honor that fell to the new president, Lyndon Baines Johnson, in December.[304] The environmental health risks to Mexican Catholics in East Chicago and El Paso remained unacknowledged at the end of 1963, and, even though Catholic and Protestant groups had condemned racism, civil rights legislation had not passed either.[305] A second wave of feminism had started to swell, as Betty Friedan published *The Feminine Mystique* in February 1963, and Kennedy's Commission on the Status of Women submitted its report in October.[306] But gender equity in the churches and the society would have to wait. The president's team had begun working on another problem, poverty, but never presented a bill to Congress.

The first US combat fatality in Vietnam happened on Eisenhower's watch, but Kennedy continued the conflict. He lived to witness a media turning point: to protest the anti-Buddhist policies of America's ally, South Vietnam, the monk Thich Quang Duc set himself on fire on a Saigon street in June 1963. As one US official said, after the photograph appeared in *Life* "the party was almost over in terms of the imagery . . . affecting American opinion," although LBJ still would escalate US involvement in the years ahead.[307]

To make things more unsettling, the "way of life" Thomas Merton mentioned was beginning to change. As the manufacturing sector slowed and the service sector quickened, postindustrial society and postindustrial religion were beginning to appear. Eisenhower's 1961 farewell address had declared that computers were ushering in a "technological revolution," and Kennedy noticed it too, even addressing the worry that computers might replace humans.[308] In a 1963 speech, Kennedy conceded computers were "extraordinary" but insisted "man is still the most extraordinary computer of all." That claim would seem less self-evident in later years as views of the human-machine relationship changed and computer metaphors circulated. An artificial intelligence pioneer had introduced the phrase "machine learning" in 1959, and by 1963 Kennedy had seen how computer-driven spacecraft, communication satellites, and business machines were changing American life.[309] The churchgoing Catholic also witnessed a spirit of change in religion. In 1959 Pope John XXIII announced an ecumenical council to "update" the church, and JFK visited the Vatican in July 1963 while bishops prepared their first document, which would end the centuries-long use of Latin at mass.[310] Other faith communities were changing too, though few Americans could have anticipated the dramatic spiritual shifts ahead as the counterculture would inspire innovation—and generate backlash—and the computer would alter everyday life as much as the field plow and the steam engine.

CHAPTER 9

Countercultural Religion

Spiritual Protests, Postponed Reckonings, and "Deep Division," 1964–1974

Visions of human flourishing and national belonging diverged even more sharply in the decade after 1964. Lyndon Johnson's vision of an egalitarian "Great Society" continued FDR's quest to provide a more "abundant life," and spiritually inspired protestors confronted inherited and emerging problems.[1] Yet LBJ's successor, Richard Nixon, who had a very different view of individual and communal well-being, warned a national audience in 1969 that the public displays of dissent were aggravating the "silent majority" and generating "deep division," a polarization evident in the letters President Nixon received after that speech—from supporters saying "we will be your silent America" to critics charging he had only "widened the chasm."[2]

Spiritual Protests

The decade between 1964 and 1974 was a tumultuous transitional period marked by more assassinations, as well as social unrest on city streets and college campuses.[3] Millions of White middle-class baby boomers challenged Cold War America's sacralizing of hierarchy and conformity and bequeathed a legacy of spiritual seeking and questioning authority.[4] Spiritually inspired activists promoted social and environmental well-being by demanding civil rights laws, organizing farmworker boycotts, and planning Earth Day "teach-ins."[5] Religious feminists reinvigorated efforts to seek gender equality in church and society.[6] Congress reversed the bigoted 1924 immigration act, and that legislation Johnson signed beside the Statue of Liberty spurred transnational crossings and diversified religious life.[7] At the same time, the Christian Right pushed back, enacting the Republican Party's "Southern strategy," which courted evangelicals, condemned feminists, and—using coded language—welcomed segregationists.[8]

The Sixties are often portrayed as a complete break with the past, a rupture generated by navel-gazing, back-to-nature hippies promoting free love, hallucinogenic trips, and rock music or—in the politics-focused version—a rupture incited by sign-carrying agitators demanding peace in Vietnam, care for the environment, and rights for the oppressed. There is some truth in the caricatures. Contemporaries did experience the changes as abrupt, and some minimized the legacy of earlier dissent, just as they underestimated the indignation of the Christian Right.[9] Religious conservatives issued early-Sixties manifestos reasserting "God-given" freedoms, challenging free-market constraints, and denouncing big-government programs.[10] They also showed their pull with early-Seventies bestsellers like the antifeminist advice book *The Total Woman,* which endorsed biblically based wifely submission, and *The Late Great Planet Earth,* which rejected the hippies' "mysticism" and predicted the coming rapture, when believers would make the "ultimate trip" to heaven.[11] William F. Buckley Jr., a Republican Catholic columnist and broadcaster, hosted a surprisingly judicious *Firing Line* episode on "The Hippies" in 1968.[12] Mainstream media, however, perpetuated caricatures by showcasing inward-focused hippies or outward-focused demonstrators—and overlooking the moon-landing generation's ambivalence about modern technology, which launched NASA astronauts but scorched Vietnamese villages. Yet many who sought change honored earlier dissenters and combined a concern for the personal and the political. They also reimagined Western faiths or appropriated alternative pieties, especially Asian and Native traditions, while holding in tension a nostalgic reverence for preindustrial lifeways and a utopian optimism about new technologies.

Countercultural Pieties and Communal Experiments

The counterculture's defining features were on display in San Francisco's Human Be-In, where Haight-Ashbury's hippies and Berkeley's Free Speech activists came together for a daylong "Gathering of the Tribes."[13] The 1967 gathering of young people in Golden Gate Park functioned as an initiation into a "new religion," one attendee recalled, a "religious rite in which nothing in particular happened."[14] But things did happen. The festival, which reimagined Fifties' multimedia performances, used Indigenous spiritual imagery and welcomed "Beat Buddhists" Gary Snyder and Alan Ginsberg, who chanted onstage.[15] "The personal is the political," young feminists proclaimed, and the Be-In planners conjoined those impulses, as political agitators shared the microphone with countercultural gurus.[16] Zen Buddhist priest Shunryu Suzuki sat cross-legged on stage, and advocates of drug-mediated spiritual experiences, Timothy Leary and Richard Alpert, addressed the crowd. The two former Harvard researchers had been ingesting and studying hallucinogens. Leary had counseled the doctoral student who conducted the 1962 "Good Friday Experiment" at Boston University's chapel, where Howard Thurman—the Black thinker who visited Gandhi—offered a prayer before seminarians tested the effects of "sacred mushrooms" in a double-blind study.[17] By 1966 Leary had founded the League of Spiritual Unity, discussed "LSD and Religion," and urged young people to "Turn On/Tune In/Drop Out."[18] The Buddha taught that first, Leary said, and Be-In attendees could tune in to Buddhism and turn on to psychedelics. A parachutist landed with free tabs of LSD (lysergic acid diethylamide), a modern synthetic psychedelic, while the event's countercultural idealism also helped generate the "digital utopianism" that would inspire Silicon Valley innovators and transform postindustrial culture.[19]

Countercultural values were soon on display at other festivals, and they circulated in other media. Woodstock (1969) popularized those values, including the Eastward turn. Swami Satchidananda, an orange-robed, India-born teacher, gave the festival's opening address. He said rock music—like a Hindu mantra—creates "celestial sound," and he ended his remarks by leading the revelers in a chanted repetition of the sacred Sanskrit syllables *Hari Om, Hari Om, Hari Om.*[20] Convention-challenging views aired on commercial underground radio (1966–1972) and spread in print culture—in underground newspapers like the *East Village Other* (1965) and the *San Francisco Oracle* (1966), and in bestsellers like *Be Here Now* (1971), a Hindu-inspired "countercultural Bible" published by Alpert under his new spiritual name Ram Dass, and in the spiritually eclectic *Whole Earth Catalog* (1968–1971), which provided "access to tools" to re-create the world, since "we are as gods and might as well get good at it."[21]

Steve Jobs remembered the *Whole Earth Catalog* as "one of the bibles of my generation," like "Google in paperback," and it offered a how-to resource for young people participating in thousands of communal experiments between 1967 and 1975.[22] Those communes included the Jesus Freaks at the Shiloh community outside Eugene, Oregon, the renewal-minded Jews at Havurat Shalom in Somerville, Massachusetts, and an Asian-inspired community near Summertown, Tennessee, called simply "The Farm."[23] That community, which had 1,500 residents by the late 1970s, showed how spiritual communes sometimes exhibited a caricature-defying blend of beliefs and practices. In some ways, the Farm fit the stereotypes. The group originated in San Francisco, where its founder Stephen Gaskin drew crowds to his free "Monday Night Classes."[24] As underground newspapers proclaimed, Stephen (as he was called) welcomed those who had tried psychedelics and had "spiritual" questions. His "raps" attracted 1,000 seekers a week by 1969, and two years later his caravan of painted buses toured the country, finally settling on farmland south of Nashville. There his marijuana-smoking followers established a vegetarian farming commune, which had its own rock band and opened its meetings with meditation.

Yet the Farm also challenged assumptions. The soy-growing commune embraced postindustrial technology, founding a solar company and doing computer consulting. Stephen even used computer analogies. He had "ransacked religions for goodies" but used a digital metaphor to explain how the group selected its mix of beliefs and practices: "If you took all the world's religions like old IBM cards and stacked them up, some of the holes would go clear through."[25] They looked for the shared sources of illumination, whether they were Buddhist, Hindu, or Christian. Although some spiritual communes focused more on self-realization than social action, the Farm valued both. It reached out to the needy, for example, creating an ambulance service for an underserved South Bronx neighborhood.[26] Discussion of "natural childbirth" had begun decades earlier, but Stephen's wife, Ina May Gaskin, also promoted natural birth control and described midwife-led deliveries in *Spiritual Midwifery,* which explained the Farm's unexpected stance on a controversial issue: "Don't have an abortion," she advised pregnant young women. "You can come to the Farm and we'll deliver your baby and take care of it, and if you ever decide you want it back, you can have it."[27] Finally, Farm residents also respectfully engaged their conservative Christian neighbors. In 1972 Al Gore Jr.—then a young reporter for a Nashville paper—offered an appreciative account of the Farm's weekly debates with local evangelical congregations. He acknowledged the stark differences between the eclectic "coed monastery" and the biblical literalists in town. But the progressive Baptist and future vice president found a much-needed openness. "The real importance of the debates," Gore wrote, "is that representatives of the two groups of people who are mortal enemies in many parts of America are learning to listen to—and like—the other."[28]

Countercultural Impulses and "Establishment" Faiths

As Gore lamented, there seemed to be little listening—and even less liking—across the cultural chasms. But even though only a small proportion joined communes or chanted mantras, many young people shared countercultural values and engaged in countercultural practices, especially concerning dress, language, and music. Millions of young believers spurned convention, favored egalitarianism, and embraced informality.[29] Young Episcopalian women who had sung hymns in pumps and pearls in 1964 wore sandals and slacks a decade later; crew-cut Catholic teens with neckties in 1964 walked to communion in 1974 with long hair and blue jeans. Tie-dyed Haight-Ashbury came to button-down Main Street, changing devotional styles. Although traditionalist Catholics like Buckley still longed for the Latin liturgy, the changes were hard to miss in Catholic parishes after 1965, not only because priests said mass in English and faced parishioners instead of the altar, but also because Vatican II–inspired liturgists organized "folk masses," with guitar-strumming vocalists singing folk favorites or new hymns like Sister Miriam Therese Winter's "Joy Is Like the Rain" (1965), an acoustic interpretation of a Gospel passage (Luke 8:22–25).[30]

Countercultural values affected Protestant and Jewish devotional life too. A Pittsburgh-based Presbyterian minister and radio host, Dennis C. Benson, published *Electric Liturgy* (1972), which had a pink-and-blue cover, stream-of-consciousness musings inside, and two LP records in the back-cover pocket. Reverend Benson recounted his attempt to create a "far out" worship service, while urging readers—and listeners—to "let your mind and spirit wander into these print-electric lines and grooves."[31] He hoped to make mainline Protestant worship "authentic," and the coeditors of *The Jewish Catalog: A Do-It-Yourself Kit* had similar ambitions. One of its editors, Richard Siegel, was a member of the Massachusetts commune Havurat Shalom, where he had tried to build a *sukkah,* a temporary dwelling for the holiday of Sukkot, Feast of the Tabernacles. He discovered he lacked the tools and skills. With that sense of frustration—and the inspiration of the *Whole Earth Catalog*—he set out to return control of building Jewish devotional life to the individual. At Siegel's community, worshippers sat on cushions around a macramé-curtained Torah ark, and the same spirit of informality pervaded *The Jewish Catalog,* which led some Reform and Conservative congregations to personalize and democratize synagogue life.[32]

Postponed Reckonings, 1964–1974

Some theological conservatives sided with those advocating change—including those who signed the 1973 Evangelical Declaration of Social Concern—but the acrimony Gore noticed arose in part from the Religious Right's denunciation of the period's social movements and political interventions.[33] Despite that opposition, by 1974 young protesters and their older allies in the churches and the government had begun to address some of the social and environmental problems they had inherited.[34]

Civil Rights

Spiritually inspired legal initiatives discussed during the Kennedy administration became civil rights laws during the Johnson administration. LBJ surprised segregationists when he spent the political capital accrued by succeeding an assassinated president to endorse the civil rights bill, which banned racial segregation in schools, workplaces, and public facilities. While Congress debated the bill, the Texas Protestant invited 177 faith leaders to the White House, urging them to "reawaken the conscience of your beloved land."[35] Johnson signed the resulting Civil Rights Act in the summer of 1964, and the following March he turned to voting rights, as King led a march from Selma to Montgomery that drew thousands of Black protesters and some White Northern ministers, rabbis, priests, and nuns.[36] Locals attacked the Alabama demonstrators, and on the day that King gave the funeral sermon for a murdered White minister in Selma, 70 million viewers watched LBJ announce support for a Voting Rights Act. Repeating the refrain of "We Shall Overcome," the Civil Rights Movement's unofficial anthem, he urged viewers to help "overcome the crippling legacy of bigotry" so all citizens could enjoy the "full blessings of American life."[37]

Those civil rights laws—along with Medicaid and Medicare—made some things better. The Black middle class expanded, educational opportunities increased, and health disparities lessened.[38] Infant mortality among African Americans was twice as high as for Whites in 1964, but access to integrated hospitals reduced the death toll by the mid-Seventies.[39] Programs targeting transgenerational poverty and food instability also helped, and

Johnson addressed residential segregation by signing the 1968 Fair Housing Act, which prohibited discrimination because of race or religion.[40] These interventions began to confront the inequities sacralized by planter piety in the first half of the nineteenth century and perpetuated by *Plessy*-endorsing churchgoers in the first half of the twentieth. Yet problems persisted—including hunger, unemployment, and police brutality.

Less than two weeks after LBJ signed the 1965 Voting Rights Act, police brutality sparked six days of rebellion in Watts, a working-class Black neighborhood in Los Angeles, and the Freedom Movement entered a less optimistic and more strident phase.[41] By 1966, as uprisings shook other cities and Hoover's FBI surveilled King's activities, some African Americans began to talk less about racial integration, national inclusion, nonviolent resistance, and legislative solutions and more about self-determination, self-defense, pan-Africanism, and Black Power.[42] Activists were increasingly impatient with nonviolent tactics, as White terrorists wore them down, including in Mississippi, where the Ku Klux Klan kidnapped, shot, and bombed African Americans.[43] There were White allies, of course. A pastor in Mississippi supported economic boycotts and bailed-out Black protestors.[44] North Carolina monks transformed a former slave auction block into a baptismal font in 1965. "Upon this rock," their church's new plaque explained, "men were once sold into slavery. Now . . . through the waters of Baptism, men become free children of God."[45] But evocative symbols and scattered allies weren't enough. More fundamental changes were needed, leaders said, especially after King's assassination in 1968. James Forman, who had challenged King's nonviolent faith-based approach, interrupted a service at New York's Riverside Church in 1969 to read a Black Manifesto demanding that White churches and synagogues pay reparations for the historic injustices of slavery and segregation.[46] But Forman avoided challenging the Black Church because he recognized its importance to many African Americans. Even the Black Panthers came to recognize the need to employ spiritual themes in community outreach, opening Oakland's Son of Man Temple in 1973.[47]

Other activists and theologians went further. Rev. Charles Koen of Cairo, Illinois, insisted that "a redefined, relevant Christianity" held the key to the Black Power movement's success.[48] The National Conference of Black Churchmen said the same in a 1966 statement on Black Power, and reaffirmed the message in a 1969 statement on "Black Theology," which reminded readers that "white theology sustained the American slave system."[49] The group wrote the document two months after seminary professor James Cone published *Black Theology and Black Power*.[50] Honoring the insights of Malcolm

X and the Black Power Movement as well as Martin Luther King Jr. and the Civil Rights Movement, Cone suggested that God is Black, and—as Latin American liberation theologians were arguing—God sided with the oppressed. To correct for inattention to gender, in the years ahead, Black churchwomen like Katie Cannon and Jacquelyn Grant would craft "womanist" theologies that challenged sexism as well as racism.[51]

Women's Rights

Black and White churchgoers played roles during the early years of the women's liberation movement, as a 1966 photograph of seven founding members of the National Organization of Women (NOW) shows (fig. 45).[52] Religious feminists like Sister Joel Read, second from the left, didn't have to create new organizations but did need to get the men in charge to take them seriously.[53] Anna Arnold Hedgeman, the Black Methodist who stood beside Read, had been the only woman to serve on the organizing committee for the March on Washington and sign the Black Power statement. She was involved in NOW's founding too.[54] So was Pauli Murray, a Black Episcopalian lawyer who is not pictured because she stepped back and nudged Hedgeman forward as participants posed for the shot.

It was neither the first nor the last time Murray worked behind the scenes for change. The Methodist Church had commissioned her to write a 1951 overview of segregation laws, which the NAACP's Thurgood Marshall called their "Bible," and she had urged Betty Friedan to create an NAACP-like organization for women.[55] Murray, who would serve on NOW's first board in 1966, also helped formulate legal strategies used in landmark civil rights and women's rights cases, including *Brown v. Board of Education* (1954), which used a tactic she proposed, and *Reed v. Reed* (1971), for which Ruth Bader Ginsburg repeated Murray's argument that arbitrary treatment because of gender violated the Fourteenth Amendment's Equal Protection Clause.[56] Murray served on the President's Commission on the Status of Women in 1962 and gave congressional testimony on behalf of the Equal Rights Amendment, which said "equality of rights" shall not be denied "on account of sex." Congress passed it in 1972, and, as the ratification process proceeded, polarized faith communities shaped the debate. The Evangelical Women's Caucus promoted an egalitarian interpretation of biblical womanhood, while Concerned Women for America, an anti-ERA group, reaffirmed women's distinct roles, as did most male-led evangelical institutions.[57] Catholics split over the ERA too. A NOW member cofounded Catholics for the

Figure 45. Seven of NOW's forty-nine founding members, including Sister Joel Read, second from left, and Anna Arnold Hedgeman, third from left, in an October 1966 photograph by Vincent J. Graas. Courtesy of the Schlesinger Library, Harvard Radcliffe Institute.

ERA, and six US bishops supported the amendment, but most diocesan leaders argued it endangered the family and the unborn.[58] There were some pro-ERA voices in the Church of Latter-day Saints, but leaders feared it might "stifle God-given feminine instincts."[59] A grassroots organization run by the Catholic Phyllis Schlafly mounted an especially effective challenge, and the ERA failed when only thirty-five of the thirty-eight required states had ratified it by the 1982 deadline, though litigators continued to rely on the Equal Protection Clause to win court battles for gender equity.[60]

Murray and other churchwomen also fought for their rights in religious institutions. By 1970 various women's caucuses and committees had issued resolutions and reports, including a report on theological education that included insights from Murray, then teaching at Brandeis and author of an article on women's liberation for *Church Woman,* and Mary Daly, a Boston College professor who wrote *The Church and the Second Sex* (1968).[61] Daly, who thanked Murray in her second book *Beyond God the Father,* would leave the church.[62] Feminists who stayed saw women's ordination as an expression of "the spirt of prophecy," as Murray put it after entering an Episcopalian seminary in 1973.[63] Congregationalists and Universalists had ordained women by the 1850s, and Methodists and Presbyterians had followed during the 1950s. The Southern Baptist Convention ordained Addie Davis in 1964, though women's leadership remained contested in the SBC.[64] Roman Catholic women imagined the opportunity to serve in new ways, including the lay theologian who chaired NOW's committee on religion, but the Vatican closed the door to ordination by the end of the Seventies.[65] Orthodox Jewish leaders did as well. Yet Sally Priesand became the first female Reform rabbi in 1972, and the first Reconstructionist rabbi followed two years later.[66] After rancorous debate, the Episcopal Church sanctioned women's clerical leadership, and in a 1977 ceremony at the Washington National Cathedral Murray became the denomination's first African American female priest. Five weeks later, Murray found "a symbol of healing" when she celebrated her first Eucharist in the Southern chapel where her grandmother, a slave, had been baptized.[67]

LGBTQ Rights

Between 1964 and 1974 the pious also turned their attention to several other causes, including the struggles for Indigenous and LGBTQ rights, as well as efforts to end the war in Indochina, treat farmworkers fairly, and care for the environment. LGBTQ rights began attracting media attention after the Stonewall Rebellion in 1969, a time when same-sex relationships were illegal and faith communities didn't welcome nonconforming worshippers. Murray, who had at least two significant romantic relationships with women, was one of those nonconforming worshippers. Scholars debate how to describe Murray's romantic history and gender identity, because her autobiography avoided the topics. But her journals acknowledged an attraction to women—though she resisted the label "lesbian"—and said she was "a girl who should have been a boy."[68] It's hard to know which identifier Murray might choose today, but given the threats she faced because of prevailing attitudes on sexuality, gender, and race, it's not surprising she once defined salvation as "feeling safe."[69] Bayard Rustin, the gay co-organizer of the March on Washington, didn't always feel safe, despite his Quaker faith. He once had been arrested for homosexual activity, and that came back to haunt him in 1963, when a segregationist trying to discredit the Civil Rights Movement outed him on the Senate floor shortly before the Washington March.[70] That didn't stop the march, and LGBTQ worshippers would agitate on the streets and in the churches in the years ahead. The first Pride parades appeared in 1970, and in

New York a marcher dressed as a bishop held a sign saying, "Gay People, *This* Is Our Church."[71]

But not everyone gave up on religious institutions. Troy Perry founded the Metropolitan Community Church, a LGBTQ-friendly denomination, in Los Angeles, and he performed the US's first same-sex marriage there in 1968.[72] The United Church of Christ ordained an openly gay minister in 1972. Dignity, an organization for LGBTQ Catholics, held a national convention in 1973, and Episcopalians founded Integrity the next year.[73] But this activism drew ire. The Jesuits expelled a Dignity member who wrote *The Church and the Homosexual,* and a "suspicious" fire burned Perry's first church in 1973.[74] Yet advocates had attracted leaders' attention, even if sexuality would remain a divisive issue in the decades ahead.

Indigenous Rights

The year 1967 marked a turning point for representations of Indigenous Peoples. As hippies wearing feathers and beads began "playing Indian," *Life's* December 1st issue announced the "Return of the Red Man" (fig. 46).[75] Its psychedelic cover included a multicolored rendering of a Haudenosaunee man, and a story entitled "Happy Hippie Hunting Ground" noted the fascination with Natives' spiritual use of hallucinogens and performance of communal ceremonies.[76] Yet, as Indian newspapers complained, representations were often disrespectful and uninformed.[77] At the center of the magazine's cover, for example, *Life*'s graphic designer placed an 1884 photograph of the Northern Arapaho chief Sharp Nose (Ta-qua-wi).[78] A story inside said the image was being projected as rock music pulsed in San Francisco's Avalon ballroom, but it omitted other key details. Sharp Nose had served as an Army scout to aid his impoverished community, and that's why he wore a military uniform. The Wyoming reservation resident, who lived in the era when the government forced acculturation and criminalized ceremonies, also agreed to send his son to Pennsylvania's Carlisle Indian School.[79] Yet Little Chief survived only two years, and Sharp Nose posed for that photo soon after his son had been buried at Carlisle without any family to mourn him in the Arapaho way.[80]

The magazine mentioned that a resurgence of Native activism was stirring in 1967. Concerns about police profiling led to the founding of the American Indian Movement (AIM) in Minneapolis in 1968, and AIM attracted media attention for its takeover of the Bureau of Indian Affairs in 1972 and occupation of Wounded Knee in 1973.[81] As important for religious

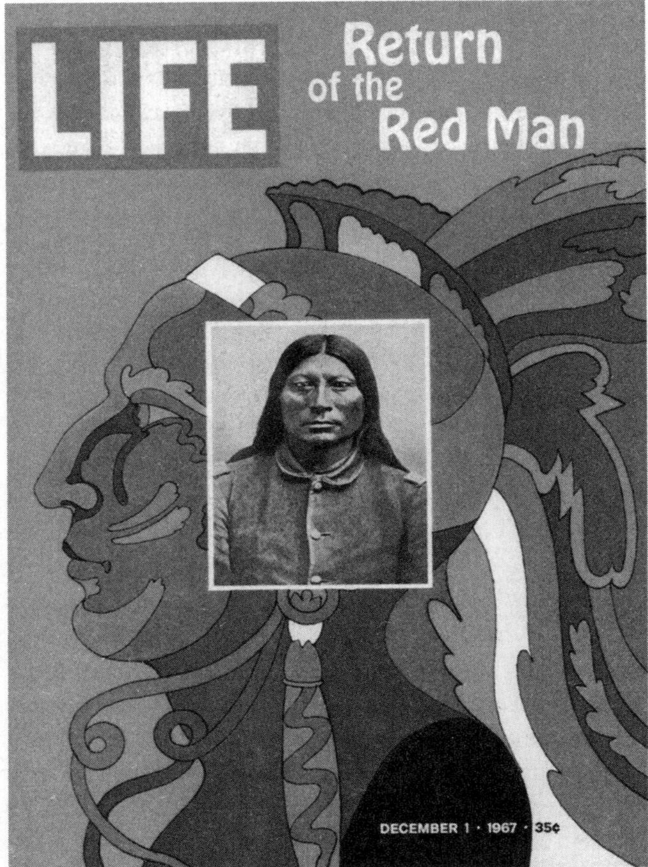

Figure 46. "Return of the Red Man," cover of *Life,* 1 December 1967. © 1967 Meredith Operations Corporation. All rights reserved. Reprinted from *LIFE* and published with permission of Meredith Operations Corporation and permission of the estate of Milton Glaser. *LIFE* and the *LIFE* logo are registered trademarks of Meredith Operations Corporation. Used under license. Reproduction in any manner in any language in whole or in part without written permission is prohibited.

history, Indigenous spiritual leaders met after a June 1967 ceremony at Bear Butte, a sacred space in South Dakota, to organize a coalition to protect holy places and to recover human remains, grave goods, and revered objects. Participants like Suzan Shown Harjo (Cheyenne and Hodulgee Muscogee) remembered that meeting as crucial for later legal advances.[82] As Harjo noted, Vine Deloria Jr., who in 1967 served as director of the National Congress of American Indians (NCAI), played a key role in those advances. He challenged Plymouth Rock narratives and revived Indigenous prophetic traditions that had gone underground because of governmental suppression. Deloria, a Standing Rock Sioux, was the son and grandson of Episcopalian missionaries, and he earned a degree in theology as well as law. But he decided Christianity no longer met Native needs and reported in his "manifesto" *Custer Died for Your Sins* (1969) that "tribal religions are making a strong comeback on most reservations."[83] The book's title came from a NCAI bumper sticker meant as a dig at the National Council of Churches.[84] It referred to the broken Sioux Treaty of 1868 and implied that just as breaches of the biblical covenant had required an atoning blood sacrifice, Custer's death had been just payment for the federal government's treaty violation. His 1973 book *God Is Red,* which recalled another bumper sticker, urged a return to place-based tribal religions, with their focus on personal healing, community preservation, and environmental responsibility. It ended with Deloria hoping that "the invaders of the North American continent will finally discover that for this land, God is Red."[85]

Equity in the Fields and the Pews

Mexican and Filipino farmworkers in California's Central Valley hoped God sided with them too, and the laborers and their allies used religious symbols, rituals, and institutions to improve conditions in the fields and demand inclusion in the churches.[86] The United Farm Workers' (UFW) cofounder César Chávez, who had worked in the fields, welcomed the aid of the Protestant-led California Migrant Ministry between 1965, when Chávez announced the Delano grape boycott, and 1970, when growers signed a contract.[87] However, Chávez wanted the Catholic Church's help too. The Delano parish refused to provide the union with a meeting space, and US bishops failed to officially support the boycott. Activist sisters and priests, including the UFW's chaplain, Mark Day, did join the cause.[88] The union incorporated Catholic Marian symbols as well as Aztec avian imagery in its banners, buttons, and publications, and Chávez valued Gandhian nonviolent resistance, papal social encyclicals, and Mexican devotional piety, especially its emphasis on the redemptive power of self-sacrifice.[89]

Those influences converged in Chávez's 1968 penitential fast. Militant strikers had been found with guns, so to reaffirm nonviolence and unify the membership, on 14 February Chávez began a fast. During the twenty-five-day fast he received encouragement from political and religious leaders, including King, who was "deeply moved," while Chávez received daily communion at the organization's headquarters, which became a pilgrimage site for farmworkers touched by his sacrifice.[90] After losing forty pounds but gaining public support, the activist ended his fast on 10 March at an open-air mass in a Delano park.[91] Thousands of farmworkers walked in the mile-long procession behind an image of the Virgin of Guadalupe and the UFW's Thunderbird banner, ending near the makeshift altar, where a weakened Chávez slouched in a chair beside Senator Bobby Kennedy, a union ally. There they heard a rabbi offer the opening prayer, a minister deliver the sermon, and a priest read Chávez's message, which explained that he fasted because he was "filled with grief and pain for the sufferings of farm workers" but wanted to remind strikers that "the justice of our cause" should be our only weapon.[92]

Other nonviolent protests—and impassioned pleas—yielded a few ecclesiastical gains. In 1969 Mexican American activists seized a Catholic campground east of San Diego to express frustration at the church's failure to serve them, while two diocesan priests in San Antonio highlighted the needs of the Mexican American residents of the city's west side.[93] Those priests founded PADRES, an organization dedicated to religious, educational, and social rights in 1969, and, two years later, fifty women religious gathered in Houston to establish Las Hermanas.[94] They demanded access to ecclesiastical power, and the Vatican named Patricio Flores, a former farmworker, as auxiliary bishop of San Antonio in 1970. Latino clerics then assumed episcopal roles in Los Angeles (1971), San Diego (1974), and Santa Fe (1974).[95] New theologies emerged too, as activists influenced by liberation theology announced "a preferential option for the poor," and Spanish-speaking women who criticized the church's sexism began to privilege their own experience as they created what some would later call *mujerista* theology.[96]

Peace Activism

Religiously inspired activists who fought for civil and ecclesiastical rights turned their attention to the Vietnam War by 1965, when most Americans supported sending troops to Southeast Asia.[97] Pacifists in the peace churches led the initial dissent. As the Johnson administration intensified the fighting and fatalities mounted—including civilian deaths—a Quaker named Norman Morrison protested in 1965 by setting himself on fire outside the Pentagon, just forty feet from the window of the pious Presbyterian Defense

Secretary Robert McNamara, who later said US policy had been "wrong, terribly wrong."[98] Principled pacifists like Morrison, who denounced all wars, were joined by Protestants, Catholics, and Jews who argued this particular conflict was unjust because the communist-backed enemy had not attacked the US, and American forces were endangering noncombatants. A Reform Jewish body proposed a ceasefire as early as 1965, and the United Presbyterian Church advocated an end to the war in 1967. Even the US Catholic bishops, who had long condemned communism and advocated military service, called for a cessation of hostilities in 1971.[99] Individuals and ad hoc groups entered the debate too. Martin Luther King joined Reinhold Niebuhr, Rabbi Abraham Heschel, and Catholic priests Philip and Daniel Berrigan to form Clergy and Laity Concerned about Vietnam in 1966.[100] The next year King delivered a sermon saying conscience led him to protest the war, and conscience led the Berrigans and the Catholic Peace Fellowship protestors to douse draft cards with blood and set them ablaze.[101]

Those rituals got protestors arrested and also drew public attention. Even more Americans paid attention after the Moratorium to End the War in Vietnam on 15 October, 1969, a nationwide event to pressure newly elected President Nixon to bring the troops home. Moratorium Day elicited divergent reactions: some praised protestors as patriotic creators of a more self-critical civil religion, while Nixon supporters dismissed the demonstrators as unpatriotic malcontents.[102] Even critics had to admit that co-organizer Sam Brown, a former divinity student, attracted a broad coalition to the marches, services, and vigils held in 268 US cities.[103] The coalition included protestors in the Boston Common crowd of 90,000 who marched from a nearby chapel, the 50,000 who heard Rev. William Sloane Coffin in New York's Bryant Park, and the 27,000 who participated in a candlelight march in Washington, where Coretta Scott King spoke (fig. 47).[104]

Moratorium Day also reached college campuses, including institutions not known as seedbeds of radicalism. At Notre Dame, one counter-demonstrator carried a sign saying "Bomb the Cong," but 2,000 worshippers attended a "peace mass" where two professors and four students walked to the altar, tore their drafts cards, and placed them in the offertory basket.[105] The next year, antiwar protestors were killed at Kent State (Ohio) and Jackson State (Mississippi), and the "credibility gap" widened as journalists reported on the conduct of the war, including the My Lai massacre, where US soldiers shot unarmed civilians.[106] When the fighting stopped in 1975 and more than 58,000 Americans had died, the polarization seemed worse, even if six in ten now told pollsters it had been a mistake to send troops to

Figure 47. Coretta Scott King (center), César Chávez (left), and Dorothy Day (right) at an ecumenical service in New York City in 1973. CNS file photo. Provided by Dorothy Day - Catholic Worker Archives, Raynor Library, Marquette University.

Vietnam.[107] The proportion would grow in the decades ahead, and in turn future US leaders would hesitate before sending uniformed personnel abroad but would sanction postindustrial warfare, launching computer-guided missiles from ships and approving remotely piloted drone strikes. After the spiritually figured antiwar protests, global conflicts would be fought in new ways.[108]

Environmental Activism

Media coverage of an oil spill off Santa Barbara's Pacific coastline and a fiery blaze on Cleveland's polluted Cuyahoga River helped to reignite public concern about ecological issues in 1969, as the late Sixties and early Seventies also became "the environmental moment."[109] Religious institutions offered little formal support, but some churched and unchurched advocates employed spiritual imagery as they warned of ecological threats, staged Earth Day events, and proposed governmental protections.

Environmentalists' spiritual imagery came from diverse sources. In 1967 historian Lynn White had blamed the Judeo-Christian theology of "dominion" over nature, but some churchgoing activists began to challenge that

Figure 48. Six-Cent Apollo 8 single stamp, issued 5 May 1969, Bureau of Engraving and Printing. Courtesy of National Postal Museum, Smithsonian.

interpretation and emphasize care for creation, while others drew on Asian and Indigenous traditions to highlight the interconnection of all life forms.[110] Spiritual resources also came from unexpected sources, most notably a photograph and broadcast by Apollo 8's crew on Christmas Eve 1968.[111] Before the astronauts blasted off to orbit the moon, NASA had told commander Frank Borman, a devout Episcopalian, to say something "appropriate" on their holiday broadcast. He decided on the biblical creation story, and on 24 December the Catholic Bill Anders read the first four lines of Genesis, starting with "In the beginning, God created the heaven and the earth." Episcopalian James Lovell read the next four lines. Borman finished with verses 6 to 10 and wished those on earth a Merry Christmas. But about ten minutes before that planned performance, the crew had a glimpse of earth rising from the lunar surface. With only mission control listening, the startled astronauts expressed delight at the sight of the aqua-blue orb suspended in tar-black space above the moon's stark landscape. Anders, who thought earth looked like a "very fragile" Christmas tree ornament, captured the moment by snapping a color photograph that came to be known as *Earthrise*.[112] After splashdown, *Life* published the image, while the religious press defended the crew's Bible reading against atheists' charge that it violated the Establishment Clause, and the Nixon administration celebrated "the first sight of the world as God sees it," issuing a commemorative stamp that paired the biblical phrase and the *Earthrise* image (fig. 48).[113]

As Anders noted later, the *Earthrise* photograph "had a lot of ecological and philosophical impact," changing conceptions of earth and invigorating the environmental movement.[114] Whole-earth images inspired symbols displayed at the first two Earth Day celebrations in 1970. On 21 March John McConnell, a preacher and activist whose grandfather had been "spirit-baptized" at the Azusa Street Revival, proposed an international ceremony to be held in San Francisco.[115] He had organized efforts to feed refugees and promote peace, and at a 1969 United Nations conference McConnell proposed an Earth Day celebration on the spring equinox, a time long reserved for communal religious rituals and a day of shared global experience, since residents of both hemispheres have equal amounts of daytime and nighttime. McConnell persuaded San Francisco's mayor to sign a proclamation reserving time to advocate world peace and encourage "interest for our planet."[116] His own ecological interest had been ignited by the *Earthrise* photograph, which "deeply stirred" him.[117] So it's not surprising that the flag McConnell designed for the March observance included the NASA image on a dark blue background, and that emblem has made an annual appearance since 1971, when UN officials began observing an hour for peace on the spring equinox.[118]

A prominent McConnell supporter praised the equinox Earth Day as "the first holy day which transcends all national borders," but the San Francisco observance was overshadowed by a national event on 22 April, the second Earth Day, which attracted 20 million participants to the teach-ins, cleanups, and public rituals coordinated by Senator Gaylord Nelson's environmental organization.[119] Nelson had suggested JFK's 1963 conservation tour and worked for environmental causes both as Wisconsin's governor (1959–1963) and, after 1963, as a US senator. While returning from the California oil spill in 1969, the Democrat hatched the idea of a national environmental "teach-in." Nelson, who had gone to Methodist Sunday School but no longer attended church, used spiritual and moral rhetoric in a major environmental speech in January 1970, praising the "great awakening" underway, and he did the same in an Earth Day address, which considered "the total eco-system" and proposed a "new American ethic" that valued "human dignity and well-being" as well as "clean air and water."[120] Nelson delivered that speech in front of a green flag with a new ecology symbol that had spiritual significance for the underground newspaper cartoonist who designed it (fig. 49).[121] The elliptical image, which also adorned buttons and bumper stickers, recalled the shape of planetary orbit and conjoined the letter *e* (for earth, Eden, and enlightenment) with the letter *o* (for organism, oneness, and *om*) to form a green planet in a white background. It alluded to whole-earth imagery, but for the designer—and, perhaps, some activists who read his widely circulated interpretation—it also symbolized the "transcendent unity" of all things, evoked the harmony of the biblical Garden of Eden, and incorporated Daoist, Hindu, and Buddhist motifs.[122]

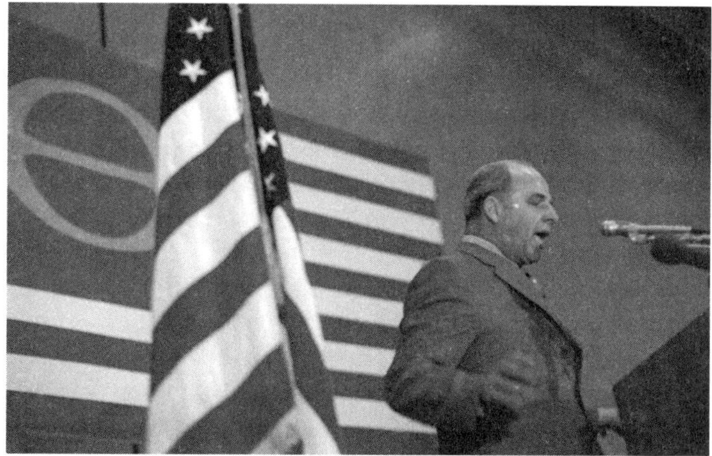

Figure 49. Gaylord Nelson at an Earth Day event with the Ecology Flag behind him, April 1970. Courtesy of the Wisconsin Historical Society, Gaylord Nelson Papers. Image ID 48017.

Religion also had a somewhat more explicit presence on Earth Day. Books published for the occasion—including *The Environmental Handbook,* which sold a million copies by April—honored the movement's unofficial patron saint, Francis of Assisi, but repeated Lynn White's condemnation of Christianity and promoted alternatives like Gary Snyder's Buddhist-inspired "Smokey the Bear Sutra" and N. Scott Momaday's Indigenous-inspired "American land ethic."[123] Even if most faith leaders and religious organizations didn't take strong stands on ecological issues, millions of Christians participated in Earth Day, from stay-at-home moms to college students. Pope Paul VI became the first pontiff to mention "the environment," warning UN officials in 1970 that pollution was triggering an ecological disaster, "a true biological death," but some in the pews were already worried, like those who attended an Earth Day "Action Mass" at Washington's Catholic University, where students carried a coffin filled with roadside litter to an outdoor altar.[124] Few evangelicals expressed support for Earth Day, though one prominent writer proposed a "Christian ecology" and a reader of *Christianity Today* wrote a letter to the editor warning that "unrestrained exploitation" threatened the environment.[125] Mainline Protestants showed more interest, attending antipollution sermons in Birmingham, which ranked second to Gary, Indiana, for the worst air quality, and protesting at a General Electric shareholders' meeting in Minneapolis and then crossing the street for a raucous service at a Methodist church.[126] A Lutheran theologian who had written an early classic published another essay in 1970, and newspaper stories about Earth Day quoted a Methodist theologian who would issue a book-length ecotheology.[127] That Methodist also supported Environment Sunday, a National Council of Churches initiative encouraging sermons the weekend before Earth Day, and a few denominations started to express concern, as when Lutherans issued a statement on "The Environmental Crisis" in 1970.[128]

Government officials responded to the crisis before and after Earth Day. Between 1963 and 1969, Stewart Udall, a less active Latter-day Saint who maintained church ties, advocated for protections both as a best-selling author who challenged the "gospel of growth" and as an Interior Secretary who favored earth-friendly legislation.[129] After Nixon took office in 1969, leading Democrats like Senator Edmund Muskie, who grew up Catholic in a polluted mill town, continued efforts to reduce pollution and preserve wilderness. By 1972, environmentalists in both parties could claim bipartisan victories. The victories were possible because voters told pollsters of their alarm about ecological degradation, and the Earth Day crowds drove home the point for politicians, including President Nixon.[130] So to attract green voters and upstage eco-friendly foes, Nixon took his advisors' counsel and reluctantly sided with environmentalists. His strategic compromises and Muskie's continuing pressure led to several advances, including the creation of the Council on Environmental Quality (1969) and the Environmental Protection Agency (EPA, 1970), as well as the passing of the Clean Air Act of 1970 and the Clean Water Act of 1972. Empowered by these new environmental laws, government officials would begin to address ecological and health problems, including in the Mexican communities in East Chicago and El Paso mentioned earlier. A 1972 study revealed that the children of El Paso's Smeltertown had dangerously high levels of lead, for example, so local leaders demolished the neighborhood in 1973, though efforts to clean up contaminants and protect residents in both cities would continue for decades.[131]

Most government officials who sponsored or enforced the legal protections were religiously active (like Senator Muskie and Interior Secretary Walter Hickel) or attended services growing up (like Senator Nelson and EPA Director William Ruckelshaus), but they said little about religion, especially how churches might aid the cause.[132] Yet Russell Train, under secretary of the interior (1969–1970) and chair of the Council on Environmental Quality (1970–1973), influenced policy and mentioned religion. His Conservation Foundation had funded a 1967 Senate study of how environmental considerations could inform policy decisions, and the next year Train chaired the

Nixon campaign's environmental task force. At a dinner with the president-elect in January 1969, he urged him to focus on the issue.[133] Nixon did for the first few years, implementing ideas that Train's task force and policy council recommended. The active Episcopalian also encouraged church leaders to join the cause.[134] In a lecture delivered as an Interior official, Train suggested, "We need the ministry, looking beyond the 'old-time religion' that called on man . . . to subdue the earth." Humans have done enough subduing, he said, and suggested "the 'old-time religion' had another message, too—Man, the Good Steward."[135]

By 1973, when Train accepted Nixon's invitation to lead the EPA, theological talk about earth stewardship and political initiatives for ecological protections had lost steam. As Train put it, "by then the bloom was off the environmental rose."[136] The Watergate scandal distracted the White House, and the Arab oil embargo shifted attention to "energy shortages."[137] But ecological degradation had continued to threaten the planet since the Great Acceleration of the 1950s, with earth-system disruptions like carbon dioxide increases and "technofossil" accumulations.[138] Few addressed the long-term problems, including the anthropogenic warming that began to be felt in the 1970s, and the legislative successes had not reduced fossil-fuel dependency or changed the car-culture infrastructure.[139] In fact, US petroleum consumption would peak around 1974 and, after a dip, would rise again.[140]

Religious leaders would mount a more vigorous environmental response later, but in this period some weren't sure that religion would even survive. Polls showed signs of eroding trust in religious institutions—and all institutions—by 1974. And atheism had gained visibility with the 1962 ban on school prayer and again in 1969, when Madalyn Murray O'Hair claimed the Bible-reading astronauts had violated the First Amendment.[141] However, a theologian's bestseller wrongly predicted religion would recede from the public arena, and *Time* overstated things when its cover story asked "Is God Dead?"[142] Across America there was more theism than atheism, more flag waving than flag burning. In fact, countercultural values and liberation movements had begun to provoke growing religious reaction and conservative counteractivism by 1974, when oil embargo gas lines replaced Depression Era bread lines as the new symbol of scarcity.[143]

PART FOUR

FIBER OPTICS

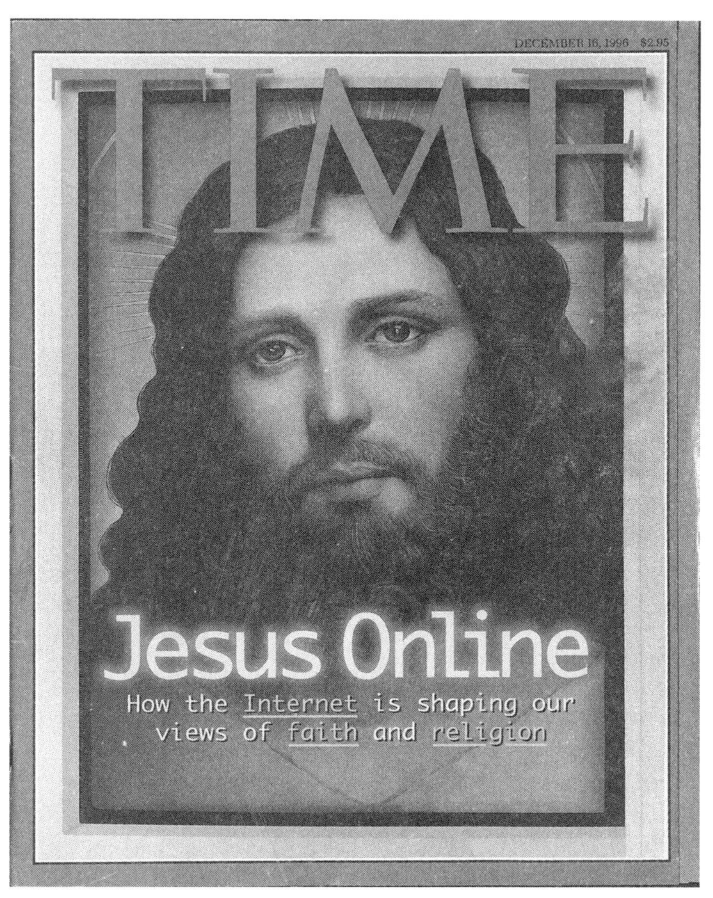

Figure 50. "Jesus Online," cover of *Time,* 16 December 1996. From *TIME.*

CHAPTER 10

Postindustrial Religion

Networked Niches, Segmented Subcultures, and Persistent Problems, 1975–2020

The withdrawal from Vietnam, President Nixon's resignation, and the economy's downturn slowed spiritual activists' momentum and heralded the counterculture's end. In this next period, when postindustrial religion emerged, suburban megachurches multiplied, and partisans exalted or denounced the Sixties' legacy, polarization, pluralism, and disaffiliation characterized America's religious restructuring.[1] While online practices and megachurch preachers sometimes brought people together, they also deepened divisions, just as media segmentation, institutional mistrust, and declining attendance made it more difficult for faith communities to resolve inherited crises and confront new problems.[2] And, as in earlier periods, religious leaders sometimes made things better and sometimes made things worse. By 2020, as Cape Cod's chamber of commerce commemorated the 400th anniversary of the Pilgrims' landing and a federal commission planned for the 250th anniversary of the nation's affirmation of the God-given right to "the pursuit of Happiness," some in the lands that had become America still struggled to meet the conditions for full flourishing (see fig. 2).[3]

Postindustrial Pieties

The Zen meditator and countercultural idealist Steve Jobs cofounded Apple in Silicon Valley in 1976, but the era of the commercially marketed computer had begun earlier—and in the Delaware Valley.[4] Philadelphia-based engineers

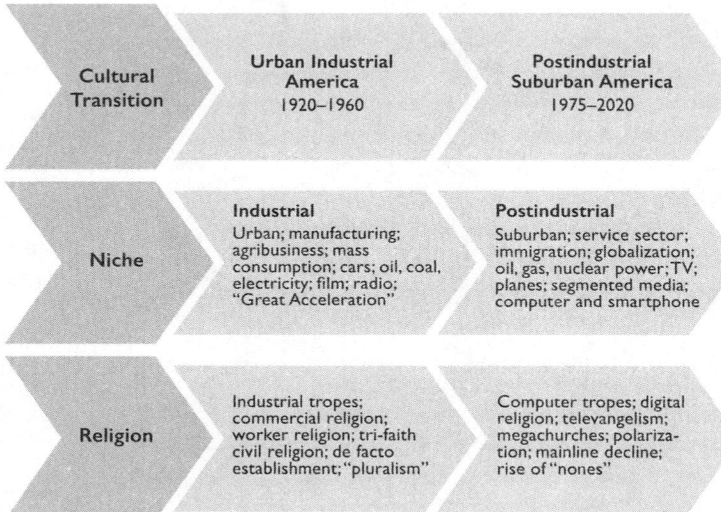

Figure 51. Transition from factories to fiber optics.

had unveiled the ENIAC in 1946, and then in a repurposed factory building they produced the first successful commercial computer, UNIVAC I, which would tabulate the 1950 Census and predict Eisenhower's unexpected victory in the 1952 election.[5] That automated divination surprised pundits, and by 1964 spiritual leaders and technology innovators were expressing worry as well as wonder about computer-mediated technologies. A Presbyterian minister declared, "Man is no UNIVAC!"[6] Christian reviewers reaffirmed that view in 1964, when Norbert Weiner, an influential mathematician raised as an Orthodox Jew, contemplated the "creative" power of machines and warned of automation's dangers.[7] The same year, a group of intellectuals and activists mailed President Johnson a memo predicting a job-stealing "cybernation revolution."[8]

The term *cybernation* never caught on, but by 1977, when mass-produced personal computers appeared, many others had noticed manufacturing's decline and the rise of the service sector, including computer technology companies (fig. 51).[9] By the late 1990s, when more than half of US adults had used a computer to search the Internet and send an email, some were calling their era the *postindustrial* age, emphasizing deindustrialization and the rising service economy, or the *information* age, highlighting the centrality of knowledge for emerging markets.[10] Others preferred the *computer* age, spotlighting digital technology's role in generating new ways of thinking, feeling, and acting.[11]

Just as earlier lifeway transitions led to changes in spiritual practice, the new computer technology began to alter religious rhetoric and practice. In midcentury America, the pious still used agricultural tropes but added Industrial Era imagery, as with Wynona Carr's 1954 gospel hit, "Get Me Jesus on the Line," which relied on a telephone analogy to suggest contact with the divine might be as easy as asking the operator to connect you.[12] By the 1970s some of the spiritually inclined began applying computer analogies—and not just the Farm's founder, who referred to IBM punched cards to describe the group's piety. Students at MIT's Artificial Intelligence Lab circulated Zen-style "AI koans," playfully recounting enlightening encounters with venerable hackers, and alarmed relatives "deprogramed" young converts to the Korean-based Unification Church.[13]

The dizzying changes quickened between 1995 and 2000, as a 1996 issue of *Time* noted (see fig. 50). Religious groups were creating web pages, chat rooms, and virtual congregations as the Internet's "high-speed spiritual bazaar" began to change what the pious did and how they thought.[14] Sister Judith Zoebelein argued that "the Internet is exploding and the Church has got to be there," and she helped improve the Vatican's web page, which launched in 1995. The next year Charles Henderson, a Presbyterian minister in New Jersey, founded the Church of Cyberspace, the first online congregation. Online experience also provided new figurative tools, tropes for reimagining the self, the world, and the divine. The engineer who proposed the World Wide Web, an interlinked space for information management, noted parallels between the nonhierarchical values of his Unitarian Universalist congregation and the decentralizing principles of the Internet Engineering Task Force.[15] Ordinary web users also turned to spiritual language, a researcher reported in 1996: "people see the Net as a new metaphor for God."[16] The Church of Cyberspace's pastor did too. Embracing the web analogy, the notion that the world is like an intricate pattern of filaments spun by a spider, Henderson revised the Gospel of John's opening verse, suggesting "In the beginning was the *Web*," and he modified Saint Anselm's eleventh-century argument for God's existence, reimaging the divine as "that *Web* greater than which none can even be conceived."[17] Information Age imagery expanded after 2000, and by 2020 Americans ranked the "technological revolution" as one of the most significant historical events of their lifetimes. Digital technologies had begun to create new ways to find meaning, form bonds, and perform rituals as religion went online.[18]

Table 2. Varieties of Postindustrial Religion and Quasi Religion, 1975–2020

Types	Stated Aim	Media	Site	Practices	Examples
Digital Religion	connectivity	computer; smartphone	home; congregation	multisensorial interaction	Virtual *Hajj;* Lourdes's "candles online"
Retail Religion	salvation; self-realization; enlightenment	print; TV; computer; podcast	bookstore; talk show; online retailer	reading; listening; buying	Christian Booksellers Association; Oprah Winfrey's media empire
Broadcast Religion	inspiration	TV; radio; smartphone	station; home	viewing; listening	CBN; EWTN; Christian radio
Workplace Religion	productivity	in-person; computer	workplace	praying; meditating	Google; Chick-fil-A; corporate "prayer rooms"
Therapeutic Religion	health	in-person; smartphone	clinic; spa; online	mindfulness; yoga; exercise	MBSR program; *Calm* app; SoulCycle
Leisure Religion	entertainment	in-person; multimedia	arena; onscreen	venerating sports and entertainment stars	NFL fandom; Graceland's "candlelight vigil"

These and other forms of religion and quasi religion emerged between 1975 and 2020 (table 2).[19] It was a period of both proliferating pluralism and escalating disaffiliation—or the rise of the religious "nones." Americans attended weekly services at a higher rate than residents of most industrialized nations, like Britain, but the proportion of US adults who didn't affiliate with a faith doubled between 1990 (8.2%) and 2006 (17%) and then continued to rise.[20] Disaffiliation was related to a broader loss of confidence in institutions, which accelerated further after the onset of the Iraq War (2003) and the Great Recession (2007).[21] Americans' rising mistrust of organized religion had multiple causes, but the popular association with misconduct and violence didn't help.[22] Mainstream media highlighted religion's role in promoting violence, as with coverage of the 1978 murder-suicide of over 900 members of Jim Jones's communal cult near Guyana's rainforest, and the 2001 attack by al-Qaeda on Manhattan's Twin Towers.[23] The coverage of televangelist scandals (from Jim Bakker in 1987 to Ted Haggard in 2006) and Catholic sexual assault cases (from the Louisiana case in 1985 to the 2002 revelations in Boston) also deepened the distrust and hastened the disaffiliation.[24]

Adding to the complexity, however, about one-third of the unaffiliated believed in God and heaven, and they prayed or meditated, including those who identified as "spiritual but not religious."[25] Many also engaged in leisure practices that offered meaning and belonging, as with the veneration of sports and entertainment stars, while others tuned to Oprah Winfrey's "Change Your Life TV," which encouraged spiritual seeking and purposeful consuming.[26] A few million Americans identified as Buddhist, but by 2020 millions more meditated regularly or tried Buddhist-inspired "stress-reduction" practices at a clinic or on their smartphone.[27] Industrial Era corporate chaplains had entered the manufacturing plant—and company-paid clergy evangelized immigrant meat processors in twenty-first-century Iowa—but postindustrial companies also brought religion into the workplace, as with Chick-fil-A's morning prayer sessions or Google's "Search inside Yourself" program, a meditation course designed to enhance productivity as well as contentment.[28]

Faith and Flourishing, 1975–2006

The first sustainability crisis, which medieval farming faiths intensified, brought social conflict, political instability, and ecological stress to high-density agricultural niches along the Upper Mississippi and in the arid Southwest, but the regional cornfield crises had been resolved before Columbus arrived (see appendix). The moral harm and environmental degradation of the second and third sustainability crises, larger in scale and magnitude, were exacerbated by imperial religion and industrial religion, and the problems earlier generations bequeathed had not been fully addressed by 1975, even if some things got better between 1964 and 1974. Faith leaders and their government allies promoted civil rights, but descendants of those displaced and disempowered during the Colonial Era—Natives and Blacks—remained disadvantaged. Just as reunion without reconciliation allowed the return of spiritually sanctioned inequity after the Civil War, Sixties activism prompted praiseworthy but partial advances. Descendants of Indigenous

Peoples displaced during the Colonial Era saw some improvements, as the federal government began to adopt policies of Indian self-determination and churches rethought their approach to Native Nations.[29] Yet Natives hadn't won full religious freedom, recovered all sacred lands, or improved well-being on the reservation or in the city, where tens of thousands had relocated under a voluntary federal program begun during the 1950s.[30] By the 1970s, officials still had not fully redressed the historic injustices. They also had done little to restore the biosphere harmed by church-sanctioned principles and state-sanctioned policies. Environmentalists had begun to confront the industrial sustainability crisis that emerged in the 1870s, during the Gilded Age, and spiked in the 1950s, during the Great Acceleration. But piecemeal attempts to slow the eco-crisis had not gone far enough. The rise in carbon dioxide, methane, and nitrates continued into the 1970s, for example, and emissions would increase between 1975 and 2006.[31]

So as Americans transitioned to a postindustrial way of life after 1975, they faced familiar problems as well as those their ancestors couldn't have foreseen, from cyberhacking to global warming. Despite important differences, there were some parallels with the Gilded Age crisis. The post-1870s decades and the post-1970s decades saw partisan stalemate, racist backlash, and nativist hostility as well as environmental damage, wealth inequality, and declining well-being, including higher rates of infant mortality among Blacks and Natives.[32] As earlier, the devout sometimes made things better. Sometimes, however, the religious deepened the problems, stressing postindustrial eco-cultural niches and making it harder to meet the conditions for full flourishing and provide the requisite environmental goods (renewable resources, favorable climate, biodiversity), communal goods (equity, freedom, political participation), and individual goods (health, meaning, and belonging).

Making Things Worse

Religious disagreements widened political divides and made it harder to address the converging problems during the post-1975 era, which interpreters have described as a time of "culture wars," when the Right and Left battled for "the soul of America," or an age of "fracture" and "fault lines," decades when something came apart.[33] There certainly was divisiveness between 1975, when the midwestern Episcopalian Gerald Ford took over for Nixon, and 2006, when outgoing President George W. Bush, a Texas Methodist, promoted "faith-based" initiatives, advocated border fencing, and waged a "war on terror" in Muslim countries.[34]

The polarization had multiple causes, expressions, and amplifiers. Diverging fears and clashing identities deepened divisions, including feelings of dislike for opponents, as White religious traditionalists in the South and the West who moved to suburban developments and endorsed Republican candidates worried their America was threatened, not only by the earlier ban on school prayer but by the lingering permissiveness of the counterculture and the unsettling clout of movements for the rights of women, homosexuals, and Blacks.[35] The suburban churchgoing family, with its stay-at-home mom and white picket fence, seemed under siege. So did the nation, at least the America they cherished. In this sense, the clashes were partly a reaction to feminism and civil rights.[36] Anti-ERA campaigns raged between 1973 and 1979, and five states even withdrew their earlier ratification. *Roe v. Wade* (1973) distressed Catholic clerics, but race was more important than abortion for the surging political resistance among conservative White Protestants. The counterrevolution stirred but didn't erupt after the Supreme Court's legalization of abortion. The evangelical Jerry Falwell, for instance, didn't preach against abortion until five years later.[37] Randall Terry's Operation Rescue started blockading abortion clinics in 1988, and the first fatal bombing at a clinic didn't happen until 1998. But White Protestants' aggrieved nationalism had begun earlier and was spiking by 1978, when the Supreme Court endorsed affirmative action policies and the Internal Revenue Service threatened to revoke the tax-exempt status of Christian schools "with an insufficient number of minority students."[38]

The polarization also concerned beliefs and values. The conversation got shrill, for instance, as evangelical anti-evolutionists weaponized older talk about "secular humanism" to challenge the teaching of Darwinian biology.[39] At a deeper level, many disputes involved competing visions of national belonging and human flourishing, and they raged *within* as well as *across* faith communities.[40] Devotees in the pews sometimes ignored clergy in the pulpit, as with US Catholics who dissented from the church's teaching on artificial contraception, and intragroup conflicts played out in other ways, creating unexpected spiritual allies as well as hurtful internal tensions.[41] Evangelical Protestants, traditionalist Catholics, and Orthodox Jews had similar reactions to controversial court decisions, museum exhibitions, and TV shows—just as mainline Protestants, progressive Catholics, and Reform Jews sometimes had more in common with each other than with coreligionists in their own communities.[42] Elite antagonists did make unreconcilable claims—for instance, about whether or not the Bible contains the Creator's inerrant message.[43] Yet they also agreed about some things, presupposing principles from the Declaration, Constitution, and Bill of Rights—equality, freedom, and justice as well as a commitment to unintrusive government and a concern for the "general welfare." Polarization sometimes arose, then, from how disputants ranked those shared principles.[44] Pious progressives tended to prize equality more highly, while traditionalists emphasized liberty. Similarly, progressives prioritized the First Amendment's Establishment Clause, which protects citizens from one faith exerting too much power, while traditionalists prioritized the Free Exercise Clause, which ensures citizens' right to practice religion as they want.

Segmented media amplified the polarization, bringing the like-minded together but limiting their capacity to engage opponents and find compromises that might address the problems they inherited and bequeathed. Audience fragmentation generated increasingly insular subcultures, or distinct lived worlds. That happened as broadcasting's midcentury "tri-faith" communications commons contracted after 1960, when the FCC abandoned public-interest religious programing and allowed local stations to sell Sunday slots to religious groups.[45] Then in 1977 Pat Robertson beamed his Christian Broadcasting Network (CBN) on cable, creating the first around-the-clock religious station, and other networks followed. After 1980, preachers exploited deregulation to create tax-free multimedia networks, which unapologetically mixed political and religious messaging. Although scandals about sex and money might have hurt televangelists' credibility briefly after 1987, televangelism recovered by the late 1990s.[46] Yet the national audience fragmented further because the 1996 Telecommunications Act allowed TV channels to multiply and media conglomerates to form.[47]

Changes in the media landscape arose in part from strategic decisions encouraged by religious conservative like Robertson, whose 1979 "action plan" said that "Christians must become aware of the awesome power of the media to mold our moral and political consensus."[48] Combatants then used that power to renew long-standing disputes about belonging and flourishing and instigate new clashes about gender and sexuality in print, radio, and television. In the early Eighties, the Republican president and Democratic speaker maintained cordial relations—and occasionally compromised—but after the Reagan administration's 1987 repeal of the FCC's Fairness Doctrine, which had required equitable on-air treatment of issues, conservative talk radio and evangelical cable television demonized opponents and deepened divides.[49] In the late Eighties and early Nineties, the right-leaning Christian politician Newt Gingrich mailed candidates instructional tapes and a glossary of terms for demeaning opponents. With the launch of the

Rush Limbaugh Show (1988) and the Fox News Channel (1996), as well as social media platforms like Facebook (2004) and Twitter (2006), increasingly targeted media intensified polarization and hindered believers trying to face old and new problems.[50] It's not surprising, then, that those with public power had not done enough to confront the inherited sustainability crises by 2006, and few were addressing the converging contemporary problems—not only ecological damage and wealth inequality, but nativist enmity, racial tension, and Muslim suspicion.[51]

National narratives multiplied before, during, and after the Bicentennial celebrations of 1976. Indigenous intellectuals like Deloria criticized the Christian colonial story and hoped "to make 1976 a celebration of independence for American Indians," while ordinary tribal citizens like Jo-Anne Big Fire, a young Ho-Chunk woman, published a six-stanza counter-narrative that began "Happy Birthday American, you who took our land."[52] But most non-Native narrators cast Christian settlers as heroic protagonists and assigned God a benevolent role, though they quarreled about whether the country was getting better or worse and disagreed about who belonged and who didn't. Religious groups maligned by White Protestants during the Centennial of 1876—Catholics, Jews, and Latter-day Saints—used the Bicentennial to reassert their claim on national belonging.[53] Yet some conservative Christians pushed back with renewed vigor, espousing narrow notions of what it means to be American. President Ford, who prayed every night, praised Billy Graham, and tried "to live by the example of Jesus Christ," preferred the Christian colonial tale.[54] His 1976 State of the Union address ignored the original US motto (*E pluribus unum*), cited the Eisenhower era alternative ("In God We Trust"), and, like Coolidge, repeated the erroneous claim that George Washington had knelt in prayer at Valley Forge.[55] Following the example of Coolidge's postmaster general, Ford's Bicentennial Commission also planned a stamp commemorating the concocted event.[56] The Post Office issued it the following year, when the born-again Baptist Jimmy Carter moved into the White House.[57] That year also saw the publication of a popular evangelical narrative, *The Light and the Glory,* which traced Christian America's history from the seventeenth-century Anglo-Protestant colonies to the growing "moral decay" of the pluralist Seventies.[58] Reverend Falwell founded the political organization Moral Majority two years later, and in 1980 he cited *The Light and the Glory* in his "conservative blueprint for America's moral rebirth."[59] More than a decade later, when White Protestants were no longer a demographic majority in the US, the Baptist Gingrich would tell a similar national story in his book *To Renew America.*[60]

Not everyone was expected to play a leading role in the country's renewal. Falwell urged women to accept their subordinate "God-given" roles as wives and mothers, and by 1982 a coalition of evangelicals, Catholics, and Latter-day Saints had defeated the ERA.[61] Five years later evangelical leaders encouraged "joyful submission" to male authority.[62] Non-Christians and people of color also had reason to worry about their roles in national revitalization. Even though a majority of Americans believed neighbors of other faiths could go to heaven, many had a hard time accepting Muslims.[63] The Iranian hostage crisis triggered hostility toward Muslims in 1979 and, though Bush denounced it, intolerance surged after the World Trade Center attack of 2001.[64] But as Bush defended the government's right to retain migrants without trial and authorized 850 miles of border fencing, many pious newcomers from Asia, Africa, and Latin America didn't feel welcome.[65] Neither did Black urban worshippers. As conservative Christians decried affirmative action and defended school segregation, some African Americans wondered whether their ancestors had been wrong to flee the Jim Crow South for fair treatment and factory jobs in the industrial North.

Those factory jobs started to disappear as deindustrialization increased and unions declined after 1975. Wealth inequality also rose again as new forms of retail religion consecrated profit-first commerce, and advocates of "Christian free enterprise" shrugged off disparities as inevitable, even God-sanctioned, tracing them to personal moral failings rather than systemic structural obstacles (fig. 52).[66] Billy Graham sided with his friend President Reagan, for example, bonding over their shared commitment to free-market capitalism, and the evangelist had a warm relationship with George H. W. Bush.[67] While some mainline Protestants said the Right's cozying up to the White House betrayed Jesus's teaching, influencers across the spiritual spectrum sidestepped public issues and directed devotees' gaze inward.[68] Right-leaning prosperity preachers updated the tranquilizing postwar "peace of mind" message, including for those unsettled by the global service economy. The disquieted sought reassurance in the gospel of health and wealth preached by televangelists like Oral Roberts, the Tulsa healer who commissioned a futuristic Prayer Tower; Robert Schuller, the Anaheim pastor who taught "possibility thinking" in his luminous Crystal Cathedral; and Joel Osteen, the cheerful Houston preacher who comforted congregants in a former basketball arena.[69] African American ministers had partnered with LBJ's White House on the War on Poverty, but the megachurch sermons of Black prosperity preachers targeted individual needs and sometimes blunted "criticism of structures of racial inequality."[70] Left-leaning spiritual seekers averted their

Figure 52. *Top 1% Net Personal Wealth Share, USA, 1913–2019*. World Inequality Lab, Paris School of Economics. https://creativecommons.org/licenses/by/4.0/.

gaze from problems too, as they bought Shirley MacLaine's *Going Within,* the actress's best-selling metaphysical guide to "inner transformation," or sought spiritual inspiration from talk-show host Oprah Winfrey, hoping they too might spark an "inner revolution" and "live their best lives."[71]

There had been some conservative support for environmental protections around 1970, but distress about degradation continued to be episodic. Public health concerns had sparked broad-based protests about air pollution and radioactive fallout between 1948 and 1961, and the 1979 accident at Pennsylvania's Three Mile Island nuclear power plant again generated bottom-up conservative dissent, especially among locals worried about the well-being of mothers and children.[72] Yet most conservative political and religious leaders downplayed the hazards of radioactive waste storage, toxic chemical dumping, and greenhouse gas emissions. Ambivalent support for Earth Day cleanups gave way to theological critiques accusing ecologists of subordinating humans to nature, even championing pantheism, and to dismissive comments from politicians, including Reagan, who asked activists trying to save redwood trees, "How many trees do you need to see?"[73] Some right-leaning critics claimed environmentalism was an elitist cause diverting attention from urban social injustices, but whatever their reasoning, from the mid-1970s to the early 2000s many neoconservative Catholics and free-market evangelicals sided with the anti-environmentalists.[74]

Making Things Better

Yet some used spiritual resources to expand the rights of the marginalized and broaden conceptions of belonging. In 1978 Indigenous activists began the Longest Walk, a march from Alcatraz Island to the Lincoln Memorial to demand "Creator-given rights." About 2,000 protesters arrived in Washington on 15 July.[75] Later that year Congress passed the American Indian Religious Freedom Act, eleven years after attendees at the Bear Butte ceremony had brainstormed about how to assert their rights.[76] That law was followed by the American Indian Gaming and Regulatory Act (1988), which had "powerful" economic benefits, as well as the National Museum of the American Indian Act (1989) and the Native American Graves Protection and Repatriation Act (1990), which had important cultural benefits.[77] But a 1990 Supreme Court decision seemed to reverse some of the legislative victories, when the justices approved the dismissal of two Oregon state employees for taking peyote during a Native American Church ritual.[78] An alarmed multifaith coalition pressured Congress to pass the Religious Freedom Restoration Act, which said government can't "substantially burden" a person's practice of religion without a "compelling interest," thereby expanding the Free Exercise Clause's reach.[79] President Bill Clinton signed the bill in 1993, and the next year he hosted 322 tribal leaders at a White House summit and signed executive orders reaffirming the nation-to-nation relationship and protecting the ceremonial use of eagle feathers.[80] Congress expanded those religious liberties with the peyote amendment to the American Indian Religious Freedom Act (1994), which protected adherents of the Native American Church. Indigenous Christians marked milestones too, as Catholics appointed their first Native bishop in 1986, and in 2002 Episcopalians consecrated their first Indigenous bishop, Carol Gallagher, a Cherokee whom Chief Wilma Mankiller praised as "a deeply spiritual woman."[81]

African Americans also found some reasons for hope. Blacks had been excluded from full participation in the LDS Church, but in 1978 the First Presidency allowed men of all races to be ordained to the priesthood, and all men and women gained access to temple rituals.[82] Black Catholics could point to the US bishops' 1979 pastoral letter, "Brothers and Sisters to Us," which condemned the "sin" of racism and called for more Black church leaders.[83] And as White televangelist Pat Robertson competed for the Republican presidential nomination in 1988, Rev. Jesse Jackson, the Baptist civil rights activist, mobilized a "rainbow coalition" of the disempowered as he campaigned for the Democratic nomination—and set the stage for Barack Obama's later victory.[84]

There also were reckonings with historic injustices. Apologies increased globally and nationally between the late 1980s and 2000, as leaders who spoke for an institution expressed regret.[85] In 1988 Congress passed a bill apologizing to Japanese Americans and authorizing compensation for the "human suffering" in World War II internment camps, which by then had become emotionally charged pilgrimage sites for former internees and their descendants.[86] Five years later, the US government apologized for the 1893 military overthrow of the Indigenous Hawaiian monarch, and in 2000 the Bureau of Indian Affairs apologized for the "ethnic cleansing" of Western tribes. Religious institutions issued statements too. Pope John Paul II offered apologies for twenty-one historical episodes of injustice committed in the name of the Catholic Church, including his 1985 apology to Africans for the church's participation in the slave trade.[87] Other churches did the same, including the Southern Baptist Convention's 1995 apology for "condoning" racism and the United Methodist Church's 2000 apology to historic Black churches and Methodists who still faced prejudice.[88]

Post-1965 immigrants faced prejudice too, but many found psychic comfort and communal belonging in repurposed or new worship spaces by 2006, when the foreign-born population reached 12 percent, lower than the 1890 peak of 14.8 percent but double the proportion in 1960.[89] More than 40 percent of the newcomers were Christian, but Muslim, Jewish, Hindu, Sikh, Jain, and Buddhist migrants added to the nation's religious diversity. By the 1990s the impact was felt from Fremont, California, to Flushing, New York.[90] Asian and Latin American migrants worshipped in Snow Belt cities that had been transformed by the migrations of 1880–1920, but post-1965 newcomers also settled in Sun Belt cities like Miami, Houston, and Los Angeles. Most striking, they altered the religious landscape across the South. In 1980 South Asian Muslims founded a mosque, Al-Farooq Masjid, in Atlanta; a Hindu priest performed a groundbreaking ceremony for Nashville's Sri Ganesha Temple in 1982; and the next year Vietnamese refugees built Chua Bo De Buddhist temple outside New Orleans. An apt symbol of the changes came from the Latin American migrants who organized a 1996 feast-day procession for the Virgin of Guadalupe in Clinton, the North Carolina town of 8,000 where the United Daughters of the Confederacy had erected a 1916 courthouse memorial to soldiers who died for the South's "lost but just" cause. Eighty years later, the Virgin, whose image rode in a pickup truck as her Spanish-speaking devotees walked behind,

Figure 53. An image of the Virgin, which adorns the back of the truck, approaches the Confederate Memorial as devotees walk behind her through the central street of Clinton, North Carolina, in 1996. Courtesy of Thomas A. Tweed.

unwittingly challenged that Southern civil religion as the procession passed the Confederate memorial (fig. 53). That ritual moment when the Old South met the New symbolized the changes underway. By the late 1990s the proportion of White residents dipped below 50 percent, while Hispanics rose to 12.5 percent. Clinton, which had welcomed antebellum planter piety and postwar Lost Cause religion, was being transformed by the new migration.[91]

Most of those migrants worked as underpaid farmworkers or meat processors, often in poor conditions, and some religious leaders addressed economic injustice. Liberal mainline Protestants, who updated the Methodists' 1908 "Social Creed," collaborated with social justice Catholics, who quoted papal encyclicals and Vatican II documents.[92] Clergy in both traditions agreed that workers deserved fair wages and safe conditions, and they challenged Reagan administration policies, including rising military spending and declining social services. The National Council of Churches condemned the president for triggering an arms race and ignoring the poor, and so did Methodist and Catholic bishops.[93] United Methodists warned of the "human costs" for the poor, the elderly, and the young; Catholics emphasized the dignity of the person and the preferential option for the poor as they promoted "economic justice for all."[94]

Despite Reagan administration resistance and continuing ecclesiastical indifference, some religious leaders also began to address environmental issues again during the Eighties. The near disaster at Three Mile Island prompted concern from central Pennsylvania clergy. A Protestant pastor told his congregation that God was warning them to "be careful" about nuclear power, and the area's Catholic bishop called for a moratorium on new plants.[95] Religious bodies, including the National Council of Churches, debated alternative energy solutions.[96] Washington-based Catholic bishops called for "a new ecological ethic," while "green sisters" established teaching centers and communal experiments like New Jersey's Genesis Farm.[97] The Women of Reform Judaism passed a 1983 resolution on "Protecting the Environment."[98] Methodists endorsed "environmental stewardship," and Congregationalists commissioned a 1987 study of waste dumps that showed people of color lived near those sites in disproportionate numbers, adding more evidence about the "slow violence" of toxic contamination in marginalized communities.[99]

Environmental concern rose a bit more after the *Exxon Valdez* oil spill of 1989, which released 10.8 million gallons of crude, polluting 1,300 miles of Alaskan coastline and killing 250,000 seabirds and 3,000 sea otters. Mainstream media coverage showcased oil-soaked otters and blamed the tanker's crew but obscured the short-term effects on the subsistence hunting and fishing of Unangax̂ (Aleut) villagers and the long-term effects of fossil-fuel consumption.[100] Nevertheless, polls showed, media attention had raised public concern for environmental protection a bit by 1990, when Congress increased the penalty for oil spills and Russell Train, the former EPA director, told attendees at a conference on religion and ecology that he remained puzzled by organized religion's "almost total obliviousness" to the problems that "threaten the very integrity of Creation."[101] Some spiritually motivated environmentalists were less oblivious. The Indigenous Environmental Network, which emphasized "the sacredness of Earth Mother," formed in 1990.[102] In 1991 the US Catholic Bishops released *Renewing the Earth*, and the next year Al Gore, former divinity student and future vice president, published *Earth in the Balance,* proposing an "environmentalism of the spirit."[103] So religious advocates had an ally in Washington, and interfaith cooperation coalesced in 1993 with the National Religious Partnership for the Environment, which included the National Council of Churches, the US Catholic Conference, the Coalition on the Environment and Jewish Life, and the Evangelical Environmental Network.[104] Those institutional partners circulated information on environmental issues in 1994, and some Catholics, Protestants, and Jews continued to attend to the problem, as with the thirty-one

Catholic religious communities engaged in sustainable land-use projects by 1996.[105] During the following decade, Americans heard about less visible sources of degradation. Awareness rose in 2006 when Gore—then a private citizen—released *An Inconvenient Truth,* a widely publicized documentary on global warming.[106]

Faith and Flourishing, 2007–2020

Familiar patterns of religious preference persisted and new ones emerged between 2007, when Richard Dawkins's *The God Delusion* topped bestseller lists but evangelicals celebrated a new Creation Museum, and 2020, when religious membership dipped below 50 percent but most Americans identified with a faith, believed in God, and imagined an afterlife.[107]

Regional differences were more important than ever. By 2020 the least religious regions were in the northwestern and northeastern corners of the mainland, and some of the most religious areas were in US commonwealths and territories in the Pacific (Guam and the Northern Mariana Islands) and the Caribbean (Puerto Rico and the US Virgin Islands).[108] The Latter-day Saints had a significant presence in the Intermountain West. New York and New Jersey had the highest proportion of Jews, and three of the four most Catholics states were in New England, including Massachusetts, which had an established Protestant church until 1833.[109] Perhaps most impactful for religious and political life, 50 percent of those who regularly attended worship services lived in the South.[110] And those regional patterns played out at the county level too. To illustrate by returning to two ancient sacred sites mentioned earlier, in the Ohio county where tourists visited the Hopewell mounds, only two out of ten residents identified with a faith, while nine out of ten were religiously affiliated in the Louisiana county that welcomed visitors to Poverty Point.[111]

White evangelical Protestants made up more than 80 percent of the affiliated in that Southern county, but nationally the proportion of mainline Protestants (23%), Catholics (23%), and Evangelicals (23%) continued to decrease.[112] Disaffiliation also continued as new preacher scandals, abuse revelations, and violent incidents eroded confidence in organized religion.[113] The proportion reporting "no religion" rose to 24 percent. Diversification continued too, with non-Christians making up at least 8 percent of the affiliated. Symbolizing the pluralism, the Congressional Prayer Room's bookshelf no longer displayed only tri-faith America's revered texts—a King James Bible, a Catholic Bible, and a Jewish Torah. By 2020 elected representatives also could consult Muslim, Buddhist, and Hindu sacred texts—even Thich Nhat Hanh's *The Miracle of Mindfulness,* which showed spiritual seekers how to calm the mind.[114]

New communal ritual styles and solitary spiritual practices emerged too. Quasi-religious practices took on greater significance, and not only among those who found shared exhilaration and collective belonging at sporting events or music concerts.[115] SoulCycle, which critics dismissed as "secular spirituality," attracted city dwellers to forty-five-minute cycling sessions in dimly lit studios with scented candles.[116] To reach the rural unchurched, clergy experimented with new forms of worship, such as the Cowboy Church movement. In ranchland south of Dallas–Fort Worth, for example, worshippers wearing jeans and boots attended horse-trough baptisms and sang country-western hymns.[117] The same informal and expressive style was transforming congregational worship across the country. Cowboy Churches included a ten-minute "howdy," and 80 percent of services nationally allowed time for congregants to greet each other. In more than six in ten congregations, worshippers also shouted "amen" or raised their hands in praise. Many churchgoers, especially Protestants, were attending more enthusiastic and less formal services.[118]

In 2007 Apple unveiled the iPhone or "Jesus phone," as one blogger called it to mock techies who anticipated its release as millennialists awaited the savior, and postindustrial technologies began to shape religious practice more fully.[119] By 2015 almost seven in ten adults owned a smartphone as well as a desktop or a laptop.[120] By 2018, 72 percent of US congregations had a website, and improved fiber-optic and cellular communication systems enabled the devout to search the times for daily Muslim prayer or Sunday Lutheran worship.[121] Some engaged in computer-mediated devotions at home. Greek Orthodox devotees lit virtual candles before online icons, for example, and Hindus performed *pūjā* online, offering flowers and burning incense at the altar of a digital deity.[122] Even before the pandemic, congregations were recording or streaming services, which left most virtual attendees feeling less "connected," but the new technologies also began to change in-person worship.[123] About half of US congregations used projection equipment, showing video clips or displaying hymn lyrics. By 2019 one-third of congregations were even encouraging attendees to use their smartphones *during* worship—to consult scripture, engage the sermon, or post on social media.[124]

Despite the shared use of new technologies, the spiritually inclined continued to promote competing visions of national belonging, human flourishing, and environmental well-being after 2007, a transitional year of alternating hope and despair. Al Gore's climate documentary won him the 2007 Nobel Peace Prize, but anti-environmentalism grew louder, including among evangelical and LDS legislators, even as the climate crisis prompted atomic scientists to move the minute hand of the Doomsday Clock two minutes closer to midnight.[125] Asian migrants began to outnumber Hispanic newcomers by 2007, further enriching the nation's ethnic and religious diversity, but nativist and Islamophobic rhetoric incited heated clashes about what it meant to be American. Barack Hussein Obama, a Black Protestant, challenged narrow notions of national identity when he announced his candidacy for president in 2007, but White Nationalist groups multiplied, officer-involved shootings continued, and Black incarceration peaked.[126] President Bush appealed to "the Author of Liberty" as he presented the 2007 troop surge as a "new way forward," but it also became the war on terror's deadliest year, and communities struggled to welcome the 900,000 disabled veterans who would return with psychic or physical wounds by the conflict's end.[127] Seventeen percent of the veterans were women, evidence that the gender revolution had broadened occupational options by 2007. Yet the gains were stalled or uneven, as women were paid less at work and did more at home.[128] Changes in mortgage financing initially made homeownership seem within reach of more buyers, but by December the Great Recession (2007–2009) began to further widen the economic inequalities and health disparities. Black household income lagged, and infant mortality rose.[129] Computer accessibility increased with the 2007 introduction of the smartphone, but a "digital divide" opened and social media's profit-driven, algorithmic microtargeting of information—and disinformation—began to amplify the polarization even more.[130]

Making Things Worse

During the Obama presidency (2009–2017) some used spiritual rhetoric to constrict conceptions of belonging and advocate policies that hampered well-being.[131] The proportion of foreign-born residents continued to rise, reaching more than 13 percent, even though immigration officials had returned 2.5 million aspiring residents by 2015. That earned Obama the title "deporter-in-chief" among Latinx advocates, but some White religious conservatives urged an even more restrictive policy.[132] Franklin Graham and Jerry Falwell Jr., heirs to their fathers' evangelical media empires, worried about both Mexicans (who had been arriving in smaller numbers) and Muslims (who had been highlighting shared American values).[133] Some conservatives, including Graham, even perpetuated a baseless conspiracy theory that claimed Obama was foreign-born (and therefore ineligible for office) and a closet Muslim (and therefore out to destroy America).[134] Obama had disclosed he was born in Hawaiʻi to religiously unaffiliated parents, an African migrant father and a White US-born mother, and that he embraced Christianity at a Black Congregational church in Chicago.[135] By 2015, however, media disinformation campaigns led 29 percent of Americans and 43 percent of Republicans to believe he was Muslim.[136]

Despite the diverting disinformation about his faith, Obama's status as a person of color was rarely far from critics' minds, and White Nationalists thrived, from churchgoing biblical literalists who avoided explicit racist language to "racial protectionists" who embraced Odinism, a Norse-inspired paganism, to fortify themselves in the battle against "white genocide."[137] While some rejected Christianity as "too Jewish," others retained an appreciation for the tradition, as with Dylann Roof, who shot nine Black Methodists attending a Wednesday-night Bible study at a Charleston church in 2015, just after the Black Lives Matter movement gained national attention. Roof, who had been raised in the Evangelical Lutheran Church in America, no longer considered himself Christian but thought the tradition deserved respect as "an extremely important part of White culture."[138] Jesus deserved respect too, he said, and, in a prison notebook, the unrepentant race warrior sketched an image of a triumphant White Christ emerging from the tomb and a large cross adorned with "In God We Trust."[139]

Religiously inflected ethnonationalism had surfaced earlier among self-described "Teavangelicals," devout White supporters of the Tea Party movement (2009–2011).[140] There were "the occasional racially tinged incidents and comments," an observer recalled, but Teavangelicals mostly targeted Obama's policies.[141] The president introduced ecological initiatives his first year, establishing "an integrated strategy towards sustainability in the Federal Government" and allocating $6 billion for renewable energy. Those green initiatives drew criticism, but Teavangelicals expressed more disdain for programs aimed at helping Americans who lost their homes or had no health insurance. Infuriated by "handouts" to the undeserving and alienated from a godless nation they no longer recognized, White, middle-class Tea Partiers bonded on social media with others hoping to reclaim lost liberties and restore pious patriotism. Only half of Tea Partiers were born-again Christians, one study found, but over 90 percent believed that America always has been a Christian nation or that it had been Christian but no longer was. Religious nationalism was evident as DC protesters carried banners reading "In God

We Trust, Not Congress" and regional Tea Party websites posted paintings like *One Nation, Under God* (2009), which featured Christ holding the Constitution.[142] The Constitution doesn't include the words "Christ" or "God." Yet Teavangelicals like David Brody, a CBN correspondent, and Wendy Wright, president of Concerned Women for America, insisted that "biblical principles are woven throughout the Constitution."[143] Both sacred texts, they believed, sanctioned their stand on myriad issues, and that was why "it's not unusual to see a fiscally conservative, gun-owning, flag-waving, home-schooling, stay-at-home Christian mom show up at a tea party event."[144]

Those faith-and-flag protestors might not have been watching TV as Obama gave his January 2017 farewell address, but, just as Dwight Eisenhower's farewell had warned of pressing problems, the speech listed four "threats" to democracy—the lack of shared economic opportunity, the divisive force of racism, the decline in institutional trust, and the partisanship produced by the "splintering of our media."[145] By the end of 2020, when the pandemic had begun to disrupt communal worship and Obama's former vice president had been elected president, many of Trump's evangelical supporters believed Trump had kept his promise. He had made America great again, as Wall Street profits, pro-Israel policies, and antiabortion judges showed. Yet it was hard to deny that those four "threats" had intensified.

Hostility toward Blacks, Natives, and migrants seemed worse by 2020, as politicians and ministers promoted even more restrictive notions of what it means to be American. That was evident in Trump's spiritual advisors and Oval Office decoration, in his executive orders banning travelers from Muslim-majority countries and approving a Mexican border wall, and in his responses to Black Lives Matter protests and White Nationalist rallies.[146] Presidents choose the art that adorns the Oval Office. Obama, for instance, had added a bust of Abraham Lincoln, who signed the Emancipation Proclamation. Blacks and Natives grew alarmed, however, when Trump hung a painting of Andrew Jackson, the Southern slaveholder who signed the Indian Removal Act. Trump's choice of spiritual advisors worried others. Among the clerics praying at his 2017 inauguration was Franklin Graham, who, like most White evangelicals, supported Trump's efforts to ban Muslims and restrict immigrants, and Paula White-Cain, the prosperity preacher who pastored a Florida megachurch, hosted a Christian TV show, and had 700,000 Twitter followers. Almost a decade after the death of Norman Vincent Peale, his first spiritual advisor, Trump reached out to White-Cain, whom he had seen on TV.[147] She would serve as a spiritual advisor during the campaign and while in office. White-Cain, who was shown praying with Trump in a posted photo-

Figure 54. Evangelical leaders lay hands on President Trump at the White House on 29 October 2019. His spiritual advisor, Paula White-Cain, stands beside him. Official White House photo by Joyce Boghosian.

graph, also would run the White House Faith and Opportunity Initiative (fig. 54). Like charismatic "prophecy voters," she believed God had chosen Trump to "restore" America, as the biblical God had used other morally imperfect men to advance the divine plan.[148] To do her part, she organized Operation Border Blessing, praying with the Texas Border Patrol and posing in front of Trump's wall.[149] Even though White-Cain had led a diverse megachurch, she also backed the president after he failed to condemn the 2017 Unite the Right rally staged by White Nationalists protesting the removal of a Confederate monument to Robert E. Lee in Charlottesville, Virginia.

Economic inequality, institutional mistrust, and media segmentation also grew worse. Trump had long cherished profit-first principles, and the self-described Presbyterian, who would identify as a "nondenominational Christian" by the end of 2020, embraced White-Cain's prosperity gospel, which proclaimed that wealth and health are available to everyone and economic inequality is the divinely sanctioned outcome of free-market competition.[150] Trump and his religious allies also deepened mistrust of the news media among Right-leaning supporters and mistrust of the executive branch among Left-leaning critics, while intensifying the polarization produced by media segmentation and disinformation. The spread of "news deserts," areas without local newspapers, reduced access to judicious reporting, so Americans were left with partisan national news or microtargeted social media, which sustained the falsehoods about Obama, for instance, as Trump challenged his birth certificate in a 2012 tweet and didn't concede the truth until 2016, when he was running for president.[151] By then, other strategic disinformation campaigns were underway, including as "the Russian government interfered in the 2016 presidential election in sweeping and systematic fashion."[152] Operatives skewed social media to favor Trump, the eventual winner, and the word *post-truth* entered the dictionary in 2017, Trump's first year in office, to describe "circumstances in which objective facts are less influential in shaping . . . public opinion."[153] "Objective facts" didn't fare better after 2017, as a now famous "deep fake" video circulated in 2018, and Trump retweeted posts associated with the QAnon conspiracy, which claimed he was battling a deep state–supported cabal of Satan-worshipping pedophiles.[154] On the eve of his failed reelection bid, the president praised those far-right sympathizers as "people who love our country."[155] So by 2020, some religious and quasi-religious beliefs circulating in segmented media had made things worse.

Making Things Better

Mobilizing religious resources to make things better was more difficult than ever by 2020, since millions raised in a faith no longer attended services, while many in the pews were disturbed by institutional failures.[156] New disclosures about the trauma suffered at Indian boarding schools reopened wounds and prompted a few attempts at reconciliation. A Diné survivor welcomed a Jesuit apology and settlement in 2011 as "a day or reckoning," for instance, while Northern Arapahos expressed relief as well as grief in 2017, when Little Chief, Sharp Nose's son who had died at Carlisle, Pennsylvania, was disinterred and made the "spiritual journey" back to Wyoming's Wind River Reservation.[157] But the reconciliation process had just begun by 2020. Non-Native institutions were sites of trauma too. In 2011 85 percent of Catholics surveyed said the sexual abuse of young people by priests had hurt the credibility of church leaders who speak out on social and political issues, and a 2018 report about the sexual abuse of Pennsylvania children convinced some that the US Bishops' 2002 Charter for the Protection of Children and Young People had not gone far enough in protecting the young or punishing the perpetrators.[158] The Southern Baptist Convention was shaken by sexual abuse disclosures in 2019, and officials would apologize for the 700 victims identified in an investigative report.[159] Yet, as a survey showed, religious leaders had more to do to regain the faithful's trust and heal the moral harm.[160]

Nonetheless, there were signs of hope. For the millions who still attended services, participation in communal worship could improve individual well-being, enhancing physical and mental health, and it could promote "pro-social behavior," like donating and volunteering.[161] As in the past, spiritual values also could motivate movements for environmental and social justice. In fact, *woke*, an adjective meaning "alert to injustice," also entered the dictionary in 2017.[162] Even if religious conservatives would repurpose the word to deride opponents, some invoked spiritual principles as they tried to redress historic injustices and face contemporary threats.

Political and religious officials confronted the legacy of Colonial Era injustices. Drawing on the Declaration's theistic imagery and moral principles, Congress apologized for slavery in 2008 and expressed regret to Indigenous Peoples in 2009. The House of Representatives' 2008 resolution said slavery's "dehumanizing atrocities" violated the principle that "all men are created equal."[163] The 2009 joint resolution apologized for "violence, maltreatment, and neglect" inflicted on Indigenous Peoples, who had been "endowed by their Creator with certain unalienable rights, and among those are life, liberty, and the pursuit of happiness."[164] Some welcomed the apologies but looked for concrete actions. Native journalists called the 2009 statement "historic" but noted that it didn't resolve any legal claims or prompt a presidential apology.[165] Indigenous Peoples and their allies found a bit more hope by 2020, as only sixteen states and the territory of American Samoa still observed the second Monday in October as an official public holiday exclusively called Columbus Day, and the Ohio city named for that Italian Catholic renamed it Indigenous Peoples Day.[166] A 2020 Supreme Court decision reaffirmed Indigenous sovereignty, and public discussion of restorative justice increased as churches rang their bells for one minute to remember the 400-year anniversary of the first enslaved Africans landing. Denominations and colleges also issued their own apologies for slavery.[167]

Racial violence also prompted some renewed attention to contemporary race relations. A number of White congregations discussed the issue, national religious groups released statements, and Roof's Lutheran denomination did some soul-searching.[168] A White Evangelical Lutheran suggested "we must confess our silent complicity in white supremacy and work to repair the harm"; a Black adherent rededicated himself to reconciliation "in this church and, through the church, the world."[169] President Obama, whom Twitter hailed as #ReverendPresident during his eulogy for the murdered

Figure 55. President Obama delivers his eulogy for Clementa Pinckney of Charleston's Emanuel AME Church, 26 June 2015. DVIDS photo by Larry Reid Jr.

Charleston minister, began by suggesting that "the Bible calls us to hope" (fig. 55).[170] He found hope in the Black Church's historic role and the multifaith support for the families of the slain Charleston nine. The congregation's public forgiveness of the shooter touched him. But, Obama said, the incident also demanded "an honest accounting," a recognition that "past injustices continued to shape the present." Two weeks later, South Carolina's governor removed the Confederate flag from the State House grounds. Soon after, however, two White men placed Confederate flags outside Atlanta's Ebenezer Baptist Church, Martin Luther King's former congregation. Its pastor, Raphael Warnock, condemned the act, saying it's "not about heritage but about hate." Warnock, who would mount a successful campaign for the US Senate in 2020, shared Obama's confidence in the Black Church but called for a renewal of its prophetic function.[171] That renewal was overdue some thought, including Black Lives Matter's female cofounders, who started the movement after a Black teen's killer was exonerated in 2013. Male preachers had been the public face of protests a half century earlier, but BLM leaders, who included a practitioner of Yorùbá religion and the daughter of a Nigerian pastor, engaged a wider range of participants and welcomed diverse spiritual views.[172]

In a 2009 address President Obama had warned that the Great Recession was the nation's economic "day of reckoning," a call to judgment prompted by Americans' valuing of "short-term gains" over "long-term prosperity."[173] FDR and his religious supporters had used similar language during the Great Depression, and they had helped to reduce inequity. That wouldn't happen between 2010 and 2020, as the economic gap widened, but some employed religious symbols, texts, and institutions to advocate economic justice. Interfaith organizations collaborated to confront disparities, and religion could be found in event spaces that seemed secular, as with Occupy Wall Street (2011), when nearby churches offered shelter and food to activists occupying a park near Wall Street.[174] Some Occupy sympathizers also served as "protest chaplains," creating temporary sacred spaces and placing themselves between the protestors and the police. Others used the symbolism of the golden calf to interpret Wall Street's bull symbol as a "false idol" (Exodus 32:1–35). Pope Francis used the same biblical image in *Evangelii Gaudium* to condemn "the new idolatry of money" and the "economy of exclusion and inequality."[175] By 2020 other groups quoting other passages were denouncing income and wealth disparities. The United Church of Christ declared there should be "a 'fair balance' between abundance for a few and the needs of many" (2 Corinthians 8:13–15), and Methodists decried "the widening gap between the rich and the poor" and rejected prosperity gospels that "view the accumulation of wealth as a sign of God's favor and poverty as a sign of God's disfavor" (Luke 6:20).[176]

Some Americans were concerned about ecological causes again after 2010, when the BP oil spill in the Gulf of Mexico became the largest US environmental disaster.[177] As with earlier eco-disasters, local clergy addressed the community's needs, like the Louisiana priest who advocated for Vietnamese fishers and shrimpers who had lost their livelihood.[178] In this decade, some argued that religious institutions were uniquely positioned to confront the environmental crisis—including Amitav Ghosh, a secular Hindu who praised "the increasing involvement of religious groups in the politics of climate change."[179] Ghosh was especially impressed by Pope Francis's 2015 encyclical *Laudato Si'*, which proposed an "integral ecology," a transgenerational ethic that linked environmental and social well-being, and the document reinvigorated Catholic green activism, including the work of the Catholic Climate Covenant.[180] Many other organizations sought solutions, including Indigenous groups. Diné CARE, for instance, drew on the principle of *hózhó,* balance or harmony, as Navajo Nation activists sought to restore the proper relation with the spirits and the environment by, for instance, seeking compensation for radiation exposure and challenging a timber-cutting program in the Chuska Mountains, which had provided planks for Chaco's great houses. Diné leaders cofounded the Indigenous Environmental Network, and by 2020 it was fighting fracking near Chaco while engaging in twenty-five other frontline protests, including against pipeline projects that crossed sacred lands.[181]

Many faith traditions issued environmental statements by 2020. More evangelicals joined the cause. Even Billy Graham urged Christians to be "stewards or trustees of God's creation," and the Evangelical Environmental Network shrewdly reframed ecological issues, as with its Pro-Life Clean Energy Campaign, which emphasized pollution's harm to children, including the unborn.[182] There were also ecumenical collaborations like Interfaith Power and Light, a national network founded by the Episcopal priest Sally Grover Bingham, and that network included more than 22,000 congregations in forty states by 2020.[183] Faith in Place, a Chicago-based affiliate, used talk about religious pluralism to advance both racial and environmental justice, and it attracted diverse supporters, including African Americans.[184] Non-Christian faiths joined the public discussion too. Jewish organizations noted their tradition's resources for thinking about earth stewardship. Buddhist leaders, including the Dalai Lama, signed a US-originated declaration on climate change. Muslims offered eco-friendly Qur'anic interpretations and formed new groups, including Green Muslims, a DC group that connected the Islamic community with climate action organizations.[185]

By 2020, the quadricentennial of the Pilgrims' landing, there were even more signs of religious pluralism in the US. Despite nativist public rhetoric, polls showed the highest level of popular support for immigration since 1965, with 70 percent of Americans saying the nation should sustain or increase the number of newcomers.[186] President Obama, an immigrant's son, had set the pluralist tone in his 2009 inaugural address, when he described America as "a nation of Christians and Muslims, Jews and Hindus, and non-believers" and praised the country's "patchwork heritage."[187] The national patchwork was on full display by 2010. The US not only had a Black president, but Catholics served as vice president (Joe Biden) and Speaker of the House (Nancy Pelosi), and the Supreme Court had no Protestants, only Jews and Catholics.[188] As Trump and his allies promoted narrower notions of national belonging at revival-like campaign rallies, Obama told the 2016 National Prayer Breakfast attendees that he had recently visited a mosque "to let our Muslim brothers and sisters know that they too are Americans and welcome here."[189] Then, after four years of fraught debate about what it means to be American, the November 2020 election results exhibited the nation's spiritual diversity and immigrant heritage. Trump again earned the votes of most anti-immigrant White evangelicals, but Irish Catholic Joe Biden won the presidency with the support of most Black Protestants and Native Americans—and the religiously unaffiliated.[190] Biden's vice president, Kamala Harris, was the daughter of a Jamaican-born father and an Indian-born mother, who had taken young Kamala to Hindu temples but raised her in a Black Baptist Church.[191] To add to the diversity, Harris would marry into a Jewish family. So, by 2020, those arguing America is—or should be—an Anglo-Saxon Protestant nation found the claim even harder to make.

Back to the Horn Shelter

Some devout Americans still thought of the country that way, of course, including in the Texas county where excavators found Horn Shelter Man, the 11,100-year-old medicine man featured in the opening chapter. Circling back to the start, then, let's end this story with digital religion, not far from where it began with foraging religion—in Clifton, a Waco suburb twenty miles east of the ancient rock-shelter burial in Bosque County. The small town was in a state that hosted booming computer and solar industries but also led the nation in greenhouse gas emissions and had one of the country's least sustainable cities.[192] The area's religious landscape had been transformed by Norwegian Lutheran migrants in the late nineteenth century and Hispanic Catholic newcomers in the late twentieth, so by 2020 the county included evangelical, mainline, and Catholic congregations, though it had a declining proportion of adherents, despite outreach efforts by the local Cowboy Church, whose website declared its members were "Riding for His Brand."[193] The town's fiber-optic Internet services allowed those who still affiliated to attend Sunday services online, and residents also could access the Bosque Museum's web page commemorating the county's most famous resident, Horn Shelter Man, while the Find a Grave app memorialized Adeline (d. 2006) and Herman Horn (d. 2007), the Baptist couple who allowed excavators to cross their land in 1966 and, four years later, uncover the holy man's grave with its shell bead offerings.[194] The Horns' children could take comfort in old-school rituals by driving to Clifton Cemetery to place a floral bouquet at the grave or, embracing a digital alternative, use an app to add virtual "flowers" to the couple's online memorial.

Yet, like those who came before them in the lands that became America, those modern mourners faced old questions, whether or not they surfaced as they honored the dead. Had the Horns' generation, which witnessed the transition from an industrial to a postindustrial lifeway, done enough to make the world better? How about their own generation? What were they doing to resolve the problems their elders bequeathed—and the ones they were unwittingly passing on to their own descendants? At a moment when few found reason for hope as the nation's 250th anniversary approached, could they and their churched and unchurched neighbors repurpose ancient figurative tools and craft new ones to rectify long-standing injustices, restore degraded niches, and build a sustainable world?[195]

Appendix

Sustainability Crises in the Lands That Became America

THE CORNFIELD CRISIS

Date: ca. 1140–1350 (resolved)

Features: A variety of elements (including climate change) reduced agricultural capacity and destabilized and depopulated maize-dependent centers. There was social hierarchy, religious conflict, increased violence, and migration.

Scale: Local and regional. At the densely populated city of Greater Cahokia (1050–1350) in the Central Mississippi Valley, and Ancestral Pueblo communities at Chaco Canyon (800–1140) and Mesa Verde (1140–1285) in the San Juan Basin of the Southwest.

Magnitude: Moderate and short-term ecological, social, political, and religious stresses.

Result: Environmental, social, political, and religious crisis was mostly resolved by migrating, scaling down, managing resources, and reducing hierarchy. Reoccupation at Chaco (1175–1250). By 1350, residents left Cahokia. Later repopulated, peaking in 1650.

THE COLONIAL CRISIS

Date: 1565–1776 (unresolved)

Features: "Columbian exchange" of biota; African slave trade; Native displacement and decimation. From the first permanent European settlement at St. Augustine to the Declaration of Independence and introduction of Watt's improved steam engine in 1776.

Scale: Regional. For slavery, the plantation niche in the South and the Caribbean; Native population loss and communal displacement in North America and the Americas.

Magnitude: Massive demographic and cultural changes, as epidemics caused population loss and colonialism shattered Native niches and enslaved African peoples. Significant change in genes, germs, plants, and animals. Ecological damage was notable but regional and reversible.

Result: Crisis insufficiently addressed. By 1789 US leaders postponed confrontation with racial inequity until the Civil War, and an expansionist nation displaced Natives during the nineteenth century. The crisis was bequeathed to later generations.

THE INDUSTRIAL CRISIS

Date: Starting 1873–1920 (unresolved)

Features: Industry-generated ecological effects began in the 1780s and increased after about 1873, when Andrew Carnegie first used the Bessemer process for making steel. Accompanied by a decline in well-being prompted by urban crowding, rising immigration, income inequality, and health disparity—and exacerbated by racism, nativism, and religious exclusivism.

Scale: Regional. Concentrated in the urban industrial North of the US, which became mostly urban by 1920. But raw materials came from the hinterlands, and ecological and social effects were seen in industrializing, segregated cities of the South, and in the West, where Native displacement also continued.

Magnitude: Unequal income and health care had notable social effects. A transgenerational impact on well-being among city-dwelling immigrants and Blacks. Fossil fuels' degrading of the land, air, and water was gradual, regional, and (mostly) reversible. But extractive industries scarred rural landscapes, like mining towns, as factories started to pollute cities.

Result: Many inequalities persisted for Blacks, Natives, and migrants, even if health disparity and income inequality declined for the general population between the 1930s and 1950s. The emerging ecological crisis was mostly ignored. Leaders did not reduce fossil-fuel dependency or admit its impact.

THE GREAT ACCELERATION

Date: Since the early 1950s (eco-crisis intensifies and social crises only partially addressed)

Features: Effects of global industrialization and urbanization sharply accelerate. Onset of the period when human intervention in natural systems is predominant. Abrupt rise in carbon dioxide, methane, and nitrates in polar ice levels. Ecological damage intensified by religious, economic, and political divides.

Scale: National and global. Global increase in industrialization, urbanization, and population. Rise of megacities. In the US, ecological effects reach beyond the nation's 4 megacities and from coast to coast. The post-Seventies inequities and divides affect local and national level.

Magnitude: Significant, sudden, and long-term ecological damage. That, in turn, threatened dramatic social, economic, political, and cultural disruptions—from food insecurity to climate migration. At the same time, economic inequality, racial injustice, and polarization destabilized institutions and eroded public trust.

Result: Ecological crisis insufficiently addressed. It might be too late to reverse biophysical changes detectable in the geological strata, but some mitigation of the harmful effects on human and nonhuman populations is possible. Inequities and divides remain.

Notes

Abbreviations

AA	*American Antiquity*
AAPSS	*Annals of the American Academy of Political and Social Science*
ACHS	*Records of the American Catholic Historical Society of Philadelphia*
AHR	*American Historical Review*
AQ	*American Quarterly*
ARA	*Annual Review of Anthropology*
CH	*Church History*
GPO	United States Government Printing Office
HMPEC	*Historical Magazine of the Protestant Episcopal Church*
JAAR	*Journal of the American Academy of Religion*
JAH	*Journal of American History*
JAR	*Journal of Archaeological Research*
JR	*Journal of Religion*
JSH	*Journal of Southern History*
JSSR	*Journal for the Scientific Study of Religion*
PMHB	*Pennsylvania Magazine of History and Biography*
PNAS	*Proceedings of the National Academy of Sciences of the United States of America*
RAC	*Religion and American Culture*
Stat.	United States Statutes at Large
WMQ	*William and Mary Quarterly*

Introduction

1. Sydney E. Ahlstrom, *A Religious History of the American People,* 2nd ed. (1972; Yale University Press, 2004). It not only won a national book award in 1973, but *Christian Century* named it "the Decade's Most Outstanding Book on Religion," and the press issued a new edition in 2004.

2. Ahlstrom, *Religious History,* 648–669. See also his chapter on "The Rise of Black Churches," where he humbly acknowledged it was a "preliminary" account because historians had only recently been awakened from their "dogmatic slumbers with regard to African American religious history" (699n1). He did the best he could with the sources he had, I concluded by the time I entered graduate school.

3. Ahlstrom, *Religious History,* 785–604, 1091–1095. Ahlstrom listed ten contemporary urban problems that seemed difficult to address without the aid of Puritan-inspired "idealism and hope" (1094–1095).

4. Thomas A. Tweed, ed., *Retelling U.S. Religious History* (University of California Press, 1997). Thomas A. Tweed, *Our Lady of the Exile: Diasporic Religion at a Cuban*

Catholic Shrine in Miami (Oxford University Press, 1997), 135–138. Thomas A. Tweed and Stephen Prothero, eds., *Asian Religions in America: A Documentary History* (Oxford University Press, 1999), 1–13. Thomas A. Tweed, "Expanding the Study of U.S. Religion: Reflections on the State of a Subfield," *Religion* 40 (2010): 250–258. I also learned from colleagues: Jon Butler, "Jack-in-the-Box Faith: The Religion Problem in Modern American History," *JAH* 90 (2004): 1357–1378. Catherine A. Brekus, "Introduction," in Catherine A. Brekus, ed., *The Religious History of American Women: Reimagining the Past* (University of North Carolina Press, 2007), 1–50. Kevin M. Schultz and Paul Harvey, "Everywhere and Nowhere: Recent Trends in American History and Historiography," *JAAR* 78.1 (2010): 129–162. John T. McGreevy, "Religious History," in Eric Foner and Lisa McGirr, eds., *American History Now* (Temple University Press, 2011). Kathryn Lofton, "Why Religion Is Hard for Historians (and How It Can Be Easier)," *Modern American History* 3.1 (2019): 1–18.

5. Jill Lepore, *The Story of America: Essays on Origins* (Princeton University Press, 2012), 3, 14.

6. Adam Goodman, "Nation of Migrants, Historians of Migration," *Journal of American Ethnic History* 34.4 (2015): 11. See also Dan Kanstroom, *Deportation Nation: Outsiders in American History* (Harvard University Press, 2007).

7. See Peter G. Mode, *The Frontier Spirit in American Christianity* (Macmillan, 1923).

8. Ahlstrom, *Religious History.* Its final section, "Toward Post-Puritan America," concluded with a reflection on the end of the "Puritan Epoch" (1094–1096). He also discussed the "Protestant establishment" (842–856). I mostly agree on this second point and refer to the de facto Protestant establishment. See William R. Hutchison, ed., *Between the Times: The Travail of the Protestant Establishment in America, 1900–1960* (Cambridge University Press, 1989).

9. "Mainline" Protestant denominations include Congregationalists, Episcopalians, Presbyterians, Disciples of Christ, United Lutherans, and the White divisions of Baptist and Methodist families. Hutchison, *Between the Times,* 4. See also Elesha J. Coffman, *The Christian Century and the Rise of the Protestant Mainline* (Oxford University Press, 2013).

10. I include elites as well as ordinary people, and ideas as well as social relations, but agree with Tilly that the task is to reconstruct how historical actors experienced the "big changes": Charles Tilly, "Retrieving European Lives," in Olivier Zunz, ed., *Reliving the Past: The Worlds of Social History* (University of North Carolina Press, 1985), 11, 31–35, 48. I add other big changes: the crises of sustainability that arose with the onset of the Little Ice Age, colonization, and industrialization.

11. The proportion of the religiously unaffiliated had risen to 30 percent by 2020. "Projecting Religious Groups' Population Shares by 2070," Pew Research Center, https://www.pewresearch.org/religion/2022/09/13/projecting-u-s-religious-groups-population-shares-by-2070/.

12. Others have imagined new Indigenous histories: Roxanne Dunbar-Ortiz, *An Indigenous Peoples' History of the United States* (Beacon, 2014); Ned Blackhawk, *The*

Rediscovery of America: Native Peoples and the Unmaking of U.S. History (Yale University Press, 2023).

13. Daniel T. Rodgers, "Exceptionalism," in Anthony Molho and Gordon S. Wood, eds., *Imagined Histories: American Historians Interpret the Past* (Princeton University Press, 1998), 21–40.

14. Ahlstrom, for example, expressed humility but said little about how his presuppositions and values shaped his selection of sources and topics. The attentive reader discovers, for instance, that he revered the "prophetic stance" that began with Puritanism, coalesced with the Social Gospel, and culminated with Neo-Orthodoxy. Presumably that tradition was among the "profounder" elements of US religion. Ahlstrom, *Religious History,* xvii, 785–804, 932–948, 1096.

15. On a continental perspective: Michael Mitgen, "Rethinking Colonial History as Continental History," *WMQ* 69.1 (2012): 527–530.

16. Michel de Certeau, *The Practice of Everyday Life* (University of California Press, 1984), 115.

17. See Daniel Lord Smail, *On Deep History and the Brain* (University of California Press, 2008); David Christian, *Maps of Time: An Introduction to Big History* (University of California Press, 2011); Jo Guldi and David Armitage, *The History Manifesto* (Cambridge University Press, 2014). See also Robert N. Bellah, *Religion in Human Evolution: From the Paleolithic to the Axial Age* (Harvard University Press, 2011), xi; David Graeber and David Wengrow, *The Dawn of Everything: A New History of Humanity* (Farrar, Straus and Giroux, 2021).

18. One of my collaborators called for long-term history: Joel W. Martin, "Indians, Contact, and Colonialism in the Deep South: Themes for a Postcolonial History of American Religion," in Tweed, *Retelling,* 149–180.

19. Daniel Rosenberg and Anthony Grafton, *Cartographies of Time: A History of the Timeline* (Princeton Architectural Press, 2010), 103–149.

20. Antonio de Alcedo, "América," in *Diccionario geográfico-histórico de las Indias Occidentales ó América* (Benito Cano, 1786), 1: 68–71.

21. Ted Goebel, Michael Waters, and Margarita Dikova, "The Archaeology of Ushki Lake, Kamchatka, and the Pleistocene Peopling of the Americas," *Science* 301.5632 (25 July 2003): 501–505.

22. William Robertson, *The History of America,* 8th ed. (1788; A. Strahan, 1800), 1: 307.

23. Thomas Jefferson, *Notes on the State of Virginia . . .* (publisher unknown, 1782), 179–180.

24. James Harvey Robinson, *The New History: Essays Illustrating the Modern Historical Outlook* (Macmillan, 1912), 85.

25. See Henry Kalloch Rowe, *The History of Religion in the United States* (Macmillan, 1924), 1. William Warren Sweet, *The Story of Religion in America* (Harper and Brothers, 1930), 11. Ahlstrom, *Religious History,* 1.

26. Rosenberg and Grafton, *Cartographies of Time,* 108–109, 147–149. See the chart by Forlong, who published *Rivers of Life,* reprinted on page 149. Philip Schaff

employed "mainstream" to describe the comingling of denominations. See David Bains and Theodore Louis Trost, "Philip Schaff: The Flow of Church History and the Development of Protestantism," *Theology Today* 71.4 (2015): 417, 420, 426–428.

27. "Upstreaming": William N. Fenton, "The Training of Historical Ethnologists in America," *American Anthropologist* 54 (1952): 333–335. For a criticism: John P. Hart and William Englebrecht, "Northern Iroquoian Ethnic Evolution: A Social Network Analysis," *Journal of Archaeological Method and Theory* 19 (2012): 332. Like Paulette Steeves, a Cree-Métis archaeologist, I consider Native oral tradition as well as archaeological evidence: Paulette F. C. Steeves, *The Indigenous Paleolithic of the Western Hemisphere* (University of Nebraska Press, 2021).

28. Robert A. Gross "The Transnational Turn: Rediscovering American Studies in a Wider World," *Journal of American Studies* 34.3 (2000): 373–393. Shelley Fisher Fishkin, "Crossroads of Cultures: The Transnational Turn in American Studies," *AQ* 57.1 (2005): 17–57. Thomas Bender, ed., *Rethinking American History in a Global Age* (University of California Press, 2002).

29. C. A. Bayly, *The Birth of the Modern World, 1780–1914: Global Connections and Comparisons* (Blackwell, 2004), 2.

30. Thomas Bender, *A Nation among Nations: America's Place in World History* (Hill and Wang, 2006), 3, 6. Some use "US Americans" to acknowledge that other hemispheric residents claim "American" identity: Dunbar-Ortiz, *Indigenous Peoples' History,* xiii–xiv. Others suggest the US is a Latin American country: Felipe Fernández-Armesto, *Our America: A Hispanic History of the United States* (W. W. Norton, 2014), 343–345.

31. See Guido Abbatista, "The English Universal History: Publishing, Authorship, and Historiography in a European Project (1736–1790)," *Storia della Storiografia* 39 (2001): 100–105. See also David Ramsay, *Universal History Americanized* (M. Carey and Son, 1819), 9: 220–330.

32. Jose C. Moya and Adam McKeown, *World Migration in the Long Twentieth Century,* Essays on Global and Comparative History (American Historical Association, 2011). See Randolph Bourne, "Trans-national America," *Atlantic Monthly* 118.7 (1916): 86–97.

33. W. E. B. Du Bois, *The Souls of Black Folk* (1903; Bantam, 1989), 136, 3.

34. Herbert E. Bolton, *Wider Horizons of American History* (1939; University of Notre Dame Press, 1969). See also William C. Binkley, George W. Brown, Edmundo O'Gorman, and German Arciniegas, "Have the Americas a Common History?," *Canadian Historical Review* 23.2 (1942): 125–156. H. Morse Stephens and Herbert E. Bolton, eds., *The Pacific Ocean in History* (Macmillan, 1917). For criticism of Bolton, see Albert L. Hurtado, *Herbert Eugene Bolton: Historian of the American Borderlands* (University of California Press, 2012), 3.

35. John T. McGreevy, *American Jesuits and the World: How an Embattled Religious Order Made Modern Catholicism Global* (Princeton University Press, 2016); David A. Hollinger, *Protestants Abroad: How Missionaries Tried to Change the World but Changed America* (Princeton University Press, 2017); Melani McAlister,

The Kingdom of God Has No Borders: A Global History of American Evangelicals (Oxford University Press, 2018).

36. The editor of the first sourcebook, Peter Mode, was born in Canada and became a US citizen in 1921. But he said little about border crossings. Mode's successor, Sweet, might have expanded the geographical frame too, since his *History of Latin America* appeared in 1919. No trace of a transhemispheric approach marked Sweet's narrative, however. Ahlstrom said little about Latin America, Canada, or the Pacific world, even though he aimed to place US history "within the larger frame of world history." Ahlstrom, *Religious History,* xxii. William Warren Sweet, *History of Latin America* (Abingdon Press, 1919). Some did trace transatlantic connections. See Winthrop Hudson, "How American Is Religion in America?," in *Reinterpretation in American Church History* (University of Chicago Press, 1968), 153–167; William R. Hutchison, "The Americanness of the Social Gospel: An Inquiry in Comparative History," *CH* 44.3 (Sept. 1975): 1–15. Mark Noll included Canada, though I don't discuss his work here since he wrote a history of "Christianity," not "religion."

37. My approach is *translocative,* which means the scale might be smaller or larger than the nation and includes the local and the regional as well as the national and transnational. I used *translocative* in *Our Lady of the Exile* and later refined my views: Thomas A. Tweed, "American Occultism and Japanese Buddhism: Albert J. Edmunds, D. T. Suzuki, and Translocative History," *Japanese Journal of Religious Studies* 32.2 (2005): 249–281; Thomas A. Tweed, "Flows and Dams: Rethinking Categories for the Study of Religion," in Philip Clart and Adam Jones, eds., *Transnational Religious Spaces: Religious Organizations and Interactions in Africa, East Asia, and Beyond* (De Gruyter, 2020), 10–32.

38. I borrow "grounded globalism" from James L. Peacock: *Grounded Globalism: How the U.S. South Embraces the World* (University of Georgia Press, 2007), 40–43. See also Karen Halttunen, "Grounded Histories: Land and Landscape in Early America," *WMQ* 68.4 (2011): 513–532.

39. Morten Rhagavan et al., "Upper Paleolithic Siberian Genome Reveals Dual Ancestry of Native Americans," *Nature* 505 (2 January 2014): 87–91.

40. Another collaborator called for attention to the Pacific: Tweed, "Introduction," *Retelling,* 12; Laurie Maffly-Kipp, "Eastward Ho! American Religion from the Perspective of the Pacific Rim," in Tweed, *Retelling,* 127–148. I argued for situating the narrative in the Indo-Pacific World in Tweed, "Expanding the Study of U.S. Religion."

41. "La Carta de Cristóbal Colón a Luis de Santángel," 15 February 1493, in Consuela Varela, ed., *Textos y documentos completos: Cristóbal Colón,* 2nd ed. (Alianza Editorial, 1992), 219–226.

42. Some surveys mention the "Pacific Rim," but emphasize the post-1960s period.

43. By *technology* I mean "the systematic, purposeful human manipulation of the physical world by some machine or tool." Barbara Hahn, "The Social in the Machine: How Historians of Technology Look beyond the Object," *Perspectives on History* 52.3 (2014): 30–31.

44. My phrasing recalls Rachel St. John's *Line in the Sand: A History of the Western U.S.–Mexican Border* (Princeton University Press, 2012).

45. Sweet, *Story of Religion*. Winthrop S. Hudson, *Religion in America* (Charles Scribner's Sons, 1965). Edwin Scott Gaustad, *A Religious History of America* (Harper and Row, 1966). Ahlstrom, *Religious History*. Martin E. Marty, *Pilgrims in Their Own Land: Five Hundred Years of Religion in America* (Little, Brown, 1984). Not all prominent survey writers were born in the middle of the continent, of course. George Marsden, one of Ahlstrom's doctoral students, was born in Pennsylvania. See George M. Marsden, *Religion and American Culture* (Harcourt Brace Jovanovich, 1990).

46. A 1918 survey located the center of the contiguous states 2.5 miles northwest of Lebanon, Kansas. In 1940, locals erected a plaque. An Episcopalian priest proposed an ecumenical chapel to mark the geographic center, and Elmer Stump funded the moving of the chapel. Lebanon's librarian, Esther Delimont, reported that by 2013 visitors left about 1,000 notecards in the chapel's box each year. See Alan Attwood, "Greetings from Lebanon USA," *The Age*, 29 August 1998. Some say that Rugby, North Dakota, is the midpoint of North America. Bell Fourche, South Dakota, became the midpoint of the United States after the 1959 boundaries were drawn. Geographer Peter Rogerson claimed the North American center is a North Dakota town called Center: Steph Yin, "North America's Geographical Center May Be in a North Dakota Town Called Center," *New York Times*, 25 January 2017. "Çoka," *Dakota-English Dictionary*, https://dictionary.swodli.com/. For local knowledge of the reference, see City of Cokato website, https://www.cokato.mn.us/community/history.php.

47. Ahlstrom, *Religious History*, xxiii.

48. The University of Notre Dame stands on the traditional homelands of the Haudenosauneega, Miami, Peoria, and especially the Pokégnek Bodéwadmik / Pokagon Potawatomi. More specifically, I live in Zénba Odan, the Potawatomi name for South Bend. See the dictionary of the Pokagan Band of the Potawatomi: http://wiwkwebthegen.com/dictionary/title/Z. See also John N. Low, *Imprints: The Pokagon Band of Potawatomi Indians and the City of Chicago* (Michigan State University Press, 2016). I try to respect Indigenous views, even when they diverge on an issue, but, as with my use of DNA evidence, I rely on most available evidence to recover the long-term history. However, I don't include sensitive sacred images and use Indigenous sources to challenge standard interpretations. My phrase "the lands that became America" attempts to acknowledge settler colonialism and Indigenous sovereignty. I hope my methodological and stylistic trade-offs prove worth the compromises. On DNA evidence: Kim TallBear, *Native American DNA: Tribal Belonging and the False Promise of Genetic Science* (University of Minnesota Press, 2013); Kim TallBear, "Genomic Articulations of Identity," in Stephanie Nohelani Teves, Andrea Smith, and Michelle H. Raheja, eds., *Native Studies Keywords* (University of Arizona Press, 2015).

49. I analyzed motifs in Tweed, *Retelling*, 13–15, and I gave a brief history of the field in Tweed, "Expanding the Study of U.S. Religion," 251–253. See also John F. Wilson, *Religion and the American Nation: Historiography and History* (University of

Georgia Press, 2003), 27–52. Survey writers influenced by Turner's emphasis on the "frontier" (Mode, Rowe, and Sweet) still told a contracted Protestant-centered tale. Frederick Jackson Turner, *The Frontier in American History* (Henry Holt, 1920). Peter G. Mode, *The Frontier Spirit in American Christianity* (Macmillan, 1923). See also Peter G. Mode, ed., *Source Book and Bibliographical Guide for American Church History* (George Banta, 1921). The pattern of emphasizing unity and diversity started with Clifton E. Olmstead, a Presbyterian minister and church historian who introduced the motif of "diversification." Clifton E. Olmstead, *History of Religions in the United States* (Prentice-Hall, 1960), 7, 27. More than a decade later, Ahlstrom used a different motif, *Puritanism,* to tell a similar story about the "Protestant Establishment" and its diverse challengers. Sweet mentioned five "creative forces" in American religion (individualism, frontier, slavery, revivalism, and nationalism), but said "frontier conditions" were most significant. Sweet, *Story of Religion,* 5.

50. By the late 1980s, several books had made the unity/diversity motif familiar: Catherine L. Albanese's *America: Religion and Religions* (Wadsworth, 1981); Mary Farrell Bednarowski's *American Religion* (Prentice-Hall, 1984); and R. Laurence Moore's *Religious Outsiders and the Making of Americans* (Oxford University Press, 1986). By the twenty-first century, four fine introductions emphasized unity and diversity, especially pluralism: Julia Corbett Heymeyer's *Religion in America,* 5th ed. (Pearson Prentice Hall, 2006); Charles H. Lippy's *Introducing American Religion* (Routledge, 2009); Peter W. Williams's *America's Religions: From Their Origins to the Twenty-First Century,* 4th ed. (University of Illinois Press, 2015); and Thomas S. Bremer's *Formed from This Soil: An Introduction to the Diverse History of Religion in America* (Wiley Blackwell, 2015).

51. In chapter 7, for instance, I suggest that three civil religions emerged after the Civil War, and discuss other contested forms of civil religion in later chapters.

52. See Thomas A. Tweed, *Crossing and Dwelling: A Theory of Religion* (Harvard University Press, 2006), 80–163. In the conclusion of *Our Lady of the Exile* and the introduction to *Asian Religions in America,* I suggested *mapping, meeting,* and *migration* were useful themes. *Contact* and *exchange,* the motifs we proposed in *Retelling,* remain helpful too. So my emphasis on *emplacement* and *displacement* builds on my earlier thinking.

53. On defining religion: Thomas A. Tweed, *Religion: A Very Short Introduction* (Oxford University Press, 2020), 1–31; Tweed, *Crossing and Dwelling,* 54–79. Discussions of flourishing have emerged in conversations about the good life, as in Aristotelian moral philosophy (*eudaimonia*): Robert C. Bartlett and Susan D. Collins, trans., Aristotle's *Nicomachean Ethics* (University of Chicago Press, 2011), 10–14 (book 1, chapter 7). Conceptions of the good life also appear in Anishinaabe spiritual discourse (*mino-bimaadiziwin*): Lawrence W. Gross, *Anishinaabe Ways of Knowing and Being* (Routledge, 2012), 205–214. See also Diné uses of *hózhó,* translated as harmony, happiness, or well-being: "Back to Harmony," *Navajo Times Today* 28.45 (7 March 1986): A11. VanderWeele suggested that flourishing means doing and being well in "five domains of human life": Tyler J. VanderWeele, "On the Promotion of Human Flourishing," *PNAS* 114.31 (2017): 8149. See also Tyler J. VanderWeele,

"Spiritual Well-being and Human Flourishing," in Adam B. Cohen, ed., *Religion and Human Flourishing* (Baylor University Press, 2020), 45; Miroslav Volf, Matthew Croasmun, and Ryan McAnnally-Linz, "Meanings and Dimensions of Flourishing: A Programmatic Sketch," in Cohen, *Religion and Human Flourishing,* 10; Charles Taylor, *Sources of the Self: The Making of Modern Identity* (Harvard University Press, 1989), 62–75; Christian Smith, *To Flourish or Destruct: A Personalist Theory of Human Goods, Motivations, Failure, and Evil* (University of Chicago Press, 2015), 181–182, 212–213.

54. I intend my focus on lifeways to align with Indigenous views: Mary Lou Fox (Anishinaabe) suggests that religion is "a way of life "or what the Anishinaabe call *anishnaabe bimaadiziwin.* Quoted in Suzanne Crawford O'Brien, with Inés Talamantez, *Religion and Culture in Native America* (Rowman & Littlefield, 2021), 2. See also Gross, *Anishinaabe Ways of Knowing and Being,* 134.

55. Tweed, *Crossing and Dwelling,* 68. Utilitarian tools are "intermediary devices that extend the range of the senses": Daniel Rothbart, *Philosophical Instruments: Minds and Tools at Work* (University of Illinois Press, 2017), 3. Thomas A. Tweed, "Space," in S. Brent Plate, ed., *Key Terms in Material Religion* (Bloomsbury, 2015), 223–229. Tweed, *Crossing and Dwelling,* 80–122. Humans actively co-create their eco-cultural niche or lived world, and its scale expands or contracts according to the reach of the group's niche-constituting practices. It can be local, regional, or transregional. On "niche construction," see F. John Odling-Smee, Kevin N. Laland, and Marcus W. Feldman, *Niche Construction: The Neglected Process in Evolution,* Monographs in Population Biology, vol. 37 (Princeton University Press, 2003), and Bruce D. Smith, "Shaping the Natural World: Patterns of Human Niche Construction by Small-Scale Societies in North America," in Bruce D. Smith, ed., *The Subsistence Economies of Indigenous North American Societies: A Handbook* (Smithsonian Institution Scholarly Press, 2011), 593–609. See also Kevin Laland and Michael J. O'Brien, "Niche Construction Theory and Archaeology," *Journal of Archaeological Method and Theory* 17 (2010): 305. Dairy farming: J. Burger et al., "Absence of the Lactase-Persistence-Associated Allele in Early Neolithic Europeans," *PNAS* 104.10 (2007): 3736–3741; Sarah A. Tishkoff et al., "Convergent Adaptation of Human Lactase Persistence in Africa and Europe," *Nature Genetics* 39.1 (2006): 31–40. Jeremy Kendal, Jamshid J. Tehrani, and John Odling-Smee, "Human Niche Construction in Interdisciplinary Focus," *Philosophical Transactions of the Royal Society—Biological Sciences* 366.1566 (2011): 785–792. "Symbolic inheritance systems": Eva Jablonka and Marion J. Lamb, *Evolution in Four Dimensions: Genetic, Epigenetic, Behavioral, and Symbolic Variation in the History of Life,* rev. ed. (MIT Press, 2014), 189–227.

56. Thomas Jefferson to James Madison, 6 January 1789, Founders Online, https://founders.archives.gov/documents/Madison/01-12-02-0248. The Haudenosaunee or Iroquois Confederacy's solemn covenant or Great Law of Peace: Arthur Caswell Parker, *The Constitution of the Five Nations; Or, the Iroquois Book of the Great Law,* New York State Museum Bulletin, no. 184 (University of the State of New York, 1916), section 28. This definition of sustainability is from a UN commission: *Report of the World Commission on Environment and Development: Our Common Future,* April 1987, p. 16 (para. 27), http://www.un-documents.net/our-common

-future.pdf. See also Paul Warde, *The Invention of Sustainability: Nature and Destiny, c. 1500–1870* (Cambridge University Press, 2018); Abby L. Goode, *Agrotopias: An American Literary History of Sustainability* (University of North Carolina Press, 2022); Jeremy L. Caradonna, *Sustainability: A History,* revised and updated ed. (Oxford University Press, 2022), 1–21. On visual models of sustainability, see Caradonna, *Sustainability,* 9–11. My model adds factors and highlights the optimal and interdependent conditions for individual, communal, and environmental flourishing. On "suitable climate," see Chi Xu et al., "Future of the Human Climate Niche," *PNAS* 117.21 (2020): 11350–11355. On the interdependence of individual, communal, and environmental well-being: Mike Hannis, "The Virtues of Acknowledged Ecological Dependence: Sustainability, Autonomy, and Human Flourishing," *Environmental Values* 24 (2015): 145–164; Hava Tirosh-Samuelson, "Human Flourishing and History: A Religious Imaginary for the Anthropocene," *Journal of the Philosophy of History* 14 (2020): 382–418. My understanding of the conditions for flourishing partially aligns with the UN's 2015 list of seventeen sustainable development goals: *Sustainable Development Goals,* adopted by the United Nations, 25 September 2015, http://www.un.org/sustainabledevelopment/sustainable-development-goals/. On religion and the goals, see Paul Freston, "Religion and the Sustainable Development Goals," in Simon Dalby, Susan Horton, and Rianne Mahon, eds., *Achieving the Sustainable Development Goals: Global Governance Challenges* (Routledge, 2019), 152–169. See also the Global Flourishing Study, which highlights six "domains" of individual flourishing, or "living in a state in which all aspects of a person's life are going well": https://globalflourishingstudy.com/.

57. I borrow "crises of sustainability" from John Brooke, "Ecology," in Daniel Vickers, ed., *A Companion to Colonial America* (Blackwell, 2006), 54. I modify its meaning, however. William Cronon suggested that sustainability discourse failed to emphasize social justice. I agree, but I refine the term's meaning to respond to that concern. William Cronon, "The Riddle of Sustainability: A Short History for the Future," plenary address, 14 April 2011, annual conference of the American Society for Environmental History, Phoenix.

58. John McConnell Jr. proposed an Earth Day on the spring equinox. See Nicole Sparks and Darrin J. Rodgers, "John McConnell Jr. and the Pentecostal Origins of Earth Day," *Assemblies of God Heritage* 30 (2010): 17–25, 69. On Nelson's Earth Day, see Thomas Jundt, *Greening the Red, White, and Blue: The Bomb, Big Business, and Consumer Resistance in Postwar America* (Oxford University Press, 2014), 190–216. Adam Rome, *The Genius of Earth Day: How a 1970 Teach-In Created the First Green Generation* (Hill and Wang, 2013). Gaylord Nelson, "Partial Text for Senator Gaylord Nelson, Denver, Colo., April 22, 1970," https://nelsonearthday.net/wp-content/uploads/2020/02/nelson-26-18-ed-denver-speech-notes.pdf.

59. Scientists disagree about how to describe and date the moment when human action became the primary force for destabilizing change. Some have proposed the term *Anthropocene* to mark the shift, but scientists debate whether it signals a geologic epoch, event, or episode. On the terminological debate: Philip Gibbard et al., "The Anthropocene as an Event, not an Epoch," *Journal of Quaternary Science* 37.3

(2022): 395–399; Martin J. Head et al., "The Proposed Anthropocene Epoch/Series Is Underpinned by an Extensive Array of Mid-20th Century Stratigraphic Event Signals," *Journal of Quaternary Science* 37.7 (2022): 1181–1187. In March 2024 a subcommission of the International Commission on Stratigraphy stated that the changes around 1950 did not constitute a new epoch or interval on the Geological Time Scale, but scholars attentive to Earth System science continued to argue for a significant shift around midcentury. See Paul Voosen, "The Anthropocene Is Dead. Long Live the Anthropocene," *Science*, 5 March 2024, https://www.science.org/content/article/anthropocene-dead-long-live-anthropocene. On the proposal that we are living in a new geological age, the Anthropocene, a time when the Earth System functioned beyond Holocene norms and human activity drove natural change, see Paul J. Crutzen and Eugene F. Stoermer, "The Anthropocene," *Global Change IGBP Newsletter* 41 (2000): 17; Paul J. Crutzen, "Geology of Mankind," *Nature* 415 (3 January 2002): 23; Colin N. Waters et al., "The Anthropocene Is Functionally and Stratigraphically Distinct from the Holocene," *Science* 351, no. 6269 (2016): 137–145; Jan Zalasiewicz et al., "The Anthropocene: Comparing Its Meaning in Geology (Chronostratigraphy) with Conceptual Approaches Arising in Other Disciplines," *Earth's Future* 9 (2021): 1–25. See also Julia Adeney Thomas, Mark Williams, and Jan Zalasiewicz, *The Anthropocene: A Multidisciplinary Approach* (Polity Press, 2020), and Julia Adeney Thomas, *Altered Earth: Getting the Anthropocene Right* (Cambridge University Press, 2022).

60. "Destroyed" niches and "negative niche construction": Odling-Smee, Laland, and Feldman, *Niche Construction*, 1, 420. "Cracked" niches: K. N. Laland, J. Odling-Smee, and M. W. Feldman, "Niche Construction, Biological Evolution, and Cultural Change," *Behavioral and Brain Sciences* 23 (2000): 131–175. I use "broken," because it signals, as the *Oxford English Dictionary* suggests, people also can be "broken."

61. Morris suggests energy structures cause or constrain the development of values: "each age gets the thought it needs" (1). Ian Morris, *Foragers, Farmers, and Fossil Fuels: How Human Values Evolve* (Princeton University Press, 2015). My categories (foraging religion, farming religion, industrial religion, and digital religion) are historical ideal types, more or less useful terms that emerge from analysis of particular times and places and are not perfectly expressed by any person or group. Max Weber, "Objectivity in the Social Sciences and Social Policy," in *Methodology in the Social Sciences*, trans. Edward A. Shils and Henry A. Finch (Free Press, 1949), 49–112.

62. Margaret A. Jodry and Douglas W. Owsley, "A New Look at the Double Burial from Horn Shelter No. 2," in Douglas W. Owsley and Richard L. Jantz, eds., *Kennewick Man: The Scientific Investigation of an Ancient American Skeleton* (Texas A&M Press, 2014), 549–604.

63. With its appeal to "Nature's God" and emphasis on equality and rights, the Declaration of Independence offers a religiously informed vision of flourishing: Thomas Jefferson et al., 4 July, copy of Declaration of Independence, 1776, https://www.loc.gov/item/mtjbib000159/. For Jefferson, as well as Adams and Franklin, happiness was *eudaimonia*, "well-being or human flourishing." See Carli N. Conklin, *The Pursuit of Happiness in the Founding Era: An Intellectual History* (University of

Missouri, 2019), 134. The US Constitution aspired to "establish Justice, insure domestic Tranquility, provide for the common defence, promote the general Welfare, and secure the Blessings of Liberty to ourselves and our Posterity," Preamble, US Constitution, https://constitution.congress.gov/constitution/.

64. Watt's steam engine patent of 1784 was especially significant. Crutzen originally dated the Anthropocene from 1784 and mentioned Watt's engine. Crutzen, "Geology of Mankind," 23.

65. On the Bessemer process and Second Industrial Revolution: John L. Brooke, *Climate Change and the Course of Global History: A Rough Journey* (Cambridge University Press, 2014), 509. The "mineral-based energy economy": E. A. Wrigley, *Continuity, Chance and Change: The Character of the Industrial Revolution in England* (Cambridge University Press, 1988). Chrisopher F. Jones, "A Landscape of Energy Abundance: Anthracite Coal Canals and the Roots of American Fossil Fuel Dependence, 1820–1860," *Environmental History* 15 (2010): 451–453.

66. The 1920 US Census marked the first time over 50 percent of the population was urban. Bureau of the Census, *Fourteenth Census of the United States Taken in the Year 1920: Population 1920* (GPO, 1921). Susan B. Carter et al., *Historical Statistics of the United States*, vol. 1, part A, *Population* (Cambridge University Press, 2006), 1: 121. On the industrialization of farming: Deborah Fitzgerald, *Every Farm a Factory: The Industrial Ideal in American Agriculture* (Yale University Press, 2003). On oil and religion: Darren Dochuk, *Anointed with Oil: How Christianity and Crude Made Modern America* (Basic Books, 2019), 273–542.

67. On the "Great Acceleration" of anthropogenetic environmental effects after 1945: Kathy Hibbard et al., "Group Report: Decadal Scale Interactions of Humans and the Environment," in Robert Costanza, Lisa Graumlich, and Will Steffen, eds., *Sustainability or Collapse? An Integrated History and Future of People on Earth* (MIT Press, 2007), 341–378; John Robert McNeill and Peter Engelke, *The Great Acceleration: An Environmental History of the Anthropocene since 1945* (Harvard University Press, 2016).

68. The service sector's employment share was already 61 percent in 1970 and rose to 76 percent by 2005. Ulrich Witt and Christian Gross, "The Rise of the 'Service Economy' in the Second Half of the Twentieth Century and Its Energetic Contingencies," *Journal of Evolutionary Economics* 30 (2020): 236. "Digital utopianism": Fred Turner, *From Counterculture to Cyberculture: Stewart Bland, the Whole Earth Network, and the Rise of Digital Utopianism* (University of Chicago Press, 2006).

69. "Nobel Peace Prize 2007," https://www.nobelprize.org/prizes/peace/2007/summary/. "Horn Shelter Exhibit," Bosque Museum, Clifton, Texas, https://www.bosquemuseum.org/hornshelter. Heidi Campbell and Antonio Pastina, "How the iPhone Became Divine: New Media, Religion and the Intertextual Circulation of Meaning," *New Media and Society* 12.7 (2010): 1191–1207. Herman Horn (1919–2007), Find a Grave, https://www.findagrave.com/memorial/17929883/herman-horn. Adeline Dennis Horn (1925–2006), Find a Grave, https://www.findagrave.com/memorial/16367156/adeline-horn.

70. Kimberly TallBear suggested Indigenous Peoples were not "ecological saints," but that "does not lessen the cruel colonial history of White America": Kimberly TallBear, "Shepard Kreech's *The Ecological Indian:* One Indian's Perspective," *Ecological Indian Review* (September 2000): 1–5. The "ecologically noble savage" debate was sparked by Shepard Krech III's *The Ecological Indian: Myth and History* (W. W. Norton, 1999). See Joy Porter, *Native American Environmentalism: Land, Spirit, and the Idea of Wilderness* (University of Nebraska Press, 2014), xiii–xix. See also Vine Deloria, *For This Land: Writings on Religion in America,* ed. James Treat (Routledge, 1999), 250–260.

71. Catherine M. Cameron and Andrew I. Duff, "History and Process in Village Formation: Context and Contrasts from the Northern Southwest," *AA* 73.1 (2008): 43–49; Severin Fowles, "The Pueblo Village in an Age of Reformation (AD 1300–1600)," in Timothy Pauketat, ed., *The Oxford Handbook of North American Archaeology* (Oxford University Press, 2012), 638–641; Jakob W. Sedig, "The Decline and Reorganization of Southwestern Complexity: Using Resilience Theory to Examine the Collapse of Chaco Canyon," in Ronald K Faulseit, ed., *Beyond Collapse: Archaeological Perspectives on Resilience, Revitalization, and Transformation in Complex Societies* (Southern Illinois University Press, 2015), 237–261. On a religious movement's effect on the population rise at Cahokia: Susan M. Alt, "The Implications of the Religious Foundations at Cahokia," in Charles H. McNutt and Ryan M. Parish, eds., *Cahokia in Context: Hegemony and Diaspora* (University Press of Florida, 2020), 32–48. On Cahokia's decline: Caitlin G. Rankin, "Testing Narratives of Ecocide with the Stratigraphic Record at Cahokia Mounds State Historic Site, Illinois, USA," *Geoarchaeology* 36.3 (2021): 369–387. On the Little Ice Age's impact: A. J. White et al., "Fecal Stanols Show Simultaneous Flooding and Seasonal Precipitation Change Correlate with Cahokia's Population Decline," *PNAS* 116.12 (2019): 5461–5466. On religious, ethnic, and political "factions": Thomas E. Emerson and Kristin M. Hedman, "The Dangers of Diversity: The Consolidation and Dissolution of Cahokia, Native North America's First Urban Polity," in Faulseit, ed., *Beyond Collapse,* 147–175.

72. For another account that conjoins African and Indigenous history, see Kyle T. Mays, *An Afro-Indigenous History of the United States* (Beacon, 2021).

73. Bob Johnson, *Carbon Nation: Fossil Fuels in the Making of American Culture* (University Press of Kansas, 2014), xviii. On the crisis between 1873 and 1920, which Brooke calls an "urban environmental crisis" and White calls "an environmental crisis": Brooke, *Climate Change,* 502; Richard White, *The Republic for Which It Stands: The United States during Reconstruction and the Gilded Age, 1865–1896* (Oxford University Press, 2017), 477–517.

74. Hibbard et al., "Group Report: Decadal Scale Interactions of Humans and the Environment," 341–378. McNeill and Engelke, *Great Acceleration.*

75. *Symbolic surplus,* an extravagant public display in ritual or architecture, resembles what some call "costly signaling." See John Kanter and Kevin J. Vaughn, "Pilgrimage as Costly Signal: Religiously Motivated Cooperation in Chaco and Nasca," *Journal of Anthropological Archaeology* 31 (2012): 66–82. *Planter piety* is what Butler called "the dominant slaveholding ethic of the colonial South." Jon

Butler, *Awash in a Sea of Faith: Christianizing the American People* (Harvard University Press, 1990), 142. I include a definition of *industrial religion* offered by Richard J. Callahan Jr., Kathryn Lofton, and Chad Seales, "Allegories of Progress: Industrial Religion in the United States," *JAAR* 78.1 (2010): 3.

76. Ahlstrom's book ended in a "somber mood" for different reasons—after chronicling the "calamities" of the Sixties and noting the loss of optimism, which had been grounded in the Puritan conviction that America, the "Redeemer Nation," "had a divine commission in the world." Ahlstrom, *Religious History,* 1094–1095.

77. James Baldwin, "As Much Truth as One Can Bear," *New York Times,* 14 January 1962, BR11. I am grateful to Eddie S. Glaude Jr., who mentioned this passage to me in 2015 and later wrote about Baldwin: Eddie S. Glaude Jr., *Begin Again: James Baldwin's America and Its Urgent Lessons for Our Own* (Crown, 2020), 4–11.

78. Efforts to reverse environmental change are called "constructive niche construction": Odling-Smee, Laland, and Feldman, *Niche Construction,* 420. On the attempts to avoid flourishing that comes at the cost of the ecosystem, see Laura M. Hartman, ed., *That All May Flourish: Comparative Religious Environmental Ethics* (Oxford University Press, 2018). On engaging religious traditions to inspire change, see Mary Evelyn Tucker and John Grim, "Moral and Spiritual Contributions to a Flourishing Earth Community," in Daniel C. Esty, ed., *A Better Planet: Forty Big Ideas for a Sustainable Future* (Yale University Press, 2019), 297–307.

Chapter 1. Foraging Religion

1. On "metaphysical anguish": Henry de Lumley, "The Emergence of Symbolic Thought: The Principal Steps of Hominisation Leading towards Greater Complexity," in Colin Renfrew and Iain Morley, eds., *Becoming Human: Innovation in Prehistoric Material and Spiritual Culture* (Cambridge University Press, 2009), 19–21. Others pointed to "the development of a metaphysics": Agustín Fuentes, "Human Evolution, Niche Complexity, and the Emergence of a Distinctively Human Imagination," *Time and Mind* 7.3 (2014): 241–257.

2. My reconstruction of this graveside ritual is based on many sources I cite below. I am disagreeing with those who suggest that big questions only would be introduced with the "theoretic culture" of the Axial Age, and with sages and prophets like Socrates, Confucius, and the Buddha. See Robert N. Bellah, *Religion in Human Evolution: From the Paleolithic to the Axial Age* (Harvard University Press, 2011), 265–282.

3. My analysis is indebted to "Reading the Layers," Horn Shelter, Texas beyond History, https://www.texasbeyondhistory.net/horn/layers.html. Some worry that the term *artifacts* risks disconnecting objects from "specific Indigenous Peoples" and "contemporary members of an Indigenous People." Gregory Younging, *Elements of Indigenous Style: A Guide for Writing by and about Indigenous People* (Brush Education, 2018), 52–53. I see the point, and where possible I refer to contemporary Native Nations. However, since I deal with so much material culture from so many communities, Native and non-Native as well as ancient and modern, I use *artifact* to refer to intentionally modified objects. In turn, I use *eco-cultural niche* or *built environment* to describe sites transformed by human use.

4. Rupert Gethin, "Cosmology," in Robert E. Buswell Jr., ed., *Encyclopedia of Buddhism* (Macmillan Reference, 2004), 1: 183–187.

5. This plot is not contained in any single text, though several works on long history tell versions of this tale, and mention some or all the milestones I note. See David Christian, *Maps of Time: An Introduction to Big History* (University of California Press, 2004); Cynthia Stokes Brown, *Big History: From the Big Bang to the Present* (New Press, 2007). The dating of cosmic, geologic, and world history milestones is always changing as new evidence appears, so these dates are approximations based on current views, as I understand the latest scholarship.

6. "Big bang" was coined on a BBC broadcast in 1948. See "Fred Hoyle: An Online Exhibition," St. John's College, University of Cambridge, http://www.joh.cam.ac.uk/library/special_collections/hoyle/exhibition.

7. Ted Goebel, Michael R. Waters, and Dennis H. O'Rourke, "The Late Pleistocene Dispersal of Modern Humans in the Americas," *Science* 319 (14 March 2008): 1497.

8. Qiaomei Fu et al., "Genome Sequence of a 45,000-Year-Old Modern Human from Siberia," *Nature* 514 (23 October 2014): 445–449.

9. David Christian, "World History in Context," *Journal of World History* 14.4 (2003): 440.

10. Unless otherwise noted, biblical quotations are from Bruce M. Metzger and Roland E. Murphy, eds., *The New Oxford Annotated Bible,* New Revised Standard Edition (Oxford University Press, 1991).

11. Christian, "World History in Context," 457.

12. On "niche construction": F. John Odling-Smee, Kevin. N. Laland, and Marcus W. Feldman, *Niche Construction: The Neglected Process in Evolution,* Monographs in Population Biology, vol. 37 (Princeton University Press, 2003).

13. Fu et al., "Genome Sequence of a 45,000-Year-Old Modern Human," 445–449.

14. See Goebel, Waters, and O'Rourke, "Late Pleistocene Dispersal," 1497–1502; Michael Bawaya, "How Won the West Was," *New Scientist* 216 (30 March 2013): 42–45; Guy Gugliotta, "The First Americans," *Smithsonian* 43.10 (2013): 38–47.

15. Luigi Luca Cavalli-Sforza, *Genes, Peoples, and Languages* (North Point Press, 2000), 61–63. Theodore G. Schurr and Stephen T. Sherry, "Mitochondrial DNA and Y Chromosome Diversity and the Peopling of the Americas: Evolutionary and Demographic Evidence," *American Journal of Human Biology* 16.4 (2004): 420–439. Reich et al., "Native American Population History," *Nature* 488 (16 August 2012): 370–374. See also Justin C. Tackney et al., "Two Contemporaneous Mitogenomes from Terminal Pleistocene Burials in Eastern Beringia," *PNAS* 112.45 (2015): 13833–13838.

16. Johanna Nichols, "The First American Languages," in Nina G. Jablonski, ed., *The First Americans* (California Academy of Sciences, 2002), 273–293. See also Reich et al., "Native American Population History." That research suggests three major streams corresponding to three major language families, and confirms what Joseph H. Greenberg proposed in *Language in the Americas* (Stanford University Press, 1987).

17. Reich et al., "Native American Population History."

18. Mark Person et al., "Pleistocene Hydrology of North America: The Role of Ice Sheets in Reorganizing Groundwater Flow Systems," *Reviews of Geophysics* 45 (2007): 4.

19. M. Waters and T. Stafford, "Redefining the Age of Clovis: Implications for the Peopling of the Americas," *Science* 315 (2007): 1122–1126. A survey of archaeologists found that two-thirds accepted human habitation in the Americas before Clovis: Bawaya, "How Won the West Was," 42.

20. Paisley Caves: Dennis L. Jenkins et al., "Geochronology, Archaeological Context, and DNA at Paisley Caves," in Kelly E. Graf, Caroline V. Ketron, and Michael R. Waters, eds., *Paleoamerican Odyssey* (Texas A&M University Press, 2014), 485–510. On the evidence from Texas: Michael R. Waters et al., "Pre-Clovis Projectile Points at the Debra L. Friedkin Site, Texas—Implications for the Late Pleistocene Peopling of the Americas," *Science Advances* 4.10 (2018): eaat4505, https://doi.org/10.1126/sciadv.aat4505; Thomas J. Williams et al., "Evidence of an Early Projectile Point Technology in North America at the Gault Site, Texas, USA," *Science Advances* 4.7 (2018): eaar5954, https://doi.org/10.1126/sciadv.aar5954.

21. On Monte Verde: Thomas D. Dillehay, *The Settlement of the Americas: A New Prehistory* (Basic Books, 2000); T. D. Dillehay, *Monte Verde: A Late Pleistocene Settlement in Chile,* vol. 1, *The Paleoenvironmental Context* (Smithsonian Institution Press, 1989); and T. D. Dillehay, *Monte Verde: A Late Pleistocene Settlement in Chile,* vol. 2, *The Archaeological Context* (Smithsonian Institution Press, 1997).

22. William R. Dickinson, "Geological Perspectives on the Monte Verde Archeological Site in Chile and Pre-Clovis Coastal Migration in the Americas," *Quaternary Research* 76.2 (2011): 201–210; Michael Balter, "Ancient Algae Suggest Sea Route for First Americans," *Science* 320 (9 May 2008): 729.

23. Jon M. Erlandson et al., "The Kelp Highway Hypothesis: Marine Ecology, the Coastal Migration Theory, and the Peopling of the Americas," *Journal of Island and Coastal Archaeology* 2.2 (2007): 161–174. See also James E. Dixon, *Bones, Boats, and Bison: Archaeology and the First Colonization of Western North America* (University of New Mexico Press, 1999); Jon M. Erlandson, "Anatomically Modern Humans, Maritime Voyaging, and the Pleistocene Colonization of the Americas," in Jablonski, *First Americans,* 59–92; Jon M. Erlandson, Madonna L. Moss, and Mathew Des Lauriers, "Life on the Edge: Early Maritime Cultures of the Pacific Coast of North America," *Quaternary Science Reviews* 27 (2008): 2232–2245.

24. On Arlington Springs: Rick Torben et al., "From Pleistocene Mariners to Complex Hunter-Gatherers: The Archaeology of the California Channel Islands," *Journal of World Prehistory* 19.3 (2005): 177. There has been some dispute about whether the remains are from a male or female, but it seems that "we are back to calling the remains 'Arlington Springs Man.'" Sally M. Walker and Douglas W. Owsley, *Their Skeletons Speak: Kennewick Man and the Paleoamerican World* (Carolrhoda Books, 2012), 38.

25. Michael Waters, quoted in Gugliotta, "First Americans."

26. John N. Low, *Imprints: The Pokagon Band of Potawatomi Indians and the City of Chicago* (Michigan State University Press, 2016), 197–199.

27. Paulette F. C. Steeves, *The Indigenous Paleolithic of the Western Hemisphere* (University of Nebraska Press, 2021), 91, xviii–xiv.

28. This rejection of archaeological narratives is from Daniel Castro Romero Jr. (Ndé Nanta' án), a social worker and US historian as well as chairman of the Lipan Apache Band of Texas. He offered this challenge in San Antonio on 19 November 2016. He elaborated in an email message to me on 20 November 2016: "Our Elders all confirm that we did not come via Alaska. We traveled up to Colorado from Chiuwau and then the Canadian border among the other Athabaskan speakers, to get the tipi, then making our way back south to share our gift of the tipi. Finally, ending up at San Louis Potosi." I am grateful for his help. Kim TallBear, *Native American DNA: Tribal Belonging and the False Promise of Genetic Science* (University of Minnesota Press, 2013), 8, 28.

29. Low, *Imprints,* 13.

30. Goebel, Waters, and O'Rourke, "Late Pleistocene Dispersal," 1500. The estimates about the dispersal from Africa (by 60,000 years ago) and the presence in Siberia (by 45,000 years ago) are earlier than the timing suggested by Goebel, but I find other evidence persuasive, including Fu et al., "Genome Sequence of a 45,000-Year-Old Modern Human," 445–449. Evidence of the earliest dispersal and occupation continues to be debated. See D. J. Meltzer, *The Great Paleolithic War: How Scientists Forged an Understanding of America's Ice Age Past* (University of Chicago Press, 2015); Michael R. Waters, "Late Pleistocene Exploration and Settlement of the Americas by Modern Humans," *Science* 365 (2019): 138.

31. Some suggest evidence does not support an occupation earlier than 17,500 years ago, and as a nonexpert I stand ready to revise my views. Waters, "Late Pleistocene Exploration and Settlement of the Americas." On older sites: Stuart J. Fiedel, "Confessions of a Clovis Mafioso," in Marcel Kornfeld and Bruce B. Huckell, eds., *Stones, Bones, and Profiles: Exploring Archaeological Context, Early American Hunter-Gatherers, and Bison* (University Press of Colorado, 2016), 32–39. Darrin L. Lowery et al., "Late Pleistocene Upland Stratigraphy of the Western Delmarva Peninsula, USA," *Quaternary Science Reviews* 29 (2010): 1472–1480. D. P. Wagner and J. M. McAvoy, "Pedoarchaeology of Cactus Hill, a Sandy Paleoindian Site in Southeastern Virginia, USA," *Geoarcheology* 19 (2004): 297–322. Loren G. Davis et al., "Late Upper Paleolithic Occupation at Cooper's Ferry, Idaho, USA, ~16,000 Years Ago," *Science* 365 (2019): 891–897.

32. Using evidence in White Sands National Park, scientists identified a 2,000-year period when humans lived with Pleistocene megafauna between 21,000 and 23,000 years ago. Matthew R. Bennett et al., "Evidence of Humans in North America during the Last Glacial Maximum," *Science* 373 (2021): 1528–1531. On the debate, see David B. Madsen et al., "Comment on 'Evidence of Humans in North America during the Last Glacial Maximum,'" *Science* 10.1126 (2022): eabm4678; Jeffrey S. Pigati et al., "Response to Comment on 'Evidence of Humans in North America during the Last Glacial Maximum,'" *Science* 10.1126 (2022): eabm6987. Confirmation of the original dating: J. S. Pigati et al., "Data Release for Independent Age Estimates

Resolve the Controversy of Ancient Human Footprints at White Sands," US Geological Survey data release, 2023, https://doi.org/10.5066/P9E36U4B.

33. Lorena Becerra-Valdivia and Thomas Higham, "The Timing and Effect of the Earliest Human Arrivals in North America," *Nature* 584 (6 August 2020): 93–97. They also mention the "well-dated footprints" at White Sands in a defense of their findings: Lorena Becerra-Valdivia and Thomas Higham, "Response to 'Current Understanding of the Earliest Human Occupations in the Americas: Evaluation of Becerra-Valdivia and Higham (2020),'" *PaleoAmerica* 8.1 (2022): 77–78.

34. Reich et al., "Native American Population History," 370–374. See also Jon Erlandson and Todd J. Braje, "Foundations for the Far West: Paleoindian Cultures of the Western Fringe of North America," in Timothy Pauketat, ed., *The Oxford Handbook of North American Archaeology* (Oxford University Press, 2012), 149, 150. Mounting evidence suggests that early movement down the coast was possible, even likely. See Alia J. Lesnek et al., "Deglaciation of the Pacific Coastal Corridor Directly Preceded the Human Colonization of the Americas," *Science Advances* 4 (30 May 2018): 1–8. The opening of the interior "corridor" was later than most thought: Jorie Clark et al., "The Age of the Opening of the Ice-Free Corridor and Implications for the Peopling of the Americas," *PNAS* 119.14 (2022): e2118558119, https://doi.org/10.1073/pnas.2118558119.

35. Michael K. Faught, "Archaeological Roots of Human Diversity in the New World: A Compilation of Accurate and Precise Radiocarbon Ages from Earliest Sites," *AA* 73.4 (2008): 670–698. Cooper's Ferry supports the Pacific coastal route theory and northeastern Asian cultural connections: Davis et al., "Late Upper Paleolithic Occupation at Cooper's Ferry, Idaho, USA, ~16,000 Years Ago."

36. Dennis J. Stanford and Bruce A. Bradley, *Across Atlantic Ice: The Origin of America's Clovis Culture* (University of California Press, 2012), 247.

37. Dennis Stanford et al., "New Evidence for a Possible Paleolithic Occupation of the Eastern North American Continental Shelf at the Last Glacial Maximum," in A. M. Evans et al., eds., *Prehistoric Archaeology on the Continental Shelf: A Global Review* (Springer, 2014), 73–93.

38. For a rebuttal, see Guy Lawrence Straus, David J. Meltzer, and Ted Goebel, "Ice Age Atlantis? A Review of Reality," *AA* 37 (2005): 507–532. See also Stephen Oppenheimer, Bruce Bradley, and Dennis Stanford, "Solutrean Hypothesis: Genetics, the Mammoth in the Room," *World Archaeology* 46.5 (2014): 752–774. On the Pacific route: Faught, "Archaeological Roots of Human Diversity," 690.

39. Faught, "Archaeological Roots of Human Diversity," 690.

40. On hunter-gather niche construction: Bruce D. Smith, "Shaping the Natural World: Patterns of Human Niche Construction by Small-Scale Societies in North America," in Bruce D. Smith, ed., *The Subsistence Economies of Indigenous North American Societies: A Handbook* (Smithsonian Institution Scholarly Press, 2011), 593–609.

41. George Crawford showed me the incised tusk at Blackwater Draw Locality No. 1. I am grateful for his help. See also Lienke Katz, *The History of Blackwater Draw* (Eastern New Mexico University Printing Services, 1997).

42. Of course, notched animal bones date to much earlier periods. See Jane M. Renfrew, "Neanderthal Symbolic Behavior?," in Renfrew and Morley, *Becoming Human*, 57.

43. Specialists have offered many accounts of religion's distant beginning. See Terrance Deacon and Tyrone Cashman, "The Role of Symbolic Capacity in the Origin of Religion," *Journal for the Study of Religion, Nature, and Culture* 3.4 (2009): 493–495.

44. On defining *religion*, see Thomas A. Tweed, *Crossing and Dwelling: A Theory of Religion* (Harvard University Press, 2006), 29–53; Thomas A. Tweed, *Religion: A Very Short Introduction* (Oxford University Press, 2020), 1–31.

45. Other scholars have made a similar point: Whitehouse argued that religious traditions "are subject to psychological and ecological constraints." Harvey Whitehouse, *Modes of Religiosity: A Cognitive Theory of Transmission* (Altamira, 2004), 7. I emphasize the role of institutions, technology, and environment more than Whitehouse, though he might agree those factors are important.

46. Mithen suggests that religion is "anchored" by things and requires "materialization." I would add that religion also requires ritualization and sonification as aids for remembering and transmitting worldviews. Ritual action and patterned sound, or music, are also important. Steven Mithen, "Out of Mind: Material Culture and the Supernatural," in Renfrew and Morley, *Becoming Human*, 131. On music, see Iain Morley, "Ritual and Music: Parallels, Practice, and the Paleolithic," in Renfrew and Morley, *Becoming Human*, 159–175.

47. Some scholars suggest compassion is also detectable in the archaeological record: P. A. Spikins, H. E. Rutherford, and A. P. Needham, "From Homininity to Humanity: Compassion from the Earliest Archaics to Modern Humans," *Time and Mind* 3.2 (2010): 303–326. Many argue for the importance of cooperation: Joseph Bulbulia, "Meme Infection or Religious Niche Construction? An Adaptationst Alternative to the Cultural Maladaptionist Hypothesis," *Method and Theory in the Study of Religion* 20 (2008): 67–107; Fuentes, "Human Evolution, Niche Complexity." On "ultrasociability," see Peter Turchin et al., "A Historical Database of Sociocultural Evolution," *Cliodynamics: The Journal of Theoretical and Mathematical History* 3 (2012): 271–293.

48. Tweed, *Crossing and Dwelling*, 73, 76–77; Tweed, *Religion*, 15–16. On routes and roots as categories of analysis, see Elizabeth M. DeLoughrey, *Routes and Roots: Navigating Caribbean and Pacific Island Literatures* (University of Hawai'i Press, 2007), 41–48.

49. "Higher order consciousness": David Lewis-Williams, "Of People and Pictures: The Nexus of Upper Palaeolithic Religion, Social Discrimination, and Art," in Renfrew and Morley, *Becoming Human*, 143. G. M. Edelman, *Wider Than the Sky: The Phenomenal Gift of Consciousness* (Allen Lane, 2004).

50. Humans' ability to move beyond the here and now contrasts with what Donald described as the "episodic culture" of nonhuman primates, who remain bound to the particular episode. Merlin Donald, *Origins of the Modern Mind: Three Stages in the Evolution of Culture and Cognition* (Harvard University Press, 1991), 149.

51. Tweed, *Crossing and Dwelling*, 85–98.

52. "Figure out": F. LeRon Shults, "Incorporating Figuration and Spirituality," in Colin Renfrew and Iain Morley, eds., *Image and Imagination* (Oxbow Books, 2007), 337. Tools that serve utilitarian functions, like spears, can also function as place-making symbols that orient users: Daniel Rothbart, *Philosophical Instruments: Minds and Tools at Work* (University of Illinois Press, 2007), 8.

53. Christopher S. Henshilwood and Curtis W. Marean, "The Origin of Modern Human Behavior: Critique of the Models and Their Test Implications," *Current Anthropology* 44.4 (December 2003): 635–636.

54. Deacon and Cashman, "Role of Symbolic Capacity in the Origin of Religion," 490–517. Donald, *Origins of the Modern Mind*. See also Bellah, *Religion in Human Evolution*, 101, 133. Adhl Agus Oktaviana et al., "Narrative Cave Art in Indonesia by 51,200 Years Ago," *Nature* 631 (25 July 2024): 814–818.

55. D. R. Hofstader, "Epilogue: Analogy as the Core of Cognition," in Dedre Genter, Keith J. Holyoak, and Boicho N. Kokinov, eds., *The Analogical Mind: Perspectives from Cognitive Science* (MIT Press, 2001), 500.

56. On Jesus as "the lamb [*amnos*] of God," see John 1:29 and John 19:36. See also 1 Cor 5:7; Heb 9:12–14; and Acts 8:32–35. See Invild Sælid Gilhus, *Animals, Gods, and Humans: Changing Attitudes to Animals in Greek, Roman, and Early Christian Ideas* (Routledge, 2006), chap. 8; Raymond E. Brown, S.S., *The Gospel According to John (I–XII)*, Anchor Yale Bible (Yale University Press, 2008), 55; C. K. Barrett, "The Lamb of God," *New Testament Studies* 1 (1954–1955): 210–218; Marco Frenschkowski, "Lamm Gottes," in Theodor Klauser, ed., *Reallexikon für Antike und Christentum*, vol. 22 (Hiersemann, 2008), 853–882. Buddhists use figurative language for Śākyamuni Buddha, the Fully Awakened One (*samyak-sambuddha*), but the direct and implied metaphor of the physician (*bhisakka*) appears in the Pali Canon and in other important Buddhist texts, just as devotion to the Master of Healing is important in Northern and Eastern Buddhism. See Raoul Birnbaum, *The Healing Buddha* (Shambhala, 1979); Peter Harvey, *An Introduction to Buddhism: Teachings, History, and Practices* (Cambridge University Press, 1990), 47, 189–195. The Islamic tradition venerates Muhammad's ninety-nine names, and one of those is "the seal [*khātam*] of the prophets" (Qur'an 33:40). It is a metaphor that compares him with the material that seals—that is, closes and authorizes—a written text, like a letter or document. So he is associated with the sealant (a stamp or sealing wax) and the act of sealing. In this sense, Muslims are affirming that he closes and confirms the prophetic tradition. See Elsaid M. Badawi and Muhammad Abdel Haleem, *Arabic-English Dictionary of Qur'anic Usage* (Brill, 2008), 254–255; Uri Rubin, "Prophets and Prophethood," in Jane Dammen McAulife, ed., *The Encyclopedia of the Qur'an* (Brill, 2004), 4: 289–306.

57. On analogical reasoning: Emmanuelle Volle et al., "Specialization of the Rostral Prefrontal Cortex for Distinct Analogy Processes," *Cerebral Cortex* 20 (2010): 2647–2659; Ann Speed, "Abstract Relational Categories, Graded Persistence, and Prefrontal Cortical Representation," *Cognitive Neuroscience* 1.2 (2010): 126–152.

58. Daniel C. Krawczyk, M. Michelle McClelland, and Colin M. Donovan, "A Hierarchy for Relational Reasoning in the Prefrontal Cortex," *Cortex* 47 (2011): 588–597.

59. In my implied distinction, I rely on Harvey Whitehouse's typology of the two "modes of religiosity," *imagistic* and *doctrinal.* Whitehouse, *Modes of Religiosity,* 63–84. I'm not suggesting, however, that the doctrinal mode is either inevitable or superior.

60. The quotation is from Colin Renfrew, "Introduction," in Renfrew and Morley, *Becoming Human,* 4. On a "symbolic explosion" see Steven Mithen, *The Prehistory of the Mind: A Search for the Origins of Art, Religion, and Science* (Phoenix, 1998), 171–210. Christopher Henshilwood, "The Origins of Symbolism, Spirituality, and Shamans: Exploring Middle Stone Age Material Culture in South Africa," in Renfrew and Morley, *Becoming Human,* 42–43. Merlin Donald, "The Roots of Art and Religion in the Ancient Material Culture," in Renfrew and Morley, *Becoming Human,* 102.

61. Lumley, "Emergence of Symbolic Thought," 17.

62. Steven Mithen, "Is Religion Inevitable? An Archaeologist's View from the Past," in Alex Bentley, ed., *The Edge of Reason: Science and Religion in Modern Society* (Continuum, 2008), 89. Christopher Henshilwood et al., "Emergence of Modern Human Behavior: Middle Stone Age Engravings from South Africa," *Science* 295 (2002): 1278–1280. Christopher Henshilwood, "The Origins of Symbolism, Spirituality, and Shamans: Exploring Middle Stone Age Material Culture in South Africa," in Renfrew and Morley, *Becoming Human,* 42–43.

63. Fuentes, "Human Evolution, Niche Complexity."

64. Vincent Formicola, "From the Sunghir Children to the Romito Dwarf: Aspects of the Upper Paleolithic Funerary Landscape," *Current Anthropology* 48.3 (2007): 446–453. Mithen, *Prehistory of the Mind,* 199.

65. Klaus Schmidt, "Göbekli Tepe, Southeastern Turkey: A Preliminary Report on the 1995–1999 Excavations," *Paléorient* 26.1 (2001): 45–54. Scholars have debated Schmidt's interpretation of the site as a sacred center for religious ritual. See Ian Kuijt, "The Materiality of Ritual on the Social Landscape: Questions and Issues," *Neo-Lithics: Newsletter of Southwest Asian Neolithic Research* (February 2005): 35–37; and E. B. Banning, "So Fair a House: Göbekli Tepe and the Identification of Temples in the Pre-Pottery Neolithic of the Near East," *Current Anthropology* 52.5 (2011): 619–660. The buildings might have been domestic structures with symbolic meanings, but ritual practice happened there. It need not have been a "temple," as Schmidt claims, to make it relevant to the history of religion.

66. Leore Grosman, Natalie D. Munro, and Anna Belfer-Cohen, "A 12,000-Year-Old Shaman Burial from the Southern Levant (Israel)," *PNAS* 105.46 (2008): 17665–17669. Natalie Munroe, Leore Grosman, and Henry T. Wright, "Early Evidence (ca. 12,000 BP) for Feasting at a Burial Cave in Israel," *PNAS* 107.35 (2010): 15362–15366. The word *shaman* is of Siberian cultural origin and perhaps from the Tungic term *šamān.* In Siberia and the Americas, and among Indigenous groups like the Ainu of Japan, the term also refers to persons who perform functions besides healing the sick and communicating with spirits; he or she also sometimes acts as a "theatrical performer" and "covert politician." See Emiko Ohnuki-Tierney, "Shamans and Imu: Among Two Ainu Groups—Toward a Cross-Cultural Model of Interpretation," *Ethos* 8.3 (1980): 208.

67. The foraging "spectrum": C. Britt Bousman and Bradley J. Vierra, eds., *From the Pleistocene to the Holocene: Human Organization and Cultural Transformations in Prehistoric North America* (Texas A&M Press, 2012), 8–10.

68. "Cal yr BP" means calibrated years before the present. Morten Rasmussen et al., "The Genome of a Late Pleistocene Human from a Clovis Burial Site in Western Montana," *Nature* 506 (13 February 2014): 225–229. There were ochre-covered artifacts at the Anzick site too, and some suggest the burial is evidence of ritual behavior: Ashley M. Smallwood, Thomas A. Jennings, and Charlotte D. Pevny, "Expressions of Ritual in the Paleoindian Record of the Eastern Woodlands: Exploring the Uniqueness of the Dalton Cemetery at Sloan, Arkansas," *Journal of Anthropological Archaeology* 49 (2018): 186.

69. Even if burials are the best evidence of religion from the period, "afterlife caches," or clusters of stone tools stored to prepare the deceased for the afterlife, also might have ritual significance: Smallwood, Jennings, and Pevny, "Expressions of Ritual in the Paleoindian Record," 186–189, 195–196.

70. Douglas W. Owsley, Margaret A. Jodry, Thomas W. Stafford Jr., C. Vance Haynes Jr., and Dennis J. Stanford, *Arch Lake Woman: Physical Anthropology and Geoarchaeology* (Texas A&M University Press, 2010), 71. Some specialists dispute that red ochre signals "symbolic behavior." But there is strong evidence for its nonutilitarian use in graves and caves. See Walker and Owsley, *Skeletons Speak,* 108. See also Wadley's argument for the utilitarian uses and Watts's argument for the symbolic purposes: Lynn Wadley, "What Is Cultural Modernity? A General View and a South African Perspective from Rose Cottage," *Archaeological Journal* 11 (2001): 201–221; I. Watts, "Ochre in the Middle Stone Age of Southern Africa: Ritualized Display or Hide Preservation?" *South African Archaeological Bulletin* 57 (2002): 15–30. See also Wil Roebroeks et al., "Use of Red Ochre by Early Neanderthals," *PNAS* 109.6 (2 February 2012): 1889–1894.

71. Arch Lake Woman is "among the oldest Paleoamerican human remains yet found." Owsley et al., *Arch Lake Woman,* 78.

72. For a comparison of these burials, see Owsley et al., *Arch Lake Woman,* 62–77. See also Ben A. Potter et al., "New Insights into Eastern Beringian Mortuary Behavior: A Terminal Pleistocene Double Infant Burial at Upward Sun River," *PNAS* 111.48 (2014): 17060–17065; Justin C. Tackney et al., "Two Contemporaneous Mitogenomes from Terminal Pleistocene Burials in Eastern Beringia," *PNAS* 112.45 (2015): 13833–13838; Mark Muniz, "Exploring Technological Organization and Burial Practices at the Paleoindian Gordon Creek Site (5LR99)," *Plains Anthropologist* 49.191 (2004): 253–279; Elisa Phelps et al., "Burial to Bronze: Excavation, Analysis, and Facial Reconstruction of a Burial from the Wilson-Leonard Site, Texas," *Bulletin of the Texas Archeological Society* 62 (1994): 75–86; Thomas J. Green et al., "The Buhl Burial: A Paleoindian Woman from Southern Idaho," *AA* 63.3 (1998): 437–456; Nicholas P. Hermann, Richard L. Jantz, and Douglas W. Owsley, "Buhl Revisited: 3-D Photographic Reconstruction and Morphometric Re-Evaluation," in José Concepción Jiménez López et al., eds., *El hombre temprano en América y sus implicaciones*

en el poblamiento de la cuenca de México (Instituto Nacional de Antropología e Historia, 2006).

73. On Horn Shelter No. 2 (41BQ46): Diane E. Young, Suzanne Patrick, and D. Gentry Steele, "An Analysis of the Paleoindian Double Burial from Horn Shelter No. 2 in Central Texas," *Plains Anthropologist* 32.117 (1987): 275–298; Albert J. Redder and John W. Fox, "Excavation and Positioning of the Horn Shelter's Burial and Grave Goods," *Central Texas Archeologist* 11 (1988): 1–12; Diane Young, "An Osteological Analysis of the Paleoindian Double Burial from Horn Shelter, Number 2," *Central Texas Archeologist* 11 (1988): 13–115; Walker and Owsley, *Skeletons Speak*, 60–69; Margaret A. Jodry and Douglas W. Owsley, " A New Look at the Double Burial from Horn Shelter No. 2," in Douglas W. Owsley and Richard L. Janz, eds., *Kennewick Man: The Scientific Investigation of an Ancient American Skeleton* (Texas A&M Press, 2014).

74. Jodry and Owsley, "A New Look at the Double Burial," 550. The Horn Shelter grave was dug about 100 years after Arch Lake Woman was interred in territory that is now New Mexico. Obituary notices for Herman and Adeline Horn suggest that they were farming the land after their 1946 marriage, and that in the early 1960s Adeline left the farm to supplement their income by working at Waco's Owens Illinois Glass Plant. The couple belonged to the First Baptist Church of Clifton, Texas, and she was devout, the obituary notice suggested.

75. Redder and Fox, "Excavation and Positioning of the Horn Shelter's Burial and Grave Goods," 8.

76. The quotation, and much of the information in this paragraph, is available from "Horn Shelter," Texas beyond History, https://www.texasbeyondhistory.net/horn/index.html. The presence of those turtle shells is not surprising, since turtle remains are the most widely occurring animal remains archaeologists have found at Clovis sites in Texas and in North America.

77. Spirit Man is most like the Ainu, and Kennewick Man is most like Moriori, according to Walker and Owsley, *Skeletons Speak*, 118. However, a 2015 DNA test indicated that Kennewick Man was most closely related to the Confederated Tribes of the Colville Reservation in Washington State, which had been arguing for rights to the 8,500-year-old remains: "Ancient 'Kennewick Man' Skeleton Was Native American: Study," *New York Times*, 19 June 2015.

78. See Jodry and Owsley, "A New Look at the Double Burial," 588.

79. On the apparently widespread human interest in special things, the exotic and the esoteric, see Thomas E. Emerson et al., "The Allure of the Exotic: Reexamining the Use of Local and Distant Pipestone Quarries in Ohio Hopewell Pipe Caches," *AA* 78.1 (2013): 48, 63.

80. For Margaret Jodry's interpretation of Horn Shelter Man as a shaman, see Walker and Owsley, *Skeletons Speak*, 66. On the other key shaman burial I mention, see Grosman, Munro, and Belfer-Cohen, "A 12,000-Year-Old Shaman Burial," 17665–17669.

81. Jodry's interpretation of the Horn Shelter Girl is in Walker and Owsley, *Skeletons Speak*, 68.

82. For this model of mobility, see Isabel C. Rivera-Collazo, "Paleoecology and Human Occupation during the Mid-Holocene in Puerto Rico: The Case of Angostura," in Corinne L. Hofman and Anne van Duijvenbode, eds., *Communities in Contact: Essays in Archaeology, Ethnohistory, and Ethnography of the Amerindian Circum-Caribbean* (Sidestone, 2011), 414.

83. Thomas A. Jennings, "San Patrice: An Example of Late Paleoindian Adaptive Versatility in South Central North America," *AA* 73.3 (2008): 553–554.

84. Jodry and Owsley, "A New Look at the Double Burial," 588.

85. E. J. Michael Witzel, *The Origins of the World's Mythologies* (Oxford University Press, 2012), x–xii, 3–7, 33–35.

86. Witzel, *Origins of the World's Mythologies*, 115, 138.

87. On Anishinaabe accounts of the origin of the name "Turtle Island," see Jennifer Graber and Pamela E. Klassen, "North America, Turtle Island, and the Study of Religion," *Numen* 67 (2020): 314. See also Basil Johnston, *Ojibway Heritage* (McClelland and Stewart, 1976), 11–20; Leanne Simpson, *Dancing on Our Turtle's Back: Stories of Nishnaabeg Re-Creation, Resurgence, and a New Emergence* (Arbeiter Ring, 2011), 65–83; Low, *Imprints*, 14; Suzanne Crawford O'Brien with Inés Talamantez, *Religion and Culture in Native America* (Rowman & Littlefield, 2021), 162. On "turtle cosmograms" in prairie-plains rock art and in Early Woodland pottery in the Upper Midwest, see David W. Benn, "Unified Theory of Cosmogram Decorations on Potteries of the Upper Midwest: Part I: Early Woodland Period," *Midcontinental Journal of Archaeology* 44.2 (2019): 124–125. Similar imagery appeared at Hopewell: Christopher Carr and Robert McCord, "Ohio Hopewell Depictions of Composite Creatures: Part I—Biological Identification and Ethnohistorical Insights," *Midcontinental Journal of Archaeology* 38.1 (2013): 68. For an account of the turtle story in the journals of a colonial Dutch traveler among the Lenape, see Jasper Danckaert, *Memoirs of the Long Island Historical Society*, vol. 1, *Journal of a Voyage to New York in 1679–1670* ("Printed by the Society," 1867), 268.

88. I borrow "symbolic locative" from Reilly: F. Kent Reilly III, "The Petaloid Motif: A Celestial Symbolic Locative in the Shell Art of Spiro," in F. Kent Reilly III and James F. Garber, eds., *Ancient Objects and Sacred Realms: Interpretations of Mississippian Iconography* (University of Texas Press, 2007), 39–55.

89. Emiko Ohnuki-Tierney, "Spatial Concepts of the Ainu of the Northwest Coast of Southern Sakhalin," *American Anthropologist*, new series, 74.3 (1972): 441–446.

90. For example, see George E. Lankford, "'The Path of Souls': Some Death Imagery in the Southeastern Ceremonial Complex," in Reilly and Garber, *Ancient Objects*, 174–212.

91. On "spirit emblems," see Owsley et al., *Arch Lake Woman*, 67–71.

92. M. Poor and K. W. Alt, "The Burial of Bad Dürrenberg, Central Germany: Osteopathology and Osteoarchaeology of a Late Mesolithic Shaman's Grave," *International Journal of Osteoarchaeology* 16 (2006): 395–406. The German burial included a deer bone used to apply red ochre and sixty-five tortoise shell fragments.

93. I use *foraging religion* here as a Weberian ideal type, a more or less useful interpretive category that doesn't mirror the practice of any particular community. I don't suggest that all foragers had the same cultural practices; I mean we can identify some patterns or features that change over time and across regions. On the climate and the number of locals: David La Vere, *The Texas Indians* (Texas A&M Press, 2004), 4–5.

94. Michael B. Collins, ed., *Wilson-Leonard: An 11,000-year Archeological Record of Hunter-Gatherers in Central Texas,* 5 vols., Studies in Archeology 31 (Texas Archeological Research Laboratory, University of Texas at Austin, and Archeology Studies Program Report 10, Texas Department of Transportation, Environmental Affairs Division, 1998); M. B. Collins et al., "The Paleoindian Sequence at the Wilson-Leonard Site, Texas," *Current Research in the Pleistocene* 10 (1993): 10–12; M. A. Masson and M. B. Collins, "The Wilson-Leonard Site (41WM235)," *Cultural Resource Management News and Views* 7.1 (1995): 6–10. On Wilson-Leonard and the Archaic transition, see C. Britt Bousman et al., "The Paleoindian-Archaic Transition in North America: New Evidence from Texas," *Antiquity* 76 (2002): 980–990.

95. I refer here to Burial 27, the adult woman, at Modoc Rock Shelter, and Burial 15, the child at Dust Cave. Jodry and Owsley, "A New Look at the Double Burial," 554. S. Homes Hogue, "The Human Skeletal Remains from Dust Cave," *Journal of Alabama Archaeology* 40 (1994): 173–191. Sydney M. Wheeler and Georgia N. Wheeler, "Cave Burials Near Fallon, Churchill County, Nevada," *Archaeological Papers* (Nevada State Museum, 1969), 70–78. Holm Wolfram Neumann, *The Paleopathology of the Archaic Mondoc Rock Shelter Inhabitants* (Illinois State Museum, 1967).

96. Dan F. Morse, *Sloan: A Paleoindian Dalton Cemetery in Arkansas* (Smithsonian Institution Press, 1997); George C. Frison, review of *Sloan: A Paleoindian Dalton Cemetery in Arkansas, AA* 63.4 (1998): 707–708; Niccole Waguespack, "Early Paleoindians, from Colonization to Folsom," in Pauketat, *Oxford Handbook,* 101; Smallwood, Jennings, and Pevny, "Expressions of Ritual in the Paleoindian Record," 184–198.

97. Morse, *Sloan,* 83–91, 140–141.

98. Li Liu, *The Archaeology of China: From the Late Paleolithic to the Early Bronze Age* (Cambridge University Press, 2012). Ian Kuijt, "The Regeneration of Life: Neolithic Structures of Symbolic Remembering and Forgetting," *Current Anthropology* 49.2 (2008): 171–197. Emma Guerrero et al., "Seated Memory: New Insights into Near Eastern Neolithic Mortuary Variability from Tell Halula, Syria," *Current Anthropology* 50.3 (2009): 379–391.

99. Martha Ann Rolingson, *Toltec Mounds: Archeology of the Mound-and-Plaza Complex,* Arkansas Archeological Survey Research Series no. 65 (Arkansas Archeological Survey, 2012). These mounds were named "Toltec" because locals assumed Mesoamerican influence.

100. The now contested assumptions about the transition to the Archaic found a classic summary in G. R. Willey and P. Phillips, *Method and Theory in American Archaeology* (University of Chicago Press, 1958), 107–111. The more recent literature on the Archaic has emphasized diversity and complexity as well as blurred boundaries

between periods and differences across regions. See Thomas E. Emerson et al., eds., *Archaic Societies: Diversity and Complexity across the Midcontinent* (State University of New York Press, 2009); Susan M. Alt, ed., *Ancient Complexities: New Perspectives in Precolumbian North America* (University of Utah Press, 2010).

101. Willey and Phillips, *Method and Theory in American Archaeology,* 107–111.

102. C. Britt Bousman and Eric Oksanen, "The Protoarchaic in Central Texas and Surrounding Areas," in Bousman and Vierra, *From the Pleistocene to the Holocene,* 198, 224.

103. See Kurt W. Carr and J. M. Adovasio, "Shades of Gray Redux: The Paleoindian/Early Archaic 'Transition' in the Northeast," in Bousman and Vierra, *From the Pleistocene to the Holocene,* 273–318.

104. Aubrey Cannon and Dongya Y. Yang, "Early Storage and Sedentism of the Pacific Northwest Coast: Ancient DNA Analysis of Salmon Remains from Namu, British Columbia," *AA* 71.1 (2006): 123–140. Amy Salomon Groesbeck, "Ancient Clam Gardens Increased Production: Adaptive Strategies from the Past Can Inform Food Security Today," master's thesis, Simon Frazer University, 2013. Dana Lepofsky et al., "Ancient Shellfish Mariculture on the Northwest Coast of North America," *AA* 80.2 (2015): 236–259. See also Herbert D. G. Maschner, "Archaeology of the Northwest Coast," in Pauketat, *Oxford Handbook,* 160–164.

105. On rock shelters and other landscape features as sacred space, see Cheryl Claassen, *Beliefs and Rituals in Archaic Eastern North America: An Interpretive Guide* (University of Alabama Press, 2015), 283–285.

106. "Climatic crossroads": Carolyn E. Boyd, *Rock Art of the Lower Pecos* (Texas A&M University Press), 10. Solveig A. Turpin, "The Cultural Significance of Seminole Sink," *Plains Anthropologist* 33.122 (1988): 119–132.

107. Boyd, *Rock Art of the Lower Pecos.* Turpin, "Cultural Significance of Seminole Sink." On rock art, pictographs, and petroglyphs at other Archaic Era sites in the Americas, see Michelle H. Hayward et al., "Rock Art of the Caribbean," in William F. Keegan, Corinne L. Hofman, and Reniel Rodríguez Ramos, eds., *The Oxford Handbook of Caribbean Archaeology* (Oxford University Press, 2013), 486–503.

108. Boyd, *Rock Art of the Lower Pecos,* 4–5.

109. Boyd, *Rock Art of the Lower Pecos,* 15.

110. Jim Zintfraff and Solveig A. Turpin, *Pecos River Arts: A Photographic Essay* (Sandy McPherson, 1991), 13–33.

111. On the use of these plants for healing and ritual, and the association between deer and peyote, including among the Huichol, see Boyd, *Rock Art of the Lower Pecos,* 67–105. See also Carolyn E. Boyd and J. Philip Dering, "Medicinal and Hallucinogenic Plants in the Sediments and Pictographs of the Lower Pecos, Texas Archaic," *Antiquity* 70.268 (1996): 256–275.

112. On these recurring motifs—the otherworldly journey, peyotism, and *Datura* shamanism—see Boyd, *Rock Art of the Lower Pecos,* 108–110.

113. Boyd, *Rock Art of the Lower Pecos,* 45–62, 67–78.

114. I follow Boyd's interpretation of Seminole Sink: Boyd, *Rock Art of the Lower Pecos,* 63.

115. Robert A. Ricklis, Richard A. Weinstein, and Douglas C. Wells, *Archaeology and Bioarchaeology of the Buckeye Knoll Site* (41VT98), Victoria County, Texas: Final Report, vol. 1 (Coastal Environments, 2012).

116. Ricklis, Weinstein, and Wells, *Archaeology and Bioarchaeology of the Buckeye Knoll Site,* 319, 345.

117. Ricklis, Weinstein, and Wells, *Archaeology and Bioarchaeology of the Buckeye Knoll Site,* 348, 356,

118. On banner stones: Richard F. Townsend, ed., *Hero, Hawk, and Open Hand: American Indian Art of the Ancient Midwest and South* (Art Institute of Chicago, in association with Yale University Press, 2004), 22–26.

119. Ricklis, Weinstein, and Wells, *Archaeology and Bioarchaeology of the Buckeye Knoll Site,* iii. On the connections with evidence from eastern sites, see also Bousman and Oksanen, "The Protoarchaic in Central Texas," 218.

120. Joe W. Saunders et al., "Watson Brake, a Middle Archaic Mound Complex in Northeast Louisiana," *AA* 70.4 (October 2005): 665.

121. Saunders et al., "Watson Brake," 663.

122. Saunders et al., "Watson Brake," 655. Joe W. Saunders, Reca Jones, Kathryn Moorhead, and Brian David, "'Watson Brake Objects': An Unusual Archaic Artifact Type from Northeast Louisiana and Southwest Mississippi," *Southeastern Archaeology* 17.1 (1998): 73–77.

123. Saunders et al., "Watson Brake," 653.

124. The earlier Archaic Era dirt mounds at the Elizabeth Mounds in Illinois were not a plaza and mound complex, as at Watson Brake. See Donald Albertson and Douglas Charles, "Archaic Mortuary Component," in D. Charles, S. Leigh, and J. Buikstra, eds., *The Archaic and Woodland Cemeteries at the Elizabeth Site in the LIV,* Kampsville Archaeological Center, Research Series vol. 7 (Center for American Archaeology, 1988), 29–40; Claassen, *Beliefs and Rituals in Archaic Eastern North America,* 68–70.

125. See Kent G. Lightfoot and Edward M. Luby, "Mound Building by California Hunter-Gatherers," in Pauketat, *Oxford Handbook,* 221.

126. See Rivera-Collazo, "Paleoecology and Human Occupation during the Mid-Holocene," 407–420; Richard G. Lesure, "Platform Architecture and Activity Patterns in an Early Mesoamerican Village in Chiapas, Mexico," *Journal of Field Archaeology* 26.4 (1999): 391–406; Thomas Pozorski and Shelia Pozorski, "Architecture and Chronology at the Site of Sechín Alto, Casma Valley, Peru," *Journal of Field Archaeology* 30.2 (2005): 143–161.

127. John E. Clark, "Surrounding the Sacred: Geometry and Design of Early Mound Groups as Meaning and Function," in Jon L. Gibson and Phillip J. Carr, eds., *Signs of Power: The Rise of Cultural Complexity in the Southeast* (University of Alabama Press, 2004), 162–213.

128. On Poverty Point's dates I rely on Diana Greenlee and Robert C. Dunnell, "Identification of Fragmentary Bone from the Pacific," *Journal of Archaeological Science* 37 (2010): 968. See also Jon L. Gibson, *Ancient Mounds of Poverty Point: Place of Rings* (University Press of Florida, 2001); Jon L. Gibson, "Broken Circles,

Owl Monsters, and Black Earth Midden: Separating Sacred and Secular at Poverty Point," in Robert C. Mainfort Jr. and Lynne P. Sullivan, eds., *Ancient Earthen Enclosures of the Eastern Woodlands* (University Press of Florida, 1998), 1–17; Jon L. Gibson, "Navels of the Earth: Sedentism in Early Mound-Building Cultures in the Lower Mississippi Valley," *World Archaeology* 38.2 (2006): 311–329; Tristram R. Kidder, "Mapping Poverty Point," *AA* 67.89 (2002): 89–101; Tristram R. Kidder, "Transforming Hunter-Gatherer History at Poverty Point," in K. E. Sassaman and D. H. Holley Jr., eds., *Hunter-Gatherer Archaeology as Historical Process* (University of Arizona Press, 2011); Tristram R. Kidder, "Poverty Point," in Pauketat, *Oxford Handbook,* 460–470.

129. Greenlee and Dunnell, "Identification of Fragmentary Bone," 968. Jon L. Gibson, *Poverty Point: A Terminal Late Archaic Culture of the Lower Mississippi Valley,* 2nd ed. (Louisiana Archaeological Survey and Antiquities Commission, 1999), 26.

130. Kidder offers a plausible estimate of the labor required to build Mound A, suggesting a minimum labor force of 1,019 individuals and, with a ratio of three dependents for every laborer, that would mean a minimum population of slightly more than 4,000 at Poverty Point for about a ninety-day period. Kidder, "Poverty Point," 466.

131. Gibson, *Ancient Mounds of Poverty Point,* 171–176.

132. Gibson offers a similar interpretation, suggesting that the anthropomorphic images and zoomorphic symbols are "charms and fetishes." Gibson, *Ancient Mounds of Poverty Point,* 187–193. But I prefer terms that have fewer negative connotations: *amulets* and *talismans.* See Theodore H. Gaster, "Amulets and Talismans," in Lindsay Jones, ed., *Encyclopedia of Religion,* 2nd ed. (Macmillan Reference, 2005), 1:297–301.

133. Gibson, *Ancient Mounds of Poverty Point,* 151–153.

134. On birds as divine figures, mythic characters, ritual components, dedicatory offerings, and status symbols at Paso de la Amada, see Katelyn Jo Bishop, "Food, Feathers, and Offerings: Early Formative Period Bird Exploitation at Paso de la Amada, Mexico," master's thesis, University of California, Los Angeles, 2014.

135. Gibson, *Ancient Mounds of Poverty Point,* 187–191.

136. Gibson, "Broken Circles, Owl Monsters, and Black Earth Midden," 26–30.

137. Gibson, "Broken Circles, Owl Monsters, and Black Earth Midden," 28–29.

138. Greenlee and Dunnell, "Identification of Fragmentary Bone," 968.

139. Anthony L. Ortmann and Tristram R. Kidder, "Building Mound A at Poverty Point, Louisiana: Monumental Public Architecture, Ritual Practice, and Implications for Hunter-Gatherer Complexity," *Geoarchaeology* 28.1 (2013): 66–86.

140. Kidder, "Poverty Point," 466–467.

141. Gibson, *Ancient Mounds of Poverty Point,* 83.

142. Kidder, "Poverty Point," 467.

143. S. Margaret Spivey, Tristram R. Kidder, Anthony L. Ortmann, and Lee J. Arco, "Pilgrimage to Poverty Point?," in Zackary I. Gilmore and Jason M. O'Donoughue, eds., *The Archaeology of Events: Cultural Change and Continuity in the Pre-Columbian Southeast* (University of Alabama Press, 2015), 141–159.

144. Lesure, "Platform Architecture and Activity Patterns in an Early Mesoamerican Village," 391–406. Pozorski and Pozorski, "Architecture and Chronology at the Site of Sechín Alto," 143–161.

Chapter 2. Farming Religion

1. On these rituals between 1050 and 1100, see Timothy R. Pauketat et al., "The Residues of Feasting and Public Ritual at Early Cahokia," *AA* 67.2 (2002): 257–279; Timothy R. Pauketat, *Cahokia: Ancient America's Great City on the Mississippi* (Penguin, 2009), 112. See also Julie Zimmermann Holt, "Rethinking the Ramey State: Was Cahokia the Center of a Theater State?" *AA* 74.2 (2009): 238–242.

2. Emile Durkheim, *The Elementary Forms of Religious Life,* trans. Karen E. Fields (Free Press, 1995), 216–225.

3. Aubrey Cannon and Dongya Y. Yang, "Early Storage and Sedentism on the Pacific Northwest Coast: Ancient DNA Analysis of the Salmon Remains from Namu, British Columbia," *AA* 71.1 (2006): 138; Dana Lepofsky et al., "Ancient Shellfish Mariculture on the Northwest Coast of North America," *AA* 80.2 (2015): 236–259. On maize agriculture in Ontario between 260 and 660 CE: G. W. Crawford, D. G. Smith, and F. E. Bowyer, "Dating the Entry of Corn (*Zea mays*) into the Lower Great Lakes Region," *AA* 62 (1997): 112–119.

4. Christopher T. Hays and Richard A. Weinstein ("Tchefuncte and Early Woodland") and Charles R. McGimsey ("Marksville and the Middle Woodland") in Mark A. Rees, ed., *Archaeology of Louisiana* (LSU Press, 2010), 97–119, 120–134. Tristram R. Kidder, "Climate Change and the Archaic to Woodland Transition (3000–2500 Cal. BP) in the Mississippi River Basin," *AA* 71.2 (2006): 203. J. Richard Shenkel, "An Early Marksville Burial Component in Southeastern Louisiana," *Midcontinental Journal of Archaeology* 9.1 (1984): 16–19.

5. Chip McGimsey, "The Rings of Marksville," *Southeastern Archaeology* 22.1 (2003): 47–62. Caves and sinkholes continued to be used for mortuary rituals: G. Crothers and P. Willey, "Mortuary Caves and Sinkholes in the Interior Low Plateaus and South Appalachian Mountains of the Eastern United States," in William Blaine White, ed., *Proceedings of the Fifteenth International Congress of Speleology,* vol. 1 (International Congress of Speleology, 2009), 74–79.

6. *Mesoamerica* refers to a cultural area that includes the southern two-thirds of Mexico, Guatemala, Belize, El Salvador, and parts of Honduras, Nicaragua, and Costa Rica. Davíd Carrasco, *Religions of Mesoamerica: Cosmovision and Ceremonial Centers* (Harper and Row, 1990), 1. On the 170 years of relative climatic stability, see Shirley Powell and Francis E. Smiley, eds., *Prehistoric Culture Change on the Colorado Plateau: Ten Thousand Years on Black Mesa* (University of Arizona Press, 2002), 66–67.

7. Dorothy K. Washburn, "Shared Image Metaphors of the Corn Lifeway in Mesoamerica and the American Southwest," *JAR* 68 (2012): 473–502.

8. Tony McMichael, *Human Frontiers, Environments, and Disease: Past Patterns, Uncertain Futures* (Cambridge University Press, 2001), 101.

9. Dylan M. Schwindt et al., "The Social Consequences of Climate Change in the Central Mesa Verde Region," *AA* 81.1 (2016): 74–96; Donna M. Glowacki, *Living*

and Leaving: A Social History of Regional Depopulation in Thirteenth-Century Mesa Verde (University of Arizona Press. 2015).

10. Christopher Carr, "Salient Issues in the Social and Political Organizations of North Hopewellian Peoples: Contextualizing, Personalizing, and Generating Hopewell," in Christopher Carr and D. Troy Case, eds., *Gathering Hopewell: Society, Ritual, and Ritual Interaction* (Springer, 2006), 75–76. Bret J. Ruby, Christopher Carr, and Douglas K. Charles, "Community Organizations in the Scioto, Mann, and Havana Regions," in Carr and Case, *Gathering Hopewell,* 119–176. Margaret M. Bender, David A. Baerreis, and Raymond L. Steventon, "Further Light on Carbon Isotopes and Hopewell Agriculture," *AA* 46.2 (1981): 346–353. Bruce D. Smith, "*Chenopodium berlandieri* ssp. *Jonesianum:* Evidence for a Hopewellian Domesticate from Ash Cave, Ohio," *Southeastern Archaeology* 4.2 (1985): 107–133. Scholars think that squash came first, then maize, and finally beans, the staples at the time of European contact.

11. Bretton T. Giles, "A Contextual and Iconographic Reassessment of the Headdress on Burial 11 from Hopewell Mound 25," *AA* 78.3 (2013): 503.

12. Douglas K. Charles, "Colorful Practices in Hopewellian Earthwork Construction," *Anthropology and Aesthetics* 61/62 (2012): 343–352.

13. Christopher Carr, "The Tripartite Ceremonial Alliance among Scioto Hopewellian Communities and the Question of Social Ranking," in Carr and Case, *Gathering Hopewell,* 258–338.

14. On Mound 25: Carr, "Tripartite Ceremonial Alliance among Scioto Hopewellian Communities," 300–307; Giles, "Contextual and Iconographic Reassessment of the Headdress on Burial 11," 503. On Hopewellian practices, see also N'omi B. Greber and Katharine C. Ruhl, *The Hopewell Site: A Contemporary Analysis Based on the Work of Charles C. Willoughby* (Westview, 1989); A. Martin Byers and DeeAnne Wymer, eds., *Hopewell Settlement Patterns, Subsistence, and Symbolic Landscapes* (University Press of Florida, 2010).

15. The chronological range I give for Mound 25 includes one of the earliest and latest dates proposed: Carr, "Tripartite Ceremonial Alliance among Scioto Hopewellian Communities," 306. Lisa Mills, "Mitochondrial DNA Analysis of the Ohio Hopewell of the Hopewell Mound Group," PhD diss., Ohio State University, 2003, 21–22. The Edict of Thessalonica in 380 established Christianity as the official religion of the Roman Empire.

16. They had four of the five mtDNA haplotypes found among the First Peoples of the Americas: Mills, "Mitochondrial DNA Analysis of the Ohio Hopewell," iii, 124.

17. Cooperation and competition: Carr, "Tripartite Ceremonial Alliance among Scioto Hopewellian Communities," 324–325; Matthew S. Coon, "Variation in Ohio Hopewell Political Economies," *AA* 74.1 (2009): 49–76.

18. Chad Thomas, Christopher Carr, and Cynthia Keller, "Animal-Totemic Clans of the Ohio Hopewellian Peoples," in Carr and Case, *Gathering Hopewell,* 339–385.

19. Cynthia Keller and Christopher Carr, "Gender, Role, Prestige, and Ritual Interaction across the Ohio, Mann, and Havana Hopewellian Regions, as Evidenced by Ceramic Figurines," in Carr and Case, *Gathering Hopewell,* 457.

20. Cherly Claassen, "Rock Shelters as Women's Retreats: Understanding Newt Kash," *AA* 76.4 (2011): 628–641. Cheryl Claassen, *Beliefs and Rituals in Archaic Eastern North America: An Interpretive Guide* (University of Alabama Press, 2015), 100–101.

21. Stephanie Field, Anne J. Goldberg, and Tina Lee, "Gender, Status, and Ethnicity in the Scioto, Miami, and Northeastern Ohio Hopewellian Regions, as Evidenced by Mortuary Practices," in Carr and Case, *Gathering Hopewell,* 397.

22. Field, Goldberg, and Lee, "Gender, Status, and Ethnicity in the Scioto, Miami, and Northeastern Ohio Hopewellian Regions," 397. H. C. Shetrone, "Explorations of the Hopewell Group of Prehistoric Earthworks," *Ohio Archaeological and Historical Quarterly* 35 (1926): 72, 189.

23. Helaine Silverman, *Cahuachi in the Ancient Nasca World* (University of Iowa Press, 1993), 300–319; Kevin J. Vaughn, "Households, Crafts, and Feasting in the Ancient Andes: The Village Context of Early Nasca Craft Consumption," *Latin America Antiquity* 15.1 (2004): 67–68, 80–81. Field, Goldberg, and Lee, "Gender, Status, and Ethnicity in the Scioto, Miami, and Northeastern Ohio Hopewellian Regions," 391. Flutes and panpipes as "definitely shamanic": Christopher Carr and D. Troy Case, "The Nature of Leadership in Ohio Hopewellian Societies: Role Segregation and the Transformation from Shamanism," in Carr and Case, *Gathering Hopewell,* 206–207.

24. Gina M. Turff and Christopher Carr, "Hopewellian Panpipes from Eastern North America: Their Social, Ritual, and Symbolic Significance," in Carr and Case, *Gathering Hopewell,* 653–654. See also Robert L. Hall, *An Archaeology of the Soul: North American Indian Belief and Ritual* (University of Illinois Press, 1997), 115–118.

25. Carr and Case, "Nature of Leadership in Ohio Hopewellian Societies," 237n28.

26. Thomas, Carr, and Keller, "Animal-Totemic Clans of the Ohio Hopewellian Peoples," 374–375. On shamans' role in corpse preparation: Amanda Jo Thompson and Kathryn A. Jakes, "Textile Evidence for Ohio Hopewell Burial Practices," *Southeastern Archaeology* 24.2 (Winter 2005): 137, 140.

27. Field, Goldberg, and Lee, "Gender, Status, and Ethnicity in the Scioto, Miami, and Northeastern Ohio Hopewellian Regions," 396–398.

28. A drawing of the antler headdress appeared in Warren K. Moorehead, *Primitive Man in Ohio* (G. P. Putnam's Sons, 1892), frontispiece.

29. On headdresses as symbols for high-status males: Coon, "Variation in Ohio Hopewell Political Economies," 61–66.

30. Warren K. Moorehead, *The Hopewell Mound Group of Ohio* (Field Museum of Natural History, 1922), 107–108.

31. See Shetrone, "Explorations of the Hopewell Group of Prehistoric Earthworks," 68–72; Giles, "A Contextual and Iconographic Reassessment of the Headdress on Burial 11," 503–507.

32. Giles, "A Contextual and Iconographic Reassessment of the Headdress on Burial 11," 504–505.

33. Stephen H. Lekson, *A History of the Ancient Southwest* (School for Advanced Research, 2008), 1–31.

34. Frank H. H. Roberts Jr., *Shabik'eshchee Village: A Late Basketmaker Site in the Chaco Canyon, New Mexico,* Smithsonian Institution, Bureau of American Ethnology,

Bulletin 92 (GPO, 1929); W. H. Wills and Thomas C. Windes, "Evidence for Population Aggregation and Dispersal during the Basketmaker III Period in Chaco Canyon, New Mexico," *AA* 54.2 (1989): 347–369; W. H. Wills, F. Scott Worman, Wetherbee Dorshow, and Heather Richards-Rissetto, "Shabik'eschee Village in Chaco Canyon: Beyond the Archetype," *AA* 77.2 (2012): 326–350; Lekson, *Ancient Southwest*, 65–68.

35. The village name: Chaco Research Archive, http://www.chacoarchive.org/cra/chaco-sites/shabikeshchee/. On burials: Roberts, *Shabik'eshchee Village*, 143–144.

36. Wills and Windes, "Population Aggregation and Dispersal," 363. Lekson, *Ancient Southwest*, 67.

37. W. H. Wills, "Pithouse Architecture and the Economics of Household Formation in the Prehistoric American Southwest," *Human Ecology* 29.4 (2001): 494. On the challenge of finding children in the record: Kathryn A. Kamp, "Where Have All the Children Gone? The Archaeology of Childhood," *Journal of Archaeological Method and Theory* 8.1 (2001): 2, 5–8, 14–15.

38. Roberts, *Shabik'eshchee Village*, 26–34.

39. Roberts, *Shabik'eshchee Village*, 73–81.

40. On whistles and ornaments: Roberts, *Shabik'eshchee Village*, 132, 142.

41. James D. Farmer, "Iconographic Evidence of Basketmaker Warfare and Human Sacrifice: A Contextual Approach to Early Anasazi Art," *Kiva* 62.4 (1997): 399. Campbell Grant, *Canyon de Chelly: Its People and Rock Art* (University of Arizona Press, 1978).

42. Farmer, "Iconographic Evidence of Basketmaker Warfare and Human Sacrifice." Nancy Marie White and Richard A. Weinstein, "The Mexican Connection and the Far West of the U.S. Southeast," *AA* 73.2 (2008): 228.

43. Moorehead, *Hopewell Mound Group*, 124–125, plate 67. Thomas Wilson, *The Swastika: The Earliest Known Symbol, and Its Migrations; with Observations on Certain Industries in Pre-historic Times* (Smithsonian Institution, 1896), 888–894.

44. Asko Parpola, *The Roots of Hinduism: The Early Aryans and the Indus Civilization* (Oxford University Press, 2015), vii, 286. "Svaskita," in Robert E. Buswell Jr. and Donald S. Lopez Jr., eds., *The Princeton Dictionary of Buddhism* (Princeton University Press, 2013), 882.

45. Alexander Statman, "Fusang: The Enlightenment Story of the Chinese Discovery of America," *Isis* 107.1 (2016): 1–25. Charles G. Leland, *Fusang; Or, the Discovery of America by Chinese Buddhist Priests in the Fifth Century* (Trübner, 1875), v–viii, 25–29, 110–120.

46. George E. Langford, "The Swirl-Cross and the Center," in George E. Lankford, F. Kent Reilly, and James Garber, eds., *Visualizing the Sacred: Cosmic Visions, Regionalism, and the Art of the Mississippian World* (University of Texas Press, 2011), 272. Wilson, *Swastika*, 981–983. Jerryl Moreno, "Petroglyphs of Lake Pleasant Regional Park," *Kiva* 68.3 (2003): 193, 195, 201. Jon Bernard Marcoux, "On Reconsidering Display Goods Production and Circulation in the Moundville Chiefdom," *Southeastern Archaeology* 26.2 (2007): 232–245. Polly Schaafsma, *Indian Rock Art of the Southwest* (School of American Research, 1980), 92, 156.

47. Patrick V. Kirch, "Peopling of the Pacific: A Holistic Anthropological Perspective," *ARA* 39 (2010): 131.

48. Helene Martinsson-Wallin, Paul Wallin, and Geoffrey Clark, "The Excavation of the Pulemelei Site, 2002–2004," *Archaeology in Oceania* 42 (2007): 41–59. Paul Wallin and Helene Martinsson-Wallin, "Settlement Patterns—Social and Ritual Space in Prehistoric Samoa," *Archaeology in Oceania* 42 (2007): 83–89. David J. Herdrich, "Towards an Understanding of Samoan Star Mounds," *Journal of the Polynesian Society* 100.4 (1991): 381–435. On dating sites in Tonga and Samoa: Jeffrey T. Clark et al., "Refining the Chronology for West Polynesian Colonization: New Data from the Samoan Archipelago," *Journal of Archaeological Science: Reports* 6 (2016): 266–274; Fiona Petchey and Patrick Kirch, "The Importance of Shell: Redating of the To'aga Site (Ofu Island, Manu'a) and a Revised Chronology for the Lapita to Polynesian Plainware Transition in Tonga and Samoa," *PloS One* 14.9 (2019): e0211990–e0211990, https://doi.org/10.1371/journal.pone.0211990.

49. Paul Rainbird, "Pacific and New Zealand," in Timothy Insoll, ed., *The Oxford Handbook of the Archaeology of Ritual and Religion* (Oxford University Press, 2011), 510.

50. On the reasons for dispersal: David A. Sear et al., "Human Settlement of East Polynesia Earlier, Incremental, and Coincident with Prolonged South Pacific Drought," *PNAS* 117.16 (2020): 8813–8819. On the settlement chronology: Jennifer G. Kahn et al., "Settlement Chronologies and Shifting Resource Exploitation in Ka'ū District, Hawaiian Islands," *Asian Perspectives* 55.2 (2016): 184–207. Marshall I. Weisler et al., "Dry, Leeward Regions Support Colonization Period Sites: Stratigraphy, Dating, and Geomorphological Setting of One of the Earliest Habitations in the Hawaiian Islands," *Journal of Island and Coastal Archaeology* (2023): 1–33, https://doi.org/10.1080/15564894.2023.2165200. Thomas S. Dye, "A Model-Based Age Estimate for Polynesian Colonization of Hawai'i," *Archaeology in Oceania* 46.3 (2011): 130–138. Janet M. Wilmshurst et al., "High-Precision Radiocarbon Dating Shows Recent and Rapid Initial Human Colonization of East Polynesia," *PNAS* 108.5 (2011): 1815–1820. The terminology to refer to Hawaiians is contested. The terms debated include *kānaka*, Hawaiian, *Kānaka 'Ōiwi, Kānaka Maoli,* and Native/Indigenous/Aboriginal Hawaiian. I use those terms and often use Hawaiian, or Indigenous Hawaiian, to refer to ethnic Hawaiians with any degree of ancestry. See Ty P. Kāwika Tengan, *Native Men Remade: Gender and Nation in Contemporary Hawai'i* (Duke University Press, 2008), xii–xiii. See also "A Note to Readers" in J. Kēhaulani Kauanui, *Hawaiian Blood: Colonialism and the Politics of Sovereignty and Indigeneity* (Duke University Press, 2008), xi–xii.

51. Dye and Pantaleo suggest the site was established between 1040 and 1219 CE: Thomas S. Dye and Jeffrey Pantaleo, "Age of the O18 Site, Hawai'i," *Archaeology and Physical Anthropology in Oceania* 45.3 (2010): 113. See also H. David Tuggle and Matthew Spriggs, "The Age of the Bellows Dune Site O18, O'ahu, Hawai'i, and the Antiquity of Hawaiian Colonization," *Asian Perspectives* 39.1–2 (2000): 165–188. Richard J. Pearson, Patrick Vinton Kirch, and Michael Pietrusewsky, "An Early Prehistoric Site at Bellows Beach, Waimanalo, Oahu, Hawaiian Islands," *Archaeology and*

Physical Anthropology in Oceania 6.3 (1971): 214. Patrick Vinton Kirch, *Feathered Gods and Fishhooks: An Introduction to Hawaiian Archaeology and Prehistory* (University of Hawai'i Press, 1985), 237.

52. Pearson, Kirch, and Pietrusewsky, "Early Prehistoric Site at Bellows Beach."

53. Tuggle and Spriggs, "Age of the Bellows Dune Site O18, O'ahu, Hawai'i," 167, 182. Pearson, Kirch, and Pietrusewsky, "Early Prehistoric Site at Bellows Beach," 211, 214.

54. Alice A. Storey et al., "Radiocarbon and DNA Evidence for a Pre-Columbian Introduction of Polynesian Chickens to Chile," *PNAS* 104.25 (2007): 10335–10339.

55. Caroline Roullier et al., "Historical Collections Reveal Patterns of Diffusion of Sweet Potato in Oceania Obscured by Modern Plant Movements and Recombination," *PNAS* 110.6 (2013): 2205–2010. Terry L. Jones et al., eds., *Polynesians in America: Precolumbian Contacts with the New World* (Altamira, 2011). R. C. Green, "A Range of Disciplines Support a Dual Origin for the Bottle Gourd in the Pacific," *Journal of the Polynesian Society* 109.2 (2000): 191–197. Andrew Christopher Clarke, "Origins and Dispersal of the Sweet Potato and Bottle Gourd in Oceania: Implications for Prehistoric Human Mobility," PhD diss., Massey University, New Zealand, 2009, v, 258.

56. Terry L. Jones and Kathryn A. Klar, "Diffusionism Reconsidered: Linguistic and Archaeological Evidence for Prehistoric Polynesian Contact with Southern California," *AA* 70.3 (2005): 457–484. Terry L. Jones and Kathryn A. Klar, "On Linguistics and Cascading Inventions: A Comment on Arnold's Dismissal of a Polynesian Contact Event in Southern California," *AA* 74.1 (2009): 173–182.

57. On Hawaiian deities (*akua*) and their powers (*mana*), as well as the primary gods (Kū, Kāne, Kanaloa, and Lono): Valerio Valeri, *Kingship and Sacrifice: Ritual and Society in Ancient Hawaii* (University of Chicago Press, 1985), 15, 43, 177–179.

58. Adrienne L. Kaeppler, "Genealogy and Disrespect: A Study of Symbolism in Hawaiian Images," *Anthropology and Aesthetics* 3 (1982): 94.

59. Katharine Luomala and Malcolm Nāea Chun, "Hawaiian Religion," in Lindsay Jones, ed., *Encyclopedia of Religion*, 2nd ed. (Macmillan Reference, 2005), 3798.

60. Glyn S. Burgess and Clara Strijbosch, eds., *The Brendan Legend: Texts and Versions* (Brill, 2006).

61. "Special Section: New Horizons in the Archaeology of the Viking Age," *SAA Archaeological Record* 18.3 (2018): 10–38. Eric Cambridge and Jane Hawkins, eds., *Crossing Boundaries: Interdisciplinary Approaches to the Art, Material Culture, Language, and Literature of the Early Medieval World* (Oxbow Books, 2017). Zanette T. Glørstad and Kjetil Loftsgarden, eds., *Viking Age Transformations: Trade, Craft, and Resources in Western Scandinavia* (Routledge, 2017).

62. J. R. S. Phillips, *The Medieval Expansion of Europe* (Oxford University Press, 1988). Angus A. Somerville and R. Andrew McDonald, eds., *The Viking Age: A Reader* (University of Toronto Press, 2010).

63. Judith Jesch, *The Viking Diaspora* (Routledge: London, 2015). Amin Tibi, "The Vikings in Arabic Sources," *Islamic Studies* 35.2 (1996): 212. Paul Lunde and Caroline Stone, eds., *Ibn Fadlan and the Land of Darkness: Arab Travelers in the Far*

North (Penguin, 2012). Neil S. Price, "Bodylore and the Archaeology of Embedded Religion: Dramatic License in the Funerals of the Vikings," in David S. Whitley and Kelley Hays-Gilpin, eds., *Belief in the Past: Theoretical Approaches to the Archaeology of Religion* (Left Coast Press, 2008), 153–156. Adam of Bremen's references to Iceland, Greenland, and "Vinland" are found in his *Gesta Hammaburgensis ecclesiae pontificum* (1075). Adam of Bremen, *History of the Archbishops of Hamburg-Bremen* (Columbia University Press, 2002), 216–220. There are multiple editions of the Icelandic sagas, including *Grænlendinga Saga* and *Erik's Saga.* See Magnus Magnusson and Hermann Pálsson, trans., *The Vinland Sagas: The Norse Discovery of America* (Penguin, 1965).

64. Kristian A. Seaver, *The Frozen Echo: Greenland and the Exploration of North America, ca. A.D. 1000–1500* (Stanford University Press, 1996), 14–43, 91–112. Joel Berglund, "The Decline of the Norse Settlements in Greenland," *Arctic Anthropology* 23.1–2 (1986): 109–135. Mario DiBacco et al., "The Effect of an Unbalanced Demographic Structure on Marriage and Fertility Patterns in Isolated Populations: The Case of Norse Settlements in Greenland," *Genus* 62.1 (2006): 99–100. Economically driven: Christian Keller, "Furs, Fish, and Ivory: Medieval Norseman at the Arctic Fringe," *Journal of the North Atlantic* 3 (2010): 1–23.

65. Thomas H. McGovern et al., "Landscapes of Settlement in Northern Iceland: Historical Ecology of Human Impact and Climate Fluctuation on the Millennial Scale," *American Anthropologist* 109.1 (2007): 32–37. Orri Vésteinsson, *The Christianization of Iceland: Priests, Power, and Social Change, 1000–1300* (Oxford University Press, 2000).

66. For a translation of this episode from *Eiríks saga rauða,* see Somerville and McDonald, *Viking Age,* 90–92.

67. Adam of Bremen, *History of the Archbishops of Hamburg-Bremen,* 216–220.

68. Claire Cavaleri, "The Vinland Sagas as Propaganda for the Christian Church: Freydís and Gudrid as Paradigms for Eve and the Virgin Mary," master's thesis, University of Oslo, 2008, 70–71.

69. Deborah Sabo and George Sabo III, "A Possible Thule Carving of a Viking from Baffin Island, N.W.T.," *Canadian Journal of Archaeology* 2 (1978): 33–42. Seaver, *Frozen Echo,* 39–41.

70. Todd J. Kristensen and Jenneth E. Curtis, "Late Holocene Hunter-Gatherers at L'Anse aux Meadows and the Dynamics of Bird and Mammal Hunting in Newfoundland," *Arctic Anthropology* 49.1 (2012): 68–87.

71. Helge Ingstad and Anne Stine Ingstad, *The Viking Discovery of America: The Excavation of a Norse Settlement in L'Anse aux Meadows, Newfoundland* (Checkmark Books, 2001). Some argue Norse activity at the base camp lasted longer, if sporadically, and there is evidence of activity in 1021. Further, Greenland Vikings might have continued to visit the camp and sites further south as they imported North American timber between 1100 and 1400. Paul M. Ledger et al., "New Horizons at L'Anse aux Meadows," *PNAS* 116.31 (2019): 15341–15343. Margot Kuitems et al., "Evidence for European Presence in the Americas in AD 1021," *Nature* 601 (2022): 388–391. Lísabet

Guðmundsdóttir, "Timber Imports to Norse Greenland: Lifeline or Luxury?," *Antiquity* 97.392 (2023): 466–468.

72. Ingstad and Ingstad, *Viking Discovery of America*, 148–158.

73. B. J. Bourque and S. L. Cox, "Maine State Museum Investigation of the Goddard Site, 1979," *Man in the Northeast* 22 (1981): 20–24. Robert W. Park, "Contact between the Norse Vikings and the Dorset Culture in Arctic Canada," *Antiquity* 82 (2008): 192. Ingeborg Marshall, *A History and Ethnography of the Beothuk* (McGill–Queen's University Press, 1996), 261–263. Svein H. Gullbekk, "The Norse Penny Reconsidered: The Goddard Coin—Hoax or Genuine?," *Journal of the North Atlantic* 33 (2017): 1–8. This coin found a few hundred miles south of the Norse camp suggests the Vikings might have made southward excursions; so does the presence of white walnuts (*Juglans cinerea*) in the Norse camp. See Birgitta Linderoth Wallace, "L'Anse aux Meadows and Vinland: An Abandoned Experiment," in James H. Barrett, ed., *Contact, Continuity, and Collapse* (Brepols, 2003), 207–238.

74. "Leif the Discoverer: The Erikson Statue Unveiled by the Boston Scandinavians," *New York Times*, 20 October 1887. David M. Krueger, *Myths of the Rune Stone: Viking Martyrs and the Birthplace of America* (University of Minnesota Press, 2015).

75. Peter Jackson with David Morgan, trans., *The Mission of Friar William of Rubruk: His Journey to the Court of the Great Khan Möngke, 1253–1255* (Hackett, 2009), 226–235.

76. Michael Mann et al., "Global Signatures and Dynamical Origins of the Little Ice Age and Medieval Climate Anomaly," *Science* 326.5957 (27 November 2009): 1256–1260. Frederick Carpenter Ljundqvist, "A New Reconsideration of Temperature Variability in the Extra-Tropical Northern Hemisphere during the Last Two Millennia," *Geografiska Annaler* 92.3 (2010): 339–351. Raymond S. Bradley, Malcolm K. Hughes, and Henry F. Diaz, "Climate in Medieval Time," *Science* 302.5644 (17 October 2003): 404–405. Valérie Trouet et al., "Persistent Positive North Atlantic Oscillation Mode Dominated the Medieval Climate Anomaly," *Science* 324.5923 (2 April 2009): 79–80. Terry L. Jones et al., "The Morro Bay Fauna: Evidence for a Medieval Droughts Refugium on the Central California Coast," *AA* 82.2 (2017): 217.

77. L. Antonio Curet and Lisa M. Stringer, eds., *Tibes: People, Power, and Ritual at the Center of the Cosmos* (University of Alabama Press, 2010).

78. A. Katharine Patton and James M. Savelle, "The Symbolic Dimensions of Whale Bone Use in Thule Winter Dwellings," *Études/Inuit/Studies* 30.2 (2006): 137–161. T. Max Friesen and Charles D. Arnold, "The Timing of the Thule Migration: New Dates from the Western Canadian Arctic," *AA* 73.3 (2008): 527–538. J. E. Arnold, *The Origins of a Pacific Coast Chiefdom: The Chumash of the Channel Islands* (University of Utah Press, 2001).

79. Dan M. Healan, "The Archaeology of Tula, Hidalgo, Mexico," *JAR* 20.1 (2012): 55, 59–61, 100–101. Alba Guadalupe Mastache and Robert H. Cobean, "Ancient Tollan: The Sacred Precinct," *Anthropology and Aesthetics* 38 (2000): 100–133. Michael E. Smith and Katharine J. Schreiber, "New World States and Empires: Politics, Religion, and Urbanism," *JAR* 14.1 (2006): 1–52.

80. Lekson, *Ancient Southwest,* 122–132.

81. Specialists disagree about Chaco's corn production: Larry V. Benson, "Factors Controlling Pre-Columbian and Early Historic Maize Productivity in the American Southwest, Part 2: The Chaco Halo, Mesa Verde, Pajarito Plateau/Bandelier, and Zuni Archaeological Regions," *Journal of Archaeological Method and Theory* 18 (2011): 61–109.

82. Chaco's political organization, which was mediated by the priestly elites' great house network, depended on "reciprocal exchange" of prestige goods and services: Timothy Earle, "Economic Support of Chaco Canyon Society," *AA* 66.1 (2001): 26–35.

83. Lekson, *Ancient Southwest,* 123.

84. Lekson, *Ancient Southwest,* 127.

85. Ryan P. Harrod, "Centers of Control: Revealing Elites among the Ancestral Pueblo during the 'Chaco Phenomenon,'" *International Journal of Paleopathology* 2 (2002): 124.

86. On the flow between Mesa Verde and Chaco: Catherine M. Cameron, "Exploring Archaeological Cultures in the Northern Southwest: What Were Chaco and Mesa Verde?" *Kiva* 70.3 (2005): 227–253.

87. Catherine M. Cameron and Andrew I. Duff, "History and Process in Village Formation: Context and Contrasts from the Northern Southwest," *AA* 73.1 (2008): 33–37. Stephen H. Lekson, "Chaco's Hinterlands," in Timothy Pauketat, ed., *The Oxford Handbook of North American Archaeology* (Oxford University Press, 2012), 597–607.

88. I borrow "foot-driven" from Lekson, "Chaco's Hinterlands," 602.

89. Ruth M. Van Dyke et al., "Great Houses, Shrines, and High Places: Intervisibility in the Chacoan World," *AA* 81.2 (2016): 205–230.

90. Randall H. McGuire, "The Mesoamerican Connection in the Southwest," *Kiva* 46.1–2 (1980): 19, 28, 31; Dorothy K. Washburn, "Pattern Symmetries of the Chaco Phenomenon," *AA* 76.2 (2011): 264–269, 277–278. On copper bells' religious uses: Scott E. Simmons and Aaron N. Shugar, "Archaeometallurgy in Ancient Mesoamerica," in Scott E. Simmons and Aaron N. Shugar, eds., *Archaeometallurgy in Mesoamerica: Current Approaches and New Perspectives* (University Press of Colorado, 2013), 2–13.

91. Washburn, "Pattern Symmetries of the Chaco Phenomenon," 278. The "corn lifeway": Washburn, "Shared Imaged Metaphors of the Corn Lifeway," 473–496.

92. Carrasco, *Religions of Mesoamerica,* 99–100.

93. Stephen Plog and Carrie Heitman, "Hierarchy and Social Inequity in the American Southwest, A.D. 800–1200," *PNAS* 107.46 (2010): 19619–19626.

94. James D. Farmer, "Astronomy and Ritual in Chaco Canyon," in Jill E. Neitzel, ed., *Pueblo Bonito: Center of the Chacoan World* (Smithsonian Books, 2003), 61–71.

95. Farmer, "Astronomy and Ritual in Chaco Canyon," 69–71.

96. Jill E. Neitzel, "Three Questions about Pueblo Bonito," in *Pueblo Bonito,* 1. The estimate of person hours: Mary P. Metcalf, "Construction Labor at Pueblo Bonito," in *Pueblo Bonito,* 76.

97. Lekson, *Ancient Southwest,* 235. John R. Stein, Dabney Ford, and Richard Friedman, "Reconstructing Pueblo Bonito," in Neitzel, *Pueblo Bonito* 59; Colin Renfrew, "Production and Consumption in a Sacred Economy: The Material Correlates of High Devotional Expression at Chaco Canyon," *AA* 66.1 (2001): 14–25. On pilgrimage's social costs: John Kanter and Kevin J. Vaughn, "Pilgrimage as Costly Signal: Religiously Motivated Cooperation in Chaco and Nasca," *Journal of Anthropological Archaeology* 31 (2012): 66–82. On challenges to claims that Chaco was a large pilgrimage center: Stephen Plog and Adam S. Watson, "The Chaco Pilgrimage Model: Evaluating the Evidence from Pueblo Alto," *AA* 77.3 (2012): 449–477.

98. Carrasco, *Religions of Mesoamerica,* 98–103. W. H. Wills, "On the Trail of the Lonesome Pine: Archaeological Paradigms and the Chaco 'Tree of Life,'" *AA* 77.3 (2012): 478–497. Stein, Ford, and Friedman, "Reconstructing Pueblo Bonito," 44–46.

99. Nancy J. Akins, "The Burials of Pueblo Bonito," in Neitzel, *Pueblo Bonito,* 94. Plog and Heitman, "Hierarchy and Social Inequity in the American Southwest."

100. On the dating of Burial 13 and Burial 14: Plog and Heitman, "Hierarchy and Social Inequity in the American Southwest."

101. Atkins, "Burials of Pueblo Bonito," 97. Harrod, "Centers of Control," 125.

102. Keith W. Kintigh, Todd L. Howell, and Andrew I. Duff, "Post-Chacoan Social Integration at the Hinkson Site, New Mexico," *Kiva* 61.3 (1996): 257–274. Benson, "Factors Controlling Pre-Columbian and Early Historic Maize Productivity in the American Southwest," 63.

103. Cameron, "Exploring Archaeological Cultures in the Northern Southwest," 231–246.

104. Donna M. Glowacki, "The Social and Cultural Contexts of the Central Mesa Verde Region during the Thirteenth-Century Migrations," in Timothy A. Kohler, Mark D. Varien, and Aaron M. Wright, eds., *Leaving Mesa Verde: Peril and Change in the Thirteenth-Century Southwest* (University of Arizona Press, 2010), 200–221; Donna M. Glowacki, "The Role of Religion in the Depopulation of the Central Mesa Verde Region," in Donna M. Glowacki and S. Van Keuren, eds., *Religious Transformation in the Late Pre-Hispanic Pueblo World* (University of Arizona Press, 2011), 66–83.

105. Glowacki, "Social and Cultural Contexts," 217–219; Glowacki, "Role of Religion," 66–78, 71–72; Glowacki, *Living and Leaving,* chap. 7.

106. Glowacki, "Role of Religion," 68–72. Bruce Bradley, "Pitchers to Mugs: Chacoan Revival at Sand Canyon Pueblo," *Kiva* 74.2 (2008): 247–262. Schwindt et al., "Social Consequences of Climate Change," 92.

107. Kintigh, Howell, and Duff, "Post-Chacoan Social Integration at the Hinkson Site," 257–274; Catherine M. Cameron and Andrew I. Duff, "History and Process in Village Formation: Context and Contrasts from the Northern Southwest," *AA* 73.1 (2008): 43–49.

108. On Pueblo stories and scholars' descriptions: Severin Fowles, "The Pueblo Village in an Age of Reformation (AD 1300–1600)," in Pauketat, *Oxford Handbook,* 638–641.

109. The new religious movement: Susan M. Alt, "The Implications of the Religious Foundations at Cahokia," in Ryan Parish and Charles H. McNutt, eds., *Cahokia in Context: Hegemony and Diaspora* (University Press of Florida, 2019), 32–48. As in Mesoamerica, they apparently performed ritual killing as payments of debts and expressions of gratitude to the gods. See Davíd Carrasco, "Human Sacrifice/Debt Payments from the Aztec Point of View," in Davíd Carrasco, ed., *The History of the Conquest of New Spain by Bernal Díaz del Castillo* (University of New Mexico Press, 2009), 458–460.

110. Thomas E. Emerson et al., "Paradigms Lost? Reconfiguring Cahokia's Mound 72 Beaded Burial," *AA* 81.3 (2016): 407, 417–418.

111. H. H. Brackenridge, *On the Population and Tumuli of the Aborigines of North America: In a Letter to Thomas Jefferson from H. H. Brackenridge . . .* (American Philosophical Society, 1813).

112. Larry V. Benson, Timothy R. Pauketat, and Edward R. Cook, "Cahokia's Boom and Bust in the Context of Climate Change," *AA* 74.3 (2009): 467–483.

113. Sarah E. Baires, *Land of Water, City of the Dead: Religion and Cahokia's Emergence* (University of Alabama Press, 2017). Alt, "Implications of the Religious Foundations at Cahokia."

114. Shawn P. Lambert and Paige A. Ford, "Understanding the Rise of Complexity at Cahokia: Evidence of Nonlocal Caddo Ceramic Specialists in the East St. Louis Precinct," *AA* 88.3 (2023): 361–385. Timothy R. Pauketat, "Resettled Farmers and the Making of a Mississippian Polity," *AA* 68.1 (2003): 39–66.

115. Andrew Lawler, "America's Lost City," *Science* 334.23 (2011): 1618, 1622. On Mound 72 and Monks Mound as pilgrimage sites: John E. Kelly and James A. Brown, "In Search of Cosmic Power: Contextualizing Spiritual Journeys between Cahokia and the St. Francois Mountains," in Kathryn Rountree, Christine Morris, and Alan A. D. Peatfield, eds., *Archaeology of Spiritualities* (Springer, 2012), 107–129. See also William Iseminger, *Cahokia Mounds: America's First City* (History Press, 2010).

116. Cahokia's comparative size: Lawler, "America's Lost City," 1622.

117. Rinita A. Dalan et al., *Envisioning Cahokia: A Landscape Perspective* (Northern Illinois University Press, 2003), 125–133.

118. James Brown, "On the Identity of the Birdman within Mississippian Period Art and Iconography," in F. Kent Reilly III and James F. Garber, eds., *Ancient Objects and Sacred Realms: Interpretations of Mississippian Iconography* (University of Texas, 2007), 56–106.

119. Some suggest the killed women were captives: Kathryn M. Koziol, "Violence, Symbols, and the Archaeological Record: A Case Study of Cahokia's Mound 72," PhD diss., University of Albany, 2002, 241–246.

120. Hall, *Archaeology of the Soul,* 171. Pauketat, *Cahokia: Ancient America's Great City,* 148. Alice Beck Kehoe, "Wind Jewels and Paddling Gods: The Mississippian Southeast in the Postclassic Mesoamerican World," in N. M. White, ed., *Gulf Coast Archaeology: The Southeastern United States and Mexico* (University Press of Florida, 2005), 260–280.

121. Melvin L. Fowler et al., *The Mound 72 Area: Dedicated and Sacred Space in Early Cahokia* (Illinois State Museum Society, 1999), 3.

122. Emerson et al., "Paradigms Lost?," 405, 413, 416. Fowler et al., *Mound 72 Area*, 167–189. James A. Brown, "The Archaeology of Ancient Religion in the Eastern Woodlands," *ARA* 26 (1997): 465–485.

123. Emerson et al., "Paradigms Lost?," 411–412, 418–422.

124. Emerson et al., "Paradigms Lost?," 421.

125. Thomas E. Emerson, "Interpreting Context and Chronology of Cahokia-Caddo Mythic Female Stone Figures," *Southeastern Archaeology* 41.4 (2022): 203–215.

126. Emerson et al., "Paradigms Lost?," 407. For another interpretation, see James A. Brown, "The Cahokia Mound 72Sub1 Burials as Collective Representation," *Wisconsin Archeologist* 84 (2003): 81–97.

127. Kanter and Vaughn, "Pilgrimage as Costly Signal," 78.

128. George E. Langford, "The 'Path of Souls': Some Death Imagery in the Southeastern Ceremonial Complex," in Reilly and Garber, *Ancient Objects*, 174–212.

129. Samuel E. Munoz et al., "Cahokia's Emergence and Decline Coincided with Shifts of Flood Frequency on the Mississippi River," *PNAS* 112.20 (2015): 6319–6324. Benson, Pauketat, and Cook, "Cahokia's Boom and Bust in the Context of Climate Change," 473.

130. T. Douglas Price, James H. Burton, and James B. Stoltman, "Place of Origin of Prehistoric Inhabitants of Aztalan, Jefferson Co., Wisconsin," *AA* 72.3 (2007): 527. Colin M. Betts, "Oneota Mound Construction: An Early Revitalization Movement," *Plains Anthropologist* 55.214 (2010): 97–110.

131. Ian W. Brown, "Plaquemine Architectural Patterns in the Natchez Bluffs and Surrounding Regions of the Lower Mississippi Valley," *Midcontinental Journal of Archaeology* 10.2 (1985): 251–305. Karl G. Lorenz, "The Natchez of Southwest Mississippi," in Bonnie G. McEwan, ed., *Indians of the Greater Southeast: Historical Archaeology and Ethnohistory* (University Press of Florida, 2000), 142–177. Robert S. Neitzel, *Archaeology of the Fatherland Site: The Grand Village of the Natchez* (Museum of National History, 1965).

132. Francis P. McManamon, James W. Bradley, and Ann L. Magennis, *The Indian Neck Ossuary: Chapters in the Archaeology of Cape Cod* (Division of Cultural Resources, National Park Service, 1986).

133. Michael Heckenberger, "The Arawak Diaspora: Perspectives from South America," in William F. Keegan, Corinne L. Hofman, and Reniel Rodríguez Ramos, eds., *The Oxford Handbook of Caribbean Archaeology* (Oxford University Press, 2013), 117. Corinne L. Hofman and Menno L. P. Hoogland, "Unravelling the Multi-Scale Networks of Mobility and Exchange in the Pre-Colonial Circum-Caribbean," in Corinne L. Hofman and Anne van Duijvenbode, eds., *Communities in Contact: Essays in Archaeology, Ethnohistory, and Ethnography of the Amerindian Circum-Caribbean* (Sidestone Press, 2011), 31.

134. Davíd Carrassco, *The Aztecs: A Very Short Introduction* (Oxford University Press, 2012), 38–46.

135. I use the low estimate for Tenochtitlán: Susan Toby Evans, *Ancient Mexico and Central America: Archaeology and Culture History,* 3rd ed. (Thames and Hudson, 2013), 549. On the population north of Mesoamerica in 1500: George Milner and George Chaplin, "Eastern North American Populations at ca. AD 1500," *AA* 75.4 (2010): 707.

136. Geoff Wade, "The Zheng He Voyages: A Reassessment," *Journal of the Malaysian Branch of the Royal Asiatic Society* 78.1 (2005): 37–58. Felipe Fernández-Armesto, *The World: A History* (Prentice Hall, 2011), 406–432.

137. See also Tim Mackintosh-Smith, ed., *The Travels of Ibn Battutah* (Picador, 2002), 270.

138. Peter Edward Russell, *Prince Henry "the Navigator": A Life* (Yale University Press, 2000).

139. Christopher Tyerman, *The Crusades: A Very Short Introduction* (Oxford University Press, 2006), 125.

140. Irving Rouse, *The Tainos: Rise and Decline of the People Who Greeted Columbus* (Yale University Press, 1992), 13, 140–145. I take creative license here, since we don't know much about the party that greeted Columbus. We do know from Columbus's accounts, and the clerics who wrote reports, that the Taíno venerated these and other *zemis* (spirits or gods).

141. "La carta de Cristóbal Colón a Luis de Santángel," 15 February 1493, in Consuela Varela, ed., *Textos y documentos completos: Cristóbal Colón,* 2nd ed. (Alianza Editorial, 1992), 219–226.

142. Ramón Pané reported this story about a *zemi* who fled: Fray Ramón Pané, *An Account of the Antiquities of the Indians,* new ed. by José Juan Arrom, trans. Susan C. Griswold (Duke University Press, 1999).

Chapter 3. Imperial Religion

1. See the 1524 report of a journey up the Atlantic coast by the French-sponsored Italian mariner Giovanni da Verrazzano: Lawrence C. Wroth, ed., *The Voyages of Giovanni da Verrazzano, 1524–1528* (Published for the Pierpont Morgan Library by Yale University Press, 1970). At this first mention of the adjective *imperial* and the implied noun *empire,* I should offer a definition. As I use it, *imperial religion* highlights the mutually supporting connections between religious institutions and expansionist states, or empires that cross terrestrial and aquatic boundaries as they control diverse local cultures and peoples and impose regime-serving hierarchical distinctions between their own people and those they control. Imperial religious institutions, which depend on the state's support and offer divine sanction in return, provide the figurative language and justifying beliefs for settler colonialism's expansionist policies and exclusionary hierarchies. But imperial religions varied. There were Catholic, Protestant, and Eastern Orthodox imperial religions. Further, Spanish and French *imperial Catholicisms* differed, as British *imperial Protestantism* differed from Dutch *imperial Protestantism.* Those imperial religions also changed over time. By my definition, Chaco and Cahokia were hierarchically arranged political realms but not full-blown empires. My view, even where it differs, is indebted to

these works: Paul A. Kramer, "Power and Connection: Imperial Histories of the United States in the World," *AHR* 116.5 (2011): 1349. Pekka Hämäläinen, *The Comanche Empire* (Yale University Press, 2009). Tisa Wenger, *Religious Freedom: The Contested History of an American Ideal* (University of North Carolina Press, 2017). James C. Scott, *Seeing Like a State: How Certain Schemes to Improve the Human Condition Have Failed* (Yale University Press, 1998), 311–316. Katherine Carté, *Religion and the American Revolution: An Imperial History* (University of North Carolina Press, 2021).

2. To read the original and an English translation of Pope Alexander VI's papal bull *Inter Caetera* dated 4 May 1493, see https://www.gilderlehrman.org/history-resources/spotlight-primary-source/doctrine-discovery-1493.

3. Twenty years later, English Protestants landed on Roanoke Island, but they sailed home to avoid starvation in 1586. The second group of would-be colonists—the so-called Lost Colony—were never heard from again. Thomas Hariot or Harriot, an associate of Sir Walter Raleigh's, was among those on Roanoke Island from 1585 to 1586. See Thomas Harriot, *A Brief and True Report of the New Found Land of Virginia* (1588; Edwards Brothers, 1931), [62]. John White, the English illustrator, also was on Roanoke with Harriot.

4. As I proposed in the introduction, for an eco-cultural niche to be fully sustainable it must provide renewable resources, meaning and purpose, safety and health, equity and productivity, and as much individual freedom and political participation as the common good permits.

5. *Industrial capitalism* began in the US in the nineteenth century and earlier in Europe, but a form of capitalism began in the 1500s with the rise of global empires, the development of plantation slavery, and the transregional trade in cash crops. Beckert calls it *war capitalism,* and I see his point. But I prefer *merchant capitalism* or *mercantile capitalism.* Sven Beckert, *Empire of Cotton: A Global History* (Vintage, 2014), xv–xvii.

6. Jane T. Merritt, *At the Crossroads: Indians and Empires on a Mid-Atlantic Frontier, 1700–1763* (University of North Carolina Press, 2003). Some have described "frontiers of inclusion," areas on the edges of empire not yet dominated by French or British imperial influences. Like Merritt, I am thinking of places like Pennsylvania before 1750.

7. Contrasting imperial knowledge with local knowledge, Scott summed up the problem with schemes at human improvement that tragically failed: Scott, *Seeing Like a State,* 343. I think that applies to the colonial period as well.

8. Kathleen Donegan, *Seasons of Misery: Catastrophe and Colonial Settlement in Early America* (University of Pennsylvania Press, 2014). During the "starving time" winter of 1609–1610, which began with three hundred colonists in the Jamestown fort and ended with only sixty, settlers resorted to cannibalism to survive.

9. I am referring to Indigenous scholars' interpretations of the destabilization. Lawrence W. Gross, *Anishinaabe Ways of Knowing and Being* (Routledge, 2016), 33–47. Gross suggests it produced "postapocalypse stress syndrome." On "historical trauma" as cumulative: Maria Yellow Horse Brave Heart, "The Return to the Sacred

Path: Healing the Historical Trauma Response among the Lakota," *Smith College Studies in Social Work* 68.3 (1998): 287–305.

10. Alan Taylor, *Colonial America: A Very Short Introduction* (Oxford University Press, 2013), 18.

11. On the high counts (18 million) and low counts (900,000) of the population between the Rio Grande and Hudson Bay at the time of European contact: Elizabeth Fenn, "Whither the Rest of the Continent?" in John Lauritz Larson and Michael A. Morrison, eds., *Whither the Early Republic: A Forum on the Future of the Field* (University of Pennsylvania Press, 2005), 21–22. The safe estimate of 1.2 to 6.1 million is from George Milner and George Chaplin, "Eastern North American Population at ca. A.D. 1500," *AA* 75.4 (2010): 707. David S. Jones, "Virgin Soils Revisited," *WMQ* 60.4 (2003): 721.

12. David Eltis and David Richardson, *Atlas of the Transatlantic Slave Trade* (Yale University Press, 2010), xviii, 13, 25–27. See David Eltis, "A Brief Overview of the Trans-Atlantic Slave Trade," https://www.slavevoyages.org/voyage/essays#interpretation/overview-trans-atlantic-slave-trade/introduction/0/en/. See also table 1 in Rik Van Welie, "Slave Trading and Slavery in the Dutch Colonial Empire: A Global Comparison," *New West Indian Guide/Nieuwe West-Indische Gids* 82.1–2 (2008): 53. Americans imported 4 percent of the total.

13. Eltis and Richardson, *Transatlantic Slave Trade,* 4, 15, 18, 19.

14. Stephen R. Berry, "Christianity," in Amanda Warnock and Toyin Falola, eds., *Encyclopedia of the Middle Passage* (Greenwood, 2007), 108–110. Stephen R. Berry, *A Path in the Mighty Waters: Shipboard Life and Atlantic Crossings to the New World* (Yale University Press, 2015).

15. On slave mortality: Eltis and Richardson, *Transatlantic Slave Trade,* 167–188.

16. A baptized Lenape told a missionary, for example, that God created people "as we find them upon earth, as red, black, and white." The quotation is from Nancy Shoemaker, "How Indians Got to Be Red," *AHR* 102.3 (1997): 629–630. William Apess used *red man*—and the tricolor metaphor—in his 1829 autobiography, *Son of the Forest:* Barry O'Connell, ed., *On Our Own Ground: The Complete Writings of William Apess, a Pequot* (University of Massachusetts Press, 1992), 3–4. On this discourse, see also James P. Howley, *The Beothuks or Red Indians* (Cambridge University Press, 1915); Alden T. Vaughan, "From White Man to Redskin: Changing Anglo-American Perceptions of the American Indian," *AHR* 87.4 (1982): 917–953; Ingebord Marshall, *A History and Ethnography of the Beothuk* (McGill–Queen's University Press, 1996), 30; Nancy Shoemaker, *A Strange Likeness: Becoming Red and White in Eighteenth-Century America* (Oxford University Press, 2004); George Milne, *Natchez Country: Indians, Colonists, and the Landscapes of Race in French Louisiana* (University of Georgia Press, 2015), 2. Milne suggests the Natchez were the first Native People to use *red man* in front of Europeans, and their revolt spread the discourse of redness through the Southeast. However, it was the discourse of elites, Native and French, as Balvay notes: Arnaud Balvay, review of *Natchez Country,* by George Milne, *WMQ* 73.3 (2016): 586–588.

17. Wheelwright's birthplace was in Massachusetts at the time but later would be part of Maine. Ann M. Little, *The Many Captivities of Esther Wheelwright* (Yale University Press, 2016). See also Emma Lewis Coleman, *New England Captives Carried to Canada between 1677 and 1760 during the French and Indian Wars,* 2 vols. (Southworth Press, 1925). For another insightful biography of a captive, see John Demos, *The Unredeemed Captive: A Family Story from Early America* (Vintage, 1995).

18. I borrow the vivid verb to describe mining's effects ("honeycombed") from J. R. McNeill and George Vrtis, eds., *Mining North America: An Environmental History since 1522* (University of California Press, 2017), 2.

19. Erik R. Seeman, *Death in the New World: Cross-Cultural Encounters, 1492–1800* (University of Pennsylvania Press, 2010), 5.

20. Peter Charles Hoffer, "Brave New Worlds: The First Century of Indian–English Encounters," in Matt Cohen and Jeffrey Glover, eds., *Colonial Mediascapes: Sensory Worlds of the Early Americas* (University of Nebraska Press, 2014), 235.

21. I prefer to talk about *boundary zones,* to avoid some assumptions associated with related but distinct scholarly categories, including *borderlands* and *middle grounds.* As I understand Richard White, "creative misunderstandings" helped to produce a French-Algonquian middle ground in Canada. Once in a while, I suggest, a few colonizers and Natives seem to actually have partially understood one another, though only after long periods of living together. Richard White, *The Middle Ground: Indians, Empires, and Republics in the Great Lakes Region, 1650–1815* (Stanford University Press, 2011). In the preface to this anniversary edition, White emphasized these "creative misunderstandings" as he defended his notion of a middle ground against critics who accused him of assuming a rosy and simplistic view of those exchanges and spaces.

22. Patrick Griffin, "The Last War of Religion or the First War for Empire? Reconsidering the Meaning of the Seven Years' War in America," unpublished essay, 2016.

23. Gregory Evans Dowd, *A Spirited Resistance: The North American Indian Struggle for Unity, 1745–1815* (Johns Hopkins University Press, 1992), 23–46.

24. I use the term *English* to describe those who came from England before 1707 and the Act of Union with Scotland, though sometimes I choose *British* if the historical actors also included those who were from Wales or Ireland. When I am speaking of the period after 1707 or discussing a span of decades, I tend to use *British.*

25. On the language of liberty and tyranny, I am indebted to Griffin's "The Last War of Religion or the First War for Empire?" and Robert Emmett Curran, *Papist Devils: Catholics in British America, 1574–1784* (Catholic University of America Press, 2014), 201–225.

26. The Danish controlled three small islands in the Lesser Antilles, starting with St. Thomas and St. John in the seventeenth century and St. Croix in 1733. In 1917 the US purchased the Danish West Indies and they became the US Virgin Islands. See C. Waldemar Westergaard, *The Danish West Indies under Company Rule (1671–1754); with a Supplemental Chapter, 1755–1917* (Macmillan, 1917); Isaac Dookhan, *A History of the Virgin Islands of the United States* (Canoe Press, 1994), 181–199.

27. I refer to *farming faiths* in the sense that I employ *foraging religion* and *factory religion.* It is a historical ideal type—Max Weber's term for scholarly concepts that are constructed by exaggerating some features of historical reality to create a category that is useful for a particular researcher's interests. Obviously, *farming religion* does not encompass all that can be said about piety in the era. Nor am I suggesting that commerce was not important. It was. Imperial commercial networks transported crops to market and returned other goods to ports adjacent to farming communities.

28. James Hansen et al., "Young People's Burden: Requirement of Negative CO_2 Emissions," *Earth System Dynamics* 8 (2017): 577–616.

29. Baker H. Morrow, trans., *A Harvest of Reluctant Souls: Fray Alonso de Benavides's History of New Mexico, 1630* (University of New Mexico Press, 2012), section 20.

30. This quotation is from Morrow, *Harvest of Reluctant Souls,* section 33. The description of women building churches occurs in section 20.

31. On John Eliot's "praying towns": John Eliot, *The Day-Breaking: If Not the Sun-Rising of the Gospell with the Indians in New England* (Printed by Richard Cotes for Fulk Clifton, 1647); Julius H. Rubin, *Tears of Repentance: Christian Indian Identity and Community in Colonial Southern New England* (University of Nebraska Press, 2013), 19–38; Richard W. Cogley, *John Eliot's Mission to the Indians before King Philip's War* (Harvard University Press, 2009).

32. Allan Greer, *The Jesuit Relations: Natives and Missionaries in Seventeenth-Century North America* (Bedford/St. Martin's, 2000), 51. Jean de Brébuf, *Relation of 1636,* in Reuben G. Thwaites, ed., *The Jesuit Relations and Allied Documents,* 73 vols. (Burrows Brothers, 1896–1901), 10: 210–235. I sometimes use the historical terms the Jesuits used for these aboriginal peoples (Huron and Montagnais) but also note the terms preferred today (Wendat and Innu). Carole Blackburn, *Harvest of Souls: Jesuit Missions and Colonialism in North America, 1632–1650* (McGill–Queen's University Press, 2000), 146n6. French contacts with the Huron-Wendat were not only aimed at saving souls: Andrew Nichols, *Fleeting Empire: Early Stuart Britain and the Merchant Adventures to Canada* (McGill–Queen's University Press, 2010), 5.

33. On gardening metaphors and "colonization as spiritual gardening" in New Spain and New England, see Jorge Cañizares-Esguerra, *Puritan Conquistadors: Iberianizing the Atlantic, 1550–1700* (Stanford University Press, 2006), 178–214.

34. Blackburn, *Harvest of Souls,* 46.

35. Richard Hakluyt, "A Discourse on Western Planting" (1584), in Leonard Woods, ed., *Documentary History of the State of Maine* (John Wilson and Son, 1877), 2: 7.

36. William T. Davis, ed., *Bradford's History of Plymouth Plantation, 1606–1646* (Scribner's Sons, 1908). The Fox passage is quoted in Kristen Block, "Cultivating Inner and Outer Plantations: Property, Industry, and Slavery in Early Quaker Migration to the New World," *Early American Studies* 8.3 (2010): 517. The passage is taken from George Fox, *The Works of George Fox,* vol. 8 (Marcus TC Gould, 1831), 218.

37. Paul Le Jeune, *Relation of 1634,* in Greer, *Jesuit Relations,* 33. See also *Jesuit Relations and Allied Documents,* 6: 228–235.

38. Quoted in Blackburn, *Harvest of Souls,* 47. The phrase was used by Paul Le Jeune and can be found in *Jesuit Relations and Allied Documents,* 10: 9, 11: 19.

39. Morrow, *A Harvest of Reluctant Souls,* section 20. The phrase "harvest of souls" is repeated in "Letter from Fray Juan de Santander to the King of Spain," which is included as the postscript in Morrow's translation.

40. On the parable of the wedding feast, see François Bovon, *Luke 2: A Commentary on the Gospel of Luke 9:51–19:27* (Fortress, 2013), 362–379.

41. On these two broad patterns in the interpretation of the parable, see Robert K. McIver, "The Parable of the Weeds among the Wheat (Matt 13:24–30, 36–43) and the Relationship between the Kingdom and the Church as Portrayed in the Gospel of Matthew," *Journal of Biblical Literature* 114.4 (1995): 643–659.

42. Stuart B. Schwartz, *All Can Be Saved: Religious Tolerance and Salvation in the Iberian Atlantic World* (Yale University Press, 2008), 1, 3.

43. This helpful definition of "toleration," which focuses on coexistence rather than conscience, is from Benjamin J. Kaplan, *Divided by Faith: Religious Conflict and the Practice of Toleration in Early Modern Europe* (Harvard University Press, 2007), 11. Locke's letter appeared first in Latin in Holland in 1689. The first English edition appeared on 3 October: John Locke, *A Letter Concerning Toleration* (Printed for Awnsham Churchill, at Black Swan, at Amen-Corner, 1689). Locke's thinking was not completely abstract, since he had a long history of thinking about religion and the state in Carolina, helped draft the 1669 Constitution, and helped edit the 1682 revision.

44. William Penn, *England's Present Interest Discovered with Honour to the Prince and Safety to the People . . .* ([n.p., 1675]), 2, 7, 38.

45. Roger Williams was banished in 1635 but did not publish his first pamphlet against John Cotton until 1644—*The Bloudy Tenent of Persecution.* Cotton responded with *The Bloudy Tenent, Washed, and Made White in the Bloud of the Lamb.* All the texts, including the letters, are collected in Edward Bean Underhill, ed., *The Bloudy Tenent of Persecution for Cause of Conscience Discussed and Mr. Cotton's Letter Examined and Answered* (J. Haddon, 1848). On Williams's interpretation of the parable: James P. Byrd Jr., *The Challenges of Roger Williams: Religious Liberty, Violent Persecution, and the Bible* (Mercer University Press, 2002), 87–127. For helpful analyses of the parable and British colonial writers, see James E. McWilliams, "Worshipping Weeds: The Parable of the Tares, the Rhetoric of Ecology and the Origins of Agrarian Exceptionalism in Early America," *Environmental History* 16 (2011): 298–302; Timothy Dwight Bozeman, "John Clarke and the Complications of Liberty," *CH* 75.1 (2006): 83–86.

46. Jonathan Edwards, *A Treatise Concerning Religious Affections . . .* (Printed for S. Kneeland and T. Green, 1746), 83–84. John Carroll, "Sermon on Membership in the Church: MT. 13:25," in Thomas O'Brien Hanley, SJ, ed., *The John Carroll Papers* (University of Notre Dame Press, 1976), 2: 373–374.

47. J. W. Cousland, "Toxic Tares: The Poisonous Weeds in Matthew's Parable of the Tares (Matthew 12.24–30, 36–43)," *New Testament Studies* 61 (2015): 395–410.

48. McWilliams, "Worshipping Weeds," 307. S. C. H. Barrett, "Crop Mimicry in Weeds," *Economic Botany* 37 (1989): 255–282. I use the term *mimicry* here and later as a shorthand way to refer to complex cultural processes. On this process, see Kathryn Lee McClure Sikes, "Peripheral Vision: Mimesis and Materiality along the James River, Virginia, 1619–1660," PhD diss., College of William and Mary, 2013, 20–43.

49. Most contemporary scholars use the plural "Reformations" to describe the reform impulses in Catholicism and Protestantism in the sixteenth and seventeenth centuries. I follow Eire in noting the importance of the printing press and the Thirty Years' War: Carlos M. Eire, *Reformations: The Early Modern World, 1450–1650* (Yale University Press, 2016), xiii–xiv. On Europe after the wars in 1648: Tim Dowley, *Atlas of the European Reformations* (Fortress, 2015), 136–137.

50. Eire, *Reformations,* 148–151. The quotation about "monkish squabble" is on p. 150. See also Brad S. Gregory, *Rebel in the Ranks: Martin Luther, the Reformation, and the Conflicts That Continue to Shape Our World* (Harper One, 2017), 39–46.

51. Kaplan, *Divided by Faith,* 343.

52. I am agreeing with Kaplan's explanations for the intensity of the religious wars: Kaplan, *Divided by Faith,* 11.

53. Hakluyt, "Discourse on Western Planting," 95, 60.

54. Don Juan de Oliván Rebolledo, report, written from "Mexico," [24 December 1717], Béxar Archives, 1717–1836, Dolph Briscoe Center for American History, University of Texas at Austin.

55. Kenneth Mills, "Religion in the Atlantic World," in Nicholas Canny and Philip Morgan, eds., *The Oxford Handbook of the Atlantic World, 1450–1850* (Oxford University Press, 2011), 434.

56. McWilliams, "Worshipping Weeds," 300.

57. On plant adaption and "biological resilience": Brian A. Mealor and Ann L. Hild, "Post-invasion Evolution of Native Plant Populations: A Test of Biological Resilience," *Oikos* 116 (2007): 1493–1500.

58. Quoted in Colin G. Calloway, *One Vast Winter Count: The Native American West before Lewis and Clark* (University of Nebraska Press, 2004), 135. That passage from Coronado's account can be found in George P. Hammond and Agapito Rey, eds., *Narratives of the Coronado Expedition, 1540–1542* (University of New Mexico Press, 1940), 168–170.

59. Judith Carney, "Seeds of Memory: Botanical Legacies of the African Diaspora," in R. Voeks and J. Rashford, eds., *African Ethnobotany in the Americas* (Springer, 2013), 13–18. Judith Ann Carney, *In the Shadow of Slavery: Africa's Botanical Legacy in the Atlantic World* (University of California Press, 2011).

60. On hybridization and gene flow between crops and weeds: John M. Burke, Keith A. Gardner, and Loren H. Rieseberg, "The Potential for Gene Flow between Cultivated and Wild Sunflower (*Helianthus annuus*) in the United States," *American Journal of Botany* 89.9 (2002): 1550–1552.

61. Anna Brickhouse proposed "unsettling" as an interpretive category: Anna Brickhouse, *The Unsettlement of America: Translation, Interpretation, and the Story of Don Luis de Velasco, 1560–1945* (Oxford University Press, 2014), 1–14.

62. On wheat and grapes for mass: Rebecca Earle, "'If You Eat Their Food . . .': Diets and Bodies in Early Colonial Spanish America," *AHR* 115.3 (2010): 699–701. Thomas Aquinas mandated wheat and grapes and ruled out other grains and berries in his *Summa Theologica* (third part, question 74): Miri Rubin, *Corpus Christi: The Eucharist in Late Medieval Culture* (Cambridge University Press, 1991), 37–49. They also brought guns: Kathleen Deagan and José María Cruxent, *Columbus's Outpost among the Taínos: Spain and America at La Isabela, 1493–1498* (Yale University Press, 2002), 168–169.

63. In 1493 Columbus started to sign his letters *Christoferens,* an inelegant Latinization meaning "Christ bearer," and his view of himself as a fulfiller of prophecies developed in the years ahead: Pauline Moffitt Watts, "Prophecy and Discovery: On the Spiritual Origins of Christopher Columbus's 'Enterprise of the Indies,'" *AHR* 90.1 (1985): 73–74, 83, 94, 100–101. He made this explicit in 1500: G. B. Spotorno, *Memorials of Columbus* (Treuttel and Wurtz, Treuttel, Jun. and Richter, 1823), 224.

64. Aboard were Friar Bernaldo Buil, a confidant of King Ferdinand, along with twelve members of religious orders and the priesthood. Deagan and Cruxent, *Columbus's Outpost,* 19. The sources describe his title as *Fray.* I use *Friar* because it is more familiar to most readers. Both terms can be traced to the Latin *frater* or brother. Unlike monks and priests, friars are itinerant, owing allegiance to a mendicant order in a province and dedicated to serving laypeople, and usually associated with the Dominicans, Franciscans, Carmelites, or Augustinians.

65. Deagan and Cruxent, *Columbus's Outpost,* 172.

66. Archaeologists use *necropolis* to describe an extensive and elaborate burial place of an ancient city. Some historians have used it to describe the mass death of Africans and Indigenous Peoples during the colonial period: Jennifer Scheper Hughes, "In the Absence of Bones," *Material Religion* 13.4 (2017): 515.

67. Deagan and Cruxent, *Columbus's Outpost,* 69.

68. Ida Altman, "Marriage, Family, and Ethnicity in the Early Spanish Caribbean," *WMQ* 70.2 (2013): 225.

69. Robert Paynter, "Historical and Anthropological Archaeology: Forging Alliances," *JAR* 8.1 (2000): 1.

70. Those who blended are harder to identify in the official records, though DNA studies show more than half of nearby island residents have Indigenous ancestries, and some today still claim Taíno heritage. See Altman, "Marriage, Family, and Ethnicity in the Early Spanish Caribbean," 250. Reséndez notes that "53 percent of contemporary Puerto Ricans have Indigenous ancestries through their maternal line": Andrés Reséndez, *A Land So Strange: The Epic Journey of Cabeza de Vaca* (Perseus Books, 2007), 231.

71. Taylor, *Colonial America,* 17.

72. Paynter, "Historical and Anthropological Archaeology: Forging Alliances," 2.

73. The political units were the Nahua *altepetl* and the Andean *ayllu.* Residents of central Mexico did not refer to themselves as Aztecs. I sometimes use *Nahua* because they were speakers of the Nahuatl language. Yet because readers will know the popular term *Aztecs,* I use that too. The residents of the capital city would have called themselves *Mexica,* and I use that to describe those in the capital. Amber

Brian, Bradley Benton, and Pablo García Loaeza, "Introduction," in *The Native Conquistador: Alva Ixtlilxochitl's Account of the Conquest of New Spain* (Pennsylvania State University Press, 2015), 1.

74. On the state religions of the Nahua and the Inca, and their comparable political units, see David Tavárez, "Religion in the Pre-Contact World: Mesoamerica and the Andes," in Virginia Garrad-Burnett, Paul Freston, and Stephen C. Dove, eds., *The Cambridge History of Religions in Latin America* (Cambridge University Press, 2016), 22–33. See Pedro Carrasco, *The Tenochca Empire of Ancient Mexico: The Triple Alliance of Tenochtitlan, Tetzcoco, and Tlacopan* (University of Oklahoma Press, 1999).

75. Sara Vicuña Guengerich, "Inca Women under Spanish Rule: *Probanzas* and *Informaciones* of the Colonial Andean Elite," in Mónica Díaz and Rocío Quispe-Agnoli, eds., *Women's Negotiations and Textual Agency in Latin America, 1500–1799* (Routledge, 2017), 108–114. Rocío Quispe-Agnoli, "Taking Possession of the New World: Powerful Female Agency of Early Colonial Accounts of Perú," *Legacy* 28.2 (2011): 257–289. Karen Vieira Powers, *Women in the Crucible of Conquest: The Gendered Genesis of Spanish American Society, 1500–1600* (University of New Mexico Press, 2005). Clara Sue Kidwell, "Women as Cultural Mediators," *Ethnohistory* 39.2 (1992): 98–99. On the "new conquest history": Matthew Restall, "The New Conquest History," *History Compass* 10.2 (2012): 151–160. On the continuities and discontinuities in Andean religion: Claudia Brosseder, *The Power of Huacas: Change and Resistance in the Andean World of Colonial Peru* (University of Texas Press, 2014).

76. Representation of the temple massacre from the Codex Durán, Diego Durán, *Historia de las Indias de Nueva España y islas de Tierra Firme,* ca. 1579–1581, paper, 30 × 21 cm, Biblioteca Nacional, Madrid. Anthony Pagden, ed., *Hernan Cortés: Letters from Mexico* (Yale University Press, 1986), 475n83. Miguel León-Portilla, ed., *The Broken Spears: The Aztec Account of the Conquest of Mexico* (Beacon, 1992), 70–82; Brian, Benton, and Loaeza, eds., *Native Conquistador,* 24–25.

77. Davíd Carrasco, *The Aztecs: A Very Short Introduction* (Oxford University Press, 2012), 16, 72–75.

78. León-Portilla, *Broken Spears,* 76.

79. The translation I quote uses *uproot:* Bartolomé de las Casas, *A Short Account of the Destruction of the Indies,* trans. Nigel Griffin (Penguin Books, 1992), 12. That is a fair rendering of *extirpar,* which means to root out or remove. It does not have all the associations of the English verb but refers to the clearing away of people from the land, as in the original: "*extirpar y raer de la haz de la tierra.*" Fray Bartolomé de las Casas, *Brevísima relación de la destrucción de las Indias* (Sebastián Trujillo, 1552), 13. In 1511 the Dominicans decided to speak out against the treatment of the Indians, and elected Antonio Montesinos to preach the first public warning. See Juan Pérez de Tudela y Bueso, ed., *Obras escogidas de Fray Bartolomé de las Casas* (Ediciones Atlas, 1957–1958), 2: 174–179.

80. Las Casas, *Destruction of the Indies,* 15.

81. Pope Paul III, *Sublimis Deus,* 29 May 1537, https://www.papalencyclicals.net/Paulo3/p3subli.htm.

82. Antonio de Herrara y Tordesillas, *Historia general de los hechos de los castellanos en las Islas y Tierra Firme del Mar Océano* (Academia de la Historia, 1935), 3: 317–326. Samuel Turner, "Juan Ponce de León and the Discovery of Florida Reconsidered," *Florida Historical Quarterly* 92.1 (2013): 1–31.

83. On Estebanico, see Reséndez, *A Land So Strange,* 55–58. See also Rukhsana Qamber, "Anti-Islamic Bias in Sources on Latin America: Preliminary Findings," *Islamic Studies* 42.4 (2003): 664. Here and below I rely on the bilingual edition of Cabeza de Vaca's 1542 *Relación* and the remarkable background and analysis in volumes 2 and 3: Rolena Adorno and Patrick C. Pautz, eds., *Álvar Núñez Cabeza de Vaca: His Account, His Life, and the Expedition of Pánfil de Navárez,* 3 vols. (University of Nebraska Press, 1999).

84. Cabeza de Vaca, "Transcription and Translation of the 1542 *Relación,*" in Adorno and Pautz, *Álvar Núñez Cabeza de Vaca,* 1: 120–121, 103, 155, 195.

85. I rely on Pedro de Castañeda de Nájera, "Relación de la jornada de Cíbola," in George Parker Winship, ed., *The Coronado Expedition, 1540–1542* (GPO, 1896), 110–127. See also Calloway, *Winter Count,* 130–145.

86. For a reconstruction of Marcos de Niza's *Relación,* see Jerry R. Craddock, "Fray Marcos de Niza, *Relación* (1539): Edition and Commentary," *Romance Philology* 53.1 (1999): 69–118. Estebanico and the Cabeza de Vaca party used "a decorated gourd" as a talisman "to enhance their shamanistic authority" (80). So a former African Muslim and converted Christian slave was using ritual implements associated with Indigenous shamans.

87. Calloway, *Winter Count,* 134–135.

88. Calloway, *Winter Count,* 135.

89. Stuart B. Schwartz, "The Iberian Atlantic to 1650," in Canny and Morgan, *Atlantic World,* 154.

90. John Calvin's ideas shaped *The French Confession of Faith* (1559), and article 24 rejects saint veneration: Philip Schaff, ed., *The Creeds of Christendom, with a History and Critical Notes,* 4th ed. (Harper and Brothers, 1919), 3: 373. On Calvinism in France between 1560 and 1562, see John T. McGrath, *The French in Early Florida: In the Eye of the Hurricane* (University Press of Florida, 2000), 40–44.

91. Theodor de Bry issued a Latin version of the narrative and drawings by Jacques Le Moyne de Morgues in 1591 as *Brevis narratio eorum quae in Florida Americae provi[n]cia Gallis acciderunt,* and an English translation appeared in 1875. It included the narrative and de Bry engravings based on the drawings. Jacques Le Moyne de Morgues, *Narrative of Le Moyne, An Artist Who Accompanied the French Expedition to Florida under Laudonnière, 1564* (James R. Osgood, 1875), 16–38, 48–60. Some challenge the accuracy of some drawings: John Hann, *A History of the Timucua Indians and Missions* (University Press of Florida, 1996), 92–93. As a Protestant publisher, de Bry emphasized the links between Native and Catholic idolatry in this and other volumes of his *America* (1590–1634). See Michael J. Zogry, "Lost in Conflation: Visual Culture and Constructions of the Category of Religion," *American Indian Quarterly* 35.1 (2011): 12.

92. Jon Butler, *The Huguenots in America: A Refugee People in New World Society* (Harvard University Press, 1983), 42. Butler also offers an account of the later history of French Protestants in Boston, New York, and Charleston. On Fort Caroline, see McGrath, *French in Early Florida,* 97–115.

93. Quoted in Alan Taylor, *American Colonies: The Settling of North America* (Penguin, 2001), 77.

94. Le Moyne de Morgues, *Narrative of Le Moyne,* 23.

95. On the French narratives and the massacre as a spur to and justification of French and English Protestant colonization, see Melissa Anderson Waldman, "A History of Remembering: The French and Spanish in Florida, 1562–1565," PhD diss., University of Michigan, 2000, 15, 35, 155, 160, 172, 190.

96. Kathleen Deagan, *Spanish St. Augustine: The Archaeology of a Colonial Creole Community* (Academic Press, 1983), 128.

97. Deagan, *Spanish St. Augustine,* 128–132.

98. On the "general deterioration in health": Clark Spencer Larsen et al., "Frontiers of Contact: Bioarchaeology of Spanish Florida," *Journal of World Prehistory* 15.1 (2001): 69–123. Deagan, *Spanish St. Augustine,* 127. Spanish-Native intermarriage "began immediately": Kathleen Deagan, "St. Augustine and the Mission Frontier," in Bonnie G. McEwan, ed., *The Spanish Missions of La Florida* (University Press of Florida, 1993), 94. Gene flow increased after 1650: Christopher M. Stojanowski, "The Bioarchaeology of Identity in Spanish Colonial Florida: Social and Evolutionary Transformation before, during, and after Demographic Collapse," *American Anthropologist* 107.3 (2005): 417–431.

99. Elizabeth J. Reitz, "Comparison of Spanish and Aboriginal Subsistence on the Atlantic Coastal Plain," *Southeastern Archaeology* 4.1 (1985): 41–50. On gene flow, see Stojanowski, "Bioarchaeology of Identity in Spanish Colonial Florida."

100. Deagan, "St. Augustine," 92–94. On epidemics and population declines: Hann, *Timucua Indians,* 145, 188, 225, 240, 318. On similarities in diet: Elizabeth J. Reitz, "Comparison of Spanish and Aboriginal Subsistence on the Atlantic Coastal Plain," *Southeastern Archaeology* 4.1 (1985): 41–50. On gene flow, see Stojanowski, "Bioarchaeology of Identity in Spanish Colonial Florida." Native pottery was used by 80 percent of Spanish households. On ceramic production and identity retention among Indigenous Peoples in St. Augustine: Gifford J. Waters, "Maintenance and Change of 18th Century Mission Indian Identity: A Multi-Ethnic Contact Situation," PhD diss., University of Florida, 2005, 167–168.

101. Deagan, "St. Augustine," 89, 94, 95.

102. Hann, *Timucua Indians,* 164, 248.

103. On burials for chiefs and others Timucuans: Hann, *Timucua Indians,* 105–106.

104. On the burials, see Lillian Seaburg, "Report on the Indian Site at the 'Fountain of Youth,'" 1951, repr. in Kathleen Deagan, ed., *America's Ancient City: A Sourcebook on First Spanish Period St. Augustine* (Garland Press, 1991).

105. Bonnie G. McEwan, Michael W. Davidson, and Jeffrey M. Mitchem, "A Quartz Crystal Cross from Mission San Luis, Florida," *Journal of Archaeological*

Science 24 (1997): 530. On San Luis, see Bonnie G. McEwan, "San Luis de Talimali: The Archaeology of Spanish-Indian Relations at a Florida Mission," *Historical Archaeology* 25.3 (1991): 36–60; Gary Shapiro and Bonnie G. McEwan, *Archaeology at San Luis, Part One, The Apalachee Council House,* and Gary Shapiro and Richard Vernon, *Archaeology at San Luis, Part Two: The Church Complex, Florida Archaeology* 6 (Bureau of Archaeological Research, 1992); John H. Hann and Bonnie G. McEwan, *The Apalachee Indians and Mission San Luis* (University Press of Florida, 1998); and Bonnie G. McEwan and John H. Hann, "Reconstructing a Spanish Mission: San Luis de Talimali," *OAH Magazine of History* 14.4 (2000): 1619.

106. Hann and McEwan, *Apalachee Indians and Mission San Luis,* 1–19. Rochelle A. Marrinan and Nancy Marie White, "Modeling Fort Walton Culture in Northwest Florida," *Southeastern Archaeology* 26.2 (2007): 292–318.

107. McEwan and Hann, "Spanish Mission," 16.

108. Elizabeth J. Reitz, "Evidence for Animal Use at the Missions of Spanish Florida," in Bonnie G. McEwan, ed., *The Spanish Missions of La Florida* (University Press of Florida, 1993), 380–383. McEwan, "San Luis de Talimali," 57.

109. The central plaza provided a stage for their ritualized athletic contest, a ball game similar to the one Cahokians played.

110. McEwan and Hann, "Spanish Mission," 17. See also Shapiro and McEwan, *Archaeology at San Luis, Part One.* On the council house, chief's house, and commoner houses, see Hann and McEwan, *Apalachee Indians and Mission San Luis,* 75–81.

111. Patricia L. Crown et al., "Ritual Black Drink Consumption at Cahokia," *PNAS* 109.35 (2012): 13944–13949. On the use of the "black drink" by Neolin in a pan-Indian restoration movement in the Ohio Valley, see Dowd, *Spirited Resistance,* 33.

112. McEwan and Hann, "Spanish Mission," 17.

113. On the church architecture: McEwan and Hann, "Spanish Mission," 17–18. See also Shapiro and Vernon, *Archaeology at San Luis, Part Two;* Hann and McEwan, *Apalachee Indians and Mission San Luis,* 84–89. On the beads and quartz, see also Jeffrey M. Mitchem, "Beads and Pendants from San Luis de Talimali: Inferences from Varying Contexts," in Bonnie G. McEwan, ed., *Spanish Missions of La Florida* (University Press of Florida, 1993), 399–417.

114. The church measured 110 feet long by 50 feet wide. McEwan, Davidson, and Mitchem, "Quartz Crystal Cross from Mission San Luis," 530.

115. McEwan, Davidson, and Mitchem, "Quartz Crystal Cross from Mission San Luis," 530–531. Mitchem, "Beads and Pendants from San Luis de Talimali," 406–410.

116. Mitchem, "Beads and Pendants from San Luis de Talimali," 406.

117. McEwan, Davidson, and Mitchem, "Quartz Crystal Cross from Mission San Luis," 532–534.

118. Taylor, *Colonial America,* 29.

119. The Spanish reaction to the failed fort is quoted in Donald E. Chipman and Harriet Denise Joseph, *Spanish Texas, 1519–1821,* rev. ed. (University of Texas Press, 2010), 84.

120. This assessment of the Caddo is from Timothy K. Perttula, "How Texas Historians Write about the Pre-A.D. 1685 Caddo Peoples of Texas," *Southwestern Historical Quarterly* 115.4 (2012): 365.

121. One ceremonial mound site the Caddo abandoned around 1300 CE is the George C. Davis Site. See Darrell Creel, *Archaeological Investigations at the George C. Davis Site, Cherokee County, Texas* (Texas A&M University and Texas Antiquities Committee, 1979). My account is based on missionary letters and an analysis by an ethnohistorian who identifies as Caddo: Cecile Elkins Carter, *Caddo Indians: Where We Come From* (University of Oklahoma Press, 1995), 83, 85, 89, 100. Mattie Austin Hatcher, trans., Francisco Casañas de Jesús María to the Viceroy of Mexico, 15 August 1691, parts 1 and 2 of "Descriptions of the Tejas or Asinai Indians, 1691–1722," *Southwestern Historical Quarterly* 30 (1927): 206–218, 283–304. Lilia M. Casis, trans., "Letter of Fray Damián Massanet to Don Carlos Sigüenza, 1690," in Herbert Eugene Bolton, ed., *Original Narratives of Early American History: Spanish Exploration in the Southwest, 1542–1706* (Charles Scribner's Sons, 1925). On the site of the first mission: Robert S. Weddle, Donald E. Chipman, and Carol A. Lipscomb, "The Misplacement of Mission San Francisco de las Tejas in Eastern Texas and Its Actual Location at San Pedro de los Nabedaches," *Southwestern Historical Quarterly* 120.1 (2016): 75–84.

122. Chipman and Joseph, *Spanish Texas,* 84–98.

123. James E. Bruseth et al., "Clash of Two Cultures: Presidio La Bahía on the Texas Coast as a Deterrent to French Incursion," *Historical Archaeology* 38.3 (2004): 78–93. Soldiers reassured Mexico City superiors by building a new fort on top of La Salle's abandoned one near the Gulf.

124. Taylor, *American Colonies,* 410–411. On the Coahiltecans' ceremonies, hallucinogens, and interactions with Cabeza de Vaca: David La Vere, *The Texas Indians* (Texas A&M Press, 2004), 66–67.

125. "Two Franciscan Documents on Early San Antonio, Texas," *The Americas* 25.2 (1968): 206.

126. Taylor, *American Colonies,* 411. On the San Antonio mission's success, see Christopher A. Dixon, "Indians in the House of God: A Socio-Economic Investigation of the San Antonio Mission Community," PhD diss., Boston University, 2004, v. *Guidelines for a Texas Mission: Instructions for the Missionary of Mission Concepción in San Antonio* (ca. 1760), transcript of the Spanish original and English trans. with notes by Fr. Benedict Leutenegger OFM (Old Spanish Missions Historical Research Library, San José Mission, 1976), 37, 54.

127. The quotation about peyote at dances: Fr. Antonio de S. Buenabentura [*sic*] Olivares to [the] Viceroy, October 1716, Biblioteca Nacional, Mexico City, Sección de Manuscritos, Caja 1, Fs. 59–60. A translation appeared in "Two Franciscan Documents on Early San Antonio, Texas," *The Americas* 25.2 (1968): 196–199. The passage suggesting missionaries "make allowances": *Guidelines for a Texas Mission,* 41.

128. Félix D. Almaráz Jr., "Harmony, Discord, and Compromise in Spanish Colonial Texas: The Río San Antonio Experience, 1691–1741," *New Mexico Historical Review* 67.4 (1992): 345. *Guidelines for a Texas Mission,* 23.

129. Fr. Benedict Leutenegger, OFM, trans., *Inventory of the Mission San Antonio de Valero: 1772* (Office of the State Archeologist, Texas Historical Commission, 1977), 26.

130. Almaráz Jr., "Harmony, Discord, and Compromise," 345.

131. Leutenegger, *Inventory of the Mission San Antonio de Valero,* 35.

132. On the Abó kiva: James E. Ivey, *In the Midst of a Loneliness: The Architectural History of the Salinas Missions,* Salinas Pueblo Missions National Monument Historic Structures Report, Professional Papers no. 15 (National Park Service, 1988), appendix 5. See also Joseph H. Toulouse Jr., *The Mission of San Gregorio de Abo: A Report on the Excavation and Repair of a Seventeenth-Century New Mexico Mission* (University of New Mexico Press, 1949). The introduction of the axe and the use of wood led to deforestation, but because the Spanish never found silver, as they did elsewhere, there was less pollution and vegetation loss: Robert MacCameron, "Environmental Change in Colonial New Mexico," *Environmental History Review* 18.2 (1994): 9, 25.

133. Lekson suggests the northern Rio Grande was within the 240 kilometer radius of outlier influence, making it part of Chaco's "hinterlands." Stephen H. Lekson, "Chaco's Hinterlands," in Timothy R. Pauketat, ed., *The Oxford Handbook of North American Archaeology* (Oxford University Press, 2012), 600. On migration from Mesa Verde to the Rio Grand Valley, see Donna M. Glowacki, "The Social and Cultural Contexts of the Central Mesa Verde Region during the Thirteenth-Century Migrations," in Timothy A. Kohler, Mark D. Varien, and Aaron M. Wright, eds., *Leaving Mesa Verde: Peril and Change in the Thirteenth-Century Southwest* (University of Arizona Press, 2010), 219; Scott G. Ortman, "Evidence of a Mesa Verde Homeland for the Tewa Pueblos," in Kohler, Varien, and Wright, *Leaving Mesa Verde,* 232–233, 256–258.

134. John L. Kessell, "Restoring Seventeenth-Century New Mexico, Then and Now," *Historical Archaeology* 31.1 (1997): 46. Matthew Liebmann, *Revolt: An Archaeological History of Pueblo Resistance and Revitalization in Seventeenth-Century New Mexico* (University of Arizona Press, 2012), 30.

135. Indian eyewitnesses later testified that the Spaniards shot first. Xunusta and Caucachi, eyewitness from Acoma Pueblo, reported the locals got angry because "the Spaniards first killed an Indian" and "the Spaniards had wounded an Acoma Indian" (466–467). For the full legal document, "Trial of the Indians of Acoma," see George P. Hammond and Agapito Rey, eds., *Don Juan de Oñate, Colonizer of New Mexico, 1595–1628* (University of New Mexico Press, 1953), 5: 428–479.

136. On the sentence as described in the legal document: Hammond and Rey, *Don Juan de Oñate,* 5: 477–478. Taylor, *American Colonies,* 80.

137. Don Juan de Oñate to the Viceroy of New Spain, 2 March 1599. The letter was published in Hammond and Rey, *Don Juan de Oñate,* 5: 480–481.

138. Juan de Escalona to the Viceroy of New Spain, 1 October 1601. The letter can be found in Hammond and Rey, *Don Juan de Oñate,* 6: 692–697.

139. The Pueblo Indians appreciated some of the colonizers' farming tools, but crops were struggling because of a prolonged drought. James E. Ivy, "'The Greatest

Misfortune of All': Famine in the Province of New Mexico, 1667–1672," *Journal of the Southwest* 36.1 (1994): 76–100. On the revolt: Andrew L. Knaut, *The Pueblo Revolt of 1680: Conquest and Resistance in Seventeenth-Century New Mexico* (University of Oklahoma Press, 1995); Robert W. Preucel, *Archaeologies of the Pueblo Revolt: Identity, Meaning, and Renewal in the Pueblo World* (University of New Mexico Press, 2002); Liebmann, *Revolt.*

140. Taylor, *American Colonies,* 88.

141. Liebmann, *Revolt,* 47–49.

142. Phil R. Geib, Carrie C. Heitman, and Ronald C. D. Fields, "Continuity and Change in Puebloan Ritual Practice: 3,800 Years of Shrine Use in the North American Southwest," *AA* 82.2 (2017): 353–373.

143. On suicide as resistance and escape: Zeb Tortorici, "Reading the (Dead) Body: Histories of Suicide in New Spain," in Martina Will de Chaparro and Miruna Achim, eds., *Death and Dying in Colonial Spanish America* (University of Arizona Press, 2011), 72–73.

144. Liebmann, *Revolt,* 48. Carla R. Van West et al., "The Role of Climate in Early Spanish-Native Interactions in the US Southwest," in C. Mathers, J. M. Mitchem, and C. M. Hæker, eds., *Native and Imperial Transformations: Sixteenth-Century Entradas in the American Southwest and the Southeast* (University of Arizona Press, 213), 95–96.

145. Liebmann, *Revolt,* 51–52.

146. Liebmann, *Revolt,* 54–55.

147. Dowd, *Spirited Resistance,* 32–36. Fred Anderson, *The War That Made America: A Short History of the French and Indian Wars* (Penguin, 2005), 236. On the Ghost Dance movement: Louis S. Warren, *God's Red Son: The Ghost Dance Religion and the Making of Modern America* (Basic Books, 2017). Laura Watterman Wittstock and Elaine J. Salinas, "A Brief History of the American Indian Movement," https://www.aimovement.org/ggc/history.html.

148. They killed as many as 380 of 1,000 colonists, and 21 of 23 Franciscans died. Liebmann, *Revolt,* 60–62.

149. One of those spared was Friar Juan Greyrobe, who has survived in Zuni oral history as the open-minded friar. Liebmann, *Revolt,* 60–61.

150. This was at Sandia Pueblo: Liebmann, *Revolt,* 60.

151. Taylor, *American Colonies,* 89.

152. David Grant Noble, ed., *Santa Fe: History of an Ancient City,* rev. ed. (School for Advanced Research Press, 2008), 39–40.

153. The 1760 report of Bishop Don Pedro Tamarón y Romeral of Durango is included in Eleanor B. Adams, trans., "Bishop Tamarón's Visitation of New Mexico, 1760," *New Mexico Historical Review* 28.4 (1953): 297–298 (on Acoma), 302 (on kivas). See also Jim Norris, *After "The Year Eighty": The Demise of Franciscan Power in Spanish New Mexico* (University of New Mexico Press, 2000), 132–135.

154. On the regional influence and historical impact of those mounted raiders on the Southern Plains, see Hämäläinen, *Comanche Empire.*

155. Overall, the French "pursued two seemingly contradictory policies toward their Indian neighbors." They negotiated "the most far-reaching system of Indian alliances" and also "developed an extensive system of Indian slavery." Brett Rushforth, "'A Little Flesh We Offer You': The Origins of Indian Slavery in New France," *WMQ* 60.4 (2003): 776.

156. On Jesuit missionaries killed in the 1640s and canonized in 1930, see Emma Anderson, *The Death and Afterlife of the North American Martyrs* (Harvard University Press, 2013).

157. Natchez after European contact: Jayur Madhusudan Mehta, "Spanish Conquistadores, French Explorers, and Natchez Great Suns in Southwestern Mississippi, 1542–1729," *Native South* 6 (2013): 33–69.

158. Taylor, *American Colonies,* 389. Barnett suggests that in the 1720s "the Natchez" was a confederation. Attached to the core Natchez-speaking group were two small tribes, the Tiou and Grigra. In the Natchez Confederacy political power was shared among the chiefs of five nearby villages. Fatherland (or the Grand Village) and Emerald Mound were ceremonial centers. See James F. Barnett Jr., *The Natchez Indians: A History to 1735* (University Press of Mississippi, 2007).

159. George Edward Milne, "Picking up the Pieces: Natchez Coalescence in the Shatter Zone," in Robbie Ethridge and Sheri M. Shuck-Hall, eds., *Mapping the Mississippian Shatter Zone: The Colonial Indian Slave Trade and Regional Instability in the American South* (University of Nebraska Press, 2009), 392.

160. Robert S. Neitzel, *Archaeology of the Fatherland Site: The Grand Village of the Natchez* (American Museum of Natural History, 1965), 50.

161. Milne, "Picking up the Pieces," 402–403.

162. Antoine Le Page du Pratz, *Histoire de la Louisiane . . .* (Chez de Bure, la veuve Delaguette, Lambert, 1758), 3: 43–60. An English translation can be found in Charles D. Van Tuyl, *The Natchez: Annotated Translations from Antoine Simon le Page du Pratz's Histoire de la Louisiane and A Short English-Natchez Dictionary* (Oklahoma Historical Society, 1979), 10–21. That translator consulted with Archie Sam, who was then the hereditary chief of Medicine Spring, near Gore, Oklahoma. Milne, "Picking up the Pieces," 401–402. On the site, see Ian W. Brown and Vincas P. Steponaitis, "The Grand Village of the Natchez Indians Was Indeed Grand: A Reconsideration of the Fatherland Site Landscape," in George A. Waselkov and Marvin T. Smith, eds., *Forging Southeastern Identities: Social Archaeology, Ethnohistory, and Folklore of the Mississippian to Early Historic South* (University of Alabama Press, 2017), 182–204. See also Ian W. Brown, "Plaquemine Culture in the Natchez Bluffs Region of Mississippi," in Mark A. Rees, Patrick C. Livingood, and Tristam Kidder, eds., *Plaquemine Archaeology* (University of Alabama Press, 2006), 145–160; John R. Swanton, *Indian Tribes of the Lower Mississippi Valley and Adjacent Coast of the Gulf of Mexico*, Bureau of American Ethnology Bulletin 43 (GPO, 1911); Neitzel, *Fatherland Site*; Robert S. Neitzel, *The Grand Village of the Natchez Revised: Excavations at the Fatherland Site, Adams County, Mississippi, 1972,* Archaeological Report no. 12 (Mississippi Department of Archives and History, 1983).

163. Gordon M. Sayre, "A Newly Discovered Manuscript Map by Antoine-Simon Le Page du Pratz," *French Colonial History* 2 (2010): 24. Le Page had lived on a nearby farm for five years with enslaved workers, including an Indian and several Africans.

164. She was a high-status woman in that society, which identified chiefs by female blood lines. I follow Milne's translation of Le Page du Pratz's *Histoire de la Louisiane.* Milne, "Picking up the Pieces," 401.

165. Le Page's visual representation of the burial is in *Histoire de la Louisiane,* 3: 55. My interpretation of it is indebted to K. T. Fields, the Great Sun or principal chief of the Natchez. I asked him about the image, and he said the motion suggested might be misleading. Most likely, the Natchez "would have moved his body to the four directions: first south, then west, then north, and then finally east, with his feet pointing that way to get a head start on his journey." K. T. "Hutke" Fields, principal chief, telephone interview with the author, 7 December 2016.

166. Taylor provides the detail about the proportion of the population: Taylor, *American Colonies,* 390.

167. Milne, "Picking up the Pieces," 408–411. Taylor suggests that the Natchez absorbed "more than two hundred African slaves": Taylor, *American Colonies,* 390.

168. Taylor, *American Colonies,* 389.

169. Silvia Marzagalli, "The French Atlantic World in the Seventeenth and Eighteenth Centuries," in Canny and Morgan, *Atlantic World,* 238–239.

170. Marzagalli, "French Atlantic World," 241. Paul Butel, *Histoire des Antilles françaises XVIIe–Xxe siècle* (Perrin, 2002).

171. On types of regional economies: David J. Keene, "Beyond Fur Trade: The Eighteenth-Century Colonial Economy of French North America as Seen from Fort De Chartes in the Illinois Country," PhD diss., University of Wisconsin-Madison, 2002, 14. On colonial Detroit: Catherine Cangany, *Frontier Seaport: Detroit's Transformation into an Atlantic Entrepôt* (University of Chicago Press, 2014).

172. Marzagalli, "French Atlantic World," 238. On Jesuit missions, see Blackburn, *Harvest of Souls,* and Dominique Deslandres, *Croire et faire croire: Les missions françaises au XVIIe siècle* (Fayard, 2003). Detroit, for example, was founded in 1701 primarily to protect the Great Lakes fur trade from the British and the Haudenosaunee, but "it also served as a Christianization center for Indians": Cangany, *Frontier Seaport,* 22–23.

173. Interpreters have offered varied accounts of the meaning of *Tekawitha.* The Saint Regis Mohawk Tribe suggests it means "putting things in order." "Saint Kateri Tekakwitha," Saint Regis Mohawk Tribe, https://www.srmt-nsn.gov/saint_kateri_tekakwitha.

174. When pronounced in French with a Mohawk accent, *Catherine* sounds like *Kateri,* which is how it entered the record in the nineteenth century, but Greer uses *Catherine* to recall her namesake, Catherine of Siena. Allan Greer, *Mohawk Saint: Catherine Tekawitha and the Jesuits* (Oxford University Press, 2005), xi. Catherine was her baptismal name, and Tekawitha was the name her Mohawk community gave her as a child.

175. On the movement of the village, see Greer, *Mohawk Saint,* 90.

176. The drawing of the mission settlement that I rely on here is "Vue de la mission du Sault St Louis" (1730), wash and watercolor, 27×37.6 cm, Bibliothèque nationale de France.

177. Greer, *Mohawk Saint,* 4.

178. Greer, *Mohawk Saint,* 4, 22–24. Claude Chauchetière, *La vie de la B. Catherine Tegakouita dite à présent la Saincte Sauvagesse* (Presse Cramoisy, 1887). Pierre Cholenec, "La vie de Catherine Tegakouita, première vierge Iroquoise," Archives de l'hôtel-dieu de Québec. See also the oil painting of Catherine Tekawitha by Father Claude Chauchetière (1690).

179. Quoted in Greer, *Mohawk Saint,* 56. The original passage: Chauchetière, *Vie de la B. Catherine Tegakouita,* 37–40.

180. Greer, *Mohawk Saint,* 10. Joseph-François Lafitau, *Customs of the American Indians Compared with the Customs of Primitive Times,* William N. Fenton and Elizabeth L. Moore, eds. (Champlain Society, 1974), 2: 227, 237–238, 251–256. On parallels in "deathways," see Erik R. Seeman, *The Huron-Wendat Feast of the Dead: Indian-European Encounters in Early North America* (Johns Hopkins University Press, 2011).

181. Greer, *Mohawk Saint,* 108–110. The observation about shamans is from Lafitau, *Customs of the American Indians,* 1: 246, 243, 133.

182. On Rouensa and Kaskaskia, see Sophie White, *Wild Frenchmen and Frenchified Indians: Material Culture and Race in Colonial Louisiana* (University of Pennsylvania Press, 2012), 8–10, 33–40, 78–92, 108–115, 122–127, 130–134, 138–139, 141, 145, 149, 151, 156, 173–174, 181, 183, 229, 231–232; David MacDonald, *Lives of Fort de Chartres: Commandants, Soldiers, and Civilians in French Illinois, 1720–1770* (Southern Illinois University Press, 2016), 125–130; Tracy Neal Leavelle, *The Catholic Calumet: Colonial Conversions in French and Indian North America* (University of Pennsylvania Press, 2012), 122–123, 156–162, 189–190, 203.

183. On the first and second generation of Jesuits: Robert Michael Morrissey, "'I Speak It Well': Language, Cultural Understanding, and the End of a Missionary Middle Ground in Illinois Country, 1673–1712," *Early American Studies* 9.3 (2011): 617–648. On intermarriage as a path to "Frenchification" and conversion, see White, *Frenchified Indians,* chap. 3.

184. The bilingual edition of Marquette's first and second journeys can be found in Thwaites, *Jesuit Relations,* 59: 109–163, 185–211. I consulted those to check the original phrasing, but I cite the narratives in John Gilmary Shea, ed., *Discovery and Exploration of the Mississippi Valley, with the Original Narratives of Marquette, Allouez, Membre, Hennepin, and Anastase Douay,* 2nd ed. (Joseph McDonough, 1903), 23–37.

185. On the calumet as the decorated stem, not the whole pipe, see Ian W. Brown, "The Calumet Ceremony in the Southeast and Its Archaeological Manifestation," *AA* 54 (1989): 312–313, 329; and Elizabeth A. Fenn, *Encounters at the Heart of the World: A History of the Mandan People* (Hill and Wang, 2014), 36.

186. The quotations in the rest of this paragraph, from the account of Marquette's second voyage, are from Shea, *Mississippi Valley,* 58–59.

187. Morrissey, "'I Speak It Well,'" 627. A later version of the prayer book was published as Claude Allouez et al., *Facsimile of Père Marquette's Illinois Prayer Book*

(Quebec Literary and Historical Society, 1908). On the prayer book: Tracy Neal Leavelle, "'Bad Things' and 'Good Hearts': Mediation, Meaning, and the Language of Illinois Christianity," *CH* 76.2 (2007): 363–394.

188. On Rouensa's will and funeral: White, *Frenchified Indians,* 112–114, 130–131; Leavelle, *Catholic Calumet,* 154–155. The inventory of Rouensa's will is included in Theodore P. Fadler and Susanne M. Fadler, *Memoirs of a French Village: Chronicles of Prairie du Rocher, Kaskaskia, and the French Triangle,* 2nd ed. (1972; Phoenix Cosmopolitan Publishing, 2016), 315–322.

189. Morrissey, "'I Speak It Well,'" 618.

190. Father Pierre-Gabriel Marest to Father Barthélemi Germon, written from the village of "the Immaculate Conception of the Holy Virgin, Cascasquias," 9 November 1712. Reprinted in Shea, *Mississippi Valley,* 27–35. The quotation is on p. 28.

191. I sometimes use the word *convert,* but in most cases religious change is more ambiguous than either the idea or the ideal of religious conversion conveys. I try to recover what Natives did and said—and what they found interesting about the faith they were offered. I emphasize the ways they *engaged* the tradition or *affiliated* with the church or *identified* with the faith. It is a small difference in language, but motives for affiliating were sometimes complex and often unrecoverable, and we should not assume that affiliation erased one way of life as devotees embraced another. See Linford D. Fisher, *The Indian Great Awakening: Religion and the Shaping of Native Cultures in Early America* (Oxford University Press, 2012), 1, 5.

192. Fadler and Fadler, *Memoirs of a French Village,* 315–322.

193. On this visit, see Leavelle, *Catholic Calumet,* 1–2. 13.

194. Leavelle, *Catholic Calumet,* 13. On that transatlantic encounter, see also Richard N. Ellis and Charles R. Steen, "An Indian Delegation in France, 1725," *Journal of the Illinois State Historical Society* 67 (1974): 385–405.

195. Quoted in Leavelle, *Catholic Calumet,* 1. For the original letter by that Jesuit, see Mathurin Le Petit to Louis d'Avaugout, 12 July 1730, in Thwaites, *Jesuit Relations,* 68: 209–211.

196. The obituary for Marie Tranchepan of St. Augustine, who died in 1733, is included in Emily Clark, ed., *Voices from an Early American Convent: Marie Madeleine Hachard and the New Orleans Ursulines, 1727–1760* (LSU Press, 2007), 108–113.

197. The Hachard quotations are from a letter to her father dated 24 April 1728. It is included in Clark, *Early American Convent,* 75–91.

198. Vernon Valentine Palmer, "The Origins and Authors of the Code Noir," *Louisiana Law Review* 56.2 (1996): 363–407. The articles of the code banned Jews and Huguenots, for example, and only Catholic marriages were recognized as valid.

199. On the Natchez orphans from Fort Rosalie, see Emily Clark, *Masterless Mistresses: The New Orleans Ursulines and the Development of a New World Society, 1727–1834* (University of North Carolina Press, 2006), 75.

200. On the 1734 Eucharistic procession, see the firsthand account by Sister Jeanne Melotte, which appears in Clark, *Early American Convent,* 124–127. See also the helpful analysis of the procession in Clark, *Masterless Mistresses,* 59–64.

201. On the confraternity, see Clark, *Masterless Mistresses,* 76–79, 64.

202. On Dubreuil, see Clark, *Masterless Mistresses,* 76. On her uncle and husband, see Virginia Meacham Gould, "Afro-Creole Women in Early New Orleans," in Richmond F. Brown, ed., *Coastal Encounters: The Transformation of the Gulf South in the Eighteenth Century* (University of Nebraska Press, 2007), 153. We cannot be certain she walked in the procession, though it is likely. On Dubreuil's role as evangelizer of her slaves, the baptismal records suggest she took it very seriously. See Mary Bernard Deggs, *No Cross, No Crown: Black Nuns in Nineteenth-Century New Orleans* (Indiana University Press, 2002), xxvii.

203. It was the largest building at that time, an architectural historian has suggested: Samuel Wilson Jr., "Religious Architecture in French Colonial Louisiana," *Winterthur Portfolio* 8 (1973): 92.

204. Leavelle, *Catholic Calumet,* 191–193. Clark, *Masterless Mistresses,* 76–79.

205. Joyce E. Chaplin, "The British Atlantic," in Canny and Morgan, *Atlantic World,* 228.

206. The quotation about New England fields and fences is from William Cronon, *Changes in the Land: Indians, Colonists and the Ecology of New England,* rev. ed. (Hill and Wang, 2003), 156. On New England as "healthier" and the lowland Carolina plantations as unhealthy—slave mortality exceeded the birth rate—see Taylor, *American Colonies,* 170, 238.

207. As Butler shows, the Huguenots settled primarily in Boston, New York, and Charleston. Butler, *Huguenots in America.* The other three towns I mention were in French territory.

Chapter 4. Plantation Religion

1. See Robert Emmett Curran, *Papist Devils: Catholics in British America, 1574–1784* (Catholic University of America Press, 2014).

2. The John Winthrop quotation is from "Reasons to Be Considered, and Objections with Answers," in *Winthrop Papers,* vol. II, 1623–1630 (Massachusetts Historical Society, 1931), 138–140.

3. Christopher Hill, *Antichrist in Seventeenth-Century England* (Oxford University Press, 1971), 40. James P. Byrd Jr., *The Challenges of Roger Williams: Religious Liberty, Violent Persecution, and the Bible* (Mercer University Press, 2002), 171–182.

4. *History of the Four Indian Kings from the Continent of America . . .* (Edward Midwinter, 1710).

5. Brendan McConville, "Pope's Day Revisited: 'Popular Culture' Reconsidered," *Explorations in Early American Culture* 4 (2000): 258–280. James Sharpe, *Remember, Remember: A Cultural History of Guy Fawkes Day* (Harvard University Press, 2005).

6. I refer again to *imperial religion,* my term for the mutually supporting connections between religious institutions and expansionist states, or empires that cross terrestrial and aquatic boundaries as they control diverse local cultures and peoples and impose regime-serving hierarchical distinctions between its own people and those it controls. On British *imperial Protestantism,* which emerged fully by the 1730s, see Katherine Carté, *Religion and the American Revolution: An Imperial History* (University of North Carolina Press, 2021), 4–6, 34, 378.

7. Jon Butler, *New World Faiths: Religion in Colonial America* (Oxford University Press, 2008), 72.

8. Thomas S. Kidd, *The Protestant Interest: New England after Puritanism* (Yale University Press, 2004), 1–13. See also Carla Gardina Pestana, *Protestant Empire: Religion and the Making of the British Atlantic World* (University of Pennsylvania Press, 2009), 6. Carté goes further, emphasizing a "shared Protestantism": Carté, *Religion and the American Revolution*, 4–6, 19.

9. Rhode Island protected freedom of *worship* but restricted the *civil* rights of Catholics and Jews in 1719. Violating the Charter of 1663, it restricted voting and office holding to "men professing Christianity . . . (Roman Catholicks only excepted)." Sidney S. Rider, ed., *The Charter and the Acts and Laws of His Majesties Colony of Rhode Island and Providence Plantations in America, 1719* (Sidney S. Rider and Burnett Rider, 1895), 3. The civil disability against Catholics was removed in 1783, and the discrimination against Jews ended in 1798. See Patrick T. Conley, "Rhode Island: Laboratory for the 'Lively Experiment,'" in *The Bill of Rights and the States: The Colonial and Revolutionary Origins of American Liberties* (Madison House, 1991), chap. 5; Patrick T. Conley, *Democracy in Decline: Rhode Island's Constitutional Development, 1776–1841* (Rhode Island Historical Society, 1977), 7–142.

10. I distinguish *statutory* and *de facto* religious establishments, those embedded in law and those maintained by the cultural power and personal networks of the dominant group. On Anglican, Presbyterian, and Congregationalist "establishments," see Carté, *Religion and the American Revolution*, 21–43. On the "institutionalization of religious inequity," with Catholics, Jews, and atheists suffering the most: Ralph E. Pyle and James D. Davidson, "The Origins of Religious Stratification in Colonial America," *JSSR* 42.1 (2003): 57–76.

11. Butler, *New World Faiths*, 73.

12. Jon Butler, *Awash in a Sea of Faith: Christianizing the American People* (Harvard University Press, 1990), 290–291.

13. Robert V. Wells, "England's Colonies in America: Old English or New Americans?," *Population Studies* 46.1 (1992): 90.

14. Daniel K. Richter, *Facing East from Indian Country: A Native History of Early America* (Harvard University Press, 2001), 7. Chinese-inspired designs influenced imports, from teapots and tea tables to chairs and wallpaper: Ellen Paul Denker, *After the Chinese Taste: Chinese Influence in America, 1730–1930* (Peabody Museum, 1985), 1–15.

15. New Englanders were complicit in the West Indies slave trade, sending planters "critical infrastructure elements like oil, candles, fish, livestock, and wood" and using the payments for English goods: Eric Kimball, "'What Have We to Do with Slavery?' New Englanders and the Slave Economies of the West Indies," in Sven Beckert and Seth Rockman, eds., *Slavery's Capitalism: A New History of American Economic Development* (University of Pennsylvania Press, 192).

16. On "muddy ground" and "middle ground": Christopher Pastore, *Between Land and Sea: The Atlantic Coast and the Transformation of New England* (Harvard University Press, 2014), 4.

17. Jean-Jacques Rousseau, *The First and Second Discourses,* Roger D. Masters, ed. (St. Martin's Press, 1964), 141–142. Rousseau was raised Protestant and converted to Catholicism. The year the Second Discourse was published he returned to Protestantism and Geneva.

18. Winthrop, "Reasons to Be Considered, and Objections with Answers." On Winthrop's understanding of "uncultivated" and "unenclosed" land: Justin B. Litke, *Twilight of the Republic: Empire and Exceptionalism in the American Political Tradition* (University of Kentucky Press, 2013), 30–31.

19. The quotation is from the section on "property" in the *Second Treatise on Civil Government:* John Locke, *Two Treatises on Government* (Hafner, 1973), 136. Locke wrote that section while he was revising the Carolina Constitution in 1682: David Armitage, "John Locke, Carolina, and the Two Treatises of Government," *Political Theory* 32.5 (2004): 602–627.

20. John R. Stilgoe, *Common Landscape of America, 1580 to 1845* (Yale University Press, 1982), 47–53. Darret Bruce Rutman, *Husbandmen of Plymouth: Farms and Villages in the Old Colony, 1620–1692* (Beacon, 1967), 29–36. Those who worked the land were called *husbandmen* until 1750 and *cultivators* or *agriculturalists* between 1750 and 1820. After 1820 *farmers* became more prevalent: Stilgoe, *Common Landscape of America,* 137. On New Haven green and its churches: Peter Williams, *Houses of God: Region, Religion, and Architecture in the United States* (University of Illinois Press, 1997), 11–12.

21. The meetinghouse was First Church or First Parish and later called Old Ship. G. E. Kidder, *The Beacon Guide to New England Houses of Worship* (Beacon, 1989), 80–81. The list of ministers: *The Commemorative Services of First Parish in Hingham on the Two Hundredth Anniversary of the Building of Its Meeting-House* (Published by the Parish, 1882), 162.

22. On Hingham's affiliation rates: Douglas L. Winiarksi, *Darkness Falls on the Land of Light: Experiencing Religious Awakenings in Eighteenth-Century New England* (University of North Carolina, 2017), 93–97.

23. Peter Benes and Philip D. Zimmerman, *New England Meeting House and Church, 1630–1850* (Boston University and the Currier Gallery of Art for the Dublin Seminar for New England Folklife, 1979), 55.

24. Benes and Zimmerman, *New England Meeting House and Church,* 21. Williams, *Houses of God,* 3–6.

25. Kidder, *New England Houses of Worship,* 60–61.

26. The sorting was based on "age, dignity of descent, place of public trust, pious disposition, estate, and peculiar serviceableness of any kind." Horton Davies, *The Worship of the American Puritans, 1629–1730* (Peter Lang, 1990), 284–285.

27. William Bradford, *A Relation or Journal of the Beginning and Proceedings of the English Plantation Settled at Plimoth in New England* (John Bellamie, 1621), 6–7.

28. Erik R. Seeman, *Death in the New World: Cross-Cultural Encounters, 1492–1800* (University of Pennsylvania, 2010), 144–146. Kathleen Donegan, *Seasons of Misery: Catastrophe and Colonial Settlement in Early America* (University of Pennsylvania Press, 2014), 119–121.

29. The seal of Massachusetts Bay Colony, used from 1629 to 1686. Commonwealth of Massachusetts, "History of the Arms and Great Seal of the Commonwealth of Massachusetts," https://www.sec.state.ma.us/divisions/public-records/history-of-seal.htm.

30. John Eliot and Thomas Mayhew, *Tears of Repentance; Or, A Further Narrative of the Progress of the Gospel Amongst the Indians in New-England* (Peter Cole, 1653). On the locals' name for the island, Noëpe: Laura Arnold Leibman, ed., *Experience Mayhew's Indian Converts: A Cultural Edition* (University of Massachusetts Press, 2008), 27.

31. Leibman, *Experience Mayhew's Indian Converts*, 232–233. The original edition: Experience Mayhew, *Indian Converts* (S. Gerrish, 1727). Those missionaries used agricultural metaphors: planting "seeds" of faith, "cultivating" pious habits, and "harvesting" souls for Christ. Mather wrote about "gospelizing the uncultivated souls," and another report was entitled *New England's First Fruits.* Just as often, however, ministers turned to metaphors about light/dark. Indigenous Peoples lived in paganism's "darkness" and needed the "light" of the gospel: Drew Lopenzina, *Red Ink: Native Americans Picking Up the Pen in the Colonial Period* (State University of New York Press, 2012), 103. Thomas Shepard, John Wilson, and John Eliot, *The Day Breaking, if Not the Sun Rising of the Gospell with the Indians in New England* (Printed by Rich. Cotes for Fulk Clifton, 1647); Thomas Shepard and John Eliot, *The Clear Sunshine of the Gospel Breaking Forth upon the Indians in New England* (J. Bellamy, 1648); Henry Whitefield, Thomas Mayhew, and John Eliot, *The Light Appearing More and More Towards the Perfect Day* (T. R. & E. M. for John Bartlet, 1651).

32. For Winthrop's description of Eliot's method, see John Winthrop, *The Journal of John Winthrop, 1630–1649* (Harvard University Press, 1996), 322–325.

33. Richard W. Cogley, *John Eliot's Mission to the Indians before King Philip's War* (Harvard University Press, 2009). Julius H. Rubin, *Tears of Repentance: Christian Identity and Community in Colonial Southern New England* (University of Nebraska Press, 2013).

34. Rachel Wheeler, *To Live upon Hope: Mohicans and Missionaries in the Eighteenth-Century Northeast* (Cornell University Press, 2008), 31.

35. Lopenzina, *Red Ink*, 93–96.

36. Wheeler, *To Live upon Hope*, 31. Lopenzina, *Red Ink*, 134. See also Lisa Brooks, *The Common Pot: The Recovery of Native Space in the Northeast* (University of Minnesota Press, 2008), 64–83, 101–103.

37. Linford D. Fisher, *The Indian Great Awakening: Religion and the Shaping of Native Cultures in Early America* (Oxford University Press, 2012), 5–7; Kevin A. McBride, "Bundles, Bears, and Bibles: Interpreting Native 'Texts,'" in Kristina Bross and Hilary E. Wyss, eds., *Early Native Literacies in New England: A Documentary and Critical Anthology* (University of Massachusetts Press, 2008), 132–141; William S. Simmons, *Cautantowwit's House: An Indian Burial Ground on the Island of Conanicut in Narragansett Bay* (Brown University Press, 1970). See also "The Mashantucket (Western) Pequot Tribal Nation," https://www.mptn-nsn.gov/default.aspx.

38. Indenture of Rebeckah Chin: Eliezer Freeman and Rebeckah Freeman, Indenture to Eleazer [i.e., Eliezer] and Rebeckah Freeman, 29 June 1731, Edward E. Ayer Collection, Newberry Library, Chicago.

39. Patricia E. Rubertone, *Grave Undertakings: An Archaeology of Roger Williams and the Narragansett* (Smithsonian Institution Press, 2001); Ryan Tripp, "Native Proprietors of the Soil: Narragansett Tribal Governance and Plantation Provisioning Politics in Colonial Rhode Island," PhD diss., University of California, Davis, 2014.

40. The quotations are from Williams's letter to John Endicott, governor of Massachusetts, dated "August 1651." Repr. in Perry Miller, *Roger Williams: His Contributions to the American Tradition* (Bobbs-Merrill, 1953), 158–164. See also Rider, ed., *Charter and Acts and Laws of His Majesties Colony of Rhode Island.* Conley, *Democracy in Decline,* 7–54. Gail I. Winson, "Researching the Laws of the Colony of Rhode Island and Providence Plantations: From Lively Experiment to Statehood," in Michael G. Chiorazzi and Marguerite Most, eds., *Prestatehood Legal Materials: A Fifty-State Research Guide . . .* (Haworth Information Press, 2005), 2: 1029–1054.

41. David D. Hall, ed., *The Antinomian Controversy, 1636–1638,* 2nd ed. (Duke University Press, 1990), 15.

42. Sandra M. Gustafson, *Eloquence Is Power: Oratory and Performance in Early America* (University of North Carolina, 2000), 25.

43. Hall, *Antinomian Controversy,* 337.

44. Horatio Rogers, *Mary Dyer of Rhode Island . . .* (Preston and Rounds, 1896), 94–97, 84–86. Catherine A. Brekus, *Strangers and Pilgrims: Female Preaching in America, 1740–1845* (University of North Carolina Press, 1998), 30.

45. The 1692 controversy concerned more than immediate revelations. Prosecutors said it was about an Indigenous slave accused of casting spells, and confirming "spectral evidence" in dreams. It also concerned the congregation's divergent opinions of their polarizing pastor, who had criticized ministers' lower standards for church membership. David D. Hall, ed., *Witch-Hunting in Seventeenth-Century New England: A Documentary History* (Northeastern University Press, 1999). On the ministerial controversy: Benjamin C. Ray, "'The Salem Witch Mania': Recent Scholarship and American History Textbooks," *JAAR* 78.1 (2010): 40–64.

46. For an environmental interpretation of the Salem crisis: Mark Fiege, *The Republic of Nature: An Environmental History of the United States* (University of Washington Press, 2012), 50–51.

47. The Middle Colonies formed amid Native–European and interimperial battles among three Protestant empires (Dutch, Swedish, and English), as Catholic France and Spain lurked in the background. The Dutch conquered New Sweden in 1655, and the English conquered the Dutch in 1664. Sweden then included part of Norway, all of Finland, and extended into Russia. See Carol E. Hoffecker et al., eds., *New Sweden in America* (University of Delaware Press, 1995).

48. Charles II had a brother, James, who was Catholic, and the king's own deathbed conversion in 1685 complicated the relationship between the monarchy and the Church of England. Scholars debate the motives for his conversion, but the charters

he approved for the colonies tolerated Catholics and dissenting Protestants. Patricia Gael, "Kingship and Catholicism in Posthumous Representations of Charles II, 1685–1714," *Seventeenth Century* 29.2 (2014): 175, 186, 189. Ronald Hutton, "The Religion of Charles II," in R. Malcolm Smuts, ed., *The Stuart Court and Europe* (Cambridge University Press, 1996), 228–248.

49. Evan Haefeli, *New Netherland and the Dutch Origins of American Religious Liberty* (University of Pennsylvania, 2012), 279–287. Dutch Brazil as pluralistic: F. L. Schalkwijk, *The Reformed Church in Dutch Brazil (1630–1654)* (Boekencentrum, 1998).

50. Kambiz GhaneaBassiri, *A History of Islam in America: From the New World to the New World Order* (Cambridge University Press, 2010), 9, 11–12. Leo Hershkowitz, "The Troublesome Turk: An Illustration of Judicial Process in New Amsterdam," *New York History* 46.4 (1965): 299–310. Susannah Shaw Romney, "Intimate Networks and Children's Survival in New Netherland in the Seventeenth Century," *Early American Studies* 7.2 (2009): 276. Ira Berlin, "From Creole to African: Atlantic Creoles and the Origins of African American Slavery in Mainland North America," *WMQ* 53 (1986): 251–288.

51. It was signed by twenty-eight residents of Flushing and two from Jamaica. On the document's limited effect: Dennis I. Maika, "Commemoration and Context: The Flushing Remonstrance Then and Now," *New York History* (2008): 29–42.

52. John Locke's *A Letter Concerning Toleration* was shaped by the author's interactions with a Dutch theologian. See Jean Le Clerc, *A Funeral Oration upon the Death of Mr. Philip Limborch . . .* (A. Baldwin, 1713). John Marshall, *John Locke, Toleration, and Early Enlightenment Culture: Religious Intolerance and Arguments for Religious Tolerance in Early Modern and "Early Enlightenment" Europe* (Cambridge University Press, 2006), 481–95. Jeremy Dupertuis Bangs, "Dutch Contributions to Religious Toleration," *CH* 79.3 (2010): 609–610.

53. The provincial charters had a provision protecting liberty of conscience in religion: section 16 of *The Charter or Fundamental Laws, of West New Jersey, Agreed Upon—1676;* section 16 of *The Fundamental Constitutions for the Province of East New Jersey in America, Anno Domini 1683;* and section 35 of *The Frame of Government of Pennsylvania May 5, 1682.* See "Colonial Charters, Grants and Related Documents," https://avalon.law.yale.edu/subject_menus/statech.asp.

54. Alf Åberg. *The People of New Sweden: Our Colony on the Delaware River* (Bokförlaget Natur och Kultur, 1988). Amandus Johnson, *The Swedish Settlements on the Delaware, 1638–1664* (Swedish Colonial Society, 1911). Hoffecker, *New Sweden in America.*

55. Quoted in Patricia U. Bonomi and Peter R. Eisenstadt, "Church Adherence in the Eighteenth-Century British American Colonies," *WMQ* 39.2 (1982): 272. The Memorial of Colonel [Lewis] Morris concerning the State of Religion in the Jerseys, 19 September 1702, Journals of the Society for the Propagation of the Gospel in Foreign Parts, appendix A, no. 2, USPG Archives, Bodleian Library, Oxford University.

56. "Ranting Quakers": "Governor Dongan's Report to the Committee of Trade on the Province of New York 22 February 1687," in E. B. O'Callahan, ed., *Documentary*

History of the State of New-York (Weed, Parsons, 1849), 1: 186. "Differences": John Miller, *New Yorke Considered and Improved A.D. 1695*, Victor Hugo Paltsits, ed. (Burrows Brothers, 1903), 55, 66.

57. Penn repeated "liberty of conscience" in several texts. See William Penn, *The Great Case of Liberty of Conscience Once More Briefly Defended and Debated* (n.p., 1670).

58. Howard M. Jenkins, *The Family of William Penn . . .* (Jenkins, 1899), 34–35. For the record of his entrance to Christ Church on 26 October 1660, see *Alumnus Aedis Christi: 1636–70*, 84, Christ Church Library Archives, Oxford University.

59. William's payment is recorded in the "Caution Book," 31 May 1662, Christ Church Library Archives, Oxford University.

60. William Penn, *William Penn's Journal of His Travels in Holland and Germany in 1677 . . .* (Darton and Harvey, 1835), 102.

61. William Penn, *No Cross, No Crown . . .* (n.p., 1669).

62. William Penn and William Mead, *The People's (Ancient and Just) Liberties Asserted in the Tryal of William Penn and William Mead . . .* (n.p., 1670).

63. S. V. Henkels, ed., *The Charter of Liberties from William Penn to the Freemen of the Province of Pennsylvania* (Printed for private circulation, 1909). *Frame of Government of Pennsylvania*, https://avalon.law.yale.edu/17th_century/pa04.asp.

64. The Wampum Belt was said to be given to William Penn by the Lenape at the time of the 1682 treaty. The belt, donated in 1857 to the Historical Society of Pennsylvania by a great-grandson of Penn, is made of white wampum with darker accent beads. See Graphics Collection, Wampum Belt, Photograph Collection, Box 58, Folder 1, Historical Society of Pennsylvania, Philadelphia. For a romanticized image of the signing, see Benjamin West's *Penn's Treaty with the Indians* (1771–1772), held in the Pennsylvania Academy of the Fine Arts, Philadelphia.

65. Jane T. Merritt, *At the Crossroads: Indians and Empires on a Mid-Atlantic Frontier* (University of North Carolina, 2003), 23–28. Voltaire praised the treaty as one that "was never infring'd." Voltaire, *Letters Concerning the English Nation* (Repr. for C. Davis, 1733), 29.

66. Penn's rectilinear urban plan was first visualized in a surveyor's map by Thomas Holme originally called *A Portraiture of the City of Philadelphia*. See *A Portraiture of the City of Philadelphia in the Province of Pennsylvania in America . . .* (Andrew Sowle, 1683). It is available in Quaker and Special Collections, Haverford College Libraries, Haverford, Pennsylvania.

67. Kurt W. Carr and Roger W. Moeller, *First Pennsylvanians: The Archaeology of Native Americans in Pennsylvania* (Pennsylvania Historical and Museum Commission, 2015), 209.

68. Randall M. Miller and William Pencak, eds., *Pennsylvania: A History of the Commonwealth* (Pennsylvania State University Press, 2002), 94.

69. The debate was different in New England. See Samuel Sewall, *The Selling of Joseph: A Memorial* (Bartholomew Green, and John Allen, 1700). Cotton Mather, *The Negro Christianized* (B. Green, 1706). Mark A. Peterson, "The Selling of Joseph:

Bostonians, Antislavery, and the Protestant International, 1689–1733," *Massachusetts Historical Review* 4 (2002): 13.

70. Gerret Hendericks, Derick up de Graeff, Francis Daniell Pastorius, and Abraham up den Graef, "First Quaker Protest against Slavery in the Americas, 1688," Haverford College Quaker and Special Collections, manuscript collection 990 B-R, 2 pages. There was another protest in 1696: Morgan Cadwalader, "Quaker Protest against Slavery, Merion (PA), 1696," Haverford College Special Collections, manuscript collection 990 B-R, 2 pages. John Woolman, *Some Considerations on the Keeping of Negroes . . .* (James Chattin, 1754). On the approval of Woolman's antislavery sentiments: "Philadelphia Yearly Meeting Epistle of Caution and Advice, 1754," Haverford College Quaker and Special Collections. There were provincial efforts to ban slavery. In 1711 Britain's Queen Anne overruled a Pennsylvania colonial law prohibiting slavery. Woolman mentioned a 1758 visit to the Meeting in Chester County: John G. Whittier, ed., *The Journal of John Woolman* (Houghton, Mifflin, 1871), 134.

71. Michael David Scholl, "The American Yeoman: An Historical Ecology of Production in Colonial Pennsylvania," PhD diss., University of North Carolina at Chapel Hill, 2008, 21, 27. See also James T. Lemon, *The Best Poor Man's Country: A Geographical Study of Early Southeastern Pennsylvania* (W. W. Norton, 1972); John Futhey Smith, *History of Chester County Pennsylvania . . .* (L. H. Everts, 1881), 229–301. On vernacular religious practices like astrology and divination: Frank Bruckerl, "The Quaker Cunning Folk: The Astrology, Magic, and Divination of Philip Roman and Sons in Colonial Chester County, Pennsylvania," *Pennsylvania History* 80.4 (2013): 479–500.

72. Muhlenberg founded Zion Lutheran in Chester County in 1743, the same year he helped purchase a lot for Philadelphia's first German Lutheran church. Theodore C. Tappert and John W. Doberstein, eds., *The Notebook of a Colonial Clergyman* (Muhlenberg Press, 1959), 12–16. Charles F. Dapp, *History of Zion's or Old Organ Church* (Inter-Borough Press, 1919), 1–16.

73. Williams, *Houses of God,* 48–49.

74. Gottlieb Mittelberger noted that in the Quaker meetinghouse "one can often hear and see a woman preach." Carl Theodor Eben, trans., *Gottlieb Mittelberger's Journey to Pennsylvania in the Year 1750 . . .* (John Joseph McVey, 1898), 50. Sophie Hutchison Drinker, *Hannah Penn and the Proprietorship of Pennsylvania* (International Publishing for the National Society of the Colonial Dames of America, 1958). Alison Duncan Hirsch, "'Instructions from a Woman': Hannah Penn and the Pennsylvania Proprietorship," PhD diss., Columbia University, 1991. Hannah had more direct political power than any other woman in the English colonies, serving for years as the leader of the province.

75. Massachusetts Bay Colony founded Harvard in 1636 to promote "a learned ministry." See George Huntston Williams, *Divinings: Religion at Harvard from Its Origins in New England Ecclesiastical History to the 175th Anniversary of the Harvard Divinity School, 1636–1992* (Vandenhoeck & Ruprecht, 2014). On Jane Fenn Hoskens (sometimes Hoskins), see Jane Hoskens, *The Life and Spiritual Sufferings of That*

Faithful Servant of Christ Jane Hoskens, A Public Preacher among the People Called Quakers (William Evitt, 1771). See Jane Fenn (later Hoskins), "A Journal of the Travels of Jane Fenn, 1727–1729," Friends Historical Library, Swarthmore College. On her role as a female preacher, see Rebecca Larson, *Quaker Women: Preaching and Prophesying in the Colonies and Abroad, 1700–1775* (University of North Carolina Press, 1999), 47–54, 56, 58, 77, 81, 82, 90, 179, 211, 283–284, 310–311. See also Brekus, *Strangers and Pilgrims.*

76. Walter F. Price, "Friends' Meeting Houses at Chester, Pennsylvania," *Bulletin of the Friends' Historical Association* 21.2 (1932): 66–68.

77. The interior of the Old Kennett Meeting House, Chester County, Pennsylvania, photography by Jack E. Boucher, Historic American Buildings Survey, Library of Congress, Prints and Photographs Division.

78. Hoskens, *Life and Spiritual Sufferings,* 21–22.

79. Hoskens, *Life and Spiritual Sufferings,* 26.

80. Jon Butler, *Becoming America: The Revolution before 1776* (Harvard University Press, 2000), 189. These denominational organizations in Philadelphia included the Presbytery of Philadelphia (1706), and later the more powerful Synod of Philadelphia (1716); the Philadelphia Baptist Association (1707); the Coetus, a "coming together" or association, of the Reformed or German Calvinist Church (1747); and the Lutheran Ministerium of Pennsylvania (1748).

81. Albert Bushnell Hart, ed., *Hamilton's Itinerarium* . . . (William K. Bixby, 1907). The entry is from 8 June 1744.

82. On the Catholic population: Sister Blanche Marie, "The Catholic Church in Colonial Pennsylvania," *Pennsylvania History* 3.4 (1936): 240.

83. For eyewitness accounts of Philadelphia's places of worship between 1750 and 1760, see Eben, trans., *Gottlieb Mittelberger's Journey,* 50, and Andrew Burnaby, *Travels through the Middle Settlements in North America in the Years 1759–1760* (T. Payne, 1775), 44.

84. On the Moravian missions, see John Heckewelder, *Narrative of the Mission of the United Brethren among the Delaware and Mohegan Indians* . . . (McCarty and Davis, 1820).

85. On the origin of the Philadelphia Baptist Church: A. D. Gillette, ed., *Minutes of the Philadelphia Baptist Association, from* A.D. *1707 to* A.D. *1807* (American Baptist Publication Society, 1851), 21–22.

86. New York City churches: Adolph S. Benson, ed., *The America of 1750: Peter Kalm's Travels in North America, the English Version of 1770,* 2 vols. (Dover, 1966). A list of the churches and account of religion around 1700 can be found in Miller, *New Yorke Considered and Improved,* 48–49, 54–55, 66–67.

87. The quotation is from Warren R. Petty, Jean Howson, and Barbara A. Bianco, *New York African Burial Ground Archaeology Final Report* (Howard University, 2006), 1: 447. Further details can be found on pp. 444–457.

88. Some call this the "First American Enlightenment." May's term, the "Moderate Enlightenment," also is useful: Henry F. May, *The Enlightenment in America*

(Oxford University Press, 1976), 2–101. "Supernatural rationalists" were the majority: Conrad Wright, *The Liberal Christians: Essays on American Unitarian History* (Unitarian Universalist Association, 1970), 5–6. One of the first to use "Great Awakening" was Joseph Tracy, *The Great Awakening: A History of the Revival of Religion in the Time of Edwards and Whitefield* (Tappan and Dennet, 1842). Butler's classic criticism of those who overemphasize the revivals' coherence and impact still has merit: Jon Butler, "Enthusiasm Described and Decried: The Great Awakening as Interpretive Fiction," *JAH* 69.2 (1982): 324.

89. Head-centered and heart-centered religion: Harry S. Stout, *The New England Soul: Preaching and Religious Culture in Colonial New England* (Oxford University Press, 2012), 257. I also contrast sudden and gradual approaches, and my interpretation applies insights from Buddhist polemics about the path (*marga*) to awakening (*bodhi*), including in the *Platform Sutra,* a classic text of Chan Buddhism. Philip B. Yampolsky, trans., *The Platform Sutra of the Sixth Patriarch* (Columbia University Press, 1967), 137. See Peter N. Gregory, "The Place of Sudden Teaching within the Hua-yen Tradition: An Investigation of the Process of Doctrinal Change," *Journal of the International Association of Buddhist Studies* 6.1 (1983): 31–60; Luis O. Gómez, "Purifying Gold: The Metaphor of Effort and Intuition in Buddhist Thought and Practice," in Peter N. Gregory, ed., *Sudden and Gradual: Approaches to Enlightenment in Chinese Thought* (University of Hawai'i Press, 1987), 131–132.

90. Edwards's work was written in 1736 and published in London the following year: Jonathan Edwards, *A Faithful Narrative of the Surprising Work of God . . .* (Printed for John Oswald, 1737). Below I quote the 1738 edition: Jonathan Edwards, *A Faithful Narrative of the Surprising Work of God . . .* (S. Kneeland and T. Green, 1738).

91. Edwards, *A Faithful Narrative,* 9, 17.

92. Richard L. Bushman, ed., *The Great Awakening: Documents on the Revival of Religion, 1740–1745* (University of North Carolina Press, 1989), xii. On Whitefield, see Harry S. Stout, *The Divine Dramatist: George Whitefield and the Rise of Modern Evangelicalism* (Eerdmans, 1991).

93. Charles Chauncy, *Seasonable Thoughts on the State of Religion in New-England* (Rogers and Fowle for Samuel Eliot, 1743), 98–99.

94. James Davenport, *The Reverend Mr. James Davenport's Confession and Retractions* (S. Kneeland and T. Green, 1744), 6–7. Thomas S. Kidd, *The Great Awakening: A Brief History with Documents* (Bedford/St. Martin's, 2008), 1. The event took place on 7 March 1743.

95. George Whitefield, *A Letter to the Reverend Doctor Charles Chauncy . . .* (W. Bradford, 1745). Charles Chauncy, *A Letter to the Reverend Mr. George Whitefield . . .* (Rogers and Fowle for S. Eliot, 1745).

96. William Temple Franklin, ed., *The Works of Benjamin Franklin . . .* (H. Gray, 1836), 1: 136–137.

97. Bushman, *Great Awakening,* 28–30.

98. Michael J. Crawford, "The Spiritual Travels of Nathan Cole," *WMQ* 33.1 (1976): 92–96.

99. George Fox urged contemporaries to look inward: "My friends . . . going over to plant, and make outward plantations in America, keep your own plantations in your hearts." Quoted in Kristen Block, "Cultivating Inner and Outer Plantations: Property, Industry, and Slavery in Early Quaker Migration to the New World," *Early American Studies* 8.3 (2010): 517.

100. Influence went in both directions. Theodorus Jacobus Frelinghuysen's Dutch Pietism influenced the Middle Colonies, for instance: Milton J. Coalter, *Gilbert Tennent, Son of Thunder: A Case Study of Continental Pietism's Impact on the First Great Awakening in the Middle Colonies* (Greenwood Press, 1986). In turn, the Pietist leader August Francke mentions Jonathan Edwards and the "Nachricht von der Erweckung in Neu England" [news about the Awakening in New England]: Gotthilf August Francke to Elisabeth Ernestine Antoinette von Sachsen-Meiningen, 16 December 1738, Franckesche Stiftungen zu Halle, https://fas.francke-halle.de/cgi-bin/gkdb.pl?t_show=x&reccheck=111906.

101. Jan Stieverman, "Faithful Translations: New Discoveries on the German Pietist Reception of Jonathan Edwards," *CH* 83.2 (2014): 324–366. Fred Van Lieburg, "Interpreting the Dutch Great Awakening," *CH* 77.2 (2008): 318–336. Roark Atkinson, "Satan in the Pulpit: Popular Christianity during the Scottish Great Awakening, 1680–1750," *Journal of Social History* 47.2 (2013): 344–370.

102. Douglas L. Winiarski, *Darkness Falls on the Land of Light: Experiencing Religious Awakenings in Eighteenth-Century New England* (University of North Carolina Press, 2017).

103. Crawford, "Spiritual Travels of Nathan Cole," 90.

104. Crawford, "Spiritual Travels of Nathan Cole," 97.

105. Jonathan Edwards, *A Divine and Supernatural Light* (1730), *Sermons and Discourses 1730–33*, in Mark Valeri, ed., *The Works of Jonathan Edwards* (Yale University Press, 1999), 17: 411. Edwards used *immediate* or *immediately* twenty-four times in that sermon. Jonathan Edwards, *The Distinguishing Marks of a Work of the Spirit of God* (S. Kneeland and T. Green, 1741), 76.

106. The passage quoted is from her conversion account: Catherine A. Brekus, ed., *Sarah Osborn's Collected Writings* (Yale University Press, 2017), 27. See also Catherine A. Brekus, *Sarah Osborn's World: The Rise of Evangelical Christianity in Early America* (Yale University Press, 2013), 4, 248–265.

107. The passage is from the first draft of Occom's autobiographical narrative, 28 November 1765: Joanna Brooks, ed., *The Collected Writings of Samson Occom, Mohegan: Leadership and Literature in Eighteenth-Century Native America* (Oxford University Press, 2006) 52.

108. Julian D. Mason Jr., ed., *The Poems of Phillis Wheatley* (University of North Carolina Press, 1989), 55–57.

109. John Tillotson, *Sermons Preached upon Several Occasions*, 5th ed. (Gellibrand, 1681). On Tillotson's sermons as "probably the most widely read works of religious literature in America between 1690 and 1750": Norman Fiering, "The First American Enlightenment: Tillotson, Leverett, and Philosophical Anglicanism," *New*

England Quarterly 54.3 (1981): 309. See also David Lundberg and Henry F. May, "The Enlightened Reader in America," *AQ* 28.2 (1976): 265, 273.

110. Thomas J. Little, *Origins of Southern Evangelicalism: Religious Revivalism in the South Carolina Lowcountry, 1670–1760* (University of South Carolina Press, 2013), esp. 116–146. See also Samuel C. Smith, *A Cautious Enthusiasm: Mystical Piety and Evangelicalism in Colonial South Carolina* (University of South Carolina Press, 2013); William Howland Kenney III, "Alexander Garden and George Whitefield: The Significance of Revivalism in South Carolina, 1738–1741," *South Carolina Historical Magazine* 71 (1970): 1–16; David T. Morgan, "The Consequences of George Whitefield's Ministry in Georgia and the Carolinas, 1739–1740," *Georgia Historical Quarterly* 55 (1971): 62–82.

111. George Whitefield, *Three Letters from the Reverend Mr. George Whitefield . . .* (James Duncan, 1740).

112. Little, *Origins of Southern Evangelicalism,* 131. Andrew Garden, *Regeneration, and Testimony of the Spirit . . .* (Peter Timothy, 1740). For Garden's criticism of Whitefield and defense of Tillotson, see also Andrew Garden, *Six Letters to the Rev. Mr. George Whitefield . . .*, 2nd ed. (T. Fleet, 1740). Andrew Garden, *Take Heed How Ye Hear: A Sermon Preached in the Parish Church of St. Philip Charles-Town, in South Carolina, on Sunday the 13th of July, 1740. With a Preface, containing some Remarks on Mr. Whitefield's Journals* (Peter Timothy, 1741).

113. As Choi shows, Whitefield was entangled in the British imperial state, including its reliance on slavery: Peter Y. Choi, *George Whitefield: Evangelist for God and Empire* (Eerdmans, 2018).

114. George Whitefield, *Three Letters from the Reverend Mr. G. Whitefield . . .* (Benjamin Franklin, 1740).

115. Little, *Origins of Southern Evangelicalism,* 143, 159.

116. Comprehensive US religious histories have underemphasized links with island "hubs of empire," and as I tried to correct that blind spot I have learned from many studies, including Katharine Gerbner, *Christian Slavery: Conversion and Race in the Protestant Atlantic World* (University of Pennsylvania Press, 2018); Matthew Mulcahy, *Hubs of Empire: The Southeastern Lowcountry and British Caribbean* (Johns Hopkins University Press, 2014); Natalie A. Zaceck, *Settler Society in the English Leeward Islands, 1670–1776* (Cambridge University Press, 2010); Nicholas M. Beasley, *Christian Ritual and the Creation of British Slave Societies, 1650–1780* (University of Georgia Press, 2009); David S. Shields, *Material Culture in Anglo-America: Regional Identity and Urbanity in the Tidewater, Lowcountry, and Caribbean* (University of South Carolina Press, 2009); Max S. Edelson, *Plantation Enterprise in Colonial South Carolina* (Harvard University Press, 2006); Larry Gragg, "The Pious and the Profane: The Religious Life of Early Barbados Planters," *Historian* 62.2 (2000): 264–283; and Sylvia R. Frey and Betty Wood, *Come Shouting to Zion: African American Protestantism in the American South and British Caribbean* to 1830 (University of North Carolina Press, 1998).

117. I borrow "hubs of empire" from Mulcahy, *Hubs of Empire.* Some refer to "the Greater United States," the territories, atolls, and archipelagos the nation has

governed or inhabited: Daniel Immerwahr, *How to Hide an Empire: A History of the Greater United States* (Farrar, Straus, and Giroux, 2019). Herbert Bolton referred to "Greater America" to gesture toward borderlands and hemispheric history: "The Epic of Greater America," *AHR* 38.3 (1932): 448–474. Some have analyzed the "Greater Caribbean." See Stuart B. Schwartz, *Sea of Storms: A History of Hurricanes in the Greater Caribbean from Columbus to Katrina* (Princeton University Press, 2015); Daniel B. Rood, *The Reinvention of Atlantic Slavery: Technology, Labor, Race, and Capitalism in the Greater Caribbean* (Oxford University Press, 2017). Here I suggest *the Greater South* to reframe the region that includes the mainland South and the British Caribbean.

118. On the plantation colonies of Barbados, Jamaica, and Carolina, and the paucity of scholarship by religious historians: Beasley, *Christian Ritual and the Creation of British Slave Societies,* 1–20. On this plantation region, see also Shields, *Material Culture in Anglo-America.* On the "reciprocal" agency of Whites and Blacks in the mainland South and the Caribbean, see Frey and Wood, *Come Shouting to Zion.*

119. Catholics would later celebrate the landing of the "Pilgrims of Maryland" and their role in establishing religious liberty: Rev. John McCaffrey, *Oration Delivered at the Commemoration of the Landing of the Pilgrims of Maryland* (H. C. Neinstedt, 1842); William George Read, *Oration Delivered at the Commemoration of the Landing of the Pilgrims of Maryland* (John Murray, 1842).

120. The defining characteristics of mainland colonial religion—and the "Christianization" of the landscape—also were evident in Barbados and Jamaica: Gragg, "The Pious and the Profane," 267.

121. My perspective is trans-hemispheric as well as continental and transatlantic. Jack Greene, "Early Modern Southeastern North America and the Broader Atlantic and American Worlds," *JSH* 73.3 (2007): 535. Michael Witgen, "Rethinking Colonial History," *WMQ* 69.3 (2012): 529.

122. I say *global empire* because the English went east as well as west, and their colonial empire was interconnected. Other imperial powers were creating transoceanic networks of exchange too. "The so-called Atlantic world, then, should not be treated as a discrete unit between 1500 and 1800 CE": Peter A. Coclanis, "Atlantic World or Atlantic/World?," *WMQ* 63.4 (2006): 734. For example, excavations in Jamestown have unearthed artifacts from China (a porcelain drinking bowl) as well as from Europe.

123. There were microregions in the Greater South where the large-scale plantation didn't take root. See Jonathan Buchanan, "Bethel: Mountain Tobacco Farming in Western North Carolina," *Appalachian Journal* 40.3 (2013): 232–234.

124. On the "plantation complex" or the "plantation system," see Philip D. Curtin, *The Rise and Fall of the Plantation Complex: Essays in Atlantic History* (Cambridge University Press, 1990); Justin Roberts, "Race and the Origins of Plantation Slavery," *Oxford Research Encyclopedia of American History,* published online March 2016, https://doi.org/10.1093/acrefore/9780199329175.013.268. The early modern plantation began in the Canary Islands and crossed to northeastern Brazil, where sugar plantations arose in the 1540s. See Trevor Burnard, "Plantation Societies," in Jerry H. Bentley,

Sanjay Subrahmanyam, and Merry E. Wiesner, eds., *The Cambridge World History: The Construction of a Global World, 1400–1800,* part 2 (Cambridge University Press, 2016), 6: 265. The British plantation, which arose in Virginia and Barbados, had parallels but was even more brutal.

125. Rolfe got the seeds from a shipmaster, who brought them from Trinidad and Venezuela: Emily Jones Salmon, "John Rolfe (d. 1622)," *Encyclopedia Virginia,* https://www.encyclopediavirginia.org/entries/rolfe-john-d-1622/.

126. On the environmental history of the mainland South, including the plantation's impact: Paul S. Sutter and Christopher J. Manganiello, eds., *Environmental History and the American South* (University of Georgia Press, 2009).

127. By *planter piety* I mean the theology, ethics, and practices that supported plantation slavery, or "the dominant slaveholding ethic of the colonial South": Butler, *Awash,* 142. On domestic religion: Lauren F. Winner, *A Cheerful and Comfortable Faith: Anglican Religious Practice in the Elite Households of Eighteenth-Century Virginia* (Yale University Press, 2010), 2, 27–59, 141–177; Rhys Isaac, *The Transformation of Virginia, 1740–1790* (W. W. Norton, 1982), 65, 68–69; Curran, *Papist Devils,* 175–184.

128. See Butler's *Awash,* especially chap. 4. In most places in the British colonies, the increase in churches and the institutional strengthening happened between the 1680s and 1750s.

129. As Butler notes, North Carolina had an Anglican establishment in 1715, the last of the territories in the Greater South. Butler, *Awash,* 103. On the SPG's missionary efforts in the Caribbean and mainland colonies, see *An Abstract of the Proceedings of the Society for the Propagation of the Gospel in Foreign Parts . . .* (Joseph Downing, 1716), 8, 18, 20, 24–25, 27, 29–30, 33. See also Rowan Strong, "A Vision of an Anglican Imperialism: The Annual Sermons of the Society for the Propagation of the Gospel in Foreign Parts, 1701–1714," *Journal of Religious History* 30.2 (2006): 175–198; Laura M. Stevens, "Why Read Sermons? What Americanists Can Learn from Sermons of the Society for the Propagation of the Gospel in Foreign Parts," *History Compass* 3 (2005): 1–19; Travis Glasson, "The Society for the Propagation of the Gospel in Foreign Parts," Oxford Bibliographies, https://doi.org/10.1093/OBO/9780199730414-0067.

130. Milton Rubincam, "Queen Henrietta Maria: Maryland's Royal Namesake," *Maryland Historical Magazine* 54.2 (1959): 137–138.

131. On Andrew White, George Calvert, Cecil Calvert, and the first decades of the settlement, see Curran, *Papist Devils,* 21–73.

132. Andrew White, *Relatio itineris in Marylandium . . .* (John Murphy, printer to the Maryland Historical Society, 1874), 24–27 (on Barbados), 32–33 (on the mass and the cross).

133. Cecilius Calvert, *Instructions from Lord Baltimore, Proprietor of Maryland . . . ,* 13 November 1633. Repr. in John Tracy Ellis, ed., *Documents of American Catholic History* (Henry Regnery, 1967), 1: 98–100.

134. *Proceedings and Acts of the General Assembly of Maryland at a Session Held at St. Mary's, February 25 to March 19, 1638–1639,* in William Hand Brown, ed., *Archives of Maryland* (Maryland Historical Society, 1883), 1: 82–83.

135. This is a passage from White's *Declaratio coloniae domini baronis de Baltimoro* (1638). It was included in the 1874 collection, along with other Jesuit missionary letters; see White, *Relatio itineris in Marylandium,* 47. See Angela Feres, "Father Andrew White, the Jesuit Order, and the Marketing of Colonial Maryland," PhD diss., Claremont Graduate University, 2011.

136. Quoted in White, *Relatio itineris in Marylandium,* 73.

137. [Father Edward Knott, SJ], *Annual Letter of 1638,* in Clayton Colman Hall, ed., *Narratives of Early Maryland, 1633–1684* (Charles Scribner's Sons, 1910), 120.

138. See Sara K. Becker, "Health Consequences of Contact on Two Seventeenth-Century Native Groups from the Mid-Atlantic Region of Maryland," *International Journal of Historical Archaeology* 17.4 (2013): 726–727.

139. Kathleen Scorza, "False Emissaries: The Jesuits among the Piscataways in Early Colonial Maryland, 1634–1648," master's thesis, College of William and Mary, 2015; Paul Cissana, "The Piscataway Indians of Southern Maryland: An Ethnohistory from Pre-European Contact to the Present," PhD diss., American University, 1986, 71–75, 84–88.

140. Georgetown University's Special Collections has the five-page manuscript of prayers in Piscataway by Andrew White, SJ. The words appeared in the beginning of the printed book *Manuale sacerdotum* (1610). *Manuale sacerdotum hoc est . . .* (Excudebat Laurentius Kellam typog. iurat sub signo Agni Paschalis, 1610). I am grateful to Scott S. Taylor for helping me see this manuscript. For a linguist's analysis: Lisa Lilly Mackie, "Fragments of Piscataway: A Preliminary Description," PhD diss., University of Oxford, 206. Curran, *Papist Devils,* 46–55.

141. Curran, *Papist Devils,* 35–36.

142. Curran, *Papist Devils,* 75.

143. Gerald P. Fogarty, SJ, "Property and Religious Liberty in Colonial Maryland Catholic Thought," *Catholic Historical Review* 72.4 (1986): 581.

144. The passage quoted from Maryland's 1649 Act Concerning Religion can be found in Ellis, *Documents of American Catholic History,* 1: 112–114.

145. Robert R. Grimes, "The Emergence of Catholic Music and Ritual in Colonial Maryland," *American Catholic Studies* 114.2 (2003): 18–19. See also James G. Gibb and Scott D. Lawrence, "Imposed and Home-Grown Colonial Institutions: The Jesuit Chapels of St. Mary's City and St. Francis Xavier, Maryland," *International Journal of Historical Archaeology* 20 (2016): 539–540.

146. Curran, *Papist Devils,* 105.

147. George Alsop, "A Character of the Province of Maryland, 1666," in Hall, *Narratives of Early Maryland,* 349.

148. Grimes, "Emergence of Catholic Music and Ritual," 19. "From the Annual Letter of 1681," in Hall, *Narratives of Early Maryland,* 143.

149. Not all Anglican clergyman on the mainland were ordained by the Bishop of London, but for the 1,600 persons in the records, including those from the Chesapeake colonies, see James B. Bell, "Anglican Clergy in Colonial America Ordained by Bishops of London," *Proceedings of the American Antiquarian Society* 83.1 (1973): 101–160.

150. Bonomi and Eisenstadt, "Church Adherence in the Eighteenth-Century British American Colonies," 236.

151. Gerald E. Hartdagen, "Vestry and Clergy in the Anglican Church of Colonial Maryland," *HMPEC* 37.4 (1968): 388.

152. John E. Booty, ed., *The Book of Common Prayer, 1559* (Folger Shakespeare Library, 1976). Daniel Swift, "The Book of Common Prayer," in Andrew Hadfield, ed., *The Oxford Handbook of English Prose, 1500–1640* (Oxford University Press, 2013), 577–578. See also Alan Jacobs, *The Book of Common Prayer: A Biography* (Princeton University Press, 2013).

153. Hartdagen, "Vestry and Clergy in the Anglican Church of Colonial Maryland," 385.

154. Hartdagen, "Vestry and Clergy in the Anglican Church of Colonial Maryland," 387.

155. Owners "entrusted with God's own Property": Rev. Thomas Bacon, *Four Sermons, Preached at the Parish Church of St. Peter, in Talbot County, in the Province of Maryland* (J. Oliver, 1753), 52. This passage is from "Sermon I: Preached to a Congregation of Black Slaves." On owners as "God's overseers," see Butler, *Awash,* 142–143. Butler cites Bacon's *Four Sermons,* 30, 31, 34.

156. Ayuba Suleiman Diallo was known as Job Ben Solomon. Thomas Bluett, *Some Memoirs of the Life of Job, the Son of Solomon . . .* (Richard Ford, 1734); and Francis Moore, *Travels into the Inland Parts of Africa . . .* (Edward Cave, 1738), 202–217, 224–225. Bluett's text is reprinted in Muhammad A. al-Ahari, ed., *Five Classic Muslim Slave Narratives* (Magrabine Press, 2006).

157. George Sale, *The Koran, Commonly Called the Alcoran of Mohamed . . .* (C. Ackers, 1734 [1733]). Alexander Ross offered the first English translation of the Qur'an in 1649, but Sale's translation would have lasting influence. Alexander Bevilacqua, "The Qur'an Translations of Marracci and Sale," *Journal of the Warburg and Courtauld Institutes* 76 (2013): 93. Bruce B. Lawrence, *The Koran in English: A Biography* (Princeton University Press, 2017), 38–43.

158. GhaneaBassiri, *Islam in America,* 30–31.

159. The Royal African Company, chartered by Charles II, "delivered some 2.5 million Africans to the Americas from 1698 to 1807": Matthew David Mitchell, "'Legitimate Commerce' in the Eighteenth Century: The Royal African Company of England under the Duke of Chandos," *Enterprise and Society* 14.2 (2013): 575.

160. "An Act to Prevent Popery within This Province" (1704), *Proceedings and Acts of the General Assembly, September 1704–April 1706,* vol. 26, 340–341. The law accused priests of evangelizing and baptizing Protestants. So there was enough outreach to worry Protestants in the Assembly. Fogarty, "Property and Religious Liberty in Colonial Maryland Catholic Thought," 585. Curran, *Papist Devils,* 146–147.

161. The veiling was at Port Tobacco, Maryland, the site of the only convent in British America at the time. See Robert Frederick Trisco, ed., *Catholics in America, 1776–1976* (United States Catholic Conference, 1976), 39. On Digges's journey, see Curran, *Papist Devils,* 185.

162. Curran, *Papist Devils,* 159.

163. Bonomi and Eisenstadt, "Church Adherence in the Eighteenth-Century British American Colonies," 236. Beatriz B. Hardy, "Papists in a Protestant Age: The Catholic Gentry and Community in Maryland, 1689–1776," PhD diss., University of Maryland, College Park, 1993, 194–204. Curran, *Papist Devils,* 177.

164. Ronald Hoffman, "'Marylando-Hibernus': Charles Carroll the Settler, 1660–1720," *WMQ* 45.2 (1988): 226.

165. Amy Speckart, "The Colonial History of Wye Plantation, the Lloyd Family, and Their Slaves on Maryland's Eastern Shore: Family, Property, and Power," PhD diss., College of William and Mary, 2011, 57. Lloyd built a chapel on one of her estates: Curran, *Papist Devils,* 108. On Maryland's Henrietta Maria (Neal) and Queen Henrietta Maria, consort of Charles I, see Rubincam, "Queen Henrietta Maria," 138–139.

166. Curran, *Papist Devils,* 173. On "saddle chalices" and itinerant Jesuit missionaries: Grimes, "Emergence of Catholic Music and Ritual." Joseph Mosley to his sister, 1 September 1759, Newton, Maryland, quoted in Curran, *Papist Devils,* 178–181.

167. "Henrietta Maria Lloyd," in *Maryland Wills and Probate Records, 1635–1777,* 26 April 1697, https://www.ancestry.com/search/collections/9068/.

168. Speckart, "Colonial History of Wye Plantation," 37–38, 50–51.

169. Speckart, "Colonial History of Wye Plantation," 43–44, 56.

170. Beth Pruitt, "Reordering the Landscape: Science, Nature, and Spirituality at Wye House," PhD diss., University of Maryland, 2015, 3, 5, 42. Speckart, "Colonial History of Wye Plantation," 188. Pruitt notes that the Lloyd family recorded the names of more than 500 enslaved persons at Wye House between 1770 and 1834. On African symbols and biblical imagery at the plantation: Jason Urbanus, "A Mix of Faiths," *Archaeology* 70.2 (2017): 18.

171. On Carroll and his manor: Curran, *Papist Devils,* 152–157. E. H. Pickering, photographer, home of Charles Carroll of Carrollton, September 1936, American Buildings Survey, Library of Congress, Prints and Photographs Division.

172. Patrick Griffin, "1607 and All That: Memory and Irish and American Exceptionalism," *History Ireland* 17.6 (2009): 48. Kathryn Webber, "Cultivating Civilized Subjects: British Agricultural 'Improvement' in Eighteenth-Century Ireland," PhD diss., University of California, Riverside, 2012.

173. Hoffman, "Marylando-Hibernus," 216.

174. Allan Kulikoff, "The Origins of Afro-American Society in Tidewater Maryland and Virginia, 1700–1790," *WMQ* 35.2 (1978): 251. Curran, *Papist Devils,* 156.

175. The first evidence of Jesuit slaveholding in Maryland: "Deed of the chattel of Newtown from Father William Hunter, S.J., to Thomas Jameson, Senior, January 30, 1717," in *History of the Society of Jesus in North America, Colonial and Federal Documents, 1605–1838* (Longmans, Green, 1908), 1: 222. Thomas Richard Murphy, SJ, "'Negroes of Ours': Jesuit Slaveholding in Maryland, 1634–1838," PhD diss., University of Connecticut, 1998, 4. Jesuits won the right to own property in Maryland but only in their own name, not the church or the order: Fogarty, "Property and Religious Liberty in Colonial Maryland Catholic Thought," 580.

176. Curran, *Papist Devils,* 37.

177. Murphy, “Negroes of Ours,” 97. Curran, *Papist Devils,* 158–159.

178. Murphy, “Negroes of Ours,” 1, 13, 97. Thomas Murphy, *Jesuit Slaveholding in Maryland, 1717–1838* (Routledge, 2001); Joseph S. Rossi, SJ, “Jesuits, Slaves, and Scholars at ‘Old Bohemia,’ 1704–1756, as Found in the Woodstock Letters,” *U.S. Catholic Historian* 26.2 (2008): 1–15. On tobacco cultivation, see Gloria L. Main, *Tobacco Colony: Life in Early Maryland, 1650–1720* (Princeton University Press, 1982).

179. Douglas Bradburn, “The Eschatological Origins of the English Empire,” in Douglas Bradburn and John C. Coombs, eds., *Early Modern Virginia: Reconsidering the Old Dominion* (University of Virginia Press, 2011), 15–56.

180. On a crucifix probably of Spanish origin, see “Crucifix,” Historic Jamestown, https://historicjamestowne.org/collections/artifacts/crucifix/.

181. John Rolfe mentioned “20 and odd Negroes” in a letter dated “January 1619/1620” to Sir Edwin Sandys, treasurer of the Virginia Company: Susan Myra Kingsbury, ed., *Records of the Virginia Company of London, 1606–1626* (GPO, 1933), 3: 241–248. John C. Coombs, “The Phases of Conversion: A New Chronology for the Rise of Slavery in Early Virginia,” *WMQ* 68.2 (2011): 340.

182. Richter, *Facing East,* 70. Helen C. Rountree, *Pocahontas, Powhatan, Opechancanough: Three Indian Lives Changed by Jamestown* (University of Virginia Press, 2005). Helen C. Rountree, *Pocahontas's People: The Powhatan Indians of Virginia through Four Centuries* (University of Oklahoma Press, 1990).

183. Ethan A. Schmidt, “Cockacoeske, Weroansqua of the Pamunkeys, and Indian Resistance in Seventeenth-Century Virginia,” *American Indian Quarterly* 36.3 (2012): 302. Helen C. Rountree, “Powhatan Confederacy,” in Frederick E. Hoxie, ed., *Encyclopedia of North American Indians* (Houghton Mifflin, 1996), 512. The Chickahominy, who moved to Pamunkey Neck, were not part of the Powhatan chiefdom, as their histories emphasize. See “Post-Contact Era,” Chickahominy Tribe, 2024, https://www.chickahominytribe.org/tribal-history/post-contact-era-1500-1900.

184. In moments of copying, meanings can be distorted and missed too. While two excavated clay pipes, Powhatan and English, look almost identical, that does not mean both communities interpreted them in the same way. See Sikes, “Peripheral Vision,” 20–43.

185. Schmidt, “Cockacoeske, Weroansqua of the Pamunkeys, and Indian Resistance,” 290. Powhatan stories and rituals seemed “Papist” to some English interpreters: Samuel Purchas, *Purchas His Pilgrimage . . .* (William Stansby, 1614), 762–769.

186. Jace Weaver, *The Red Atlantic: American Indigenes and the Making of the Modern World, 1000–1927* (University of North Carolina Press, 2014), 144–151. The nickname, Weaver notes, seems to have meant *playful* or *mischievous.* See also Paula Gunn Allen, *Pocahontas: Medicine Woman, Spy, Entrepreneur, Diplomat* (HarperSanFrancisco, 2004), 255–256.

187. Schmidt, “Cockacoeske, Weroansqua of the Pamunkeys, and Indian Resistance,” 299–301.

188. See Martin H. Quitt, “Trade and Acculturation at Jamestown, 1607–09: The Limits of Understanding,” *WMQ* 52 (1995): 227–258; Camilla Townsend, *Pocahontas*

and the Powhatan Dilemma (Hill and Wang, 2004). See also Richter, *Facing East,* 69–78; Weaver, *Red Atlantic,* 142–152.

189. Richter, *Facing East,* 73. Schmidt, "Cockacoeske, Weroansqua of the Pamunkeys, and Indian Resistance," 301.

190. John Rolfe, "Letter of John Rolfe, 1614," in Lyon Gardiner Tyler, ed., *Narratives of Early Virginia* (Charles Scribner's Sons, 1907), 240, 242. The letter appeared originally in Ralph Hamor, ed., *A True Discourse of the Present State of Virginia . . .* (John Beale, 1615), 61–68.

191. Helen C. Rountree, "Powhatan Priests and English Rectors: World Views and Congregations in Conflict," *American Indian Quarterly* 16.4 (1992): 490. Schmidt, "Cockacoeske, Weroansqua of the Pamunkeys, and Indian Resistance," 300.

192. Weaver, *Red Atlantic,* 142–144, 149.

193. Coombs, "Phases of Conversion," 347. Lorena S. Walsh, *Motives of Honor, Pleasure, and Profit: Plantation Management in the Colonial Chesapeake, 1607–1763* (University of North Carolina Press, 2010).

194. Coombs, "Phases of Conversion," 347.

195. David Brown and Clive Webb, "Red, White, and Black? Native Americans, Europeans, and Africans Meet in the Chesapeake," *Race in the American South: From Slavery to Civil Rights* (Edinburgh University Press, 2007), 23–31; Linda Heywood and John K. Thornton, *Central Africans, Atlantic Creoles, and the Foundation of the Americas, 1585–1660* (Cambridge University Press, 2007), 242–248. On the flow of slaves to the Chesapeake: David Eltis and David Richardson, *Atlas of the Transatlantic Slave Trade* (Yale University Press, 2010), 212. On these African Indigenous practices: Christina Frances Mobley, "The Kongolese Atlantic: Central African Slavery and Culture from Mayombe to Haiti," PhD diss., Duke University, 2015, iv.

196. Heywood and Thornton, *Central Africans,* 283–284.

197. Heywood and Thornton, *Central Africans,* 247. Robin Law, "Religion, Trade, and Politics on the 'Slave Coast': Roman Catholic Missions in Allada and Whydah in the Seventeenth Century," *Journal of Religion in Africa* 21.1 (1991): 43–46. Rosalind I. J. Hackett, *Religion in Calabar: The Religious Life and History of a Nigerian Town* (De Gruyter, 1989), 20–23, 27–29. On the slave trade from Calabar: Eltis and Richardson, *Atlas of the Transatlantic Slave Trade,* 129–131, 212. On African religions, see Jacob K. Olupona, *African Religions: A Very Short Introduction* (Oxford University Press, 2014).

198. Both the quoted passage and the Eastern Shore reference can be found in Brent Tarter, "Evidence of Religion in Seventeenth-Century Virginia," in Paul Rasor and Richard E. Bond, eds., *From Jamestown to Jefferson: The Evolution of Religious Freedom in Virginia* (University of Virginia Press, 2011), 21.

199. On slave quarters: Heywood and Thornton, *Central Africans,* 248. On slave codes: Brown and Webb, "Red, White, and Black?," 24–28.

200. On a shared African culture: Allan Kulikoff, "The Origins of Afro-American Society in Tidewater Maryland and Virginia, 1700–1790," *WMQ* 35.2 (1978): 229.

201. Tarter, "Evidence of Religion," 38. One scholar has called this "ecclesiastical localism": Edward L. Bond, *Damned Souls in a Tobacco Colony: Religion in Seventeenth-Century Virginia* (Mercer University Press, 2000), 133.

202. Tarter, "Evidence of Religion," 32.

203. Coombs, "Phases of Conversion," 350, 352–353, 359–360. The office-holding gentry in the best tobacco-growing areas started to assemble larger numbers of enslaved workers before 1698.

204. Louis B. Wright and Marion Tinling, eds., *The Secret Diary of William Byrd of Westover, 1709–1712* (Dietz Press, 1941). Fiering, "First American Enlightenment," 344. On Bryd's beliefs, see also Catherine L. Albanese, *A Republic of Mind and Spirit: A Cultural History of American Metaphysical Religion* (Yale University Press, 2007), 75.

205. The council also commissioned a group to pursue runaway slaves earlier. See the minutes for 9 July 1640: H. R. McIlwaine, ed., *Minutes of the Council and General Court of Colonial Virginia, 1622–1632, 1670–1676* (Library of Virginia, 1924), 466. Those minutes are available online at "The Practise of Slavery," *Virtual Jamestown,* http://www.virtualjamestown.org/practise.html. The passage about plots and funerals is from a November 1687 proclamation of Governor Effingham of Virginia: *York County Deeds, Orders, and Wills* 8: 99–100, 24 January 1688.

206. "Spiritual holocaust": Butler, *Awash,* 130. Some suggest it became a global tradition: Jacob K. Olupona and Terry Rey, eds., *Òrìṣà Devotion as World Religion: The Globalization of Yorùbá Religious Culture* (University of Wisconsin Press, 2008). Young avoids the binaries of the "survivals" debate and reframes religion as "resistance": Jason R. Young, *Rituals of Resistance: African American Religion in Kongo and the Lowcountry South in the Era of Slavery* (LSU Press, 2007), introduction.

207. On the yam harvest festival of the Yorùbá, see E. Thomas Lawson, *Religions of Africa* (HarperSanFrancisco, 1984), 69. Many enslaved Muslims came from urban settings: Paul E. Lovejoy, "The Urban Background of Enslaved Muslims in the Americas," *Slavery and Abolition* 26.3 (2005): 349–376.

208. This passage from a 1680 Virginia legal document is quoted in Seeman, *Death in the New World,* 105.

209. The quotations are from Morgan Godwyn, *The Negro's and Indians' Advocate . . .* (Printed for the author, 1680), 1, 9, 11, 87, The sermon preached at Westminster Abbey: Morgan Godwyn, *Trade Preferr'd before Religion . . .* (B. Took, 1685).

210. *The Loyal Address of the Clergy of Virginia* (Printed for Fr. Maggot, 1702). The author of this parody is unknown, though it was probably a Virginia resident: Herman Teerink, *Bibliography of the Writings of Jonathan Swift,* 2nd ed. (University of Pennsylvania Press, 1963), 315; Richard Beale Davis, "The Colonial Virginia Satirist: Mid-Eighteenth-Century Commentaries on Politics, Religion, and Society," in *Transactions of the American Philosophical Society* 57.1 (1967): 7.

211. Cary Carson, "Banqueting Houses and the 'Need of Society' among Slave-Owning Planters in the Chesapeake Colonies," *WMQ* 70.4 (2013): 725–780. See also Edmund Berkeley Jr., ed., "The Diary, Correspondence, and Papers of Robert 'King' Carter of Virginia, 1701–1732," https://christchurch1735.org/robert-king-carter-papers/.

212. The mention of Madagascar Jack is brief in his diary—"brot home"—but the context is explained in the Lancaster County Order Book, as note 32 explains in

the Carter diary, 3 September 1722. Both are found in Berkeley, "Diary, Correspondence, and Papers of Robert 'King' Carter."

213. Carter diary, 9 November 1727 and 11 November 1727. He sold three slaves that Friday and went to church that Sunday. Berkeley, "Diary, Correspondence, and Papers of Robert 'King' Carter."

214. On Christ Church: Alan Gowans, *King Carter's Church: Being a Study in Depth of Christ Church, Lancaster County, Virginia* . . . (University of Victoria, 1969). William Meade, *Old Churches, Ministers, and Families of Virginia* (J. B. Lippincott, 1897), 1: 117–123; Williams, *Houses of God,* 106.

215. Isaac, *Transformation of Virginia,* 21.

216. By the mid-1780s, the owner of Shirley Plantation was Virginia's largest slaveholder, Charles Carter, who owned more than 35,000 acres and 785 slaves. See Theodore R. Reinhart and Judith A. Habicht, "Shirley Plantation in the Eighteenth Century: A Historical and Archaeological Study," *Virginia Magazine of History and Biography* 92.1 (1984): 29–49; Theodore R. Reinhart, *The Archaeology of Shirley Plantation* (University Press of Virginia, 1984).

217. Carson, "Banqueting Houses," 730–736. Carson also uses the phrase "over-the-top displays."

218. Bureau of the Census, *Historical Statistics of the United States: Colonial Times to 1970* (US Department of Commerce, Bureau of the Census, 1975). In 1750 enslaved persons made up 43.9 percent of Virginia's total population. They were 30.8 percent for Maryland. South Carolina's slaves constituted more than half the population in 1750 (60.9%).

219. John Brooke, "Ecology," in Daniel Vickers, ed., *A Companion to Colonial America* (Blackwell, 2006), 55, 60, 61. Isaac, *Transformation of Virginia,* 18–42. Lorena S. Walsh, "'Till Death Us Do Part': Marriage and Family in Seventeenth-Century Maryland," in Thad W. Tate and David Ammerman, eds., *The Chesapeake in the Seventeenth Century: Essays on Anglo-American Society* (W. W. Norton, 1979), 126–152. Wells, "Old English or New Americans?," 97. On inequitable land distribution: Ewout Frankema, "The Colonial Roots of Land Inequity: Geography, Factor Endowments, or Institutions?" *Economic History Review* 63.2 (2010): 418–451.

220. Coombs, "Phases of Conversion," 358.

221. Coombs, "Phases of Conversion," 343.

222. The Washington quotations are from J. M. Toner, ed., *The Daily Journal of Major George Washington in 1751–52, Kept While on a Tour from Virginia to the Island of Barbadoes* . . . (Joel Munsell's Sons, 1892), 48, 42, 62, 61, 53–54.

223. On Native presence: S. M. Fitzpatrick, "Verification of an Archaic Age Occupation of Barbados, Southern Lesser Antilles," *Radiocarbon* 53.4 (2011): 595–604; Hilary Beckles, *A History of Barbados: From Amerindian Settlement to Nation-State* (Cambridge University Press, 1990), 1–6; George Gmelch and Sharon Bohn Gmelch, "Barbados's Amerindian Past," *Anthropology Today* 12.1 (1996): 11–15. Jerome S. Handler, "Aspects of Amerindian Ethnography in Seventeenth-Century Barbados," *Caribbean Studies* 9.4 (1970): 50–72; Keven Farmer, "Barbados," in Basil A. Reid and

R. Grant Gilmore III, eds., *Encyclopedia of Caribbean Archaeology* (University Press of Florida, 2014), 64–66. On the interaction sphere: Corinne L. Hofman et al., "Island Rhythms: The Web of Social Relationships and Interaction Networks in the Lesser Antillean Archipelago between 400 B.C. and A.D. 1492," *Latin American Antiquity* 18.3 (2007): 242–268.

224. Kevin Farmer, "Forward Planning: The Utilization of GIS in the Management of Archaeological Resources in Barbados," in Basil A. Reid, ed., *Archaeology and Geoinformatics: Case Studies from the Caribbean* (University of Alabama Press, 2009), 76. On the uses of red ochre in the Caribbean: Joshua M. Torres, "Hematite," in Reid and Gilmore, *Encyclopedia of Caribbean Archaeology*, 177. On the white-on-red paint used in pottery: Peter L. Drewett, "Excavations at Heywoods, Barbados, and the Economic Basis of the Suazoid Period in the Lesser Antilles," *Proceedings of the Prehistoric Society* 59 (1993): 117.

225. The "Indian Bridge" was used until 1654: Frederick H. Smith and Karl Watson, "Urbanity, Sociability, and Commercial Exchange in the Barbados Sugar Trade: A Comparative Colonial Archaeological Perspective on Bridgetown, Barbados, in the Seventeenth Century," *International Journal of Historical Archaeology* 13 (2009): 71. Early European settlers in Barbados bartered with Dutch settlers to acquire Indigenous labor: Douglas Armstrong, "New Directions in Caribbean Historical Archaeology," in William F. Keegan, Corinne L. Hofman, and Reniel Rodríguez Ramos, eds., *The Oxford Handbook of Caribbean Archaeology* (Oxford University Press, 2013), 528.

226. Griffith Hughes, *Natural History of Barbados* (Printed for the Author, 1750), 50.

227. Olaudah Equiano, *The Interesting Narrative of the Life of Olaudah Equiano, or Gustavus Vassa . . .* (Printed by T. Wilkins, 1789). The account by Ashy was reported to John Ford in 1789; I quote from the full document in Jerome S. Handler, "Life Histories of Enslaved Africans in Barbados," *Slavery and Abolition* 19.1 (1998): 133–134. Venture Smith, *A Narrative of the Life and Adventures of Venture . . .* (C. Holt, 1798). On Smith, see James Brewer Stewart, ed., *Venture Smith and Business of Slavery and Freedom* (University of Massachusetts Press, 2010), 13–14, 260.

228. Jerome S. Handler, "An African-Type Healer/Diviner and His Grave Goods: A Burial from a Plantation Slave Cemetery in Barbados, West Indies," *International Journal of Historical Archaeology* 1.2 (1997): 91–130.

229. Washington was a "lifelong Anglican" who went to church regularly and knew his Bible. He stopped taking communion but never disaffiliated. Mary V. Thompson, *"In the Hands of a Good Providence": Religion in the Life of George Washington* (University of Virginia Press, 2008), 185–186.

230. Smith and Watson, "Urbanity, Sociability, and Commercial Exchange in the Barbados Sugar Trade," 74. On the six meetinghouses by 1671, see Stephen W. Angell, "An Early Version of George Fox's 'Letter to the Governor of Barbados,'" *Quaker Studies* 19.2 (2015): 277–278. For an image with thirty ships anchored in the Bay, see Samuel Copen, *A Prospect of Bridge Town in Barbados, 1695*, print, Library of Congress, Prints and Photographs Division. Bridgetown had one of the earliest synagogues in the hemisphere: Barry L. Stiefel, "Life at the Corner of Swan and Prince

William Henry Streets: A Snapshot from Bridgetown, Barbados," *American Jewish History* 101.2 (2017): 241–243. On the Irish, see Alison Donnell et al., eds., *Caribbean Irish Connections: Interdisciplinary* Perspectives (University of the West Indies Press, 2015).

231. Gragg, "The Pious and the Profane," 267–268.

232. Mulcahy, *Hubs of Empire,* 163–166. William Cleland, *The Present State of the Sugar Plantations Consider'd . . .* (John Morphew, 1713), 3–4.

233. Architects' and builders' adaptations: Mulcahy, *Hubs of Empire,* 164–166.

234. Richard Ligon, *True and Exact History of the Island of Barbadoes* (Peter Parker, 1673), 82. Susan Scott Parrish, "Richard Ligon and the Atlantic Science of Commonwealths," *WMQ* 67.2 (2010): 239.

235. George Fox, Epistle 153, "To Friends beyond Sea, that have Blacks and Indian Slaves" (1657), in *A Collection of Many Select and Christian Epistles, Letters, and Testimonies, Written on Sundry Occasions* (T. Sowle, 1698), 117. Block, "Cultivating Inner and Outer Plantations," 521.

236. Gragg, "The Pious and the Profane," 280.

237. Gerbner, *Christian Slavery,* 91–92, 96–100.

238. On his will: John A. Schultz, "Christopher Codrington's Will: Launching the S.P.G. into the Barbadian Sugar Business," *Pacific Historical Review* 15.2 (1946): 195. See also William Gordon, *A Sermon Preach'd at the Funeral of the Honourable Colonel Christopher Codrington . . .* (G. Strahan, 1710), esp. 20–21.

239. Larry Gragg, *The Quaker Community on Barbados: Challenging the Culture of the Planter Class* (University of Missouri Press, 2009), 125. See also Katharine Gerbner, "The Ultimate Sin: Christianizing Slaves in Barbados in the Seventeenth Century," *Slavery and Abolition* 31.1 (2010): 57–73.

240. Carla Gardina Pestana, *The English Atlantic in an Age of Revolution, 1640–1661* (Harvard University Press, 2004), 191. Parrish, "Richard Ligon and the Atlantic Science of Commonwealths," 215.

241. On 27 September 1661 the Assembly of Barbados passed two acts about the island's laborers: "An Act for the better ordering of Negroes" and "An Act for the good governing of Servants." Taylor, *American Colonies,* 213. Gerbner, "Christian Slavery," 41–42.

242. See "The Manner of Making Sugar in the Sugar-Mills," 1671, Lionel Pincus and Princess Firyal Map Division, New York Public Library. The image appeared in John Ogilby, *America: Being the Latest, and Most Accurate Description of the New World* (T. Johnson, 1671).

243. An eighteenth-century Jamaican planter, Simon Taylor, worried he was "murdering the Negroes." Quoted in Mulcahy, *Hubs of Empire,* 127.

244. Kristrina A. Shuler et al., "Sugar, Health, and Slavery: Forty Years of Bioarcheological Research of Newton Plantation, Barbados," *American Journal of Physical Anthropology* 147.54 (2012): 269. Michael Blakey, "Bioarcheology of the African Diaspora in the Americas: Its Origins and Scope," *ARA* 30 (2001): 408. See also Jerome S. Handler, *Plantation Slavery in Barbados: An Archaeological and Historical Investigation* (Harvard University Press, 1978).

245. Taylor, *American Colonies,* 212.

246. Zaceck, *Leeward Islands,* 131.

247. Hamilton's Jewish teacher in Nevis: Zaceck, *Leeward Islands, 1776,* 133; Ron Chernow, *Alexander Hamilton* (Penguin, 2004), 17. See Jon Sensbach, *Rebecca's Revival: Creating Black Christianity in the Atlantic World* (Harvard University Press, 2005).

248. Anonymous [Thomas Parkhurst], *The Truest and Largest Account of the Late Earthquake in Jamaica, June the 7th 1692* (Printed for Thomas Parkhurst, 1693), 2. On Jamaica's slave society: Jack P. Greene, *Settler Jamaica in the 1750s: A Social Portrait* (University of Virginia Press, 2016).

249. Jack P. Greene, *Imperatives, Behaviors, and Identities: Essays in Early American Cultural History* (University of Virginia Press, 1992), 68–69.

250. Louis P. Nelson, "Anglican Church Building and Local Context in Early Jamaica," in *Perspectives in Vernacular Architecture,* vol. 10, *Building Environments* (2005): 70. Philip Wright, ed., *Lady Nugent's Journal of Her Residence in Jamaica from 1801 to 1805* (Institute of Jamaica, 1966), 165.

251. Nathaniel Samuel Murrell, *Afro-Caribbean Religions: An Introduction to Their Historical, Cultural, and Sacred Traditions* (Temple University Press, 2010), 246–257. Shirley Gordon, "'God Is Dumb until the Drum Speaks': Religious Life in Jamaica before Emancipation," *Comparative Studies of South Asia, Africa, and the Middle East* 17.1 (1997): 145–156.

252. Brent Russell Fortenberry, "Church, State, and the Space in Between: An Archaeological and Architectural Study of St. George's, Bermuda," PhD diss., Boston University, 2013, 202–203.

253. On St. Philip's Church in Charles Town: Eliza Lucas [Pinckney] to Thomas Lucas (her brother), 22 May 1742, in Elise Pinkney, ed., *The Letterbook of Eliza Lucas Pickney, 1739–1762* (University of North Carolina Press, 1972), 39–40. On the architecture, see Williams, *Houses of God,* 108.

254. On Stephen and William Bull: M. Eugene Sirmans Jr., "Masters of Ashley Hall: A Biographical Study of the Bull Family of Colonial South Carolina, 1670–1737," PhD diss., Princeton University, 1959.

255. On Stephen Bull: Sirmans, "Masters of Ashley Hall," 27–48.

256. Edelson, *Plantation Enterprise,* 2–4. Alan Taylor, *Colonial America: A Very Short Introduction* (Oxford University Press, 2013), 77–89.

257. Anthony Ashley Cooper, Early of Shaftesbury, *Characteristicks of Men, Manners, Opinions, and Times,* 3 vols. (John Darby, 1711).

258. *The Fundamental Constitutions of Carolina,* 1 March 1669, https://avalon.law.yale.edu/17th_century/nc05.asp. John Locke was secretary to Cooper and the Proprietors from 1669 to 1675, and he helped draft that document. There would be revisions in 1682 and 1698, and Locke was one of several editors of the 1682 version as well. Another editor of the 1682 version was the absentee owner of a Barbadian sugar plantation, Sir Peter Colleton, so the interests of planters were well represented. See David Armitage, "John Locke, Carolina, and the 'Two Treatises of Government,'" *Political Theory* 32.5 (2004): 603, 607–609.

259. Charles H. Lippy, "Chastized by Scorpions: Christianity and Culture in Colonial South Carolina, 1669–1740," *CH* 79.2 (2010): 259–266. A congregation from Dorchester, Massachusetts, relocated.

260. "Letter of Judith Giton Manigault," trans. Charles W. Baird, in *History of the Huguenot Emigration to America* (Dodd, Mead, and Company, 1885), 2: 112–114. See Bertrand Van Ruymbeke, "Judith Giton: From Southern France to the Carolina Lowcountry," in Marjorie Julian Spruill et al., eds., *South Carolina Women: Their Lives and Times* (University of Georgia Press, 2009), 1: 26–39.

261. Stephen Bull to Lord Ashley, 12 September 1670, in *Collections of the South Carolina Historical Society* (William Ellis Jones, 1897), 5: 192–196.

262. See Peter A. Coclanis, *The Shadow of a Dream: Economic Life and Death in the South Carolina Low Country, 1670–1920* (Oxford University Press, 1989). The rice industry declined when the European market dried up: Peter A. Coclanis, "Bitter Harvest: The South Carolina Low Country in Historical Perspective," *Journal of Economic History* 45.2 (1985): 251–259.

263. For the watercolor and a brief description of Rice Hope, the seat of Dr. William Read on the Cooper River, see Charles Fraser, *A Charleston Sketchbook, 1796–1806* (Carolina Art Association, 1940), 30. On Ashley Hall, see Henry DeSaussure Bull, "Ashley Hall Plantation," *South Carolina Historical Magazine* 53.2 (1952): 61–67.

264. The typical Carolina rice plantation was 500 acres. On the comparison, see Edelson, *Plantation Enterprise,* 113–114.

265. On the plantations along the Ashley River and the personal interconnections: Paul Porwoll, *Yesterday and Today: Four Centuries of Change at Old S. Andrew's* (Saint Andrew's Parish Church, 2015), 28. The connection: Charlotta Bull Drayton, the daughter of William Bull, was the wife of John Drayton. On Drayton Hall, see also Samuel Gaillard Stoney, *Plantations of the Carolina Low Country,* 4th ed. (Carolina Art Association, 1955), 61; Lauren Elizabeth Golden, "Unlocking Drayton Hall: A Survey and Analysis of Hardware at a Southern Plantation," PhD diss., Clemson University, 13–21.

266. S. Max Edelson, "Clearing Swamps, Harvesting Forests: Trees and the Making of a Plantation Landscape in the Colonial South Carolina Lowcountry," *Agricultural History* 81.3 (2007): 381–406. On the population of St. Andrew's Parish in 1728, which then had 800 Whites and 1,800 enslaved persons, see Michael S. Reynolds, "St. Andrew's Parish," in *South Carolina Encyclopedia,* https://www.scencyclopedia.org/sce/entries/st-andrews-parish/.

267. David Eltis, Philip Morgan, and David Richardson, "Agency and Diaspora in Atlantic History: Reassessing the African Contribution to Rice Cultivation in the Americas," *AHR* 112.5 (2007): 1335. See also Judith A. Carney, *Black Rice: The African Origins of Rice Cultivation in the Americas* (Harvard University Press, 2001).

268. On conditions in South Carolina as only marginally better, see Mulcahy, *Hubs of Empire.* On slave flows to Charleston: Eltis and Richardson, *Atlas of the*

Transatlantic Slave Trade, 216. On the plantation region: J. R. McNeill, "The Ecological Atlantic," in Nicholas Canny and Philip Morgan, eds., *The Oxford Handbook of the Atlantic World, 1450–1850* (Oxford University Press, 2011), 289–291. McNeill proposed that "an ecological history of the Atlantic world" from the fifteenth to the eighteenth centuries might be framed in terms of eight regions, including the plantation region from the Chesapeake to Bahia, and southern Brazil and Argentina.

269. Mulcahy, *Hubs of Empire,* 156–157.

270. Samuel Quincy, *Twenty Sermons on the Following Subjects . . . Preach'd in St. Philip, Charles-Town, South Carolina* (John Draper, 1750), 38–54. Bradford Wood, "'A Constant Attendance on God's Alter': Death, Disease, and the Anglican Church in Colonial South Carolina, 1706–1750," *South Carolina Historical Magazine* 100.3 (1999): 216.

271. Edelson, *Plantation Enterprise,* 157–161.

272. Paul Kelton, "The Great Southeastern Smallpox Epidemic, 1696–1700: The Region's First Major Epidemic?," in Robbie Ethridge and Charles Hudson, eds., *The Transformation of Southeastern Indians, 1540–1760* (University Press of Mississippi, 2002), 21–38.

273. On the Cusabos, see Edelson, *Plantation Enterprise,* 24–33.

274. Stephen Bull to Lord Ashley, 12 September 1670, in *Collections of the South Carolina Historical Society,* 192–196.

275. Those who traded with the Natives were called "Indian traders," and one study identified 695 licensed by Carolina: Eirlys Mair Barker, "'Much Blood and Treasure': South Carolina's Indian Traders, 1670–1755," PhD diss., College of William and Mary, 1993. See also Edward J. Cashin, *Lachlan McGillivray, Indian Trader: The Shaping of the Southern Colonial Frontier* (University of Georgia Press, 1992); William L. Ramsey, *The Yamasee War: A Study of Culture, Economy, and Conflict in the Colonial South* (University of Nebraska Press, 2008), 35–53.

276. Sirmans "Masters of Ashley Hall," 34.

277. Henry Woodward to the Earl of Shaftesbury [formerly Lord Ashley], 31 December 1674, Grand Council Journal, in *Collections of the South Carolina Historical Society,* 5: 460.

278. Ramsey, *Yamasee War,* 36–37.

279. On slaving and violence: Richter, *Facing East,* 161–164; Matthew H. Jennings, "Violence in a Shattered World," in Robbie Ethridge and Sheri M. Shuck-Hall, eds., *Mapping the Mississippian Shatter Zone: The Colonial Indian Slave Trade and Regional Instability in the American South* (University of Nebraska Press, 2009), 280–291.

280. Sheri M. Shuck-Hall, "Alabama and Coushatta Disapora and Coalescence in the Mississippian Shatter Zone," in Ethridge and Shuck-Hall, *Mississippian Shatter Zone,* 264–265.

281. Richter, *Facing East,* 163.

282. John Lawson, *A New Voyage to Carolina,* ed. Hugh Talmage Lefler (1709; University of North Carolina Press, 1967), 244–246.

283. Shuck-Hall, "Alabama and Coushatta Disapora and Coalescence," 266.

284. John E. Worth, "Razing Florida: The Indian Slave Trade and the Devastation of Spanish Florida, 1659–1715," in Ethridge and Shuck-Hall, *Mississippian Shatter Zone*, 308–309. On the continuation of artistic traditions: James A. Nyman, "The Ashley Series as Native American Persistence: Lowcountry Indians in the Period of European Expansion," master's thesis, University of South Carolina, 2011.

285. H. D. Bull, "Ashley Hall Plantation," 65–67.

286. "Act for the Establishment of Religious Worship in this Province . . . ," Act no. 236 of 1706, SC Stat. 282 (Cooper 1837). In 1716 the assembly banned Catholic migrants, and the Irish in particular. See Lippy, "Chastized by Scorpions," 267–268.

287. I reconstructed William's church activity from several sources, including Sirmans, "Masters of Ashley Hall," 154, 178–190.

288. Porwoll, *Yesterday and Today.*

289. This pastor, Ebenezer Taylor, was awarded an MA at Glasgow University and ordained in London in 1711. He later served at other congregations, including St. Thomas Church in Bathe, North Carolina. Bell, "Anglican Clergy in Colonial America," 153.

290. Ira Berlin, "From Creole to African," in Edward Countryman, ed., *How Did American Slavery Begin?* (Macmillan, 1999), 41. Peter Charles Hoffer, *Cry Liberty: The Great Stono River Slave Rebellion of 1739* (Oxford University Press, 2012), 58,

291. On early-eighteenth-century Anglican justifications of the slave plantation: Little, *Origins of Southern Evangelicalism*, 71. Prince William's Church, Sheldon (1757) rested on land adjoining William Bull's Sheldon Plantation. He funded much of it and is buried there. See Stoney, *Plantations of the Carolina Low Country*, 61. For context, see Suzanne Cameron Linder, *Anglican Churches in Colonial South Carolina: Their History and Architecture* (Wyrick, 2000).

292. William Bull to the Board of Trade (London), 5 October 1739, South Carolina Department of Archives and History, Columbia, South Carolina. The quotations from Bull are from this letter. On the Stono Rebellion, see Hoffer, *Cry Liberty.*

293. Bull's friend, Georgia's governor James Oglethorpe, identified the leader, whom he called their "captain," as Jemmy. "An Account of the Negroe Insurrection in South Carolina," in Alan D. Candler et al., eds., *Colonial Records of the State of Georgia* (Byrd, 1913), 22: 232–236. On Jemmy as the rebel leader, see also Hoffer, *Cry Liberty*, 104, 109, 153–155

294. On the rebel encounter with the riders: William Bull to the Board of Trade (London), 5 October 1739. On the claim they "shouted liberty," see "Report of the Committee Appointed to Enquire into the Causes of the Disappointment in the Late-Expedition against St. Augustine, July 1, 1741," in J. H. Esterby, ed., *The Colonial Records of South Carolina: Journal of the Commons House of Assembly, May 18, 1741–July 10, 1742* (South Carolina Historical Commission, 1953), 84.

295. The rider, probably Fenwick Golightly, went to the Willtown Presbyterian Church to sound the alarm for the local militia: Hoffer, *Cry Liberty*, 110–113.

296. William Bull to the Board of Trade (London), 5 October 1739.

297. On the Kongolese Catholic connection: John K. Thornton, "African Dimensions of the Stono Rebellion," *AHR* 96 (1991): 1101–1113; John K. Thornton, *A*

Cultural History of the Atlantic World, 1250–1820 (Cambridge University Press, 2012), esp. 412–419, 462; Mark K. Smith, "Remembering Mary, Shaping Revolt: Reconsidering the Stono Rebellion," *JSH* 67.3 (2001): 513–534.

298. Alida C. Metcalf, "Millenarian Slaves? The Santidade de Jaguaripe and Slave Resistance in the Americas," *AHR* 10 (1999): 1531–1559.

299. Smith, "Remembering Mary," 531.

300. For visual evidence of a priest blessing warriors and weapons, see the reproduction of *Missione in prattica, Padri cappuccini ne Regni di Congo, Angola, et adiacenti,* in Thornton, *Cultural History of the Atlantic World,* 96.

301. Kathleen Deagan and Darice MacMahon, *Fort Mose: Colonial America's Black Fortress of Freedom* (University Press of Florida, 1995), vii, 35–36.

Chapter 5. Rebellious Religion

1. Both the Declaration of Independence and the Preamble of the US Constitution sketch a vision of human flourishing. On "the pursuit of happiness" as well-being or human flourishing: Carli N. Conklin, *The Pursuit of Happiness in the Founding Era: An Intellectual History* (University of Missouri, 2019), 134.

2. Thomas Paine, *Common Sense . . .* (W. and T. Bradford, 1776).

3. Kathleen DuVal, *Independence Lost: Lives on the Edge of the American Revolution* (Random House, 2016), ix–ix. See also Claudio Saunt, *West of the Revolution: An Uncommon History of 1776* (W. W. Norton, 2014); Alan Taylor, *American Revolutions: A Continental History, 1750–1804* (W. W. Norton, 2016). Patrick Spero, *Frontier Rebels: The Fight for Independence in the American West, 1765–1776* (W. W. Norton, 2018). "Landward turn": Felipe Fernández-Armesto, *The Americas: A Hemispheric History* (Modern Library, 2005), 105–106.

4. Nikolai N. Bolkhovitinov, "The Declaration of Independence: The View from Russia," *JAH* 85.4 (1999): 1389–1398. Frank Li, "East Is East and West Is West: Did the Twain Ever Meet? The Declaration of Independence in China," *JAH* 85.4 (1999): 1432–1448.

5. "Treaty of Peace and Friendship between the United States of America and the Bey and Subjects of Tripoli of Barbary," ratified by the Senate, 10 June 1797, https://avalon.law.yale.edu/18th_century/bar1796t.asp. I quote from article 11. Richard Buel Jr., *Joel Barlow: Citizen in a Revolutionary World* (Johns Hopkins University Press, 2011), 196–214. Rob Boston, "Joel Barlow and the Treaty with Tripoli: A Tangled Tale of Pirates, a Poet, and the True Meaning of the First Amendment," *Church and State* 50.6 (1997): 11–14. The "Age of Revolutions": R. R. Palmer, *The Age of Democratic Revolutions: A Political History of Europe and America, 1760–1800* (Princeton University Press, 1959); Lester D. Langley, *The Americas in the Age of Revolution, 1750–1850* (Yale University Press, 1996); John Charles Chasteen, *Americanos: Latin America's Struggle for Independence* (Oxford University Press, 2008); Wim Klooster, *Revolutions in the Atlantic World: A Comparative History* (New York University, 2009); David Armitage and Sanjay Subrahmanyam, eds., *The Age of Revolutions in Global Context, c. 1760–1840* (Palgrave Macmillan, 2010); Janet L. Polasky, *Revolutions without Borders: The Call to Liberty in the Atlantic World* (Yale University

Press, 2015.) My approach is multiscalar, considering local, regional, continental, hemispheric, and global contexts, though my focus often is on the continent.

6. "Use of the word 'nation' was rejected in Philadelphia in 1787, and Madison described the work of the convention as writing a '*federal,* and not a *national* Constitution'": Thomas Bender, *A Nation among Nations: America's Place in World History* (Hill and Wang, 2006), 155. On the US as a *state-nation:* David Armitage, "Interchange: Nationalism and Internationalism in the Era of the Civil War," *JAH* 98.2 (2011): 478. I add "nationalist sentiment," since shared feelings were among the features of the nation-state between 1848 and the 1860s. A geographer called it "geopiety" or attachment to the homeland: John K. Wright, "Notes on Early American Geopiety," in *Human Nature in Geography: Fourteen Papers, 1962–65* (Harvard University Press, 1966), 250–285.

7. "Empire of liberty": Thomas Jefferson to George Rogers Clarke, 25 December 1780, in Julian P. Boyd, ed., *Papers of Thomas Jefferson* (Princeton University Press, 1951), 4: 237–238.

8. The two clauses of the First Amendment state, "Congress shall make no law respecting an establishment of religion, or prohibiting the free exercise thereof." US Constitution, First Amendment, https://constitution.congress.gov/constitution/amendment-1/.

9. Jon Butler, "Why Revolutionary America Wasn't a Christian Nation," in James H. Hutson, ed., *Religion and the New Republic: Faith in the Founding of America* (Rowman & Littlefield, 2000), 187–202; Chris Beneke, *Beyond Toleration: The Religious Origins of American Pluralism* (Oxford University Press, 2006), 159; Katherine Carté, *Religion and the American Revolution: An Imperial History* (University of North Carolina Press, 2021), 5. Washington said "religion and morality are indispensable supports": "Washington's Farewell Address, 1796," https://avalon.law.yale.edu/18th_century/washing.asp.

10. *Civil religion* is a loosely linked set of beliefs, values, symbols, and rituals found outside of traditional worship spaces and used to interpret political life in spiritual terms. It is evident in presidential inaugurations, Memorial Day parades, and July Fourth celebrations. The concept has a long history, and it has been controversial but influential since Robert Bellah's "Civil Religion in America," *Daedalus* 96 (1967): 1–21. See the positive evaluations, as with Philip Gorski, *American Covenant: A History of Civil Religion from the Puritans to the Present* (Princeton University Press, 2017) as well as the critiques, such as Walter A. McDougall's *The Tragedy of U.S. Foreign Policy: How America's Civil Religion Betrayed the National Interest* (Yale University Press, 2016). See also Ronald Beiner, *Civil Religion: A Dialogue in the History of Political Philosophy* (Cambridge University Press, 2011); Michael Lienesch, "Contesting Civil Religion: Religious Responses to American Patriotic Nationalism, 1919–1929," *RAC* 28.1 (2018): 92; Vine Deloria Jr., "Completing the Theological Circle: Civil Religion," in Vine Deloria Jr., *For This Land: Writings on Religion in America* (Routledge, 1999), 166–174; and Charles Long, "Civil Rights—Civil Religion: Visible People and Invisible Religion," in Russell E. Richey and Donald G. Jones, eds., *American Civil Religion* (Harper and Row, 1974), 211–221.

11. On biblical themes: Thomas S. Kidd, *God of Liberty: A Religious History of the American Revolution* (Basic Books, 2010), 3; Mark A. Noll, *In the Beginning Was the Word: The Bible in American Public Life, 1492–1783* (Oxford University Press, 2016).

12. A "niche" is a material and symbolic lived world that is inherited, modified, and bequeathed. McConville complained about the "poverty of theorization" in writing on the Revolution, and here I suggest historians engage niche construction theory, sustainability studies, and the cross-disciplinary scholarship on human flourishing to enrich analysis of the Revolutionary Era. Brendan McConville, "Going Continental? Romantic Transnationalism and Contemporary Interpretation of the American Revolution," *Journal of the Early American Republic* 39 (2019): 545.

13. Thomas Jefferson to James Madison, 6 January 1789, Founders Online, https://founders.archives.gov/documents/Madison/01-12-02-0248. For a United Nations definition of sustainability: *Report of the World Commission on Environment and Development: Our Common Future,* April 1987, 16 (paragraph 27), http://www.un-documents.net/our-common-future.pdf. See also Jeremy L. Caradonna, *Sustainability: A History,* rev. and updated ed. (Oxford University Press, 2022), 1–21.

14. I quote a 1916 version of the Haudenosaunee Great Law of Peace: Arthur Caswell Parker, *The Constitution of the Five Nations; Or, the Iroquois Book of the Great Law,* New York State Museum Bulletin no. 184 (University of the State of New York, 1916), section 28.

15. On *bimaadiziwin:* Lawrence W. Gross, *Anishinaabe Ways of Knowing and Being* (Routledge, 2012), 205–214. See also Diné uses of *hózhó,* translated as harmony, happiness, or well-being: "Back to Harmony," *Navajo Times Today* 28.45 (7 March 1986): A11.

16. With its appeal to "Nature's God" and emphasis on equality and rights, the Declaration of Independence offers a religiously informed vision of flourishing: Thomas Jefferson et al., copy of Declaration of Independence, 4 July 1776, Thomas Jefferson Papers, Library of Congress, https://www.loc.gov/item/mtjbib000159/. See Conklin, *Pursuit of Happiness,* 134. Pursuing happiness, as Jefferson understood it, was seeking our greatest good. John Locke, whose portrait hung in Jefferson's parlor, used "the pursuit of happiness" in his *Essay Concerning Human Understanding* (1689): John Locke, *The Works of John Locke: In Nine Volumes,* 12th ed. (Printed for C. and J. Rivington, 1824), 1: 252–253. The Preamble of the Constitution also presents a model of flourishing as the framers set out to "establish Justice, insure domestic Tranquility, provide for the common defence, promote the general Welfare, and secure the Blessings of Liberty to ourselves and our Posterity." Preamble, US Constitution, https://constitution.congress.gov/constitution/preamble/. As Kloppenberg argues, "the Constitution is, above all, concerned with the search for the common good." James T. Kloppenberg, "To Promote the General Welfare: Why Madison Matters," *Supreme Court Review* 2019.1 (2020): 384. On "the pursuit of happiness" in the metaphysical tradition: Catherine L. Albanese, *The Delight Makers: Anglo-American Metaphysical Religion and the Pursuit of Happiness* (University of Chicago Press, 2023), 45, 56, 127–128, 146, 163, 179, 208, 230, 254, 263, 296, 311–315.

17. William Cronon, *Changes in the Land: Indians, Colonists, and the Ecology of New England,* 20th anniversary ed. (1983; Hill and Wang, 2003), 159–170. Matthew Dennis, "Cultures of Nature: To ca. 1810," in Douglas Cazaux Sackman, ed., *A Companion to American Environmental History* (Wiley-Blackwell, 2010), 225–237. David C. Hsiung, "Food, Fuel, and the New England Environment in the War for Independence, 1775–1776," *New England Quarterly* 80.4 (2007): 614–654. On Jefferson, the Declaration, and "nature," see Mark Fiege, *The Republic of Nature: An Environmental History of the United States* (University of Washington Press, 2012), 57–99.

18. Jefferson penned the Declaration at his rented second-floor accommodation in Philadelphia in 1776. Watt's partner, Matthew Boulton, told a visitor to their "manufactory" in 1776 that they were selling "what all the world desires to have—POWER." James Patrick Muirhead, *The Life of James Watt with Selections from His Correspondence* (J. Murray, 1859), 259. Jefferson, who favored agriculture over manufacturing until 1812, was impressed with Watt's engine when he visited the manufactory in 1786: Thomas Jefferson to Charles Thomson, 22 April 1786, Founders Online, https://founders.archives.gov/documents/Jefferson/01-09-02-0353. Crutzen originally dated the "Anthropocene" from Watt's steam engine improvements of 1784: Paul J. Crutzen, "Geology of Mankind," *Nature* 415 (3 January 2002): 23.

19. Fred Anderson, *Crucible of War: The Seven Years' War and the Fate of Empire in British North America, 1754–1766* (Vintage, 2001). A *sphere* is a territory or, metaphorically, a realm of life within or beyond an eco-cultural niche. An *interaction sphere* is a group's network of contact and exchange, and we can distinguish a *symbolic* or *ceremonial sphere,* including imagined sites above, below, or beyond its lived world.

20. Anderson, *Crucible of War,* 199, 374–375. Harry S. Stout, *The New England Soul: Preaching and Religious Culture in Colonial New England* (Oxford University Press, 2012), 248–255. On the Ohio Company and the intrusion of Pennsylvania traders: Fred Anderson, *The War That Made America: A Short History of the French and Indian War* (Penguin, 2005), 25–36.

21. Philip Reading, *The Protestant's Danger, and the Protestant's Duty: A Sermon on the Occasion of the Present Encroachments of the French, Preached at Christ Church, Philadelphia . . .* (Benjamin Franklin, 1755). A missionary of the Society for the Propagation of the Gospel, he was ordained in London on 7 April 1746 and started his duties in Delaware: James B. Bell, "Anglican Clergy in Colonial America Ordained by Bishops of London," *Proceedings of the American Antiquarian Society* 83.1 (1973): 147. Dorothy Rowlett Colburn, ed., *St. Anne's Church in Apoquinimy: A History of One of Delaware's Oldest Churches from Its Founding in 1704* (St. Anne's Church, 2011), 97–99. See also Nelson R. Burr, "The Welsh Episcopalians of Colonial Pennsylvania and Delaware," *HMPEC* 8.2 (1939): 119–120.

22. On British casualties: Colin G. Calloway, *The Scratch of a Pen: 1763 and the Transformation of North America* (Oxford University Press, 2006), 4.

23. On 2 May 1760 Reading mentioned Catholics at Bohemia, which was five miles away in Maryland. The nearby Jesuit presence "seemed to haunt Philip

throughout his ministry": Colburn, *St. Anne's Church in Apoquinimy,* 107–108. His 1760 remarks about Bohemia: Philip Reading, "Mission at Apoquiniminck, Delaware," *American Catholic Historical Researches* 3.4 (1887): 52.

24. The quotations are from Reading, *The Protestant's Danger,* 19, 6, 7, 24, 19, 7.

25. On slave baptisms and 1748 attendees: Colburn, *St. Anne's Church,* 100, 103–104.

26. The quotations about Africans in Reading's October 1752 and October 1748 reports are from Colburn, *St. Anne's Church,* 105, 102, 103.

27. Philip Reading, 6 September 1778, *Wills of New Castle County, Delaware, 1682–1854,* District and Probate Courts, vol. L–N, 1777–1794. Delaware had 9,000 enslaved residents in 1790. On slavery there, see Gary B. Nash and Miles Albrook Stanley, "The Travail of Delaware Slave Families in the Early Republic," *Slavery and Abolition* 40.1 (2018): 19.

28. On slavery among SPG ministers, see Travis Gleason, *Mastering Christianity: Missionary Anglicanism and Slavery in the Atlantic World* (Oxford University Press, 2012).

29. In 1756 Stiles sent rum on a ship bound for Guinea and received in return a ten-year-old African boy he named "Newport." Edmund S. Morgan, *The Gentle Puritan: A Life of Ezra Stiles, 1727–1795* (W. W. Norton, 1962), 125.

30. Ezra Stiles, "Sermon on 2 Chronicles 20:6–7," 25 September 1760, Ezra Stiles Papers, Yale University. Ezra Stiles, Thanksgiving Sermon [on the fall of Montreal], 20 November 1760, Ezra Stiles Papers, Yale University. Much of the second sermon is included in Morgan, *Gentle Puritan,* 210–212. See also Stout, *New England Soul,* 258–262.

31. G. Adolf Koch, *Religion of the American Enlightenment* (Thomas Y. Crowell, 1968), 16–17. As Walters suggested, *deism* emphasized reason and "natural philosophy" and affirmed a benevolent creator. In its more iconoclastic forms, it rejected all supernatural sources of authority, while advocating tolerance based on "natural rights" and the authority of "conscience." The clergy overestimated deism's influence, but they were right to be alarmed at its reception, even if few spoke up before 1784, when Ethan Allen published the first "full-blown American defense of deism." Kerry Walters, *Revolutionary Deists: Early America's Rational Infidels* (Prometheus Books, 2010), 7–9, 35, 19, 273. On the types of Enlightened thought, see Henry F. May, *The Enlightenment in America* (Oxford University Press, 1976).

32. Morgan, *Gentle Puritan,* 267. Kerry S. Walters, *The American Deists: Voices of Reason and Dissent in the Early Republic* (University of Kansas, 1992), 16.

33. Quoted in Morgan, *Gentle Puritan,* 213. Walters, *American Deists,* 24.

34. Boston's slave population: Jared Ross Hardesty, *Unfreedom: Slavery and Dependence in Eighteenth-Century Boston* (NYU Press, 2016), 5.

35. On Mayhew, see J. Patrick Mullins, *Father of Liberty: Jonathan Mayhew and the Principles of the American Revolution.* (University Press of Kansas, 2017).

36. Jonathan Mayhew, *A Discourse Concerning Unlimited Submission and Non-Resistance to Higher Powers . . .* (D. Fowle, D. Gookin, 1750). John Adams called it the "catechism" of the Revolution: Stout, *New England Soul,* 248.

37. Jonathan Mayhew, *A Sermon Preach'd in the Audience of His Excellency William Shirley, Esq; Captain General, Governour and Commander in Chief* . . . (Samuel Kneeland, 1754), 38. Stout, *New England Soul,* 251–252. On anti-Catholic themes in political rhetoric, see also Noll, *In the Beginning Was the Word,* 261–269.

38. The bishop's letter: E. B. O'Callaghan and Berthold Fernow, eds., *Documents Relative to the Colonial History of the State of New York* (Weed, Parsons, 1859), 10: 1057–1059. See also Thomas J. Shannon, *The Seven Years' War in North America: A Brief History with Documents* (Bedford/St. Martin's, 2014), 147–149.

39. Robert Emmett Curran, *Papist Devils: Catholics in British America, 1574–1783* (Catholic University of America Press, 2014), 226.

40. [Benjamin Franklin], *The Interest of Great Britain Considered, with Regard to Her Colonies, and the Acquisition of Canada and Guadaloupe* (William Bradford, 1760). On Franklin's view of the expanding continental empire: Alberto Lena, "Benjamin Franklin's 'Canada Pamphlet' or 'The Ravings of a Mad Prophet': Nationalism, Ethnicity, and Imperialism," *European Journal of American Culture* 20.1 (2001): 38, 42–43.

41. Jonathan Mayhew, *Two Discourses Delivered October 25th, 1759* (Draper, Edes, Gill, and Fleet, 1759), 23–24, 57–61.

42. Anderson, *The War That Made America,* 203.

43. Anderson, *Crucible of War,* 373.

44. "Quebeck Reduced," *New Hampshire Gazette,* 19 October 1759, https://americainclass.org/sources/makingrevolution/crisis/text1/britainvictorious1763.pdf, p. 3.

45. On African resistance on ships and plantations in the 1750s: Gerald Horne, *The Counter-Revolution of 1776: Slave Resistance and the Origins of the United States of America* (NYU Press, 2014), 165–166.

46. "The Converted Algerine," *The Panoplist and Missionary Magazine* 12.12 (1816): 545. William Meade, *Old Churches, Ministers, and Families of Virginia* (J. B. Lippincott, 1897), 1: 340–348. See Kambiz GhaneaBassiri, *A History of Islam in America* (Cambridge University Press, 2010), 43–46.

47. Linford D. Fisher, *The Indian Great Awakening: Religion and the Shaping of Native Cultures in Early America* (Oxford University Press, 2012), 148.

48. Mechal Sobel, *The World They Made Together: Black and White Values in Eighteenth-Century Virginia* (Princeton University Press, 1987), 189. Stephanie Reiss, "Religion and Resistance: African Baptist Churches in Virginia," master's thesis, College of William and Mary, 1997, 19–20.

49. Fisher, *Indian Great Awakening,* 107–135.

50. The entry was dated 10 January 1757: Carol F. Karlsen and Laurie Crumpacker, eds., *The Journal of Esther Edwards Burr* (Yale University Press, 1984), 239.

51. Ann M. Little, *The Many Captivities of Esther Wheelwright* (Yale University Press, 2016), 186–197.

52. Horne, *Counter-Revolution of 1776,* 161–183.

53. On the Treaty of Paris and other events of 1763, see Calloway, *Scratch of a Pen.*

54. On the Spanish in the Pacific: Rainer F. Buschmann, Edward R. Slack Jr., and James B. Tueller, *Navigating the Spanish Lake: The Pacific in the Iberian World, 1521–1898* (University of Hawai'i Press, 2014). See also David Armitage and Alison Bashford Basingstoke, eds., *The Pacific and Its Place in Global History* (Palgrave Macmillan, 2013).

55. Anderson, *The War That Made America*, 228–229.

56. For a history of the missions: James A. Sandos, *Converting California: Indians and Franciscans in the Missions* (Yale University Press, 2004). On attempts to counter Russian and British "incursions": Buschmann, Slack, and Tueller, *Navigating the Spanish Lake*, 9.

57. Fisher makes a similar point about the forms of resistance, but doesn't use my labels: Fisher, *Indian Great Awakening*, 11–12.

58. For a comparative study of two communities that sought to preserve "important elements of what defined them as a people," see Rachel Wheeler, *To Live upon Hope: Mohicans and Missionaries in the Eighteenth-Century Northeast* (Cornell University Press, 2008), 7.

59. Anderson, *Crucible of War*, 535–553. Gregory Evans Dowd, *War under Heaven: Pontiac, the Indian Nations, and the British Empire* (Johns Hopkins University Press, 2002).

60. On the parallels with the Southwestern Pueblo Rebellion: Anderson, *The War That Made America*, 236.

61. On this as a "revitalization" movement: Cave, "The Delaware Prophet Neolin: A Reappraisal." Anthony F. C. Wallace, "Revitalization Movements," *American Anthropology* 58 (1956): 265.

62. John W. Jordan, ed., "Journal of James Kenny, 1761–1763," *PMHB* 37.2 (1913): 152.

63. On Detroit before and after this period: Catherine Cangany, *Frontier Seaport: Detroit's Transformation into an Atlantic Entrepôt* (University of Chicago Press, 2014).

64. Gregory Evans Dowd, *A Spirited Resistance: The North American Indian Struggle for Unity, 1745–1815* (Johns Hopkins University Press, 1992), 30.

65. Anderson, *Crucible of War*, 535–536. On the number of Lenape in the Upper Ohio Valley: Taylor, *American Revolutions*, 73.

66. On Neolin: Jordan, "Journal of James Kenny," 171, 175, 188; John Heckewelder, *History, Manners, and Customs of the Indian Nations Who Once Inhabited Pennsylvania . . .* (Historical Society of Pennsylvania, 1876), 291–293. John McCullough, "A Narrative of the Captivity of John McCullough, Esq., Written by Himself," in Archibald Loudon, ed., *Selection of Some of the Most Interesting Narratives of Outrages, Committed by the Indians . . .* (A. Loudon, 1808), 271–272. *Journal ou dictation d'un conspiration* (1763) described a speech Pontiac gave recounting the teachings of Neolin; see M. Agnes Burton, ed., *Journal of Pontiac's Conspiracy, 1763* (Speaker-Hines, 1912), 20–32. The author might have been an unlearned French trader or traveler who disliked Pontiac and wanted to gain favor with the newly ascendant British. See Milo Milton Quife, ed., *The Siege of Detroit in 1763* (Lakeside Press, 1958), xxvi. See also Dowd, *War under Heaven*, 94–105; Dowd, *Spirited Resistance*, 27–36; Alfred A. Cave, "The Delaware Prophet Neolin: A Reappraisal," *Ethnohistory* 46.2

(1999): 265–290. On the Potawatomi during the war: Gregory Evans Dowd, "Indigenous Catholicism and St. Joseph Potawatomi Resistance in 'Pontiac's War,'" *Ethnohistory* 63.1 (2016): 143–166.

67. Neolin's chart (drawn by John M'Cullough, who was held captive during Pontiac's Rebellion), depicts two spiritual paths: the first, now guarded by evil forces and blocked by White corruption, is impassable. The second offers Natives who give up White ways a direct route to the Master of Life. Other missionaries used diagrams to preach: Dowd, *War under Heaven,* 99.

68. Charles Hudson, ed., *Black Drink: A Native American Tea* (University of Georgia Press, 1979). See also Edwin M. Hale, Ilex cassine, *the Aboriginal North American Tea: Its History, Distribution, and Use among the Native American Indians* (US Department of Agriculture, 1891).

69. Jordan, "Journal of James Kenny," 172.

70. Jordan, "Journal of James Kenny," 188.

71. Mark A. Noll, *A History of Christianity in the United States and Canada* (Eerdmans, 1992), 123.

72. Benjamin Franklin, *The Narrative of the Late Massacres* . . . (Franklin and Hall, 1764), 27. Richter, *Facing East,* 201, 203, 205, 206, 208.

73. Matthew Smith, *A Declaration and Remonstrance of the Distressed and Bleeding Frontier Inhabitants of the Province of Pennsylvania* . . . (William Bradford, 1764). Peter Butzin, "Politics, Presbyterians, and the Paxton Riots, 1763–1764," *Journal of Presbyterian History* 51.1 (1973): 70–84; Patrick Griffin, "Migrants and Identity Formation in Eighteenth-Century Pennsylvania," *WMQ* 63.3 (2001): 587–614; George William Franz, "Paxton: A Study of Community Structure and Mobility in the Colonial Pennsylvania Back Country," PhD diss., Rutgers University, 1974.

74. Franz, "Paxton," 107. On the church and John Elder, pastor from 1738 to 1792: M. W. McAlakney, *History of the Sesqui-centennial of Paxtang Church, September 18, 1890* (Harrisburg Publishing, 1890).

75. Franz, "Paxton," 108.

76. John Smolenski, "Murder on the Margins: The Paxton Massacre and the Remaking of Sovereignty in Colonial Pennsylvania," *Journal of Early Modern History* 19 (2015): 513–518. Richter, *Facing East,* 201–208. Anderson, *Crucible of War,* 611–612.

77. On the colony's changes: Kevin Kenny, *Peaceable Kingdom Lost: The Paxton Boys and the Destruction of William Penn's Holy Experiment* (Oxford University Press, 2009).

78. See Alison Olson, "The Pamphlet War over the Paxton Boys," *PMHB* 123.1 (1999): 31–55. The differences expressed in the public statements were along religious lines. See Peter A. Butzin, "Politics, Presbyterians and the Paxton Riots, 1763–64," *Journal of Presbyterian History* 51.1 (1973): 70–84.

79. Butzin, "Politics, Presbyterians and the Paxton Riots," 77–78.

80. I describe Franklin as a deist since he rejected most traditional Christian doctrines but believed in God and an afterlife. Hart interprets him as a "cultural Protestant." Both labels capture something important about Franklin. D. G. Hart, *Benjamin Franklin: Cultural Protestant* (Oxford University Press, 2021), 4–10.

81. Andrew J. O'Shaughnessy, "The Stamp Act Crisis in the British Caribbean," *WMQ* 51.2 (1994): 203–226.

82. Paul Leicester Ford, ed., *The Writings of John Dickinson: Political Writings, 1764–1774* (Historical Society of Pennsylvania, 1895), 1: 259–276.

83. Jonathan Mayhew, *The Snare Broken. A Thanksgiving-Discourse, Preached at the Desire of the West Church in Boston, N.E. Friday May 23, 1766. Occasioned by the Repeal of the Stamp-Act* (R. and S. Draper, 1766). Mayhew began with Psalm 124: "Our soul is escaped as a bird from the snare of the fowlers."

84. See Edmund Morgan and Helen M. Morgan, *The Stamp Act Crisis: Prologue to Revolution,* rev. ed. (Collier, 1963).

85. Zachary McCleod Hutchins, "Introduction," in Hutchins, ed., *Community without Consent: New Perspectives on the Stamp Act* (Dartmouth College Press, 2016), xiii–xiv. O'Shaughnessy, "Stamp Act Crisis."

86. The Stamp Act also reinforced the view that civic order required virtuous actors. See Nathan O. Hatch, *The Sacred Cause of Liberty: Republican Thought and the Millennium in Revolutionary New England* (Yale University Press, 1977).

87. For a protesting Presbyterian voice, see the Reverend David Caldwell's 1775 sermon "The Character and Doom of the Sluggard," in Robert M. Calhoon, ed., *Religion and the American Revolution in North Carolina* (North Carolina Department of Cultural Resources, 1976), 7–16.

88. On this 1765 print and the transatlantic discourse: Clay Zuba, "Redness and the Contest of Anglo-American Empires," in Hutchins, *Community without Consent,* 199–203. See also Cécile R. Ganteaume, *Officially Indian: Symbols That Define the United States* (Smithsonian Institution, National Museum of the American Indian, 2017).

89. Mary Beth Norton, *Liberty's Daughters: The Revolutionary Experience of American Women, 1750–1800* (Cornell University Press, 1996), 156. Caroline Wigginton, "Letters from a Woman in Pennsylvania, or Elizabeth Graeme Fergusson Dreams of John Dickinson," in Hutchins, *Community without Consent,* 89.

90. "The Dream (1768, 1790) by Elizabeth Graeme Fergusson," *Common-Place: The Journal of Early American Life* 16.4 (2016), https://commonplace.online/article/dream-1768-1790-elizabeth-graeme-fergusson/. See also Anne M. Ousterhout, *The Most Learned Woman in America: A Life of Elizabeth Graeme Fergusson* (Pennsylvania State University Press, 2004). The biography's title repeats a claim made in Anne Hollingsworth Wharton, *Salons Colonial and Republican* (J. B. Lippincott, 1900), 13.

91. Molly Perry, "Buried Liberties and Hanging Effigies: Imperial Persuasion, Intimidation, and Performance during the Stamp Act Crisis," in Hutchins, *Community without Consent,* 51–52.

92. John Dickinson, *Letters from a Farmer in Pennsylvania . . .* (Mein and Fleeming, 1768). On Dickinson's response to the acts, see Patrick Griffin, *The Townshend Moment: The Making of Empire and Revolution in the Eighteenth Century* (Yale University Press, 2017), 151–164.

93. His song appeared also as a single sheet: John Dickinson, *A New Song. To the Tune of "Hearts of Oak, &c."* (David Hall and William Sellers, 1768).

94. See Benjamin Carp, *Defiance of the Patriots: The Boston Tea Party and the Making of America* (Yale University Press, 2010).

95. George Washington to George William Fairfax, 10–15 June 1774, Founders Online, https://founders.archives.gov/documents/Washington/02-10-02-0067.

96. My analysis relies on the daily records kept by the secretary, Charles Thomson: Worthington C. Ford et al., eds., *Journals of the Continental Congress, 1774–1789* (GPO, 1904–1937).

97. Derek H. Davis, *Religion and the Continental Congress, 1774–1789: Contributions to Original Intent* (Oxford University Press, 2000). See also James H. Hutson, *Religion and the Founding of the American Republic* (Library of Congress, 1998), 49–74. Peter Harrison, *"Religion" and the Religions in the English Enlightenment* (Cambridge University Press, 1990), 39. On the classification of religions: Thomas A. Tweed, "Introduction," in Hannah Adams, *A Dictionary of All Religions and Religious Denominations . . .* (1817; Scholars Press and Oxford University Press, 1992), xiv.

98. "Morals of Confucius," *Pennsylvania Gazette,* 7 and 21 March 1738. John Adams, *Thoughts on Government, Applicable to the Present State of the American Colonies . . .* (John Dunlap, 1776), 5. See also Dave Wang, "Confucius in the American Founding: The Founders' Efforts to Use Confucian Moral Philosophy in Their Endeavor to Create New Virtue for the Nation," *Virginia Review of Asian Studies* 16 (2014): 11–26.

99. As Sarna notes, "the Constitutional Convention and most state discussions concerning the place of religion in American life, ignored Jews." Jonathan D. Sarna, *American Judaism: A History* (Yale University Press, 2004), 31–32, 37.

100. John Jay drafted the document: *Journals of the Continental Congress,* 1: 88.

101. Charles Carroll authored a series of letters as "First Citizen" in the *Maryland Gazette* starting 4 February 1773. See Kate Mason Rowland, *The Life of Charles Carroll of Carrollton, 1737–1832 . . .* (G. P. Putnam's Sons, 1898), 1: 284–85, 316. John Adams to Abigail Adams, 9 October 1774, Founders Online, https://founders.archives.gov/documents/Adams/04-01-02-0111.

102. *Journals of the Continental Congress,* 1:26. Davis, *Religion and the Continental Congress,* 74. John Adams mentioned the denominations represented in the room: John Adams to Abigail Adams, 16 September 1774, Founders Online, https://founders.archives.gov/documents/Adams/04-01-02-0101.

103. Silas Deane to Elizabeth Deane, 7 September 1774, in Paul H. Smith et al., eds., *Letters of Delegates to Congress, 1774–1789* (Library of Congress, 1976–2000), 1: 34. Davis, *Religion and the Continental Congress,* 74–75.

104. Edmund C. Burnett, ed., *Letters of Members of the Continental Congress* (Carnegie Institution, 1921–1936), 1: 19.

105. *Journals of the Continental Congress,* 1: 27. Davis, *Religion and the Continental Congress,* 74–75.

106. Davis, *Religion and the Continental Congress,* 65.

107. Elise Marienstras and Naomi Wulf, "French Translations and Reception of the Declaration of Independence," *JAH* 85.4 (1999): 313, 322. As the authors note, some early French translations of the Declaration omitted the reference to "Nature's God."

108. Catharine A. Brekus, ed., *Sarah Osborn's Collected Writings* (Yale University Press, 2017), 240.

109. Jane Hoskens, *The Life and Spiritual Sufferings of That Faithful Servant of Christ Jane Hoskens . . .* (William Evitt, 1771). On Jane (Fenn) Hoskens and other Quaker female preachers, see Rebecca Larson, *Daughters of Light: Quaker Women Preaching and Prophesying in the Colonies and Abroad, 1700–1775* (University of North Carolina Press, 1999), 47–50, 56, 58, 77, 81, 128, 175, 211, 241, 283, 310–311. On female preaching: Catherine A. Brekus, *Strangers and Pilgrims: Female Preaching in America, 1740–1845* (University of North Carolina Press, 1998). On Ann Lee and the Shakers: Stephen J. Stein, *The Shaker Experience in America: A History of the United Society of Believers* (Yale University Press, 1992).

110. For a comparative analysis of how they imagined race: Katy L. Chiles, "Becoming Colored in Occom and Wheatley's Early America," *Proceedings of the Modern Language Association* 123. 5 (2008): 1398–1417.

111. Julian D. Mason Jr., ed., *The Poems of Phillis Wheatley* (University of North Carolina Press, 1989), 53, 54, 55–57, 122–127, 174–177.

112. Occom's popular 1772 sermon was "A Sermon Preached at the Execution of Moses Paul, an Indian." See Joanna Brooks, ed., *The Collected Writings of Samson Occom, Mohegan: Leadership and Literature in Eighteenth-Century Native America* (Oxford University Press, 2006), 176–195.

113. The letter from Phillis Wheatley to Rev. Samson Occom was dated 11 February 1774. It first appeared in the *Connecticut Gazette* 11.539, 11 March 1774. It was reprinted in more than ten other newspapers. Mason, *Poems of Phillis Wheatley,* 203–204. John C. Shields, ed., *The Collected Works of Phillis Wheatley* (Oxford University Press, 1988), 315.

114. Patrick Griffin, *America's Revolution* (Oxford University Press, 2013), 125.

115. Lord Dunmore, governor of Virginia, issued a proclamation in April 1775 promising freedom to those slaves who fought with him. Woody Holton, *Forced Founders: Indians, Debtors, Slaves, and the Making of the American Revolution in Virginia* (University of North Carolina Press, 1999), 133–163.

116. Griffin, *America's Revolution,* 127.

117. Taylor, *American Revolutions,* 210–211.

118. Sarna, *American Judaism,* 31, 35.

119. Theodore C. Tappert and John W. Doberstein, eds., *The Notebook of a Colonial Clergyman* (Muhlenberg Press, 1959), 161–162.

120. John Wesley, *A Calm Address to Our American Colonies* (R. Hawes, 1775). See Allan Raymond, "'I Fear God and Honour the King': John Wesley and the American Revolution," *CH* 45.3 (1976): 316–328.

121. In a letter dated 25 August 1776, Philip Reading noted the dilemma about whether to include prayers for the king and said he decided to "shut up" his Delaware church: W. S. Perry, ed., *Historical Collections Relating to the American Colonial Church* (AMS Press, 1969), 483–486. On Duché, a loyalist during the war who returned to England when it ended: Davis, *Religion and the Continental Congress,*

75–76. See also Nancy L. Rhoden, *Revolutionary Anglicanism: The Colonial Church of England Clergy during the American Revolution* (NYU Press, 1999).

122. Thomas Hutchins and T. Cheevers, *A New Map of the Western parts of Virginia, Pennsylvania, Maryland, and North Carolina* . . . (Thomas Hutchins, 1778). Thomas Hutchins, *A Topographical Description of Virginia, Pennsylvania, Maryland, and North Carolina* . . . (John Norman, 1787).

123. John Spaulding, *From the Plow to the Pulpit* (Robert Carter and Brothers, 1874), 13.

124. Hannah Adams, *A Memoir of Miss Hannah Adams* . . . (Gray and Bowen, 1832), 11. Hannah Adams, *Alphabetical Compendium of the Various Sects* . . . (B. Edes and Sons, 1784). See also Thomas A. Tweed, "An American Pioneer in the Study of Religion: Hannah Adams (1755–1831) and Her *Dictionary of All Religions*," *JAAR* 60.3 (1992): 437–464.

125. See Katherine Carté Engel, *Religion and Profit: Moravians in Early America* (University of Pennsylvania, 2009).

126. The Single Sisters Diary, entries for 24 June and 4 July 1776: Bethlehem Digital History Project, http://bdhp.moravian.edu/community_records/catalogs_diary/single_sisters/singlesisters1776.html.

127. On the rebellion as "one of the most causeless, unprovoked and *unnatural* that ever disgraced any Country," see Charles Inglis to the Secretary of the Society for the Propagation of the Gospel, 31 October 1776, in John Wolfe Lydekker, ed., *The Life and Letters of Charles Inglis* (Society for Promoting Christian Knowledge, 1936), 157–161. On the theologies I discuss here, see Mark Noll, *America's God: From Jonathan Edwards to Abraham Lincoln* (Oxford University Press, 2002), chaps. 4–8.

128. Patrick Henry, "Give Me Liberty or Give Me Death," 23 March 1775, https://avalon.law.yale.edu/18th_century/patrick.asp. There were also "biblical echoes" in Henry's speech; see Noll, *In the Beginning Was the Word,* 276.

129. *Journals of the Continental Congress,* 1: 128–157. The document is reprinted as appendix A in Davis, *Religion and the Continental Congress,* 231–237.

130. The original edition of *Common Sense* appeared on 14 February. I refer to the revised edition: Thomas Paine, *Common Sense; Addressed to the Inhabitants of America* . . . (W. and T. Bradford, 1776). On the number of copies sold: Griffin, *America's Revolution,* 134.

131. Paine, *Common Sense,* 27.

132. Paine, *Common Sense,* 9, 26.

133. "Declaration of Independence: A Transcription," America's Founding Documents, https://www.archives.gov/founding-docs/declaration-transcript. The Declaration, as Armitage notes, asserted the new state's place in "the law of nations": David Armitage, "The Declaration of Independence and International Law," *WMQ* 59.1 (2002): 42. Pauline Maier, *American Scripture: Making the Declaration of Independence* (Alfred A. Knopf, 1997). Maier argues that the document became revered as an antislavery text during the early nineteenth century and remained so after the Civil War.

134. On what the Declaration did not say: Griffin, *America's Revolution,* 136; David Armitage, *The Declaration of Independence: A Global History* (Harvard University Press, 2008), 19.

135. The Confederate constitution mentioned "Almighty God": *The Constitution of the Confederate States of America,* 11 March 1861, https://avalon.law.yale.edu/19th_century/csa_csa.asp. See Katharine Mary Batlan, "Christ in the Constitution: Contesting Amendment Proposals and Religious Liberty in the United States, 1863–1975," PhD diss., University of Texas, 2018, 34–35.

136. See the works by Nicholas Street, Ezra Stiles, Samuel Langdon, and Thomas Jefferson in Conrad Cherry, ed., *God's New Israel: Religious Interpretations of American Destiny,* rev. and updated ed. (University of North Carolina Press, 1998), 61–112.

137. Armitage, *Declaration of Independence,* 17, 49.

138. Abel Buell, *A New and Correct Map of the United States of North America . . .* (Abel Buell, 1784). This landmark map is on deposit at the Library of Congress.

139. Manasseh Cutler, *An Explanation of the Map Which Delineates That Part of the Federal Lands . . .* (Dabney and Cushing, 1787), 14. Andrew R. L. Cayton, "Introduction: The Significance of Ohio in the Early American Republic," in Andrew R. L. Cayton and Stuart D. Hobbs, eds., *The Center of a Great Empire: The Ohio Country in the Early American Republic* (Ohio University Press, 2005), 1.

140. Thomas Jefferson, draft of the Declaration of Independence, 28 June 1776, *Journals of the Continental Congress* (1906), 5: 498. Griffin, *America's Revolution,* 136–137. Annette Gordon-Reed and Peter S. Onuf, *"Most Blessed of the Patriarchs": Thomas Jefferson and the Empire of the Imagination* (Liveright, 2016), 60. On the drafts, see Julian P. Boyd, *The Declaration of Independence: The Evolution of the Text,* rev. ed. (University Press of New England, 1999).

141. Abraham Lincoln to Henry L. Pierce and others, 6 April 1859, in Roy P. Basler, ed., *Collected Works of Abraham Lincoln* (Rutgers University Press, 1953), 3: 375–376.

142. Willi Paul Adams, "German Translations of the American Declaration of Independence," *JAH* 85.4 (1999): 1327. For a famous criticism, see [John Lind with Jeremy Bentham], *An Answer to the Declaration of the American Congress* (T. Cadell, J. Walter, and T. Sewell, 1776).

143. This sermon preached on 13 December 1776 was by "the chaplain in ordinary to His Majesty": Henry Stebbing, *A Sermon on the Late General Fast . . .* (W. Flexney, 1776), 3.

144. *Experience Preferable to Theory: Remarks on Dr. Price's Observations on the Nature of Civil Liberty . . .* (G. Kearsley, 1776), 66. Scholars suggest the author was either Adam Ferguson or Thomas Hutchison. Another British text suggested the idea of independence was "a baneful Weed": An Englishman, *An Address to the People of Great Britain . . .* (Bristol: T. Cocking, 1776), 78.

145. Robert J. Taylor, ed., *Papers of John Adams,* vol. 4, *February–August 1776* (Harvard University Press, 1979), 4: 130–133.

146. Taylor, *American Revolutions,* 479. "The Revolution roiled a society that mixed exploitation with opportunity, hierarchy with mobility, and slavery with freedom": Alan Taylor, *Writing Early American History* (University of Pennsylvania Press, 2005), 224.

147. On the Great Seal: US Department of State, *The Great Seal of the United States* (Bureau of Public Affairs, US Department of State, 2003); Richard Sharpe Patterson and Richardson Dougall, *The Eagle and the Shield: A History of the Great Seal of the United States* (Office of the Historian, US Department of State, 1978); "Report on the Seal of the United States" and other visual representations and verbal accounts in the Papers of the Continental Congress, 1774–1789, Letters and Papers of Charles Thomson, 1781–1789, National Archives, Washington DC.

148. The first committee's work: Patterson and Dougall, *The Eagle and the Shield,* 6–31. The source of *E pluribus unum* was the *Gentleman's Magazine,* published in London. The motto was on its title page: Patterson and Dougall, *The Eagle and the Shield,* 22–25.

149. Thomson was an elder in Philadelphia's First Presbyterian Church, though his religious views were complex. See Lewis R. Harley, *The Life of Charles Thomson* (George W. Jacobs, 1900), 63.

150. On the contributions of each committee: US Department of State, *Great Seal,* 2–4. A copy of his "Remarks and Explanation" that was adopted by the Continental Congress on 20 June 1782 is also reprinted on p. 5.

151. On the reverse, Thomson also placed two mottos inspired by Virgil: David M. Pollio, "Virgil and American Symbolism," *Classical Outlook* 87.4 (2010): 137.

152. Patterson and Dougall, *The Eagle and the Shield,* 74–82.

153. Homer, *Iliad,* vol. II, books 13–24, Loeb Classical Library 171 (Harvard University Press, 1925), 585–586. The passage is 24:311. On raptors in Scandinavian myths: G. Roland Murphy, SJ, *Tree of Salvation: Yggdrasil and the Cross in the North* (Oxford University Press, 2013), 4, 6. On Charles V's symbol: Stephanie Schrader, "'Greater Than Ever He Was': Ritual and Power in Charles V's 1558 Funeral Procession," *Nederlands Kunsthistorisch Jaarboek / Netherlands Yearbook for History of Art* 49 (1998): 77.

154. Davíd Carrasco, *The Aztecs: A Very Short Introduction* (Oxford University Press, 2012), 40–41, 44–45.

155. Elizabeth A. Fenn, *Encounters at the Heart of the World: A History of the Mandan People* (Hill and Wang, 2014), 71–74.

156. Edward J. Lenik, "The Thunderbird Motif in Northeastern Indian Art," *Archaeology of Eastern North America* 40 (2012): 163–185. Michael Edmonds, "Flights of Fancy: Birds and People in the Old Northwest," *Wisconsin Magazine of History* 83.3 (2000): 162–163. John E. Kelly, "The Context of Post Pit and Meaning of the Sacred Pole at the East S. Louis Mound Group," *Wisconsin Archaeologist* 84.1–2 (2003): 112. Andrew W. Hickok et al., "Mortuary Evidence of Coast Salish Shamanism?," *Canadian Journal of Archaeology* 34 (2010): 251. Stephen Plog and Julie Solometo, "The Never-Changing and Ever-Changing: The Evolution of Western Pueblo Ritual,"

Cambridge Archaeological Journal 7.2 (1997): 172. Sergei Kan, "Memory Eternal: Orthodox Christianity and the Tlingit Mortuary Complex," *Arctic Anthropology* 24.1 (1987): 42.

157. James A. Brown, "The Archaeology of Ancient Religion in the Eastern Woodlands," *ARA* 26 (1997): 476. John E. Kelly, James A. Brown, and Lucretia S. Kelly, "The Context of Religion at Cahokia: The Mound 34 Case," in Lars Fogelin, ed., *Religion, Archaeology, and the Material World* (Center for Archaeological Investigations, Southern Illinois University, 2008), 311. Sissel Schroeder, "Current Research on Late Precontact Societies of the Midcontinental United States," *JAR* 12.4 (2004): 339.

158. Charles Thomson, trans., *The Holy Bible* . . . (Jane Aitken, 1808). See J. Ramsey Michaels, "Charles Thomson and the First American New Testament," *Harvard Theological Review* 104.3 (2011): 349–365.

159. Patterson and Dougall, *The Eagle and the Shield,* 96–99.

160. Harley, *Life of Charles Thomson,* 46–58. Charles Thomson, *An Enquiry into the Causes of the Alienation of the Delaware and Shawanese Indians from the British Interest* . . . (J. Wilkie, 1759), 56, 75.

161. "An Act to encourage national industrial recovery . . . June 16, 1933," Enrolled Acts and Resolutions of Congress, 1789–1996, General Records of the United States Government, Record Group 11, National Archives. On the thunderbird image: Graphic of NRA Blue Eagle, ca. 1933, Records of the National Recovery Administration [NRA], 1927–1937, Records Group 9 (NWDNS-9-X), National Archives. The quotation is from "The Thunderbird Spreads Its Wings," *El Malcriado,* no. 34, 21 April 1966, 9.

162. Patterson and Dougall, *The Eagle and the Shield,* 425–429 (Rutherford), 402–407 (Roosevelt). "Congressional Prayer Room," Office of the Chaplain, https://chaplain.house.gov/religion/prayer_room.html.

163. Taylor, *American Revolutions,* 73.

164. "Narrative of John Heckewelder's Journey to the Wabash in 1792 (continued)," *PMHB* 12.1 (1888): 49–50. The land speculator who told this story was John Cleves Symmes (1742–1814). On Symmes, see "Life and Services of John Cleves Symmes," *New Jersey Historical Society Proceedings* 2.5 (1879): 22–43.

165. This remark by the Shawnee chief and the others quoted below can be found in "Narrative of John Heckewelder's Journey," 50. On Shawnee religion: Jerry E. Clark, *The Shawnee* (University of Kentucky Press, 2007), chap. 5.

166. The probable authors of the 1787 Northwest Ordinance were two Harvard-trained lawyers, Nathan Dane and Rufus King.

167. *An Ordinance for the Government of the Territory of the United States, North-West of the River Ohio, 1787,* broadside, Continental Congress, 1787, Rare Book and Special Collections Division, Library of Congress.

168. Jefferson drafted the proposed statute for religious freedom in 1779, though it was not passed until 1785: Thomas Jefferson, "A Bill for Establishing Religious Freedom," 18 June 1779, Founders Online, https://founders.archives.gov/documents/Jefferson/01-02-02-0132-0004-0082. Act for Establishing Religious Freedom, 31

October 1785, Founders Online, https://founders.archives.gov/documents/Madison/01-08-02-0206.

169. See "The Contract of the Ohio Company with the Honorable Board of Treasury of the United States of America, Made by the Rev. Mr. Manasseh Cutler and Major Winthrop Sargent, as agents for the Directors of said Company, at New York, October 7, 1787," in Charles M. Walker, *History of Athens County, Ohio* (Robert Clarke, 1869), appendix C, 555–561. A reference to religion is on p. 555: "lot number 29 to be appropriated to the purposes of religion." William Parker Cutler and Julia Perkins Cutler, *Life, Journals, and Correspondence of Rev. Manasseh Cutler, LL.D.* (Robert Clarke, 1888), 253–334, 335–373. On Story, see S. P. Hildreth, *Memoirs of the Early Pioneer Settlers of Ohio* (H. W. Derby, 1852), 325–329.

170. The new Massachusetts state constitution, for example, perpetuated a Congregational establishment.

171. Joel Barlow, *The Vision of Columbus: A Poem in Nine Books* (Hudson and Goodwin, 1787), lines 151–152. See Danielle E. Conger, "Native American Nationalism: Joel Barlow's Vision of Columbus," *New England Quarterly* 72.4 (1999): 558–576; Joseph L. Blau, "Joel Barlow, Enlightened Religionist," *Journal of the History of Ideas* 10.3 (1949): 430–444. The quotations from his poem: Barlow, *Vision of Columbus,* lines 158, 160, 167–169, 175, 235, 239, 71, 91–94, 95, 100, 101–110.

172. Buel, *Joel Barlow,* 94–95. Most of the 785 subscribers to the book received their copies in May as the Constitutional Convention was meeting in Philadelphia. Buel, *Joel Barlow,* 84.

173. Steven C. Bullock, *Revolutionary Brotherhood: Freemasonry and the Transformation of the American Social Order, 1730–1840* (University of North Carolina Press, 1996), 53.

174. Surviving accounts agree that about 5,000 processed and 17,000 observed the festivities. The city's 1790 population was 42,520. Francis Hopkinson, "An Account of the Grand Federal Procession, Performed at Philadelphia on Friday the 4th of July 1788," in *The Miscellaneous Essays and Occasional Writings of Francis Hopkinson, Esq.* (T. Dobson, 1792), 349–422. [Benjamin Rush], "Observation on the Federal Procession on the Fourth of July, 1788, in the City of Philadelphia," in "A Letter from a Gentleman in this City to his Friend in a Neighboring State," *The American Museum, or Universal Advertiser* 4 (July 1788): 77. See also Beneke, *Beyond Toleration,* 3–4.

175. William Penn, "Letter from William Penn to the Committee of the Free Society of Traders, 1683," in Albert Cook Myers, ed., *Narratives of Early Pennsylvania, West New Jersey and Delaware, 1630–1707* (Charles Scribner's Sons, 1912), 234.

176. Amy C. Schutt, *Peoples of the River Valleys: The Odyssey of the Delaware Indians* (University of Pennsylvania Press, 2007), 142. Jean R. Soderlund, *Lenape Country: Delaware Valley Society before William Penn* (University of Pennsylvania Press, 2015).

177. Johannes and Sophia, the Moravian Indians, appear on a list of "Departures and Burials on the Common Burial Ground of Indians departed in the Barracks at

Philadelphia, 1764," Moravian Archives, Box-Philadelphia I, p. 208, Bethlehem, Pennsylvania. They died from smallpox. On the fifty-six Christian Lenape who died in 1764: John Heckewelder, *A Narrative of the Mission of the United Brethren among the Delaware and Mohegan Indians . . .* (M'Carty and David, 1820), 88. On taverns and civic life, including the Indian Queen, see Peter Thompson, *Rum Punch and Revolution: Taverngoing and Public Life in Eighteenth-Century Philadelphia* (University of Pennsylvania, 1999), 59, 62, 87–88. On convention attendees at the Indian Queen, see George Washington's diary entry for 7 June 1787: "Attended Convention as usual. Dined with a Club of Convention Members at the Indian Queen." George Washington, 7 June 1787, Washington Papers, Founders Online, https://founders.archives.gov/documents/Washington/01-05-02-0002-0006.

178. On some of the city's 300 enslaved Africans and greater number of Free Blacks watching the parade: Hopkinson, "Grand Federal Procession."

179. Shane White, "'It Was a Proud Day': African Americans, Festivals, and Parades in the North, 1741–1834," *JAH* 81.1 (1994): 33. On the Black Masons' parade in 1797: Elaine Forman Crane, ed., *The Diary of Elizabeth Drinker,* vol. 2 (Northeastern University Press, 1991), 935. On Freemasonry, see David G. Hackett, *That Religion in Which All Men Agree: Freemasonry in American Culture* (University of California Press, 2014).

180. Francis Hopkinson, *An Ode for the 4th of July 1788* (Matthew Carey, 1788). The ode is from the Constitutional Convention Broadside Collection, Library of Congress, https://www.loc.gov/item/90898122/.

181. Rush, "Observation on the Federal Procession." On Rush's own creed, see Benjamin Rush to John Adams, 5 April 1808, Founders Online, https://founders.archives.gov/documents/Adams/99-02-02-5236.

182. The *Almanac* for 1789 listed sixteen congregations in 1788, including Catholics, Jews, Lutherans, Moravians, Presbyterians, Episcopalians, German Reformed, Baptists, and Quakers. "A List of the Births and Deaths of the Various Religious Societies in the City of Philadelphia . . . ," in *Poulson's Town and Country Almanac for the Year of Our Lord, 1789* (Zachariah Poulson Jr.). On the probable identity of the rabbi: Sarna, *American Judaism,* 38; Alan D. Corré and Malcolm H. Stern, "The Record Book of the Reverend Jacob Raphael Cohen," *American Jewish Historical Quarterly* 59.1 (1969): 23.

183. Sarna, *American Judaism,* 38.

184. Laura Rigal, "'Raising the Roof': Authors, Spectators and Artisans in the Grand Federal Procession of 1788," *Theatre Journal* 48.3 (1996): 253–277.

185. James Wilson's speech was printed in Hopkinson, "Account of the Grand Federal Procession," 20–24. On religion and the deliberations, see Davis, *Religion and the Continental Congress.*

186. On the reciprocal relationship between the urban and the agrarian, see Peter Bess, "City Stories of Nature and Grace: An Urban Pilgrim's Progress," *Communio* 43 (2016): 573.

187. On labels for the social classes: Steve Rosswurm, "Equality and Justice: Philadelphia's Popular Revolution," in Billy G. Smith, ed., *Life in Early Philadelphia:*

Documents from the Revolutionary and Early National Periods (Pennsylvania State University Press, 1995), 247.

188. On Powel and his wife Elizabeth, see the Powel Family Papers, Abstract and Background Note, Historical Society of Pennsylvania, Collection 1582, Philadelphia. Powel was a founding member of the society; so were Benjamin Rush and Charles Thomson. The full list of founding members: Simon Baatz, *"Venerate the Plough": A History of the Philadelphia Society for Promoting Agriculture, 1785–1985* (Philadelphia Society for the Promotion of Agriculture, 1985), 109–111.

189. Drew Lopenzina, *Red Ink: Native Americans Picking Up the Pen in the Colonial Period* (State University of New York Press, 2013).

190. Brooks, *Collected Writings of Samson Occom,* 306. Occom visited Brotherton in 1785 and moved his family there in 1789.

191. Lisa Brooks, *The Common Pot: The Recovery of Native Space in the Northeast* (University of Minnesota Press, 2008), 51–53. Mohegan historian Melissa Tantaquidgeon Zobel suggested this Mohegan narrative was a "strategic romanticization," but the changes in the landscape and lifeways are indisputable (p. 52).

192. Taylor, *American Revolutions,* 72.

193. Valerio Valeri, *Kingship and Sacrifice: Ritual and Society in Ancient Hawaii* (University of Chicago Press, 1985), 103, 215.

194. Thomas A. Tweed and Stephen Prothero, eds., *Asian Religions in America: A Documentary History* (Oxford University Press, 1999), 25–26, 392.

195. Jürgen Heideking, "The Federal Processions of 1788 and the Origins of American Civil Religion," *Soundings* 77.3/4 (1994): 367–387.

196. Nothing was inevitable, including the fate of Natives and Africans after the Revolutionary and Early National period: Gary B. Nash, "Native Americans, the National Parks, and the Concept of Historical Inevitability," *American Indian Culture and Research Journal* 35.1 (2011): 75–80.

197. Quoted in Len Travers, *Celebrating the Fourth: Independence Day and the Rites of Nationalism in the Early Republic* (University of Massachusetts, 1997), 78. See Anna Clifford to Sarah Clifford, 11 July 1788, Clifford Family Papers, 8:279, Historical Society of Pennsylvania, Philadelphia.

198. George Washington to Colonel Benedict Arnold, 14 September 1775, Founders Online, https://founders.archives.gov/documents/Washington/03-01-02-0355.

199. A Catholic Clergyman [John Carroll], *An Address to the Roman Catholics of the United States of America* (Frederick Green, 1784), 11. [Charles Henry Wharton], *A Reply to an Address to the Roman Catholics of the United States of America . . .* (Charles Cist, 1785), 87.

200. Sarna, *American Judaism,* 40.

201. Taylor, *American Revolutions,* 437–438, 452–454.

202. Elizabeth Powel received Franklin's famous reply when she asked what form of government the Convention had just produced—"A republic, madam, if you can keep it"—and she is credited with persuading Washington to serve a second term. On Powel and the political salon: Susan Branson, *These Fiery Frenchified Dames: Women and Political Culture in Early National Philadelphia* (University of

Pennsylvania Press, 2010), 133–135, 142. Elizabeth sent Washington new lamps to use in Virginia, and he sent her books, including Joel Barlow's *The Vision of Columbus*. George Washington to Elizabeth Powel, 6 June 1787, Founders Online, https://founders.archives.gov/documents/Washington/04-05-02-0201. Elizabeth Powel to George Washington, 8 September 1787, Founders Online, https://founders.archives.gov/documents/Washington/04-05-02-0293.

203. "Petition of Belinda an African, to the Honourable Senate and House of Representatives in General Court Assembled, February 14, 1783," in Revolution Resolves, 239: 11–14, Massachusetts Archives. See Roy E. Finkenbine, "Belinda's Petition: Reparations for Slavery in Revolutionary Massachusetts," *WMQ* 64.1 (2007): 94–98, 101–102.

204. Billy G. Smith and Richard Wojtowicz, *Blacks Who Stole Themselves: Advertisements for Runaways in the Pennsylvania Gazette, 1728–1790* (University of Pennsylvania Press, 1989), 5.

205. Gary Nash, *Forging Freedom: Philadelphia's Black Community, 1720–1840* (Harvard University Press, 1988), 98–126. An Act for the Gradual Abolition of Slavery, 1780, https://avalon.law.yale.edu/18th_century/pennst01.asp.

206. The Declaration's phrase "all men are created equal" sustained some dissenters, but the Constitution was "as anti-Indian as it was proslavery": Gregory Evans Dowd, "Indigenous Peoples without the Republic," *JAH* 104.1 (2017): 36.

207. Charles Thomson to Thomas Jefferson, 2 November 1785, Founders Online, https://founders.archives.gov/documents/Jefferson/01-09-02-0005.

208. I side with those who say the Revolution didn't end in 1787, 1795, 1812, or 1815. The unfinished work was taken up again in the Civil War. See David Armitage, "The American Revolution in Atlantic Perspective," in Nicholas Canny and Philip Morgan, eds., *The Oxford Handbook of the Atlantic World, 1450–1850* (Oxford University Press, 2011), 529. See also Griffin, *America's Revolution*, 258–259.

Chapter 6. Expansionist Religion

1. Susan Sleeper-Smith, *Indigenous Prosperity and American Conquest: Indian Women of the Ohio River Valley, 1690–1792* (University of North Carolina Press, 2018), 285–320. Chief de Coigne's speech: Rowena Buell, ed., *The Memoirs of Rufus Putnam . . .* (Houghton, Mifflin, 1903), 342.

2. Putnam described the earthworks in a 1788 letter: William Parker Cutler, ed., *Life, Journals, and Correspondence of Rev. Manasseh Cutler, LL.D.* (R. Clarke, 1888), 1: 376–380. Marietta had Woodland Era mounds from both Adena (800 BCE–100 CE) and Hopewell (100 BCE–400 CE) cultures. Marietta's conical burial mound was an Adena mound. See Evan Bevins, "Mounds Offer a Glimpse of History Predating Marietta," *Parkersburg News and Sentinel*, 10 September 2022. Whitney A. Martinko, "'So Majestic a Monument of Antiquity': Landscape, Knowledge, and Authority in the Early National West," *Buildings and Landscapes: Journal of the Vernacular Architecture Forum* 16.1 (2009): 29–61.

3. *An Ordinance for the Government of the Territory of the United States, North-West of the River Ohio, 1787*, Continental Congress; "The Contract of the

Ohio Company with the Honorable Board of Treasury of the United States of America . . . October 7, 1787," in Charles M. Walker, *History of Athens County, Ohio* (Robert Clarke, 1869), 555–561.

4. Thomas Jefferson Summers, *History of Marietta* (Leader Publishing, 1903), 198–242. Barbara A. Terzian, "Ohio's Constitutions: An Historical Perspective," *Cleveland Law Review* 51.3–4 (2003): 357–370. On Putnam and slavery: Buell, *Memoirs of Rufus Putnam,* xxxvi.

5. Willia Dawson Cotton, *Sketch of Mound Cemetery, Marietta, Ohio* (Marietta Register Printing, 1900). On this period, I am indebted to John Lauritz Larson and Michael A. Morrison, eds., *Whither the Early Republic: A Forum on the Future of the Field* (University of Pennsylvania Press, 2005); Daniel Walker Howe, *What Hath God Wrought: The Transformation of America, 1815–1848* (Oxford University Press, 2007).

6. "Empire of liberty": Thomas Jefferson to George Rogers Clarke, 25 December 1780, in Julian P. Boyd, ed., *Papers of Thomas Jefferson* (Princeton University Press, 1951), 4: 237–238.

7. Sweet and Ahlstrom emphasized westward movement as well as territorial and ecclesiastical expansion, while mentioning Marietta's founding. William Warren Sweet, *The Story of Religion in America* (Harper and Brothers, 1939), 298–321. Sydney E. Ahlstrom, *A Religious History of the American People,* 2nd ed. (1972; Yale University Press, 2004), 455–471. Ahlstrom wrote that the founders arrived "in a flatboat they named the *Mayflower* and on landing reenacted the arrival of the Pilgrim Fathers at Plymouth." The flatboat was called *Adventure Galley,* and Putnam's account did not refer to the *Mayflower* or to Plymouth. See Buell, *Memoirs of Rufus Putnam,* 103–104. Perhaps Ahlstrom read Thomas Wickes, *A Historical Discourse Commemorative of the Organization of the Congregational Church in Marietta . . .* (Intelligencer Office, 1847), 4. Ahlstrom also noted that "the region retained its New England flavor." Sweet described Marietta's settlers as "typical representatives of the New England movement westward." Neither mentioned mounds. They also deemphasized the slow pace of church building and the area's increasing religious diversity. Ahlstrom, *Religious History,* 455–456. Sweet, *Story of Religion,* 299–300.

8. Charles Boewe, ed., *John Clifford's Indian Antiquities* (University of Tennessee Press, 2000); Albert Gallatin, *A Synopsis of the Indian Tribes within the United States . . . ,* in *Archaeologia Americana,* American Antiquarian Society, vol. 2 ("the University Press," 1836); Alexander W. Bradford, *American Antiquities and Researches into the Origin and History of the Red Race* (Dayton and Saxton, 1841); R. Tripp Evans, *Romancing the Maya: Mexican Antiquity in the American Imagination, 1820–1915* (University of Texas Press, 2004); Andrew J. Lewis, *A Democracy of Facts: Natural History in the Early Republic* (University of Pennsylvania Press, 2011); Terry A. Barnhart, *American Antiquities: Revisiting the Origins of American Archaeology* (University of Nebraska Press, 2015); Leonard Wilson, *Lyell in America: Transatlantic Geology, 1841–1853* (Johns Hopkins University Press, 1998); Thomas A. Tweed and Stephen Prothero, eds., *Asian Religions in America: A Documentary History* (Oxford University Press, 1999), 25–59.

9. Three Legs, a Piankashaw war chief, made this comment to Washington: Thomas Jefferson, "Minutes of a Conference with the Illinois and Wabash Indians," 1–4 February 1793, https://founders.archives.gov/documents/Jefferson/01-25-02-0120.

10. Gregory Evans Dowd, *A Spirited Resistance: The North American Indian Struggle for Unity, 1745–1815* (Johns Hopkins University Press, 1992), 116–119. Steven Stoll, *Larding the Lean Earth: Soil and Society in Nineteenth-Century America* (Hill and Wang, 2003). Margaret Washington, "Religion, Reform, and Antislavery," in Ellen Hartigan-O'Connor and Lisa G. Materson, eds., *The Oxford Handbook of American Women's and Gender History* (Oxford University Press, 2018), 417–442. Manisha Sinha, *The Slave's Cause: A History of Abolition* (Yale University Press, 2016).

11. The first Columbus Day: *National Gazette,* 17 October 1792. Jefferson, "Minutes of a Conference with the Illinois and Wabash Indians."

12. Nancy F. Cott, *The Bonds of Womanhood: "Woman's Sphere" in New England, 1780–1835* (1977; Yale University Press, 2021), xi–xvii, xix–xxxvi.

13. Some Protestants challenged nationalism: Sam Haselby, *The Origins of American Religious Nationalism* (Oxford University Press, 2015), 2–5.; Mark Y. Hanley, *Beyond a Christian Commonwealth: The Protestant Quarrel with the American Republic, 1830–1860* (University of North Carolina Press, 1994).

14. The US Census of 1850 counted 38,183 worship spaces in the US. J. D. B. DeBow, *Statistical View of the United States . . .* (Beverly Tucker, 1854), 133–134. Jon Butler emphasized "Christianization" in *Awash in a Sea of Faith: Christianizing the American People* (Harvard University Press, 1990). On the "metaphysical" tradition: Catherine L. Albanese, *A Republic of Mind and Spirit: A Cultural History of American Metaphysical Religion* (Yale University Press, 2007), 121–176. See also Amanda Porterfield, *Religion and Politics in the New American Nation* (University of Chicago Press, 2012); Kerry Walters, *Revolutionary Deists: Early America's Infidels* (Prometheus, 2011), 19–46; Leigh Eric Schmidt, *Village Atheists: How America's Unbelievers Made Their Way in a Godly Nation* (Princeton University Press, 2016), 4–5; John Lardas Modern, "Evangelical Secularism and the Measure of Leviathan," *CH* 77.4 (2008): 868.

15. Nathan O. Hatch, *The Democratization of American Christianity* (Yale University Press, 1989). Porterfield, *Religion and Politics in the New American Nation.* Christine Leigh Heyrman, *Southern Cross: The Beginnings of the Bible Belt* (University of North Carolina Press, 1997), 254–255.

16. Sarah Barringer Gordon, "The First Disestablishment: Limits on Church Power and Property before the Civil War," *University of Pennsylvania Law Review* 162.2 (2014): 307–372. On the three "constitutional periods," see Sarah Barringer Gordon, *The Spirit of the Law: Religious Voices and the Constitution in Modern America* (Harvard University Press, 2010), 3–13.

17. Shari Rabin, *Jews on the Frontier: Religion and Mobility in Nineteenth-Century America* (NYU Press, 2017), 7, 125.

18. John R. Dichtl, *Frontiers of Faith: Bringing Catholicism to the West in the Early Republic* (University of Kentucky Press, 2008). William W. Warner, *At Peace with All Their Neighbors: Catholics and Catholicism in the National Capital, 1787–1860* (Georgetown University Press, 1994), 81–165.

19. Daniel Webster, *A Discourse Delivered at Plymouth, December 22, 1820 . . .*, 2nd ed. (Wells and Lilly, 1821). William Apess, *Eulogy on King Philip* ("Published by the Author," 1836), 53–54. John McCaffrey, *Oration Delivered at the Commemoration of the Landing of the Pilgrims of Maryland* (H. C. Neinstedt, 1842); William George Read, *Oration Delivered at the First Commemoration of the Landing of the Pilgrims of Maryland . . .* (John Murray, 1842). William Grimes, *Life of William Grimes, the Runaway Slave . . .* (W. Grimes, 1825).

20. The US as a *state-nation:* David Armitage, "Interchange: Nationalism and Internationalism in the Era of the Civil War," *JAH* 98.2 (2011): 478. Thomas Bender, *A Nation among Nations: America's Place in World History* (Hill and Wang, 2006), 150–155. Emma Willard, *History of the United States or Republic of America . . .* (White, Gallaher, and White, 1828), 3. Between 1819 and 1824 four paintings by John Trumbull were placed in the rotunda; four more were added by 1855. Architect of the Capitol, "Capitol Rotunda," https://www.aoc.gov/explore-capitol-campus/buildings-grounds/capitol-building/rotunda. Susan Strong, "Great Seal" quilt, probably made in Ohio, where her family moved in 1820; see National Quilt Collection, National Museum of American History, Smithsonian Institution, https://americanhistory.si.edu/collections/object-groups/national-quilt-collection.

21. *Symbolic surplus* refers to an extravagant public display in ritual or architecture. *Civil religion* is a loosely linked set of beliefs, values, symbols, and rituals found outside of traditional worship spaces and used to interpret political life in spiritual terms. Robert Bellah, "Civil Religion in America," *Daedalus* 96 (1967): 1–21.

22. Simon P. Newman, "Principles or Men? George Washington and the Political Culture of National Leadership, 1776–1801," *Journal of the Early Republic* 12.4 (1992): 501–502. *Gazette of the United States,* 27 December 1799. Joseph Dana, *A Discourse on the Character and Death of General George Washington . . .* (Edmund M. Blunt, 1800); Frederick W. Hotchkiss, *An Oration Delivered at Saybrook on Saturday February 22nd, 1800 . . .* (S. Green, 1800). See also Andrew Burstein, "Immortalizing the Founding Fathers: The Excesses of Public Eulogy," in Nancy Isenberg and Andrew Burstein, eds., *Mortal Remains: Death in Early America* (University of Pennsylvania Press, 2003), 91–107.

23. Richard Allen, *Philadelphia Gazette and Universal Daily Advertiser,* 31 December 1799, p. 2. Richard S. Newman, "'We Participate in Common': Richard Allen's Eulogy of Washington and the Challenge of Interracial Appeals," *WMQ* 64.1 (2007): 117–128. Chief Joseph Bryant and Chief Bloody Fellow, who visited Washington in 1792, returned disappointed. See Collin G. Calloway, *The Indian World of George Washington: The First President, the First Americans, and the Birth of the Nation* (Oxford University Press, 2018).

24. The *Apotheosis of Washington,* a fresco on the canopy of the dome, was painted by Constantino Brumidi. Architect of the Capitol, "Apotheosis of Washington," https://www.aoc.gov/explore-capitol-campus/art/apotheosis-washington.

25. Charles L'Enfant's plan first appeared in *Dunlop's American Daily Advertiser,* 26 December 1791. See also Kenneth R. Bowling, *The Creation of Washington, D.C.: The Idea and Location of an American Capital* (George Mason University Press, 1991).

26. Richard F. Grimmett, *St. John's Church, Lafayette Square: The History and Heritage of the Church of the Presidents, Washington, D.C.* (Hillcrest Publishing Group, 2009).

27. Ernest Lee Tuveson, *Redeemer Nation: The Idea of America's Millennial Role* (University of Chicago Press, 1968). Walter A. McGougall, *The Tragedy of U.S. Foreign Policy: How America's Civil Religion Betrayed the National Interest* (Yale University Press, 2016).

28. On *statutory* and *de facto* religious establishments: Mark deWolfe Howe, *The Garden and the Wilderness: Religion and Government in American Constitutional History* (University of Chicago Press, 1965), 11. The de facto establishment lasted into the mid-twentieth century. See also Winnifred Fallers Sullivan, "FORUM: Mark deWolfe Howe, *The Garden and the Wilderness*, Introduction," *CH* 79.4 (2010): 860–862.

29. Frederick L. Harvey, *History of the Washington Monument and Washington National Monument Society* (GPO, 1903). Jean Barman and Bruce McIntyre Watson, *Leaving Paradise: Indigenous Hawaiians in the Pacific Northwest, 1787–1898* (University of Hawaiʻi Press, 2006). Ilya Vinkovetsky, *Russian America: An Overseas Colony of a Continental Empire, 1804–1867* (Oxford University Press, 2011). John Demos, *The Heathen School: A Story of Hope and Betrayal in the Age of the Early Republic* (Vintage, 2014). Laurie F. Maffly-Kipp, "Eastward Ho! American Religion from the Pacific Rim," in Thomas A. Tweed, ed., *Retelling US Religious History* (University of California Press, 1997), 128–133.

30. "Annexation," *Democratic Review* 17 (1845): 5. Most attributed the phrase to John L. O'Sullivan. Hudson suggests that the journalist Jane McManus Storm Cazneau originated it: Linda Hudson, *Mistress of Manifest Destiny* (University of Texas Press, 2001), 60–62. Robert Sampson, *John L. O'Sullivan and His Times* (Kent State University Press, 2003), 244–245. Howe, *What Hath God Wrought*, 703.

31. William Earl Weeks, *The New Cambridge History of American Foreign Relations: Dimensions of the Early American Empire, 1754–1865* (Cambridge University Press, 2013), 122–123.

32. J. T. Leerssen, "Notes towards a Definition of Romantic Nationalism," *Romantik* 2.1 (2013): 9–35.

33. Drew R. McCoy, *The Elusive Republic: Political Economy in Jeffersonian America* (University of North Carolina Press, 1980), 9. John Craig Hammond, "President, Planter, Politician: James Monroe, the Missouri Crisis, and the Politics of Slavery," *JAH* 105.4 (2019): 845. See also David L. Holmes, "The Religion of James Monroe," *Virginia Quarterly Review* 79 (2003): 557–578.

34. Thomas Jefferson, "Second Inaugural Address," *Papers of Thomas Jefferson*, vol. 45, *11 November 1804 to 8 March 1805* (Princeton University Press, 2021), 625–663. Thomas Jefferson, *The Jefferson Bible* (Beacon, 1989).

35. Thomas Jefferson to George Rogers Clarke, 25 December 1780, in Boyd, *Papers of Thomas Jefferson*, 4: 237–238.

36. *Johnson v. McIntosh*, 22 Ill.21 U.S. 543, 8 Wheat. 543, 5 L. Ed. 681 (1823). Roxanne Dunbar-Ortiz, *An Indigenous Peoples' History of the United States* (Beacon,

2014), 200. See also *Cherokee Nation v. Georgia,* 30 U.S. 1, 8 L. Ed. 25 (1831). The so-called "discovery doctrine" appeared in Pope Alexander VI's papal bull *Inter Caetera,* dated 4 May 1493. See https://www.gilderlehrman.org/history-resources/spotlight-primary-source/doctrine-discovery-1493.

37. "State of the Union Addresses of Andrew Jackson," https://www.gutenberg.org/files/5016/5016-h/5016-h.htm.

38. See William Dusinberre, *Slavemaster President: The Double Career of James Polk* (Oxford University Press, 2003).

39. James Belich, *Replenishing the Earth: The Settler Revolution and the Rise of the Anglo-World, 1783–1939* (Oxford University Press, 2009), 65.

40. Joan Mulholland, "Patchwork: The Evolution of a Women's Genre," *Journal of American Culture* 19.4 (1996): 57–69. Laurel Thatcher Ulrich, *A House Full of Females: Plural Marriage and Women's Rights in Early Mormonism, 1835–1870* (Alfred A. Knopf, 2017), 338–343. D. W. Meinig, "The Beholding Eye: Versions of the Same Scene," in D. W. Meinig, ed., *The Interpretation of Ordinary Landscapes: Geographical Essays* (Oxford University Press, 1979), 35.

41. G. Malcolm Lewis, "Indian Maps: Their Place in the History of Plains Cartography," *Great Plains Quarterly* 4.2 (1984): 94. Selwyn Dewdney, *The Sacred Scrolls of the Southern Ojibway* (University of Toronto Press, 1975). Martin D. Mitchell, "Using Mental Map Principles to Interpret American Indian Cartography," *Journal of Geography* 113.1 (2014): 3–9.

42. Christopher Arris Oakley, "The Center of the World: The Principle People and the Great Smoky Mountains," in Jessica Joyce Christie, ed., *Landscapes of Origin in the Americas: Creation Narratives Linking Ancient Places and Present Communities* (University of Alabama Press, 2009), 3–14.

43. David Igler, *The Great Ocean: Pacific Worlds from Captain Cook to the Gold Rush* (Oxford University Press, 2013), 99–102; Mary Brewster, *"She Was a Sister Sailor": The Whaling Journals of Mary Brewster, 1845–1851* (Mystic Seaport Museum, 1992).

44. Mary Hill's album quilt, National Quilt Collection, National Museum of American History, the Smithsonian Institution, https://americanhistory.si.edu/collections/object-groups/national-quilt-collection?page=2.

45. Connecticut Missionary Society, *A Summary of Christian Doctrine and Practice . . .* (Hudson and Goodwin, 1804). See also Amy DeRogatis, *Moral Geography: Maps, Missionaries, and the American Frontier* (Columbia University Press, 2003).

46. Seth Pease, "The Original Plan of the Town and Village of Cleveland," 1 October 1796. Edmund H. Chapman, *Cleveland: Village to Metropolis: A Case Study of Problems of Urban Development in Nineteen-Century America* (Western Reserve Historical Society, 1964), frontispiece.

47. Michael J. McTighe and Jimmy E. W. Meyer, "Religion," *Encyclopedia of Cleveland History,* https://case.edu/ech/articles/r/religion. DeRogatis, *Moral Geography,* 21–24.

48. For a quilter's reflections, see "Annette," "The Patchwork Quilt," *Lowell Offering,* September 1845, 5. The distinction between "homespun" and "broadcloth" informed religious discourse. See "Pulpit Eloquence," *German Reformed Messenger,* 8

May 1839, 3; "The Pilgrim: Charity Thinketh No Evil," *Connecticut Observer,* 27 November 1826, 1.

49. Deborah Vansau McCauley, *Appalachian Mountain Religion: A History* (University of Illinois Press, 1995), 6.

50. David Hurst Thomas, "A Shoshonean Prayerstone Hypothesis: Ritual Cartographies of Great Basin Incised Stones," *AQ* 84.1 (2019): 1–25.

51. Pekka Hämäläinen, "The Rise and Fall of the Plains Indian Horse Cultures," *JAH* 90.3 (2003): 833–862; Pekka Hämäläinen, *Lakota America: A New History of Indigenous Power* (Yale University Press, 2019).

52. Frederick Jackson Turner, *The Frontier in American History* (Henry Holt, 1921), 12.

53. Patricia Nelson Limerick, "What on Earth Is the New Western History?," in Patricia Nelson Limerick, Clyde A. Milner II, and Charles E. Rankin, eds., *Trails: Toward a New Western History* (University of Kansas Press, 1991), 81–88. David M. Wrobel, "What on Earth Has Happened to the New Western History?," *Historian* 66.3 (2004): 437–441. Robert V. Hine, John Mack Faragher, and Jon Coleman, *The American West: A New Interpretive History,* 2nd ed. (Yale University Press, 2017). See also Danae Jacobson, "Spiritual Geographies: How Nuns Changed the U.S. West," PhD diss., University of Notre Dame, 2019, 4.

54. "Scatter zone": John N. Low, *Imprints: The Pokagon Band of Potawatomi Indians and the City of Chicago* (Michigan State University Press, 2006), 6. Sleeper-Smith, *Indigenous Prosperity and American Conquest,* 319–320. Mark R. Schurr, "Archaeological Indices of Resistance: Diversity in the Removal Period Potawatomi of the Western Great Lakes," *AA* 75.1 (2010): 44–60.

55. Turner, *Frontier in American History,* 162. Amy Hill Shevitz, *Jewish Communities on the Ohio River: A History* (University of Kentucky Press, 2007), 3.

56. Shevitz, *Jewish Communities,* 3.

57. Matthew Salafia, *Slavery's Borderland: Freedom and Bondage along the Ohio River* (University of Pennsylvania Press, 2013).

58. The city had more than 100 congregations, including 23 Catholic and 6 Jewish spaces, by 1869: Matthew Smith, *The Spires Still Point to Heaven: Cincinnati's Religious Landscape, 1788–1873* (Temple University Press, 2023), 69. See also the churches visible in this view of Cincinnati's riverfront in 1848: "Panorama of Progress: Building a City in the Photographic Age," Public Library of Cincinnati and Hamilton County, https://1848.cincinnatilibrary.org/.

59. Gerard W. Gawalt, "James Monroe, Presidential Planter," *Virginia Magazine of History and Biography* 101.2 (1993): 263.

60. Robert H. Bishop, ed., *An Outline of the History of the Church in the State of Kentucky . . . Containing the Memoirs of Rev. David Rice* (T. T. Skillman, 1824), 68. See also Andrew M. McGinnis, "Between Enthusiasm and Stoicism: David Rice and Moderate Revivalism in Virginia and Kentucky," *Register of the Kentucky Historical Society* 106.2 (2008): 165–190.

61. David Barrow, "Diary" (1795), David Barrows Papers, Library Special Collections, Western Kentucky University. The quotations are from pp. 26 and 24 of the diary.

62. *The Farmer's Almanac Calculated for Pennsylvania, Delaware, Maryland, Virginia, and Kentucky for the Year of Our Lord, 1801* (Warner and Hanna, 1801). There is no page number for the astrological chart.

63. Walters, *Revolutionary Deists,* 19–22.

64. B. H. Roberts, ed., *History of the Church of Jesus Christ of Latter-day Saints,* 2nd ed. (Deseret Books, 1964), 2: 4–6.

65. James C. Klotter and Craig Thompson Friend, *A New History of Kentucky* (University of Kentucky Press, 2018), 105. David Barrow, *Involuntary, Unmerited, Perpetual, Absolute, Hereditary Slavery . . .* (D. and C. Bradford, 1808).

66. *A Short Abridgement of Christian Doctrine, Newly Revised for the Use of the Catholic Church in the United States of America . . .* (James Doyle, 1793).

67. *The Biography of Elder Barton Warren Stone, Written by Himself . . .* (J. A. and U. P. James, 1847), 37. Haselby, *Origins of American Religious Nationalism,* 170. See also Paul Conkin, *Cane Ridge: America's Pentecost* (University of Wisconsin Press, 1990); Ellen Eslinger, *Citizens of Zion: The Social Origins of Camp Meeting Revivalism* (University of Tennessee Press, 1999); John R. Stilgoe, *Common Landscape of America, 1580 to 1845* (Yale University Press, 1982), 231–238. On the history of "revivalism," see William G. McLoughlin, *Revivals, Awakenings, and Reform: An Essay on Religion and Social Change in America, 1607–1977* (University of Chicago Press, 1978).

68. "Autobiography of William Burke," in James B. Finley, ed., *Sketches of Western Methodism* (R. P. Thompson, 1854), 42; *Biography of Elder Barton Warren Stone,* 9–42; Haselby, *Origins of American Religious Nationalism,* 170.

69. Richard McNemar, *The Kentucky Revival . . .* (E. and E. Hosford, 1808), 61–65.

70. Quoted in John Marshall Barker, *History of Ohio Methodism . . .* (Curts and Jennings, 1898), 181.

71. Cane Ridge as "the most important religious gathering": Conkin, *Cane Ridge,* 3.

72. "Rev. D. H. of Ohio," "Wyandott Indians," *Christian Watchman and Baptist Register* 1.13 (11 March 1820): 2. The pastor was probably John Stewart, "a freeborn mulatto who was part Indian himself": Henry Warner Bowden, *American Indians and Christian Missions: Studies in Cultural Conflict* (University of Chicago Press, 1981), 168.

73. Martin John Spalding, *Sketches of the Early Catholic Missions of Kentucky from Their Commencement in 1787 to the Jubilee of 1826–1827* (B. J. Webb, 1844), 100.

74. McNemar, *Kentucky Revival.* Steven J. Stein, *The Shaker Experience in America* (Yale University Press, 1992), 166.

75. The estimate by Francis Asbury is quoted in Haselby, *Origins of American Religious Nationalism,* 170–171.

76. *Plan of the Camp,* 8 August 1809, *Journal of Benjamin Latrobe,* sketch by Benjamin Henry Latrobe, Latrobe Papers, Maryland Historical Society. See also *Camp Meeting* (c. 1829), lithography by Hugh Bridgeport, Kennedy and Lucas Lithography, Library of Congress.

77. See Gorham B. Weed, *Camp Meeting Manual* (Degen, 1854).

78. Charles G. Finney, *Lectures on Revivals of Religion* (Fleming H. Revell, 1868). Grant Wacker, *America's Pastor: Billy Graham and the Shaping of a Nation* (Harvard University Press, 2014).

79. Spalding, *Sketches of the Early Catholic Missions of Kentucky,* 105. Badin's letter about Cane Ridge appears in Sister Mary Ramona Mattingly, "The Catholic Church on the Kentucky Frontier," PhD diss., Catholic University of America, 1936, 191. Badin's 1805 letter to the Congregatio de Propaganda Fide is quoted in Mattingly, "Kentucky Frontier," 192–193. See also Dichtl, *Frontiers of Faith,* 119, 122–123.

80. Joan Campbell, SL, *Loretto: An Early American Congregation in the Antebellum South* (Bluebird Publishing, 2015), 36.

81. The quotation is from Nerinckx's 30 June 1808 letter to John Carroll, which is in Campbell, SL, *Loretto,* 340.

82. Quoted in Campbell, SL, *Loretto,* 38.

83. Quoted in Campbell, SL, *Loretto,* 39.

84. "Kentucky's Holy Land": *Loretto Magazine* (Fall–Winter 2009): 12. C. Walker Gollar, "The Role of Father Badin's Slaves in Frontier Kentucky," *American Catholic Studies* 115.1 (2004): 4.

85. Gollar, "Father Badin's Slaves in Frontier Kentucky," 1, 13, 16, 17, 22. Gollar notes that some slaves, like Uncle Harry, were respected for their devotion (18).

86. See Badin's account: *Origine et progrès de la mission du Kentucky* (Adrien Le Clere, 1821). Carroll also gave Badin a copy of the *Holy Bible,* 3 vols. (Carey, Stewart, and Co., 1790); this was the first Douai version of the Bible printed in the United States.

87. Carroll was "moved even to tears" at the dedication: Jean Dilhet, *Beginnings of the Catholic Church in the United State*s (Salve Regina Press, 1922), 32–33. Michael DeStefano, "John Carroll, the Amplitude Apologetic and the Baltimore Cathedral," *American Catholic Studies* 122.2 (2011): 46. Peter W. Williams, *Houses of God: Region, Religion, and Architecture in the United States* (University of Illinois Press, 1997), 61.

88. W. Barksdale Maynard, "The Greek Revival: Americanness, Politics, and Economics," in Keith L. Eggener, ed., *American Architectural History: A Contemporary Reader* (Routledge, 2004), 132–141. John T. McGreevy, *Catholicism: A Global History from the French Revolution to Pope Francis* (W. W. Norton, 2022), 58–80. Thomas A. Tweed, *America's Church: The National Shrine and Catholic Presence in the Nation's Capital* (Oxford University Press, 2011), 157–191.

89. DeStefano, "John Carroll," 32–44.

90. DeStefano, "John Carroll," 38–44.

91. Dichtl, *Frontiers of Faith,* 14.

92. The institutions: Saint Thomas Seminary (1811), the Sisters of Loretto (1812), the Sisters of Charity of Nazareth (1812), Saint Joseph College (1820), Saint Mary College (1821), and the Dominican Sisters at Springfield (1822).

93. Campbell, *Loretto.* Mother Seton's rule was based on an existing French model. See Catherine O'Donnell, *Elizabeth Seton: American Saint* (Cornell University Press, 2018), 368. On the Kentucky abbey founded in 1848, see Right Rev. Edmund N. Obrecht, ORC, "History of the Trappists in Kentucky," *Register of the Kentucky State Historical Society* 18.52 (1920): 45, 47–49.

94. G. J. Garraghan, SJ, "The Trappists of Monks Mound," *ACHS* 36.1 (1925): 70–110. Henry Marie Brackenridge, *Views of Louisiana: Together with a Journal of a Voyage up the Missouri River, in 1811* (Cramer, Spear and Eichbaum, 1814), 187. Henry M. Brackenridge to Thomas Jefferson, 25 July 1813, https://founders.archives.gov/documents/Jefferson/03-06-02-0269. Avocational archaeologists sent artifacts to Charles Willson Peale's Philadelphia Museum, and Lexington, Cincinnati, and St. Louis opened museums displaying "antiquities." Charles Coleman Sellers, *Mr. Peale's Museum: Charles Willson Peale and the First Popular Museum of Natural Science and Art* (W. W. Norton, 1980).

95. Martinko, "'So Majestic a Monument of Antiquity."

96. Caleb Atwater, "Description of the Antiquities Discovered in the State of Ohio and Other Western States," *Archaeologia Americana,* American Antiquarian Society 1 (1820): 105–267. William Henry Harrison, *Discourse on the Aborigines of the Valley of the Ohio* (G. W. Bradbury, 1838). Ephraim Squier and Edwin Davis, *Ancient Monuments of the Mississippi Valley* (Smithsonian Institution, 1848). On Circleville, see John W. Reps, "Urban Redevelopment in the Nineteenth Century: The Squaring of Circleville," *Journal of the Society of Architectural Historians* 14.4 (1955): 23–26.

97. Lewis's entry is from 10 September 1803. The most inclusive edition is Gary E. Moulton, ed., *The Journals of the Lewis and Clark Expedition* (University of Nebraska Press, 1983). See Thomas Townsend, "Grave Creek Mound," *Cincinnati Chronicle,* 2 February 1839; Mr. Schoolcraft and J. E. Alexander, "Account of the Mound at Grave Creek Flats in Virginia," *Journal of the Royal Geographical Society of London* 12 (1842): 259–60; E. Thomas Hemmings, "Investigations at Grave Creek Mound, 1975–76: A Sequence for Mound and Moat Construction," *West Virginia Archaeologist* 362 (1984): 3–49.

98. Garraghan, "Trappists of Monks Mound," 70–110. As noted in chapter 3, there is evidence of the ceremonial black drink in Greater Cahokia. It seems that a twelfth-century agricultural cult associated with female fertility and world renewal dominated before 1200. See Thomas E. Emerson, Brad H. Koldehoff, and Tamira K. Brennan, eds., *Revealing Greater Cahokia, North America's First Native City: Rediscovery and Large-Scale Excavations of the East St. Louis Precinct* (Illinois State Archaeological Survey, 2018), 406, 517–521.

99. The "Big Mound" was demolished in 1869. Patricia Cleary, "The Destruction of the Big Mound: Possessing and Defining Native American Places in Early St. Louis," *Missouri Historical Review* 113.1 (2018): 1–21. "Greater Cahokia" refers to the region that extended to East St. Louis and across the Mississippi to St. Louis. See Emerson, Koldehoff, and Brennan, *Revealing Greater Cahokia.*

100. Stephen Aron, *American Confluence: The Missouri Frontier from Borderland to Border State* (Indiana University Press, 2006), esp. 233–243. On the lifeway changes

in St. Louis and the region, see also John Reda, *From Furs to Farms: The Transformation of the Mississippi Valley, 1762–1825* (Northern Illinois University Press, 2016).

101. Quoted in Reda, *From Furs to Farms,* 1.

102. Aron, *American Confluence,* 235–236.

103. Lucas P. Volkman, "Church Property Disputes, Religious Freedom, and the Ordeal of African Methodists in Antebellum St. Louis: Farrar v. Finney (1855)," *Journal of Law and Religion* 27.1 (2011–2012): 90. Anna K. Roberts, "Crossing Jordan: The Mississippi River in the Black Experience in Greater St. Louis, 1815–1860," *Missouri Historical Review* 113.1 (2018): 22–23. See also Anne Twitty, *Before Dred Scott: Slavery and Legal Culture in the American Confluence, 1787–1857* (Cambridge University Press, 2016), chap. 7.

104. On Lovejoy as a "martyr": Edward Beecher, *Narrative of Riots at Alton: In Connection with the Death of Rev. Elijah P. Lovejoy* (George Holton, 1838), 2. *The Liberator:* "Obituary," *Liberator* 7, 8 December 1837, 1. "Commemoration of the Death of Elijah P. Lovejoy," *Liberator* 8, 5 January 1838, 1. See also Sinha, *Slave's Cause,* 237.

105. J. B. D. DeBow, *Statistical View of the United States . . . Being a Compendium of the Seventh Census* (Beverly Tucker, "Senate Printer," 1854), 82–86 (on the slave population), 176 (on agricultural products and acres cultivated).

106. Sinha, *Slave's Cause,* 76–77.

107. Sven Beckert, *Empire of Cotton: A Global History* (Vintage, 2014), 202–204.

108. Edward Ball, "Retracing Slavery's Trail of Tears: America's Forgotten Migration: The Journeys of a Million African-Americans from the Tobacco South to the Cotton South," *Smithsonian* 46.7 (2015): 58–82.

109. Brian W. Thomas, "Power and Community: The Archaeology of Slavery at the Hermitage Plantation," *AA* 63.4 (1998): 546.

110. Kambiz GhaneaBassiri, *A History of Islam in America* (Cambridge University Press, 2010), 80–81.

111. Ala Alryyes, ed., *A Muslim American Slave: The Life of Omar Ibn Said* (University of Wisconsin Press, 2011). On his "broken Arabic" and "mid-level knowledge": GhaneaBassiri, *Islam in America,* 78.

112. On Umar's plural religious identity: GhaneaBassiri, *Islam in America,* 80–91. The passage might have been a critique of slaveholding. Alryyes, *Muslim American Slave,* 18–22, 51, 77.

113. Pope Gregory XVI's apostolic letter, *In Supremo,* was issued on 3 December 1839, https://w2.vatican.va/content/gregorius-xvi/it/documents/breve-in-supremo-apostolatus-fastigio-3-dicembre-1839.html. John F. Quinn, "'Three Cheers for the Abolitionist Pope!': American Reaction to Gregory XVI's Condemnation of the Slave Trade, 1840–1860," *Catholic Historical Review* 90.1 (2004): 67–93.

114. Charles F. Irons, *The Origins of Pro-Slavery Christianity: White and Black Evangelicals in Colonial and Antebellum Virginia* (University of North Carolina Press, 2008), 81, 86.

115. Robert S. Starobin, ed., *Blacks in Bondage: Letters of American Slaves* (Marcus Wiener, 1988), 116–117.

116. William L. Andrews, ed., *Sisters of the Spirit: Three Black Women's Autobiographies of the Nineteenth Century* (Indiana University Press, 1986), 64–67.

117. "B.," "The Black Preacher," *Boston Recorder* 7.12 (1822): 46.

118. About 13,000 migrants arrived in Liberia by 1860. On the ACS: Douglas Egerton, "A New Look at the American Colonization Society," *Journal of the Early Republic* 5 (1985): 463–480. Howe, *What Hath God Wrought*, 260–266.

119. Paul Cuffee, *A Black Colonist: Memoir of Captain Paul Cuffee, A Man of Colour . . .* (W. Alexander, [1817]).

120. "Letter from Bishop Allen," *Freedom's Journal*, 2 November 1827, 134.

121. Michael P. Johnson, "Denmark Vesey and His Co-Conspirators," *WMQ* 58.4 (2001): 915–976.

122. William L. Andrews and Regina E. Mason, eds., *Life of William Grimes, the Runaway Slave* (Oxford University Press, 2008), 103.

123. Robert S. Levine, "African American Literary Nationalism," in Gene Andrew Jarrett, ed., *A Companion to African American Literature* (Wiley-Blackwell, 2010), 123.

124. David Walker, *Walker's Appeal, in Four Articles . . . written in Boston, State of Massachusetts, September 28, 1829*, DocSouth Books ed. (University of North Carolina Press, 2011), 45.

125. *The Confessions of Nat Turner, the Leader of the Late Insurrection in Southampton, Va . . . , Nov. 5, 1831, for his trial* (T. R. Gray, 1831), 9–11.

126. Sinha, *Slave's Cause*, 213.

127. William Lloyd Garrison, *Thoughts on African Colonization . . .* (Garrison and Knapp, 1832). Donald M. Jacobs, "David Walker and William Lloyd Garrison: Racial Cooperation and the Shaping of Boston Abolition," in Donald M. Jacobs, ed., *Courage and Conscience: Black and White Abolitionists in Boston* (Indiana University Press, 1993), 7–17. Sinha, *Slave's Cause*, 214–227. [Francis Jackson Garrison and Wendell Phillips Garrison], *William Lloyd Garrison, 1805–1879: The Story of His Life Told by His Children*, vol. 1 (Century Company, 1885). Henry Mayer, *All on Fire: William Lloyd Garrison and the Abolition of Slavery* (St. Martin's, 1998).

128. Donald G. Mathews, *Religion in the Old South* (University of Chicago Press, 1977), 182.

129. The *summa* quotation: Walter Johnson, *River of Dark Dreams: Slavery and Empire in the Cotton Kingdom* (Harvard University Press, 2013), 201. David Christy, *Cotton Is King; Or the Culture of Cotton . . .* (Moore, Wilstach, and Keys, 1855). E. N. Elliot, *Cotton Is King: Pro-Slavery Arguments . . .* (Pritchard, Abbott, and Loomis, 1860). Starobin, *Blacks in Bondage*, 42. Jones spoke of "subordination" in all his writings, including Charles Colcock Jones, "The Religious Instruction of the Negroes," *Boston Recorder* 20, 9 October 1835, 161. On Jones and the "slaveholding ethic," see Mathews, *Religion in the Old South*, 139–154. See also Drew Gilpin Faust, ed., *The Ideology of Slavery: Proslavery Thought in the Antebellum South, 1830–1860* (LSU Press, 1981).

130. For Jones's account of slavery and religion in Liberty County, Georgia, see *Proceedings of the Meeting in Charleston, S.C., May 13–15, 1845, on the Religious Instruction of Negroes . . .* (B. Jenkins, 1845), 59–61.

131. Jones, "Religious Instruction of the Negroes."

132. Charles Colcock Jones, *The Religious Instruction of the Negroes in the United States* (Thomas Purse, 1842). Charles Colcock Jones, *Catechism of Scripture, Doctrine, and Practice: For Families and Sabbath Schools. Designed Also for the Oral Instruction of Colored Persons,* 2nd ed. (T. Purse, 1837).

133. Mrs. Child [Lydia Maria Child], *Anti-Slavery Catechism* (Charles Whipple, 1836), 3. See also Lydia Maria Child, *An Appeal in Favor of that Class of Americans Called Africans* (Allen and Ticknor, 1833). On Child as a Unitarian, see Daniel Walker Howe, *The Unitarian Conscience: Harvard Moral Philosophy, 1805–1861* (Wesleyan University Press, 1988), xii. Jones, *Catechism.* Jones's volume went through at least ten editions by the 1850s.

134. Jones, *Catechism,* 142–143.

135. Jones, *Catechism,* 127–131. On African Americans' use of the Exodus story: Eddie S. Glaude, *Exodus! Religion, Race, and Nation in Early Nineteenth-Century Black America* (University of Chicago Press, 2000).

136. Starobin, *Blacks in Bondage,* 47–50, 53–55.

137. Starobin, *Blacks in Bondage,* 52–55, 169. Karen B. Bell, "Rice, Resistance, and Forced Transatlantic Communities: (Re)envisioning the African Diaspora in Low Country Georgia, 1750–1800," *Journal of African American History* 95.2 (2010): 169. For a "gendering" of slave religion, see Alexis Wells-Oghoghomeh, *The Souls of Womenfolk: The Religious Cultures of Enslaved Women in the Lower South* (University of North Carolina Press, 2021).

138. Starobin, *Blacks in Bondage,* 49.

139. Dusinberre, *Slavemaster President,* 14–16, 26. Polk's plantation was near Coffeeville, Mississippi, in the Yazoo–Mississippi Delta northeast of Natchez. See Beckert, *Empire of Cotton,* 113.

140. William Henry Sparks, *The Memories of Fifty Years . . .* (1870; E. Claxton, 1882), 364. Sparks moved to Mississippi, just above Natchez. He owned a sugar plantation across the river in Louisiana and referred to his occupation as planter. Alexander Barrow Daspit, "Sparks from a Smoldering Ember: Some Incidents from the Life of William H. Sparks (1880–1882)," *Sparks Quarterly* 29.4 (1981): 2353–2362.

141. Christian Pinnen, *Colonial Mississippi: A Borrowed Land* (University Press of Mississippi, 2021), 129–138, 139–152. Brandon Layton, "Indian Country to Slave Country: The Transformation of Natchez during the American Revolution," *JSH* 82.1 (2016): 27–58. David J. Libby, *Slavery and Frontier Mississippi, 1720–1835* (University Press of Mississippi, 2004), 37–59. Martha Jane Brazy, *An American Planter: Stephen Duncan of Antebellum Natchez and New York* (LSU Press, 2006). J. Michael Crane, "Controlling the Night: Perceptions of the Slave Patrol System in Mississippi," *Journal of Mississippi History* 61.2 (1999): 119–136. "cotton-bale religion": Randy J. Sparks, *Religion in Mississippi* (University Press of Mississippi, 2001), 106. Sylvester Johnson, "Religion and Empire in Mississippi, 1790–1833," in Michael Pasquier, ed., *Gods of the Mississippi* (Indiana University Press, 2013), 36–55.

142. Trent Brown, "Myths and Representations," *Mississippi Encyclopedia,* https://mississippiencyclopedia.org/overviews/myths-and-representations/.

143. T. H. Gallaudet, *A Statement with Regard to the Moorish Prince, Abduhl Rahhahman* (D. Fanshaw, 1828). GhaneaBassiri, *Islam in America*, 19–21, 34–36, 61, 63. See also Terry Alford, *Prince among Slaves*, 30th anniversary ed. (Oxford University Press, 2007).

144. Dow's popularity: Hatch, *Democratization of American Christianity*, 36. On Dow and the 1804 camp meeting: Henry Gabriel Hawkins, *Methodism in Natchez* (Hawkins Foundation, 1937), 205. On local apathy: *Weekly Chronicle* [Natchez], 23 April 1810. Dow wondered whether there were "three Christians in town": Lorenzo Dow, *History of Cosmopolite; or The Four Volumes of Lorenzo's Journal Concentrated in One . . .* (Joseph Rakestraw, 1815). 212. Hawkins, *Methodism in Natchez*, 205.

145. Dennis J. Mitchell, *A New History of Mississippi* (University Press of Mississippi, 2014), 150. Joseph Bowen, *The American Almanac and Repository of Useful Knowledge for 1836* (Charles Bowen, 1835), 239. The most prominent free Black, William Johnson, listened to Methodist preachers and was memorialized in the Methodist Church. See William Ransom Hogan and Edwin Adams Davis, eds., *The Ante-Bellum Diary of a Free Negro* (LSU Press, 1951), 1: 58–59, 231a.

146. Morton Rothstein, "The Antebellum South as a Dual Economy: A Tentative Hypothesis," *Agricultural History* 41.4 (1967): 378. Cory James Young, "North to Natchez during the Age of Gradual Abolition," *PMHB* 143.2 (2019): 117–139. Christopher Morris, "The Intellectual Lives of Natchez and Concord, and the Legacies of Slavery," *Southern Quarterly* 54.2 (2017): 49–70.

147. Arthur H. DeRosier Jr., *The Removal of the Choctaw Indians* (University of Tennessee Press, 1970), 104–105. Charles M. Hudson, *The Southeastern Indians* (University of Tennessee Press, 1976), 453. Tim Alan Garrison, "Inevitability and the Southern Opposition to Indian Removal," in Garrison, ed., *The Native South* (University of Nebraska Press, 2017), 129–147.

148. The quotation: Sparks, *Memories of Fifty Years*, 268. Ian W. Brown and Vincas P. Steponaitis, "The Grand Village of the Natchez Indians Was Indeed Grand: A Reconsideration of the Fatherland Site Landscape," in Gregory A. Waselkov et al., eds., *Forging Southeastern Identities: Social Archaeology, Ethnohistory, and Folklore of the Mississippian to Early Historic South* (University of Alabama Press, 2017), 185. Montroville W. Dickeson, "Opening of Mounds on the Plantation of Col. A. L. Bingaman," *Lotus* 1.9 (27 May 1848): 129–131. Fatherland's owner, Adam Bingaman, was a vestryman at Trinity Episcopal Church. His wife, Julia Murray Bingaman, was the daughter of a Universalist minister, John Murray, and a women's rights advocate, Judith Sargent Murray.

149. "Cherokee Women Petition" (1818), in Theda Perdue and Michael D. Green, eds., *The Cherokee Removal: A Brief History with Documents* (St. Martin's Press, 1995), 125–126.

150. James Monroe, Second Annual Message, 16 November 1818, https://millercenter.org/the-presidency/presidential-speeches/november-16-1818-second-annual-message.

151. An Act Making Provision for the Civilization of the Indian Tribes Adjoining the Frontier Settlements, 3 March 1819, 3 Stat. 516b, Chap. 85. Noah Webster,

The American Spelling Book . . . (Holbrook and Fessenden, 1826). Sean P. Harvey, "'Must Not Their Languages Be Savage and Barbarous Like Them?' Philology, Indian Removal, and Race Science," *Journal of the Early Republic* 30 (2010): 506–507.

152. Gallatin, *A Synopsis of the Indian Tribes* 2 (1836): 158.

153. Rowena McClinton, "Cherokee and Christian Expressions of Spirituality through First Parents Eve and Selu," in Garrison, *Native South*, 92–105. See also Theda Perdue, *Cherokee Women: Gender and Culture Change, 1700–1835* (University of Nebraska Press, 1998).

154. Isaac McCoy, *History of the Baptist Indian Missions* . . . (William M. Morrison, 1840), 197. Isaac McCoy, *Remarks on the Practicability of Indian Reform* . . . (Lincoln and Edmands, 1827). See also Emory J. Lyons, *Isaac McCoy: His Plan of Work for Indian Colonization* (Kansas State Printing, 1945), 20; William S. Belko, "John C. Calhoun and the Creation of the Bureau of Indian Affairs: An Essay on Political Rivalry, Ideology, and Policymaking in the Early Republic," *South Carolina Historical Magazine* 105.3 (2004): 170–197.

155. Thomas L. McKenney, *Memoirs, Official and Personal* . . . (Paine and Burgess, 1846), 34. Francis Paul Prucha, "Thomas L. McKenney and the New York Indian Board," *Mississippi Valley Historical Review* 48.4 (1962): 635–655. Richard Drinnon, *Facing West: The Metaphysics of Indian-Hating and Empire-Building* (University of Minnesota Press, 1980), 165–190. McKenney, *Memoirs*, 237.

156. Henry David Thoreau, *Walden: A Fully Annotated Edition*, Jeffrey S. Cramer, ed. (Yale University Press, 2004), 71.

157. George Morton, *Crania Americana* . . . (John Pennington, 1839). See also Albanese, *Republic of Mind and Spirit*, 195–197. Henry Clay said an analysis of Jackson's head would find a propensity for "destructiveness"; Clay, speech before the US Senate, 30 April 1834, in William Jennings Bryan, ed., *The World's Famous Orations* (Funk and Wagnalls, 1906).

158. Howe, *What Hath God Wrought*, 352.

159. Christina Synder, "Andrew Jackson's Indian Son: Native Captives and American Empire," in Garrison, *Native South*, 90–93. Alfred A. Cave, "Abuse of Power: Andrew Jackson and the Indian Removal Act of 1830," *Historian* 65.6 (2003): 1330–1353.

160. Frelinghuysen's and Crockett's speeches: *Speeches on the Passage of the Bill for the Removal of the Indians* . . . (Perkins and Marvin), 1: 1–30, 251–253.

161. Howe, *What Hath God Wrought*, 350. On Beecher's piety, see Colleen McDannell, *The Christian Home in Victorian America, 1840–1900* (Indiana University Press, 1986), 128.

162. Sinah, *Slave's Cause*, 378, 414.

163. "William Penn" [Jeremiah Evarts], "Essays on the Present Crisis in the Condition of the American Indians," *Christian Examiner* 9 (1830): 108.

164. Ralph Waldo Emerson, "Letter to Martin Van Buren, President of the United States, A Protest against the Removal of the Cherokee Indians from the State of Georgia," in *The Complete Works of Ralph Waldo Emerson: Miscellanies* (Houghton, Mifflin, [1903–1904]), 11: 90–96.

165. John K. Mahon, *History of the Second Seminole War, 1835–1842* (University Press of Florida, 1967). Michael D. Green, *The Politics of Indian Removal: Creek Government and Society in Crisis* (University of Nebraska Press, 1982). Walter H. Conser Jr., "John Ross and the Cherokee Resistance Campaign, 1833–1838," *JSH* 44.2 (1978): 191–212. John Taylor Carson, *Searching for the Bright Path: The Mississippi Choctaws from Prehistory to Removal* (University of Nebraska Press, 1999). Cecil L. Summers, *Chief Tishomingo: A History of the Chickasaw Indians and Some Historical Events of their Era* (Amory Advertiser, 1974), 116–125.

166. Conser, "John Ross."

167. Gary E. Moulton, *John Ross: Cherokee Chief* (University of Georgia Press, 1982), 34–105.

168. Quoted in Conser Jr., "John Ross," 211.

169. Chief Whitepath died on a farm that had been owned by John and Nancy Latham. Those living there in 1838–1839 gave food and water to the Cherokee. The site is now the Trail of Tears Commemorative Park in Hopkinsville, Kentucky. On his burial: Rick Williams, "The Seal of the Cherokee Nation," *Cherokee Observer*, 31 May 1999, 3. I am grateful to Kristina Scott, a citizen of the Cherokee Nation and a guide at the Heritage Center.

170. Four Bears' final speech: Francis A. Chardon, *Chardon's Journal at Fort Clark, 1834–1839 . . .* (Department of History, State of South Dakota, 1932), 124–125. Elizabeth A. Fenn, *Encounters at the Heart of the World: A History of the Mandan People* (Hill and Wang, 2014), 322–325.

171. Congress mandated that the superintendent live in St. Louis: An Act to Provide for the Organization of the Department of Indian Affairs, 30 June 1834, Chap. 162, 4 Stat. 735.

172. The notice from the *St. Louis Gazette* was reprinted: "Missionaries at St. Louis," *Boston Recorder*, 5 July 1834. Richard E. Jensen, ed., *The Pawnee Mission Letters, 1834–1851* (University of Nebraska Press, 2010), 49. For a portrait, see George Catlin, *Shón-ka-ki-he-ga, Horse Chief, the Grand Pawnee Head Chief* (1832), oil on canvas, Smithsonian American Art Museum, Washington, DC.

173. Jensen, *Pawnee Mission Letters*, 77.

174. Hämäläinen, *Lakota America*, 206.

175. Hiram Martin Chittenden and Alfred Talbot Richardson, eds., *Life, Letters, and Travels of Father Pierre-Jean De Smet, S.J.* (Francis P. Harper, 1905), 1: 396.

176. Colin G. Calloway, *One Vast Winter Count: The Native American West before Lewis and Clark* (University of Nebraska Press, 2003), 425–426. Robert Hellyer, "The West, the East, and the Insular Middle: Trading Systems, Demand, and Labour in the Integration of the Pacific, 1750–1875," *Journal of Global History* 8.3 (2013): 391–413.

177. Thomas M. Gilbert et al., "DNA from Pre-Clovis Human Coprolites in Oregon, North America," *Science* 320.5877 (2008): 786–789. John Erlandson and Todd J. Braje, "Foundations for the Far West: Paleoindian Cultures of the Western Fringe of North America," in Timothy R. Pauketat, ed., *The Oxford Handbook of*

North American Archaeology (Oxford University Press, 2012), 149–159. Douglas W. Owsley and Richard L. Jantz, eds., *Kennewick Man: The Scientific Investigation of an Ancient American Skeleton* (Texas A&M University Press, 2014). Sally M. Walker and Douglas W. Owsley, *Their Skeletons Speak: Kennewick Man and the Paleoamerican World* (Carolrhoda Books, 2012), 118.

178. Matthias D. Bergmann, "'We Should Lose Much by Their Absence': The Centrality of Chinookans and Kalapuyans to Life in Frontier Oregon," *Oregon Historical Quarterly* 109.1 (2008): 2. Henry B. Zenk, "Kalapuyans," in Alvin M. Josephy Jr., ed., *The Northwest Coast* (Alfred A. Knopf, 1966), 547. Robert Boyd, "Strategies of Indian Burning in the Willamette Valley," in Robert Boyd, ed., *Indians, Fire, and the Land in the Pacific Northwest* (Oregon State University Press, 1999), 95, 97–98, 103. Helen N. Norton et al., "The Klikitat Trail of South-Central Washington: A Reconstruction of Seasonally Used Resource Sites," in Boyd, *Indians, Fire, and the Land*, 69. On the river, see Richard White, *The Organic Machine: Remaking the Columbia River* (Hill and Wang, 1995).

179. R. T. Boyd, "Demographic History, 1774–1874," in W. P. Suttles, ed., *Handbook of North American Indians* (Smithsonian Institution, 1990), 7: 135–147.

180. Alexander Ross, *Adventures of the First Settlers on the Oregon or Columbia River . . .* (Smith, Elder, 1849). Michael E. La Salle, *Emigrants on the Oregon Trail: The Wagon Train of 1848* (Truman State University Press, 2011), xv. See also Francis Parkman Jr., *The California and Oregon Trail* (Putnam, 1849) and Clifford Merrill Drury, ed., *On to Oregon: The Diaries of Mary Walker and Myra Eells* (University of Nebraska Press, 1998).

181. See J. B. Z. Bolduc's account in Father P. J. De Smet, *Oregon Missions and Travels over the Rocky Mountains, in 1845–46* (Edward Dunigan, 1847), 31, 35, 66–87.

182. Gray H. Whaley, "'Trophies' for God: Native Mortality, Racial Ideology, and the Methodist Mission of Lower Oregon, 1834–1844," *Oregon Historical Quarterly* 107.1 (2006): 6–35. Clifford Drury, *Marcus and Narcissa Whitman and the Opening of Old Oregon*, 2 vols. (Arthur H. Clark, 1973). Cameron Addis, "The Whitman Massacre: Religion and Manifest Destiny on the Columbian Plateau, 1809–1858," *Journal of the Early Republic* 25 (2005): 222.

183. On earlier contacts, see Terry L. Jones et al., eds., *Polynesians in America: Pre-Columbian Contacts with the New World* (Altamira, 2011). On terms that refer to Hawaiians, I follow Ty Kāwika Tengan and use multiple terms to refer to ethnic Hawaiians with some ancestry: *Kānaka Maoli, Kānaka ʻŌiwi, Hawaiian,* and *Native/Indigenous/Aboriginal Hawaiian.* Ty Kāwika Tengan, *Native Men Remade: Gender and Nation in Contemporary Hawaiʻi* (Duke University Press, 2008), xii–xiii. See also J. Kēhaulani Kauanui, *Hawaiian Blood: Colonialism and the Politics of Sovereignty and Indigeneity* (Duke University Press, 2008), xi–xii.

184. Quoted in Jean Barman and Bruce McIntyre Watson, "Hawaiians in the Oregon Country," *Oregon Encyclopedia,* 18 May 2023, https://oregonencyclopedia.org/articles/hawaiians_in_the_oregon_country/. See Barman and Watson, *Leaving Paradise.* Douglas C. Wilson and Theresa E. Langford, eds., *Exploring Fort Vancouver* (University of Washington Press, 2011). Tamara Bray, "Ethnic Differences in the

Archaeological Assemblages at Kanaka Village" (appendix C), in Bryn Thomas et al., *Report of Investigations of Excavations at Kanaka Village/Vancouver Barracks, Washington* (Washington State Department of Transportation, 1980–1981).

185. Vinkovetsky, *Russian America,* 163. Russian traders exported more than 2 million fur seals between 1743 and 1823: Vasilii Nikolaevich Berkh, *A Chronological History of the Discovery of the Aleutian Islands . . .* (Limestone Press, 1974), 93. See Igler, *Great Ocean,* 99–128.

186. Jesse D. Murray, "Together and Apart: The Russian Orthodox Church, the Russian Empire, and Orthodox Missionaries in Alaska, 1794–1917," *Russian History* 40 (2013): 91–110.

187. Quoted in John H. Erickson, *Orthodox Christians in America* (Oxford University Press, 2008), 23–24. See also Gregory L. Freeze, "Russian Orthodoxy: Church, People, and Politics in Imperial Russia," in Dominic Lieven, ed., *The Cambridge History of Russia,* vol. 2, *Imperial Russia, 1689–1917* (Cambridge University Press, 2006), 284–305.

188. For a 1909 Tlingit story about how they came to "New Archangel" (later Sitka): John R. Swanton, ed., *Tlingit Myths and Texts* (Smithsonian Institution, 1909), 295–296. Alexey Postnikov and Marvin Falk, *Exploring and Mapping Alaska: The Russian American Era, 1741–1867* (University of Alaska Press, 2015).

189. Sergei Kan, *Memory Eternal: Tlingit Culture and Russian Orthodox Christianity through Two Centuries* (University of Washington Press, 2014), 95–102.

190. James R. Gibson, "Russia in California, 1833: Report of Governor Wrangel," *Pacific Northwest Quarterly* 60.4 (1969): 205–215. Benjamin Madley, *An American Genocide: The United States and the California Indian Catastrophe* (Yale University Press, 2017), 36. Igler, *Great Ocean,* 76. Aleksandr Iu. Petrov, Metropolitan Kliment of Kaluga and Borov, and Aleksei N. Ermolaev, "The Sale of Fort Ross, Russia's Colony in California," *Russian Studies in History* 54.1 (2015): 43. For a history that takes a different perspective, see Damon B. Akins and William J. Bauer Jr., *We Are the Land: A History of Native California* (University of California Press, 2021).

191. Kent G. Lightfoot, Antoinette Martinez, and Ann M. Schiff, "Daily Practice and Material Culture in Pluralistic Social Settings: An Archaeological Study of Culture Change and Persistence from Fort Ross, California," *AA* 63.2 (1998): 199–222. Kent G. Lightfoot, "Oral Traditions and Material Things: Constructing Histories of Native People in Colonial Settings," in James F. Brooks, Christopher R. N. DeCorse, and John Walton, eds., *Small Worlds: Method, Meanings, and Narrative in Microhistory* (School for Advanced Research Press, 2008), 265–288.

192. Diane Spencer-Hancock and William E. Pritchard, "The Chapel at Fort Ross: Its History and Reconstruction," *California History* 61.1 (1982): 2–17.

193. Quoted in George O. Schanzer, "A Russian Visit to the Spanish Franciscans in California, 1836," *The Americas* 9.4 (1953): 456. See also Ioann Veniaminov, *Journals of the Priest Ioann Veniaminov in Alaska, 1823–1836,* trans. Jerome Kisslinger (University of Alaska Press, 1993).

194. James A. Sandos, *Converting California: Indians and Franciscans in the Missions* (Yale University Press, 2004), 14–32. Lynn Gamble, *The Chumash World at*

European Contact: Power, Trade, and Feasting among Complex Hunter-Gatherers (University of California Press, 2008), 275–301. E. A. Okladnikova, "The California Collection of I. G. Voznesensky and the Problems of Ancient Cultural Connections between Asia and America," *Journal of California and Great Basin Anthropology* 5.1–2 (1983): 224–239. Alfred Kroeber, "The Patwin and Their Neighbors," *University of California Publications in American Archaeology and Ethnology* 29 (1930–1932): 312–340. Edwin Loeb, "The Creator Concept among the Indians of North Central California," *American Anthropologist* 28 (1926): 467–493. William J. Bauer Jr., *California through Native Eyes: Reclaiming History* (University of Washington Press, 2016), 10–27, 49–62.

195. Madley, *American Genocide,* 3.

196. Igler, *Great Ocean,* 135–143. Quincy D. Newell, *Constructing Lives at Mission San Francisco: Native Californians and Hispanic Colonists, 1776–1821* (University of New Mexico Press, 2009). On the longer history: Alan Levanthal et al., *Final Report on the Burial and Archaeological Data Recovery Program Conducted on a Portion of an Early Bay Period Ohlone Indian Cemetery . . .* (Muwekma Ohlone Tribe, 2014). James A. Sandos, *Converting California: Indians and Franciscans in the Missions* (Yale University Press, 2004), 28.

197. Hine, Faragher, and Coleman, *American West,* 191–201. See also Ernesto Chávez, ed., *The U.S. War with Mexico: A Brief History with Documents* (Bedford/St. Martin's, 2008).

198. Jamie M. Starling, "'He Does Not Profess, Until Today, any Religion': Catholic Clergy and Intermarriage in Paso del Norte during the Nineteenth Century," *American Catholic Studies* 126.1 (2015): 45–57.

199. "Mexicans to Catholic Irishmen," [184?], broadside, Beinecke Rare Book and Manuscript Library, Yale University, https://collections.library.yale.edu/catalog/2065161.

200. Starling, "'He Does Not Profess, Until Today, any Religion,'" 45–57. Fenton, *Religious Liberties,* 9–11; Robert Ryal Miller, *Shamrock and Sword: The Saint Patrick's Battalion in the U.S.-Mexico War* (University of Oklahoma Press, 1989); Michael Hogan, *Irish Soldiers of Mexico* (Fondo Editorial Universitario, 1997).

201. "Treaty of Guadalupe Hidalgo," 2 February 1848, https://avalon.law.yale.edu/19th_century/guadhida.asp. Richard Griswold del Castillo, *The Treaty of Guadalupe Hidalgo: A Legacy of Conflict* (University of Oklahoma Press, 1990).

202. Madley, *American Genocide,* 3.

203. Howe, *What Hath God Wrought,* 62. Richard Carwardine, "Antebellum Reform," in Heath W. Carter and Laura Rominger Porter, eds., *Turning Points in the History of American Evangelicalism* (Eerdmans, 2017), 65–83. On the contrasting theological views, see E. Brooks Holifield, *Theology in America: Christian Thought from the Age of the Puritans to the Civil War* (Yale University Press, 2003), 361–368.

204. On artisans: Sean Wilenz, *Chants Democratic: New York City and the Rise of the Working Class, 1788–1850* (Oxford University Press, 2004), 145–171. On the Sailors' Home: John Spaulding, *From the Plow to the Pulpit* (Robert Carter and Brothers, 1874), 97. "The Floating Church of Our Savior for Seamen," 15 February 1844, steel engraving, Library of Congress, https://www.loc.gov/item/2002737223/.

205. William Still, *The Underground Railroad . . .* (Porter and Coates, 1872), 623–624. See also James A. McGowan, *Station Master on the Underground Railroad: The Life and Letters of Thomas Garrett*, rev. ed. (McFarland, 2005), 115–128. On Catholics traveling to hear the abolitionist: C[atherine] S. Brown, *Memoir of Rev. Abel Brown . . .* (Published by the author, 1849), 194–195. See also Tom Calarco, *The Underground Railroad in the Adirondack Region* (McFarland, 2004), 90.

206. Sarna, *American Judaism*, 47–50. Evelyn Bodek, "Making Do: Jewish Women and Philanthropy," in Murray Friedman, ed., *Jewish Life in Philadelphia* (Institute for the Study of Human Issues, 1983), 145–150.

207. Ira V. Brown, "Cradle of Feminism: The Philadelphia Female Anti-Slavery Society, 1833–1840" *PMHB* 102.2 (1978): 143–166. Washington, "Religion, Reform, and Antislavery," 417–437. Elizabeth J. Clapp and Julie Roy Jeffrey, eds., *Women, Dissent, and Anti-Slavery in Britain and America, 1790–1865* (Oxford University Press, 2011). Elsa Barkley Brown, "Womanist Consciousness: Maggie Lena Walker and the Independent Order of Saint Luke," *Signs* 14.3 (1989): 610–633. Melissa V. Harris-Perry, *Sister Citizen: Shame, Stereotypes, and Black Women in America* (Yale University Press, 2013). Anne Braude, "Women, Gender, and Religion," in Hartigan-O'Connor and Materson, *Oxford Handbook of American Women's and Gender History*, 391–414.

208. Elizabeth Heyrick, *Immediate Not Gradual Abolition . . .* (Hatchard, 1824).

209. Margaret Washington, *Sojourner Truth's America* (University of Illinois Press, 2009). Gerda Lerner, *The Grimké Sisters from South Carolina: Pioneers for Women's Rights and Abolition* (Houghton Mifflin, 1967).

210. Angelina Grimké, *Appeal to the Christian Women of the South* (American Anti-Slavery Society, 1836).

211. In 1837 the Congregational Association of Massachusetts issued a "pastoral letter" condemning female speakers. Sarah Grimké's response: Larry Ceplair, ed., *The Public Years of Sarah and Angelina Grimké: Selected Writings, 1835–1839* (Columbia University Press, 1989), 212–216.

212. G. H. Barnes and D. L. Dumond, eds., *Letters of Theodore Dwight Weld, Angelina Grimké Weld, and Sarah Grimké, 1822–1844* (D. Appleton-Century), 1: 411–412, 414–416.

213. Sarah Moore Grimké, *Letters on the Equality of the Sexes . . .* (I. Knapp, 1838). The first book-length defense of women's rights in Britain was Mary Wollstonecraft, *Vindication of the Rights of Woman . . .* (J. Johnson, 1792).

214. Her diary entries about the London meeting: Lucretia Mott, *Slavery and "The Woman Question": Lucretia Mott's Diary of Her Visit to Great Britain to Attend the World's Anti-Slavery Convention of 1840* (Friends Historical Association, 1952), 29–30, 33, 35–37, 53, 57. See also Beverly Wilson Palmer, Holly Byers Ochoa, and Carol Faulkner, eds., *Selected Letters of Lucretia Coffin Mott* (University of Illinois Press, 2002), 77–81.

215. Mott said Stanton proposed the idea of a women's rights convention in 1841: Lucretia Mott to Elizabeth Cady Stanton, 16 March 1855, repr. in Palmer, Ochoa, and Faulkner, *Selected Letters of Lucretia Coffin Mott*, 233–237. See also Carol Faulkner, *Lucretia Mott's Heresy: Abolition and Women's Rights in Nineteenth-Century America*

(University of Pennsylvania Press, 2011). Judith Wellman, *The Road to Seneca Falls: Elizabeth Cady Stanton and the First Women's Rights Convention* (University of Illinois Press, 2004).

216. *The First Convention Ever Called to Discuss the Civil and Political Rights of Women, Seneca Falls, New York, July 19, 20, 1848,* Library of Congress, https://www.loc.gov/item/27007548/. "The Declaration of Sentiments," https://sourcebooks.fordham.edu/mod/senecafalls.asp. Mott had influenced the Anti-Slavery Society's 1833 "Declaration of Sentiments." See Washington, "Religion, Reform, and Antislavery," 421.

217. Stoll, *Larding the Lean Earth.* See also Richard F. Nation, *At Home in the Hoosier Hills: Agriculture, Politics, and Religion in Southern Indiana, 1810–1870* (Indiana University Press, 2005). During this period horticulturists were interested in adapting "American fruits," and that movement had its organizations and periodicals. See Philip J. Pauly, *Fruits and Plains: The Horticultural Transformation of America* (Harvard University Press, 2007), 51–79.

218. Jesse Buel, *The Farmer's Companion; or, Essays on the Principles and Practice of American Husbandry* (Marsh, Capen, Lyon, and Webb, 1839), 21–33. Stoll, *Larding the Lean Earth,* 89–90. Harry J. Carman, *Jesse Buel, Agricultural Reformer* (Columbia University Press, 1947). Harry J. Carman, "Jesse Buel, Early Nineteenth-Century Agricultural Reformer," *Agricultural History* 17.1 (1943): 11.

219. Philip Mills Herrington, "Agricultural and Architectural Reform in the Antebellum South: Fruitland at Augusta, Georgia," *JSH* 78.4 (2012): 855–886.

220. William Apess, *Indian Nullification of the Unconstitutional Laws of Massachusetts Relative to the Mashpee Tribe . . .* (Jonathan Howe, 1835). Barry O'Connell, ed., *On Our Own Ground: The Complete Writings of William Apess, a Pequot* (University of Massachusetts Press, 1992), 166–274. See also Robert Warrior, *The People and the Word: Reading Native Nonfiction* (University of Minnesota Press, 2005), 32–36. Philip F. Gura, *The Life of William Apess, Pequot* (University of North Carolina Press, 2015), 77–99. Drew Lopenzina, *Through an Indian's Looking-Glass: A Cultural Biography of William Apess, Pequot* (University of Massachusetts Press, 2017), 212–221, 253–260. Drew Lopenzina, "Letter from Barnstable Jail: William Apess and the 'Memorial of the Mashpee Indians,'" *Native American and Indigenous Studies* 3.2 (2016): 105–127.

221. See David J. Silverman, *Red Brethren: The Brothertown and Stockbridge Indians and the Problem of Race in Early America* (Cornell University Press, 2010).

222. Antonio McDaniel, *Swing Low Sweet Chariot: The Mortality Cost of Colonizing Liberia in the Nineteenth Century* (University of Chicago Press, 1995).

223. William H. Pease and Jane H. Pease, *Black Utopia: Negro Communal Experiments in America* (State Historical Society of Wisconsin, 1963), 4, 22–108. Kerry Walters, *The Underground Railroad: A Reference Guide* (ABC-CLIO, 2012), 99–119.

224. John Lobb, ed., *Uncle Tom's Story of His Life: An Autobiography of the Reverend Josiah Henson* (University of North Carolina at Chapel Hill Library, 2011). Jared A. Brock, *The Road to Dawn: Josiah Henson and the Story That Sparked the Civil War* (Public Affairs, 2018).

225. The quotation is from "American Health Convention," *Graham Journal of Health and Longevity* 2.14 (1838): 209–210. Quoted in Jonathan D. Riddle, "Prospering Body and Soul: Health Reform, Religion, and Capitalism in Antebellum America," PhD diss., University of Notre Dame, May 2019, 29. See also Sylvester Graham, *Lectures on the Science of Human Life,* 2 vols. (Marsh, Capen, Lyon, and Webb, 1839).

226. "History of a Graham Boarding House," *Graham Journal of Health and Longevity* 3.25 (1839): 3. David Cambell, "Rules of a Graham House," *Graham Journal of Health and Longevity* 1.6 (1837): 47. Riddle, "Prospering Body and Soul," 263.

227. Donald E. Pitzer, ed., *America's Communal Utopias* (University of North Carolina Press, 1997). Robert P. Sutton, *Communal Utopias and the American Experience: Religious Communities, 1732–2000* (Praeger, 2003). Lawrence Foster, *Religion and Sexuality: The Shakers, The Mormons, and the Oneida Community* (University of Illinois Press, 1984).

228. On separatist communities, including Zoar: Sutton, *Communal Utopias,* 37–65; Kathleen M. Fernandez, *Zoar: The Story of an Intentional Community* (Kent State University Press, 2019).

229. Joseph Michael Bimeler, *Die wahre Separation, oder Die Wiedergeburt: Dargestellet in geistreichen und erbaulichen Versammlungsreden und Betrachtungen . . .* [1831, 1832, 1834], 4 vols. (Press of the Society of Separatists, 1856–60). The leader's name was changed to Bimeler, as it appeared in this work.

230. "Reminiscences of a Traveller: A Visit to the Shakers," *Southern and Western Literary Messenger and Review* 12 (1846): 60. Stein, *Shaker Experience in America,* 39–222.

231. Rufus Bishop and Seth Y. Wells, *Testimonies of the Life, Character, Revelations and Doctrines of Our Ever Blessed Mother Ann Lee . . .* (J. Talcott and J. Deming, 1816), vi.

232. *Summary View of the Millennial Church or United Society of Believers, Commonly Called Shakers . . .* (Packard and Van Benthuysen, 1823); Stein, *Shaker Experience in America,* 87–92, 114; Priscilla J. Brewer, "The Shakers of Mother Ann Lee," in Pitzer, *America's Communal Utopias,* 37–56; William Sims Bainbridge, "The Decline of the Shakers: Evidence from the United States Census," *Communal Societies* 4 (1984): 4.

233. Jean McMahon Humez, ed., *Gifts of Power: The Writings of Rebecca Jackson, Black Visionary, Shaker Eldress* (University of Massachusetts Press, 1981). Shakers dancing during service with Black believers in the back row: "Shakers Near Lebanon, Their Mode of Worship," anonymous artist, lithograph, ca. 1835, W. E. B. Du Bois Institute, Harvard University. See also Robert P. Emlen, "Black Shaker Minstrels and the Comic Performance of Shaker Worship," *American Communal Societies Quarterly* 4.4 (2010): 191–217.

234. On Brook Farm: Octavius Brooks Frothingham, *Transcendentalism in New England: A History* (G. P. Putnam's Sons, 1876), 157–175. Anne C. Rose, *Transcendentalism as a Social Movement, 1830–1850* (Yale University Press, 1981), 130–161.

235. "The divinity of labor": O. B. Frothingham, *George Ripley* (Houghton, Mifflin, 1882), 307–312. [Sophia Ripley,] "Woman," *Dial* 1 (1841): 362–366.

236. Hawthorne reflected on his Brook Farm experience in Nathaniel Hawthorne, *The Blithedale Romance* (Ticknor, Reed, and Fields, 1852).

237. The quotation: Lindsay Swift, *Brook Farm: Its Members, Scholars, and Visitors* (Macmillan, 1900), 203.

238. Henry David Thoreau, *"Walden," "Civil Disobedience," and Other Writings*, 3rd ed., William Rossi, ed. (W. W. Norton, 2008), chap. 1 ("Walden") and chap. 4 ("Civil Disobedience" and "Slavery in Massachusetts"). Laura Dassow Walls, *Henry David Thoreau: A Life* (University of Chicago Press, 2017), 248–254, 313–355.

239. Henry David Thoreau, *Wild Fruits: Thoreau's Rediscovered Last Manuscript*, Bradley P. Dean, ed. (W. W. Norton, 2000). See also Henry David Thoreau, *Faith in a Seed: "The Dispersion of Seeds" and Other Late Natural History Writing*, Bradley P. Dean, ed. (Island Press, 1993).

240. Walls, *Henry David Thoreau*, xiv–xvii, 404–456.

241. Christopher F. Jones, "A Landscape of Energy Abundance: Anthracite Coal Canals and the Roots of American Fossil Fuel Dependence, 1820–1860," *Environmental History* 15 (2010): 449–484; Michael Nies, *Coal on the Lehigh, 1790–1827: Beginnings and Growth of the Anthracite Industry in Carbon Country Pennsylvania* (Canal History and Technology Press, 2001); *History of the Lehigh Coal and Navigation Company . . .* (William S. Young, 1840).

242. During a 1770 trip, Washington visited a mine and commented on the coal: Donald Jackson, ed., *The Diaries of George Washington* (University Press of Virginia, 1976), 2: 287–291.

243. Eleanor Morton, *Josiah White, Prince of Pioneers* (Stephen Daye Press, [1946]), 52, 65, 69. "Sketch of the Life of Josiah White," *Friends Intelligencer*, 21 December 1850, 7, 39. Solomon W. Roberts, *Memoir of Josiah White* (Bixler and Corwin, 1860). Josiah White, *Josiah White's History, Given by Himself* (G. H. Buchanan, 1909), 9–11, 14, 69. Jones, "Landscape of Energy Abundance," 456–458.

244. Jones, "Landscape of Energy Abundance," 456–458. Eighty percent of the coal produced before 1865 came from Pennsylvania, either southwestern bituminous coal, which is less efficient but easier to ignite, or northeastern anthracite coal, a slow-lighting fuel that burns hotter: Frederick M. Binder, "Pennsylvania Coal and the Beginnings of American Steam Navigation," *PMHB* 83.4 (1959): 445.

245. Jones, "Landscape of Energy Abundance," 459.

246. Jones, "Landscape of Energy Abundance," 472–473.

247. Anthony F. C. Wallace, *Rockdale: The Growth of an American Village in the Early Industrial Revolution*, new ed. (University of Nebraska Press, 2005), 33–69 (on Rockdale in 1850), 394–397 (on Christian industrialism). The son of Matthew Carey, a Catholic publisher, Henry converted to Episcopalianism in 1819. Frank Gerrity and Anne M. Gerrity, "The Joseph R. Chandler–Henry C. Carey Correspondence: Five Letters from Naples, 1858–1859," *ACHS* 92.1 (1981): 98. On the family's interfaith experience: Anne C. Rose, *Beloved Strangers: Interfaith Families in Nineteenth-Century America* (Harvard University Press, 2001), 16–18, 33–35. Henry C. Carey, *The Harmony of Interests, Agricultural, Manufacturing, and Commercial*, 2nd ed. (Finch, 1852). Wallace, *Rockdale*, 394–397.

248. On the Cedar Grove mill village: Mary McConaghy, "The Whitaker Mill, 1813–1843: A Case Study of Workers, Technology, and Community in Early Industrial Philadelphia," *Pennsylvania History: A Journal of Mid-Atlantic Studies* 51.1 (1984): 30–63.

249. McConaghy, "Whitaker Mill," 42, 52–55.

250. One pastor was William Smith, who later founded the University of Pennsylvania: George Harrison Fisher, "Trinity Church, Oxford, Philadelphia," *PMHB* 27.3 (1903): 292–293.

251. There had been "camp meetings" at least since the 1820s. A Methodist camp meeting held twelve miles from Philadelphia included about 500 Philadelphians: *Boston Recorder* 9.36, 4 September 1824, 443.

252. On earlier Native presence: Brian S. Robinson, "A Regional Analysis of the Moorhead Burial Tradition, 8500–3700 B.P.," *Archaeology of Eastern North America* 24 (1996): 135. David Stewart-Smith, "The Penacook: Lands and Relations, An Ethnography," *New Hampshire Archaeologist* 33/34.1 (1994): 66–80. It was also the site of a "praying town." Linford D. Fisher, "Native Americans, Conversion, and Christian Practice in Colonial New England, 1640–1730," *Harvard Theological Review* 102.1 (2009): 101.

253. See Patrick M. Malone, *Waterpower in Lowell: Engineering and Industry in Nineteenth-Century America* (Johns Hopkins, 2009).

254. Joshua B. Freeman, *Behemoth: A History of the Factory and the Making of the Modern World* (W. W. Norton, 2018), 1, 28–35. Alan Kidd, *Manchester: A History,* 4th ed. (Carnegie Publishing, 2012). Maxine Berg, *The Age of Manufactures: Industry, Innovation, and Work in Britain, 1700–1820* (Barnes and Noble, 1985).

255. It would be like Robert Owen's New Lanark, the rural, water-powered mill Bostonians toured in Scotland. See Ted Steinberg, *Nature Incorporated: Industrialization and the Waters of New England* (Cambridge University Press, 1991), 40–41.

256. Jefferson suggested "those who labour in the earth are the chosen people of God." Thomas Jefferson, *Notes on the State of Virginia* (Prichard and Hall, 1788), 175. Annette Gordon-Reed and Peter S. Onuf, *"Most Blessed Patriarchs": Thomas Jefferson and the Empire of the Imagination* (Liveright, 2016), 51–57.

257. George S. White, *Memoir of Samuel Slater, the Father of American Manufactures . . . ,* 2nd ed. (Printed at No. 46 Carpenter Street, Philadelphia, 1836). White notes that Jefferson changed his mind about manufacturing and devotes a chapter to the "moral influence of manufacturing establishments" (201). Slater, the founder of cotton manufacturing in America, "abundantly demonstrated" they might serve "the most moral purpose" (117).

258. Thomas Jefferson to Benjamin Austin, 9 January 1816, https://founders.archives.gov/documents/Jefferson/03-09-02-0213. His letter was also published in Boston's *Independent Chronicle,* 19 February 1816, and used by the friends of manufacturing against those who opposed the industrial turn. On Jefferson's change of mind: Gordon S. Wood, *Empire of Liberty: A History of the Early Republic, 1789–1815* (Oxford University Press, 2009), 705.

259. Wood, *Empire of Liberty,* 702–703.

260. On Lowell in comparative perspective, see Freeman, *Behemoth,* 43–79.

261. Hannah Williamson (Lowell) to [Mary S. Fraser] (Stockbridge, Vermont), 3 April 1836, Center for Lowell History, University of Massachusetts Lowell Libraries, https://libguides.uml.edu/c.php?g=542883&p=3735368.

262. Massachusetts House Document, no. 50, March 1845. It was reprinted in John R. Commons et al., eds., *A Documentary History of American Industrial Society* (Arthur H. Clark Company, 1910), 8: 133–151. The Special Committee reported that 2,139 names appeared on the petitions, including 1,151 people from Lowell (133). The quotation about noise: "A Visit by an Associationist," *Harbinger,* 14 November 1846, 366. It was reprinted in Commons et al., *Documentary History of American Industrial Society,* 7: 132–135.

263. Steinberg, *Nature Incorporated,* 99–134. Ted Steinberg, "Down to Earth: Nature, Agency, and Power in History," *AHR* 107.3 (2002): 806–808. The Concord Farmers' Club commissioned Thoreau to survey the river from Concord to Lowell for a case against the company that erected the dam, which caused floods downriver in the Concord area. Walls, *Henry David Thoreau,* 441–443.

264. Henry A. Miles, *Lowell, As It Was, and As It Is,* 2nd ed. (Nathaniel L. Dayton; Merrill and Heywood, 1846), 48.

265. Miles, *Lowell, As It Was, and As It Is,* 48. Thomas Dublin, *Women at Work: The Transformation of Work and Community in Lowell, Massachusetts, 1826–1860* (Columbia University Press, 1992), 132–134.

266. Charles Dickens, *American Notes for General Circulation* (Chapman and Hall, 1842), 164. Freeman, *Behemoth,* 43.

267. Henry A. Miles, *Thanksgiving Discourse: A Glance at Our History, Prospects, and Duties* (Stearns and Taylor, 1844), 9.

268. Miles, *Lowell, As It Was, and As It Is,* 142. Ure, a British writer, described the "moral economy" of the factory system as well as "religion in the factory": Andrew Ure, *The Philosophy of Manufactures: Or, an Exposition of the Scientific, Moral, and Commercial Economy of the Factory System of Great Britain* (C. Knight, 1835), 277, 404–429. E. P. Thompson analyzed factories' "moral machinery": E. P. Thompson, *The Making of the English Middle Class* (1963; Vintage, 1966), 350–374.

269. The rules included this: "The company will not employ anyone who is habitually absent from public worship on the Sabbath or known to be guilty of immorality." "Hamilton Company Factory Rules," from *Handbook to Lowell,* 1848, Center for Lowell History, University of Massachusetts at Lowell Libraries, https://libguides.uml.edu/c.php?g=529205&p=3619725.

270. Eric Baldwin, "Religion and the American Industrial City: Protestant Culture and Social Transformation in Lowell, Massachusetts, 1824–1890," PhD diss., Boston University, 2009, 239–250.

271. Hannah Williamson (Lowell) to [Mary S. Fraser] (Stockbridge, VT), 3 April 1836.

272. Sarah White (Lowell) to "the Brethren and Sisters of the John St. Church" (Lowell), 15 April 1843, Center for Lowell History, University of Massachusetts Lowell Libraries, https://libguides.uml.edu/c.php?g=542883&p=3735249.

273. Mary Ann Cowles (Lowell) to Miss Adeline Cowles (Wethersfield, CT), 6 December 1847, Center for Lowell History, University of Massachusetts Lowell Libraries, https://libguides.uml.edu/c.php?g=542883&p=3734984. Sarah Hodgdon (Lowell) to [Mary Hodgdon] "Dearly beloved mother" (Rochester, NH), n.d., Center for Lowell History, University of Massachusetts Lowell Libraries, https://libguides.uml.edu/c.php?g=542883&p=3733249. See also Thomas Dublin, ed., *Farm to Factory: Women's Letters, 1830–1860* (Columbia University Press, 1993).

274. "Letters from Susan," Letter First, *Lowell Offering,* series 4, no. 7 (May 1844): 145–148. This epistolary fiction was based on the author's experience working in the mills. It was written by Harriet Farley using the pseudonym "Susan." The magazine can be found at the Center for Lowell History, University of Massachusetts Lowell Libraries, https://www.uml.edu/docs/finished-cl-docs_tcm18-313033.pdf.

275. Mary H. Blewett, ed., *Caught between Two Worlds: The Diary of a Lowell Mill Girl* (Lowell Museum, 1984), 28.

276. Blewett, *Caught between Two Worlds,* 47.

277. Lucy Larcom, *A New England Girlhood* (Houghton, Mifflin, 1889). The passages quoted are from pp. 248, 250, 248, 248, 251, 251.

278. Larcom joined Philips Brooks's congregation when attendees like William Sturgis Bigelow were declaring their allegiance to Buddhism. Larcom, *New England Girlhood,* vii.

Chapter 7. Industrial Religion

1. Lucy Larcom, *A New England Girlhood* (Houghton, Mifflin, 1889), 251 "Death of Lucy Larcom," *New York Times,* 19 April 1893, 11.

2. Lucy Larcom, "A Loyal Woman's No," *Poems of Lucy Larcom* (Fields, Osgood, 1869), 144–147.

3. R. Laurence Moore, *In Search of White Crows: Spiritualism, Parapsychology, and American Culture* (Oxford University Press, 1977). Beryl Satter, *Each Mind a Kingdom: American Women, Sexual Purity, and the New Thought Movement, 1875–1920* (University of California Press, 1999), 57–78.

4. William Hutchison, *Errand to the World: American Protestant Thought and Foreign Missions* (University of Chicago Press, 1987).

5. Lucy Larcom, "American Factory Life: Past, Present, and Future," *Journal of Social Science* 16 (1882): 141–146. Thomas Dublin, *Women at Work: The Transformation of Work and Community in Lowell, Massachusetts, 1826–1860* (Columbia University Press, 1979), 139. George F. O'Dwyer, *Irish Catholic Genesis of Lowell* (Sullivan Brothers, 1920). Frederick A. Bushee, "The Growth of the Population of Boston," *Publications of the American Statistical Association* 6.46 (1899): 1–2.

6. Paul A. Carter, *The Spiritual Crisis of the Gilded Age* (Northern Illinois University Press, 1971); D. H. Meyer, "American Intellectuals and the Victorian Crisis of Faith," in Daniel Walker Howe, ed., *Victorian America* (University of Pennsylvania Press, 1976), 59–77. In Britain, the "spiritual crisis" started in the 1850s: Frederick W. Gibbs and Daniel J. Cohen, "A Conversation with Data: Prospecting Victorian

Words and Ideas," *Victorian Studies* 54.1 (2011): 70–73. In the US, it emerged between 1870 and 1900.

7. Lucy Larcom, *The Unseen Friend* (Houghton, Mifflin, 1892), vii–viii. Daniel Dulany Addison, ed., *Lucy Larcom: Life, Letters, and Diary* (Houghton, Mifflin, 1894), 252–253. See Brooks's letter to her dated 14 April 1879 repr. in Addison, *Lucy Larcom*, 86. Peter W. Williams, "Phillips Brooks and Trinity Church: Symbols for an Age," in *Religion, Art, and Money: Episcopalians and American Culture from the Civil War to the Great Depression* (University of North Carolina Press, 2016), 27–50.

8. Her final poem, "Dreaming and Waking," was printed in her obituary: "Death of Lucy Larcom," *New York Times*, 19 April 1893, 11.

9. Quoted in Karen L. Kilup, *Fallen Forests: Emotion, Embodiment, and Ethics in American Women's Environmental Writing, 1781–1924* (University of Georgia Press, 2013), 186. See also "Factory Life in Lowell: Miss Lucy Larcom Describes What It Was Thirty Years Ago," *New York Times*, 27 April 1884, 6. As Kilup notes (189), Larcom downplayed environmental concerns because of her audience and "financial fragility."

10. Captain Richard H. Pratt, "The Advantages of Mingling Indians with Whites," in *Proceedings of the National Conference of Charities and Correction . . .* (George Ellis, 1892), 46. "Friends of the Indian" was a self-designation: Jennifer Graber, *Gods of Indian Country: Religion and the Struggle for the American West* (Oxford University Press, 2018), xx, 9–12, 77–81, 176–179; Michael D. McNally, *Defend the Sacred: Native American Religious Freedom beyond the First Amendment* (Princeton University Press, 2020), 37–39.

11. Richard White, *The Republic for Which It Stands: The United States during Reconstruction and the Gilded Age, 1865–1896* (Oxford University Press, 2017), 477–517.

12. Richard J. Callahan Jr., Kathryn Lofton, and Chad Seales, "Allegories of Progress: Industrial Religion in the United States," *JAAR* 78.1 (2010): 3.

13. The 1920 US Census marked the first time over 50 percent of the US population was classified as urban: Bureau of the Census, *Fourteenth Census of the United States Taken in the Year 1920: Population 1920* (GPO, 1921). Susan B. Carter et al., *Historical Statistics of the United States*, vol. 1, part A, *Population* (Cambridge University Press, 2006), 121.

14. On the Civil War and other wars of "national consolidation": C. A. Bayly, *Birth of the Modern World, 1780–1914: Global Connections and Comparisons* (Blackwell, 2004), 161–169. Thomas Bender, *A Nation among Nations: America's Place in World History* (Hill and Wang, 2006), 116–181. Don Harrison Doyle, *American Civil Wars: The United States, Latin America, Europe, and the Crisis of the 1860s* (University of North Carolina Press, 2017).

15. Randall M. Miller, "Religion and the Civil War," in Stephen J. Stein, ed., *The Cambridge History of Religions in America* (Cambridge University Press, 2000), 2: 203. George C. Rable, *God's Almost Chosen Peoples: A Religious History of the American Civil War* (University of North Carolina Press, 2010), 49, 397. Randall M. Miller, Harry S. Stout, and Charles Reagan Wilson, eds., *Religion and the American Civil War*

(Oxford University Press, 1998). Harry S. Stout, *Upon the Altar of the Nation: A Moral History of the American Civil War* (Viking, 2006).

16. Lenoir Chambers, "The South on the Eve of the Civil War," *North Carolina Historical Review* 39.2 (1962): 181–194. Donghyu Yang, "Notes on the Wealth Distribution of Farm Households in the United States, 1860: A New Look at Two Manuscript Census Samples," *Explorations in Economic History* 21.1 (1984): 88–102. Zachary Liscow, "Why Fight Secession? Evidence of Economic Motivations from the American Civil War," *Public Choice* 153.1 (2012): 37–54. Elizabeth R. Varon, *Disunion! The Coming of the American Civil War, 1789–1859* (University of North Carolina Press, 2008). Edward L. Ayers and Carolyn R. Martin, *America on the Eve of the Civil War* (University of Virginia Press, 2010). Mark Fiege, *The Republic of Nature: An Environmental History of the United States* (University of Washington Press, 2012), 199–227; Lisa M. Brady, *War upon the Land: Military Strategy and the Transformation of Southern Landscapes during the American Civil War* (University of Georgia Press, 2012).The war as a religious crisis: Daniel W. Stowell, *Gospel of Disunion: Religion and Separatism in the Antebellum South* (Cambridge University Press, 1993); Mark A. Noll, *The Civil War as a Theological Crisis* (University of North Carolina Press, 2006).

17. Eric Foner, *Give Me Liberty! An American History,* 5th ed. (W. W. Norton, 2017), 524.

18. N. B. Cloud, "Editor's Table," *American Cotton Planter and the Soil of the South* 12.12 (December 1858): 381. James Tackach, *Lincoln and the Natural Environment* (Southern Illinois University Press, 2019), 82. Fiege, *Republic of Nature,* 201–209.

19. Adam Wesley Dean, *An Agrarian Republic: Farming, Antislavery Politics, and Nature Parks in the Civil War Era* (University of North Carolina Press, 2015); R. Douglas Hurt, *Agriculture and the Confederacy: Policy, Productivity, and Power in the Civil War South* (University of North Carolina Press, 2015).

20. George Fitzhugh, *Cannibals All!; Or, Slaves without Masters,* C. Vann Woodward, ed. (1857; Harvard University Press, 1988), 8–13. See also George Fitzhugh, *Slavery Justified by a Southerner* (Recorder Printing Office, 1850). George Fitzhugh, *Sociology for the South . . .* (Burt Franklin, 1854).

21. James Henley Thornwell, "The Christian Doctrine of Slavery," in John B. Adger and John L. Giradeau, eds., *The Collected Writings of James Henley Thornwell, D.D, LL.D.* (Presbyterian Committee of Publication, 1873), 398–436. James Henley Thornwell, "Our National Sins," in *Fast Day Sermons; Or, The Pulpit on the State of the Country* (Rudd and Carleton, 1861), 9–56. B. M. Palmer, *The Life and Letters of James Henley Thornwell . . .* (Whittet and Shepperson, 1875), 167–169. See also William Freehling, "James Henley Thornwell's Mysterious Antislavery Moment," *JSH* 57.3 (1991): 385–392.

22. Fugitive Slave Act of 1850, 9 Stat. 462. Kansas–Nebraska Act of 1854, 10 Stat. 277. Jeremy J. Tewell, "A Difference of Complexion: George Fitzhugh and the Birth of the Republican Party," *Historian* 73.2 (2011): 235–254.

23. Tubman as "Moses": "Harriet Tubman Is Dead," *Auburn Citizen,* 11 March 1913; "Death of Aunt Harriet: Moses of Her People," *Auburn Daily Advertiser,* 11 March 1913.

See also Milton Sernett, *Harriet Tubman: Myth, Memory, and History* (Duke University Press, 2007). Frederick Douglass, *My Bondage and My Freedom* (Miller, Orton, and Mulligan, 1855). On sales figures and "Jeremiah": David Blight, *Frederick Douglass: Prophet of Freedom* (Simon & Schuster, 2018), 253–254.

24. Harriet Beecher Stowe, *Uncle Tom's Cabin, Or, Life among the Lowly* (J. P. Jewett, 1852).

25. The Brown quotation: F. B. Sanborn, ed., *John Brown: Liberator of Kansas and Martyr of Virginia: Life and Letters* (Torch Press, 1910), 517.

26. Brown "will make the gallows glorious, like a cross": Moncure Daniel Conway, *Emerson at Home and Abroad* (J. R. Osgood, 1882), 310–311. John J. McDonald, "Emerson and John Brown," *New England Quarterly* 44.3 (1971): 386–389.

27. J. D. Hacker, "A Census-Based Count of the Civil War Dead," *Civil War History* 57.4 (2011): 307–348.

28. "The Firing on the 'Star of the West,'" *Harper's Weekly*, 26 January 1861, 52, 54.

29. Elizabeth R. Varon, *Armies of Deliverance: A New History of the Civil War* (Oxford University Press, 2019). "Deliverance": Peter Cooper, *Letter of Peter Cooper on Slave Emancipation* (W. C. Bryant, 1863), 5.

30. Lifeway and identity: Jon L. Wakelyn, *Southern Pamphlets on Secession, November 1860–April 1861* (University of North Carolina Press, 1996). See B. M. Palmer, *The South: Her Peril and Her Duty* (True Witness and Sentinel, 1860).

31. "Heresy": Cooper, *Letter of Peter Cooper on Slave Emancipation*, 6. See "A Letter from Peter Cooper to His Excellency Abraham Lincoln," 1862, https://www.gilderlehrman.org/collection/glc06853.

32. Confederate States of America, *Constitution of the Confederate States of America* (Syme and Hall, 1861). See Colleen E. Mitchell, "'Decidedly Better Than the Old'? A Comparative Analysis of the Confederate and United States Constitutions," *Constitutional Studies* 5 (2019): 107–140.

33. Rable, *God's Almost Chosen Peoples*, 397. See also Stout, *Upon the Altar of the Nation;* Drew Gilpin Faust, *This Republic of Suffering: Death and the American Civil War* (Alfred A. Knopf, 2008).

34. The peace churches (Quakers, Brethren, and Mennonites) refused to endorse the war and sought conscientious objector status. See Miller, "Religion and the Civil War," 215. On centers of anti-Confederate sentiment: Victoria Bynum, *The Long Shadow of the Civil War: Southern Dissent and Its Legacies* (University of North Carolina Press, 2010).

35. Stephen W. Stathis and Daniel Canfield Strizek, "Ella Elvira Hobart Gibson: Nineteenth-Century Teacher, Lecturer, Author, Poet, Feminist, Spiritualist, Free Thinker, and America's First Woman Military Chaplain," *Journal of Church and State* 58.1 (2014): 1–37. Hobart had been ordained by the Religio-Philosophical Society of St. Charles, Illinois. Louis Nelson, with Company M of the 7th Tennessee Cavalry, went to war as a "cook" for his owner and got a Confederate pension. See Louis Nelson, "Colored Man's Application for Pension," 25 January 1921, State of Tennessee, no. 32, https://deadconfederates.com/wp-content/uploads/2012/12

/louisnelsonpensionfile.pdf. It identifies him as "a cook and servant for the company."

36. Isaac Mayer Wise, "No Political Preaching," *Israelite,* 1 February 1861, 244. Sefton D. Temkin, "Isaac Mayer Wise and the Civil War," *American Jewish Archives* 15.2 (1963): 125–127.

37. David Einhorn, "Two Civil War Sermons," in Marc Saperstein, ed., *Jewish Preaching in Times of War, 1800–2001* (Liverpool University Press, 2008), 201. Einhorn alludes to E. N. Elliot, ed., *Cotton Is King and Proslavery Arguments . . .* (Pritchard, Abbott, and Loomis, 1860).

38. See C. C. Goen, *Broken Churches, Broken Nation: Denominational Schisms and the Coming of the American Civil War* (Mercer University Press, 1985); Drew Gilpin Faust, *The Creation of Confederate Nationalism: Ideology and Identity in the Civil War South* (LSU Press, 1988), 22–40; Stowell, *Gospel of Disunion;* Noll, *The Civil War as Theological Crisis.* See *Proceedings of the Southern Baptist Convention . . .* (H. K. Ellyson, 1845).

39. *Address of the General Assembly of the Presbyterian Church in the Confederate States of America . . . December 1861* ("Published by order of the Assembly," [1861]), 9. See also Protestant Episcopal Church in the Confederate States of America, *Proposed Constitution and Digest of Revised Canons for the Government of the Protestant Episcopal Church in the Confederate States of America* (R. W. Gibbes, 1861).

40. Jonathan D. Sarna, *American Judaism: A History* (Yale University Press, 2004), 112–124.

41. Bertram W. Korn, "Jewish Chaplains during the Civil War," *American Jewish Archives Journal* 1.1 (1948): 14. Sarna, *American Judaism,* 119.

42. Benjamin J. Blied, *Catholics and the Civil War* (self-pub., 1945); John T. McGreevy, *Catholicism and American Freedom* (W. W. Norton, 2003), 68–90; Michael Hochgeschwender, *Wahrheit, Einheit, Ordnung: Die Sklavenfrage und der amerikanische Katholizismus, 1835–1870* (Ferdinand Schöningh, 2006); Mark A. Noll, "The Catholic Press, the Bible, and Protestant Responsibility for the Civil War," *Journal of the Civil War Era* 7.3 (2017): 355–376.

43. In 1864 Jefferson Davis commissioned Charleston's bishop to ask Pius IX to recognize the Confederacy. The pope refused: John Tracy Ellis, ed., *Documents of American Catholic History* (Henry Regnery, 1967), 1: 347–356. Michael V. Gannon, *Rebel Bishop: The Life and Era of Augustin Verot* (Bruce, 1964), 31; McGreevy, *Catholicism and American Freedom,* 82; Carl C. Creason, "United, Yet Divided: An Analysis of Bishops Martin John Spalding and John Baptist Purcell during the Civil War Era," *American Catholic Studies* 124.2 (2013): 49–69.

44. For his defense of the faith: James Gibbons, *The Faith of Our Fathers . . .* (John Murphy, 1876).

45. On just war theory: Stout, *Upon the Altar of the Nation,* xiii–xv, xvii, 9–15, 20–22, 42, 79, 175, 278, 376, 461; Marcus Schulzke, *Just War Theory and Civilian Casualties: Protecting the Victims of War* (Cambridge University Press, 2017), 1–17; Seth Lazar and Helen Frowe, eds., *The Oxford Handbook of Ethics of War* (Oxford

University Press, 2016); Gardiner Shattuck, *A Shield and Hiding Place: The Religious Life of the Civil War Armies* (Mercer University Press, 1987); Steven E. Woodworth, *While God Is Marching On: The Religious World of Civil War Soldiers* (University Press of Kansas, 2001).

46. See the photograph of the 69th Infantry regiment of the New York State Militia, with Father Thomas Mooney saying mass at Fort Corcoran, Virginia, on 1 June 1861, Library of Congress, https://www.loc.gov/item/00652518/.

47. "God of Battles" is from Lee's aide: A. L. Long, *Memoirs of Robert E. Lee* (J. M. Stoddart, 1886), 317–318. J. William Jones, *Christ in the Camp; or Religion in Lee's Army* (B. F. Johnson, 1887). On Lee, see Allen C. Guelzo, *Robert E. Lee: A Biography* (Alfred A. Knopf, 2021).

48. The "conjure doctor": Emmaline Heard, *Federal Writers' Project: Slave Narrative Project,* vol. 4, *Georgia,* part 4, *Telfair-Young (with combined interviews of others),* 1936, manuscript/mixed material, https://www.loc.gov/item/mesn044/. The quotations are from p. 158. See also Alexis Wells-Oghoghomeh, *The Souls of Womenfolk: The Religious Cultures of Enslaved Women in the Lower South* (University of North Carolina Press, 2021).

49. Recollections of Uncle Shang Harris in *Federal Writers' Project: Slave Narrative Project,* vol. 4, *Georgia,* part 4, *Telfair-Young.* The quotation is on p. 120.

50. "Gospel Train": *Federal Writers' Project: Slave Narrative Project,* vol. 4, *Georgia,* part 4, *Telfair-Young.* The quotations and song lyrics are on pp. 17–27.

51. See photo by Thomas W. Bankes, RG 3323-06-12, Nebraska State Historical Society, Lincoln; Thavolia Glymph, "Refugee Camp at Helena, Arkansas," in J. Matthew Gallman and Gary W. Gallagher, eds., *Lens of War: Exploring Iconic Photographs of the Civil War* (University of Georgia Press, 2015), 133–140. See also Abigail Cooper, "'Away I Goin' to Find My Mamma': Self-Emancipation, Migration, and Kinship in Refugee Camps in the Civil War Era," *Journal of African American History* 102.4 (2017): 447–449.

52. Lizzie Hart, a Methodist, exhorted Blacks to pray for their troops: Eric Gardner, "Remembered (Black) Readers: Subscribers to the *Christian Recorder,* 1864–1865," *American Literary History* 23.2 (2011): 248–249.

53. White corresponded with the *Christian Recorder:* Gardner, "Remembered (Black) Readers," 241–242. See also Edward A. Miller Jr., "Garland H. White, Black Army Chaplain," *Civil War History* 43.3 (1997): 201–218. Morgan W. Carter to "Friend Charles," 3 December 1864, Fort Ward Museum and Historic Site, Alexandria, Virginia. Dianna Penner, "Black Soldier's Letter Offers Rare View of Civil War," *Indianapolis Star,* 4 March 2013. See also "Recruitment Poster for Civil War Soldiers" (ca. 1863), Indiana Civil War Visual Collection, Indiana Historical Society, https://images.indianahistory.org/digital/collection/dc008/id/230/.

54. Abraham Lincoln, "Address Delivered at the Dedication of the Cemetery at Gettysburg," in Roy P. Basler, ed., *Collected Works of Abraham Lincoln* (Rutgers University Press, 1953), 7: 18–23.

55. Abraham Lincoln, "Second Inaugural Address," in Basler, *Collected Works of Abraham Lincoln,* 8: 332–333.

56. Booth as "instrument": Terry Alford, "Testimony Relating to John Wilkes Booth, and the Circumstances Attending the Assassination," in Edward Steers, ed., *The Trial: The Assassination of President Lincoln and the Trial of the Conspirators* (University Press of Kentucky, 2003), 40. Stout, *Upon the Altar of the Nation,* 448–466.

57. "Benediction": Ida Tarbell, "Disbanding the Union Army," *McClure's Magazine* 16.5 (1901): 405. See also "Review of the Armies," *New York Times,* 24 May 1865, 1.

58. Gregory P. Downs and Kate Masur, "Introduction," in Downs and Masur, eds., *The World the Civil War Made* (University of North Carolina Press, 2015), 1–21. Eric Foner, *Reconstruction: America's Unfinished Revolution, 1863–1877* (Harper and Row, 1988). W. E. B. Du Bois, *Black Reconstruction: An Essay toward a History of the Part Which Black Folk Played in the Attempt to Reconstruct Democracy in America, 1860–1880* (Harcourt Brace, 1935). Leon Fink, *The Long Gilded* Age (University of Pennsylvania Press, 2015). Forum on "The Future of Reconstruction Studies," *Journal of the Civil War Era* 7.1 (2017). Joshua Paddison, *American Heathens: Religion, Race, and Reconstruction in California* (University of California Press, 2012). Moon-Ho Jung, *Coolies and Cane: Race, Labor, and Sugar in the Land of Emancipation* (Johns Hopkins University Press, 2006). Lucy M. Cohen, *Chinese in the Post–Civil War South: A People without a History* (LSU Press, 1984).

59. Quoted in Blight, *Frederick Douglass,* 461. Caroline E. Janney, *Remembering the Civil War: Reunion and the Limits of Reconciliation* (University of North Carolina Press, 2013), 5–10. Daniel Philpott, *Just and Unjust Peace: An Ethic of Political Reconciliation* (Oxford University Press, 2012). Schulzke, *Just War Theory and Civilian Casualties,* 1–4. See also Jeremi Suri, *Civil War by Other Means: America's Long and Unfinished Fight for Democracy* (Public Affairs, 2022).

60. Paul A. Cimbala and Randall M. Miller, *The Freedmen's Bureau and Reconstruction: Reconsiderations* (Fordham University Press, 1999).

61. Abraham Lincoln, "Proclamation of Amnesty and Reconstruction, December 8, 1863," in Basler, *Collected Works of Abraham Lincoln,* 7: 54–56.

62. Sherman's theological interpretation of firing into residential districts: Stephen E. Bower, "The Theology of the Battlefield: William Tecumseh Sherman and the U.S. Civil War," *Journal of Military History* 64 (2000): 1021–1024.

63. Philpott, *Just and Unjust Peace,* 4. See also Schulzke, *Just War Theory and Civilian Casualties,* 3.

64. Scott Nesbit, "A Sharecropper's Millennium: Land and the Perils of Forgiveness in Post–Civil War South Carolina," in Ben Wright and Zachary W. Dresser, eds., *Apocalypse and the Millennium in the American Civil War Era* (LSU Press, 2013), 176.

65. R. Scott Huffard, *Engines of Redemption: Railroads and the Reconstruction of Capitalism in the New South* (University of North Carolina Press, 2019), 83.

66. "Letter from Mr. H. S. Beals," *American Missionary* 16.3 (1872): 50. "Chinese Labor," *American Missionary,* 16.3 (1872): 54.

67. Madeline Y. Hsu, *Dreaming of Gold, Dreaming of Home: Transnationalism and Migration between the United States and South China, 1882–1942* (Stanford University Press, 2000), 10.

68. On the Chinese in Carroll Parish: Jung, *Coolies and Cane,* 198. On the preacher E. C. Manning and his plantation workers: E. C. Manning, *Tenth Census of the United States: 1880,* Records of the Bureau of the Census, Record Group 29, National Archives, Washington, DC. The funeral: "Death of a 'Heathen Chinee,'" *Carroll Watchman,* 29 January 1876, repr. in Sandy L. Schmitz, ed., *Murder, Mayhem, and Misc. of Carroll Parish, La., 1866–1876* (S and S Press, 2001), 301.

69. Edward Cary Royce, *The Origins of Southern Sharecropping* (Temple University Press, 1993). Mark Reinberger, "The Architecture of Sharecropping: Extended Farms of the Georgia Piedmont," *Perspectives in Vernacular Architecture* 9 (2003): 116–134. Stanley Engerman, "Slavery and Its Consequences for the South in the Nineteenth Century," in Stanley L. Engerman and Robert E. Gallman, eds., *The Cambridge Economic History of the United States* (Cambridge University Press, 1996), 357. Sven Beckert, *Empire of Cotton: A Global History* (Vintage, 2014), 285–292. Susan E. O'Donovan, *Becoming Free in the Cotton South* (Harvard University Press, 2007).

70. W. E. B. Du Bois, "The Problem of Housing the Negro," *Southern Workmen* 30.7 (1901): 390–395; 30.9 (1901): 486–493; 30.10 (1901): 535–542; 30.11 (1901): 601–604; 30.12 (1901): 688–693.

71. Stout, *Upon the Altar of the Nation,* 459. Stout recognized that "civil religion would not include the very freedmen and women so many thousands died to liberate." Stout, *Upon the Altar of the Nation,* xxii. Wilson saw "two well developed civil religions," and I add a third. Imani Perry identified practices I discuss but did not use the term. Imani Perry, *May We Forever Stand: A History of the Black National Anthem* (University of North Carolina Press, 2018), 7–24. Blight identifies "three overall visions of Civil War memory." David W. Blight, *Race and Reunion: The Civil War in American Memory* (Harvard University Press, 2003), 2. See also Elaine A. Peña, "More than a Dead American Hero: Washington, the Improved Order of Red Men, and the Limits of Civil Religion," *American Literary History* 26.1 (2013): 63.

72. "Whole": Gilbert Haven, *The Uniter and Liberator of America: A Memorial Discourse on the Character and Career of Abraham Lincoln* (J. P. McGee, 1865), 27.

73. "Ruins": Conwell quoted in Reiko Hillyer, *Designing Dixie: Tourism, Memory, and Urban Space in the New South* (University of Virginia Press, 2015), 24. Megan Kate Nelson, "George N. Barnard: Charleston, S.C., View of Ruined Buildings through Porch of the Circular Church (150 Meeting Street), 1865," in Gallman and Gallagher, *Lens of War,* 231–238.

74. K. Stephen Prince, "The Burnt District: Making Sense of Ruins in the Postwar South," in Downs and Masur, *The World the Civil War Made,* 113–126.

75. Quotation from Henry Ward Beecher, *Oration at the Raising of "The Old Flag" at Sumter and Sermon on the Path of Abraham Lincoln, President of the United States* (Alexander Ireland, 1865), 31. Beecher on seeing the "ruins" of Charleston: T. J. Ellinwood, ed., *Autobiographical Reminiscences of Henry Ward Beecher* (Frederick A. Stokes, 1898), 27.

76. Richard Allen, *Philadelphia Gazette and Universal Daily Advertiser,* 31 December 1799, 2. Black wartime views of Washington, who "was no friend to slavery":

Reverend Dr. Wylie, "Washington's Views on Slavery," *Christian Recorder,* 26 April 1862.

77. "In Memory of Abraham Lincoln: The Reward of the Just," 1865, D. T. Wiest, William Smith, lithograph, Lincoln Financial Foundation Collection, courtesy of the Indiana State Museum, https://www.lincolncollection.org/collection/curated-groupings/item/?node=3236&item=22700. "Abraham Lincoln, the martyr, victorious, designed by W. H. Hermans; engraved by John Sartain, Phila.," 2 May 1866, Library of Congress, https://www.loc.gov/pictures/item/2006678341/. See also Lincoln and Washington together: Joseph Ward, Looking Glasses and Picture Frames, 125 Washington St., Boston, "The Apotheosis," https://rememberinglincoln.fords.org/node/240. "Relics" like Lincoln's blood-stained pillow became venerated objects: Richard Wightman Fox, *Lincoln's Body: A Cultural History* (W. W. Norton, 2015), 62–63.

78. Julia Ward Howe, "The Battle Hymn of the Republic," *Atlantic Monthly* 9.52 (1862): 10. See John Stauffer and Benjamin Soskis, *The Battle Hymn of the Republic: A Biography of the Song That Marches On* (Oxford University Press, 2013). Memorial Day was originally called Decoration Day because mourners decorated graves with flowers.

79. Edward A. Pollard, *The Lost Cause: A New Southern History of the War of the Confederates . . .* (E. B. Treat, 1866), 750. Janney, *Remembering the Civil War.* Grand Army of the Republic, *Services for the Use of the Grand Army of the Republic* (Burk and McFetridge, 1894).

80. "Eternally wrong": "Speech by William Warner of Missouri, Senior Vice-Commander-in-Chief," in *Journal of the Eighteenth Annual Session of the National Encampment, Grand Army of the Republic* (Town Book and Job Printing House, 1884), 258–260. See also Janney, *Remembering the Civil War,* 110. The 1884 Union memorials with Warner's phrase are in Mishawaka, Indiana, and Vanceburg, Kentucky. President Garfield was a Disciples of Christ minister and, so far, America's only president to be an ordained minister.

81. Martin Luther King Jr., "I Have a Dream," speech delivered at the March on Washington for Jobs and Freedom, 28 August 1963, in Eric J. Sundquist, *King's Dream* (Yale University Press, 2009), 229–234.

82. Blight, *Race and Reunion,* 64–97.

83. On Tubman's status as prophet and patriot, see Sernett, *Harriet Tubman,* 165–194. "Aunt Harriet's Funeral," *Auburn Daily Advertiser,* 13 March 1913. "Harriet Tubman Davis," *New York Times,* 14 March 1913. "Describes Tablet to Be Unveiled in Memory of Harriet Tubman," *Auburn Advertiser-Journal,* 25 May 1914.

84. Perry, *May We Forever Stand,* especially xvi, 1–24, 36–38.

85. Charles Reagan Wilson, *Baptized in Blood: The Religion of the Lost Cause, 1865–1920* (University of Georgia Press, 1980), 8.

86. Wright and Dresser, *Apocalypse and the Millennium in the American Civil War Era,* esp. vii–ix, 1–12, 110–128, and 217–252. Nicholas Guyatt, *Providence and the Invention of the United States, 1607–1876* (Cambridge University Press, 2007).

87. The entry is from 30 May 1865: Henry William Ravenel, "Private Journal, 1865–1866," 5, Henry William Ravenel Papers Collection, University of South Carolina, https://digital.tcl.sc.edu/digital/collection/rav/id/5437/rec/6. See also Tamara Miner Haygood, *Henry William Ravenel, 1814–1887: South Carolina Scientist in the Civil War Era* (University of Alabama Press, 1987).

88. The quotations are from his diary: Bobbie Swearingen Smith, ed., *A Palmetto Boy: Civil War–Era Diaries and Letters of James Adams Tillman* (University of South Carolina Press, 2010), 148–188.

89. Quoted in Luke E. Harlow, "The Long Life of Proslavery Religion," in Downs and Masur, *The World the Civil War Made,* 143–144. See also Wilson, *Baptized in Blood;* Paul Harvey, *Redeeming the South: Religious Cultures and Racial Identities among Southern Baptists, 1865–1925* (University of North Carolina Press, 1997); Edward J. Blum, *Reforging the White Republic: Race, Religion, and American Nationalism, 1865–1898* (LSU Press, 2005).

90. The 1866 sermon by William B. W. Howe is quoted in Wilson, *Baptized in Blood,* 67. See also Maurice D. McInnis, "Conflating Past and Present in the Reconstruction of Charleston's St. Philip's Church," *Perspectives in Vernacular Architecture* 9 (2003): 39–53.

91. Abram Joseph Ryan, "The March of the Deathless Dead," in *Poems: Patriotic, Religious, Miscellaneous* (P. J. Kennedy, 1898), 76–77. On Ryan as "poet-priest of the Lost Cause": Wilson, *Baptized in Blood,* 58.

92. "Truthful" history: Article II, Constitution of the United Daughters of the Confederacy (1895), https://www.encyclopediavirginia.org/Confederacy_Constitution_of_The_United_Daughters_of_the_1895. The war's cause was the North's "disregard" for the "rights" of Southern states. Cornelia B. Stone, *U.D.C. Catechism for Children* (1904; J. E. B. Stuart Chapter No. 10, United Daughters of the Confederacy, 1912). See also Karen L. Cox, *Dixie's Daughters: The United Daughters of the Confederacy and the Preservation of Confederate Culture* (University Press of Florida, 2003). On the North Carolina memorial: Thomas A. Tweed, "Our Lady of Guadeloupe Visits the Confederate Memorial: Latino and Asian Religions in the South," in Corrie E. Norman and Don S. Armentrout, eds., *Religion in the Contemporary South: Changes, Continuities, and Contexts* (University of Tennessee Press, 2005), 139–158.

93. David Gleeson, "Another Lost Cause: The Irish in the South Remember the Confederacy," *Southern Cultures* 17.1 (2011): 53, 63. Blight suggests that public memorialization began in 1875, with the unveiling of the first significant monument to a Confederate hero (Stonewall Jackson) in Richmond: Blight, *Race and Reunion,* 80.

94. Roadside signs pointed travelers to Jackson's "shrine" until 2019, when it became the Stonewall Jackson Death Site: https://www.nps.gov/frsp/learn//historyculture/jds.htm.

95. Katherine Grafton Miller, *Natchez of Long Ago and the Pilgrimage* (Relimake Publishing, 1938), 5. John Michael Vlach, *The Planter's Prospect: Privilege and Slavery in Plantation Paintings* (University of North Carolina Press, 2002). Steven

Hoelscher, "Making Place, Making Race: Performances of Whiteness in the Jim Crow South," *Annals of the Association of American Geographers* 93.3 (2003): 657–686.

96. The takeover as "redemption": Stephen Kantrowitz, "Ben Tillman and Hendrix McLane, Agrarian Rebels: White Manhood, the Farmers, and the Limits of Southern Populism," *JSH* 66.3 (2000): 500, Harvey, *Redeeming the South,* 11. On "re-subjugation": Blight, *Race and Reunion,* xxii.

97. Frederick Douglass, "Composite Nation," lecture in the Parker Fraternity Course, Boston, 1867, Frederick Douglass Papers, Library of Congress, mss11879, box 22, reel 14, https://www.loc.gov/item/mss1187900407. Blight, *Frederick Douglass,* 528. In *Brown v. Board of Education of Topeka,* 347 U.S. 483 (1954), the Supreme Court overruled *Plessy v. Ferguson,* 163 U.S. 537 (1896), as it used the Due Process Clause to outlaw school segregation. The "rights revolution": Lawrence M. Friedman and Grant M. Hayden, *American Law: An Introduction* (Oxford University Press, 2017), 181, 195–196, 201. Christian G. Samito, *Becoming American under Fire: Irish Americans, African Americans, and the Politics of Citizenship* (Cornell University Press, 2009), 1–12.

98. George Sewell, "Hiram Rhodes Revels: Another Evaluation," *Negro History Bulletin* (1 December 1974): 336–339. Julius E. Thompson, "Hiram Rhodes Revels, 1827–1901: A Reappraisal," *Journal of Negro History* 79.3 (1994): 297–303. See also Eric Foner, *Freedom's Lawmakers: A Directory of Black Officeholders during Reconstruction,* rev. ed. (LSU Press, 1996); Steven Hahn, *A Nation under Our Feet: Black Political Struggles in the Rural South, from Slavery to the Great Migration* (Harvard University Press, 2003).

99. Robert Tristano, "Holy Family Parish: The Genesis of an African-American Catholic Community in Mississippi," *Journal of Negro History* 83.4 (1998): 266. Laylon Wayne Jordan, "The New Regime: Race, Politics, and Police in Reconstruction Charleston, 1865–1875," in Michael Brem Bonner and Fritz Hamer, eds., *South Carolina in the Civil War and Reconstruction Eras* (University of South Carolina Press, 1994), 174–180.

100. Congress of Colored Catholics of the United States, *Three Catholic Afro-American Congresses: A Short Resume of the Work That Has Been Done since the Third Plenary Council of Baltimore* (American Catholic Tribune, 1893).

101. Wilbert L. Jenkins, *African Americans in Post–Civil War Charleston* (Indiana University Press, 1998), 118. Harvey, *Redeeming the South,* 46.

102. AME growth: Julius H. Bailey, *Race Patriotism: Protest and Print Culture in the AME Church* (University of Tennessee Press, 2012), xvi.

103. See Evelyn Brooks Higginbotham, *Righteous Discontent: The Women's Movement in the Black Baptist Church, 1880–1920* (Harvard University Press, 1993).

104. Curtis Evans, "W. E. B. Du Bois: Interpreting Religion and the Problem of the Negro Church," *JAAR* 75.2 (2007): 276. W. E. B. Du Bois, *The Negro Church . . .* (1903; Altamira Press, 2003). The "Black Church" came to be seen as a cluster of seven denominations in C. Eric Lincoln and Lawrence H. Mamiya, *The Black Church in the African-American Experience* (Duke University Press, 1990). But, as Warnock

suggests, the definition should include small Black denominations and nondenominational communions: Raphael G. Warnock, *The Divided Mind of the Black Church: Theology, Piety, and Public Witness* (NYU Press, 2013), 9.

105. [Buckner H. Payne], *The Negro: What Is His Ethnological Status?* ("Published for the Proprietor," 1867). See also Charles Carroll, *The Negro a Beast or in the Image of God* . . . (American Book and Bible House, 1900), 339. "Death of Col. Buckner H. Payne," *New York Times*, 8 June 1883; Blum, "To Doubt This Would Be to Doubt God," in Wright and Dresser, *Apocalypse and the Millennium in the American Civil War Era*, 221–223; Mason Stokes, "Someone's in the Garden with Eve: Race, Religion, and the American Fall," *AQ* 50.4 (1998): 722–724. *Plessy v. Ferguson*, 163 U.S. 537 (1896).

106. Quoted in Harvey, *Redeeming the South*, 53.

107. Morgan Kousser, *The Shaping of Southern Politics: Suffrage Restrictions and the Establishment of the One-Party South, 1880–1910* (Yale University Press, 1974).

108. B. R. Tillman, *The Negro Problem and Immigration* . . . (Gonzales and Bryan, 1908), 22.

109. On the number of lynchings: Equal Justice Initiative, "Reconstruction in America: Racial Violence after the Civil War," https://eji.org/reports/reconstruction-in-america-overview/. Luke P. Poland and John Scott, *Report of the Joint Select Committee Appointed to Inquire into the Condition of Affairs in the Late Insurrectionary States* . . . (GPO, 1872).

110. W. Scott Poole, "Religion, Gender, and the Lost Cause in South Carolina's 1876 Governor's Race: 'Hampton or Hell!,'" *JSH* 68.3 (2002): 573–598.

111. "Strike terror": B. R. Tillman, *Struggles of 1876: How South Carolina Was Delivered from Carpet-bag and Negro Rule* . . . (n.p., 1909), 24.

112. Article II, *Constitution of the State of South Carolina, Ratified in Convention, December 4, 1895* (Hugh Wilson Printer, 1900), 9–12.

113. "Speech of Senator Benjamin R. Tillman, March 23, 1900," *Congressional Record, 56th Congress, 1st Session*, 3223–3224. Stephen Kantrowitz, *Ben Tillman and the Reconstruction of White Supremacy* (University of North Carolina Press, 2000).

114. J. Allen Kirk, *A Statement of Facts Concerning the Bloody Riot in Wilmington, N.C.* . . . (n.p., 1898). One observer saw ten Black corpses in the morgue; another said "more than one hundred" African Americans died in the riot (15).

115. Kirk, *A Statement of Facts Concerning the Bloody Riot in Wilmington*.

116. J. W. Kramer was quoted in Timothy B. Tyson, "The Ghosts of 1898: Wilmington's Race Riot and the Rise of White Supremacy," *Raleigh News and Observer*, 17 November 2006, 12.

117. The phrase *national belonging* combines what others think of as *cultural belonging* and *political belonging*. See Renato Rosaldo, "Cultural Citizenship and Educational Democracy," *Cultural Anthropology* 9.3 (1994): 402–411. Some call this the "Era of Citizenship," when Americans debated the requirements for becoming American: Paddison, *American Heathens*, 6. The "Whiteness" discourse also appeared in the Northeast: Ralph Waldo Emerson, *English Traits*, rev. ed. (1856; James R. Osgood, 1876), 37–60, 163–176. Nell Irvin Painter, *The History of White People* (W. W. Norton,

2010), 151, 166, 173, 183. On the printmaker, see Charlotte Streifer Robinson, "The Early Career of Frances Flora Bond Palmer (1812–1876)," *American Art Journal* 17.4 (1985): 74.

118. The first environmental protest: Tackach, *Lincoln and the Natural Environment,* 94–95. On 7 June 1853 miners chopped down a giant sequoia in California. A year later they axed another redwood. By December 1855 the *New York Herald* urged that citizens should "preserve these California monuments of the capabilities of our American soil."

119. Alex Ruuska, "Ghost Dancing and the Iron Horse: Surviving through Tradition and Technology," *Technology and Culture* 52.3 (2011): 574–597. Fiege, *Republic of Nature,* 254–258, 260–261.

120. The iconic image of the 1869 golden spike ceremony didn't reveal all the diversity, including Chinese, Irish, and Latter-day Saints workers. See Andrew Russell, *East Shakes Hands with West at Laying Last Rail,* 10 May 1869, photographic print, Library of Congress, https://www.loc.gov/pictures/item/2005677835/.

121. Gordon H. Chang and Shelley Fisher Fishkin, eds., *The Chinese and the Iron Road: Building the Transcontinental Railroad* (Stanford University Press, 2019). Paddison, *American Heathens,* 131–136.

122. On Latter-day Saints officials welcoming the railroad and members constructing it, see David Walker, *Railroading Religion: Mormons, Tourists, and the Corporate Spirit of the West* (University of North Carolina Press, 2019). Edmunds-Tucker Act, 2 March 1887, 24 Stat. 635, Chap. 397. Sarah Barringer Gordon, *The Mormon Question: Polygamy and Constitutional Conflict in Nineteenth-Century America* (University of North Carolina Press, 2002). See also Fiege, *Republic of Nature,* 228–230, 261–262.

123. Andrew C. Isenberg, *The Destruction of the Bison* (Cambridge University Press, 2000), 143. Jeffrey Ostler, "'The Last Buffalo Hunt' and Beyond: Plains Sioux Economic Strategies in the Early Reservation Period," *Great Plains Quarterly* 21.2 (2001): 117. Louis S. Warren, *God's Red Son: The Ghost Dance Religion and the Making of Modern America* (Basic Books, 2017), 45, 146–159.

124. Tisa Wenger, *We Have a Religion: The 1920s Pueblo Indian Dance Controversy and American Religious Freedom* (University of North Carolina Press, 2009), 31–38. Graber, *Gods of Indian Country,* 77–115. On Catholics, see Wenger, *We Have a Religion,* 47–58; Peter J. Rahill, *Catholic Indian Missions and Grant's Peace Policy, 1870–1884* (Catholic University of America Press, 1953); Amanda Bresie, "Mother Katharine Drexel's Benevolent Empire: The Bureau of Catholic Indian Missions and the Education of Native Americans, 1885–1935," *U.S. Catholic Historian* 32.3 (2014): 1–24.

125. Quoted in Douglas Firth Anderson, "'More Conscience Than Force': U.S. Indian Inspector William Vandever, Grant's Peace Policy, and Protestant Whiteness," *Journal of the Gilded Age and Progressive Era* 9.2 (2010): 177.

126. "First Inaugural Address of Ulysses S. Grant," 4 March 1869, https://avalon.law.yale.edu/19th_century/grant1.asp.

127. Thomas C. Battey, *Life and Adventures of a Quaker among the Indians* (Lee and Shepard, 1875), 318.

128. Stout, *Upon the Altar of the Nation,* 460–461.

129. De facto establishment: Mark deWolfe Howe, *The Garden and the Wilderness: Religion and Government in American Constitutional History* (University of Chicago Press, 1965), 11.

130. For accounts of the experiences of Carlisle students between 1890 and 1918, see Arnold Krupat, ed., *Boarding School Voices: Carlisle Indian School Students Speak* (University of Nebraska Press, 2021). "Indian Education," in *Annual Report of the Commissioner of Indian Affairs . . . for the Year 1879* (GPO, 1879), 7–9. For a study that places child removal in a broader context, see Margaret D. Jacobs, *White Mother to a Dark Race: Settler Colonialism, Maternalism, and the Removal of Indigenous Children in the American West and Australia, 1880–1940* (University of Nebraska Press, 2009).

131. An Act to Provide for the Allotment of Lands in Severalty to Indians on the Various Reservations [General Allotment Act or Dawes Act], 8 February 1887, 24 Stat. 388. Hiram Price, Commissioner of Indian Affairs, to Henry Teller, Secretary of the Interior, "Rules Governing the Court of Indian Offenses," US Office of Indian Affairs, 30 March 1883. *Annual Report of the Commissioner of Indian Affairs . . . for the Year 1883* (GPO, 1883), xiv–xv, 27, 42, 58, 86, 110, 146. McNally, *Defend the Sacred,* 33–68.

132. Carolyn E. Boyd, *Rock Art of the Lower Pecos* (Texas A&M University Press), 67–105. See also Carolyn E. Boyd and J. Philip Dering, "Medicinal and Hallucinogenic Plants in the Sediments and Pictographs of the Lower Pecos, Texas Archaic," *Antiquity* 70.268 (June 1996): 256–275.

133. Omer Call Stewart, *Peyote Religion: A History* (University of Oklahoma Press, 1987). Thomas Maroukis, *The Peyote Road: Religious Freedom and the Native American Church* (University of Oklahoma Press, 2011).

134. James Mooney, *The Ghost Dancing Religion and the Sioux Outbreak of 1890 . . .* (GPO, 1896); Brad Logan, "The Ghost Dance among the Paiute: An Ethnohistorical View of the Documentary Evidence, 1889–1893," *Ethnohistory* 27.3 (1980): 267–288; Gregory E. Smoak, *Ghost Dances and Identity: Prophetic Religion and American Indian Ethnogenesis in the Nineteenth Century* (University of California Press, 2006), 152–190; Ruuska, "Ghost Dancing and the Iron Horse"; Warren, *God's Red Son,* 2–18, 56–68, 93–96, 148–150, 289–294; McNally, *Defend the Sacred,* 51–54; Alex K. Carroll et al., "Landscapes of the Ghost Dance: A Cartography of Numic Ritual," *Journal of Archaeological Method and Theory* 11.2 (2004): 127–156.

135. A Boston spiritualist said Sitting Bull's spirit transmitted a posthumous poem, pleading for "fairer dealing": [Mrs. Kate R. Stiles], *Sitting Bull's Message from Spirit Life* (n.p., 1891), 6.

136. Jennifer Graber, "Religion in Kiowa Ledgers: Expanding the Canon of American Religious Literature," *American Literary History* 26.1 (2014): 42–60.

137. Quoted in Phillip Earenfight, ed., *A Kiowa's Odyssey: A Sketchbook from Fort Marion* (University of Washington Press, 2007), 51. On Éttàlyìdònmàui's death: *The Indian Helper* 3.38 (4 May 1888): 2; "Died: Etahdleuh Doanmoe," *Red Man* 8.7 (May 1888): 3, 6.

138. Sergei Kan, *Memory Eternal: Tlingit Culture and Russian Orthodox Christianity through Two Centuries* (University of Washington Press, 2014); Sergei Kan,

"Memory Eternal: Orthodox Christianity and the Tlingit Mortuary Complex," *Arctic Anthropology* 24.1 (1987): 32–55; John R. Swanton, ed., *Tlingit Myths and Texts* (Smithsonian Institution, 1909); Thomas F. Johnston, "The Socio-Mythic Contexts of Music in Tlingit Shamanism and Potlach Ceremonials," *World of Music* 34.2 (1992): 43–71.

139. Ilya Vinkovetsky, *Russian America: An Overseas Colony of a Continental Empire, 1804–1867* (Oxford University Press, 2011); Patrick Daley and Beverly James, "Missionary Voices as the Discursive Terrain for Native Resistance," *Journal of Communication Inquiry* 22.4 (1998): 365–384; John H. Erickson, *Orthodox Christians in America* (Oxford University Press, 2008). See also Sheldon Jackson, *Alaska and Missions on the North Pacific Coast* (Dodd, Mead, 1880), 129–130, 138–139.

140. "A Letter to the Right Reverend Nikolai, Bishop of the Aleutian Islands and Alaska, from Hieromonk Anatolii Kamenskii of Sitka," 21 January 1897, *Russian Orthodox American Messenger* 1.12 (1897): 226–239.

141. Quoted in "Letter to the Right Reverend Nikolai."

142. Quoted in Bender, *Nation among Nations,* 219, 220. Theodore Roosevelt, *The Winning of the West* (G. P. Putnam's Sons, 1900), 1: vii. For global perspectives on religion: Bayly, *Birth of the Modern World,* 325–365; Jürgen Osterhammel, *The Transformation of the World: A Global History of the Nineteenth Century* (Princeton University Press, 2014), 873–901; John T. McGreevy, *Catholicism: A Global History from the French Revolution to Pope Francis* (W. W. Norton, 2022), 111–155.

143. Robert W. Rydell, *All the World's a Fair* (University of Chicago Press, 1984), 60–71. Richard Hughes Seager, ed., *The Dawn of Religious Pluralism: Voices from the World's Parliament of Religions, 1893* (Open Court, 1993).

144. US presidents sent troops to Cuba, Haiti, Nicaragua, China, Korea, Mexico, Panama, Samoa, Honduras, and the Dominican Republic. Donna R. Gabaccia, *Foreign Relations: American Immigration in Global Perspective* (Princeton University Press, 2012), 89.

145. Jonathan H. Ebel, *Faith in the Fight: Religion and the American Soldier in the Great War* (Princeton University Press, 2010).

146. The Danish West Indies sales treaty signed by Wilson: Danish National Archives, Treaty Collection, 1901–1920, United States of America, no. VII, 120.

147. "President's Instructions and Proclamation of General Otis," in *Elihu Root Collection of United States Documents, Relating to the Philippine Islands* (GPO, 1902), 776. Bender, *Nation among Nations,* 221. Rebecca Tinio McKenna, *American Imperial Pastoral: The Architecture of US Colonialism in the Philippines* (University of Chicago Press, 2017), 26. See also Anne M. Martinez, *Catholic Borderlands: Mapping Catholicism onto American Empire, 1905–1935* (University of Nebraska Press, 2014); John T. McGreevy, *American Jesuits and the World: How an Embattled Religious Order Made Modern Catholicism Global* (Princeton University Press, 2016), 179–209.

148. "Second Inaugural Address of William McKinley," 1 March 1901, https://avalon.law.yale.edu/19th_century/mckin2.asp. See also Ian Tyrell, *Reforming the World: The Creation of America's Moral Empire* (Princeton University Press, 2010); Paul A. Kramer, "Empires, Exceptions, and Anglo-Saxons: Race and Rule between

the British and United States Empires, 1880–1910," *JAH* 88.4 (2002): 1315–1353; Walter A. McDougall, *The Tragedy of U.S. Foreign Policy: How America's Civil Religion Betrayed the National Interest* (Yale University Press, 2016), 112–116; Ernest Lee Tuveson, *Redeemer Nation: The Idea of America's Millennial Role* (University of Chicago Press, 1968), 127–136, 165–175.

149. Lilian D. Powers, ed., *Proceedings of the Twenty-Third Annual Meeting of the Lake Mohonk Conference of Friends of the Indian and Other Dependent Peoples: 1905* (Lake Mohonk Conference, 1905). Graber, *Gods of Indian Country,* 198. James S. Dennis et al., eds., *World Atlas of Christian Missions* (Student Volunteer Movement for Foreign Missions, 1911), 89. Emily Conroy-Krutz, *Christian Imperialism: Converting the World in the Early American Republic* (Cornell University Press, 2015).

150. "Perishing millions": Thomas A. Tweed and Stephen Prothero, eds., *Asian Religions in America: A Documentary History* (Oxford University Press, 1999), 38–42. Anne Tuttle Jones Bullard, *Louisa Ralston, or, What Can I Do for the Heathen?* (Massachusetts Sabbath School Society, 1831). Anne Tuttle Jones Bullard, *Wife for a Missionary* (Truman, Smith, 1834).

151. Dana Lee Robert, *American Women in Mission: A Social History of Their Thought and Practice* (Mercer University Press, 1996), 128–130. Helen Barrett Montgomery, *Western Women in Eastern Lands: An Outline Study of Fifty Years of Woman's Work in Foreign Missions* (Macmillan, 1910). Regina D. Sullivan, *Lottie Moon: A Southern Baptist Missionary to China in History and Legend* (LSU Press, 2011).

152. William R. Hutchison, "Protestantism as Establishment," in Hutchison, ed., *Between the Times: The Travail of the Protestant Establishment in America, 1900–1960* (Cambridge University Press, 1989), 3–13. Elesha Coffman, "The Measure of a Magazine: Assessing the Influence of the *Christian Century,*" *RAC* 22.1 (2012): 55, 59–61, 74–75, 77n8. John R. Mott, *The Evangelization of the World in This Generation* (Student Volunteer Movement, 1900).

153. Anna L. Peterson and Manuel A. Vásquez, ed., *Latin American Religions: Histories and Documents in Context* (NYU Press, 2008), 170–176.

154. Angelyn Dries, "The Foreign Mission of the American Catholic Church, 1893–1925," *International Bulletin of Missionary Research* 15.2 (1991): 61–66.

155. Hutchison, *Errand to the World,* 126–127.

156. Quoted in M. L. Gordon, *An American Missionary in Japan* (Houghton, Mifflin, 1892), 209–220. David A. Hollinger, *Protestants Abroad: How Missionaries Tried to Change the World but Changed America* (Princeton University Press, 2017), 3.

157. Deborah Fitzgerald, *Every Farm a Factory: The Industrial Ideal in American Agriculture* (Yale University Press, 2003), 7. An American Sugar Mill, Ewa Sugar Plantation, Oahu, Hawaiian Islands (1902), photograph, print on card mount, Library of Congress. Benjamin Franklin Dillingham, who leased the land for the Ewa Sugar Plantation and founded the railroad that transported the crop to Honolulu, married into a missionary family in 1869 and helped overthrow the queen in 1893.

158. J. Kēhaulani Kauanui, *Hawaiian Blood: Colonialism and the Politics of Sovereignty and Indigeneity* (Duke University Press, 2008), 25–29.

159. Lydia Kualapai, "The Queen Writes Back: Lili'uokalani's *Hawaii's Story by Hawaii's Queen*," *Studies in American Indian Literatures* 17.2 (2005): 32–62. Lili'uokalani of Hawai'i, *The Kumulipo: An Hawaiian Creation Myth* (Lee and Shepard, 1897). Lili'uokalani of Hawai'i, *Hawaii's Story by Hawaii's Queen* (Lee and Shepard, 1898). Cristy Dwyer, "Queen Lili'uokalani's Imprisonment Quilt: Indomitable Spirits in Protest Cloth," *Femspec* 9.2 (2008): 2–17.

160. The island's diversity: Rev. Edward P. Baker, "The Hawaiian Islands," in John Henry Barrows, ed., *The World's Parliament of Religions . . .* (Parliament Publishing Company, 1893), 2: 1070–1072. On Mary Foster: Thomas A. Tweed, *The American Encounter with Buddhism, 1844–1912: Victorian Culture and the Limits of Dissent* (University of North Carolina Press, 2000), 53, 89, 185n11.

161. "Register of the Ewa Plantation Company," Plantation Archives, University of Hawai'i at Manoa Library, https://www2.hawaii.edu/~speccoll/p_ewa.html. George Tanabe and Willa Jane Tanabe, *Japanese Buddhist Temples of Hawai'i: An Illustrated Guide* (University of Hawai'i Press, 2013), 52–53.

162. Quoted in Margaret Miki, "Mother and Her Temple," *Social Process in Hawaii* 12 (1948): 19.

163. G. L. Morrill, *Hawaiian Heathen and Others* (M. A. Donohue, 1919), 212–213, 239. Y. Iwamura, *Democracy According to the Buddhist Viewpoint* (Hongwanji Mission in Hawaii, 1918).

164. Sōen Shaku represented Zen at the Parliament in 1893 and sent his translator D. T. Suzuki. Swami Vivekanada promoted Vedānta and founded the Ramakrishna Mission (1897). Inayat Khan promoted an Islamic mystical tradition, Sufism, and by 1912 he had attracted disciples to his Sufi Order of the West. Tweed, *American Encounter with Buddhism*, 31–33. Carl T. Jackson, *Vedanta for the West: The Ramakrishna Movement in the United States* (Indiana University Press, 1994), 23–36. Kambiz GhaneaBassiri, *A History of Islam in America: From the New World to the New World Order* (Cambridge University Press, 2010), 127–132.

165. Immigration statistics in this paragraph: Carter et al., *Historical Statistics*, esp. 1: 20–23 and table Aa1884–1895.

166. John Higham, *Strangers in the Land: Patterns of American Nativism, 1860–1925* (Atheneum, 1968), 4.

167. Josiah Strong, *Our Country: Its Possible Future and Its Present Crisis* (American Home Missionary Society, 1885).

168. The "huddled masses" were mentioned in the 1883 sonnet "The New Colossus" by Emma Lazarus, a Jewish poet. In 1903 the poem was affixed to the Statue of Liberty.

169. US Bureau of Immigration, *Annual Report of the Commissioner of Immigration* (GPO, 1907), 62. Douglas C. Baynton, "Defect: A Selective Reinterpretation of American Immigration History," in Nancy J. Hirschmann and Beth Linker, eds., *Civil Disabilities: Citizenship, Membership, and Belonging* (University of Pennsylvania Press, 2015), 45–51. Douglas C. Baynton, *Defectives in the Land: Disability and Immigration in the Age of Eugenics* (University of Chicago Press, 2016), 1. The scientist who coined

the term *eugenics* saw it as a "secular religion"; see Francis Galton, *Inquiries into Human Faculty and Its Development* (Macmillan, 1883), 25, 27, 44–45, 307, 323–324.

170. "Leif the Discoverer: The Erikson Statue Unveiled by the Boston Scandinavians," *New York Times,* 30 October 1887.

171. Julian Nordstrom, *Danger on the Doorstep: Anti-Catholicism and American Print Culture in the Progressive Era* (University of Notre Dame Press, 2006).

172. Bureau of the Census, *Religious Bodies: 1906* (GPO, 1910), 17–50.

173. Sarna, *American Judaism,* 375. GhaneaBassiri, *Islam in America,* 136. Bureau of the Census, *Chinese and Japanese in the United States: 1910,* Bulletin 127 (GPO, 1914), 7.

174. GhaneaBassiri, *Islam in America,* 140, 144.

175. Adam Mintz, "Halakhah in America: The History of City Eruvin, 1894–1962," PhD diss., New York University, 2011, 229–282. This *eruv* was contested by other rabbis, but Seigel was still revered: "Throng at Rabbi's Funeral," *New York Times,* 25 February 1910.

176. Trinity Church, *Trinity's Tenements: A Report on the Condition of All Residence Buildings Owned and Controlled by Trinity Church . . .* (Tenement House Committee, 1909), 12. On Trinity Church: Jon Butler, *God in Gotham: The Miracle of Religion in Modern Manhattan* (Harvard University Press, 2020), 86–88.

177. Butler, *God in Gotham,* 80–83. Sarna, *American Judaism,* 178–179.

178. James T. Fisher, *Communion of Saints: A History of Catholics in America* (Oxford University Press, 2002), 79.

179. Robert S. Carr, *Digging Miami* (University Press of Florida, 2012), 96–98. Thomas A. Tweed, "An Emerging Protestant Establishment: Religious Affiliation and Public Power on the Urban Frontier in Miami, 1896–1904," *CH* 64.3 (1995): 412–414.

180. "Colored Town" churches: *Official City Directory of Miami and Nearby Towns: 1904* (repr., Historical Association of Southern Florida, 1974), 252. Raymond Mohl, "Black Immigrants: Bahamians in Early Twentieth-Century Miami," *Florida Historical Quarterly* 65.3 (1987): 275–276.

181. Larry Ten Harmsel, *Dutch in Michigan* (Michigan State University Press, 2002), 1–19. The tulip festival began in 1920.

182. Gunther Barth, *Instant Cities: Urbanization and the Rise of San Francisco and Denver* (University of New Mexico Press, 1988). Cabrini's order in Colorado: Thomas A. Tweed, *America's Church: The National Shrine and Catholic Presence in the Nation's Capital* (Oxford University Press, 2011), 206.

183. Strong, *Our Country,* 149–150.

184. "Hindoos Plan to Float Burning Body Down River," *San Francisco Chronicle,* 6 July 1909, 3. See also Stephen R. Prothero, *Purified by Fire: A History of Cremation in America* (University of California Press, 2001).

185. Jeanne Halgren Kilde, *When Church Became Theatre: The Transformation of Evangelical Architecture and Worship in Nineteenth-Century America* (Oxford University Press, 2005), 113–114.

186. Gabaccia, *Foreign Relations,* 92–106. Roger Daniels, *Coming to America: A History of Immigration and Ethnicity in American Life,* 2nd ed. (Perennial, 2002); John

Bodnar, *The Transplanted: A History of Immigrants in Urban America* (Indiana University Press, 1985). GhaneaBassiri, *Islam in America,* 136, 140.

187. Gabriel Brillante: Tweed, *America's Church,* 113, 274.

188. "Soe Sonoda" [Shūe Sonoda]: Bureau of the Census, *Twelfth Census of the United States: 1900,* San Francisco, California. See also Thomas A. Tweed, "Tracing Modernity's Flow: Buddhist Currents in the Pacific World," *Eastern Buddhist* 43.1–2 (2012): 50.

189. Joshua Seigel: Bureau of the Census, *Twelfth Census of the United States: 1900,* Borough of Manhattan, New York.

190. Paul Rhode and Julian Zutchkofski [Ziuchkovski]: Bureau of the Census, *Thirteenth Census of the United States: 1910,* Chicago Ward 8, Cook County, Illinois.

191. Dominic A. Pacyga, *Polish Immigrants and Industrial Chicago: Workers on the South Side, 1880–1922* (Ohio State University Press, 1991). Dominic A. Pacyga, "To Live amongst Others: Poles and Their Neighbors in Industrial Chicago, 1865–1930," *Journal of American Ethnic History* 16.1 (1996): 55–73. Victoria Granacki, "The Architecture of Polish Catholic Churches in Chicago," Loyola University, 14 November 2015, https://ecommons.luc.edu/cgi/viewcontent.cgi?article=1057&context=ccic.

192. White, *Republic for Which It Stands,* 477–517. John L. Brooke, *Climate Change and the Course of Global History: A Rough Journey* (Cambridge University Press, 2014), 502.

193. Christopher F. Jones, "A Landscape of Energy Abundance: Anthracite Coal Canals and the Roots of American Fossil Fuel Dependence, 1820–1860," *Environmental History* 15 (2010): 451–453, 473. Thomas Parke Hughes, *Networks of Power: Electrification in Western Society, 1880–1930* (Johns Hopkins University Press, 1983). Donald Worster, *Under Western Skies: Nature and History in the American West* (Oxford University Press, 1992), 57–63.

194. William Buckland, *Geology and Mineralogy Considered with Reference to Natural Theology* (William Pickering, 1836), 1: 524–538.

195. "Christian industrialism": Anthony F. C. Wallace, *Rockdale: The Growth of an American Village in the Early Industrial Revolution,* new ed. (University of Nebraska Press, 2005), 4, 394–397.

196. Bob Johnson, *Carbon Nation: Fossil Fuels in the Making of American Culture* (University Press of Kansas, 2014), xviii. George Vrtis and J. R. McNeill, eds., *Mining North America: An Environmental History since 1522* (University of California Press, 2017), 1–16.

197. David B. Danbom, *Born in the Country: A History of Rural America,* 3rd ed. (Johns Hopkins University Press, 2017), 121–174.

198. William Cronon, *Nature's Metropolis: Chicago and the Great West* (W. W. Norton, 1991).

199. Elizabeth A. Walsh, "Ellen Swallow Richards and the 'Science of Right Living': Nineteenth-Century Foundations for Practice Research Supporting Individual, Social and Ecological Resilience and Environmental Justice," *Journal of Urban Management* 7.3 (2018): 131–140. On "human ecology": Ellen Swallow Richards, *Sanitation in Daily Life* (Whitcomb & Barrows, 1907), v. See also Theodore Steinberg,

Nature Incorporated: Industrialization and the Waters of New England (University of Massachusetts Press, 1991), 205–239.

200. Jonathan Wlasiuk, "A Company Town on Common Waters: Standard Oil in the Calumet," *Environmental History* 19 (2014): 690.

201. Svante Arrhenius, "On the Influence of Carbonic Acid in the Air upon the Temperature of the Ground," *London, Edinburgh, and Dublin Philosophical Magazine and Journal of Science* 41.251 (1896): 237–276. Nerilie J. Abram et al., "Early Onset of Industrial-Era Warming across the Oceans and Continents," *Nature* 536 (2017): 411–418.

202. On religion and industry in Monessen: John Newton Boucher, *History of Westmoreland County, Pennsylvania* (Lewis Publishing, 1906), 1: 523–525.

203. Edward T. O'Donnell, *Henry George and the Crisis of Inequality: Progress and Poverty in the Gilded Age* (Columbia University Press, 2015). C. S. Denny, "The Whipping Post for Tramps," *Century* 40 (1895): 794. Economic inequality had persisted during and after the Civil War for Blacks in the urban North: Jacqueline Jones, *No Right to an Honest Living: The Struggles of Boston's Black Workers in the Civil War Era* (Basic Books, 2023). For a broader view, see also Thomas Piketty, *Capital in the Twenty-First Century,* trans. Arthur Goldhammer (Harvard University Press, 2014), 31–33.

204. Alan M. Kraut, "The Perennial Fear of Foreign Bodies," *Modern American History* 2.1 (2019): 53–57.

205. "Over-Density of Population in Cities," *Scientific American* 40.3 (1879): 32. US population density increased from 7.9 residents per square mile in 1850 to 35.6 residents per square mile in 1920. On the "urban mortality penalty": Louis Cain and Sok Chul Hong, "Survival in 19th Century Cities: The Larger the City, the Smaller Your Chances," *Explorations in Economic History* 46 (2009): 450–463.

206. White, *Republic for Which It Stands,* 477–481.

207. John Fabian Witt, *The Accidental Republic: Crippled Workingmen, Destitute Widows, and the Remaking of American Law* (Harvard University Press, 2004); Mark Aldrich, *Death Rode the Rails: American Railroad Accidents and Safety, 1828–1965* (Johns Hopkins University Press, 2006), 97–180. Carroll Davidson Wright, *A Report on Marriage and Divorce in the United States, 1867–1886* (GPO, 1889). To confront the problem, Congregationalist ministers founded an organization: Samuel W. Dike, *The National Divorce Reform League* (Our Day, 1888).

208. New York Legislature, *Report of the Tenement House Committee* (James B. Lyon, 1895). See also *The Pittsburgh Survey: Findings in Six Volumes* (Charities Publication Committee, 1909–1914).

209. Edward K. Muller and Joel A. Tarr with Timothy M. Collins, "Pittsburgh's Three Rivers: From Industrial Infrastructure to Environmental Assets," in Edward K. Muller et al., eds., *Making Industrial Pittsburgh Modern* (University of Pittsburgh Press, 2019), 92–98. Samuel R. Haythorn and Harry B. Miller, "Necropsy Evidences on the Relation of Smoky Atmosphere to Pneumonia," *American Journal of Public Health* 28 (1938): 479–486. Cliff Davidson, "Air Pollution in Pittsburgh: A Historical Perspective," *Journal of the Air Pollution Control Association* 29.10 (1979): 1035–1038.

See also Erin Stewart Mauldin, "The United States in Global Environmental History," in J. R. McNeill and Erin Stewart Mauldin, eds., *A Companion to Global Environmental History* (Wiley, 2012), 141.

210. "At Chapel, Brooklyn Navy Yard," Detroit Publishing Co. no. 32378, ca. 1900, Library of Congress, https://www.loc.gov/item/2016807178/.

211. Kathryn Lofton, *Consuming Religion* (University of Chicago Press, 2017), 203–208.

212. James Connolly, "Bringing the City Back In: Space and Place in the Urban History of the Gilded Age and Progressive Era," *Journal of the Gilded Age and Progressive Era* 1.3 (2002): 258–278. Kenneth T. Jackson, *Crabgrass Frontier: The Suburbanization of the United States* (Oxford University Press, 1985), 73–137. See also Kevin M. Kruse and Thomas J. Sugrue, eds., *The New Suburban History* (University of Chicago Press, 2006).

213. Butler, *God in Gotham,* 112. On "live options": William James, "The Will to Believe," in Ralph Barton Perry, ed., *Essays on Faith and Morals: William James* (Meridian, 1962), 33–34.

214. F. Max Müller, *Origin and Growth of Religion* (Charles Scribner's Sons, 1879).

215. Mark A. Lause, *Free Spirits: Spiritualism, Republicanism, and Radicalism in the Civil War Era* (University of Illinois Press, 2016), 14.

216. Willard defended women's ordination using the metaphor of a stereoscope: Frances Willard, *Woman in the Pulpit* (D. Lothrop, 1888), 21. Lisa Zimmerelli, "'The Stereoscopic View of Truth': The Feminist Theological Rhetoric of Frances Willard's *Woman in the Pulpit,*" *Rhetoric Society Quarterly* 42.4 (2012): 353–374.

217. Harriet Earhart Monroe, *Twice-Born Men in America; Or the Psychology of Conversion in Rescue Mission Work* (Lutheran Publication Society, 1914), 38, 42, 94.

218. On the "cultural work of suppression": Johnson, *Carbon Nation,* xx.

219. "*Frank Leslie's Illustrated Newspaper* 1858 Cable News," *History of the Atlantic Cable and Undersea Communications,* 17 October 2014, https://atlantic-cable.com/Article/1858Leslies/index.htm.

220. Bishop Matthew Simpson: "Formal Opening of the International Exposition of 1876," *Detroit Free Press,* 11 May 1876, 1. See also Homer L. Calkin, "The Methodists and the Centennial of 1876," *Methodist History* 14 (1976): 95–96; Rydell, *All the World's a Fair,* 11–16; George R. Crooks, ed., *Sermons by Bishop Matthew Simpson . . .* (Harper and Brothers, 1885), 189–190, 230–231.

221. Rossiter Johnson, ed., *A History of the World's Columbian Exposition Held in Chicago in 1893* (D. Appleton, 1897), 1: 302.

222. Camden M. Cobern, *The Stars and the Book: Sermons Preached in St. James Methodist Episcopal Church, Chicago* (Jennings and Graham, 1904), 92.

223. Quoted in Roger Burlingame, *Henry Ford* (Hutchinson, 1957), 62.

224. Frank Morton Todd, *The Story of the Exposition; Being the Official History of the International Celebration Held at San Francisco in 1915 . . .* (G. P. Putnam's Sons, 1921), 2: 290–293, 4: 247. The wonders of industrial progress: "The Edge of the Future," *McClure's Magazine* 2.2 (1894): 199–216. See also Kati Curts, "Temples and Turnpike

in 'The World of Tomorrow': Religious Assemblage and Automobility at the 1939 New York World's Fair," *JAAR* 83.3 (2015): 739.

225. I quote the definition in Callahan Jr., Lofton, and Seales, "Allegories of Progress," 3. I add that it varied by industry, changed over time, and employed at least four spiritual frameworks. Industrial religion also includes such venerated objects as "the Menlo Park Relic," a light bulb from Thomas Edison's Laboratory, and the "First Ford Model T Production Card, September 27, 1908," https://www.thehenryford.org/collections-and-research/digital-collections/artifact/312908/.

226. See William R. Hutchison, *The Modernist Impulse in American Protestantism* (Oxford University Press, 1976); George M. Marsden, *Fundamentalism and American Culture: The Shaping of Twentieth-Century Evangelicalism, 1870–1925* (Oxford University Press, 1980); Grant Wacker, *Heaven Below: Early Pentecostals and American Culture* (Harvard University Press, 2001); Timothy E. W. Gloege, *Guaranteed Pure: The Moody Bible Institute, Business, and the Making of Modern Evangelicalism* (University of North Carolina Press, 2015), 13.

227. Darren Dochuk, *Anointed with Oil: How Christianity and Crude Made Modern America* (Basic Books, 2019), 12–13, 41–51, 141–181. B. M. Pietsch, "Lyman Stewart and Early Fundamentalism," *CH* 82.3 (2013): 617–646.

228. Quoted in Dochuk, *Anointed with Oil,* 42.

229. Washington Gladden, *Working People and Their Employers* (1876; Funk and Wagnalls, 1894), 14, 15, 21.

230. Andrew Carnegie, "A Confession of Religious Faith," in Burton J. Hendrick, ed., *Miscellaneous Writings of Andrew Carnegie* (Doubleday, Doran, 1933), 2: 297, 303, 307. Herbert Spencer, *Ecclesiastical Institutions: Being Part VI of the Principles of Sociology* (Williams and Norgate, 1885), 843. Herbert Spencer, *First Principles* (Williams and Norgate, 1862).

231. Andrew Carnegie, *The Autobiography of Andrew Carnegie and His Essay "The Gospel of Wealth"* (1920; Signet Classics, 2006), 179.

232. Andrew Carnegie, *Notes of a Trip Round the World* ("private circulation," 1880), 185. "Carnegie Exalted by Bahaist Leader," *New York Times,* 5 September 1915, 9.

233. Carnegie, "Confession of Religious Faith," 297.

234. Burton J. Hendrick, *The Life of Andrew Carnegie* (Doubleday Doran, 1932), 1: 183.

235. Ralph Waldo Trine, *In Tune with the Infinite: Or, Fullness of Peace, Power, and Plenty* (T. Y. Crowell, 1897), 72. Catherine L. Albanese, *A Republic of Mind and Spirit: A Cultural History of American Metaphysical Religion* (Yale University Press, 2007), 394–399; Sydney E. Ahlstrom, *A Religious History of the American People,* 2nd ed. (Yale University Press, 2004), 1019, 1026–1029.

236. The Ford quotations: A. M. Smith, "Magnate and Mystic Meet," *Detroit Free Press,* 7 February 1926, 1–2. See also Samuel S. Marquis, *Henry Ford: An Interpretation* (Little, Brown, 1923), 88–92; Williams, *Religion, Art, and Money,* 200–204.

237. *American Magazine* 131 (February 1941), https://www.thehenryford.org/collections-and-research/digital-resources/popular-topics/henry-ford-quotes/.

238. "The Requirements of the Hardwareman," *Industrial World* 47 (13 August 1896): 17. "Notes and Queries," *Industrial World* 47 (5 November 1896): 1. See also "Missionary Work in Export Trade," *American Trade,* 15 September 1900, 181. This discourse points to a related form of piety, "commercial religion": Daniel Vaca, *Evangelicals Incorporated: Books and the Business of Religion in America* (Harvard University Press, 2019), 2–7, 231–234.

239. Andrew Carnegie, "Wealth," *North American Review* 148.391 (1889): 653–664. Peter Marsh, *The New Industrial Revolution* (Yale University Press, 2012), 8.

240. Quoted in Ralph Waldo Trine and Henry Ford, "The Religion of a Practical Man: He Builds His Own Creed if He Gets the Most Out of Life," *New McClure's* 62.2 (1929): 66–67, 88. See also Ralph Waldo Trine, *The Power That Wins: Henry Ford and Ralph Waldo Trine in an Intimate Talk on Life . . .* (Bobbs-Merrill, 1929).

241. Albert Hatcher Smith, *The Life of Russell H. Conwell, Preacher, Lecturer, Philanthropist; with an Appendix Containing Mr. Conwell's Lecture "Acres of Diamonds" and His Oration "Let There Be Light"* (Silver, Burdett, 1899). Carnegie provided funds for 7,689 church organs at a cost of about $6 million. On Rockefeller's donations: Kenneth W. Rose and Darwin H. Stapleton, "Rockefeller, Religion, and Philanthropy in Gilded Age Cleveland," Rockefeller Archive Center, https://rockarch.issuelab.org/resource/rockefeller-religion-and-philanthropy-in-gilded-age-cleveland.html.

242. "Moral machinery": Henry A. Miles, *Lowell, As It Was, and As It Is,* 2nd ed. (Nathaniel L. Dayton; Merrill and Heywood, 1846), 142; E. P. Thompson, *The Making of the English Middle Class* (1963; Vintage, 1966), 350–374. See also Andrew Ure, *The Philosophy of Manufactures . . .* (C. Knight, 1835), 277, 404–429.

243. Paul Krause, *The Battle for Homestead, 1880–1892: Politics, Culture, and Steel* (University of Pittsburgh Press, 1992). On the ways that industrialists and their defenders framed labor conflict as about non-Protestant immigrant agitators, including in the discourse about the Homestead strike, see Robert F. Zeidel, *Robber Barons and Wretched Refuse: Ethnic and Class Dynamics during the Era of American Industrialization* (Cornell University Press, 2020), 83–106.

244. The service: "Worshipped in the Mill: Chaplain Adams Preaches to the Non-Union Workmen in Homestead," *Chicago Daily Tribune,* 1 August 1892, 1. "Preaching in the Mills," *Indianapolis Journal,* 1 August 1892, 5.

245. Quoted in Herbert G. Gutman, "Protestantism and the American Labor Movement: The Christian Spirit in the Gilded Age," *AHR* 72.1 (1966): 93.

246. Ida M. Tarbell, *The History of the Standard Oil Company* (McClure, Phillips, 1904). Upton Sinclair, *The Jungle* (Doubleday, Page, 1906).

247. "Redeeming the Rivers," *New York Times,* 4 January 1902, 10. Charles Hatch Sears, *The Redemption of the City* (Griffith & Rowland, 1911).

248. Martin E. Marty, *Modern American Religion* (University of Chicago Press), 1: 283. Mary Austin, *Earth Horizon* (Houghton Mifflin, 1932), 268. See also Henry F. May, *Protestant Churches and Industrial America* (Harper and Brothers, 1949).

249. The quotation is on p. 7: Robert Schilling, "Preamble of the Constitution of the Knights of Labor, 1885," *American Catholic History Classroom,* https://cuomeka.wrlc.org/items/show/15.

250. Heath W. Carter, *Union Made: Working People and the Rise of Social Christianity in Chicago* (Oxford University Press, 2015).

251. Pope Leo XIII, *Rerum Novarum*, 15 May 1891, https://www.vatican.va/content/leo-xiii/en/encyclicals/documents/hf_l-xiii_enc_15051891_rerum-novarum.html. Deirdre M. Moloney, *American Catholic Lay Groups and Transatlantic Social Reform* (University of North Carolina Press, 2002), 6. John A. Ryan, *A Living Wage* (Macmillan, 1906). National Catholic War Council, *Social Reconstruction: A General Review of the Problems and Survey of the Remedies*, Reconstruction Pamphlets no. 1 (Committee on Special War Activities, National Catholic War Council, 1919). See also McGreevy, *Catholicism and American Freedom*, 127–146; Carol K. Coburn and Martha Smith, *Spirited Lives: How Nuns Shaped Catholic Culture and American Life, 1836–1920* (University of North Carolina Press, 1999), 189–219. Daniel T. Rogers, *Atlantic Crossings: Social Politics in a Progressive Age* (Harvard University Press, 1998), 63–75.

252. The "Social Gospel" got its name in 1886: Marty, *Modern American Religion*, 1: 286.

253. George Hodges, *Faith and Social Service* (Thomas Whittaker, 1896). Williams, *Religion, Art, and Money*, 132. Keith A. Zahniser, *Steel City Gospel: Protestant Laity and Reform in Progressive-Era Pittsburgh* (Routledge, 2005). Charles Monroe Sheldon, *In His Steps: What Would Jesus Do?* (Fleming H. Revell, 1897). Vida Dutton Scudder, *A Listener in Babel . . .* (Houghton, Mifflin, 1903).

254. Susan Hill Lindley, "The Social Gospel," in Rosemary Skinner Keller et al., eds., *Encyclopedia of Women and Religion in North America* (Indiana University Press, 2006), 3: 1069–1076.

255. Walter Rauschenbusch, *Christianity and the Social Crisis* (Macmillan, 1907). Walter Rauschenbusch, *A Theology for the Social Gospel* (Macmillan, 1917). "The 1908 Social Creed of the Methodist Episcopal Church," United Methodist Church, https://www.umcjustice.org/articles/the-1908-social-creed-of-the-methodist-episcopal-church-822. Federal Council of the Churches of Christ in America, *The Church and Modern Industry* (Federal Council of the Churches of Christ in America, 1908), 9.

256. "Reform Judaism: The Pittsburgh Platform (November 1885)," https://www.jewishvirtuallibrary.org/the-pittsburgh-platform. Quoted in Leonard J. Mervis, "The Social Justice Movement and the American Reform Rabbi," *American Jewish Archives* 7.3 (1955): 178. See Sarna, *American Judaism*, 150, 172, 178–179.

257. Louis Grossman, "Religion from Social Standpoint," *Cincinnati Enquirer*, 8 January 1900, 5.

258. "New Social Religion 'Device of Hell,' He Says," *Detroit Free Press*, 10 January 1911, 11.

259. Gloege, *Guaranteed Pure*. John M. Giggie and Diane Winston, eds., *Faith in the Market: Religion and the Rise of Urban Commercial Culture* (Rutgers University Press, 2002), 13–34, 49. "Soap, soup, and salvation": Priscilla Pope-Levinson, *Building the Old-Time Religion: Women Evangelicals in the Progressive Era* (NYU Press, 2014), 139–171.

260. Art Young, *Jesus Wanted,* a political cartoon depicting Jesus as a socialist agitator, in *The Masses* (1917), Vanderbilt Divinity Library, https://diglib.library.vanderbilt.edu/act-imagelink.pl?RC=55832. "Service for Art Young," *New York Times,* 5 January 1944, 15. See also Jacob H. Dorn, "'In Spiritual Communion': Eugene V. Debs and the Socialist Christians," *Journal of the Gilded Age and Progressive Era* 2.3 (2003): 303–325.

261. Henry George, *Progress and Poverty . . .* (1879; Kegan Paul, Trench, 1882), 11, 416. See also O'Donnell, *Henry George and the Crisis of Inequality,* 3–32.

262. Edward Bellamy, *Looking Backward: 2000–1887* (1888; Penguin, 1984), 22, 194.

263. John Muir, "Letter from John Muir to [Ralph Waldo] Emerson," 18 March 1872, in *John Muir Correspondence,* https://scholarlycommons.pacific.edu/muir-correspondence/1435. Catherine L. Albanese, *Nature Religion in America: From the Algonkian Indians to the New Age* (University of Chicago Press, 1990), 95–105. Lynn Ross-Bryant, "Sacred Sites: Nature and Nation in the U.S. National Parks," *RAC* 15.1 (2005): 31–62.

264. Quotations are from Frederick Law Olmsted, *Public Parks and the Enlargement of Towns: Read before the American Social Science Association . . . 1870* (Riverside Press, 1870), 341. Bellamy's futuristic city also had "large open squares filled with trees." Bellamy, *Looking Backward,* 55.

265. Patrick M. Malone and Charles A. Parrott, "Greenways in the Industrial City: Parks and Promenades along the Lowell Canals," *Journal of the Society for Industrial Archeology* 24.1 (1998): 35–37.

266. Quoted in Harry Silcox, "Henry Disston's Model Industrial Community: Nineteenth-Century Paternalism in Tacony, Philadelphia," *PMHB* 114.4 (1990): 514.

267. Rachel McBride Lindsey, *A Communion of Shadows: Religion and Photography in Nineteenth-Century America* (University of North Carolina Press, 2017), 228. *Cliff Dwellings of Prehistoric Men, Mesa Verde, National Park, Colorado,* Underwood and Underwood, 1911, Library of Congress, https://www.loc.gov/pictures/item/2018647906/. An Act Creating the Mesa Verde National Park, 29 June 1906, Public, No. 353, Chap. 3607.

268. Booker T. Washington, "An Address before the White House Conference on the Care of Dependent Children," [25 January 1909], in Louis R. Harlan et al., eds., *Booker T. Washington Papers* (University of Illinois Press, 1981), 10: 21.

269. Robert P. Sutton, *Communal Utopias and the American Experience: Religious Communities, 1732–2000* (Praeger, 2003), 52–56 (Amana), 67–86 (Oneida), 128–133 (Point Loma).

270. On Shiloh, as well as Zion (1900), see Jonathan R. Baer, "Holiness and Pentecostalism," in Philip Goff, ed., *The Blackwell Companion to Religion in America* (Wiley-Blackwell, 2010), 574.

271. Oneida Community, *Hand-Book of the Oneida Community with a Sketch of Its Founder . . .* (Office of the Circular, Wallingford Community, 1867).

272. Heather D. Curtis, *Holy Humanitarians: American Evangelicals and Global Aid* (Harvard University Press, 2018), 49. Danbom, *Born in the Country,* 152.

273. "New Jersey Jewish Colonies: Their Part in Redeeming the Wild Lands of the State," *Atlanta Constitution*, 27 January 1902, 7.

274. John Lancaster Spalding, *The Religious Mission of the Irish People and Catholic Colonization* (Catholic Publication Society, 1880), 80. "Catholic Colonization," *Boston Daily Globe*, 25 March 1881, 2. See also Moloney, *American Catholic Lay Groups*, 69–91.

275. Danbom, *Born in the Country*, 151–174; R. Douglas Hurt, *American Agriculture: A Brief History*, rev. ed. (Purdue University Press, 2002), 221–279. A movement to plant trees across the grasslands helped erosion control, but there was no environmental restoration of the rural prairie: Philip J. Pauly, *Fruits and Plains: The Horticultural Transformation of America* (Harvard University Press, 2007), 80–98.

276. Jacob A. Riis, *How the Other Half Lives: Studies among the Tenements of New York* (Charles Scribner's Sons, 1890).

277. *Standard Oil Company of New Jersey v. United States*, 221, US 1 (1911).

278. On citizenship demands, see the Yankton-Dakota writer Zitkála-Šá: Z. S., "The Red Man's America," *American Indian Magazine* 5.1 (1917): 64.

279. Rosalyn R. LaPier, *Invisible Reality: Storytellers, Storytakers, and the Supernatural World of the Blackfeet* (University of Nebraska Press, 2017), 3–6.

280. Elizabeth Cady Stanton, "Has Christianity Benefitted Woman?" *North American Review* 140 (1885): 389–399. See also Elizabeth Cady Stanton and Lillie Devereux Blake, *The Woman's Bible* (European Publishing, 1895). Francis E. Willard, *Occupations for Women* (Success Company, 1897), 204–208.

281. Susan Ware, *Why They Marched: Untold Stories of the Women Who Fought for the Right to Vote* (Harvard University Press, 2019). Cathleen D. Cahill, *Recasting the Vote: How Women of Color Transformed the Suffrage Movement* (University of North Carolina Press, 2020). Cathleen D. Cahill, "Marie Louise Bottineau Baldwin: Indigenizing Federal Indian Service," *Studies in American Indian Literatures* 25.2 (2013): 63–86. See also Kathleen Sprows Cummings, *New Women of the Old Faith: Gender and American Catholicism in the Progressive Era* (University of North Carolina Press, 2009).

282. Rory McVeigh, *The Rise of the Ku Klux Klan: Right-Wing Movements and National Politics* (University of Minnesota Press, 2009). Linda Gordon, *The Second Coming of the KKK: The Ku Klux Klan of the 1920s and the American Political Tradition* (Liveright, 2017). Health disparities persisted in the South after 1865, and that played a role in the Great Migration too. On the disparities, see Maria Franklin and Samuel M. Wilson, "A Bioarchaeological Study of African American Health and Mortality in the Post-Emancipation U.S. South," *AA* 85.4 (2020): 652–675.

283. Bonnie Maas Morrison, "Ninety Years of U.S. Household Energy History: A Quantitative Update," *Proceedings of the American Council for an Energy-Efficient Economy*, 10.125 (1992), https://www.aceee.org/files/proceedings/1992/data/papers/SS92_Panel10_Paper17.pdf. See also "History of Energy Consumption in the United States, 1775–2009," US Energy Information Administration, 9 February 2011, https://www.eia.gov/todayinenergy/detail.php?id=10.

284. Nettie P. McGill, "Trend of Child Labor in the United States, 1913 to 1920," *Monthly Labor Review* 12.4 (1921): 1–14.

285. A. P. Duafala, "The Historiography of the West Virginia Mine Wars," *West Virginia History* 12.1–2 (2018): 71–89.

286. Christine Arnold-Lourie, "Baby Pilgrims, Sturdy Forefathers, and One Hundred Percent Americanism: The Mayflower Centenary of 1920," *Massachusetts Historical Review* 17 (2015): 35–66. On "Whiteness," see also W. E. B. Du Bois, *Darkwater: Voices from within the Veil* (Harcourt, Brace and Howe, 1920), 33–59.

287. Horace M. Kallen, "Democracy versus the Melting Pot: A Study of American Nationality," *Nation* 100 (18 February 1915): 190–194. See also this commentary by a Presbyterian-turned-Unitarian social critic who read Kallen and proposed an alternative: Randolph Bourne, "Trans-national America," *Atlantic Monthly* 118.7 (1916): 86–97.

288. See Abram C. Van Engen, *City on a Hill: A History of American Exceptionalism* (Yale University Press, 2020), 113–129, 183–196. Monroe E. Deutsch, "E Pluribus Unum," *Classical Journal* 18.7 (1923): 387–407.

289. *Church of the Holy Trinity v. United States,* 143 U.S. 457 (1892). See also David J. Brewer, *The United States a Christian Nation* (Winston, 1905), 47, 70, 80. For a Jewish critique: Isaac Hassler and Josiah H. Banton, *A Reply to Justice Brewer's Lectures "The United States a Christian Nation"* (L. H. Cahan, 1908). See also Steven K. Green, *The Second Disestablishment: Church and State in Nineteenth-Century America* (Oxford University Press, 2010); Katharine Batlan, "Christ in the Constitution: Contesting Amendment Proposals and Religious Liberty in the United States, 1863–1975," PhD diss., University of Texas at Austin, 2018.

290. Baynton, *Defectives in the Land,* 1–10. Medha D. Makhlouf, "Destigmatizing Disability in the Law of Immigration Admissions," in E. Glenn Cohen et al., eds., *Disability, Health, Law, and Bioethics* (Cambridge University Press, 2020), 190–191. For an opposing view, see [Randolph Bourne], "The Handicapped: By One of Them," *Atlantic Monthly* 108.3 (1911): 320–329.

291. 34 Stat. 596 (Pub. Law 59-338). Quotations from the 1917 immigration law are from section 3: 39 Stat. 874 (Pub. Law 64-301).

292. Nordstrom, *Danger on the Doorstep,* 1–4, 19–144; Higham, *Strangers in the Land,* 178–182. *The Fundamentals: A Testimony to the Truth . . . ,* 12 vols. (Testimony Publishing, 1910–1915); T. W. Medhurst's "Is Romanism Christianity?" (100–112) and J. M. Foster's "Rome, The Antagonist of the Nation" (113–126), in *The Fundamentals,* vol. 11. Marsden, *Fundamentalism,* 4, 118–123.

293. *Birth of a Nation,* directed by D. W. Griffith (Triangle Film Corporation, 1915). See also *Fighting a Vicious Film: Protest against "The Birth of a Nation"* (Boston Branch, National Association for the Advancement of Colored People, 1915).

294. "Address of President Woodrow Wilson," in *Reunion of United Confederate Veterans . . .* (GPO, 1918), 22–24. C. R. Wilson, *Baptized in Blood,* 174–182.

295. Warren G. Harding, "Americanism" speech recorded in New York, 29 June 1920 (Columbia Graphophone, 1920). Harding's letter to Protestant clergy stated

that America was "a Christian nation" and reaffirmed the principles that "marked the Pilgrim settlement." "Harding Opposes 'Recall' of Dry Law," *New York Times,* 26 October 1920, 3. Coolidge also encouraged citizens "to look to the Pilgrims" and Plymouth Rock: Calvin Coolidge, "Law and Order," recorded 2 March 1920, in New York (Columbia Graphophone, 1920).

296. The Coolidge and Lodge quotations are from "Tributes Paid to the Pilgrims in Prose and Poem," *Christian Science Monitor,* 22 December 1920, 1.

297. Arnold-Lourie, "Baby Pilgrims," 56.

298. See Spanish-language newspapers in the US, including *La Prensa* from San Antonio. "Las Cividades mas Antiguas de los Estados Unidos," *La Prensa,* 12 March 1919, 20. "Los Puritanos no Puristas," *La Prensa,* 18 November 1920, 6. "Harding tiene fe en que se lograra implantar la Paz permanente en el Mundo," *La Prensa,* 2 August 1921, 2.

299. "Fight over Milwaukee Pilgrim Pageant Ends," *Detroit Free Press,* 29 May 1921, 9.

300. Some Catholics welcomed the fraudulent stories about the "Kensington Rune Stone," which claimed evidence of Marian devotion among fourteenth-century Vikings in Minnesota. See Francis J. Schaefer, "The Kensington Rune Stone," *Catholic Historical Review* 6.3 (1920): 330–334. Japanese Buddhists claimed national belonging by publishing testimonies of White converts: *Why I Became a Buddhist* (Kyodan Times Sha, "with Headquarters at the Buddhist Mission of North America" [1 January 1920]).

301. Tweed, *America's Church,* 157–191.

302. More than 50,000 Civil War veterans returned for a reunion at Gettysburg in 1913, but only 10,000 remained by 1938.

303. For signs that might worry advocates of immigration and diversity, see "Check Alien Horde, Wallis Demands," *New York Times,* 20 November 1920, 22.

Chapter 8. Reassuring Religion

1. The "Four Freedoms" speech: Franklin D. Roosevelt, annual message to Congress (State of the Union address), 6 January 1941, https://www.fdrlibrary.org/four-freedoms.

2. Martin E. Marty, *Modern American Religion,* vol. 2, *The Noise of Conflict, 1919–1941* (University of Chicago Press, 1991).

3. Warren G. Harding, inaugural address, 4 March 1921, https://avalon.law.yale.edu/20th_century/harding.asp. Daniel L. Dreisbach, "Micah 6:8 in the Literature of the American Founding Era: A Note on Religion and Rhetoric," *Rhetoric and Public Affairs* 12.1 (2009): 91–106. William McKinley, Theodore Roosevelt, Richard Nixon, and Bill Clinton all expressed appreciation for Micah 6:8.

4. George Washington, "Circular to the States," 8 June 1783, in John C. Fitzpatrick, ed., *The Writings of George Washington* (GPO, 1931–1940), 26: 483–484. Jimmy Carter, inaugural address, 20 January 1977, https://avalon.law.yale.edu/20th_century/carter.asp. Carter, like Harding, had his Bible opened to Micah 6:8: Randall Balmer, *Redeemer: The Life of Jimmy Carter* (Basic Books, 2014), 75.

5. *Plessy v. Ferguson,* 163 U.S. 537 (1896).

6. The Native American Citizenship Act: 2 June 1924, Public Law 68-175, 43 Stat. 253. Scott H. Peters and the Grand Council Fire of American Indians, "Memorial and Recommendations of the Grand Council Fire of American Indians presented to the Hon. William Hale Thompson, mayor of Chicago, December 1, 1927," in Robert Costo and Jeanette Henry, eds., *Textbooks and the American Indian* (Indian Historians Press, 1970), 2–4. See also John N. Low, *Imprints: The Pokagon Band of Potawatomi Indians and the City of Chicago* (Michigan State University Press, 2016), 92–93.

7. Harding repeated "America First" in this campaign speech: Warren G. Harding, "Americanism," recorded in New York, 29 June 1920 (Columbia Graphophone, 1920). John Bright, *Hizzoner Big Bill Thompson: An Idyll of Chicago* (Jonathan Cape and Harrison Smith, 1930), 65, 207, 230, 235, 248, 252–253, 265, 278–280.

8. John Higham, *Strangers in the Land: Patterns of American Nativism, 1860–1925* (Atheneum, 1968), 204–212, 242–250; Hiram Wesley Evans, "The Klan's Fight for Americanism," *North American Review* 223.830 (1926): 52.

9. Indigenous communities also used religion to assert their rights: Tisa Wenger, *We Have a Religion: The 1920s Pueblo Indian Dance Controversy and American Religious Freedom* (University of North Carolina Press, 2009).

10. "Thompson Inaugurated," *Chicago Defender,* 1 May 1915, 1; "Plans Complete for 75,000 to March Monday," *Chicago Daily Tribune,* 22 April 1915, 4; "Hail Prosperity Chief," *Washington Post,* 27 April 1915, 3.

11. An Act to Limit the Immigration of Aliens into the United States, 19 May 1921, Ch. 8, 42 Stat. 5.

12. The National Origins Act (Johnson-Reed Act), 26 May 1924, 43 Stat. 153. "Quarreling" led to the delayed implementation of the national origins clause until 1929: Higham, *Strangers in the Land,* 324.

13. William Stell, "Guess Who's Coming to Church: The *Chicago Defender,* the Federal Council of Churches, and Rethinking Shared Faith in Interracial Religious Practice," *CH* 92 (2023): 607–625. On Abbott's newspaper: Ethan Michaeli, *The Defender: How the Legendary Black Newspaper Changed America* (Houghton Mifflin Harcourt, 2016). See also Wallace D. Best, *Passionately Human, No Less Divine: Religion and Culture in Black Chicago, 1915–1952* (Princeton University Press, 2005).

14. David J. Goldberg, "Unmasking the Ku Klux Klan: The Northern Movement against the KKK, 1920–1925," *Journal of American Ethnic History* 15.4 (1996): 39–42. On similar tactics elsewhere: Shawn Lay, *Hooded Knights on the Niagara: The Ku Klux Klan in Buffalo* (NYU Press, 1995).

15. Robert Abbott, editorial, *Chicago Defender,* 19 August 1922, 1.

16. Charles A. McMahon, "Christ's Eucharistic Triumph," *National Catholic Welfare Conference Bulletin* 8.2 (July 1926): 4–6, 26.

17. Lerone A. Martin, T*he Gospel of J. Edgar Hoover: How the FBI Aided and Abetted the Rise of White Christian Nationalism* (Princeton University Press, 2023), 4.

18. Katherine Grafton Miller, *Natchez of Long Ago and the Pilgrimage* (Rellimak Publishing, 1938).

19. Harding and Coolidge attended "Plymouth Day" in 1921: "Plymouth Day, Old Colony Memorial (Plymouth)," 5 August 1921. Christine Arnold-Lourie, "Baby Pilgrims, Sturdy Forefathers, and One Hundred Percent Americanism: The Mayflower Tercentenary of 1920," *Massachusetts Historical Review* 17 (2015): 57–58. Architect Henry Bacon modeled the Lincoln Memorial after the Parthenon, dedicated to the goddess Athena.

20. Harding, inaugural address, 4 March 1921.

21. Calvin Coolidge, inaugural address, 4 March 1925, https://www.presidency.ucsb.edu/documents/inaugural-address-50. Hoover also called on "Almighty God" and encouraged "religious spirit": inaugural address, 4 March 1929, https://avalon.law.yale.edu/20th_century/hoover.asp.

22. Albert Edward Wiggam, *The New Decalogue of Science* (Bobbs-Merrill, 1923), 22, 110. Christine Rosen, *Preaching Eugenics: Religious Leaders and the American Eugenics Movement* (Oxford University Press, 2004). Douglas C. Baynton, "Defect: A Selective Reinterpretation of American Immigration History," in Nancy J. Hirschmann and Beth Linker, eds., *Civil Disabilities: Citizenship, Membership, and Belonging* (University of Pennsylvania Press, 2015), 45–46.

23. Alma White, *The Ku Klux Klan in Prophecy* (Good Citizen, 1925). See Lynn S. Neal, "Christianizing the Klan: Alma White, Branford Clarke, and the Art of Religious Intolerance," *CH* 78.2 (2009): 350–378.

24. Evans, "Klan's Fight for Americanism," 33–63. "Ku Klan Thousands in Colorful Review as Conclave Opens," *Washington Post,* 14 September 1926, 1, 4, 5.

25. "What Is Americanism? Forum Definitions," *Forum* 75.6 (1926): 801–806.

26. For a photograph of the 4 July 1917 graduation ceremony, see https://www.thehenryford.org/collections-and-research/digital-collections/artifact/254569/.

27. Henry Pratt Fairchild, *Melting-Pot Mistake* (Little, Brown, 1926), 9–12. "Pluralism": Horace M. Kallen, *Culture and Democracy in the United States: Studies in the Group Psychology of the American Peoples* (Boni and Liveright, 1924), 43. "Percentage Americanism," *Jewish Advocate* 18 June 1925, A4. See also "True Americanism: A Lesson for the Fourth of July," *Methodist Review* 37.4 (1921): 611; "Dakota Bishop Assails Klan at K. of C. Session," *New York Times,* 7 August 1924, 8; John A. O'Brien, *The Light That Shall Not Fail: An Interpretation of the Mission of America* (International Catholic Truth Society, 1925), 20–21, 26, 30.

28. Calvin Coolidge, "The Spiritual Unification of America," in *Foundations of the Republic: Speeches and Addresses* (Charles Scribner's Sons, 1926), 201–218. *The International Jew: The World's Foremost Problem, Being a Reprint of a Series of Articles Appearing in the Dearborn Independent,* 4 vols. (Dearborn Independent, 1920–1922). Jonathan D. Sarna, *American Judaism* (Yale University Press, 2004), 217. See also Deborah Dash Moore, *At Home in America: Second Generation New York Jews* (Columbia University Press, 1981).

29. William H. J. Kennedy and Sister Mary Joseph Dunn, *America's Story: A History of the United States for the Lower Grades of Catholic Schools* (Benziger Brothers, 1926), ii. Thomas A. Tweed, *America's Church: The National Shrine and*

Catholic Presence in the Nation's Capital (Oxford University Press, 2011), 198. "Alfred E. Smith's Reply to Charles C. Marshall," *Atlantic Monthly* 39 (1927): 728.

30. "Text of President's Address to Holy Name Crusaders," *Washington Post,* 22 September 1924, 4. Tweed, *America's Church,* 170–171.

31. Calvin Coolidge, "Discriminating Benevolence" [26 October 1924], in *Foundations of the Republic,* 169–172.

32. See Herbert Hoover, *American Individualism* (Doubleday, 1922). Herbert Hoover, inaugural address, 4 March 1929. Herbert Hoover, *The Memoirs of Herbert Hoover: The Cabinet and the Presidency, 1920–1933* (Macmillan, 1952), 222–223.

33. Harding, inaugural address, 4 March 1921. See also Marina Moskowitz, *Standard of Living: The Measure of the Middle Class in Modern America* (Johns Hopkins University Press, 2004).

34. Coolidge, inaugural address, 4 March 1925.

35. Coolidge, *Foundations of the Republic,* 39. Calvin Coolidge, "Address to the American Society of Newspaper Editors, Washington, DC," 17 January 1925, https://www.presidency.ucsb.edu/documents/address-the-american-society-newspaper-editors-washington-dc.

36. John L. Brooke, *Climate Change and the Course of Global History: A Rough Journey* (Cambridge University Press, 2014), 403, 411, 526.

37. David J. Goldberg, *Discontented America: The United States in the 1920s* (Johns Hopkins University Press, 1999), 57. Deborah Fitzgerald, *Every Farm a Factory: The Industrial Ideal in American Agriculture* (Yale University Press, 2003), 106–129. R. Douglas Hurt, *American Agriculture: A Brief History,* rev. ed. (Purdue University Press, 2022), 221–277. See also William E. Leuchtenburg, *The Perils of Prosperity, 1914–1932,* 2nd ed. (University of Chicago Press, 1993).

38. Hoover, *Memoirs,* 266. Mary E. McDowell, "Hovels or Homes?," *Opportunity: A Journal of Negro Life* 7.3 (1929): 74–77, 100. H. L. Harris Jr., "A High Mortality Rate—Why?," *Opportunity: A Journal of Negro Life* 7.3 (1929): 8.

39. Thomas Piketty, *Capital in the Twenty-First Century,* trans. Arthur Goldhammer (Harvard University Press, 2014), 30–33.

40. Slowed mainline growth: Bureau of the Census, *Religious Bodies: 1926* (GPO, 1930), 1: 46–69. Robert Handy, *A Christian America: Protestant Hopes, Historical Realities,* 2nd ed. (Oxford University Press, 1984), 174–179.

41. "Kinship between Music and Motor Cars He Finds," *Washington Post,* 24 August 1924, AA6; "Widespread Use of Autos Brings 'Motion Mindedness,'" *Washington Post,* 26 July 1925, R2.

42. Bishop William Bertrand Stevens: "Jazz in Religion Held Modern Church Curse," *Los Angeles Times,* 8 September 1924, A3.

43. Robert S. Lynd and Helen Merrell Lynd, *Middletown: A Study in Modern American Culture* (Harcourt Brace, 1929), 258.

44. Christopher W. Wells, *Car Country* (University of Washington Press, 2012), 125–129. Erin Stewart Mauldin, "The United States in Global Environmental History," in J. R. McNeill and Erin Stewart Mauldin, eds., *Companion to Global Environmental History* (Blackwell, 2012), 144. The quotation: Hoover, *Memoirs,* 183.

45. Margaret Bendroth, "Fundamentalism," in Stephen J. Stein, ed., *The Cambridge History of Religions in America* (Cambridge University Press, 2000), 2: 584; George M. Marsden, *Fundamentalism and American Culture: The Shaping of Twentieth-Century Evangelicalism, 1870–1925* (Oxford University Press, 1980), 4; Daniel R. Bare, *Black Fundamentalists: Conservative Christianity and Racial Identity in the Segregation Era* (NYU Press, 2021); William R. Hutchison, *The Modernist Impulse in American Protestantism* (Oxford University Press, 1976), 2; Thomas A. Tweed, "Tracing Modernity's Flows: Buddhist Currents in the Pacific World," *Eastern Buddhist* 42.1–2 (2012): 46; R. Scott Appleby, *Church and Age Unite: The Modernist Impulse in American Catholicism* (University of Notre Dame Press, 1992).

46. "Commercial religion": Daniel Vaca, *Evangelicals Incorporated: Books and Business of Religion in America* (Harvard University Press, 2019), 2–7, 231–234. See also R. Laurence Moore, *Selling God: American Religion in the Marketplace of Culture* (Oxford University Press, 1994), 204–237; Una M. Cadegan, *All Good Books Are Catholic Books: Print Culture, Censorship, and Modernity in Twentieth-Century America* (Cornell University Press, 2013), 4–5; Leigh Eric Schmidt, *Consumer Rites: The Buying and Selling of American Holidays* (Princeton University Press, 1995); Bethany Moreton, *To Serve God and Wal-Mart: The Making of Christian Free Enterprise* (Harvard University Press, 2009); Timothy E. W. Gloege, *Guaranteed Pure: The Moody Bible Institute, Business, and the Making of Modern Evangelicalism* (University of North Carolina Press, 2015); Amanda Porterfield, Darren Grem, and John Corrigan, eds., *The Business Turn in American Religious History* (Oxford University Press, 2017); Kathryn Lofton, *Consuming Religion* (University of Chicago Press, 2017), 1–13, 197–219; Kristin Kobes Du Mez, *Jesus and John Wayne: How White Evangelicals Corrupted a Faith and Fractured a Nation* (Liveright, 2020), 7–10, 12–18, 29–30, 48, 63–64, 69–70, 81, 190–191, 246, 294, 299–300. By 1925 there were sixty-three church-owned radio stations: Colleen McDannell, "Christianity in the United States during the Inter-War Years," in Hugh McLeod, ed., *The Cambridge History of Christianity* (Cambridge University Press, 2006), 9: 250.

47. "God-given powers": "The Requirements of the Hardwareman," *Industrial World* 47 (13 August 1896): 17. Lew Wallace, *Ben-Hur: A Tale of the Christ* (Harper and Brothers, 1880). Ben-Hur perfume (1904): Andrew Jergens Company, Cincinnati, National Museum of American History, https://americanhistory.si.edu/collections/nmah_1298006. Ben-Hur flour (1903): Howard Miller, "The Charioteer and the Christ: From the Gilded Age to the Culture Wars," *Indiana Magazine of History* 104.2 (2008): 158–159.

48. Bruce Barton, *The Man Nobody Knows: A Discovery of the Real Jesus* (Review of Reviews, 1925). *The Man Nobody Knows,* directed by Errett Leroy Kenepp, black-and-white silent film, Pictorial Clubs, 1925. Erin A. Smith, *What Would Jesus Read? Popular Religious Books and Everyday Life in Twentieth-Century America* (University of North Carolina Press, 2015), 106–132.

49. Richard M. Fried, *The Man Everybody Knew: Bruce Barton and the Making of Modern America* (Ivan R. Dee, 2005), 84–113. The General Motors campaign: Roland

Marchand, "The Corporation Nobody Knew: Bruce Barton, Alfred Sloan, and the Founding of the General Motors 'Family,'" *Business History Review* 65 (1991): 851–853. "Autos Called Great Help to Rural Church," *New York Tribune,* 1 April 1923, A8. Phillip Maciak, "The Resurrection Is in Technicolor: Cecil B. DeMille," in *The Disappearing Christ* (Columbia University Press, 2019), 178–184.

50. Fried, *The Man Everybody Knew,* 99–101. Richard Wightman Fox, *Jesus in America: Personal Savior, Cultural Hero, National Obsession* (HarperSanFrancisco, 2004), 321–322.

51. [Reinhold Niebuhr], "Jesus as Efficiency Expert," *Christian Century* 85 (1925): 851–852.

52. "Monkey Trial a Publicity Stunt, Says Press Agent in $15,000 Suit," *New York Times,* 22 June 1925, 1. *Little Girls with Monkey Dolls,* W. C. Robinson Collection of Scopes Trial Photographs, University of Tennessee, https://digital.lib.utk.edu/collections/islandora/object/scopes%3A161. Michael Lienesch, *In the Beginning: Fundamentalism, the Scopes Trial, and the Making of the Antievolution Movement* (University of North Carolina Press, 2007), 139–170. Shantá Robinson, "A Crusader and an Advocate: The Black Press, the Scopes Trial, and Educational Progress," *Journal of Negro Education* 87.1 (2018): 5–21.

53. Leigh Eric Schmidt, *Village Atheists: How America's Unbelievers Made Their Way in a Godly Nation* (Princeton University Press, 2016), 253–266. R. Laurence Moore, *Godless Citizens in a Godly Republic: Atheists in American Public Life* (W. W. Norton, 2018).

54. Joel A. Carpenter, *Revive Us Again: The Reawakening of American Fundamentalism* (Oxford University Press, 1997), 11.

55. Saima Akhtar, "Immigrant Island Cities in Industrial Detroit," *Journal of Urban History* 41.2 (2015): 182. Sally Howell, *Old Islam in Detroit: Rediscovering the Muslim American Past* (Oxford University Press, 2014), 36–50. Ralph Waldo Trine and Henry Ford, *The Power That Wins: Henry Ford and Ralph Waldo Trine in an Intimate Talk . . .* (Bobbs-Merrill, 1929). Ralph Waldo Trine and Henry Ford, "The Religion of a Practical Man: An Amazing Discussion of an Age-Old Topic by Two Great Minds," *New McClure's* 62.2 (1929): 66–69. Norman Vincent Peale, *The Power of Positive Thinking* (Prentice-Hall, 1952).

56. Philip Deslippe, "The Swami Circuit: Mapping the Terrain of Early American Yoga," *Journal of Yoga Studies* 1 (2018): 5–44. Mersene Sloan, *The Indian Menace . . .* (Way Press, 1929). Michael J. Altman, "The Business of Asian Religions: Guru Entrepreneurs and Godmen CEOs," in Porterfield, Grem, and Corrigan, *The Business Turn in American Religious History,* 159–163.

57. Harold M. Kingsley, "The Negro Goes to Church," *Opportunity: A Journal of Negro Life* 7.3 (1929): 90–91.

58. Quoted in Susan Nance, "Respectability and Representation: The Moorish Science Temple, Morocco, and Black Public Culture in 1920s Chicago," *AQ* 54.4 (2002): 628–629. See also Edward E. Curtis IV, ed., *The Columbia Sourcebook of Muslims in the United States* (Columbia University Press, 2008), 53–64.

59. Jon Butler, *God in Gotham: The Miracle of Religion in Modern Manhattan* (Harvard University Press, 2020), 104–108. Tona J. Hangen, *Redeeming the Dial: Radio, Religion, and Popular Culture in America* (University of North Carolina Press, 2002). Lerone A. Martin, *Preaching on Wax: The Phonograph and the Shaping of Modern American Religion* (NYU Press, 2014). Stephen Lippman, "The Institutional Context of Industry Consolidation: Radio Broadcasting in the United States, 1920–1934," *Social Forces* 86.2 (2007): 469–471, 489–490.

60. The "day of reckoning" meant both Judgment Day, when God will assess a person's or a community's actions, and a financial accounting, a calculation of what has been paid and what is owed. Americans associated it with Genesis 9:5, Genesis 42.22, Leviticus 25:52, Isaiah 10:3–4, Hosea 5:9, Hosea 7:2, and Hebrews 4:12–13.

61. "Slavery in Georgia, A.D. 1921!," *Gazette* (Cleveland), 21 May 1921, 1. M. A. Majors, "Between the Devil and the Deep Blue Sea," *Broad Axe* (Chicago), 5 August 1922, 2.

62. John A. Ryan, "Unemployment: Causes and Remedies," *Catholic World* 128 (1929): 535–542. See also John A. Ryan, *A Living Wage* (Macmillan, 1920). On religion during the Great Depression: Robert T. Handy, "The American Religious Depression, 1925–1935," *CH* 29.1 (1960): 3–16; Alan Brinkley, *Voices of Protest: Huey Long, Father Coughlin, and the Great Depression* (Vintage Books, 1983); Beth S. Wenger, *New York Jews and the Great Depression* (Yale University Press, 1996); Carpenter, *Revive Us Again;* Kenneth J. Heineman, *A Catholic New Deal: Religion and Reform in Depression Pittsburgh* (Pennsylvania State University Press, 1999); McDannell, "Christianity in the United States during the Inter-War Years," 236–251; Darren Dochuk, *From Bible Belt to Sunbelt: Plain-Folk Religion, Grassroots Politics, and the Rise of Evangelical Conservatism* (W. W. Norton, 2011); "Forum: American Religion and the Great Depression," *CH* 80.3 (2011): 575–610.

63. "Girl, Starving to Death, Collapses in Bread Line," *Pittsburgh Courier,* 30 April 1932, 2. Hoover, *American Individualism.*

64. Kenneth J. Heineman, "Religiously Informed Social Reform and Reaction in the Era of the Great Depression," in Stein, *Cambridge History of Religions in America,* 2: 601.

65. Quoted in Kieran W. Taylor, ed., *Charleston and the Great Depression: A Documentary History, 1929–1941* (University of South Carolina Press, 2018), xix.

66. "Address of Governor Franklin D. Roosevelt, Forbes Field, Pittsburgh, Pennsylvania," 19 October 1932, p. 18, typescript, Franklin D. Roosevelt Library and Museum, https://www.fdrlibrary.org/documents/356632/390886/smCampaign_10-19-1932.pdf/eda3f690-4176-4d1f-8fbf-7b432964f34f.

67. Alice Carpenter, "The Day of Reckoning," *New York Herald Tribune,* 16 May 1937, A13. On Carpenter: "Alice Caroline Carpenter," in Mabel Ward Cameron, ed., *Biographical Cyclopedia of American Women* (Halvord Publishing, 1924–1925). See also Adrian Troy, *Day of Reckoning* (1939), woodcut print, Art Institute of Chicago, https://www.artic.edu/artworks/40254/day-of-reckoning. James Truslow Adams, *The Epic of America* (Little, Brown, 1931). Moskowitz, *Standard of Living,* 235.

68. "Money changers": Franklin D. Roosevelt, first inaugural address, 4 March 1933, https://avalon.law.yale.edu/20th_century/froos1.asp. On FDR's religion: Gary Scott Smith, "Franklin Delano Roosevelt and the Quest to Achieve an Abundant Life," in *Faith and the Presidency from George Washington to George W. Bush* (Oxford University Press, 2006), 191–220; Merlin Gustafson and Jerry Rosenberg, "The Faith of Franklin Roosevelt," *Presidential Studies Quarterly* 19 (1989): 559–566; Ronald Isetti, "'The Moneychangers of the Temple': FDR, American Civil Religion, and the New Deal," *Presidential Studies Quarterly* 26 (1996): 678–693. See also Frances Perkins, *The Roosevelt I Knew* (1946; Penguin, 2011), 133–142.

69. Franklin D. Roosevelt, acceptance speech to the Democratic Convention, 2 July 1932, https://www.fdrlibrary.org/dnc-curriculum-hub. Franklin D. Roosevelt, "Campaign Address on Progressive Government at the Commonwealth Club in San Francisco, California," 23 September 1932, https://www.presidency.ucsb.edu/documents/campaign-address-progressive-government-the-commonwealth-club-san-francisco-california.

70. Phillips Brooks, *The More Abundant Life: Lenten Readings . . .* (E. P. Dutton, 1897). "Crowd Turned Away at Riverside Church," *New York Times,* 6 October 1930, 11. Franklin D. Roosevelt, "Address before the Federal Council of Churches of Christ in America," https://www.presidency.ucsb.edu/documents/address-before-the-federal-council-churches-christ-america. Franklin D. Roosevelt, "Letter to the Chief of Chaplains of the War Department," 13 February 1934, https://www.presidency.ucsb.edu/documents/letter-the-chief-chaplains-the-war-department. Franklin D. Roosevelt, "Extemporaneous Speech at the Subsistence Homes Exhibition," 24 April 1934, in Samuel I. Rosenman, comp., *The Public Papers and Addresses of Franklin D. Roosevelt* (Random House, 1938), 3: 199.

71. Arthur Krok, "'More Abundant Life' President's Final Goal," *New York Times,* 7 January 1934, E1. Cyril Brown, "A More Abundant Life," letter to the editor, *New York Times,* 22 April 1935, 20.

72. David M. Kennedy, *Freedom from Fear: The American People in Depression and War, 1929–1945* (Oxford University Press, 1999), 364–365, 775.

73. Quoted in Mauldin, "Environmental History," 144.

74. "Address of Governor Franklin D. Roosevelt, Forbes Field," 19 October 1932, p. 1. Franklin D. Roosevelt, first inaugural address, 4 March 1933. Roosevelt, annual message to Congress, 6 January 1941. Kennedy, *Freedom from Fear,* 379. William Leuchtenberg, *Franklin D. Roosevelt and the New Deal, 1932–1940* (Harper and Row, 1963), 1–26.

75. *Cantwell v. Connecticut,* 310 U.S. 296 (1940). Michael D. McNally, *Defend the Sacred: Native American Religious Freedom beyond the First Amendment* (Princeton University Press, 2020), 61–68. On Native complaints: American Indian Federation, "A Memorial by American Indians," 21 December 1934, in *Indian Conditions and Affairs: Hearings before the Subcommittee on General Bills of the Committee on Indian Affairs, House of Representatives, Seventy-fourth Congress, First Session, on H.R. 7781, and Other Matters* (GPO, 1935), 19–21.

76. Kennedy, *Freedom from Fear,* 364.

77. Waldemar Kaempffert, "Power for the Abundant Life," *New York Times,* 23 August 1936, SM 1–2.

78. Kennedy, *Freedom from Fear,* 290–291, 297. On Perkins's faith: Michelle L. Kew, "Frances Perkins: Private Faith, Public Policy," https://francesperkinscenter.org/wp-content/uploads/2022/08/Frances-Perkins-Private-Faith-Public-Policy-by-Michelle-Kew.pdf. Social Security Act of 1935, 14 August 1935, Public Law 74-271, 49 Stat. 620.

79. Many of the fireside chats are archived at the Franklin Delano Roosevelt Library and Museum, https://www.fdrlibrary.org/utterancesfdr. Eleanor's column ran from 1935 to 1961. For her religious views: Mrs. Franklin D. Roosevelt, "The Place of the Spiritual Forces in the Life of the Nation," *Journal of the Department of History* ("Presbyterian Church in the USA"), 15.7 (1933): 392–395; "What Religion Means to Me," *Forum* 88 (December 1932): 322–324.

80. "Minister, Rabbi, Priest to Make Tolerance Tour," *New York Times* 19 October 1933, 7. Kevin M. Schultz, *Tri-Faith America: How Catholics and Jews Held Postwar America to Its Protestant Promise* (Oxford University Press, 2011), 35–41. Benny Kraut, "Towards the Establishment of the National Conference of Christians and Jews: The Tenuous Road to Religious Goodwill in the 1920s," *American Jewish History* 77.3 (1988): 388–412.

81. Jennifer Wingate, "Framing Race in Personal and Political Spaces: New Deal Photographs of Franklin Delano Roosevelt Portraits in Domestic Settings," *Winterthur Portfolio* 52.2–3 (2018): 137–166.

82. Stephen Wise, *Challenging Years: The Autobiography of Stephen Wise* (G. P. Putnam's Sons, 1949), 221–223. Rafael Medoff, *The Jews Should Keep Quiet: Franklin D. Roosevelt, Rabbi Stephen S. Wise, and the Holocaust* (Jewish Publication Society, 2019), 56. "Texts of Prayers at Inauguration," *New York Times,* 21 January 1937, 17. Ryan also gave the benediction at the 1945 inauguration. On FDR and Catholics, see also Leslie Tentler, *American Catholics: A History* (Yale University Press, 2020), 270; George Q. Flynn, *American Catholics and the Roosevelt Presidency, 1932–1936* (University Press of Kentucky, 1968), 17.

83. Monroe Billington and Cal Clark, "The Episcopal Clergy and the New Deal: Clerical Responses to Franklin D. Roosevelt's Letter of Inquiry, September 1935," *HMPEC* 52.3 (1983): 295, 297. Mary E. Stuckey, *Political Vocabularies: FDR, the Clergy Letters, and the Elements of Political Argument* (Michigan State University Press, 2018), xxvi.

84. "Moses": Quoted in Taylor, *Charleston and the Great Depression,* xxvii. "Word": Quoted in Wayne Flynt, "Religion for the Blues: Evangelicalism, Poor Whites, and the Great Depression," *JSH* 61.1 (2005): 37.

85. Robert S. Lynd and Helen Merrell Lynd, *Middletown in Transition: A Study in Cultural Conflicts* (Harcourt, Brace, 1937). James J. Connolly, "The Legacies of Middletown: Introduction," *Indiana Magazine of History* 101.3 (2005): 217.

86. Heineman, "Religiously Informed Social Reform," 609–613. Darren Dochuk, *Anointed with Oil: How Christianity and Crude Made Modern America* (Basic Books, 2019), 261–263.

87. "Message of the First Presidency to the Church," *One Hundred Seventh Semi-Annual Conference* . . . (Church of Jesus Christ of Latter-day Saints, 1936), 2–3.

88. J. B. Haws, "Mormons at Midcentury," in Keith A. Erekson, Brent M. Rogers, and Spencer W. McBride, eds., *Contingent Citizens: Shifting Perceptions of Latter-day Saints in American Political Cultures* (Cornell University Press, 2020), 202.

89. Sarna, *American Judaism,* 226. Mordecai Menahem Kaplan, *Judaism as a Civilization: Toward a Reconstruction of American-Jewish Life* (1934; Jewish Publication Society, 2010).

90. Handy, *A Christian America,* 174–179. The US Religious Census suggested that White mainline Protestant denominations either grew slowly or declined between 1925 and 1935: *Census of Religious Bodies, 1936: Congregational and Christian Churches: Statistics, Denominational History, Doctrine, and Organization* (GPO, 1940).

91. Miles Mark Fisher, "Negro Churches in Illinois: A Fragmentary History with Emphasis on Chicago," *Journal of the Illinois State Historical* Society 56.3 (1963): 561. Wallace Best, "Olivet Baptist Church," *Encyclopedia of Chicago,* https://encyclopedia.chicagohistory.org/pages/929.html.

92. Christopher Buck, "The Baha'i 'Race Amity' Movement and the Black Intelligentsia in Jim Crow America: Alain Locke and Robert S. Abbott," *Bahá'í Studies Review* 17.1 (2011): 3–46.

93. Judith Weisenfeld, *New World A-Coming: Black Religion and Racial Identity during the Great Migration* (NYU Press, 2016). Jacob S. Dorman, *Chosen People: The Rise of American Black Israelite Religions* (Oxford University Press, 2013). Edward E. Curtis, *Islam in Black America: Identity, Liberation, and Difference in African-American Islamic Thought* (State University of New York Press, 2002). Kambiz GhaneaBassiri, *History of Islam in America: From the New World to the New World Order* (Cambridge University Press, 2010), 193–207. "Howard and Sue Bailey Thurman Meet Mahatma Gandhi (1936)," in Thomas A. Tweed and Stephen Prothero, eds., *Asian Religions in America: A Documentary History* (Oxford University Press, 1999), 215–218.

94. John Vachon for the Farm Security Administration, *Berrien County, Michigan, July 1940, Migrant Agricultural Workers, 'Fruit Tramps' and Families* . . . , Library of Congress, https://www.loc.gov/pictures/item/2004678146/. "Storm Climax . . . Some People Thought the End of the World Was at Hand . . . ," *Liberal News* (Kansas), 15 April 1935. Brad Lookingbill, "'A God-Forsaken Place': Folk Eschatology and the Dust Bowl," *Great Plains Quarterly* 14.4 (1994): 278–280.

95. Robert E. Geier, an Associated Press reporter, used "dust bowl" in "Another Dust Blow Felt," *Lubbock Evening Journal,* 15 April 1935. "Legendary 'Messiah' Service Is Held in Kansas Dust Storm," *Washington Post,* 15 April 1935.

96. Donald Worster, *Dust Bowl: The Southern Plains in the 1930s,* 25th anniversary ed. (1979; Oxford University Press, 2004), 93–94. Jeffrey K. Stine, "A Sense of Place: Donald Worster's 'Dust Bowl,'" *Technology and Culture* 48.2 (2007): 382. Siegfried D. Schubert et al., "On the Cause of the 1930s Dust Bowl," *Science* 303 (19 March 2004): 1855–1859. See also the government-produced documentary *The Plow That Broke the Plains* (1936), which 10 million Americans watched in 1937.

97. John Steinbeck, *The Grapes of Wrath* (Viking, 1939).

98. James Gregory identified 286,746 Southern Plains migrants in California by the 1940 US Census: "The Dust Bowl Migration to California," America's Great Migrations Project, University of Washington, https://depts.washington.edu/moving1/dustbowl_migration.shtml. Many ended up in the labor camps established by the Farm Security Administration. On their religious lives, see Jonathan H. Ebel, *From Dust They Came: Government Camps and the Religion of Reform in New Deal California* (NYU Press, 2023).

99. Carey McWilliams, *Factories in the Field: The Story of Migratory Farm Labor in California* (1939; University of California Press, 1999), 306.

100. Matthew Garcia, *From the Jaws of Victory* (University of California Press, 2012). Nelson Lichtenstein, "Introduction: Symposium on César Chávez and the United Farm Workers," *International Labor and Working-Class History* 83.83 (2013): 143–145. Dochuk, *Bible Belt to Sunbelt.*

101. Frank L. Wright, "Broadacre City, a New Community Plan," *Architectural Record* 77.4 (1935): 243–254. Frank Lloyd Wright, *The Disappearing City* (William Farquhar Payson, 1932), 17, 75–76. See also Ella Wise, "A Gradual Reawakening: Broadacre City and a New American Agrarianism," *Berkeley Planning Journal* 26.1 (2013): 133–149; Courtney Bender, "How and Why to Study Up: Frank Lloyd Wright's Broadacre City and the Study of Lived Religion," *Nordic Journal of Religion and Society* 29.2 (2016): 100–116.

102. Stephen J. Stein, *The Shaker Experience in America* (Yale University Press, 1992), 344–351.

103. Robert P. Sutton, *Communal Utopias and the American Experience, 1732–2000* (Praeger, 2003), 155–157. See also Jill Watts, *God, Harlem U.S.A: The Father Divine Story* (University of California Press, 1992).

104. John C. Rawe, SJ, "Life, Liberty, and the Pursuit of Happiness in Agriculture," in *Catholic Rural Life Objectives: A Second Series of Discussions on Some Elements of Major Importance in the Philosophy of Agrarianism* (National Catholic Rural Life Conference, 1936), 35–45.

105. Luigi G. Ligutti and John C. Rawe, SJ, *Rural Roads to Security: America's Third Struggle for Freedom* (Bruce Publishing Company, 1940), 171–185, 332–336. Christopher Hamlin and John T. McGreevy, "The Greening of America, Catholic Style, 1930–1950," *Environmental History* 11 (2006): 471–472.

106. Paul V. Stock, "The Perennial Nature of the Catholic Worker Farms: A Reconsideration of Failure," *Rural Sociology* 79.2 (2014): 143–173. Dorothy Day, *The Long Loneliness* (Harper and Row, 1952), 222–235.

107. Lizbeth Cohen, *Making a New Deal: Industrial Workers in Chicago, 1919–1939* (Cambridge University Press, 1990), 5–7.

108. Herman Horn grew up on a farm in Eastland, Texas. By 1940 he had moved to Borger and was working for Danube Oil Corporation: Herman L. Horn, World War II Draft Cards, 1940–1947, 16 October 1940, Borger, Texas, National Archives and Records Administration.

109. Ira M. Powell, "Baptist Leaders Overcome Chaotic Conditions to Build Fine Church," *Borger Daily Herald*, 25 July 1940, 4. *St. John the Evangelist Catholic Church:*

Celebrating 90 Years of Catholic Presence in Borger, Texas, 1926–2016 (St. John the Evangelist Church, 2016), 12–14. Hutchison County Historical Commission, *History of Hutchison County, Texas: 104 Years, 1876–1980* (Hutchison County Historical Commission, 1980), 432.

110. Thomas Hart Benton, *Boomtown* (1928), egg yolk and oil on canvas, Marion Stratton Gould Fund, the Encyclopedia Britannica Collection, Memorial Art Gallery, University of Rochester, https://magart.rochester.edu/objects-1/info/211.

111. Hutchison County Historical Commission, *History of Hutchison County,* 30–31. Borger's dusters were worse because of carbon black, a dark powdered material resulting from the combustion of a hydrocarbon in a space fueled by air and natural gas. It had ten carbon black plants.

112. "Mail Bombs Deal Death," *Los Angeles Times* 11 April 1936, 1. "Asserts Religion Dulls Conscience," *New York Times,* 9 May 1932, 13.

113. Mrs. Franklin D. Roosevelt, "Place of the Spiritual Forces in the Life of the Nation," 394.

114. Kennedy, *Freedom from Fear,* 297. Lewis didn't attend services but donated to the Restored Latter-day Saints: Ron Roberts, "A Waystation from Babylon: Nineteenth-Century Saints in Lucas, Iowa," *John Whitmer Historical Association Journal* 11 (1991): 69.

115. George Korson, *Coal Dust on the Fiddle: Songs and Stories of the Bituminous Industry* (University of Pennsylvania Press, 1943), 311–312.

116. Richard J. Callahan Jr., *Work and Faith in the Kentucky Coal Fields: Subject to Dust* (Indiana University Press, 2009), 2.

117. Philip Murray, "Labor's Stake in the Principle of the Dignity of Man," in *Democracy: Should It Survive?* (Bruce Publishing, 1945), 82–83. Melvyn Dubofsky, *Forging a Union of Steel: Philip Murray, SWOC, and the United Steelworkers* (Cornell University Press, 1987), 31, 44. Irving Bernstein, *Turbulent Years: A History of the American Worker, 1933–1941* (Houghton Mifflin, 1970), 444. Kenneth J. Heineman, "Charles Owen Rice and Philip Murray: Irish Apostles of Pennsylvania Labor," *Pennsylvania Legacies* 14.2 (2014): 29. John T. McGreevy, *Catholicism and American Freedom* (W. W. Norton, 2003), 163.

118. *Church Also Used for Union Hall in Coal Mining Town, Caples, West Virginia,* photograph by Marion Post Wolcott, 1938, Farm Security Administration Collection, Library of Congress, https://www.loc.gov/pictures/item/2017752527/. Alessandro Portelli, *They Say in Harlan County: An Oral History* (Oxford University Press, 2010), 211.

119. Edward Brett, "A Monument to Catholic Social Justice: The Maxo Vanka Murals of St. Nicholas Croatian Church, Pittsburgh, Pennsylvania," *American Catholic Studies* 122.1 (2011): 101–107. Jo Ann Bedic Aftanas, *An Historical Introduction to the First Croatian Parish in America: Saint Nicholas Church, 1894–1976* (Saint Nicholas Church, 1976). Gavin Moulton, "Max Vanka's Radical Gaze," 18 September 2023, *Belt Magazine,* https://beltmag.com/maxo-vankas-radical-gaze/.

120. David Spencer, *We Shall Not Be Moved / No Nos Moverán: Biography of a Song of Struggle* (Temple University Press, 2016), 42. It appeared in Edward Boatner's

Spirituals Triumphant, Old and New (Sunday School Publishing Board, 1927) and was recorded by the Taskiana Four, Victor Talking Machine Company, 21 July 1926.

121. "Rebel Unions Hint Plan for Rival to A.F. of L.," *Los Angeles Times,* 23 November 1936, 5.

122. The Homestead ritual: "State Aid Pledged if Unionized Men Lose Steel Jobs," *New York Times,* 6 July 1936, 1; Bernstein, *Turbulent Years,* 434.

123. "Union Leaders Hurl Challenge to Steel Heads," *Washington Post,* 5 July 1936, M4; Jerold Auerbach, ed., *American Labor: The Twentieth Century* (Bobbs-Merrill, 1969), 320–323.

124. Kenneth J. Heineman, "A Catholic New Deal: Religion and Labor in 1930s Pittsburgh," *PMHB* 118.4 (1994): 373.

125. Richard Walker, "Industry Builds the City: The Suburbanization of Manufacturing in the San Francisco Bay Area, 1850–1940," *Journal of Historical Geography* 27.1 (2001): 45–50. "Stella Adoa Baptista: Recollections on Life in the Canneries," conducted by Don Warrin in 2004, Regional Oral History Office, Bancroft Library, University of California, Berkeley, https://digitalassets.lib.berkeley.edu/roho/ucb/text/baptista_stella_adoa.pdf. João Leal, "Festivals, Group Making, Remaking and Unmaking," *Ethnos* 81.4 (2016): 589.

126. Will Prather interview, Sloss Furnaces National Historic Landmark, Birmingham, 1983, https://uab.contentdm.oclc.org/digital/collection/oralhistory/id/799/rec/43. *Polk's Birmingham City Directory: 1938* (Birmingham Chamber of Commerce and R. L. Polk, 1938), 779. Michael W. Fazio, *Landscape Transformations: Architecture and Birmingham, Alabama* (University of Tennessee Press, 2010), 52–57, 127.

127. Francisco Arturo Rosales and Daniel T. Simon, "Mexican Immigrant Experience in the Urban Midwest: East Chicago, Indiana, 1919–1945," *Indiana Magazine of History* 77.4 (1981): 333–357. John H. Flores, *The Mexican Revolution in Chicago: Immigration Policies from the Early Twentieth Century to the Cold War* (University of Illinois Press, 2018), 56–58, 65–68. Emiliano Aguilar, "East Chicago's Failed Utopian Visions," *Belt Magazine,* 1 July 2021, https://beltmag.com/1920s-east-chicago-failed-utopian-vision-segregation-industrialization/. See also Julia G. Young, *Mexican Exodus: Emigrants, Exiles, and Refugees of the Cristero War* (Oxford University Press, 2015).

128. Monica Perales, *Smeltertown: Making and Remembering a Southwest Border Community* (University of North Carolina Press, 2010). Marcia Hatfield Daudistel and Mimi R. Gladstein, *The Women of Smeltertown* (Texas Christian University Press, 2018), 75–94.

129. "Gigantic Statue of Savior Dedicated at Border Shrine," *Los Angeles Times,* 18 October 1940, 22. "Christ upon the Mountain," *Newsweek* 16.18 (28 October 1940): 64–65. Sister M. Lilliana Owens et al., *Most Reverend Anthony J. Schuler, SJ, First Bishop of El Paso . . .* (Revista Católica Press, 1953), 386–416. Young, *Mexican Exodus,* 150–154. I am indebted to my former student: Bailey Kendall, "Patrolling Pilgrimage: Sacred Space on the US–Mexico Border," senior thesis, University of Notre Dame, 2019.

130. Sheen's sermon: Owens et al., *Most Reverend Anthony J. Schuler,* 515–517. Alexander Pavuk, "Constructing a Catholic Church Out of Thin Air: Catholic Hour's Early Years on NBC Radio," *American Catholic Studies* 118.4 (2007): 37–67.

131. FDR's letter: Owens et al., *Most Reverend Anthony J. Schuler,* 412.

132. "Franklin D. Roosevelt, Day by Day," 29 October 1940, Franklin D. Roosevelt Presidential Library and Museum, http://www.fdrlibrary.marist.edu/daybyday/daylog/october-29th-1940/. Smeltertown's residents named streets after fallen World War II soldiers, and they continued to be remembered: "Honoring the Veterans of Foreign Wars Willie Barraza Post 9173," *Congressional Record,* vol. 162, no. 20, 3 February 2016, p. E104.

133. Warner Sallman, *Head of Christ* (1941), Kriebel and Bates, Warner Sallman Collection, Anderson University, https://www.warnersallman.com/collection/images/head-of-christ/. David Morgan, "Warner Sallman and the Visual Culture of American Protestantism," in David Morgan, ed., *Icons of American Protestantism: The Art of Warner Sallman* (Yale University Press, 1996), 52.

134. "Day of Infamy," Franklin D. Roosevelt Presidential Library and Museum, https://www.fdrlibrary.org/pearl-harbor-exhibit. Sandra Yocum Mize, "'We Are Still Pacifists': Dorothy Day's Pacificism during World War II," *ACHS* 108.1–2 (1997): 1–12. Gregory Allen Barnes, *A Centennial History of the American Friends Service Committee* (Friends Press, 2016). Paul R. Dekar, *Dangerous People: The Fellowship of Reconciliation Building a Nonviolent World of Freedom, Justice, and Peace* (Donning Publishers, 2016).

135. Deborah Dash Moore, *GI Jews* (Harvard University Press, 2009); Tweed, *America's Church,* 161–165; Tentler, *American Catholics,* 278–280; "Victory and Peace," statement issued by the Administrative Board of the National Catholic Welfare Conference, 14 November 1942, 175–177.

136. Schultz, *Tri-Faith America,* 3–7. Moore, *GI Jews,* 118–121. William R. Hutchison, *Religious Pluralism in America: The Contentious History of a Founding Ideal* (Yale University Press, 2003), 198–199.

137. "Chaplains at War," *The Living Bible,* no. 3 (1946), https://fourchaplains.org/wp-content/uploads/2020/03/CH-at-WAR.pdf.

138. Franklin D. Roosevelt, "Text of Radio Address—Prayer on D-Day," 6 June 1944, Franklin D. Roosevelt Presidential Library and Museum, https://www.fdrlibrary.org/d-day.

139. Kennedy, *Freedom from Fear,* 856. The estimate of 60 million global fatalities includes 15 to 20 million combat deaths, 35 to 45 million civilians killed by belligerents, and 10 to 20 million who died from famine or disease. Allan Reed Millett, *A War to Be Won: Fighting the Second World War* (Harvard University Press, 2000), 554–556; Gerhard L. Weinberg, *A World at Arms* (Cambridge University Press, 2005), 894; Antony Beevor, *The Second World War* (Little, Brown, 2012).

140. Kennedy, *Freedom from Fear,* 856.

141. Frank S. Adams, "American Minorities," *New York Times,* 7 October 1945. See also Wallace Stegner, *One Nation* (Houghton Mifflin, 1945); Carey McWilliams, *Prejudice: Japanese Americans: Symbol of Racial Intolerance* (Little, Brown, 1944).

142. *Personal Justice Denied: Report of the Commission on Wartime Relocation and Internment of Civilians: Report for the Committee on Interior and Insular Affairs* (GPO, 1982), 18. See also President Gerald R. Ford's "Proclamation 4417, Confirming the Termination of the Executive Order Authorizing Japanese-American Internment during World War II," 19 February 1976, Gerald R. Ford Library and Museum, https://www.fordlibrarymuseum.gov/library/speeches/760111p.htm. Civil Liberties Act of 1988, 10 August 1988, Public Law 100-383, 102 Stat. 903, as codified at 50 U.S.C. app. 1989b *et seq.* FDR's Executive Order 9006 (1942) is reprinted in Tweed and Prothero, *Asian Religions,* 164–166.

143. "National Unity Urged in Plea against Bigotry," *New York Herald Tribune,* 4 July 1940, 14.

144. Greg Robinson, *By Order of the President: FDR and the Internment of Japanese Americans* (Harvard University Press, 2001), 240–248.

145. Galen M. Fisher, "What Race-Baiting Costs America," *Christian Century,* 8 September 1943, 1009–1011. Robert Shaffer, "Opposition to Internment: Defending Japanese American Rights during World War II," *Historian* 61.3 (1999): 597–620. Sarah M. Griffith, *The Fight for Asian American Civil Rights: Liberal Protestant Activism, 1900–1950* (University of Illinois Press, 2018), 103–126. On the White Buddhists: Michihiro Ama, "The First White Buddhist Priestess," in Scott A. Mitchell and Natalie E. F. Quli, eds., *Buddhism beyond Borders: New Perspectives on Buddhism in the United States* (State University of New York Press, 2015), 62. Michihiro Ama, "A Jewish Buddhist Priest: The Curious Case of Julius A. Goldwater and the Hompa Hongwanji Buddhist Temple in 1930s and 1940s Los Angeles," *Southern California Quarterly* 100.3 (2018): 307–310.

146. Duncan Ryūken Williams, *American Sutra: A Story of Faith and Freedom in the Second World War* (Harvard University Press, 2019), 122–148.

147. Tweed and Prothero, *Asian Religions,* 168.

148. Tweed and Prothero, *Asian Religions,* 171. See also Shigeo Kikuchi, *Memoirs of a Buddhist Woman Missionary in Hawaii,* trans. Florence Okada (Buddhist Study Center Press, 1991).

149. Wise, *Challenging Years,* 294. Sarna, *American Judaism,* 258–271.

150. "Other Faiths Join In, Crowd Overflowing Garden Hears Leaders Assail Persecution," *New York Times,* 28 March 1933, 1.

151. "22,000 Nazis Hold Rally in Garden," *New York Times,* 21 February 1939, 1. Maria Mazzenga, "Condemning the Nazi's Kristallnacht: Father Maurice Sheehy, the National Catholic Welfare Conference, and the Dissent of Father Charles Coughlin," *U.S. Catholic Historian* 26.4 (2008): 71–87. Leslie Tentler, *Seasons of Grace: A History of the Catholic Archdiocese of Detroit* (Wayne State University Press, 1990), 336–342. Wise, *Challenging Years,* 246, 293, 294. Stephen S. Wise, *As I See It* (Jewish Opinion Publishing, 1944), 77, 92–97, 251–254. Thomas M. Keefe, "The Mundelein Affair: A Reappraisal," *ACHS* 89.1 (1978): 71–81. Carl Hermann Voss, *Rabbi and Minister: The Friendship of Stephen S. Wise and John Haynes Holmes* (World Publishing, 1964). Rafael Medoff, "American Responses to the Holocaust: New Research, New

Controversies," *American Jewish History* 100.3 (2016): 406. Medoff, *The Jews Should Keep Quiet,* 15–16.

152. The World Jewish Congress representative in Geneva sent Wise a cable on 8 August 1942, and Wise urged FDR to make a statement: Stephen Wise to Franklin D. Roosevelt, 12/2/1942, OF 76-c: Jewish 1942–July 1943 (Church Matters), Collection FDR-FDRPOF: President's Official Files (Roosevelt Administration), Record Group Franklin D. Roosevelt President's Official Files, 1933–1945, Franklin D. Roosevelt Presidential Library and Museum.

153. Ryan's contribution appeared in Stephen S. Wise, ed., *Never Again! Ten Years of Hitler: A Symposium* (Jewish Opinion Publishing, 1943), 16.

154. Wise, *Challenging Years,* 295. Rafael Medoff, *The Anguish of a Jewish Leader: Stephen S. Wise and the Holocaust* (David S. Wyman Institute for Holocaust Studies, 2016); Medoff, *The Jews Should Keep Quiet.* See also Melvin I. Urofsky, *A Voice That Spoke for Justice: The Life and Times of Stephen S. Wise* (State University of New York Press, 1982).

155. Elie Wiesel, *Night* (Bantam, 1982), 32.

156. Mark Fiege, "The Atomic Scientists, the Sense of Wonder, and the Bomb," *Environmental History* 12 (2007): 578–613.

157. "Atomic Age": William L. Laurence, "Drama of the Atomic Bomb Found Climax in July 16 Test," *New York Times,* 26 September 1945, 1. Ferenc Morton Szasz, *The Day the Sun Rose Twice: The Story of the Trinity Site Nuclear Explosion, July 16, 1945* (University of New Mexico Press, 1984), 28–31. On the White Sands footprints (fig. 4), see Matthew R. Bennett et al., "Evidence of Humans in North America during the Last Glacial Maximum," *Science* 373 (2021): 1528–1531.

158. Szasz, *Day the Sun Rose Twice,* 41–42. James A. Hijiya, "The 'Gita' of J. Robert Oppenheimer," *Proceedings of the American Philosophical Society* 144.2 (2000): 161–164.

159. Felix Adler, *Creed and Deed* (G. P. Putnam's Sons, 1880), 1. Richard Polenberg, "The Ethical Responsibilities of the Scientist: The Case of J. Robert Oppenheimer," in William H. Chafe, ed., *The Achievement of American Liberalism: The New Deal and Its Legacies* (Columbia University Press, 2002), 131–133. Arthur W. Ryder helped him read the *Gita* in Sanskrit. See Arthur W. Ryder, trans., *The Bhagavad-Gita* (University of Chicago Press, 1929).

160. My quotation of the first passage (11:12) uses Ryder's 1929 translation. The second passage (11:32) reproduces Laurence's published recollection and Oppenheimer's phrasing in a *Time* story and an NBC documentary. Other translators render the word as "Time," not "Death." Ryder, *Bhagavad-Gita,* 84, 88. Laurie Patton, trans., *The Bhagavad Gita* (Penguin, 2008), 126, 131. William L. Laurence, *Men and Atoms: The Discovery, the Uses, and the Future of Atomic Energy* (Simon & Schuster, 1959), 118. "The Eternal Apprentice," *Time,* 8 November 1948, 77. Fred Freed and Len Giovannitti, *NBC White Paper: The Decision to Drop the Bomb* (NBC Universal, 1965). Hijiya, "'Gita' of J. Robert Oppenheimer," 123–125, 130–133, 151–153, 161–165. Polenberg, "Ethical Responsibilities of the Scientist," 135.

161. "Groves and Farrell Watching Trinity," Atomic Heritage Foundation, https://ahf.nuclearmuseum.org/ahf/key-documents/groves-farrell-watching-trinity/.

162. Victor Frederick Weisskopf, *The Joy of Insight: Passions of a Physicist* (Basic Books, 1991), 152. He was referring to Matthias Grünewald, *Isenheim Altarpiece: Resurrection* (ca. 1515), oil on wood, 269 × 141 cm, Musée d'Unterlinden, Colmar, France.

163. Laurence, "Drama of the Atomic Bomb Found Climax in July 16 Test," 16.

164. Beevor, *Second World War,* 774.

165. Hersey's reporting appeared as a 1946 *New Yorker* issue and as a book: John Hersey, *Hiroshima* (Alfred A. Knopf, 1946). See also David A. Hollinger, *Protestants Abroad: How Missionaries Tried to Change the World but Changed America* (Princeton University Press, 2017), 46–58; Michael J. Yavenditti, "John Hersey and the American Conscience: The Reception of 'Hiroshima,'" *Pacific Historical Review* 43.1 (1974): 24–49; Paul S. Boyer, *By the Bomb's Early Light: American Thought and Culture at the Dawn of the Atomic Age* (Pantheon, 1985), 203–210. The quotation is from the report of the Commission on the Relation of the Church to the War in the Light of the Christian Faith, which was appointed by the Federal Council of Churches: *Atomic Warfare and the Christian Faith* (Federal Council of Churches, [1946]), 11–12.

166. Joseph Papalia, "William Downey's Interview—Part 1," 1987, Voices of the Manhattan Project, https://ahf.nuclearmuseum.org/voices/oral-histories /william-downeys-interview-part-1.

167. Peter N. Kirstein, "Hiroshima and Spinning the Atom: America, Britain, and Canada Proclaim the Nuclear Age," *Historian* 71.4 (2009): 805–827.

168. "Press Release by the White House, August 6, 1945," Harry S. Truman Library and Museum, https://www.trumanlibrary.gov/library/research-files/press-release-white-house.

169. W. H. Laurence, "2nd Big Aerial Blow . . . Result Called Good," *New York Times,* 9 August 1945, 1.

170. David W. Moore, "Majority Supports Use of Atomic Bomb on Japan in WWII," https://news.gallup.com/poll/17677/majority-supports-use-atomic-bomb-japan-wwii.aspx; Those poll numbers declined to 59 percent by the fiftieth anniversary of Hiroshima.

171. Press Department, NCWS News Service, "Moral Aspects of Using Atomic Power in Warfare Reviewed by Theologians," *National Catholic Welfare Conference News Service,* 13 August 1945, 1–2. "Use of Atom Bomb Assailed by Sheen; Only Effective Control Is by Moral Education, He Tells St. Patrick's Audience," *New York Times,* 8 April 1946, 20.

172. "Atom Bombing 'an Atrocity,' Churchmen Say," *New York Herald Tribune,* 20 August 1945, 9.

173. *Atomic Warfare and the Christian Faith,* 11–12.

174. *Atomic Warfare and the Christian Faith,* 11–12.

175. Quoted in "Thanks for Peace Given in Churches," *New York Times,* 23 November 1945, 34.

176. W. H. Auden, *The Age of Anxiety* (Random House, 1947). Arthur M. Schlesinger, *The Vital Center: The Politics of Freedom* (Houghton Mifflin, 1949), 1–2. George Cotkin, *Existential America* (Johns Hopkins University Press, 2003), 54–87.

177. Cover, *Bulletin of the Atomic Scientists* 3.6 (June 1947).

178. Harry S. Truman to Mrs. Haydon Klein Jr., 4 August 1964, Folder: The Decision to Drop the Atomic Bomb, Series: Post-Presidential File, Harry S. Truman Library and Museum. "Text of President Truman's Address to Federal Council of Churches," *New York Times,* 7 March 1946, 14.

179. Harry S. Truman, "Radio and Television Remarks on Election Eve," 3 November 1952, Harry S. Truman Library and Museum, https://www.trumanlibrary.gov/soundrecording-records/sr59-263-radio-and-television-remarks-election-eve-president-truman-kansas.

180. Jonathan P. Herzog, *The Industrial-Spiritual Complex: America's Religious Battle against Communism in the Early Cold War* (Oxford University Press, 2011), 19–120. Federal Civil Defense Administration, Alert America/Federal Civil Defense Administration/GPO, 1952 O-999841, Poster Series 1B-6, artist's signature, Lee D+P, Harry S. Truman Library and Museum. George Hansen, "Alert America! Retailers Are Invited to Help the Nation Prepare Its Civil Defense," *Stores: The Bulletin of the National Retail Dry Goods Association* 34 (1952): 21–23.

181. Document 153, Memorandum of a Conference with the President, White House, Washington, 4 November 1957, in William Klingaman, David Patterson, and Ilana Stern, eds., *Foreign Relations of the United States, 1955–1957,* vol. 19, *National Security Policy* (GPO, 1990), https://history.state.gov/historicaldocuments/frus1955-57v19/d153.

182. "Enter the Survival Merchants," *Consumer Reports* 27.1 (January 1962): 47. Thomas Bishop, "'The Struggle to Sell Survival': Family Fallout Shelters and the Limits of Consumer Citizenship," *Modern American History* 2 (2019): 132. See also Kenneth D. Rose, *One Nation Underground: The Fallout Shelter in American Culture* (NYU Press, 2004).

183. Howard Thurman, *Jesus and the Disinherited* (1949; Beacon, 1996), 26–47.

184. Steven Mintz, *Huck's Raft: A History of American Childhood* (Harvard University Press, 2004), 285–295.

185. "Gilbert U-238 Atomic Energy Lab (1950–1951)," Museum of Radiation and Radioactivity, Oakridge Associated Universities, https://www.orau.org/health-physics-museum/collection/toys/gilbert-u-238-atomic-energy-lab.html.

186. Gladwin Hill, "Atomic-Age Sight-Seeing Way Out West," *New York Times,* 15 April 1951, 266. Karen R. Jones and John Wills, "Turn Here for 'The Sunny Side of the Atom': Tourism, the Bomb and Popular Culture in the Nuclear West," in *The American West: Competing Visions* (Edinburgh University Press, 2009), 284–304.

187. Elaine Tyler May, *Homeward Bound* (Basic, 1999), 23. *If the Bomb Falls: A Recorded Guide to Survival,* 33⅓ rpm LP recording, David Wiley, narrator (Tops Records, 1961.)

188. Andrea Tone, *The Age of Anxiety: A History of America's Turbulent Affair with Tranquilizers* (Basic Books, 2009), 52. David Herzberg, *Happy Pills in America: From Milltown to Prozac* (Johns Hopkins University Press, 2009).

189. Lizbeth Cohen, *A Consumers Republic: The Politics of Mass Consumption in Postwar America* (Vintage, 2004), 257–289.

190. By 1960 one-third of Americans lived in suburbs: Kevin M. Kruse and Thomas I. Sugrue, eds., *The New Suburban History* (University of Chicago Press, 2006), 1. Herbert J. Gans, *The Levittowners: Ways of Life and Politics in a New Suburban Community* (Vintage Books, 1967). On suburban religion: Gibson Winter, *The Suburban Captivity of the Churches* (Doubleday, 1961); James Hudnut-Beumler, "Suburbanization and Religion," in Stein, *Cambridge History of Religions in America,* 3: 106–125; Stephen M. Koeth, CSC, "Crabgrass Catholicism: U.S. Catholics and the Historiography of Postwar Suburbia," *U.S. Catholic Historian* 37.4 (2019): 1–27; Mauri and Florence E. Edwards, "The New Suburbanite: What's He Think of It All?" *New York Herald Tribune,* 30 March 1958, F6. On economic inequality in the suburbs: Tim Keogh, *In Levittown's Shadow: Poverty in America's Wealthiest Suburb* (University of Chicago Press, 2023).

191. A. Roy Eckardt, *The Surge of Piety in America: An Appraisal* (Association Press, 1958).

192. The statistics from the Princeton Religious Research Index (PRRI) are cited in Schultz, *Tri-Faith America,* 74.

193. Bureau of the Census, "Religion Reported by the Civilian Population of the United States: March 1957," *Current Population Reports: Population Characteristics,* series P-20, no. 79, 2 February 1958 (GPO, 1958). See also Hazel Gaudet Erskine, "The Polls: Church Attendance," *Public Opinion Quarterly* 28.4 (1964): 672; Sidney Goldstein, "Socioeconomic Differentials among Religious Groups in the United States," *American Journal of Sociology* 74.6 (1969): 615–617; Samuel A. Mueller and Angela V. Lane, "Tabulations from the 1957 Current Population Survey on Religion: A Contribution to the Demography of American Religion," *JSSR* 11.1 (1972): 76–98; Kevin M. Schultz, "Religion as Identity in Postwar America: The Last Serious Attempt to Put a Question on Religion in the United States Census," *JAH* 93.2 (2006): 359–384.

194. Jonathan Herzog, "America's Spiritual-Industrial Complex and the Policy of Revival in the Early Cold War," *Journal of Policy History* 22.3 (2010): 337–365. R. Laurence Moore, "Top-Down Religion and the Design of Post–World War II American Pluralism," *Modern Intellectual History* 10.1 (2013): 233–243.

195. Harry S. Truman, inaugural address, 20 January 1949, https://www.presidency.ucsb.edu/documents/inaugural-address-4. Harry S. Truman, "Proclamation 2978—National Day of Prayer, 1952," 17 June 1952, https://www.presidency.ucsb.edu/documents/proclamation-2978-national-day-prayer-1952.

196. William Lee Miller, *Piety along the Potomac: Notes on Politics and Morals in the Fifties* (Houghton Mifflin, 1964). Ike's pastor responded to Miller: "President's Pastor Strikes Back," *Washington Post,* 12 January 1959, B1. See also William Inboden, *Religion and American Foreign Policy, 1945–1960* (Cambridge University Press, 2008);

Hutchison, *Religious Pluralism;* Herzog, *Industrial-Spiritual Complex;* Schultz, *Tri-Faith America;* James C. Wallace, "A Religious War? The Cold War and Religion," *Journal of Cold War Studies* 15.3 (2013): 162–180; Kevin M. Kruse, *One Nation under God: How Corporate America Invented Christian America* (Basic Books, 2015).

197. Dwight D. Eisenhower, inaugural address, 20 January 1953, https://www.presidency.ucsb.edu/documents/inaugural-address-3.

198. *The National Presbyterian Church: The First 200 Years, 1795–1995* (National Presbyterian Church, 1996), 22. He was annoyed at the publicity: Dwight D. Eisenhower, Diaries Files, Box 1, 1953 [DDE] Desk Diary, NAID #575354, Dwight D. Eisenhower Presidential Library, Museum, and Boyhood Home. On Ike's faith: David L. Holmes, *The Faiths of the Postwar Presidents from Truman to Obama* (University of Georgia Press, 2012), 24–44. "Mainline" Protestantism: Elesha Coffman, "The Measure of a Magazine: Assessing the Influence of the *Christian Century,*" *RAC* 22.1 (2012): 55, 59–61, 74–75, 77n8; William R. Hutchison, ed., *Between the Times: The Travail of the Protestant Establishment in America, 1900–1960* (Cambridge University Press, 1989), 3–13.

199. "'Back to God' Drive Enlists President," *New York Times,* 2 February 1953, 13. "God and Country" and "one hundred percent Americanism" are from the preamble to their constitution. See *Condensed History of American Legion* (National Publicity Division, American Legion, 1945).

200. Ike's appointment book records that he met with the NAE at 9 a.m. on 2 July. For his endorsements, see "Ike Approves Evangelicals' Aim," *Washington Post,* 3 July 1953, 11; "Eisenhower Signs Tract Telling Religion's Role," *New York Herald Tribune,* 3 July 1953, 5. See also Carpenter, *Revive Us Again,* 147–150.

201. Hayes B. Jacobs, "Oral Roberts: High Priest of Faith Healing," *Harper's,* 224.1341 (1962): 40, 41. Oral Roberts, *Expect a New Miracle Every Day* (Oral Roberts Evangelic Association, 1963), 31. See also Kate Bowler, *Blessed: A History of the American Prosperity Gospel* (Oxford University Press, 2013), 48.

202. Louis Fisher and Nada Mourtada-Sabbah, "Adopting 'In God We Trust' as the U.S. National Motto," *Journal of Church and State* 44.4 (2002): 680–683. Tweed, *America's Church,* 182, 340n37. On the "contrived" image of Washington kneeling: Sheila Brennan, *Stamping American Memory* (University of Michigan Press, 2018), 118–121. Challenging the image: W. E. Woodward, *George Washington, the Image and the Man* (Boni and Liveright, 1926); Mary V. Thompson, *"In the Hands of a Good Providence": Religion in the Life of George Washington* (University of Virginia Press, 2008), 91–100; "Protests against Washington Stamp," *Daily Boston Globe,* 8 May 1928, 6; Isaac R. Pennypacker, "Valley Forge," *American Mercury,* March 1926, 341–345; Thomas F. Rzeznik, "'Representatives of All That Is Noble': The Rise of the Episcopal Establishment in Early-Twentieth-Century Philadelphia," *RAC* 19.1 (2009): 81–87.

203. I am indebted to my student: Madeline Doctor, "From Shared Meanings to Shattered Solidarity: The History, Representations, and Uses of the Congressional Prayer Room, 1952–2000," senior thesis, University of Notre Dame, 2019. David Judson and Steffie Nelson, *Judson: Innovation in Stained Glass* (Angel City Press, 2020).

Opened to Psalm 23: Rev. Margaret Grun Kibben, "Congressional Prayer Room," Office of the Chaplain, https://chaplain.house.gov/religion/prayer_room.html.

204. A Unitarian minister criticized the Prayer Room, noting that "Washington never was known to kneel in prayer": "Prayer Room Scored," *New York Times,* 28 March 1955, 20.

205. Paul Hutchison, "Have We a New Religion?," *Life,* 11 April 1955, 138, 140, 143–144, 147, 150, 155, 157–158. Eckardt, *Surge of Piety.* Martin E. Marty, *The New Shape of American Religion* (Harper and Row, 1958). Miller, *Piety along the Potomac.* John Cogley, ed., *Religion in America: Original Essays on Religion in a Free Society* (Meridian, 1958). Carol V. R. George, *God's Salesman* (Oxford University Press, 2019), 136–144. On "excessive nationalism": "Text of Catholic Bishops' Statement on 'Freedom and Peace,'" *New York Times,* 22 November 1959, 76. See also Abraham Joshua Heschel, "The Religious Message," in Cogley, *Religion in America,* 244–271.

206. Kay Starr, "The Man Upstairs," Capitol Records, T415, 1954, written by Dorinda Morgan, Harold Stanley, and Gerry Manners. "God and the Juke-Box," *Christian Century,* 22 December 1954, 1543–1544. Cecil B. DeMille et al., *The Ten Commandments,* 1923 and 1956 versions (Paramount Pictures).

207. Grant Wacker, *America's Pastor: Billy Graham and the Shaping of a Nation* (Harvard University Press, 2014), 13–15, 21, 65, 84, 124–125.

208. Norman Vincent Peale, "Drivers Find God at Filling Station," *Washington Post,* 7 August 1954, 15. Patrick Peyton, CSC, who promoted the Family Rosary Crusade, inspired him.

209. I refer to the John E. Mitchell Company: Elizabeth Fones-Wolf and Ken Fones-Wolf, "Managers and Ministers: Instilling Christian Free Enterprise in the Postwar Workplace," *Business History Review* 89.1 (2015): 110, 116. See also Chad E. Seales, "Corporate Chaplaincy and the American Workplace," *Religion Compass* 6.3 (2012): 195–203.

210. *The Catholic World in Pictures,* 28 January 1952, 1. National Catholic Welfare Conference, "Back from 32-Day Global Tour, Cardinal Spellman Takes Part in Boston Airport Chapel Rites," *NCWC News Service,* 21 January 1952, 14. See also Wendy Cadge, "The Evolution of American Airport Chapels: Local Negotiations in Religiously Plural Contexts," *RAC* 28.1 (2018): 135–165. "Chapel Is Dedicated at Shopping Center," *Catholic Transcript* 42.40 (4 February 1960): 7.

211. Mary Ann Watson, "Bishop Sheen's Show *Life Is Worth Living* in the 1950s," *Television Quarterly* 30.2 (1999): 80–85.

212. Fulton J. Sheen, *Life Is Worth Living* (McGraw-Hill, 1953). See Smith, *What Would Jesus Read?,* 157–198.

213. Harry Emerson Fosdick, *On Being a Real Person* (Harper, 1943).

214. Joshua Loth Liebman, *Peace of Mind* (Simon & Schuster, 1946). Andrew R. Heinze, "*Peace of Mind* (1946): Judaism and the Therapeutic Polemics of Postwar America," *RAC* 12.1 (2002): 32.

215. Fulton J. Sheen, *Peace of Soul* (McGraw-Hill, 1949). Billy Graham, *Peace with God* (Doubleday, 1953). Wacker identifies Ruth Graham and the ghostwriter, Janet Baird, as coauthors: Wacker, *America's Pastor,* 159–161.

216. Peale, *Positive Thinking.*

217. Hutchison, "Have We a New Religion?," 148. See also Eckardt, *Surge of Piety,* 75; Donald Meyer, *The Positive Thinkers: Popular Religious Psychology from Mary Baker Eddy to Norman Vincent Peale and Ronald Reagan,* rev. ed. (Wesleyan University Press, 1988), 262; George, *God's Salesman,* 4–5, 123–136.

218. Bowler, *Blessed,* 59. Dochuk, *Bible Belt to Sunbelt,* 168–195. Connections with Nixon, Trump, and Reagan: George, *God's Salesman,* 157–229. On Nixon and Peale, see Holmes, *Faiths of the Postwar Presidents,* 99–123. On Reagan, see Meyer, *Positive Thinkers,* 368–393. "Christian libertarianism": Gerardo Martí and Mark T. Mulder, "Capital and the Cathedral: Robert H. Schuller's Continual Fundraising for Church Growth," *RAC* 30.1 (2020): 66.

219. Norman Vincent Peale, "Only Earned Tranquility Is Permanent," *Chicago Daily Tribune* 9 November 1957, 20.

220. Catherine L. Albanese, *A Republic of Mind and Spirit: A Cultural History of American Metaphysical Religion* (Yale University Press, 2007), 442–447. Ralph Waldo Trine, *The Power That Wins: Henry Ford and Ralph Waldo Trine in an Intimate Talk on Life . . .* (Bobbs-Merrill, 1929). See also Trine and Ford, "Religion of a Practical Man."

221. Jack Kerouac, *The Dharma Bums* (Viking, 1958). Thomas A. Tweed, "Buddhism, Art, and Transcultural Collage: Toward a Cultural History of Buddhism in the United States, 1945–2000," in Charles L. Cohen and Ronald L. Numbers, eds., *Gods in America: Religious Pluralism in the United States* (Oxford University Press, 2013), 193–227. Cotkin, *Existential America,* 35–87. R. Gordon Wasson, "Seeking the Magic Mushroom," *Life,* 13 May 1957, 100–120.

222. Norman Vincent Peale, *Stay Alive All Your Life* (1957; Fireside, 2003), 96.

223. Eckardt, *Surge of Piety,* 82.

224. Kennedy, *Freedom from Fear,* 857. James T. Patterson, *Grand Expectations: The United States, 1945–1974* (Oxford University Press, 1996), 68, 320–326.

225. Dwight D. Eisenhower, second inaugural address, 21 January 1957, https://www.presidency.ucsb.edu/documents/second-inaugural-address. Howard R. Bowen, *The Social Responsibilities of the Businessman* (Harper, 1953). For evangelical criticism, see "Ten Books on Ethics and Economics," *Christianity Today* 3.19 (3 June 1959): 12.

226. Billy Graham, "The Sin of Tolerance," *Christianity Today* 3.9 (2 February 1959): 3–4. L. C. Hugh, SJ, "Working Definitions: Our Post-Protestant Pluralism," *America* 102 (5 March 1960): 675. Amanda Brown, *The Fellowship Church: Howard Thurman and the Twentieth-Century Religious Left* (Oxford University Press, 2021).

227. "Letter to President Harry Truman from Representatives of the Hopi Indian Empire, Hopi Indian Empire," in Armin W. Geertz, *The Invention of Prophecy: Continuity and Meaning in Hopi Indian Religion* (University of California Press, 1994), 441–443. John F. Kennedy, "Remarks to Representatives of the National Congress of American Indians, 5 March 1963," https://www.jfklibrary.org/asset-viewer/archives/jfkwha-168-006.

228. "Trio Sentenced for Peyote Use," *Desert Sun* 36.181 (30 November 1962): 11.

229. An Act to Revise the Laws Relating to Immigration, Naturalization, and Nationality, 27 June 1952, 66 Stat., 163.

230. On Ike, oil, and religion: Dochuk, *Anointed with Oil,* 323, 369, 379–388.

231. On Taft: Matthew L. Harris, *Thunder from the Right* (University of Illinois Press, 2019). John H. Erickson, *Orthodox Christians in America: A Short History* (Oxford University Press, 2008), 91.

232. Sarna, *American Judaism,* 272–306.

233. George, *God's Salesman,* 185–194. McGreevy, *Catholicism and American Freedom,* 166–169. See also Paul Blanshard, *American Freedom and Catholic Power* (Beacon, 1949).

234. Tweed, *America's Church,* 157–191.

235. Darren Dochuk, "Religion in Post-1945 America," *Oxford Research Encyclopedia of American History,* https://doi.org/10.1093/acrefore/9780199329175.013.37.

236. Elesha J. Coffman, *The Christian Century and the Rise of the Protestant Mainline* (Oxford University Press, 2013), 206. Bowler, *Blessed,* 41–60. Carpenter, *Revive Us Again,* 154–159, 176, 187–210. Daniel Silliman, "An Evangelical Is Anyone Who Likes Billy Graham: Defining Evangelicalism with Carl Henry and Networks of Trust," *CH* 90 (2021): 621–643.

237. Coffman, *Christian Century,* 218–224. Hutchison, *Between the Times.* James D. Davidson, Ralph E. Pyle, and David V. Reyes, "Persistence and Change in the Protestant Establishment, 1930–1992," *Social Forces* 74.1 (1995): 157–175. See also Robert P. Jones, *The End of White Christian America* (Simon & Schuster, 2016), 257.

238. Quoted in George, *God's Salesman,* 186–187.

239. Martin Marty, "The New Establishment," *Christian Century* (15 October 1958): 1179. See also John Courtney Murray, "The Problem of Pluralism in America," *Catholic Lawyer* 1.3 (1955): 223–241. Thurston N. Davis, SJ, "Cabots and Kennedys: Our Post-Protestant Pluralism," *America* 102 (5 March 1960): 675–677. Reinhold Niebuhr, "A Note on Pluralism," in Cogley, *Religion in America,* 42–50.

240. Ruby Jo Kennedy, "Single or Triple Melting Pot? Intermarriage Trends in New Haven, 1870–1940," *American Journal of Sociology* 49.4 (1944): 331–339. Will Herberg, *Protestant–Catholic–Jew: An Essay in Religious Sociology* (Doubleday, 1955), 32–33. On the chapel: Hutchison, *Religious Pluralism,* 209–213.

241. Martin E. Marty, "The New Establishment," third in a series entitled "The New Shape of American Religion," *Christian Century* 75.42 (15 October 1958): 1176–1179. The essays also appeared as Marty, *New Shape of American Religion.* John Courtney Murray, SJ, "America's Four Conspiracies," in J. Cogley ed., *Religion in America* (Meridian 1958), 12–41. John Courtney Murray, SJ, *We Hold These Truths: Catholic Reflections on the American Proposition* (Sheed and Ward, 1960), 5–24. Herberg rejected the category "secular humanists": Herberg, *Protestant–Catholic–Jew,* 32–33; Schultz, *Tri-Faith America,* 89. Justice Hugo Black didn't cite Murray or Marty when he used "secular humanism" in footnote 11 of his decision in *Torcaso v. Watkins,* 367 US 488 (1961). Yet a brief quoted Murray as proposing "Secularist" (p. 12): *Torcaso v. Watkins,* 1961 WL 102251 (Appellate Brief) (U.S. Jan. 20, 1961), Brief for the American Ethical Union as Amicus Curiae (No. 373). See also

Joseph L. Blau, "Who First Used the Words 'Secular Humanism'?," *New York Times,* 19 June 1985, A22. The phrase reappeared in the "creationism" debate: Lienesch, *In the Beginning,* 212–219; Kathleen M. Sands, *America's Religious Wars: The Embattled Heart of Our Public Life* (Yale University Press, 2019), 211–212.

242. Ed Cray, *Chief Justice: A Biography of Earl Warren* (Simon & Schuster, 1997), 61–62.

243. *Engel v. Vitale,* 370 US 321 (1962). *Abington v. Schempp,* 374 US 203 (1963). Schempp and Unitarianism: Kimberly French, "A Victory for the Heretics," *UU World* (January/February 2003), https://www.uuworld.org/articles/ellery-schempp-stood-religious-mi.

244. Sarah Imhoff, "The Creation Story, or How We Learned to Stop Worrying and Love 'Schempp,'" *JAAR* 84.2 (2016): 466–497. Corinna Barrett Lain, "God, Civic Virtue, and the American Way: Reconstructing *Engel,*" *Stanford Law Review* 67.3 (2015): 479–555. On "secularism," the larger issues, and the later cases, see Winnifred Fallers Sullivan, *The Impossibility of Religious Freedom,* new ed. (Princeton University Press, 2018), xv–xxvii, 63, 67, 106, 108, 109, 153, 199, 266n39.

245. Andrew Preston, *Sword of the Spirit, Shield of Faith: Religion in American War and Diplomacy* (Alfred A. Knopf, 2012). Inboden, *Religion and American Foreign Policy.* Gene Zubovich, "For Human Rights Abroad, against Jim Crow at Home: The Political Mobilization of American Ecumenical Protestants in the World War II Era," *JAH* 105.2 (2018): 267–290. *Universal Declaration of Human Rights* (GPO, 1949).

246. On the government's stated aims, see President Millard Fillmore's letter in Francis L. Hawks, ed., *Narrative of the Expedition of an American Squadron to China and Japan, Performed in the Years 1852, 1853, and 1854, under the Command of Commodore M. C. Perry United States Navy . . .* (A. O. P. Nicholson, Printer, 1856), 1: 256–259. On Perry's flag: Millett, *War to Be Won,* 525–526. "General MacArthur's Speech at the Surrender of Japan," 2 September 1945, Naval History and Heritage Command, https://www.history.navy.mil/research/archives/digital-exhibits-highlights/vj-day/surrender/macarthur-speech.html.

247. Donna R. Gabaccia, *Foreign Relations: American Immigration in Global Perspective* (Princeton University Press, 2012), 146–149.

248. An Act to Revise the Laws Relating to Immigration, Naturalization, and Nationality, 27 June 1952, 66 Stat., 163.

249. Gráinne McEvoy, "'Operation Migratory Labor': Braceros, Migrants, and the American Catholic Bishops' Committee for the Spanish Speaking," *U.S. Catholic Historian* 34.3 (2016): 75–98. Brett Hendrickson, "Catholic Social Policy and Resistance to the Bracero Program," in Christopher D. Cantwell, Heath W. Carter, and Janine Giordano Drake, eds., *The Pew and the Picket Line: Christianity and the American Working Class* (University of Illinois Press, 2016), 192. See Ana María Díaz-Stevens, *Oxcart Catholicism on Fifth Avenue: The Impact of the Puerto Rican Migration upon the Archdiocese of New York* (University of Notre Dame Press, 1993).

250. James P. Niessen, "God Brought the Hungarians," *Hungarian Historical Review* 6.3 (2017): 566–596. Michael J. McNally, *Catholicism in South Florida, 1868–1968*

(University Presses of Florida, 1982), 127–166. Thomas A. Tweed, *Our Lady of the Exile: Diasporic Religion at a Cuban Catholic Shrine in Miami* (Oxford University Press, 1997), 13–40.

251. Tom W. Smith, "The Polls: America's Most Important Problems, Part I: National and International," *Public Opinion Quarterly* 49.2 (1985): 266.

252. "Reckoning": Sherwood Ross, "To Have and Have Not," *Chicago Defender,* 25 September 1963, 8. C. L. Washington, "Saluting 100 Years of Progress," *Los Angeles Sentinel,* 31 January 1963, A1.

253. William P. Jones, *The March on Washington: Jobs, Freedom, and the Forgotten History of Civil Rights* (W. W. Norton, 2013). Cynthia Taylor, *A. Philip Randolph: The Religious Journey of an African American Labor Leader* (NYU Press, 2006). Taylor Branch, *Parting the Waters: America in the King Years, 1954–1963* (Simon & Schuster, 1989). Eddie S. Glaude Jr., *African American Religion: A Very Short Introduction* (Oxford University Press, 2014), 66–76. Paul Harvey, *Bounds of Their Habitation: Race and Religion in American History* (Rowman & Littlefield, 2017), 159–175. David L. Chappell, *A Stone of Hope: Prophetic Religion and the Death of Jim Crow* (University of North Carolina, 2004). See also A. J. Muste, *What the Bible Teaches about Freedom: A Message to the Negro Churches* (Fellowship of Reconciliation, 1943).

254. Executive Order 8802, dated 25 June 1941, in which President Franklin D. Roosevelt prohibited discrimination in the defense program, National Archives, https://www.archives.gov/milestone-documents/executive-order-8802. *Brown et al. v. Board of Education of Topeka, Kansas et al.*, 17 May 1954, 347 U.S. 483, 349 U.S. 294.

255. On Oliver Brown, assistant pastor of Topeka's St. Mark's AME Church, and his eldest daughter, Linda: William Barry Furlong, "The Case of Linda Brown," *New York Times,* 12 February 1961, SM63; Isabell Masters, "The Life and Legacy of Oliver Brown . . . ," PhD diss., University of Oklahoma, 1980, 47–48, 55–61.

256. Patterson, *Grand Expectations,* vii. Jane Dailey, "Sex, Segregation, and the Sacred after *Brown,*" *JAH* 91.1 (2004): 119–144. Stephen M. Stookey, "Brooks Hays: Civil Politician in an Uncivil Parish," *Baptist History and Heritage* 55.1 (2020): 19–33. "The Christian Life Commission Report," *Annual of the Southern Baptist Convention, St. Louis, Missouri, June 2–5, 1954* (Executive Committee of the Southern Baptist Convention, 1954), 407 (recommendation 3).

257. Quoted in Martin Luther King Jr., "Our Struggle: The Story of Montgomery," *Liberation* 1.2 (April 1956): 3–6. Rosa Parks and James Haskins, *Rosa Parks: My Story* (Dial Books, 1992), 108–160; Parks "didn't often attend" MLK's church (131). See also George Barrett, "'Jim Crow, He's Real Tired,'" *New York Times,* 3 March 1957, 196. Jo Ann Gibson Robinson and David J. Garrow, *The Montgomery Bus Boycott and the Women Who Started It: The Memoir of Jo Ann Gibson Robinson* (University of Tennessee Press, 1987).

258. Robert S. Bird, "Dixie Tolerates Resurgent KKK," *Washington Post,* 5 May 1957, E3. On Rustin: John D'Emilio, *Lost Prophet: The Life and Times of Bayard Rustin* (Free Press, 2003).

259. Telegram from W. E. B. Du Bois to Martin Luther King Jr., ca. March 1956, W. E. B. Du Bois Papers, MS 312, Special Collections and University Archives,

University of Massachusetts Amherst Libraries, https://credo.library.umass.edu/view/full/mums312-b145-i418.

260. "Montgomery, Alabama's, Reverend Martin Luther King Jr.," cover, *Time,* 18 February 1957. Wacker, *America's Pastor,* 125.

261. Alfred S. Levitt, "A Community Builder Looks at Community Planning," *Journal of the American Institute of Planners* 17.2 (1951): 80–88. Daisy D. Myers, *Sticks 'n Stones: The Myers Family in Levittown* (York County Historical Trust, 2005). See also John T. McGreevy, *Parish Boundaries: The Catholic Encounter with Race in the Twentieth-Century Urban North* (University of Chicago Press, 1996); Thomas J. Sugrue, *Sweet Land of Liberty: The Forgotten Struggle for Civil Rights in the North* (Random House, 2008).

262. An Act to Provide Means of Further Securing and Protecting the Civil Rights of Persons within the Jurisdiction of the United States, 9 September 1957, 71 Stat. 634.

263. Martin Luther King Jr., "My Pilgrimage to Nonviolence," *Fellowship* 24 (September 1958): 4–9. Martin Luther King Jr., "My Trip to the Land of Gandhi," *Ebony* (July 1959): 84–92.

264. "New Twist: 'Kneel-In' at 6 Ga. Churches," *Daily Defender,* 9 August 1960, 1; "'Kneel-In' Extended: Negroes Turned Away at 4 of 10 Atlanta Churches," *New York Times,* 15 August 1960, 20. See also Stephen R. Haynes, *The Last Segregated Hour: The Memphis Kneel-Ins and the Campaign for Southern Church Desegregation* (Oxford University Press, 2012); Joseph Kip Kosek, "'Just a Bunch of Agitators': Kneel-Ins and the Desegregation of Southern Churches," *RAC* 23.2 (2013): 232–261.

265. Fred Shuttlesworth and N. H. Smith, "Birmingham Manifesto," 3 April 1963, Alabama Christian Movement for Human Rights, *Southern Christian Leadership Conference Newsletter* 1.10 (July 1963): 2, 4.

266. Andrew M. Manis, *A Fire You Can't Put Out: The Civil Rights Life of Birmingham's Reverend Fred Shuttlesworth* (University of Alabama Press, 1999), 208.

267. The American Friends Service Committee published King's 16 April "Letter" in May 1963 and circulated copies before the march. It also appeared in *Christianity and Crisis* 23 (27 May 1963), *Christian Century* 80 (12 June 1963), and *Ebony* 10.10 (August 1963): 23–33.

268. The official program included a "Tribute to Negro Women Fighters for Freedom," and Marian Anderson and Mahalia Jackson sang. See "March on Washington (Program)," 28 August 1963, Bayard Rustin Papers, John F. Kennedy Library, National Archives and Records Administration, https://www.archives.gov/milestone-documents/official-program-for-the-march-on-washington. Joan Baez also sang "We Shall Overcome" before King spoke. But some complained about the absence of a major female speaker: "Pauli Murray Lashes Out at Back Row Role," *Afro-American,* 23 November 1963, 7.

269. King feared a "racial holocaust" without federal action: Martin Luther King Jr. to John F. Kennedy, 15 September 1963, telegram from Atlanta to Washington; "Statement by the President—Birmingham—16 September 1963," https://civilrights.jfklibrary.org/media-assets/the-bombing-of-the-16th-street-baptist-church.html#Pressure. John F. Kennedy, "Televised Address to the Nation on Civil

Rights," 11 June 1963, John F. Kennedy Presidential Library, TNC-262-EX, https://www.jfklibrary.org/learn/about-jfk/historic-speeches/televised-address-to-the-nation-on-civil-rights. Kennedy's approval rating was 70 percent in February; after the March on Washington, 50 percent said he was moving too fast on civil rights: Andrew Kohut, "From the Archives: JFK's America," Pew Research Center, 5 July 2019, https://www.pewresearch.org/short-reads/2019/07/05/jfks-america/.

270. Thurgood Marshall, *Thurgood Marshall Oral History: July 10, 1969* (Alexander Street Press, 2003), 4.

271. John F. Kennedy, "Remarks at the Convention Center in Las Vegas, Nevada," 28 September 1963, https://www.presidency.ucsb.edu/documents/remarks-the-convention-center-las-vegas-nevada.

272. J. R. McNeill and Peter Engelke, *The Great Acceleration: An Environmental History of the Anthropocene since 1945* (Harvard University Press, 2014). See also Brooke, *Climate Change*, 529–558.

273. Scientists disagree about how to describe and date the moment when human action became the primary force for destabilizing global change. Some proposed the term *Anthropocene* to mark the shift, but scientists debate whether it signals a geologic epoch, event, or episode. On the terminological debate, see Philip Gibbard et al., "The Anthropocene as an Event, not an Epoch," *Journal of Quaternary Science* 37.3 (2022): 395–399; Martin J. Head et al., "The Proposed Anthropocene Epoch/Series Is Underpinned by an Extensive Array of Mid-20th Century Stratigraphic Event Signals," *Journal of Quaternary Science* 37.7 (2022): 1181–1187. In 2024 a subcommission of the International Commission on Stratigraphy stated that the changes around 1950 did not constitute a new epoch on the Geological Time Scale, but scholars attentive to Earth System science still argued for a shift around midcentury. Paul Voosen, "The Anthropocene Is Dead. Long Live the Anthropocene," *Science*, 5 March 2024, https://www.science.org/content/article/anthropocene-dead-long-live-anthropocene. See also Jan Zalasiewicz et al., "The Anthropocene: Comparing Its Meaning in Geology (Chronostratigraphy) with Conceptual Approaches Arising in Other Disciplines," *Earth's Future* 9.3 (2021), https://doi.org/10.1029/2020EF001896; Kathy Hibbard et al., "Group Report: Decadal Scale Interactions of Humans and the Environment," in Robert Costanza, Lisa Graumlich, and Will Steffen, eds., *Sustainability or Collapse? An Integrated History and Future of People on Earth* (MIT Press, 2007), 341–378; Julia Adeney Thomas, *Altered Earth: Getting the Anthropocene Right* (Cambridge University Press, 2022).

274. Robert S. Bird, "Neglect of Natural Resources: Day of Reckoning Seen at Hand," *New York Herald Tribune*, 1 November 1948, 12.

275. Bird, "Neglect of Natural Resources," 12. Fairfield Osborn, *Our Plundered Planet* (Little, Brown, 1948).

276. *Sixty Years' Growth of the Petroleum Tree*, advertisement, Socony-Vacuum Oil Company, *Fortune* 28.5 (November 1943): ii. "Refinery Shutdown Demanded until Smog Siege Terminates," *Los Angeles Times*, 3 December 1949, 1; "Worst Smog of Year Hits Los Angeles," *Los Angeles Times*, 8 March 1957, 1.

277. Kenneth Jackson, *Crabgrass Frontier: The Suburbanization of the United States* (Oxford University Press, 1985), 157–189, 246–271; Wells, *Car Country,* 251–258.

278. *Oiltown, USA,* 72 minutes, directed by Dick Ross, World Wide Pictures, released 27 February 1953. Dochuk, *Anointed with Oil,* 354–357.

279. "Mass for Oil Progress Week," *New York Times,* 12 October 1949, 31. Dochuk, *Anointed with Oil,* 370–371. See also William R. Callahan, "Catholic Petroleum Guild to Hear Abp. Cushing," *Daily Boston Globe,* 21 April 1956, 13.

280. Reinhold Niebuhr, *The Nature and Destiny of Man: Human Destiny* (Charles Scribner's Sons, 1943), 2: 1–3, 96, 294–295.

281. Rachel Carson, *Silent Spring* (Houghton Mifflin, 1962), 15–16. See also Bob Johnson, *Carbon Nation: Fossil Fuels in the Making of American Culture* (University Press of Kansas, 2014), xx.

282. On postwar environmentalism: Hal R. Rothman, *The Greening of a Nation? Environmentalism in the United States since 1945* (Harcourt Brace, 1998); Thomas Jundt, *Greening the Red, White, and Blue: The Bomb, Big Business, and Consumer Resistance in Postwar America* (Oxford University Press, 2014); Ellen Griffith Spears, *Rethinking the American Environmental Movement Post-1945* (Routledge, 2019), 55–88; Thomas Robertson, "Total War and the Total Environment," in Richard P. Tucker et al., eds., *Nature at War* (Cambridge University Press, 2020), 325–358. On religion and environmentalism: Robert Booth Fowler, *The Greening of Protestant Thought* (University of North Carolina Press, 1995); Bron Raymond Taylor, *Ecological Resistance Movements: The Global Emergence of Radical and Popular Environmentalism* (State University of New York Press, 1995); Evan Berry, *Devoted to Nature: The Religious Roots of American Environmentalism* (University of California Press, 2015); Mark Stoll, *Inherit the Holy Mountain: Religion and the Rise of American Environmentalism* (Oxford University Press, 2015).

283. Joseph Sittler, "A Theology for Earth," *Christian Scholar* 37.3 (1954): 367–374. See also Joseph Sittler, *The Ecology of Faith* (Fortress, 1961).

284. Teilhard de Chardin, *The Divine Milieu: An Essay on the Interior Life* (1957; Harper and Row, 1960). See Susan Kassman Sack, *America's Teilhard: Christ and Hope in the 1960s* (Catholic University of America Press, 2019).

285. Aldo Leopold, "Thinking Like a Mountain," in Curt Meine, ed., *Aldo Leopold: A Sand County Almanac and Other Writings on Ecology and Conservation* (1949; Library Classics of the United States, 2013), 114–117.

286. Anne Ford, "Rachel Carson Called 'A Nun of Nature,'" *Boston Globe,* 19 April 1964, A1. "Rachel Carson's Funeral Set," *New York Times,* 16 April 1964. Robert K. Musil, *Rachel Carson and Her Sisters: Extraordinary Women Who Have Shaped America's Environment* (Rutgers University Press, 2014), 123–129. John Mizzoni, "A Case Study in Environmental Conflict: The Two Pennsylvania Environmentalists Rachel Carson and Gifford Pinchot," *Environmental Philosophy* 2.2 (2005): 20–22.

287. Rachel Carson, "Help Your Child to Wonder," *Women's Home Companion* 83 (July 1956): 43.

288. "Six Groups Rap Plan for Dam at Echo Park," *Washington Post,* 17 June 1954, 39. Mark W. T. Harvey, *A Symbol of Wilderness: Echo Park and the American Conservation Movement* (University of Washington Press, 2000).

289. Roger Revelle and Hans E. Suess, "Carbon Dioxide Exchange between Atmosphere and Ocean and the Question of an Increase of Atmospheric CO_2 during the Past Decades," *Tellus* 9.1 (1957): 18–27. Committee on Public Works, *A Study of Pollution—Air* (GPO, 1963).

290. "Death Smog 'Act of God,' Says Steel Company," *Donora Herald American,* 29 September 1949, 1. "Editorial: God Didn't Do It," *Monessen Daily Independent* 48, 1 October 1949, 4.

291. "'God-Sent' Rain Drives Out Smog and Saves Thousands, Doctor Says," *Los Angeles Times,* 2 November 1948, 2. See Lynne Page Snyder, "'The Death-Dealing Smog over Donora, Pennsylvania': Industrial Air Pollution, Public Health Policy, and the Politics of Expertise, 1948–1949," *Environmental History Review* 18.1 (1994): 117–139.

292. "Hits Indiana Smoke: Asks 10 Times Number of Inspectors Here," *Chicago Daily Tribune,* 10 February 1949, 10. F. W. McNamara, "Smog Abatement Put First on Health Problem List," *Los Angeles Times,* 12 October 1949, A4.

293. J. R. Oppenheimer drafted a memorandum for Brigadier General Thomas Farrell on 11 May 1945. See Sean L. Malloy, "'A Very Pleasant Way to Die': Radiation Effects and the Decision to Use the Atomic Bomb against Japan," *Diplomatic History* 36.3 (2012): 531–535.

294. W. K. Wyant Jr., *Nation,* 13 June 1959, 535–537.

295. Charles Bazerman, "Nuclear Information: One Rhetorical Moment in the Construction of the Information Age," *Written Communication* 18.3 (2001): 259–295.

296. "Women Strike for Peace Milk Campaign, 1961," in James W. Feldman, ed., *Nuclear Reactions: Documenting American Encounters with Nuclear Energy* (University of Washington Press, 2017), 144–148.

297. Zyoyue Wang, *In Sputnik's Shadow: The President's Advisory Committee and Cold War America* (Rutgers University Press, 2008), 199–203.

298. Mamie Ella Roach Plyler (1896–1977), https://www.findagrave.com/memorial/72009645/mamie_ella_plyler, Brewton Cemetery, Evans County, Georgia. Elena Conis, "DDT Disbelievers: Health and the New Economic Poisons in Georgia after World War II," *Southern Spaces,* 28 October 2016, https://doi.org/10.18737/M7038M.

299. Courtney I. P. Thomas, *In Food We Trust: The Politics of Purity in American Food Regulation* (University of Nebraska Press, 2014), 41–57.

300. Stewart L. Udall, *The Quiet Crisis* (Holt, Rinehart and Winston, 1963).

301. "Who Killed Cock Robin?," *Christian Century,* 1 August 1962, 928–929.

302. Quoted in Monica Weis, *The Environmental Vision of Thomas Merton* (University Press of Kentucky, 2011), 14–15.

303. Patterson, *Grand Expectations,* 517–523.

304. Clean Air Act, 17 December 1963, Public Law 88-206.

305. National Catholic Welfare Conference, "Discrimination and Christian Conscience" (1958), in Hugh J. Nolan, ed., *Pastoral Letters of the United States Catholic Bishops* (US Catholic Conference, 1984), 2: 201–206.

306. Betty Friedan, *The Feminine Mystique* (W. W. Norton, 1963). *American Women: Report of the President's Commission on the Status of Women* (GPO, 1963).

307. *Self-Immolation of Thich Quang Duc,* 11 June 1963, in Saigon, AP photo by Malcolm Brown, https://www.worldpressphoto.org/collection/photo-contest/1963/malcolm-w-browne/1. William E. Colby, CIA director, quoted in Tweed, "Buddhism, Art, and Transcultural Collage," 196–197.

308. Dwight D. Eisenhower, "Farewell Address," 17 January 1961, https://www.eisenhowerlibrary.gov/research/online-documents/farewell-address. John F. Kennedy, "Remarks upon Presenting the NASA Distinguished Service Medal to Astronaut L. Gordon Cooper," 21 May 1963, in *Public Papers of the Presidents of the United States: John F. Kennedy, 1963* (GPO 1964), 416–417.

309. Arthur Lee Samuel, "Some Studies in Machine Learning Using the Game of Checkers," *IBM Journal of Research and Development* 3.3 (1959): 210–229.

310. Kennedy met Pope Paul VI on 2 July 1963. See Pope Paul VI, oral history interview, circa 1964, pp. 1–4, John F. Kennedy Presidential Library and Museum, https://www.jfklibrary.org/asset-viewer/archives/ jfkoh-pop-01. Pope Paul VI, *The Constitution on the Sacred Liturgy (Sacrosanctum Concilium)*, 4 December 1963, https://www.vatican.va/archive/hist_councils/ii_vatican_council/documents/vat-ii_const_19631204_sacrosanctum-concilium_en.html. The documents were interpreted and enacted differently: Kathleen Sprows Cummings, Timothy Matovina, and Robert A. Orsi, eds., *Catholics in the Vatican II Era: Local Histories of a Global Event* (Cambridge University Press, 2018).

Chapter 9. Countercultural Religion

1. Lyndon B. Johnson, "Remarks at the University of Michigan," 22 May 1964, https://www.presidency.ucsb.edu/documents/remarks-the-university-michigan.

2. Richard M. Nixon, "Address to the Nation on the War in Vietnam," 3 November 1969, https://www.presidency.ucsb.edu/documents/address-the-nation-the-war-vietnam. "Silent Majority Reaction Letters," Richard Nixon Presidential Library and Museum, https://www.nixonlibrary.gov/silent-majority-reaction-letters.

3. James T. Patterson, *Grand Expectations: The United States, 1945–1974* (Oxford University Press, 1996), 442–790. Glenda Elizabeth Gilmore and Thomas J. Sugrue, *These United States: A Nation in the Making, 1890 to the Present* (W. W. Norton, 2015), 371–494.

4. Wade Clark Roof, *A Generation of Seekers: The Spiritual Journeys of the Baby Boom Generation* (HarperSanFrancisco, 1993).

5. Civil Rights Act of 1964, 2 July 1964, Public Law 88-352 (78 Stat. 241). "ENACT Teach-In and Earth Day, Spring 1970," https://michiganintheworld.history.lsa.umich.edu/environmentalism/exhibits/show/main_exhibit/earthday.

6. Ann Braude, "A Religious Feminist—Who Can Find Her? Historical Challenges from the National Organization of Women," *JR* 84.4 (2004): 555–572.

7. Lyndon B. Johnson, "Remarks at the Signing of the Immigration Bill, Liberty Island, New York," https://www.presidency.ucsb.edu/documents/remarks-the-signing-the-immigration-bill-liberty-island-new-york.

8. Tim Galsworthy, "Carpetbaggers, Confederates, and Richard Nixon: The 1960 Presidential Election, Historical Memory, and the Republican Southern Strategy," *Presidential Studies Quarterly* 52.2 (2022): 260–289. Angie Maxwell and Todd Shields, *The Long Southern Strategy: How Chasing White Voters in the South Changed American Politics* (Oxford University Press, 2019).

9. The sense of abrupt change: Peter Marshall and David Manuel, *The Light and the Glory* (Revell, 1977), 13.

10. "God-given" freedoms: See, for example, the 1960 Sharon Statement by M. Stanton Evans of the Young Americans for Freedom, who met at Buckley Jr.'s estate: https://yaf.org/news/the-sharon-statement-a-timeless-declaration-of-conservative-principles/. Rebecca E. Klatch, *A Generation Divided: The New Left, the New Right, and the 1960s* (University of California Press, 1999), 341–342.

11. Hal Lindsey with C. C. Carlson, *The Late Great Planet Earth* (Zondervan, 1970). Marabel Morgan, *The Total Woman* (Fleming Revell, 1973).

12. See "The Hippies," 3 September 1968, *Firing Line* broadcast records, Hoover Institution Library and Archives, https://digitalcollections.hoover.org/objects/6047/the-hippies. Buckley hosted *Firing Line* from 1966 to 1999. On Buckley: Grace Elizabeth Hale, *A Nation of Outsiders: How the White Middle Class Fell in Love with Rebellion in Postwar America* (Oxford University Press, 2011), 135–147.

13. Damon R. Bach, *The American Counterculture: A History of Hippies and Cultural Dissidents* (University Press of Kansas, 2020). *The Human Be-In: A Gathering of the Tribes* (1967), poster designed by Stanley Mouse and Michael Bowen, with a photograph of an itinerant Hindu holy man by Casey Sonnabend. See Michael Parke-Taylor, "Images of Natives Americans in Rick Griffin's Psychedelic Posters," *Journal of Popular Culture* 53.5 (2020): 1121, 1126.

14. Helen Swick Perry, *The Human Be-In* (Basic Books, 1970), 88.

15. On "happenings": David Revill, *The Roaring Silence: John Cage, a Life* (Arcade, 1992), 161. Jack Kerouac, *The Dharma Bums* (Penguin Books, 1958). David Chadwick, *Crooked Cucumber: The Life and Zen Teaching of Shunryu Suzuki* (Broadway Books, 1999), 307–310.

16. Carol Hanisch, "The Personal Is Political," in Shulamith Firestone and Anne Koedt, eds., *Notes from the Second Year: Women's Liberation: Major Writings of the Radical Feminists* (Radical Feminism, 1970). See also Ram Dass, *The Only Dance There Is* (Anchor Press, 1974), 37–41.

17. Timothy Leary, *High Priest* (World Publishing, 1968), 303–318. Walter Pahnke, "Drugs and Mysticism," PhD diss., Harvard University, 1963.

18. "Timothy Leary, "An Interview with Timothy Leary: LSD and Religion," *Innisfree* 2 (December 1966): 14–21. Timothy Leary, "Turn On/Tune In/Drop Out," *East*

Village Other 1.12 (15 May–1 June 1966): 5. Timothy Leary, *The Politics of Ecstasy* (Putnam, 1968), 304–309.

19. Fred Turner, *From Counterculture to Cyberculture: Steward Brand, the Whole Earth Network, and the Rise of Digital Utopianism* (University of Chicago Press, 2006). Roszak discussed "the shamanistic worldview" but said less about the celebration of postindustrial technologies: Theodore Roszak, *The Making of a Counter Culture: Reflections on the Technocratic Society and Its Youthful Oppositions* (Anchor Books, 1969), 5, 264–265.

20. Sri Swami Satchidananda, "The Woodstock Opening Address," https://swamisatchidananda.org/life/woodstock-guru/swami-satchidanandas-woodstock-address/. On Satchidananda, see Thomas A. Tweed and Stepehen Prothero, eds., *Asian Religions in America: A Documentary History* (Oxford University Press, 1999), 253–254. On the eastward turn: Roszak, *Making of a Counter Culture,* 124–154. A mantra is a sacred word or phrase, often in Sanskrit, repeated by the devotee.

21. Michael C. Keith, "Commercial Underground Radio and the Sixties: An Oral History and Narrative," PhD diss., University of Rhode Island, 1998, 301. John Campbell McMillian, *Smoking Typewriters: The Sixties Underground Press and the Rise of Alternative Media in America* (Oxford University Press, 2011). Ram Dass, *Be Here Now* (Lama Foundation, 1971). "Countercultural Bible": Timothy Miller, *The 60s Communes: Hippies and Beyond* (Syracuse University Press, 1999), 117. "We are as gods": *The Last Whole Earth Catalog: Access to Tools* (Portola Institute, 1971), "Purpose," 1. See also Andrew G. Kirk, *Countercultural Green: The Whole Earth Catalog and American Environmentalism* (University Press of Kansas, 2007).

22. Steve Jobs, commencement address, Stanford University, 12 June 2005, https://news.stanford.edu/2005/06/youve-got-find-love-jobs-says. There were "thousands, probably tens of thousands" of communes: Miller, *60s Communes,* xviii.

23. On Gaskin and the Farm, see Miller, *60s Communes,* 118–124.

24. "Questions Answered," *High Times* 2.36 (18 September 1969): 13. Stephen Gaskin and William Myers, *Monday Night Class* (Book Farm, 1970). See also Stephen Gaskin, *Hey Beatnik! This Is the Farm Book* (Farm Book Publishing, 1974).

25. Arthur Versluis and Morgan Shipley, "Stephen Gaskin Interview," *Journal for the Study of Radicalism* 4.1 (2010): 142. The hole-filled punch card was known as the "IBM card."

26. Morgan Shipley "'This Season's People': Stephen Gaskin, Psychedelic Religion, and a Community of Social Justice," *Journal for the Study of Radicalism* 9.2 (2015): 41–92.

27. Ina May [Gaskin] and the Farm Midwives, *Spiritual Midwifery* (Farm Book Publishing, 1975), 375. Jane Simonsen, "Neither 'Baby Factories' nor Squatting 'Primitives': Defining Women Workers through Alternative Childbirth Methods in the United States, 1945–1965," *Journal of Women's History* 27.2 (2015): 134–158.

28. Albert Gore Jr., "Church Group Swaps Views with Gaskin's," *Tennessean,* 13 March 1972.

29. Mark Oppenheimer, *Knocking on Heaven's Door: American Religion in the Age of Counterculture* (Yale University Press, 2003).

30. William F. Buckley Jr., "The Non-Latin Mass: Reflections on the Final Solution," *Commonweal* 87.6 (1967): 167. The lyrics of "Joy Is Like the Rain": Mark Oppenheimer, "Folk Music in the Catholic Mass," in Colleen McDannell, ed., *Religions of the United States in Practice* (Princeton University Press, 2001), 2: 103–111. James P. McCartin, *Prayers of the Faithful: The Shifting Spiritual Life of American Catholics* (Harvard University Press, 2010), 115–116.

31. Dennis C. Benson, *Electric Liturgy* (John Knox Press, 1972), 2.

32. Richard Siegel, Michael Strassfeld, and Sharon Strassfeld, eds., *The Jewish Catalog: A Do-It-Yourself Kit* (Jewish Publication Society of America, 1973). Jonathan D. Sarna, *American Judaism: A History* (Yale University Press, 2004), 318–322. Ari Y. Kelman, "Reading a Book like an Object: The Case of *The Jewish Catalog*," in Ken Koltun-Fromm, ed., *Thinking Jewish Culture in America* (Lexington Books, 2014), 109–128.

33. David R. Swartz, *Moral Minority: The Evangelical Left in an Age of Conservatism* (University of Pennsylvania Press, 2012), 267–270. Joseph Crespino, *In Search of Another Country: Mississippi and the Conservative Counterrevolution* (Princeton University Press, 2007). See also Andrew Hartman, *A War for the Soul of America: A History of the Culture Wars*, 2nd ed. (University of Chicago Press, 2019).

34. The Disability Rights Movement also began in 1969, and the Rehabilitation Act of 1973 offered the first antidiscrimination law: Scot Danforth, "Becoming the Rolling Quads: Disability Politics at the University of California, Berkeley, in the 1960s," *History of Education Quarterly* 58.4 (2018): 506–536.

35. Quoted in Ben A. Franklin, "Johnson Exhorts Clerics on Rights," *New York Times*, 30 April 1964, 1.

36. The Civil Rights Act of 1964, 2 July 1964, Public Law 88-352 (78 Stat. 241). "Selma to Montgomery March," 21–25 March 1965, Martin Luther King Jr. Research and Education Institute, Stanford University, https://kinginstitute.stanford.edu/encyclopedia/selma-montgomery-march. See also Paul Harvey, *Bounds of Their Habitation: Race and Religion in American History* (Rowman & Littlefield, 2017), 183–189; Amy L. Koehlinger, *The New Nuns: Racial Justice and Religious Reform in the 1960s* (Harvard University Press, 2007).

37. "President Lyndon Johnson's Speech to Congress on Voting Rights, March 15, 1965," National Archives, https://www.archives.gov/legislative/features/voting-rights-1965/johnson.html. On "We Shall Overcome": Imani Perry, *May We Forever Stand: A History of the Black National Anthem* (University of North Carolina Press, 2018), 158. The Voting Rights Act of 1965, 6 August 1965, Public Law 89-110 (79 Stat. 437).

38. Eddie S. Glaude Jr., *African American Religion: A Very Short Introduction* (Oxford University Press, 2014), 80–81.

39. Douglas V. Almond, Kenneth Y. Chay, and Michael Greenstone, "Civil Rights, the War on Poverty, and Black-White Convergence in Infant Mortality in Mississippi," Center for Labor Economics, University of California, Berkeley, Working Paper no. 43, September 2001, p. 1.

40. Fair Housing Act: Civil Rights Act of 1968, 11 April 1968, Public Law 90-284 (82 Stat. 73).

41. Elizabeth Hinton, *America on Fire: The Untold Story of Police Violence and Black Rebellion since the 1960s* (W. W. Norton, 2021).

42. Lauren F. E. Galloway, "'A Conspiracy of the Nation': Case Study of Stokely Carmichael's and H. Rap Brown's Arguments in Support of Black Power," *Journal of Black Studies* 5.1 (2020): 83–102. Peniel E. Joseph, *Waiting 'til Midnight Hour: A Narrative History of Black Power in America* (Holt, 2006), 303. Lerone A. Martin, *The Gospel of J. Edgar Hoover: How the FBI Aided and Abetted the Rise of White Christian Nationalism* (Princeton University Press, 2023), 159, 229–258.

43. Randy J. Sparks, *Religion in Mississippi* (University Press of Mississippi, 2001), 221–247.

44. Sparks, *Religion in Mississippi,* 240–241.

45. The quotation: *Abbey Church of Mary, Help of Christians,* pamphlet, Belmont Abbey, Belmont, North Carolina, 1990, pp. 3–4. See also Paschal Baumstein, OSB, *My Lord of Belmont: A Biography of Leo Haid* (Herald House, 1985), 36; Paschal Baumstein, OSB, *A Carolina Basilica: A History of the Monastic Church at Belmont Abbey* (Belmont Abbey, 1990), 14–15.

46. R. S. Lecky and H. E. Wright, eds., *Black Manifesto: Religion, Racism, and Reparations* (Sheed and Ward, 1969), 125–126.

47. "Bobby Seale Dedicates New Youth Institute and Son of Man Temple to Community," *Black Panther,* 27 October 1973, 4–5, 16. "Son of Man Temple," *Co-Evolution Quarterly* 3 (1974): 17–18. Huey Newton was raised in and memorialized in the Black Church. See *Funeral of Dr. Huey P. Newton* (Dr. Huey P. Newton Foundation, 2015), video, 122 mins.

48. Quoted in Kerry Pimblott, *Faith in Black Power: Religion, Race, and Resistance in Cairo, Illinois* (University Press of Kentucky, 2017), 106. *Hearing before the United States Commission on Civil Rights: Hearing Held in Cairo, Illinois, 23–24 March 1972* (GPO, 1972), 330. See also Albert B. Cleage, *Black Christian Nationalism: New Directions for the Black Church* (W. Morrow, 1972).

49. Milton C. Sernett, ed., *African American Religious History: A Documentary Witness,* 2nd ed. (Duke University Press, 1999), 555–566.

50. James H. Cone, *Black Theology and Black Power* (Seabury, 1969). James H. Cone, "Some Brief Reflections on Writing *Black Theology and Black Power,*" *Black Theology* 8.3 (2010): 264–265. See also James H. Cone, *God of the Oppressed* (Seabury Press, 1975). Gustavo Gutiérrez's *Teología de la liberación* appeared in 1971, and a translation appeared as *A Theology of Liberation: History, Politics, and Salvation* (Orbis Books, 1973). Gutiérrez's book was based on papers presented earlier, including at a July 1968 meeting in Chimbote, Peru.

51. Katie G. Cannon, *Black Womanist Ethics* (Scholars Press, 1988). Jacquelyn Grant, *White Women's Christ and Black Women's Jesus: Feminist Christology and Womanist Response* (Scholars Press, 1989). The adjective *womanist* is from Alice Walker, *In Search of Our Mothers' Gardens: Womanist Prose* (Harcourt Brace Jovanovich, 1983), xi–xii.

52. My analysis of the NOW photograph is indebted to Braude's "A Religious Feminist—Who Can Find Her?" NOW lists forty-nine founding members: "Honoring Our Founders and Pioneers," National Organization for Women, https://now.org/about/history/honoring-our-founders-pioneers/.

53. Sister Mary Joel Read, later a college president, was a member of the School Sisters of Saint Francis (SSSF). Two other Catholics were "strong early supporters": Elizabeth Farians, the lay theologian who chaired its Task Force on Women and Religion, and Sister Austin Doherty, SSSF, who attended the October 1966 meeting. Jewish women were founders and supporters too, including Sonia Pressman Fuentes.

54. Jennifer Scanlon, *Until There Is Justice: The Life of Anna Arnold Hedgeman* (Oxford University Press, 2016).

55. Quoted in Paul L. Edenfield, "American Heartbreak: The Life of Pauli Murray," *Legal Studies Forum* 27.2 (2003): 763. Pauli Murray, ed., *States' Laws on Race and Color* (Women's Division of Christian Service, Methodist Church, 1951). Pauli Murray, *Song in a Weary Throat: An American Pilgrimage* (Harper and Row, 1987), 365–368.

56. Brief for Appellant, *Reed v. Reed,* 404 U.S. 71 (1971) (no. 70-4). See also Rosalind Rosenberg, *Jane Crow: The Life of Pauli Murray* (Oxford University Press, 2017); Troy R. Saxby, *Pauli Murray: A Personal and Political Life* (University of North Carolina Press, 2020).

57. Chelsea Griffis, "'In the Beginning was the Word': Evangelical Christian Women, the Equal Rights Amendment, and Competing Definitions of Womanhood," *Frontiers* 38.2 (2017): 148–172.

58. Farians, cofounder of Catholics for the ERA, also testified about the ERA: "Statement of Dr. Elizabeth Farians, Joint Committee of Organizations Concerned about the Status of Women in the Church," in *Hearings before Subcommittee No. 4 of the Committee on the Judiciary, House of Representatives, Ninety-Second Congress . . .* serial no. 2 ("Printed for use of the Committee on the Judiciary," 1971), 463–469. George Vecsey, "Bishops' Unit Rejects Rights Law Backing," *New York Times,* 2 May 1978, 18.

59. "First Presidency Issues Statement Opposing Equal Rights Amendment," December 1976, Church of Jesus Christ of Latter-day Saints, https://www.churchofjesuschrist.org/study/ensign/1976/12/news-of-the-church/first-presidency-issues-statement-opposing-equal-rights-amendment?lang=eng#title1. See also Sonia Johnson, *From Housewife to Heretic* (Doubleday, 1981), 276–280.

60. "What's Wrong with 'Equal Rights' for Women?" *Phyllis Schlafly Report* 5.7 (1972). Schlafly's essay is reprinted in Mark Massa, SJ, and Catherine Osborne, eds., *American Catholic History: A Documentary Reader* (NYU Press, 2008), 181–184.

61. For the report, see Sarah Doely, ed., *Women's Liberation and the Church: The New Demand for Freedom in the Life of the Christian Church* (Association Press, 1970), 147–154. Mary Daly, *The Church and the Second Sex* (Harper and Row, 1968).

62. Mary Daly, *Beyond God the Father: Toward a Philosophy of Women's Liberation* (Beacon, 1973), xii, 57, 207n16, 217n11.

63. Pauli Murray, "Sermon on the Ordination of Women," in Anthony B. Pinn, ed., *Pauli Murray: Selected Sermons and Writings* (Orbis, 2006), 61.

64. Elizabeth H. Flowers, *Into the Pulpit: Southern Baptist Women and Power since World War II* (University of North Carolina Press, 2012), 27–29.

65. *Declaration on the Question of the Admission of Women to the Ministerial Priesthood* (United States Catholic Conference, 1977). John Paul II reaffirmed that view in *Ordinatio Sacerdotalis: Apostolic Letter of His Holiness Pope John Paul II on Reserving Priestly Ordination to Men Alone* (United States Catholic Conference, 1994).

66. Pamela S. Nadell, *Women Who Would Be Rabbis: A History of Women's Ordination, 1889–1985* (Beacon, 1998). See also Sarna, *American Judaism*, 340–344.

67. Murray, *Song in a Weary Throat*, 432–435.

68. Quoted in Kathryn Schulz, "Saint Pauli," *New Yorker*, 17 April 2017, 67–73. See also Rosenberg, *Jane Crow*, and Saxby, *Pauli Murray*.

69. Murray, "The Dilemma of the Minority Christian," in Pinn, *Pauli Murray: Selected Sermons and Writings*, 8. I follow other scholars' practice by using female pronouns.

70. Joshua H. Miller, "Bolstering Bayard Rustin: Collaborative Apologia, Heteronormativity, and the 1963 March on Washington," *Southern Communication Journal* 87.1 (2022): 44–55.

71. The activist's sign at the first New York City Pride March can be seen in *Gay and Proud*, a documentary film by Lilli Vincenz, 28 June 1970, Library of Congress, "LGBTQIA+ Studies: A Resource Guide," https://guides.loc.gov/lgbtq-studies/stonewall-era.

72. "Hope for the Homosexual," *Time*, 13 July 1970, 46, 49. Melissa M. Wilcox, "Of Markets and Missions: The Early History of the Universal Fellowship of Metropolitan Community Churches," *RAC* 11.1 (2001): 83–108. Robert Ridinger, "Rising in Witness: The Metropolitan Community Church in the Religious Press," *Journal of Religious and Theological Information* 18.1 (2019): 1–22.

73. Oppenheimer, *Knocking on Heaven's Door*, 30–60. Homosexuality was no longer criminalized as laws changed, and it was no longer medicalized: The American Psychiatric Association removed "homosexuality" from its *Diagnostic and Statistical Manual of Mental Disorders* in 1973.

74. John J. McNeill, *The Church and the Homosexual* (Sheed, Andrews, and McMeel, 1976). "Suspicious fire": *Reverend Troy Perry and Jerry Small Standing amid Fire Damage at Metropolitan Community Church in Los Angeles, Calif., 1973*, 14 February 1973, *Los Angeles Times* Photographic Collection, UCLA Library Special Collections, https://digital.library.ucla.edu/catalog/ark:/21198/zz0002p4nw.

75. "Return of the Red Man," cover, *Life*, 1 December 1967. Philip Joseph Deloria, *Playing Indian* (Yale University Press, 1998). The cover art was by graphic designer Milton Glaser.

76. Robin Richman, "Happy Hippie Hunting Ground," *Life*, 63.22, 1 December 1967, 67–69. Michael Parke-Taylor, "Images of Native Americans in Rick Griffin's Early Psychedelic Posters," *Journal of Popular Culture* 53.5 (2020): 1105–1134.

77. "Hippies, Hippies, Hooray!!!," *Hopi Action News*, 29 September 1967, 8; "Be Careful, 'Hippies,'" *Navajo Times*, 24 August 1967, 2.

78. *Sharp Nose (Ta-qua-wi), a Northern Arapaho Chief . . . Wearing US Army Captain's Bars,* 1884, Department of Defense, Record Group 111, Records of the Chief Signal Officer, 1860–1985, National Archives, https://catalog.archives.gov/id/530817. Sharp Nose served as a scout between 1876 and 1890: Trevor K. Plante, "Lead the Way: Researching US Army Indian Scouts, 1866–1914," *Genealogy Notes* 41.2 (2009): 2–3. He got an Army pension: "Sharp Nose, Indian Scout," HR Rep. No. 1352, 53rd Congress, 2nd series (1894). His projected image appeared in *Life,* 1 December 1967, 57.

79. Richard H. Pratt, "The Advantages of Mingling Indians with Whites," in *Proceedings of the National Conference of Charities and Correction . . .* (George Ellis, 1892), 46. See also Richard Henry Pratt, *Battlefield and Classroom: Four Decades with the American Indian* (University of Oklahoma Press, 2003). On Little Chief (Dickens Nor), see https://carlisleindian.dickinson.edu/student_files/dickens-student-information-card.

80. The records state Little Chief died of pneumonia at age fifteen in 1883, two years after his arrival. The "Arapaho way" was changing, as Catholics established a mission at the Wind River Reservation in 1884. See Jeffrey D. Anderson, "Northern Arapaho Conversion of a Christian Text," *Ethnohistory* 48.4 (2001): 697–698.

81. "Trail of Broken Treaties Twenty-Point Position Paper," October 1972, Minneapolis, Minnesota, https://www.aimovement.org/ggc/trailofbrokentreaties.html. Bette Crouse Mele, "Wounded Knee Seen as Symbol of Resistance," *Wassaja* 1.2 (February/March 1973): 1. "1973 Wounded Knee," *Native Nevadan* 8.20 (March/April 1973): 1. Laura Waterman Wittstock and Elaine J. Salinas, "A Brief History of the American Indian Movement," https://www.aimovement.org/ggc/history.html. See also Paul Chaat Smith and Robert Allen Warrior, *Like a Hurricane: The American Indian Movement from Alcatraz to Wounded Knee* (New Press, 1996).

82. Michael D. McNally, *Defend the Sacred: Native American Religious Freedom beyond the First Amendment* (Princeton University Press, 2020), 171–195. Suzan Shown Harjo, "American Indian Religious Freedom Act after Twenty-Five Years: An Introduction" and "Keynote Address: The American Indian Religious Freedom Act: Looking Back and Looking Forward," *Wicazo Sa Review* 19.2 (2004): 129–136, 143–151.

83. Vine Deloria Jr., *Custer Died for Your Sins: An Indian Manifesto* (Avon, 1969), 109, 115–116. Harjo, "Keynote Address," 146.

84. Deloria, *Custer Died for Your Sins,* 150.

85. Bumper sticker: Deloria, *Custer Died for Your Sins,* 126. "For this land": Vine Deloria Jr., *God Is Red* (Grosset and Dunlap, 1973), 301.

86. "The Plan of Delano," *El Malcriado* 33 (1966): 9.

87. Ronald A. Wells, "Cesar Chavez's Protestant Allies: The California Migrant Ministry and the Farm Workers," *Journal of Presbyterian History* 87.1 (2009): 5–16.

88. Mark Day, *Forty Acres: Cesar Chavez and the Farm Workers* (Praeger, 1971). See also Allan J. Watt, *Farm Workers and the Churches: The Movement in California and Texas* (Texas A&M University Press, 2010), 67–106; Harvey, *Bounds of Their Habitation,* 175–181; Jacques E. Levy, *Cesar Chavez: Autobiography of La Causa* (University

of Minnesota Press, 2007); Matt Garcia, *From the Jaws of Victory: The Triumph and Tragedy of Cesar Chavez and the Farm Worker Movement* (University of California Press, 2012); "Symposium on César Chávez and the United Farm Workers," *International Labor and Working Class History* 83 (2013): 143–169; Miriam Pawel, *The Crusades of Cesar Chavez: A Biography* (Bloomsbury Press, 2014). On Dolores Huerta, UFW cofounder: Mario T. García, ed., *A Dolores Huerta Reader* (University of New Mexico Press, 2008); Marlene Targ Brill, *Dolores Huerta Stands Strong* (Ohio University Press, 2018).

89. The UFW's banner included an avian image that recalled the bird on the Aztec *Codex Mendoza* and has been interpreted as the thunderbird revered across Indigenous North America. Davíd Carrasco, *The Aztecs: A Very Short Introduction* (Oxford University Press, 2012), 40–41, 44–45; Edward J. Lenik, "The Thunderbird Motif in Northeastern Indian Art," *Archaeology of Eastern North America* 40 (2012): 163–185. On devotion and activism, see Gastón Espinosa, Virgilio Elizondo, and Jesse Miranda, eds., *Latino Religions and Civic Activism in the United States* (Oxford University Press, 2005); Gastón Espinosa, *Mexican American Religions: Spirituality, Activism, and Culture* (Duke University Press, 2008); Felipe Hinojosa, Maggie Elmore, and Sergio M. González, eds., *Faith and Power: Latino Religious Politics since 1945* (NYU Press, 2022), 3–5.

90. Photograph of Chávez receiving communion: *Twenty-Five Day Fast 1968: Father Eugene Boyle, Cesar Chavez,* Farmworker Movement Documentation Project, University of California at San Diego, https://libraries.ucsd.edu/farmworkermovement/gallery/displayimage.php?album=45&pid=1255#top_display_media. Martin Luther King Jr. to César Chávez, 5 March 1968, United Farm Workers, https://ufw.org/dr-kings-telegram-to-cesar-chavez-during-his-1968-fast-for-nonviolence/.

91. The quotations from Chávez and descriptions of the ritual: "10,000 Mass in Gran Fiesta," *El Malcriado* 11.3 (1 April 1968): 3. That account said Chávez lost forty pounds, while the *Times* said thirty-five pounds; the UFW suggested there were 10,000 attendees and the *Times* mentioned 4,000. See Wallace Turner, "Head of Farm Workers Union Ends 25-Day Fast in California," *New York Times,* 11 March 1968, 22.

92. César E. Chávez, "The Mexican-American and the Church," a paper prepared during his fast for the Second Annual Mexican Conference in Sacramento on 8–10 March 1968. See the Farmworker Movement Documentation Project, UC San Diego Library, https://libraries.ucsd.edu/farmworkermovement/essays/essays/Cesar%20Chavez%20-%20The%20Mexican-American%20and%20the%20Church.pdf.

93. The San Diego protestors from Católicos por La Raza saw *la raza* (meaning "the people" and not "the race") as more inclusive than *Chicano:* Mario T. García, *Católicos* (University of Texas Press, 2008), 137. See also Mario T. García, *Chicano Liberation Theology: The Writings and Documents of Richard Cruz and Católicos por la Raza* (Kendall Hunt, 2009).

94. Richard Edward Martínez, *PADRES: The National Chicano Priest Movement* (University of Texas Press, 2005). Lara Medina, *Las Hermanas: Chicana/Latina Religious-Political Activism in the U.S. Catholic Church* (Temple University Press, 2004).

95. Martin McMurtrey, *Mariachi Bishop: The Life Story of Patrick Flores* (Corona, 1987). "Hispanic/Latino Bishops in the United States since 1970," US Conference of Catholic Bishops, https://www.usccb.org/committees/hispaniclatino-affairs/hispaniclatino-bishops-united-states-1970.

96. "Preferential option for the poor" appeared in the documents of CELAM, the organization of Latin American Bishops, from Medellín (1968): *Medellín, conclusiones: Segunda Conferencia General del Episcopado Latinoamericano, Bogotá, 24 de agosto, Medellín, agosto 26–septiembre 6, Colombia, 1968* (Secretariado General del CELAM, 1984), paragraph 14.9. María Pilar Aquino, Daisy L. Machado, and Jeanette Rodriguez, eds., *A Reader in Latina Feminist Theology: Religion and Justice* (University of Texas Press, 2002). Ada María Isasi-Díaz, *Mujerista Theology: A Theology for the Twenty-First Century* (Orbis Books, 1996), 1–2.

97. Tom Rosentiel, "Polling Wars: Hawks vs. Doves," Pew Research Center, 23 November 2009, https://www.pewresearch.org/2009/11/23/polling-wars-hawks-vs-doves/. See also Michael H. Hunt, *A Vietnam War Reader: A Documentary History from American and Vietnamese Perspectives* (University of North Carolina Press, 2010); Scott Laderman and Edwin A. Martini, eds., *Four Decades On: Vietnam, the United States, and the Legacies of the Second Indochina War* (Duke University Press, 2013).

98. Robert S. McNamara, *In Retrospect: The Tragedy and Lessons of Vietnam* (Times Books, 1995), 216–217. Nicholas Patler, "Norman's Triumph: The Transcendent Language of Self-Immolation," *Quaker History* 104.2 (2015): 18–39. Anne Morrison Welsh, *Fire from the Heart: Norman Morrison's Legacy in Vietnam and at Home*, pamphlet 381 (Pendle Hill, 2005). Martin Luther King Jr., "Beyond Vietnam," 4 April 1967, https://kinginstitute.stanford.edu/encyclopedia/beyond-vietnam. On religion and the Vietnam War, see Gilmore and Sugrue, *These United States*, 428–429.

99. National Conference of Catholic Bishops, "Resolution on Southeast Asia, November 1971," in *In the Name of Peace: Collective Statements of the United States Catholic Bishops on War and Peace, 1919–1980* (United States Catholic Conference, 1983), 59–62. Catholics suffered the most fatalities (16,817): "Vietnam War US Military Fatal Casualty Statistics," https://www.archives.gov/research/military/vietnam-war/casualty-statistics.

100. Mitchell K. Hall, *Because of Their Faith: CALCAV and Religious Opposition to the Vietnam War* (Columbia University Press, 1990).

101. Penelope Adams Moon, "'Peace on Earth—Peace in Vietnam': The Catholic Peace Fellowship and Antiwar Witness, 1964–1976," *Journal of Social History* 36.4 (2003): 1033–1057. "Conscience" and the CPF: Peter Cajka, *Follow Your Conscience: The Catholic Church and the Spirit of the Sixties* (University of Chicago Press, 2021).

102. George Dugan, "Religious Leaders Endorse Vietnam Moratorium," *New York Times*, 11 October 1969, 25. Edward B. Fiske, "War Protest Viewed as 'Civil Religion,'" *New York Times*, 19 October 1969, 92. Lorena Oropeza, *¡Raza Sí! ¡Guerra No! Chicano Protest and Patriotism during the Vietnam War Era* (University of California Press, 2005). Army recruiters reported "a record enlistment": "Enlistment Mark Set on Moratorium Day," *Washington Post*, 17 October 1969, A12.

103. David Rosenbaum, "Moratorium Organizer: Samuel Winfred Brown Jr.," *New York Times,* 16 October 1969, 18. Brown on how to use churches for activism: Sam W. Brown Jr., *Storefront Organizing: A Mornin' Glories' Manual* (Pyramid Books, 1972), 29.

104. For crowd estimates I rely on this intelligence report: Arthur K. Nishimoto, LTC, Chief, Special Operations Division, "After Action Report: Vietnam Moratorium, 15 October 1969," 24 October 1969, pp. 1–5, ProQuest History Vault: *American Politics and Society from JFK to Watergate, 1960–1975.* Thomas M. Gannon, "A Report on the Vietnam Moratorium," *America* 121.14 (1969): 380–383. E. W. Kenworthy, "Thousands Mark Day," *New York Times,* 16 October 1969, 1. A photograph of the Boston University marchers: Jeff Albertson, *Moratorium to End the War in Vietnam: Demonstrators Walking Down Commonwealth Ave. on the Way to the Boston Common, October 15, 1969,* Jeff Albertson Photograph Collection (PH 57), Special Collections and University Archives, University of Massachusetts Amherst Libraries, https://credo.library.umass.edu/view/full/mupho57-b002-sl238-i028.

105. Cliff Wintrode, "Moratorium Day Protests Spreading," and "Candle-light Walk by Students," *Observer* 4.22 (15 October 1969): 1; William J. Mitchell, "How They Observed M-Day at Notre Dame," *National Catholic Reporter* 5.51 (22 October 1969): 1, 9. Three officials supported the events: "Catholic Officials Comment on Vietnam Peace Moratorium," Press Department, US Catholic Conference, *NC News Service,* 3 October 1969, 13–14.

106. Murrey Marder, "Credibility Gap: Greater Skepticism Greets Administration Declarations," *Washington Post,* 5 December 1965, A21. David Schoenbrun, "Behind the Credibility Gap," *New York Times,* 7 July 1968, BR1. Hal Wingo, "The Massacre at My Lai," *Life,* 5 December 1969, 36–45. The photograph of Phan Thị Kim Phúc: *Napalm Girl,* AP Images, https://apimagesblog.com/blog/2017/3/31/napalm-girl-photographer-retires-after-51-years.

107. Rosentiel, "Polling Wars: Hawks vs. Doves"; "Vietnam War US Military Fatal Casualty Statistics."

108. The war's legacies: Andrew Preston, "The Irony of Protest: Vietnam and the Path to Permanent War," in Martin Halliwell and Nick Witham, eds., *Reframing 1968: American Politics, Protest, and Identity* (Edinburgh University Press, 2018), 70, 76.

109. David Stradling, ed., *The Environmental Moment* (University of Washington Press, 2013). David J. Webber, "Earth Day and Its Precursors: Continuity and Change in the Evolution of Midtwentieth-Century U.S. Environmental Policy," *Review of Policy Research* 25.4 (2008): 316. See also Teresa Sabol Spezio, *Slick Policy: Environmental and Science Policy in the Aftermath of the Santa Barbara Oil Spill* (University of Pittsburgh Press, 2018). "The Cities: The Price of Optimism," *Time,* 1 August 1969, 41; David Stradling and Richard Stradling, "Perceptions of the Burning River: Deindustrialization and Cleveland's Cuyahoga River," *Environmental History* 13.3 (2008): 515–535.

110. Lynn White, "The Historical Roots of Our Ecologic Crisis," *Science* 155 (1967): 1203–1207. On the reception of White's argument: Jeremy Cohen, *Be Fertile and Increase, Fill the Earth and Master It: The Ancient and Medieval Career of a*

Biblical Text (Cornell University Press, 1989); Peter Harrison, "Subduing the Earth: Genesis 1, Early Modern Science, and the Exploitation of Nature," *JR* 79 (1999): 86–109; Christopher Hamlin and David M. Lodge, "Beyond Lynn White: Religion, the Contexts of Ecology, and the Flux of Nature," in David M. Lodge and Christopher Hamlin, eds., *Religion and the New Ecology: Environmental Responsibility in a World in Flux* (University of Notre Dame Press, 2006), 1–25; Willis Jenkins, "After Lynn White: Religious Ethics and Environmental Problems," *Journal of Religious Ethics* 37 (2009): 285–309; Elspeth Whitney, "The Lynn White Thesis," *Environmental Ethics* 35.3 (2013): 313–331; Bron Taylor et al., "Lynn White Jr. and the Greening-of-Religion Hypothesis," *Conservation Biology* 30.5 (2016): 1000–1009.

111. The Genesis reading was recommended by a Catholic woman: "Why Astronaut Borman Decided to Read Story of Creation," *Witness* 54.2 (23 January 1969): 3; James P. Moore, *One Nation under God: A History of Prayer in America* (Doubleday, 2005), 380–381. Borman also recorded a prayer for St. Christopher Episcopal Church in League City, Texas: a selection by G. F. Weld in *Prayers for the Church Service League of the Diocese of Massachusetts*, 7th ed. (Riverside Press, 1952), 15. The transcript and audio of Borman's in-flight prayer for his congregation (74:50), Earthrise photograph (75:48), and Genesis reading (85:39): Hamish Lindsay, "Apollo 8," 21–28 December 1968 (updated 2018), Honeysuckle Creek Tracking Station, Canberra, Australia, https://honeysucklecreek.net/msfn_missions/Apollo_8_mission/index.html.

112. William A. Anders, interview by Paul Rollins, NASA Johnson Space Center Oral History Project, Houston, Texas, 8 October 1997, https://historycollection.jsc.nasa.gov/JSCHistoryPortal/history/oral_histories/AndersWA/AndersWA_10-8-97.htm. Anders later said the sight "undercut my religious beliefs": Ian Sample, "Earthrise: How the Iconic Image Changed the World," *Guardian*, 24 December 2018.

113. Richard Nixon, first inaugural address, 20 January 1969, https://www.presidency.ucsb.edu/documents/inaugural-address-1. Robert Poole, *Earthrise: How Man First Saw the Earth* (Yale University Press, 2008), 1–35, 128–140. Benjamin Lazier, "Earthrise; Or, the Globalization of the World Picture," *AHR* 116.3 (2011): 602–630. The publication of *Earthrise:* "Discovery," *Life*, 10 January 1969, 20–22. Religious responses: Edward B. Fiske, "'Modern Magi' Put Moon Flight into Scriptural Perspective," *Christianity Today*, 17 January 1969, 36. "The View from Apollo 8," *Christian Century* 86.2 (8 January 1969): 37; "Thanks, Apollo 8," *Catholic Transcript* 52.36 (26 December 1969): 1. See also Kendrick Oliver, *To Touch the Face of God: The Sacred, the Profane, and the American Space Program, 1957–1975* (Johns Hopkins University Press, 2013).

114. Anders, interview by Rollins. See also "Earthrise at 50," *Nature* 564 (27 December 2018): 301.

115. Nicole Sparks and Darrin J. Rodgers, "John McConnell Jr. and the Pentecostal Origins of Earth Day," *Assemblies of God Heritage* 30 (2010): 17–25, 69.

116. Poole, *Earthrise*, 152–153. The John McConnell Papers, Collection DG 212, Swarthmore College Peace Collection, https://archives.tricolib.brynmawr.edu/repositories/8/resources/8625. That collection contains McConnell's Earth Day

proclamation: https://www.swarthmore.edu/news-events/original-earth-day-proclamation-arrives-campus-time-years-celebration.

117. John McConnell, "The History of the Earth Flag," *Flag Bulletin* 93 (1982): 57–62.

118. U Thant rings the peace bell at a 1971 ceremony: "Secretary General Attends Earth Day Proclamation Ceremony," United Nations Audiovisual Library, https://www.unmultimedia.org/avlibrary/en/asset/d636/d2636557/.

119. Margaret Mead, "Earth Day," *EPA Journal* 4.3 (1978): 31.

120. Gaylord Nelson, "Senate Joint Resolution 169—Introduction of a Joint Resolution Relating to an Environmental Agenda for the 1970s," *Congressional Record,* Senate, 19 January 1970, 81–85, https://www.govinfo.gov/content/pkg/GPO-CRECB-1970-pt1/pdf/GPO-CRECB-1970-pt1-1-1.pdf. The quotations are from Nelson's speeches in Madison and Denver: Gaylord Nelson, Earth Day speech, University of Wisconsin, 21 April 1970, videotape, visual materials archive, Wisconsin Historical Society; Gaylord Nelson, "Partial Text for Senator Gaylord Nelson, Denver, Colorado, April 22, 1970," https://michiganintheworld.history.lsa.umich.edu/environmentalism/files/original/f94eb1f6b6eb3dfd65c33eb862dab290.pdf. On Nelson's Sunday School attendance and moral outlook: Bill Christofferson, *The Man from Clear Lake: Earth Day Founder Senator Gaylord Nelson* (University of Wisconsin Press, 2004), 44. See also Thomas Jundt, *Greening the Red, White, and Blue: The Bomb, Big Business, and Consumer Resistance in Postwar America* (Oxford University Press, 2014), 190–216; Adam Rome, *The Genius of Earth Day: How a 1970 Teach-In Created the First Green Generation* (Hill and Wang, 2013).

121. In Denver, Nelson was a panelist at a "teach-in," and this source identifies the photograph of Nelson with the Ecology Flag as taken during that address: "Gaylord Nelson, Founder of Earth Day," Wisconsin Historical Society and the Nelson Institute for Environmental Studies, University of Wisconsin, https://nelsonearthday.net/april-22-1970-first-earth-day/. For Nelson's recollections: Gaylord Nelson, "Earth Day '70: What It Meant," *EPA Journal,* April 1980, https://www.epa.gov/archive/epa/aboutepa/earth-day-70-what-it-meant.html.

122. The ecology symbol was designed by cartoonist Ron Cobb of the *Los Angeles Free Press,* and his one-page description of its meanings circulated. See Ron Cobb, *Ecology: A Symbol,* Sawyer Press, 25 October 1969, https://web.archive.org/web/20110724044747/http://roncobb.net/ecology-symbol/. William Cronon, "Foreword: The Myriad Tributaries of a Watershed Moment," in Stradling, *Environmental Moment,* xi–xiii. See also Adam Rome, "This Homemade Flag from the '70s Signals the Beginning of the Environmental Movement," *Smithsonian Magazine,* April 2020, https://www.smithsonianmag.com/smithsonian-institution/homemade-flag-from-70s-signals-beginning-environmental-movement-180974373/; "Environmental Button," National Museum of American History, https://americanhistory.si.edu/collections/search/object/nmah_333284.

123. Garett De Bell, ed., *The Environmental Handbook: Prepared for the First Environmental Teach-In* (Ballantine Books, 1970), 1–3 (Gary Snyder's poem), 12–26

(Lynn White's essay), 24–26 (on Saint Francis). De Bell was Notre Dame's keynote Earth Day speaker: "De Bell Opens Earth Day; *Observer* 4.114 (22 April 1970): 1, 6. "A million copies": Adam Rome, "The Genius of Earth Day," *Environmental History* 15.2 (2010): 202. See also John G. Mitchell, ed., *Ecotactics: The Sierra Club Handbook for Environmental Activists* (Trident Press, 1970); Pat Smith and Mariana Gosnell, "That Snyder Sutra," in Mitchell, *Ecotactics,* 84–87. N. Scott Momaday, "An American Land Ethic," in Mitchell, *Ecotactics,* 97–105.

124. "Visit of Pope Paul VI to the FAO on the 25th Anniversary of Its Institution," 16 November 1970, https://www.vatican.va/content/paul-vi/en/speeches/1970/documents/hf_p-vi_spe_19701116_xxv-istituzione-fao.html. Pope Paul also mentioned "the Environment" (section 21) in Pope Paul VI, *Octogesima Adveniens,* apostolic letter on the eightieth anniversary of *Rerum Novarum,* 14 May 1971, https://www.vatican.va/content/paul-vi/en/apost_letters/documents/hf_p-vi_apl_19710514_octogesima-adveniens.html. "Earth Day Mass," *NC News Service,* 27 April 1970, 6–7. For other Catholic participation, see E. D. Duarte, "Earth Day," *NC News Service,* 24 April 1970, 12–15. Linda B. Major, "Pollution Umbrella to Protect Nation from Rain of Garbage, *NC News Service,* 2 December 1970, 1–2. See also Theodore Lai and Cecilia Tortajada, "The Holy See and the Global Environmental Movements," *Frontiers in Communication* 6 (2021), https://doi.org/10.3389/fcomm.2021.715900.

125. Francis A. Schaeffer, *Pollution and the Death of Man: The Christian View of Ecology* (Tyndale House, 1970). Wayne Cosby, letter to the editor, "Balancing Science," *Christianity Today,* 10 April 1970, 19–20. Editorial, "Terracide," *Christianity Today,* 23 April 1971, 26–27. James M. Houston, "The Environmental Movement: Five Causes of Confusion," *Christianity Today,* 15 September 1972, 8–10. Sarah Pulliam Bailey, "Earth Day's Pentecostal Origins," *Christianity Today,* 22 April 2010, https://www.christianitytoday.com/news/2010/april/earth-days-pentecostal-origins.html.

126. On the Greater Birmingham Alliance to Stop Pollution (GASP): Rome, "Genius of Earth Day," 202–203. On the disproportionate impact on the Northside's Black communities: Shauntice Allen et al., "The Search for Environmental Justice: The Story of North Birmingham," *International Journal of Environmental Research and Public Health* 16 (12): 2117 (14 June 2019), doi:10.3390/ijerph16122117. The service in Minneapolis: Peter Ackerberg, "Blaring of Kazoos Symbolizes Earth Day Protest at Church," *Minneapolis Star*, 23 April 1970, https://libnews.umn.edu/2020/04/slow-down-make-the-good-earth-last/.

127. Joseph A. Sittler, "Ecological Commitment as Theological Responsibility," *Zygon* 5 (1970): 172–181. Sittler had published "A Theology for Earth," *Christian Scholar* (1954): 367–374. John B. Cobb Jr., *Is It Too Late? A Theology of Ecology* (1972; Fortress, 2021).

128. Cobb's endorsement of Environment Sunday: Dan L. Thrapp, "Ecology in Need of Church's Help, Theologian Says," *Los Angeles Times,* 19 April 1970, A1. Mainline Protestants' endorsement of efforts "to redeem the air, the water, and the landscape": "The New Politics of the Environment," *Christian Century,* 14 January 1970, 36. See also Richard M. Fagley, "Earth Day and After," *Christian Century,* 15 April 1970,

440–442; Roger L. Shinn, "Population and the Dignity of Man," *Christian Century,* 15 April 1970, 442–448. Lutheran environmental statement: Robert Booth Fowler, *The Greening of Protestant Thought* (University of North Carolina Press, 1995), 16.

129. Stewart L. Udall, *1976: Agenda for Tomorrow* (Harcourt, Brace, and World, 1968), 67. See also Stewart L. Udall, *The Quiet Crisis* (Holt, Rinehart and Winston, 1963); Stewart L. Udall, Charles Conconi, and David Osterhout, *The Energy Balloon* (McGraw-Hill, 1974). On Udall: Scott Raymond Einberger, *With Distance in His Eyes: The Environmental Life and Legacy of Stewart Udall* (University of Nevada Press, 2018). For help in describing Udall's relation to the Latter-day Saints, I'm indebted to Reid Neilson of Brigham Young University and Philip Barlow of Utah State University.

130. On Nixon's decision to side with environmentalists: John Ehrlichman, *Witness to Power: The Nixon Years* (Pocket Books, 1982), 52, 182. Persuaded by the Earth Day crowds: Christina Pazzanese, "How Earth Day Gave Birth to Environmental Movement," *Harvard Gazette,* 17 April 2020, https://news.harvard.edu/gazette/story/2020/04/denis-hayes-one-of-earth-days-founders-50-years-ago-reflects/. On opinion polls and Earth Day crowds: John C. Whitaker, "Earth Day Recollections: What It Was Like When the Movement Took Off," *EPA Journal* (July/August 1988), https://www.epa.gov/archive/epa/aboutepa/earth-day-recollections-what-it-was-when-movement-took.html. Nixon's first EPA administrator, Ruckelshaus, also said Nixon "never asked me about anything going on in EPA. Never." "William D. Ruckelshaus: Oral History Interview," EPA, interview conducted by Michael Gorn, January 1993, https://www.epa.gov/archive/epa/aboutepa/william-d-ruckelshaus-oral-history-interview.html.

131. Dale L. Morse et al., "EI Paso Revisited: Epidemiological Follow Up of an Environmental Lead Problem," *Journal of the American Medical Association* 242 (1979): 739–741. Mary Romero, "The Death of Smeltertown: A Case Study of Lead Poisoning in a Chicano Community," in Theresa Cordova, John A. Garcia, and Juan R. Garcia, eds., *The Chicano Struggle: Analyses of Past and Present Efforts* (National Association for Chicano Studies, 1984), 26–41. Monica Perales, "Fighting to Stay in Smeltertown: Lead Contamination and Environmental Justice in a Mexican American Community," *Western Historical Quarterly* 39.1 (2008): 41–63. An EPA-ordered cleanup of lead-contaminated soil in El Paso would not be completed until 2008, and in 2009 the EPA added East Chicago to the national priority list and began to clean up the polluted soil. See US Environmental Protection Agency, "USS Superfund Site," 1 December 2022, https://www.epa.gov/uss-lead-superfund-site.

132. Ruckelshaus, who was raised Catholic, said, "I am not a particularly religious man, but my father was": "William D. Ruckelshaus: Oral History Interview." On Muskie as "a good Catholic," see Don Nicoll, "Muskie, Jane Gray oral history interview," 3 May 2000, Edmund S. Muskie Oral History Collection, https://scarab.bates.edu/muskie_oh/293. See also Jim Ross, "Muskie, Edmund S. oral history interview," 14 August 1985, Edmund S. Muskie Oral History Collection, https://scarab.bates.edu/muskie_oh/291. Walter Hickel, Nixon's first secretary of the interior

(1969–1970), was baptized, married, and memorialized in the Catholic Church, and the Sisters of Providence remembered him as a "staunch supporter": John C. Shideler and Hal K. Rothman, *Pioneering Spirit: The Sisters of Providence in Alaska* (Providence Hospital, 1987), 70. John Ehrlichman also was raised as a Christian Scientist and turned to the faith for comfort during his time in the White House: Harold K. Steen, "An Interview with Russell E. Train," July 1993, Forest History Society, p. 11, https://foresthistory.org/wp-content/uploads/2016/12/Train_Russell_E.ohi_.pdf.

133. On Train and Nixon: "Russell E. Train: Oral History Interview," interview by Michael Gorn, 5 May 1992, https://www.epa.gov/archive/epa/aboutepa/russell-e-train-oral-history-interview.html.

134. He was a "relatively active layman in the Episcopal Church here in Washington," but by 1990 had become "something of a backslider": Russell E. Train, "Caring for Creation," delivered before the North American Conference on Religion and Ecology, Washington, DC, 18 May 1990, *Vital Speeches of the Day* 56.21 (1990): 664.

135. Russell E. Train, "Prescription for a Planet: The Ninth Bronfman Lecture," *American Journal of Public Health* 60.3 (1970): 433–440. Russell E. Train, *Politics, Pollution, and Pandas: An Environmental Memoir* (Island Press, 2003). J. Brooks Flippen, *Conservative Conservationist: Russell E. Train and the Emergence of American Environmentalism* (LSU Press, 2006), 47–184. "Interview with John Ehrlichman," episode 16, 7 February 1999, National Security Archive, https://nsarchive2.gwu.edu/coldwar/interviews/episode-16/ehrlichman1.html.

136. "Russell E. Train: Oral History Interview."

137. Mark Fiege, *The Republic of Nature: An Environmental History of the United States* (University of Washington Press, 2012), 358–402. The Arab oil embargo was a response to US support for Israel: Thomas A. Tweed, *Religion: A Very Short Introduction* (Oxford University Press, 2020), 99–100.

138. US Energy Information Administration, "History of Energy Consumption in the United States, 1775–2009," 9 February 2011, https://www.eia.gov/todayinenergy/detail.php?id=10.

139. J. R. McNeill and Peter Engelke, *The Great Acceleration: An Environmental History of the Anthropocene since 1945* (Harvard University Press, 2014). Will Steffen et al., "The Trajectory of the Anthropocene: The Great Acceleration," *Anthropocene Review* 2 (2015): 81–98.

140. US Energy Information Administration, "History of Energy Consumption in the United States, 1775–2009."

141. *Engel v. Vitale,* 25 June 1962, 370 U.S. 421.

142. Harvey Gallagher Cox, *The Secular City: Secularization and Urbanization in Theological Perspective* (Macmillan, 1965). "Is God Dead?," cover, *Time,* 8 April 1966. See also Thomas J. J. Altizer and William Hamilton, *Radical Theology and the Death of God* (Bobbs-Merrill, 1966).

143. Megan Rosenfeld, "Gas Lines Stretch On and On," *Washington Post,* 19 February 1974, C1.

Chapter 10. Postindustrial Religion

1. Robert Wuthnow, *The Restructuring of American Religion* (Princeton University Press, 1988). A "megachurch" is a congregation with at least 1,500 attendees. There were precedents, like Russell Conwell's Baptist Temple (1891) and Aimee Semple McPherson's Angelus Temple (1923), but megachurches multiplied from only 50 in 1970 to more than 1,200 by 2005. David E. Eagle, "Historicizing the Megachurch," *Journal of Social History* 48.3 (2015): 589–604. See also Jeanne Halgren Kilde, "Reading Megachurches: Investigating the Religious and Cultural Work of Church Architecture," in Louis P. Nelson, ed., *American Sanctuary: Understanding Sacred Spaces* (Indiana University Press, 2006), 225–249.

2. See Warren Bird and Scott Thumma, *Megachurch 2020: The Changing Reality in America's Largest Churches* (Hartford Institute for Religion Research, 2020).

3. Cape Cod Chamber of Commerce, "400th Anniversary of the Pilgrims' Landing: Key 2020 Events," https://www.capecodchamber.org/articles/post/key-2020-events/. America250, the federal commission planning the 2026 anniversary of the Declaration, was established in 2016: https://america250.org/about-america250/. Declaration of Independence, https://www.archives.gov/founding-docs/declaration-transcript.

4. Steve Jobs "dropped out," found a Hindu guru in India, and went on to practice Zen meditation: Walter Isaacson, *Steve Jobs* (Simon & Schuster, 2011), 31–55.

5. Martin Campbell-Kelly and Daniel D. Garcia-Swartz, *From Mainframes to Smartphones: A History of the International Computer Industry* (Harvard University Press, 2015), 11–41. The UNIVAC was built in a former factory: see *3747 Ridge Avenue* (industrial property), photograph by Parker and Mullikin, 6 December 1948, Print and Picture Collection, Free Library of Philadelphia, https://libwww.freelibrary.org/digital/item/pdcm00303a.

6. John Pitts, "Man Is No Univac!" *Christianity Today* 6.22 (3 August 1962): 6–8.

7. Norbert Wiener, *God and Golem, Inc.: A Comment on Certain Points Where Cybernetics Impinges on Religion* (MIT Press, 1964). Weiner died that year, and *Newsweek* mentioned his new book in an obituary: "The Cyberneticist," *Newsweek*, 30 March 1964, 48. Reviews by Christian scholars: A. M. Frazier, rev. of *God and Golem, Inc., JR* 45.4 (1965): 355–356; Robert McAfee Brown, rev. of *God and Golem, Inc., Technology and Culture* 6.3 (1965): 531–532. Norbert Wiener, "Cybernetics," *Scientific American* 179.5 (1948): 14–19.

8. *The Triple Revolution* (Ad Hoc Committee on the Triple Revolution, 1964).

9. William J. Regan, "The Service Revolution," *Journal of Marketing* 27.3 (1963): 57–62. *Economic Report to the President, Transmitted to Congress January 1963* (GPO, 1963), 32. Francisco J. Buera and Joseph P. Kaboski, "The Rise of the Service Economy," *American Economic Review* 102.6 (2012): 2540–2569. Ulrich Witt and Christian Gross, "The Rise of the 'Service Economy' in the Second Half of the Twentieth Century and Its Energetic Contingencies," *Journal of Evolutionary Economics* 30 (2020): 236.

10. Susannah Fox and Lee Rainie, "The Web at 25 in the U.S.: Part 1: How the Internet Has Woven Itself into American Life," Pew Research Center, 27 February 2014, https://www.pewresearch.org/internet/2014/02/27/part-1-how-the-internet-has-woven-itself-into-american-life/. Kristen Purcell, "Search and Email Still Top the List of Most Popular Online Activities," Pew Research Center, 9 August 2011, https://www.pewresearch.org/internet/wp-content/uploads/sites/9/media/Files/Reports/2011/PIP_Search-and-Email.pdf. Daniel Bell, *The Coming of Post-Industrial Society: A Venture in Social Forecasting* (Basic Books, 1973). Marion Harper Jr., "A New Profession to Aid Management," *Journal of Marketing* 23 (1961): 1–6. Alex Sayf Cummings, "Of Sorcerers and Thought Leaders: Marketing the Information Revolution in the 1960s," *The Sixties* 9.1 (2016): 1–25. George McGovern, "The Information Age," *New York Times*, 9 June 1977, 21.

11. David Gonzalez, "The Computer Age Bids Religious World to Enter," *New York Times*, 24 July 1994, 1.

12. On Sister Wynona Carr: W. K. McNeil, *Encyclopedia of American Gospel Music* (Routledge, 2005), 247, 363, 430.

13. Eric S. Raymond, *The Hacker's Dictionary*, 3rd ed. (MIT Press, 1996), 513–514. Margaret Montagno, "Is Deprogramming Legal?" *Newsweek*, 21 February 1977, 44; David G. Bromley and Anson D. Shupe Jr., *Strange Gods: The Great American Cult Scare* (Beacon, 1981), 32–38, 177–204.

14. Joshua Cooper Rao, "Finding God on the Web," *Time*, 16 December 1996, 52–59.

15. Tim Berners-Lee's proposal can be found at "History of the Web," World Wide Web Foundation, https://webfoundation.org/about/vision/history-of-the-web/. He was raised in the Church of England but joined a Unitarian Universalist congregation, and his reflections on the parallels can be found in Tim Berners-Lee, "The World Wide Web and the 'Web of Life,'" 1998, https://www.w3.org/People/Berners-Lee/UU.html. See also Brett T. Robinson, *Appletopia: Media Technology and the Religious Imagination of Steve Jobs* (Baylor University Press, 2013), 12.

16. Quoted in the *Time* story, saying the Internet had become "a new metaphor for God." See also Sherry Turkle, *Life on the Screen: Identity in the Age of the Internet* (Simon & Schuster, 1995), 167.

17. Charles P. Henderson Jr., "The Future of ARIL in the Information Age," *Cross Currents* 46.2 (1996): 190. Charles P. Henderson Jr., "The Internet as a Metaphor for God?," *Cross Currents* 50.1–2 (2000): 83. On Henderson, see https://www.godweb.org/?page_id=2.

18. On digital religion: Thomas A. Tweed, *Religion: A Very Short Introduction* (Oxford University Press, 2020), 102–110. TV script writers used Facebook imagery to describe "friending" God: *God Friended Me*, CBS series created by Steven Lilien and Bryan Wynbrandt, 2018–2020. Claudia Deane, Maeve Duggan and Rich Morin, "Americans Name the 10 Most Significant Historic Events of Their Lifetimes," Pew Research Center, 15 December 2016, https://www.pewresearch.org/politics/2016/12/15/americans-name-the-10-most-significant-historic-events-of-their

-lifetimes/. Respondents ranked September 11 first, Barack Obama's election second, and the tech revolution third.

19. By *quasi religion* I mean beliefs, practices, and institutions that have some features of religion.

20. On the "nones," see the 2014 Religious Landscape Study, Pew Research Center, https://www.pewresearch.org/dataset/pew-research-center-2014-u-s-religious-landscape-study/. The proportion of "nones" rose to 30 percent by 2020: "Projecting U.S. Religious Groups' Population Shares by 2070," Pew Research Center, https://www.pewresearch.org/religion/2022/09/13/projecting-u-s-religious-groups-population-shares-by-2070/. A 2018 study identified the "non-religious" (29%), but noted that some unaffiliated engage in practices and report beliefs resembling those of the affiliated: "The Religious Typology: A New Way to Categorize Americans by Religion," Pew Research Center, 29 August 2018, https://www.pewresearch.org/religion/2018/08/29/the-religious-typology/. See also Stephen Sebastian Bullivant, *Nonverts: The Making of Ex-Christian America* (Oxford University Press, 2022), 9.

21. Carroll Doherty and Jocelyn Kiley, "A Look Back at How Fear and False Beliefs Bolstered U.S. Public Support for War in Iraq," Pew Research Center, 14 March 2023, https://www.pewresearch.org/politics/2023/03/14/a-look-back-at-how-fear-and-false-beliefs-bolstered-u-s-public-support-for-war-in-iraq/. Bush's decision: Melvyn P. Leffler, *Confronting Saddam Hussein: George W. Bush and the Invasion of Iraq* (Oxford University Press, 2023).

22. Seymour Martin Lipset and William Schneider, "The Decline of Confidence in American Institutions," *Political Science Quarterly* 98.3 (1983): 379–402. Tom W. Smith, *Trends in Confidence in Institutions, 1973–2006,* NORC/University of Chicago, August 2008, GSS Social Change Report no. 54, https://gss.norc.org/Documents/reports/social-change-reports/SC54%20Trends%20in%20Confidence%20in%20Institutions.pdf. Jeffrey M. Jones, "Confidence in US Institutions Down; Average at New Low," Gallup, 5 July 2022, https://news.gallup.com/poll/394283/confidence-institutions-down-average-new-low.aspx. Declining trust in "organized religion": Tom W. Smith and Jasesok Son, *General Social Survey 2012 Final Report: Trends in Public Attitudes about Confidence in Institutions,* NORC/University of Chicago, May 2013, https://www.norc.org/content/dam/norc-org/pdfs/Trends%20in%20Confidence%20Institutions_Final.pdf, pp. 2, 8.

23. Jonestown's "cult of death": Sean McCloud, *Making the American Religious Fringe: Exotics, Subversives, and Journalists, 1955–1993* (University of North Carolina Press, 2004), 153–159. Brian A. Monahan, *The Shock of the News: Media Coverage and the Making of 9/11* (NYU Press, 2010), 55–69.

24. William V. D'Antonio, Michelle Dillon, and Mary Gautier, *American Catholics in Transition* (Rowman & Littlefield, 2013), 83–86. Tom W. Smith, "The Impact of the Televangelist Scandals of 1987–88 on American Religious Beliefs and Behaviors," NORC, University of Chicago, GSS Social Change Report no. 34, April 1991, p. 6. Jason Berry, *Lead Us Not into Temptation: Catholic Priests and the Sexual Abuse of Children* (Doubleday, 1992). Thomas R. Reilly, "The Sexual Abuse of Children in

the Roman Catholic Archdiocese of Boston: A Report by the Attorney General," Office of the Attorney General, Commonwealth of Massachusetts, 23 July 2003, https://www.mass.gov/doc/the-sexual-abuse-of-children-in-the-roman-catholic-archdiocese-of-boston/download. "Church Allowed Abuse for Years," part 1, *Boston Globe,* 6 January 2002; "Geoghan Preferred Preying on Poorer Children," part 2, *Boston Globe,* 7 January 2002.

25. The proportion of Americans who are "more spiritual than religious" increased from 18.5 percent in 1998 to 33.0 percent in 2018: *Spirituality and Religion in the United States, 1998–2020,* presented by Tom W. Smith and Benjamin Schapiro of NORC/University of Chicago, to the Fetzer Institute, 11 May 2021, https://www.norc.org/content/dam/norc-org/pdfs/Spirituality%20and%20Religion%20in%20the%20United%20States,%201998-2020.pdf, p. 2.

26. Randall Balmer, *Passion Plays: How Religion Shaped Sports in North America* (University of North Carolina Press, 2022), 2. Kathryn Lofton, *Oprah: Gospel of an Icon* (University of California Press, 2011), 4.

27. By 2014, 40 percent of Americans said they meditated weekly: David Masci and Conrad Hackett, "Meditation Is Common across Many Religious Groups in the U.S.," 2 January 2018, Pew Research Center, https://www.pewresearch.org/short-reads/2018/01/02/meditation-is-common-across-many-religious-groups-in-the-u-s/. Jeff Wilson, *Mindful America: The Mutual Transformation of Buddhist Meditation and American Culture* (Oxford University Press, 2014), 75–103.

28. Kristy Nabhan-Warren, *Meatpacking America: How Migration, Work, and Faith Unite and Divide the Heartland* (University of North Carolina Press, 2021), 107–121. Bethany Moreton, *To Serve God and Wal-Mart: The Making of Christian Free Enterprise* (Harvard University Press, 2009). Kathryn Lofton, *Consuming Religion* (University of Chicago Press, 2017). Daniel Vaca, *Evangelicals Incorporated: Books and the Business of Religion in America* (Harvard University Press, 2019). Chade-Meng Tan, "Search Inside Yourself," talks at Google, 26 April 2012, https://www.youtube.com/watch?v=r8fcqrNO7so. Carolyn Chen, *Work Pray Code: When Work Becomes Religion in Silicon Valley* (Princeton University Press, 2022), 54. S. Truett Cathy, *Chick-fil-A, Inc.: A History Maker in Foodservice* (Newcomen Society of America, 1998).

29. McNally, *Defend the Sacred,* 179.

30. Larry W. Burt, "Roots of the Native American Urban Experience: Relocation Policy in the 1950s," *American Indian Quarterly* 10.2 (1986): 85–99.

31. T.A. Boden, G. Marland, and R. J. Andres, *Global, Regional, and National Fossil-Fuel CO_2 Emissions,* Carbon Dioxide Information Analysis Center, Oak Ridge National Laboratory (US Department of Energy, 2017).

32. Richard White, "Gilded Ages," *Journal of the Gilded Age and Progressive Era* 19 (2020): 314–320. Richard White, *The Republic for Which It Stands: The United States during Reconstruction and the Gilded Age, 1865–1896* (Oxford University Press, 2017), 477–517. Gopal K. Singh and Stella M. Yu, "Infant Mortality in the United States, 1915–2017: Large Social Inequities Have Persisted for Over a Century," *International Journal of MCH and AIDS* 8.1 (2019): 19–31. See also US Department of Health

and Human Services, *Health, United States, 1983; and Prevention Profile, [PHS] 84-1232* (GPO, 1983); B. D. Smedley, A. Y. Stith, and A. R. Nelson, *Unequal Treatment: Confronting Racial and Ethnic Disparities in Healthcare* (National Academies Press, 2003). The ratio improved for Blacks 1965 to 1975, and then rose again.

33. James Davison Hunter, *Culture Wars: The Struggle to Define America* (Basic Books, 1992). James E. Campbell, *Polarized: Making Sense of a Divided America* (Princeton University Press, 2016). On the culture wars, see Andrew Hartman, *A War for the Soul of America: A History of the Culture Wars,* 2nd ed. (University of Chicago Press, 2019). Hartman quotes Pat Buchanan's 1992 speech declaring a war "for the soul of America" (p. 1). For a volume that complicates the story, see Darren Dochuk, ed., *Religion and Politics beyond the Culture Wars: New Directions in a Divided America* (University of Notre Dame Press, 2021). See also Jason Bivins, *Embattled America: The Rise of Anti-politics and America's Obsession with Religion* (Oxford University Press, 2022). On "fracture" and "fault lines": Daniel T. Rodgers, *Age of Fracture* (Harvard University Press, 2011); Kevin M. Kruse and Julian E. Zelizer, *Fault Lines: A History of the United States since 1974* (W. W. Norton, 2019). See also R. Marie Griffith, *Moral Combat: How Sex Divided American Christians and Fractured American Politics* (Basic Books, 2017); Kristin Kobes Du Mez, *Jesus and John Wayne: How White Evangelicals Corrupted a Faith and Fractured a Nation* (Liveright Publishing, 2020).

34. George W. Bush, "Establishing the Office of Faith-Based and Community Initiatives," 29 January 2001, https://georgewbush-whitehouse.archives.gov/news/releases/2001/01/print/20010129-2.html. George W. Bush, "The Global War on Terrorism: The First 100 Days," https://2001-2009.state.gov/s/ct/rls/wh/6947.htm. Casey argues that "willful ignorance of religion" made things worse: Shaun A. Casey, *Chasing the Devil at Foggy Bottom: The Future of Religion in American Diplomacy* (Eerdmans, 2023), 17–30.

35. Lilliana Mason, *Uncivil Agreement: How Politics Became Our Identity* (University of Chicago Press, 2018). Matthew D. Lassiter, *The Silent Majority: Suburban Politics in the Sunbelt South* (Princeton University Press, 2006). Joseph Crespino, *In Search of Another Country: Mississippi and the Conservative Counterrevolution* (Princeton University Press, 2007). Kevin Michael Kruse, *White Flight: Atlanta and the Making of Modern Conservatism* (Princeton University Press, 2007). Darren Dochuk, *From Bible Belt to Sunbelt: Plain-Folk Religion, Grassroots Politics, and the Rise of Evangelical Conservatism* (W. W. Norton, 2011).

36. As a response to feminism and civil rights: Hartman, *War for the Soul of America,* 102–133, 171–199; Angie Maxwell and Todd Shields, *The Long Southern Strategy: How Chasing White Voters in the South Changed American Politics* (Oxford University Press, 2019).

37. Race, not abortion, as key: Randall Balmer, *Bad Faith: Race and the Rise of the Religious Right* (Eerdmans, 2021), 37, 45. See also Anthea Butler, *White Evangelical Racism: The Politics of Morality in America* (University of North Carolina Press, 2021), 57–95. The Voting Rights Act (1965) triggered an increase in white registration rates: Andrea Bernini et al., *Black Empowerment and White Mobilization: The Effects*

of the Voting Rights Act, Working Paper 314125, July 2023, National Bureau of Economic Research, https://www.nber.org/papers/w31425.

38. Randall A. Terry, "Operation Rescue: The Civil Rights Movement of the Nineties," *Policy Review* 47 (1989): 82–83. Eric Rudolph, who admitted to the 1998 clinic bombing, cited abortion as the motive. Pro-life groups condemned it: Art Toalston, "Fatal Abortion Clinic Bombing Condemned by Pro-Life Leaders," *Baptist Press,* 20 January 1998, https://www.baptistpress.com/resource-library/news/fatal-abortion-clinic-bombing-condemned-by-pro-life-leaders/. Teresa Malcolm, "Birmingham Bombing Condemned," *National Catholic Reporter* 34.15 (1998): 8. *Regents of the University of California v. Bakke,* 438 US 265 (1978). See also Andrew L. Whitehead and Samuel L. Perry, *Taking America Back for God: Christian Nationalism in the United States* (Oxford University Press, 2020).

39. Michael Lienesch, *In the Beginning: Fundamentalism, the Scopes Trial, and the Making of the Antievolution Movement* (University of North Carolina Press, 2007), 212–219; Kathleen M. Sands, *America's Religious Wars: The Embattled Heart of Our Public Life* (Yale University Press, 2019), 211–212.

40. Wuthnow, *Restructuring.*

41. Andrew M. Greeley, *Religious Change in America* (Harvard University Press, 1989), 47–52, 71–75. D'Antonio, Dillon, and Gautier, *American Catholics in Transition,* 155.

42. About half of Orthodox Jews reported they have "not much" (23%) or "nothing at all" (26%) in common with Reform Jews, and a majority of Reform Jews felt the same way: "Jewish Americans in 2020," Pew Research Center, 11 May 2021, www.pewresearch.org/religion/2021/05/11/jewish-americans-in-2020/. On protests: the American Family Association organized boycotts in the 1980s; see Edward C. Brewer and Kay Taylor, "Managing Collaboration in the Thirty Years War: Culture, Politics and the Influence of Donald Wildmon," *Journal of Religion and Popular Culture* 23.1 (2011): 1–13.

43. John D. Inazu, *Confident Pluralism: Surviving and Thriving through Deep Difference* (University of Chicago Press, 2016), 5.

44. Sands, *America's Religious Wars,* 6–8. See Reagan's 1988 Proclamation on the National Day of Prayer; the 697-word document did not mention *equality* but mentioned *freedom* six times and *liberty* six times. Ronald Reagan, "Proclamation 5767: National Day of Prayer 1988," 3 February 1988, https://www.reaganlibrary.gov/archives/speech/proclamation-5767-national-day-prayer-1988.

45. John Fraim, "Mass to Segmented Culture: From One Reality to Alternative Realities," *Explorations in Media Ecology* 20.3 (2021): 329–332. Social media segmentation increased with the founding of Facebook (2004) and Twitter (2006). By a "communication commons," I mean a media ecosystem for public service communication in a democratic society that is free of advertisements and surveillance. See Christian Fuchs, "The Digital Commons and the Digital Public Sphere: How to Advance Digital Democracy Today," *Westminster Papers in Communication and Culture* 16.1 (2021): 9–26. See also Shoshana Zuboff, *The Age of Surveillance Capitalism: The Fight for a Human Future at the New Frontier of Power* (Public Affairs, 2019). John

Lauer and Kenneth Lipartito, eds., *Surveillance Capitalism in America* (University of Pennsylvania Press, 2021).

46. Jeffrey K. Hadden, "The Rise and Fall of American Televangelism," *AAPSS* 527 (1993): 113–130. Mark Ward Sr., "Televangelism, Audience Fragmentation, and the Changing Coverage of Scandal," in Hinda Mandell and Gina Masullo Chen, eds., *Scandal in a Digital Age* (Palgrave Macmillan, 2016), 53–68.

47. The Telecommunications Act of 1996 (Public Law 104-104, 8 February 1996) aimed to "promote competition and reduce regulation" to aid consumers and encourage new technologies.

48. Pat Robertson, "Action Plan for the 1980s" (1979), in Matthew Avery Sutton, ed., *Jerry Falwell and the Rise of the Religious Right: A Brief History with Documents* (Bedford/St. Martin's, 2013), 122.

49. Christopher Matthews, *Tip and the Gipper: When Politics Worked* (Simon & Schuster, 2013). Du Mez, *Jesus and John Wayne*, 147–148.

50. Gingrich sent tapes and memos, including a 1990 memo ("Language: A Key Mechanism of Control") listing 133 words to demean opponents and elevate candidates: Stephen Gillon, "GOPAC Strategy and Instructional Tapes (1986–1994)," Library of Congress, https://www.loc.gov/static/programs/national-recording-preservation-board/documents/GOPACtapes.pdf. Michael Oreskes, "For GOP Arsenal, 133 Words to Fire," *New York Times*, 9 September 1990, 30; "Accentuate the Negative," *Harper's* 281 (1990): 17.

51. Putnam and Campbell's "Faith Matters Survey" of 2006 found that Americans felt least warmly toward Muslims. See Robert D. Putnam and David E. Campbell, with the assistance of Shaylyn Romney Garrett, *American Grace: How Religion Divides and Unites Us* (Simon & Schuster, 2010).

52. Vine Deloria Jr., "1976: The Desperate Need for Understanding," *Cross Talk* 3.4, part 8 (December 1974–February 1975). See also Vine Deloria Jr., "Why Aren't Indians Celebrating the Bicentennial?" *Learning Magazine*, 14 November 1975; Vine Deloria Jr., "Completing the Theological Circle: Civil Religion in America," *Religious Education* 71.3 (1976): 278–287. JoAnne Big Fire, "Happy Bicentennial American," *Wassaja*, July 1976, 5. We cannot be sure how she understood her religious affiliation, but she wore a silver cross in her senior yearbook photograph: "Joanne Big Fire, Winnebago, Winnebago, Nebraska," *Spirit 76: Flandreau Indian School*, 38.

53. Hartman, *War for the Soul of America*, 253–284. Robert Trisco, ed., *Catholics in America, 1776–1976* (National Conference of Catholic Bishops Committee for the Bicentennial, 1976). Emanuel Feldman et al., "Bicentennial Symposium: The Jew in America," *Tradition: A Journal of Orthodox Jewish Thought* 16.2 (1976): 7–15. Jacob R. Marcus, *The Jew and the American Bicentennial* (American Jewish Archives, 1976). L. Tom Perry, "God's Hand in the Founding of America," Church of Jesus Christ of Latter-day Saints, 1976, https://www.churchofjesuschrist.org/study/new-era/1976/07/gods-hand-in-the-founding-of-america?lang=eng.

54. The self-characterization comes from a handwritten reflection of 1977 or 1978: Gerald R. Ford, "What Religion Means to Me," Gerald R. Ford Presidential

Library and Museum, https://www.fordlibrarymuseum.gov/library/document/0065/atth-religion.pdf.

55. Gerald R. Ford, "Address before a Joint Session of the Congress, Reporting on the State of the Union," 19 January 1976, Gerald R. Ford Presidential Library and Museum, https://www.fordlibrarymuseum.gov/library/speeches/760019.asp.

56. On the Washington at Valley Forge thirteen-cent stamp, see "1977 Christmas Issue," National Postal Museum, https://postalmuseum.si.edu/exhibition/about-us-stamps-modern-period-1940-present-commemorative-issues-1970-1979-1976-1977-27.

57. On Carter: Randall Herbert Balmer, *Redeemer: The Life of Jimmy Carter* (Basic Books, 2014).

58. Peter Marshall and David Manuel, *The Light and the Glory* (Revell, 1977).

59. Jerry Falwell, *Listen, America!* (Doubleday, 1980). Ruth Tomczak coauthored the book, and *The Light and the Glory* is cited on p. 236. An evangelical counterpoint: Mark A. Noll, Nathan O. Hatch, and George M. Marsden, *The Search for a Christian America* (Crossway Books, 1983). On Falwell, see Dirk Smillie, *Falwell Inc.: Inside a Religious, Political, Educational, and Business Empire* (St. Martin's, 2008). See also Susan B. Ridgely, "Conservative Christianity and the Creation of Alternative News: An Analysis of Focus on the Family's Multimedia Empire," *RAC* 30.1 (2020): 1–25. On hemispheric parallels: Benjamin A. Cowan, *Moral Majorities across the Americas: Brazil, the United States, and the Creation of the Religious Right* (University of North Carolina Press, 2021).

60. Newt Gingrich, *To Renew America* (HarperCollins, 1995), 7. Hartman, *War for the Soul of America*, 6. The last year of the White Protestant demographic majority was 1993: Robert P. Jones, *The End of White Christian America* (Simon & Schuster, 2016), 257. Gingrich, who later converted to Catholicism, also published Newt Gingrich, *Rediscovering God in America* (Thomas Nelson, 2006).

61. Falwell, *Listen, America!*, 130. Some Catholics and Evangelicals signed an influential document: "Evangelicals and Catholics Together: The Christian Mission in the Third Millennium," *First Things* 43 (1994): 15–22.

62. The Council on Biblical Manhood and Womanhood (CBMW), "The Danvers Statement," 1987. The final form appeared in November 1988: https://cbmw.org/about/danvers-statement/.

63. The majority of respondents in the 2006 "Faith Matters Survey," including 54 percent of evangelicals, said people of other faiths can go to heaven: Putnam and Campbell, *American Grace*; "American Grace: How Religions Divides and Unites Us," 16 December 2010, https://www.pewresearch.org/religion/2010/12/16/american-grace-how-religion-divides-and-unites-us/.

64. George W. Bush, "Address at the Islamic Center of Washington," 17 September 2001, https://www.americanrhetoric.com/speeches/gwbush911islamispeace.htm.

65. Bush signed the Enhanced Border Security Act and the Secure Fence Act: Dan Kanstroom, *Deportation Nation: Outsiders in American History* (Harvard University Press, 2007), 230.

66. Moreton, *God and Wal-Mart,* 125–144.

67. Grant Wacker, *America's Pastor: Billy Graham and the Shaping of a Nation* (Harvard University Press, 2014), 216–217. "Christianity and Capitalism: New Light in an Old Debate," *Christianity Today* 27.2 (21 January 1983): 43.

68. Stanley Hauerwas and William H. Willimon, *Resident Aliens: Life in the Christian Colony* (Abingdon Press, 1989). Carter, a Baptist, also challenged free-market Christianity in his 1979 "Crisis of Confidence" speech: Darren Dochuk, "Religion in Post-1945 America," *Oxford Research Encyclopedia of American History,* https://doi.org/10.1093/acrefore/9780199329175.013.37

69. Kate Bowler, *Blessed: A History of the American Prosperity Gospel* (Oxford University Press, 2013). Tony Tian-Ren Lin, *Prosperity Gospel Latinos and Their American Dream* (University of North Carolina Press, 2020). David Edwin Harrell, *Oral Roberts: An American Life* (Indiana University Press, 1985). Roberts's Prayer Tower (1967) and building campaign: Margaret M. Grubiak, "An Architecture for the Electronic Church: Oral Roberts University in Tulsa, Oklahoma," *Technology and Culture* 57.2 (2016): 380–413. Robert H. Schuller, *Peace of Mind through Possibility Thinking* (Spire Books, 1977). Philip Johnson's Crystal Cathedral (1980) and Schuller's megachurch empire: Mark T. Mulder, *The Glass Church: Robert H. Schuller, the Crystal Cathedral, and the Strain of Megachurch Ministry* (Rutgers University Press, 2020). Philip Luke Sinitiere, *Salvation with a Smile: Joel Osteen, Lakewood Church, and American Christianity* (NYU Press, 2015), 11.

70. Omar M. McRoberts, "The Rise of the Public Religious Welfare State: Black Religion and the Negotiation of Church/State Boundaries during the War on Poverty," in James T. Sparrow, William J. Novak, and Stephen W. Sawyer, eds., *Boundaries of the State in US History* (University of Chicago Press, 2019), 233–258. Eddie S. Glaude Jr., *African American Religion: A Very Short Introduction* (Oxford University Press, 2014), 93.

71. Shirley MacLaine, *Going Within: A Guide for Inner Transformation* (Bantam, 1989). Lofton, *Oprah,* 6–7.

72. James W. Feldman, *Nuclear Reactions: Documenting American Encounters with Nuclear Energy* (University of Washington Press, 2017), 144–148. Natasha Zaretsky, *Radiation Nation: Three Mile Island and the Political Transformation of the 1970s* (Columbia University Press, 2018). Sherry Cable, Edward J. Walsh, and Rex H. Warland, "Differential Paths to Political Activism: Comparisons of Four Mobilization Processes after the Three Mile Island Accident," *Social Forces* 66.4 (1988): 964.

73. Thomas H. Harris, "How Many Trees Do You Need to See? Said the Governor," *New York Times,* 24 June 1973, 418, 437.

74. Mark Fiege, *The Republic of Nature: An Environmental History of the United States* (University of Washington Press, 2012), 422–425. Keith Makoto Woodhouse, "In Defense of People: Environmentalism and the Religious Right in Late Twentieth-Century American Politics," in Dochuk, *Religion and Politics,* 267–289. The decline of bipartisanship: Ellen Griffith Spears, *Rethinking the American Environmental Movement Post-1945* (Routledge, 2019), 10–11. Richard Neuhaus, a Lutheran who later

converted to Catholicism, wrote *In Defense of People: Ecology and the Seduction of Radicalism* (Macmillan, 1971). James Schall, "Ecology—An American Heresy?" *America,* 27 March 1971, 309.

75. "These Are Our Inherent Rights (1978)," in Daniel M. Cobb, ed., *Say We Are Nations: Documents of Politics and Protest in Indigenous America since 1887* (University of North Carolina Press, 2015), 184–188. The Walk as "spiritual": Banks Explains 'Longest Walk,'" *Navajo Times,* 9 February 1973, 13; "What Does the Longest Walk Mean to You?" *Navajo Times,* 20 April 1978, 29; "Longest Walk Concludes with Demonstrations," *Cherokee Advocate,* July 1978, 10.

76. McNally, *Defend the Sacred,* 172, 180. Suzan Shown Harjo, "American Indian Religious Freedom Act after Twenty-Five Years: An Introduction" and "Keynote Address: The American Indian Religious Freedom Act: Looking Back and Looking Forward," *Wicazo Sa Review* 19.2 (2004): 129–136, 143–151. Suzan Shown Harjo, "Our Vision for a Living Museum," *Indian Country Today,* 22 September 2004, A7.

77. "Powerful" benefits: Ned Blackhawk, *The Rediscovery of America: Native Peoples and the Unmaking of U.S. History* (Yale University Press, 2023), 443.

78. *Employment Division v. Smith,* 494 U.S. 872 (1990).

79. The Religious Freedom Restoration Act of 1993, Public Law 103-141, 107 Stat. 1488, codified at 42 U.S.C. § 2000bb through 42 U.S.C. § 2000bb-4. A later decision extended rights to corporations: *Burwell v. Hobby Lobby Stores, Inc.*, 573 U.S. 682 (2014). On issues in the third "Constitutional era," see Sarah Barringer Gordon, *The Spirit of the Law: Religious Voices and the Constitution in Modern America* (Harvard University Press, 2010), 12. See also Winnifred Fallers Sullivan, *The Impossibility of Religious Freedom*, new ed. (Princeton University Press, 2018); Winnifred Fallers Sullivan, *A Ministry of Presence: Chaplaincy, Spiritual Care, and the Law* (University of Chicago Press, 2014).

80. Bunty Anquoe, "President Promises Hope," *Indian Country Today* 13.45 (1994): A1.

81. Quoted in Bobbie Whitehead, "Cherokee Bishop Brings American Indian Perspective to the Episcopal Church," *Indian Country Today* 24.13 (2004): B1. See also Wilma Mankiller, ed., *Every Day Is a Good Day: Reflections by Contemporary Indigenous Women* (Fulcrum, 2011), 16–23.

82. Edward L. Kimball, "Spencer W. Kimball and the Revelation on Priesthood," *BYU Studies* 47.2 (2008): 5–78. Udall argued for a more egalitarian position earlier: F. Ross. Peterson, "'Do Not Lecture the Brethren': Stewart L. Udall's Pro–Civil Rights Stance, 1967," *Journal of Mormon History* 25.1 (1999): 272–287.

83. US Catholic Bishops, *Brothers and Sisters to Us: Pastoral Letter on Racism* (US Conference of Catholic Bishops, 1979).

84. Quoted in Michael Oreskes, "Jackson Enters Race for the Presidency," *New York Times,* 8 September 1987, A16. Obama's candidacy was indebted to Shirley Chisholm's 1972 campaign and Jackson's 1984 and 1988 campaigns. See Evelyn M. Simien, *Historic Firsts: How Symbolic Empowerment Changes U.S. Politics (*Oxford University Press, 2015).

85. The rise of apologies: Aaron Lazare, *On Apology* (Oxford University Press, 2004), 6–7. The UN identified four kinds of "reparations": *Basic Principles and Guidelines on the Right to a Remedy and Reparation for Victims of Gross Violations of International Human Rights Law and Serious Violations of International Humanitarian Law,* General Assembly Resolution 60/147, 16 December 2005, https://www.ohchr.org/en/instruments-mechanisms/instruments/basic-principles-and-guidelines-right-remedy-and-reparation. Daniel Philpott, *Just and Unjust Peace: An Ethic of Political Reconciliation* (Oxford University Press, 2012), 175–285.

86. Civil Liberties Act, 10 August 1988, Stat. 903, Public Law 100-383. Reagan said the bill helped "to right a grave wrong": "Remarks on Signing the Bill Providing Restitution for the Wartime Internment of Japanese-American Civilians," 10 August 1988, https://www.reaganlibrary.gov/archives/speech/remarks-signing-bill-providing-restitution-wartime-internment-japanese-american. On "pilgrimages" to internment camps: Jane Naomi Iwamura, "Critical Faith: Japanese Americans and the Birth of a New Civil Religion," *AQ* 59.3 (2007): 937–968.

87. E. J. Dionne Jr., "Pope Apologizes to Africans for Slavery," *New York Times,* 14 August 1985, 3. Luigi Accatolli, *When a Pope Asks for Forgiveness: The Mea Culpas of John Paul II* (Pauline Books and Media, 1998).

88. Keith Hinson, "Resolutions Committee Frames Racism Statement," *Baptist Press* [news service of the Southern Baptist Convention], 19 June 1995, 1–2. Timothy C. Morgan, "Southern Baptists Racist No More? Black Leaders Ask," *Christianity Today* 39.9 (1 August 1995): 53. Southern Baptist Convention, "Resolution on Racial Reconciliation on the 150th Anniversary of the Southern Baptist Convention," 1 June 1995, https://www.sbc.net/resource-library/resolutions/resolution-on-racial-reconciliation-on-the-150th-anniversary-of-the-southern-baptist-convention/. Linda Bloom, "United Methodists Repent for Racism," United Methodist General Conference, 5 May 2000, http://gc2000.org/gc2000news/stories/gc019.htm.

89. Phillip Connor and Abby Budiman, "Immigrant Share in U.S. Nears Record High but Remains Below That of Many Other Countries," Pew Research Center, 30 January 2019, https://www.pewresearch.org/short-reads/2019/01/30/immigrant-share-in-u-s-nears-record-high-but-remains-below-that-of-many-other-countries/.

90. *Fremont, USA* (2009), film directed by Rachel Antell and Elinor Pierce, 57 minutes, Pluralism Project, Harvard University. R. Scott Hanson, *City of Gods: Religious Freedom, Immigration, and Pluralism in Flushing, Queens* (Empire State Editions, 2016).

91. Thomas A. Tweed, "Our Lady of Guadeloupe Visits the Confederate Memorial," *Southern Cultures* 8.2 (2002): 72–93.

92. Federal Council of Churches, "The Social Creed of the Churches," adopted 4 December 1908, https://nationalcouncilofchurches.us/common-witness-ncc/the-social-creed-of-the-churches/. Pope Leo XIII, *Rerum Novarum,* 15 May 1891, https://www.vatican.va/content/leo-xiii/en/encyclicals/documents/hf_l-xiii_enc_15051891_rerum-novarum.html.

93. Christopher Winans, "National Council of Churches Condemns Reagan," UPI Archives, 16 May 1981, https://www.upi.com/Archives/1981/05/16/National-Council-of-Churches-condemns-Reagan/2641358833600/. Ecumenical collaboration in Los Angeles: Sean T. Dempsey, *City of Dignity: Christianity, Liberalism, and the Making of Global Los Angeles* (University of Chicago Press, 2023).

94. United Methodists Council of Bishops, *In Defense of Creation: The Nuclear Crisis and a Just Peace* (Graded Press, 1986), 57. United States Catholic Bishops, *Economic Justice for All: Pastoral Letter on Catholic Social Teaching and the U.S. Economy* (National Conference of Catholic Bishops, 1986).

95. Quoted in a story dated 8 April 1979: https://apnews.com/article/ca23009e-a5b54f21a3fed04065cacc7e. The quoted minister, Dick Deardorff of the Churches of God, pastored a church across the river from the plant. The bishop's call for a moratorium: Jim Castelli, "'Nuclear Plants OK, but Not Near My House,'" *St. Louis Review* 38.46 (16 November 1979): 12.

96. Marjorie Hyer, "Church Groups Study Religious Aspects of Energy," *Washington Post,* 27 April 1979. For articles in Protestant magazines, see J. George Butler, "Christian Ethics and Nuclear Power," *Christian Century,* 18 April 1979, 438–441; Nancy M. Tischler, "Three Mile Island," *Christianity Today,* 4 May 1979, 35. See also Finis Dunaway, *Seeing Green: The Use and Abuse of American Environmental Images* (University of Chicago Press, 2015), 138–153.

97. United States Catholic Bishops, *Economic Justice for All,* 3, paragraph 12. Sarah McFarland Taylor, *Green Sisters: A Spiritual Ecology* (Harvard University Press, 2007), xi, xvii, 2, 51, 197–204.

98. Women of Reform Judaism, "Protecting the Environment," 1983, https://wrj.org/what-we-believe/resolutions/protecting-environment.

99. Commission for Racial Justice, *Toxic Wastes and Race in the United States* (United Church of Christ, 1987). See also their follow-up study: Justice and Witness Ministries, *Toxic Wastes and Race at Twenty, 1987–2007* (United Church of Christ, 2007). Rob Nixon, *Slow Violence and the Environmentalism of the Poor* (Harvard University Press, 2011), 2. Spears, *Rethinking the American Environmental Movement,* 5. Josiah Rector, "The Spirit of Black Lake: Full Employment, Civil Rights, and the Forgotten Early History of Environmental Justice," *Modern American History* 1.1 (2018): 45–66.

100. On Native Alaskan counternarratives: Patrick Daley with Dan O'Neill, "'Sad Is Too Mild a Word': Press Coverage of the *Exxon Valdez* Oil Spill," *Journal of Communications* 41.4 (1991): 42–57. On the sudden violence of the Exxon Valdez, see also Dunaway, *Seeing Green,* 223–238.

101. "Environment," Gallup Historical Trends, https://news.gallup.com/poll/1615/environment.aspx. Russell E. Train, "Caring for Creation," delivered before the North American Conference on Religion and Ecology, Washington, DC, 18 May 1990, *Vital Speeches of the Day* 56.21 (1990): 664–666. Other speakers included Al Gore, Jürgen Moltmann, and Carl Sagan: Bennett J. Sims, "The North American Conference on Religion and Ecology . . . ," *Anglican and Episcopal History* 59.4 (1990): 441–452.

102. On the Indigenous Environmental Network, see https://www.ienearth.org/about/.

103. US Conference of Catholic Bishops, *Renewing the Earth: An Invitation to Reflection and Action on Environment in Light of Catholic Social Teaching,* 14 November 1991, https://www.usccb.org/resources/renewing-earth. Al Gore, *Earth in the Balance: Ecology and the Human Spirit* (Houghton Mifflin, 1992), 238–265. He advocated "a new reverence" for the environment: Gore, *Earth in the Balance,* 204–205, 258–265, 368. Gore identified as a "born-again" Baptist but studied at the National Cathedral and spent three semesters at Vanderbilt Divinity School.

104. Mark A. Shibley and Jonathon L. Wiggins, "The Greening of Mainline American Religion: A Sociological Analysis of the Environmental Ethics of the National Religious Partnership for the Environment," *Social Compass* 44.3 (1997): 333–348.

105. The sustainable projects: Taylor, *Green Sisters,* 35.

106. Albert Gore et al., *An Inconvenient Truth,* widescreen film (Paramount Classics, 2006).

107. "Atheist books," "the Creation Museum," and Ted Haggard's admission of "sexual immorality" were top stories: David Van Biema, "Top 10 Religion Stories," *Time,* 9 December 2007, https://content.time.com/time/specials/2007/article/0,28804,1686204_1690170_1692386,00.html. *Time* mentioned three atheist manifestos, including Richard Dawkins's *The God Delusion* (Houghton Mifflin, 2006). The Creation Museum opened in Petersburg, Kentucky, in May 2007; see https://creationmuseum.org. On "religious preference" and the patterns I report, see the 2018 General Social Survey (GSS), which was conducted before the start of the COVID-19 pandemic: https://gss.norc.org.

108. The proportion of the "non-religious" ranged from only 1.1 percent (Northern Mariana Islands) to 4.0 percent (US Virgin Islands). The data on "national/regional profiles" were downloaded from the Association of Religion Data Archives, www.theARDA.com, and were collected by Todd M. Johnson and Brian J. Grim, eds., *World Religion Database* (Brill, 2024). The regional distribution of Catholics, Latter-day Saints, and non-religious: "The Religiously Distinct States of America," 9 February 2018, https://news.gallup.com/poll/226844/religiously-segregated-states-america.aspx.

109. "Religiously Distinct States of America." On Jews, see also Pew Research Center, "Jewish Americans in 2020," 11 May 2021, https://www.pewresearch.org/religion/2021/05/11/jewish-americans-in-2020/.

110. Michael Hout, *A New Compendium of Trends in the General Social Survey, 1972–2018,* GSS Social Change Report no. 64, NORC/University of Chicago, May 2020, 11–12.

111. I rely on the "National Congregational Study" from 2018–2019: Mark Chaves, Joseph Roso, Anna Holleman, and Mary Hawkins, *Congregations in 21st Century America* (Duke University, Department of Sociology, 2021).

112. On "religious preference" patterns, see the 2018 General Social Survey, https://gss.norc.org.

113. Megan Brenan, "Americans' Confidence in Major U.S. Institutions Dips," 14 July 2021, https://news.gallup.com/poll/352316/americans-confidence-major-institutions-dips.aspx. On religious scandals and declining confidence: Tom W. Smith and Jaesok Son, *General Social Survey 2012 Final Report: Trends in Public Attitudes about Confidence in Institutions,* NORC/University of Chicago, May 2013, 2. Researchers disagree about the impact of the sexual abuse crisis. A 2008 Pew survey found a quarter of former Catholics said the sexual abuse scandal was a reason they had left, but other studies reported lower numbers. Pew Research Center, "Americans See Catholic Clergy Sex Abuse as an Ongoing Problem," 11 June 2019, note 1, https://www.pewresearch.org/religion/2019/06/11/americans-see-catholic-clergy-sex-abuse-as-an-ongoing-problem/. See also Robert J. McCarty and John M. Vitek, *Going, Going, Gone: The Dynamics of Disaffiliation in Young Catholics* (Saint Mary's Press, 2017). On the findings of a grand jury investigation of six Pennsylvania dioceses: https://www.attorneygeneral.gov/report/. The *Boston Globe* and the *Philadelphia Inquirer* collaborated for an article that examined how US bishops had failed to police themselves since 2002: Jeremy Roebuck et al., "Failure at the Top," *Philadelphia Inquirer,* 4 November 2018. On declining trust, attendance, and donations after the report, see Pew Research Center, "Clergy Sex Abuse."

114. On the Prayer Room's bookshelf: Madeline Doctor, "From Shared Meanings to Shattered Solidarity: The History, Representations, and Uses of the Congressional Prayer Room, 1952–2000," senior thesis, University of Notre Dame, 2019, 2. Thich Nhat Han, *The Miracle of Mindfulness: A Manual of Meditation* (1975; Beacon, 1987).

115. By interpreting sporting events and musical concerts as sites of exhilaration and belonging, I'm rephrasing Durkheim's insight about the "collective effervescence" experienced in communal rituals. I'm suggesting these events have some features associated with religion. See Emile Durkheim, *The Elementary Forms of Religious Life,* trans. Karen E. Fields (1912; Free Press, 1995), xli–xlii, 386–387, 398–399. Attending sporting events may generate some of the well-being benefits of communal worship: Helen Keyes et al., "Attending Live Sporting Events Predicts Subjective Well-being and Reduces Loneliness," *Frontiers in Public Health* 10 (2023): 989706.

116. David Zahl, "The Great American Religious Remix," *Christianity Today* 64.6 (2020): 71. On its popularity, see Nicole Hong, "How I Built It: Cycling Chain SoulCycle Spins into Fast Lane," *Wall Street Journal,* 18 September 2013, https://www.wsj.com/articles/SB10001424127887323342404579081680434969954.

117. I allude to the Cowboy Church of Ellis County; see https://www.cowboyfaith.org. See also Marie W. Dallam, *Cowboy Christians* (Oxford University Press, 2017).

118. On the informality and expressiveness of congregational worship, see Chaves et al., *Congregations,* 17–20, 76–77.

119. Heidi Campbell and Antonio Pastina, "How the iPhone Became Divine: New Media, Religion and the Intertextual Circulation of Meaning," *New Media and Society* 12.7 (2010): 1191–1207.

120. "Mobile Fact Sheet," Pew Research Center, 7 April 2021, https://www.pewresearch.org/internet/fact-sheet/mobile/.

121. On videotaping, streaming services, web pages, and projection equipment and smartphones in worship: Chaves et al., *Congregations,* 20–23, 95–97 (table 2).

122. The "Light a Candle" program was developed by the Greek Orthodox Archdiocese of America. See "Light a Candle," https://www.constantineandhelen.org/our-faith/candle. *Puja,* mobile phone application by Panagola, released 20 November 2014; updated 23 November 2020, https://play.google.com/store/apps/details?id=com.panagola.app.puja&hl=en_US&gl=US&pli=1. See also Toledo First Seventh-Day Adventists, who announced "Google Hangout Bible Studies" in 2019, https://www.toledofirstadventist.org/toledo-first-blog/toledo-first-headline-news--april-25-2019; Ann Gleig, *American Dharma: Buddhism beyond Modernity* (Yale University Press, 2019), 176–208.

123. One 2022 study found that 28 percent reported "a strong connection with people who are attending a service in person while they, themselves, are watching on a screen." Michelle Faverio et al., "Online Religious Services Appeal to Many Americans, but Going in Person Remains More Popular," 2 June 2023, Pew Research Center, https://www.pewresearch.org/religion/2023/06/02/online-religious-services-appeal-to-many-americans-but-going-in-person-remains-more-popular/.

124. Chaves et al., *Congregations,* 20–23, 95–97 (table 2).

125. "The Nobel Peace Prize 2007," https://www.nobelprize.org/prizes/peace/2007/summary/. "'Doomsday Clock' Moves Two Minutes Closer to Midnight," *Bulletin of the Atomic Scientists,* 17 January 2007, https://thebulletin.org/2007/01/doomsday-clock-moves-two-minutes-closer-to-midnight/. On Latter-day Saints' and evangelical legislators' reduced support: Brian Newman et al., "Religion and Environmental Politics in the US House of Representatives," *Environmental Politics* 25.2 (2016): 290.

126. David Holthouse and Mark Potok, "2007: A Year Marked by Staggering Levels of Racist Hate," *Intelligence Report,* 1 March 2008, Southern Poverty Law Center, https://www.splcenter.org/fighting-hate/intelligence-report/2008/2007-year-marked-staggering-levels-racist-hate. Jessica T. Simes, *Punishing Places: The Geography of Mass Imprisonment* (University of California Press, 2021), 1. See also Michelle Alexander, *The New Jim Crow: Mass Incarceration in the Age of Colorblindness* (New Press, 2020). The peak around 2007: James Cullen, "The History of Mass Incarceration," Brennan Center for Justice, 20 July 2018, https://www.brennancenter.org/our-work/analysis-opinion/history-mass-incarceration.

127. Congressional Research Service, "Trends in Active-Duty Military Deaths from 2006 through 2021," *In Focus,* 9 September 2022, https://sgp.fas.org/crs/natsec/IF10899.pdf. George W. Bush, "President's Address to the Nation," 10 January 2007, https://georgewbush-whitehouse.archives.gov/news/releases/2007/01/20070110-7.html.

128. Paula England, "The Gender Revolution: Uneven and Stalled," *Gender and Society* 24 (2010): 149–166.

129. Robert Rich, "The Great Recession," *Federal Reserve History,* 22 November 2013, https://www.federalreservehistory.org/essays/great-recession-of-200709. US Census Bureau, "Figure 2," Current Population Survey, 1968 to 2021, Annual Social

and Economic Supplements, https://www.census.gov/content/dam/Census/library/visualizations/2021/demo/p60-273/figure2.pdf. Black households lost twice as much income after the crisis of 2008 than White households: Hartman, *War for the Soul of America,* 286. Gopal K. Singh and Stella M. Yu, "Infant Mortality in the United States, 1915–2017: Large Social Inequalities Have Persisted for Over a Century," *International Journal of MCH and AIDS* 8.1 (2019): 1931.

130. Shoshana Zuboff, "The Coup We Are Not Talking About," *New York Times,* 29 January 2021. See also Zuboff, *The Age of Surveillance Capitalism.* Monica Anderson and Andrew Perrin, "Nearly One-in-Five Teens Can't Always Finish Their Homework Because of the Digital Divide," Pew Research Center, 26 October 2018, https://www.pewresearch.org/short-reads/2018/10/26/nearly-one-in-five-teens-cant-always-finish-their-homework-because-of-the-digital-divide/.

131. Juan M. Floyd-Thomas and Anthony B. Pinn, eds., *Religion in the Age of Obama* (Bloomsbury Academic, 2018).

132. Miguel A. De La Torre, "Deporter-in-Chief: Why Reject Christian Hospitality?," in Floyd-Thomas and Pinn, *Age of Obama,* 152, 154.

133. For Muslims emphasizing shared American values since the press releases by the Council for Islamic American Relations and the Islamic Circle of North America on 11 September 2001, see the One America Campaign, US Council of Muslim Organizations (founded 2013), https://uscmo.org/one-america/.

134. About 12 percent said they believed Obama was Muslim in 2008. That number rose to 18 percent by 2010 and to 29 percent by 2015. "Growing Number of Americans Say Obama Is a Muslim," Pew Research Center, 18 August 2010, https://www.pewresearch.org/religion/2010/08/18/growing-number-of-americans-say-obama-is-a-muslim-2/.

135. Obama worshipped for two decades at the Trinity United Church of Christ (UCC) in Chicago. On his religious perspective, see Floyd-Thomas and Pinn, "Introduction," in *Age of Obama,* 3–11. See also Barack Obama, *Dreams from My Father: A Story of Race and Inheritance* (Times Books, 1995).

136. The 2015 CNN/ORC poll: Jennifer Agiesta, "Misperceptions about Obama's Faith Persist, but Aren't So Widespread," CNN Politics, 14 September 2015, https://www.cnn.com/2015/09/13/politics/barack-obama-religion-christian-misperceptions/index.html.

137. Damon T. Berry, *Blood and Faith: Christianity in American White Nationalism* (Syracuse University Press, 2017), 2–4.

138. Dylann Roof, notebook, "Religion," Government Exhibit 2A, US-001649, p. 16, F. Supp. 3d 419 (D.S.C. 2016) [*United States v. Dylann Storm Roof*].

139. The sketch of Jesus (p. 7) and the cross with "In God We Trust" (p. 6): Dylann Roof, prison notebook, "Contents of Cell Search 8-3-15," Government Exhibit 500, US-060652. F. Supp. 3d 419 (D.S.C. 2016) [*United States v. Dylann Storm Roof*].

140. David Brody, *The Teavangelicals: The Inside Story of How the Evangelicals and the Tea Party Are Taking Back America* (Zondervan, 2012). Nella Van Dyke and David S. Meyer, eds., *Understanding the Tea Party Movement* (Routledge, 2016).

141. David P. Gushee, "On the Outside," contribution to "What Place Do Christians Have in the Tea Party Movement?," *Christianity Today* 54.10 (27 October 2010): 55.

142. Theda Skocpol and Vanessa Williamson, "What They Believe: Ideas and Passions," in *The Tea Party and the Remaking of Republican Conservatism* (Oxford University Press, 2012), 50–52. For the LDS artist's explanation of the painting, see Jon McNaughton, "One Nation under God," McNaughton Fine Art Company, https://jonmcnaughton.com/one-nation-under-god/. DC protestors carrying the banner "In God We Trust, Not Congress": Photograph by Nickolas Kamm, AFP/Getty Images, 12 September 2010, "The Tea Party's Tension: Religion's Role in Politics," National Public Radio, https://www.npr.org/2010/09/30/130238835/the-tea-partys-tension-religions-role-in-politics. Ruth Braunstein and Malena Taylor, "Is the Tea Party a 'Religious' Movement? Religiosity in the Tea Party versus the Religious Right," *Sociology of Religion* 78.1 (2017): 51. See also Tony Keddie, *Republican Jesus: How the Right Has Rewritten the Gospels* (University of California Press, 2020), 104–132.

143. "Wendy Wright, "On the Inside," contribution to "What Place Do Christians Have in the Tea Party Movement?," *Christianity Today* 54.10 (27 October 2010): 54–55.

144. David Brody, "In the Front Row," contribution to "What Place Do Christians Have in the Tea Party Movement?," *Christianity Today* 54.10 (27 October 2010): 54.

145. "Threats": Barack Obama, "Farewell Address," 10 January 2017, https://obamawhitehouse.archives.gov/farewell.

146. Gregory A. Smith, "Most White Evangelicals Approve of Trump Travel Prohibition and Express Concerns about Extremism," Pew Research Center, 27 February 2017, https://www.pewresearch.org/short-reads/2017/02/27/most-white-evangelicals-approve-of-trump-travel-prohibition-and-express-concerns-about-extremism/.

147. On White-Cain, see Paula White Ministries, https://paulawhite.org/.

148. Damon T. Berry, *The New Apostolic Reformation, Trump, and Evangelical Politics: The Prophecy Voter* (Bloomsbury, 2023). Franklin Graham also said God chose Trump, as did Jonathan Cahn, the pastor of Beth Israel Worship Center in Wayne, New Jersey.

149. Operation Border Blessing: https://paulawhite.org/teaching-articles/paula-white-ministries-brings-hope-and-happiness-to-border-patrol-families/.

150. Trump self-identified as Presbyterian until October 2020, when he said in response to written questions submitted by the Religion News Service (and presented to the president by Paula White-Cain) that he now considered himself a "non-denominational Christian." See "President Trump's Q&A with Religion News Service," 26 October 2020, https://trumpwhitehouse.archives.gov/articles/president-trumps-qa-religion-news-service/?utm_source=link. The White House allegedly refused to answer questions about his connections to Peale in that RNS interview, but on Peale and Trump (as well as Nixon and Reagan), see Carol V. R. George, *God's Salesman* (Oxford University Press, 2019), 157–229. The prosperity gospel was preached by about one-quarter of congregations: Chaves et al., *Congregations,* 64. On religion and the 2016 election: Jessica Martínez and Gregory A. Smith, "How the

Faithful Voted: A Preliminary Analysis," Pew Research Center, 29 November 2016, https://pewrsr.ch/2fSNWBY. Gregory A. Smith, "Among White Evangelicals, Regular Churchgoers Are the Most Supportive of Trump," Pew Research Center, 26 April 2017, https://pewrsr.ch/2q521NP. Randall Balmer et al., "Forum," *RAC* 27.1 (2017): 2–56.

151. Penelope Muse Abernathy, *The Expanding News Desert* (University of North Carolina Press, 2018). Henry E. Brady and Thomas B. Kent, "Fifty Years of Declining Confidence and Increasing Polarization in Trust in American Institutions," *Daedalus* 151.4 (2022): 43–66. Brent Kitchens, Steve L. Johnson, and Peter Gray, "Understanding Echo Chambers and Filter Bubbles: The Impact of Social Media on Diversification and Partisan Shifts in News Consumption," *MIS Quarterly* 44.4 (2020): 1619–1649. R. Kelly Garrett, "The 'Echo Chamber' Distraction: Disinformation Campaigns Are the Problem, Not Audience Fragmentation," *Journal of Applied Research in Memory and Cognition* 6 (2017): 370–376. W. Lance Bennett and Steven Livingston, eds., *The Disinformation Age: Politics, Technology, and Disruptive Communication in the United States* (Cambridge University Press, 2021).

152. Robert S. Mueller III, *Report on the Investigation into Russian Interference in the 2016 Presidential Election,* vol. 1 (Department of Justice, March 2019), 1.

153. Lei Guo and Chris Vargo, "'Fake News' and Emerging Online Media Ecosystem: An Integrated Intermedia Agenda-Setting Analysis of the 2016 U.S. Presidential Election," *Communications Research* 47.2 (2020): 178–200. See also Andie Tucher, *Not Exactly Lying: Fake News and Fake Journalism in American History* (Columbia University Press, 2022). "Post-truth, adj.," *OED Online,* Oxford University Press, https://www.oed.com/dictionary/post-truth_adj.

154. Jeffrey T. Hancock and Jeremy N. Beilenson, "The Social Impact of Deepfakes," *Cyberpsychology, Behavior, and Social Networking* 24.3 (2021): 149–152. Mark Juergensmeyer, "QAnon as Religious Terrorism," *Journal of Religion and Violence* 10.1 (2022): 89–100. Mia Bloom and Sophia Moskalenko, *Pastels and Pedophiles: Inside the Mind of QAnon* (Stanford University Press, 2021).

155. Brandon Carter, "Trump, Addressing Far-Right QAnon Conspiracy, Offers Praise for Its Followers," National Public Radio, 19 August 2020, https://www.npr.org/2020/08/19/904055593/trump-addressing-far-right-qanon-conspiracy-offers-praise-for-its-followers

156. Some suggest the association of religion with the political right also has diminished religious leaders' ability "to speak prophetically on important public issues." David E. Campbell, "The Perils of Politicized Religion," *Daedalus* 149.3 (2020): 87–104.

157. Quoted in Donna Gordon Blankenship, "Jesuits Settle NW US Sex Abuse Claims for $166 Million," *Navajo Times* 1.13 (31 March 2011): C5. In August 2017 the remains of Dickens Nor (Little Chief) were repatriated: Carlisle Indian School Digital Resource Center, https://carlisleindian.dickinson.edu/cemetery-info/dickens-little-chief. Yufna Soldier Wolf, the tribal historic preservation officer and a relative of Little Chief, called the process "a spiritual journey" and discussed the repatriation in a roundtable and documentary called *Home from School:* National Native

American Boarding School Healing Coalition, "Boarding School Healing Coalition to Host Tribal Roundtable on Carlisle Repatriation," press release, 13 October 2017, https://boardingschoolhealing.org/wp-content/uploads/2017/10/Press-Release_NABS-to-Host-Tribal-Roundtable-on-Carlisle-Repatriation_10-13-17.pdf.

158. D'Antonio, Dillon, and Gautier, *American Catholics in Transition,* 84. The bishops revised the charter: US Conference of Catholic Bishops, *Promise to Protect, Pledge to Heal: Charter for the Protection of Children and Young People* (US Conference of Catholic Bishops, 2018).

159. Robert Downen, Lise Olsen, and John Tedesco, "Abuse of Faith," *Houston Chronicle,* part 1, 10 February 2019, https://www.chron.com/news/investigations/article/Investigation-reveals-700-victims-of-Southern-13591612.php. David Bumgardner, "SBC Executive Committee Publicly Apologizes to Sexual Abuse Survivor," *Baptist News Global,* 23 February 2022, https://baptistnews.com/article/sbc-executive-committee-publicly-apologizes-to-sexual-abuse-survivor/.

160. Claire Gecewicz, "Key Takeaways about How Americans View the Sexual Abuse Scandal in the Catholic Church," Pew Research Center, 11 June 2019, https://www.pewresearch.org/short-reads/2019/06/11/key-takeaways-about-how-americans-view-the-sexual-abuse-scandal-in-the-catholic-church/.

161. Adam B. Cohen, ed., *Religion and Human Flourishing* (Baylor University Press, 2020), esp. 95–104 ("pro-social behavior"), 145–163 (health and happiness). "Religion's Relationship to Happiness, Civic Engagement, and Health around the World," Pew Research Center, 31 January 2019, https://www.pewresearch.org/religion/2019/01/31/religions-relationship-to-happiness-civic-engagement-and-health-around-the-world/. Frank Newport, "Religion and Wellbeing in the US: Update," Gallup, 4 February 2022, https://news.gallup.com/opinion/polling-matters/389510/religion-wellbeing-update.aspx.

162. "Woke, adj.2," *OED Online,* Oxford University Press, https://www.oed.com/dictionary/woke_adj2.

163. Apologizing for the Enslavement and Racial Segregation of African-Americans, 27 February 2007, H. Res. 194, https://www.govinfo.gov/content/pkg/BILLS-110hres194ih/pdf/BILLS-110hres194ih.pdf.

164. To Acknowledge a Long History of Official Depredations and Ill-Conceived Policies by the Federal Government Regarding Indian Tribes and Offer an Apology to All Native Peoples on Behalf of the United States, 30 April 2009, S.J. Res. 14 (IS), https://www.govinfo.gov/app/details/BILLS-111sjres14is.

165. Rob Capriccioso, "A Sorry Saga: Obama Signs Native American Apology Resolution; Fails to Draw Attention to It," *Indian Country Today,* 13 January 2010, https://indianlaw.org/node/529. See also Rick Smith, "US Formally Apologizes to Indians," *Win Awenen Nisitotung* 31.1 (8 January 2010): 6.

166. Drew DeSilver, "Working on Columbus Day or Indigenous Peoples Day? It Depends on Where Your Job Is," Pew Research Center, 5 October 2023, https://www.pewresearch.org/short-reads/2023/10/05/working-on-columbus-day-or-indigenous-peoples-day-it-depends-on-where-your-job-is/.

167. A key Supreme Court case ruled that land in northeastern Oklahoma reserved for the Creek Nation since the nineteenth century remained "Indian Country." *McGirt v. Oklahoma,* 591 U.S. (2020). "H.R. 40 and the Path to Restorative Justice," Hearing before the Subcommittee on the Constitution, Civil Rights, and Civil Liberties, 116th Congress, 19 June 2019, serial no. 116–27, https://www.govinfo.gov/content/pkg/CHRG-116hhrg41178/html/CHRG-116hhrg41178.htm. "Cathedral to Ring Funeral Bell to Mark 400th Anniversary of Slavery," Washington National Cathedral, 21 August 2019, https://cathedral.org/about/news-media/cathedral-to-toll-funeral-bell-to-mark-400th-anniversary-of-american-slavery/. Georgetown, for example, began a process of "memorialization and reconciliation" for selling slaves to Louisiana plantations in 1838. See Adam Rothman and Elsa Barraza Mendoza, *Facing Georgetown's History: A Reader on Slavery, Memory, and Reconciliation* (Georgetown University Press, 2021).

168. Jacey Fortin, "In Quick Reversal, Southern Baptists Denounce White Nationalists," *New York Times,* 15 June 2017. US Conference of Catholic Bishops, *Open Wide Our Hearts: The Enduring Call to Love—A Pastoral Letter against Racism* (US Conference of Catholic Bishops, 2018).

169. "Dylann Roof Is in Our Congregation," Luther Seminary (St. Paul, MN), blog, 23 June 2020, accessed 1 June 2021, https://www.luthersem.edu/context/2020/06/23/dylann-roof-is-in-our-congregation/. Lenny Duncan, *Dear Church: A Love Letter from a Black Preacher to the Whitest Denomination in the US* (Fortress Press, 2019), 62.

170. Natelege Whaley, "Twitter Reacts to Obama's Charleston Speech with #ReverendPresident," Black Entertainment Television, 26 June 2015, https://www.bet.com/article/s3cw71/twitter-reacts-to-obama-s-speech-with-reverendpresident. Barack Obama, "Remarks by the President in Eulogy for the Honorable Reverend Clementa Pinckney," Charleston, 26 June 2015, https://obamawhitehouse.archives.gov/the-press-office/2015/06/26/remarks-president-eulogy-honorable-reverend-clementa-pinckney.

171. "Confederate Flags Placed outside MLK's Atlanta Church," 31 July 2015, Religion News Service, https://religionnews.com/2015/07/31/confederate-flags-placed-outside-mlks-atlanta-church/. See Raphael G. Warnock, *The Divided Mind of the Black Church* (NYU Press, 2013). Warnock's book responded, in part, to Eddie Glaude Jr., "The Black Church Is Dead," *Huffington Post,* 26 August 2010 (updated 23 August 2012), https://www.huffpost.com/entry/the-black-church-is-dead_b_473815.

172. On BLM and its cofounders, Patrisse Cullors, Alicia Garza, and Opal Tometi: "Religion and Black Lives Matter," Berkley Forum, Berkley Center, Georgetown University, 31 October 2016, https://berkleycenter.georgetown.edu/forum/religion-and-black-lives-matter. See Christopher Cameron and Phillip Luke Sinitiere, eds. *Race, Religion, and Black Lives Matter: Essays on a Moment and a Movement* (Vanderbilt University Press, 2021).

173. Barak Obama, "Address before a Joint Session of the Congress," 24 February 2009, https://www.presidency.ucsb.edu/documents/address-before-joint-session-the-congress-1.

174. Paul Cloke, Callum Sutherland, and Andrew Sullivan, "Postsecularity, Political Resistance, and Protest in the Occupy Movement," *Antipode* 48.3 (2016): 497–523. Ruth Braunstein, *Prophets and Patriots: Faith in Democracy across the Political Divide* (University of California Press, 2017). See also Matt Sheedy, "The Occupy Movement, Religion, and Social Formations," *Bulletin for the Study of Religion* 43.1 (2014): 17–24.

175. Pope Francis, *Evangelii Gaudium,* apostolic exhortation, 24 November 2013, 45–47, https://www.vatican.va/content/francesco/en/apost_exhortations/documents/papa-francesco_esortazione-ap_20131124_evangelii-gaudium.html.

176. United Church of Christ, "Economic Justice Movement," United Church of Christ, https://www.ucc.org/what-we-do/justice-local-church-ministries/efam/economic-justice/economic-justice-movement/. United Methodist Church, *Revised Social Principles: 2024,* 15–19, https://www.umcjustice.org/documents/124. See also "Jewish Views on Economic Justice," https://reformjudaism.org/jewish-views-economic-justice.

177. By 2018, 18 percent of congregations discussed the environment, up from 7 percent in 1998: Chaves et al., *Congregations,* 64. America spends "too little" on the environment: General Social Survey, NORC/University of Chicago, https://gssdataexplorer.norc.org/trends?category=Current%20Affairs&measure=natenvir. The proportion favoring environmental protection: Gallup, "Environment," https://news.gallup.com/poll/1615/environment.aspx. By 2020 about 75 percent believed water pollution was very or extremely dangerous, and 66 percent were somewhat or very worried about climate change. See National Science Foundation, "Environment" and "Climate Change," *Science and Technology: Public Attitudes, Knowledge, and Interest,* May 2020, https://ncses.nsf.gov/pubs/nsb20207/public-attitudes-about-specific-s-t-issues.

178. Brentin Mock, "A Pastor Takes on BP in New Orleans," *Religion Dispatches,* 9 June 2010, https://religiondispatches.org/a-pastor-takes-on-bp-in-new-orleans/.

179. Amitav Ghosh, *The Great Derangement: Climate Change and the Unthinkable* (University of Chicago Press, 2016), 150–158.

180. Spears, *Rethinking the American Environmental Movement,* 14. "Integral ecology": Pope Francis, *Laudato Si': On Care for Our Common Home,* encyclical letter (Our Sunday Visitor, 2015), 93–108. On the Catholic Climate Covenant, founded in 2006, see https://catholicclimatecovenant.org.

181. The Diné C.A.R.E. (Citizens against Ruining Our Environment) vision was "to practice our sacred duty and responsibility" by "revering and protecting *hózhó* of the natural world for future life," as well as its past and current projects: https://www.dine-care.org. *Hózhó* has been used to discuss "well-being" for persons and for the natural environment. On the Network's twenty-six "frontline struggles," including at the Chaco Canyon and San Juan Oil and Gas Basin, see *Indigenous Resistance against Carbon* (Oil Change International, August 2021), https://www.ienearth.org/indigenous-resistance-against-carbon/.

182. The "Greening of Evangelicalism" was one of *Time*'s top religion stories for 2007, but by 2020 the majority still told pollsters that climate change was not human-made. Van Biema, "Top 10 Religion Stories." Billy Graham, "Should Christians Work to Protect the Environment? Billy Graham's Answer," Billy Graham Evangelistic Association, 22 April 2020, https://billygraham.org/story/billy-grahams-my-answer-global-warming-and-the-environment/. "Pro-Life Clean Energy Campaign," Evangelical Environmental Network, https://creationcare.org/what-we-do/initiatives-campaigns/pro-life-clean-energy-campaign.html.

183. Interfaith Power and Light, "Our History," https://interfaithpowerandlight.org/about/.

184. On Faith in Place and its proportion of African American members (19%) in 2014: Amanda J. Baugh, *God and the Green Divide: Religious Environmentalism in Black and White* (University of California Press, 2017), 165.

185. For the "Buddhist Declaration on Climate Change," published in 2009 and revised in 2015: David R. Loy, *Ecodharma: Buddhist Teachings for the Ecological Crisis* (Wisdom Publications, 2018), 181–185. See also "The Time to Act Is Now," One Earth Sangha, 20 September 2015, https://oneearthsangha.org/articles/buddhist-declaration-on-climate-change/. Green Muslims, Living the Environmental Spirit of Islam, https://www.greenmuslims.org.

186. Mohamed Younis, "Americans Want More, Not Less, Immigration for First Time," Gallup, 1 July 2020, https://news.gallup.com/poll/313106/americans-not-less-immigration-first-time.aspx.

187. Barack Obama, inaugural address, 20 January 2009, https://obamawhitehouse.archives.gov/blog/2009/01/21/president-Barack-obamas-inaugural-address.

188. Pelosi's family was "devoutly Catholic," and the nuns at her school had "a commitment to social justice." Nancy Pelosi and Amy Hill Hearth, *Know Your Power: A Message to America's Daughters* (Doubleday, 2008), 10–11.

189. Barack Obama, "Remarks at the National Prayer Breakfast," 4 February 2016, https://www.presidency.ucsb.edu/documents/remarks-the-national-prayer-breakfast-25.

190. Biden's Irish Catholic heritage: Joseph R. Biden, "Remarks at a Virtual Irish Community Event," https://www.presidency.ucsb.edu/documents/remarks-virtual-irish-community-event.

191. Harris's religious influences: Yonat Shimron, "5 Faith-facts about VP-elect Kamala Harris, a Black Baptist with a Hindu Family," 7 November 2020, Religion News Service, https://religionnews.com/2020/11/07/5-faith-facts-about-vp-elect-kamala-harris-a-black-baptist-with-a-hindu-family/. See also Maina Mwaura, "Kamala Harris Talks about Her Own Faith . . . ," 28 October 2020, Religion News Service, https://religionnews.com/2020/10/28/kamala-harris-talks-about-her-own-faith-and-how-it-might-influence-a-biden-harris-white-house/.

192. McAllen, Texas, was one of the least sustainable US cities (99th of 105) and Austin, Texas, one of the most sustainable (9th of 105): Alainna Lynch, Anna LoPresti and Caroline Fox, *The 2019 US Cities Sustainable Development Report* (Sustainable Development Solutions Network, 2019), 12–13.

193. Bosque County (founded 1854) is the "Norwegian Capital of Texas," and Lutherans have worshipped there since 1869. See "Our Savior's Lutheran at Norse," https://oursaviorsnorse.org/index.html. For a list, see "Churches," Bosque County Historical Commission, https://www.bosquechc.org/churches.shtml. The county's membership report data were downloaded from the Association of Religion Data Archives, www.theARDA.com, and were collected by the Association of Statisticians of American Religious Bodies, who reported fifty-seven Bosque County congregations in 2020. Many were evangelical, but there also were mainline Protestant and Roman Catholic congregations. Evangelicals made up 32.1 percent of adherents, while mainline Protestants were 10.4 percent and Catholics 4.1 percent. Only 47.4 percent of the county's population were adherents who associated with local congregations: "Bosque, County, Texas, County Membership Report (2020)," Association of Religion Data Archives, https://www.thearda.com/us-religion/census/congregational-membership?y=2020&y2=0&t=0&c=48035. "Riding": Bosque County Cowboy Church, https://www.bosquecountycowboychurch.com.

194. "Horn Shelter Exhibit," Bosque Museum, Clifton, Texas, https://www.bosquemuseum.org/hornshelter. That page included a facial reconstruction. The Bosque Museum's recorded history of the county also mentioned him. See "Bosque County History," https://www.youtube.com/watch?v=9jyp6xrrZ4Q. On virtual mourning: Candi K. Cann, *Virtual Afterlives: Grieving the Dead in the Twenty-First Century* (University Press of Kentucky, 2014), 105–131. Find-a-Grave attracted millions of users by 2013, when it became a subsidiary of Ancestry.com and introduced iOS (2013) and Android (2014) mobile phone applications. A redesigned website appeared in August 2018. Herman Horn (1919–2007), Find-a-Grave, https://www.findagrave.com/memorial/17929883/herman-horn. Adeline Dennis Horn (1925–2006), Find-a-Grave, https://www.findagrave.com/memorial/16367156/adeline-horn. Adeline's memorial includes a "flower," a cross with entwined flowers with an attached obituary. It was added in 2006. The couple was survived by two sons, but they also had lost a three-month-old daughter, Sherry Lou Horn, in 1948, and in 2008 an online site was created for her. Sherry Lou Horn (31 December 1947–16 March 1948), Find-a-Grave, https://www.findagrave.com/memorial/31728474/sherry-lou-horn.

195. America250, the federal commission planning the 2026 anniversary of the Declaration, was established in 2016, and by 2020 Texas had a commission member, Lynn Forney Young, a churchgoing former president of the Daughters of the American Revolution who lived on a cattle ranch about 100 miles south of Clifton, and who hoped that the 250th might unify a divided country. See "Service, Voting, and Texas Pride: A Commissioner Spotlight on Lynn Forney Young," America250, 29 September 2020, https://america250.org/news/service-voting-texas-pride-a-commissioner-spotlight-on-lynn-forney-young/. The Bosque County Historical Commission planned America250 celebrations highlighting the area's Norwegian heritage: Elaine Bakke Bell, chair, email message to the author, 8 January 2024.

Acknowledgments

I've been working on this book for a long time, and many people and institutions helped as I researched and wrote it. I'll mention some of them, though the book's flaws are not their fault.

I'm grateful to the University of Notre Dame, where I hold the Harold and Martha Welch Professorship in American Studies and serve as professor of history. I'm also affiliated with the Institute for Latino Studies, the Ansari Institute for Global Engagement with Religion, and the Kroc Institute for International Peace Studies. The Institute for Scholarship in the Liberal Arts provided financial support, and the Institute for Advanced Study gave me time and space to write. John McGreevy did more than anyone. Our semesters co-teaching a graduate seminar were invaluable, and so were our many conversations about this book. We also participated in the Colloquium on Religious History, and the graduate students, staff members, and faculty colleagues who attended offered helpful advice. Colleagues in American Studies and History at Notre Dame provided encouragement along the way.

I'm grateful to former students and colleagues at the University of Texas at Austin, where the Shive, Lindsay, and Gray Professorship supported some early research trips. With funding from the Lilly Endowment and the Pew Charitable Trusts, I began the *Retelling U.S. Religious History* project at the University of Miami. I experimented with new narratives in classes at the University of North Carolina at Chapel Hill, and the Duke–UNC Colloquium and the Living Room Group sustained me. Scholars at Oxford's School of Anthropology offered crucial early encouragement, and so did participants in the University of London's Global History Seminar. I tried out ideas in the Thomas Lamb Eliot Lecture at Reed College, and appreciated advice I got at the University of Virginia's Americas Center/Centro de las Américas.

Contributors and respondents helped refine my initial ideas in *Retelling U.S. Religious History,* which we dedicated to our teachers and students. My students have meant so much to me, and not just the many who read draft chapters. My teachers and mentors deserve thanks too, including Catherine L. Albanese, Conrad Cherry, William Clebsch, Edwin Gaustad, Daniel Walker Howe, William Hutchison, and Martin Marty.

The anonymous reviewers for Yale University Press, as well as Jennifer Banks, Ann-Marie Imbornoni, and Duke Johns, improved the manuscript, and many scholars of history and religion offered suggestions or read chapters, including Philip Barlow, Catherine Brekus, Jon Butler, Philip Byers, Julie Byrne, Jorge Canizares-Esguerra, Jon Coleman, Darren Dochuk, Robbie Ethridge, Felipe Fernández-Armesto, Pieter Francois, Virginia Garrard, Philipp Gollner, Jennifer Graber, Brad Gregory, Patrick Griffin, Pekka Hämäläinen, Anna Holdorf, Danae Jacobson, Greg Johnson, Fredrik Albritton Jonsson, Stephen M. Koeth, CSC, Kathryn Lofton, Dana Logan, Semion Lyandres, Michael McNally, Lynn Neal, Reid Neilson, Mark Noll, Stephen Prothero, Emily Remus, Susan Ridgely, Jonathan Sarna, Sarah Shortall, Ann Taves, Julia Thomas, Daniel Vaca, and Tisa Wenger. Sociologists (including Mark Chaves, Roger Finke, Conrad Hackett, and Christian Smith) helped with the last chapter.

Staff at many archives, libraries, museums, archaeological sites, and tribal offices gave indispensable aid, and the endnotes and illustration credits don't begin to show my debts. Librarians at Notre Dame, including Jean McManus, were extraordinary. At the start and the end of my research, staff at the Bosque County Museum were kinder than they had to be. Archaeologists graciously received me, and I'm especially indebted to John E. Kelly, who welcomed me to his dig at Cahokia; Donna M. Glowacki, who showed me Mesa Verde; and Joe W. Saunders, who walked me around Watson Brake. Many others read chapters or made suggestions, including Cheryl Classen, Agustín Fuentes, Ian Kuijt, Iain Morley, F. Kent Reilly III, Mark Schurr, and Vincas P. Steponaitis. Staff at the Shirley Plantation Foundation helped me find the 1742 plan of the slave quarters, and East Carroll Parish Public Library staff helped me locate a nineteenth-century plantation.

Many helped with Indigenous history, including Zada Ballew, Ashlee Bird, Roxanne Dunbar-Ortiz, K. T. Fields, Mikaela Murphy, Daniel Castro Romero Jr., Kristina Scott, Paulette Steeves, and Marcus Winchester. Inés Talamantez and Lawrence Gross offered crucial advice, and John Low kindly commented on most of the chapters. Notre Dame's Native American and Indigenous Initiative, and conversations with citizens of the Pokagon Band of Potawatomi, also taught me a great deal.

Finally, I'm grateful to my family. Kevin, Bryn, Leticia, and Ignacio helped me to remember the next generation—and the generations after that. Margaret McNamee, my wife, helped more than I can say. It seems insufficient to dedicate the book to her. But, for now, it will have to be enough.

Index

Illustrations are indicated by page numbers in italics.